The Human Odyssey
Volume 1
Prehistory Through the Middle Ages

Contributing Writers

Robin Currie
Chief Writer

Rebecca Jones
Mary Lyons
Mara Rockliff

Academic Reviewers

Kathryn Bard
Boston University

John A. Brinkman
University of Chicago

Patricia Buckley Ebrey
University of Washington

Michael H. Fisher
Oberlin College

Ronald Herzman
State University of New York, Geneseo

David Kelley
Oberlin College

Susan Lape
University of California, Irvine

Byron McCane
Wofford College

Joseph C. Miller
University of Virginia

James M. Quillin
Lake Forest Academy

The Human Odyssey is based in part upon *Ancient Civilization, Four World Views, Greek and Roman Civilization*, and *Medieval Civilization*, four volumes in The Human Adventure series. The Human Adventure series was prepared by the Social Science Staff of the Educational Research Council of America: Raymond English, Director; Mary Catherine McCarthy, Editor-in-Chief; Agnes M. Michnay, Managing Editor. Writers for The Human Adventure included: Nancy Bostick, Constance Burton, Nancy Henderson, Michael Joyce, Marilyn McLaughlin, Agnes Michnay, James Packard, Marie Richards, Mary Ritley, Judith Wentz, and Marlene Zweig.

The editors of The Human Odyssey wish to thank Rose Schaffer, HM, and The Center for Learning for kindly granting permission to K12 Inc. to use and adapt text from The Human Adventure series. The Center for Learning (www.centerforlearning.org) is a nonprofit educational publisher committed to integrating academic learning and universal values through the humanities.

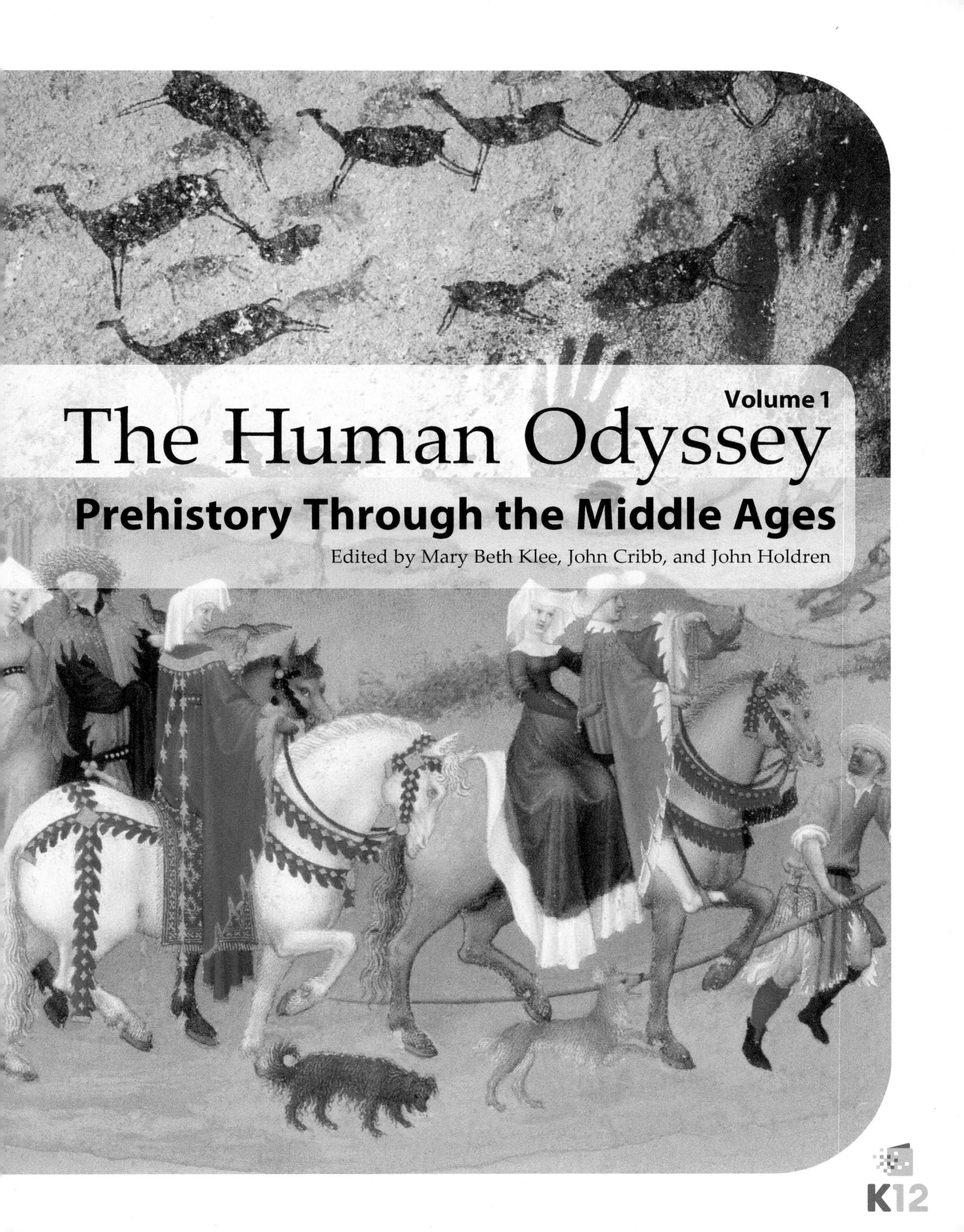

Volume 1

The Human Odyssey

Prehistory Through the Middle Ages

Edited by Mary Beth Klee, John Cribb, and John Holdren

K12

Cover images:
Front cover and title page top: Prehistoric cave art c. 11,000 B.C.
Front cover and title page bottom: Painting of a falcon hunt in medieval France
Back cover: Detail of a fourteenth-century map of North Africa

Library of Congress Cataloging-in-Publication Data

The human odyssey / edited by John Cribb, Mary Beth Klee, and John Holdren.
p. cm.
Includes index.
ISBN 978-1-931728-53-9
1. World history--Juvenile literature. I. Cribb, John. II. Klee, Mary Beth, 1953- III. Holdren, John, 1954-
D20.H88 2004
909--dc22

2004007909

Printed by Quad Graphics, Versailles, KY, USA, May 2019

Contents

Part 3

Part 4

Introduction

Our Human Odyssey

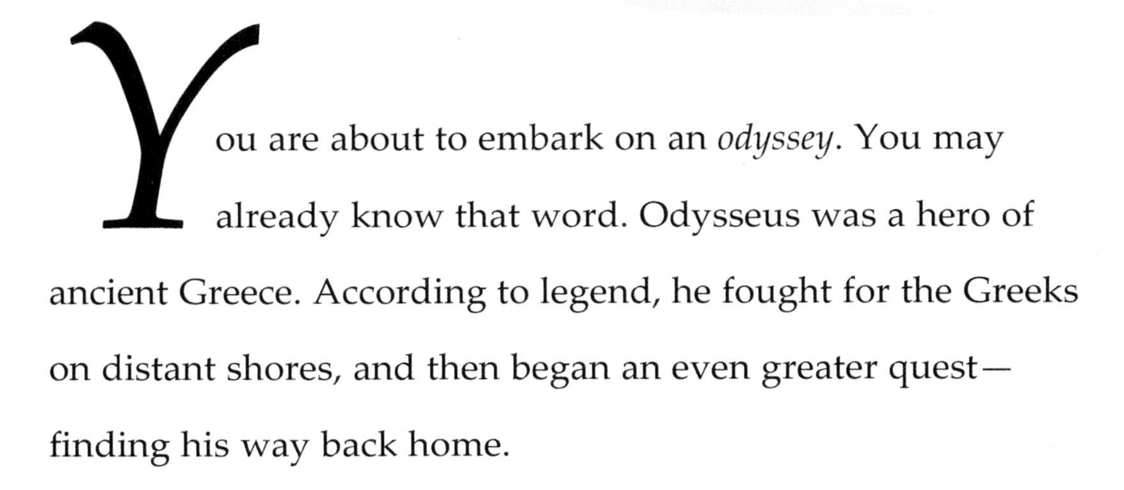

You are about to embark on an *odyssey*. You may already know that word. Odysseus was a hero of ancient Greece. According to legend, he fought for the Greeks on distant shores, and then began an even greater quest—finding his way back home.

The journey of Odysseus took ten long years. It was perilous and thrilling. The hero battled sea monsters, tricked a one-eyed giant, and fled from the sirens—beautiful women who sang sweet songs that lured sailors to their deaths on the rocks. He even traveled to the mythical underworld, the land of the dead, a place no living man had seen before. Through it all, Odysseus was determined to find his way back home. His perseverance paid off, and after many trials he steered his ship into his home port and returned to his wife and son.

Odysseus's long, adventuous journey became known as "the Odyssey." The voyage was named after him. Now we use the word *odyssey* to mean any long and daring voyage.

You are about to study the *human odyssey*, the journey of human beings through time. It has been the greatest quest of all, spanning thousands of years, taking us from pyramids and mummies to space flight. You'll find this human journey has had its heroes, monsters, and giants. It has been marked by moments of peril and times of triumph, times when perseverance and determination have been rewarded, when human beings have been, as the Bible puts it, "little lower than the angels."

If you squint through the prism of time, you'll be able to make out the shape of the human past. When you do, you'll also understand better where we are now, in the present.

Looking back through tim and space, studying what men and women have been and done, is like locating ourselves on a map. It shows where we have been, and how we got where we are. History, the story of the human odyssey, doesn't predict the future, but it shows how we have changed and how we've stayed the same. It shows which paths have been fruitful and which ones should be shunned. It gives us a glimpse of who we might be and who we never want to become. It not only shows us what happened, but also makes us consider how things might have happened differently. The human journey has been an extraordinary odyssey indeed.

At every point in this odyssey we'll need to know where we are in time. Are we talking about time one hundred years ago, or one thousand years ago, or six thousand years ago? We'll also need to know where we are in space. Are we in Mesopotamia or China or the United States? Let's go over a few terms that will help us bring some order to the story of the past.

Help with Pronunciation

In this book you will encounter words that may be new to you. To help you pronounce those words, we have "respelled" them to show how you say them. For example, in this chapter you will come upon the words *odyssey* and *Odysseus*. They are respelled as (AH-duh-see) and (oh-DIH-see-us). The capital letters indicate which syllable to accent. For a closer look at how to pronounce the respelled words, see the Pronunciation Guide on page 650.

How We Keep Track of the Years

You probably know that we call ten years a *decade*. Ten decades equal 100 years, and we call that much time a *century*. Ten centuries equal 1,000 years, and we call that much time a *millennium*.

- How many years are there in four decades?
- How many years are there in seven and one-half centuries?
- The plural of millennium is *millennia*. How many years are there in six millennia?

The words *decade, century*, and *millennium* are tools that help us measure time. But we need a starting point. Before we can use a map to take a trip, we must be able to find the place where we're beginning our travels. It's the same with time—when we want to measure it, we have to know where we are starting.

You might say, "What's the problem? We're starting from today!" True, we know what the date is today. But how did we get that date? When did people start counting to make today the date it is, and not some other date?

In the past, people have used many different calendars, but most of them had different starting points. Today, most people use the same calendar, which measures time from the year when people thought Jesus Christ was born. That year is called A.D. 1. The letters A.D. are short for the Latin words *anno Domini* (a-noh DAH-muh-nee), which mean "in the year of the Lord." So A.D. 1 means "in the year of the Lord, number one." Notice that A.D. goes before the year. That's an old Latin convention and it's still used today.

Why, you may ask, is the calendar we use today pegged to the time of Christ's birth? It's because nearly fifteen centuries ago, a monk named Dionysius Exiguus (diy-uh-NIS-ee-us eg-ZIG-yuh-wus) sat down and invented a system to keep track of years. In his day, the Christian Church carried on most scholarship in Western Europe. So it wasn't at all surprising that this studious monk decided to make the birth of Christ a starting point for his system of keeping track of time. Later on, other church leaders began using a calendar based on the year of Christ's birth, according to Dionysius Exiguus's system. That tradition spread and has lasted to this day.

Sometimes, instead of the letters A.D., you'll see the letters C.E. Those letters stand for "common era" and are simply another way to say the same thing without referring specifically to Christ. The initials A.D. and C.E. are interchangeable. For example, the dates A.D. 1492 and 1492 C.E. mean the same year. (In this book, we will use A.D.)

So, to recap:

- The calendar we use today begins counting the years from the time of the birth of Christ.
- The letters A.D. stand for the Latin words *anno Domini,* which mean "in the year of the Lord."
- Instead of A.D., you can also use the letters C.E., which stand for "common era."
- When you use A.D., the letters come before the date. When you use C.E., the letters come after the date. You say or write A.D. 1215 or 1215 C.E.

Now, what about the years before A.D. 1? Millions of people lived before that time. We date those years by numbering them *backward,* beginning from A.D. 1. The year before A.D.1 is 1 B.C.—*B.C.* stands for *before Christ.* Notice that we write A.D. *before* a number and B.C. *after* a number. To see how this works, look at the time line in **Figure 1** on the next page.

Compare this time line with a number line for mathematics showing positive and negative integers. Do you see a difference? There's no "year zero" on the time line. That's because the monk who developed the system began with

A.D. 1. All the time before that was "before Christ," so the first year before Christ became 1 B.C.

At times, instead of the letters B.C., you will see the letters B.C.E. Those letters stand for "before the common era." B.C. and B.C.E. are inter changeable. For example, the dates 750 B.C. and 750 B.C.E. mean the same year. (In this book, we will use B.C.)

- Which of these dates is written correctly: 800 B.C. or B.C. 800?

Figure 1

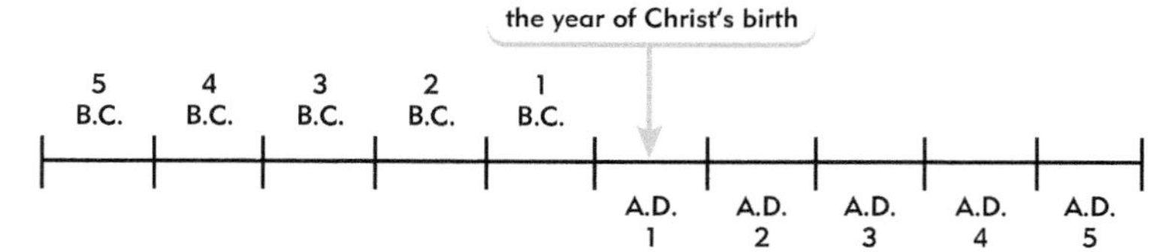

Figure 2

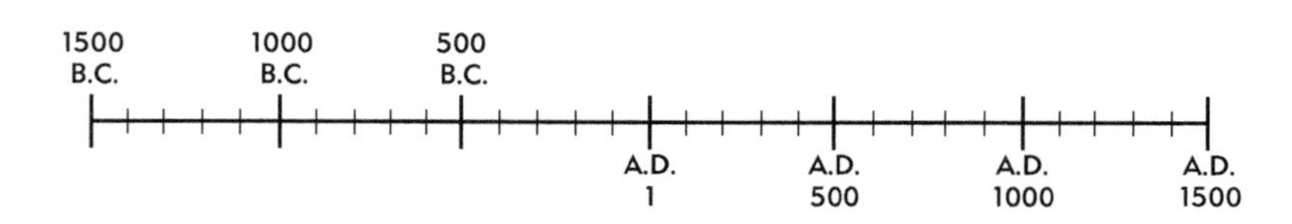

Figure 3

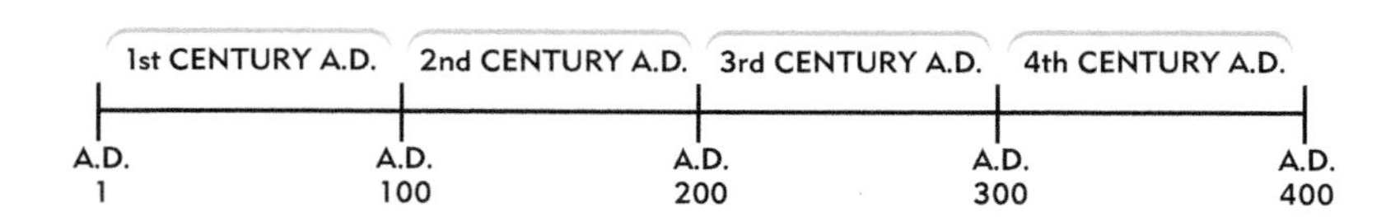

Figure 4

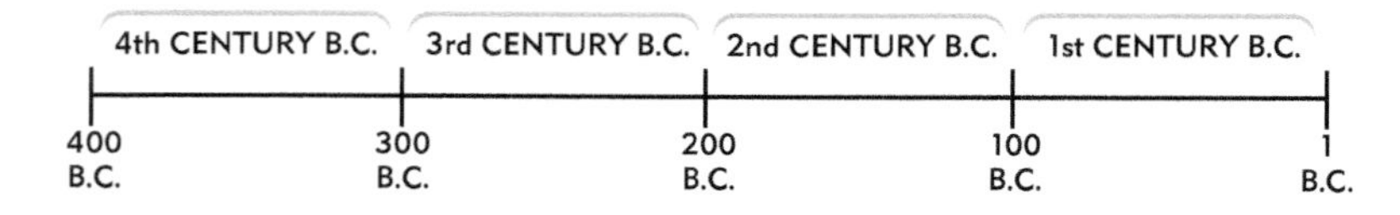

- Human beings first landed on the moon in A.D. 1969. What does that date mean?
- World War II ended in 1945 C.E. What does C.E. stand for?
- Julius Ceasar died in the year 44 B.C. What does B.C. stand for? What's another way to express that year?

How We Number the Centuries

Let's look at a time line that shows longer periods of time. **Figure 2** shows *centuries*.

- Show where 800 B.C. is on the time line. Then show where these dates are:

  A.D. 400 A.D. 975
  A.D. 1250 A.D. 250
  1125 B.C. 300 B.C.

How old are you? If you are twelve, then you are in your *thirteenth* year of life. If you are fourteen, you are in your *fifteenth* year of life. Why? Think of newborn babies just a few weeks old. They are in their *first* year of life. On their first birthday, they begin the *second* year of their life. Still, we say they are only one year old. It is almost as if they were a year ahead of themselves. We number centuries the same way. Look at the time line in **Figure 3** to see how this works.

All the years from A.D. 1 *through* A.D. 100 are part of the first century A.D. All the years from A.D. 101 *through* A.D. 200 are part of the second century A.D. All the years from A.D. 1901 *through* the year A.D. 2000 are in the twentieth century A.D.

- What years make up the fourteenth century A.D.? The ninth century A.D.? The sixth century A.D.?

- Imagine you were born in 1992. In what century was that year?

The same system is used for naming the centuries that came before Christ. See **Figure 4**.

All the years from 100 B.C. *through* 1 B.C. are in the first century B.C. All the years from 200 B.C. *through* 101 B.C. are in the second century B.C.

- What years make up the eighth century B.C.? The thirteenth century B.C.? The fifth century B.C.?

Figure 5

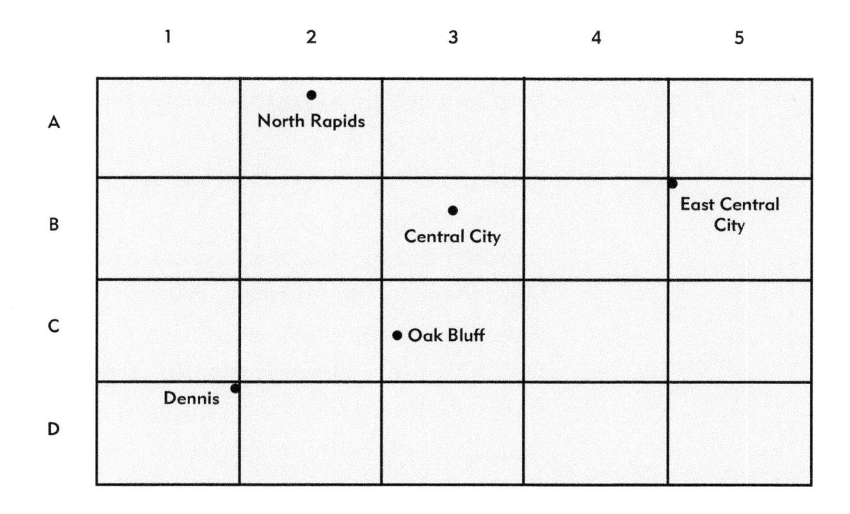

Figure 6

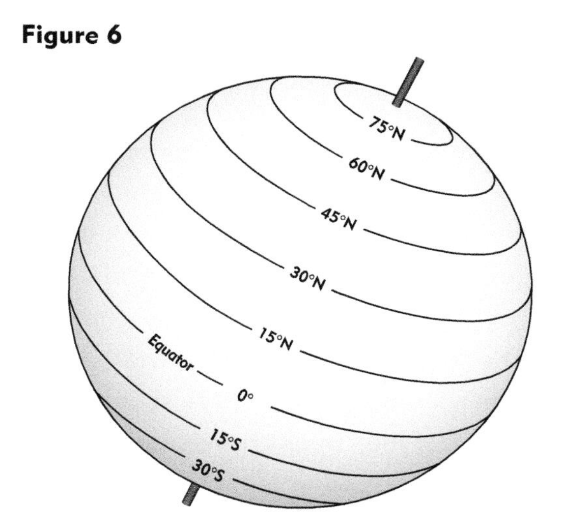

Locating Ourselves in Space: Grid Lines

We're almost ready to begin our odyssey through time and space. But first, we have to be sure we can locate ourselves on the Earth's surface. We'll need another reference system for that.

You've probably used a road map to find a city or some other place. Most road maps have lines that run north-south and east-west. Those crisscrossing lines make a grid. The lines are called grid lines, and maps with grid lines on them are called grid maps.

The grid lines divide the map into sections and make the map look something like a large checkerboard. The spaces between the lines are numbered or lettered. The numbers help us find cities according to their east-west location. The letters help us find cities according to their north-south location. Together, they give us reference points that help describe the location of any place on a grid. For example, on the grid map in **Figure 5**, Oak Bluff is located at C3.

- On the grid map in **Figure 5**, what is the location of Central City? Of North Rapids? Of East Central City?

Locating Ourselves on the Globe: Longitude and Latitude

We can use a similar grid system to find points on a globe. Let's start with the imaginary line known as the equator, which runs around the Earth halfway between the North Pole and the South Pole. *Equator* comes from the word *equal*. As you may already know, the equator is an equal distance from each of the poles. See **Figure 6**.

When you hold a globe and look straight down on the North Pole, you can see most of the Northern Hemisphere. If you look toward the equator from the North Pole, you will see that the circles running around the globe get larger as they get closer to the equator. We call these circles *parallels of latitude.*

All points along a parallel are the same distance from the equator. The parallels tell how far north or south any given point is from the equator. We use the parallels as reference lines. Each parallel has its own number, from zero (the equator) to 90 (each pole). Its number tells how far north or south it is from the equator.

Now look at the globe again, and you'll see a second set of lines that cross the parallels. Rather than running east and west, as lines of latitude do, these lines run north and south. They divide the globe into sections like an orange. The lines are called *meridians.* If we label one of these meridians zero, we can use it to tell how far east or west we are. We do that by simply counting how many meridians east or west of the "zero" meridian we are. The meridians are called the *lines of longitude.* See **Figure 7**.

We saw that the parallels are numbered from 0 to 90 north and from 0 to 90 south. The distances north and south from the equator are called *degrees of latitude.* The distances east or west from the zero meridian are also called degrees, but they are *degrees of longitude.* The lines of longitude run from pole to pole. Zero meridian is also called the *prime meridian.* There are 180 degrees (180°) of longitude west of the prime meridian. There are also 180° of longitude east of the prime meridian.

These intersecting lines of latitude and longitude make a useful grid system to help us find any point on the globe. We can take the same system and use it on flat maps of the Earth, as well.

Imagining the Past

Nothing helps us understand the past quite like good stories. Maybe that's because history *is* the great ongoing human story, one made of countless smaller tales of adventure, struggle, and triumph. These stories whisk us across oceans and ages, and sweep us over continents and centuries. They help us see, in our mind's eye, what happened long ago. They let us put ourselves in the place of people long gone, walk around in their shoes for a while, and glimpse what they might have seen and thought.

In this book, you'll find lots of stories, including some stories in special sections called "Imagining the Past." Some of these stories are myths important to an ancient civilization. Other stories in "Imagining the Past" sections are fiction, but they are based on historical truth. Sometimes they involve imaginary characters in likely historical situations. Sometimes they depict real historical figures whose exact thoughts and words may be lost, but whose thinking we can imagine based on the evidence we have.

As you read these stories, let your mind travel back through time. Pretend for a moment that you're there, standing beside these characters, living as they might have lived. Spend some time in their world. Look around. Live their stories. Imagine the past. That's one way to bring history to life.

Figure 7

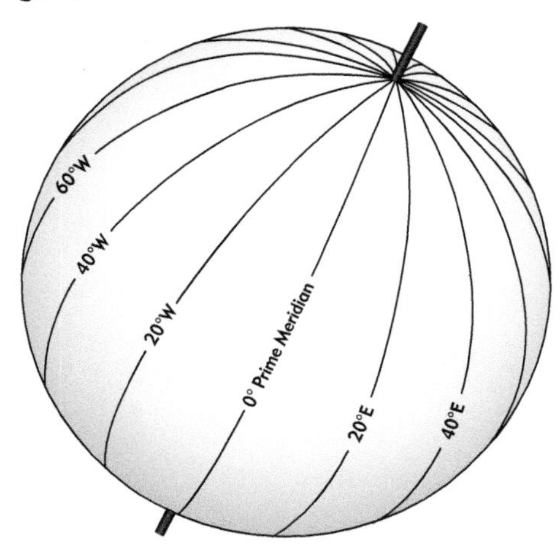

Figure 8

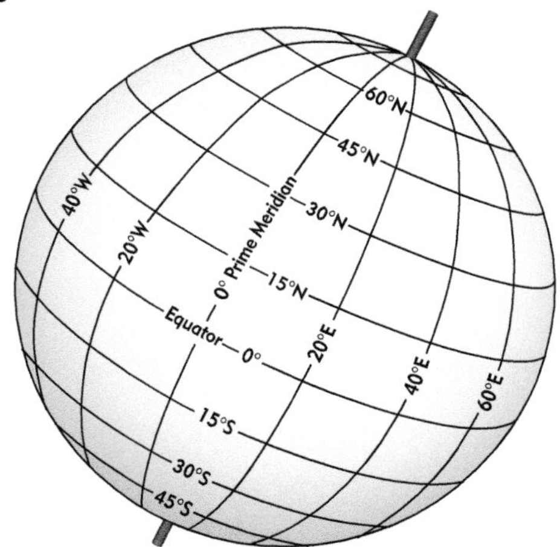

- Look at the picture of the globe in **Figure 8**. Which lines are the lines of latitude? Which lines are the lines of longitude?
- What does *parallel* mean? Why are the lines of latitude called parallels?
- Look again at **Figure 8**, and you'll see the prime meridian. Now pick up your globe and find the prime meridian there.
- On your globe, put your finger on latitude 35° N and longitude 40° E. This is part of the area called the Middle East. Now find the same place on the map in **Figure 9**.
- The city of Baghdad is closest to which of these four locations?
  a) 39° N, 45° E c) 40° N, 35° E
  b) 33° N, 44° E d) 45° N, 33° E
- Look at a globe again. What major city of the world is located near 30° N, 30° E? Now locate that city on the map in **Figure 9**.
- Look at a globe or map of the United States. Which of these four cities is located at about the same latitude as Baghdad?
  New York New Orleans
  Chicago Los Angeles

Now you know how to locate yourself in both time and space. With that information, and with a bit of healthy curiosity, you're ready to begin *The Human Odyssey*.

Figure 9

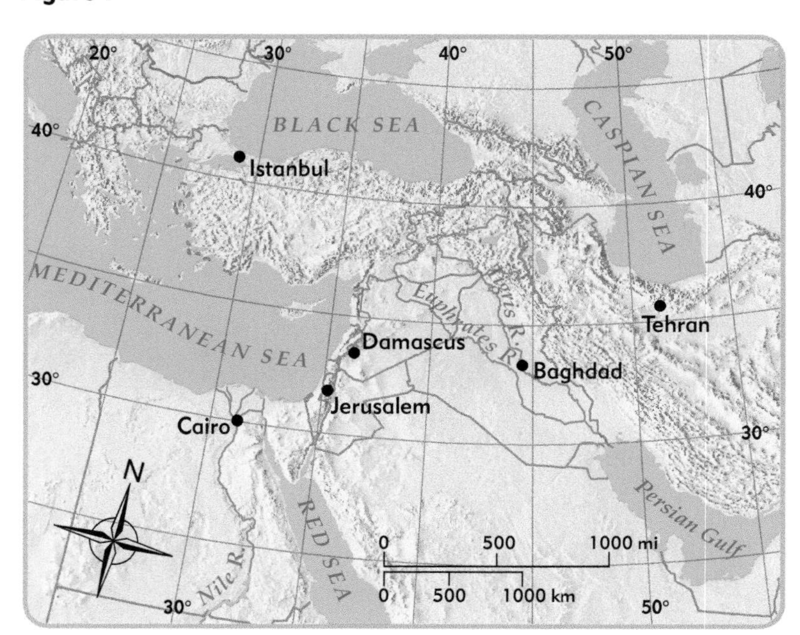

Ice Age paintings of horses and a great bull adorn the wall of a cave in south-western France.

How Civilized! From Hunter-Gatherers to City-Builders

Our human odyssey stretches over many millennia and begins not with history but "prehistory." *Pre-* is a Latin prefix that means "before." Prehistory is the long period of time before human beings could write.

History is the period from which we have written records. The human journey from prehistory to history, from cave dweller to city-builder, was a very long one. In this chapter we'll explore the life of early human beings as they began that journey.

It might surprise you to learn that prehistory is a lot longer than history. For many years, perhaps more than two million years, people inhabited the Earth but had no form of writing. They may not even have had a fully developed language. But that didn't stop early people from figuring out how to make good use of the world about them.

We still don't know a lot about that distant prehistoric age, but what we do know is fascinating. It was a time when human beings became very resourceful indeed. In 1940, four teenagers found that out firsthand.

Stampede on the Wall

One fall day in 1940, four boys in southwestern France made a discovery that amazed the world. In pursuit of their straying dog, they squeezed into a deep hole on a hillside that eventually opened up into a huge cavern. Striking matches, the boys peered around. The flickering light showed they were surrounded by an astonishing array of wild animals. Images of wild oxen, black horses, and red deer raced across the walls of the cave.

Above: This graceful horse gallops across a wall of the Lascaux Grotto in France. Horses were often depicted in cave art.

Right: Many early humans lived in deep caves that offered shelter from the elements.

Only after careful study did it become clear what the boys had discovered. They had stumbled upon nothing less than a prehistoric gallery of art. Who had created these marvelous images on the cave wall? What kind of people lived here? What do we know about their daily lives?

Overcoming Ice and Shaping Stone

The paintings of the Lascaux (lah-SKOH) Grotto, as the cave is now known, were made sometime between 15,000 and 13,000 B.C. This was during the last major Ice Age. The Earth's temperatures had dropped, and vast sheets of ice spread out from the ice caps of the North Pole. The ice shrouded more than a quarter of the Earth's land surface. In some places it was almost two miles deep. Beyond the ice sheets lay semi-frozen tundra and steppe, where long, bitter winters thawed into short, cool summers.

Large herds of animals—the bulls and horses pictured in the Lascaux cave—roamed across this forbidding landscape. Other large creatures strode the steppe as well—bison, mammoths, magnificent two-horned woolly rhinoceroses, and giant deer with antler spans of 10 feet or more.

Early human beings lived here, too. People had been sharing this unfriendly world with the bison, bulls, and deer for thousands of years. While they left no written records, they were adept at surviving in harsh conditions. These people dwelt in caves, in rock shelters of cliffs, and in tents. They used fire to warm themselves and cook. Fire—created by

Ice Ages

From a variety of evidence, scientists have concluded that during the last 570 million years, the climate of the Earth has gone back and forth between warm periods and cool periods. The cooler periods are called "ice ages" because huge sheets of ice covered large areas of the planet. These periods have sometimes lasted several million years. The last major ice age, which began about two million years ago and ended about eleven to twelve thousand years ago, is often called "*The* Ice Age." During this time, glaciers repeatedly advanced over much of Northern Europe, North America, South America, and parts of Asia.

striking two very hard rocks against each other or by drilling a pointed stick into a wooden base—also offered protection against the ever-present danger of wild animals. Lions, bears, and saber-toothed tigers, which often attacked at night, were terrified of fire and kept their distance.

Early human beings made tools out of a variety of materials, especially stone. That's why we call this era the Stone Age. These early humans made finely worked stone spear points and knives, some as sharp and thin as modern steel blades. They also devised scrapers, cutters, perforators, and sewing needles—more than 100 types of tools in all. Using fine animal sinews as thread, they stitched hides and furs together into comfortable clothing and snug tents.

Not everything these people produced was for survival. The people of the Stone Age also took time to fashion necklaces from shells, animal teeth, ivory, and colored pebbles. They sculpted and etched images of animals onto chunks of horn or bone. They made musical instruments, such as flutes, from the bones of birds, bears, and reindeer. And, by the light of lamps that burned animal fat for fuel, they mixed pigments and applied them to the walls of caves like Lascaux to depict the power—and perhaps the religious importance—of the animals of the hunt.

Human Beings on the Move

For the most part, the people of the Stone Age were people on the move. They were *nomadic*, wandering from place to place in search of food. We are still discovering new

Distribution of Tundra Today

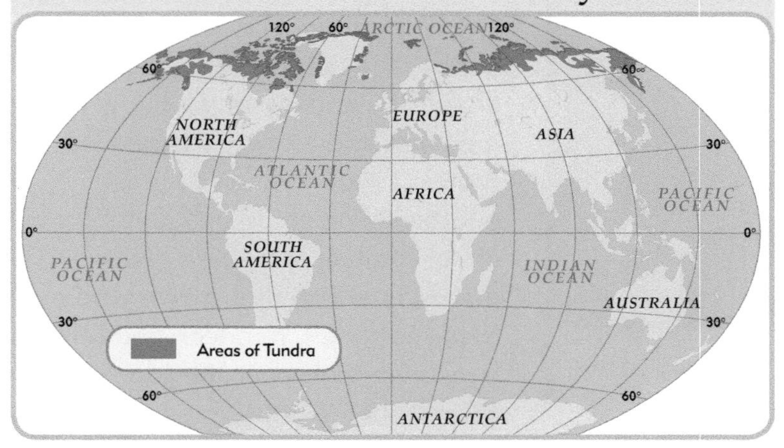

Vast, treeless plains called tundra cover much of the Earth's arctic and subarctic regions.

things about Stone Age people, but we have evidence that they traveled in bands of perhaps 30 men, women, and children.

The members of such bands wore hooded tunics made of hide or fur, and leggings that could be tucked inside hide boots. Spears at the ready, the men usually walked at the head of the band, on the lookout for predators and prey. Women and children followed, sometimes stopping to collect berries, fruits, seeds, roots, or nuts. On their backs the women carried infants and the hides that would provide shelter for the night.

People of the Stone Age were skillful hunters. Working as a group, they could bring down even the

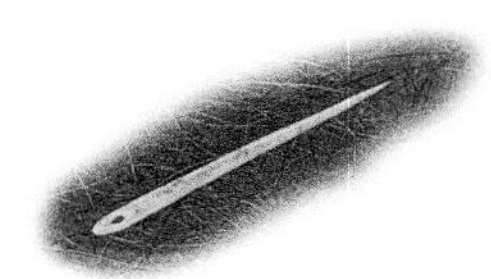

Important Stone Age tools—a flint hand ax, bone needle, and stone mortar and pestle.

How Long Was the Stone Age?

Really long. The Stone Age began about two and a half million years ago, when early people first used small stones to make tools. It would last until nearly 3000 B.C. in Mesopotamia when people began using bronze to make their tools. (You'll soon learn a lot more about the land and people of Mesopotamia.)

Above: Barbed bone harpoons were used for fishing.

Below: Woolly mammoths weighed 8 tons and stood 12 feet tall.

largest prey, such as woolly mammoths. They observed the habits of animals and lay in wait at watering holes and along well-traveled routes. To kill animals in greater numbers than could be killed by direct combat, they used game drives, in which they drove whole herds of horses, reindeer, and other large mammals over the edges of cliffs to their deaths.

Over time, bands of hunter-gatherers began to organize their life according to seasonal patterns. They moved with the migrations of the animals they hunted. They learned when fish and shellfish were most plentiful in the rivers or seas. They speared the fish with sharply barbed harpoons, and caught the shellfish in nets held down with small stones. They knew when and where certain fruits or vegetables would ripen, and year after year, these nomadic peoples regularly returned to gather what gifts the land gave them.

The First Americans

During the last ice age, sea levels were far lower than they are now. Because so much water was frozen in the ice sheets, the oceans shrank and large parts of the seabed lay uncovered. This allowed people to walk between land areas that are today separated by seas.

At that time small nomadic bands crisscrossed the Eurasian landmass, seeking their prey. Their travels took them from Asia to North America. They may have walked across a land bridge about 50 miles long, where there is now a body of water, the Bering Strait. These early transcontinental travelers were probably following big game that had crossed the land bridge before them. But in so doing, they became the first humans to set foot on the North American continent.

North America underwent great change as people spread out across the continent. But the whole Stone Age world was beginning to change —once again, as a result of a shift in climate. Vegetation began to change and life for the hunter-gatherers—for early humans like the cave artists of Lascaux—was about to change forever.

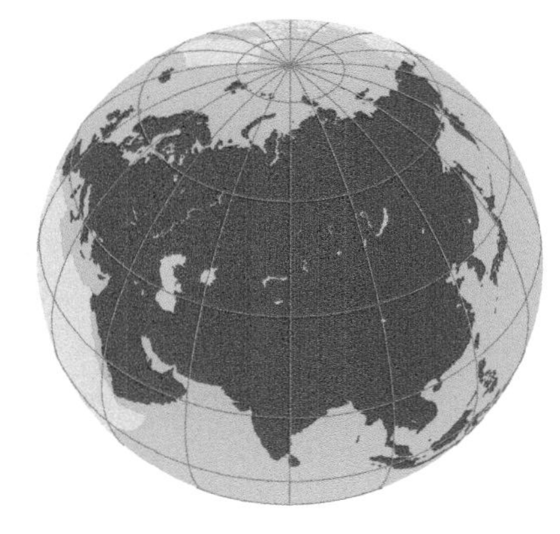

Eurasia *is the name for the landmass formed by the continents of Europe and Asia.*

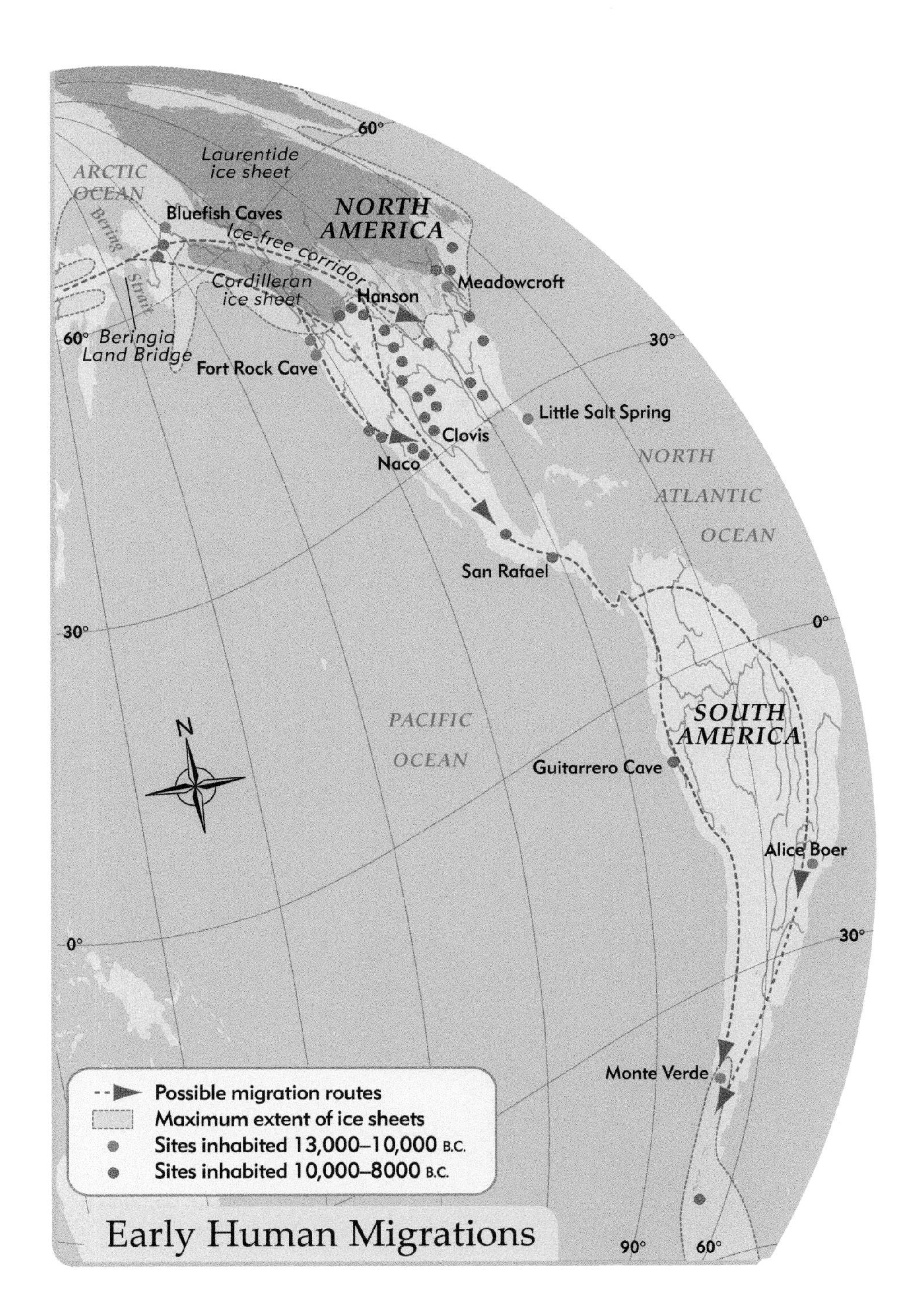

The Move to Mesopotamia

By 10,000 B.C., the Ice Age was drawing to a close. The last of the vast ice sheets had melted. The air warmed and the climate changed. Lands that had been cold and arid grew warm and moist. Thick forests sprang up in northern Eurasia, where ice had once covered the ground. Meanwhile, the grasslands south and southeast of the Mediterranean Sea dried up and disappeared, forming today's great deserts of the Sahara and Arabian Peninsula.

Between these two regions—the forest region in northern Eurasia and the desert region south of the Mediterranean Sea—lay another region. This region was located *east* of the Mediterranean Sea. Ancient Greek travelers called it Mesopotamia (meh-suh-puh-TAY-mee-uh), and we still use that name.

The name *Mesopotamia* comes from Greek words that mean "between rivers." This important region was given that name because it lay between two rivers—the Tigris (TIY-grus) in the east and the Euphrates (yoo-FRAY-teez) in the west.

Mesopotamia is part of an area that today we call the Middle East. The Middle East is situated at the crossroads of three continents—Europe, Asia, and Africa. The Middle East is usually defined as stretching from Turkey in the north to Yemen in the south, and from Egypt in the west to Iran in the east.

- On the map below, locate the Middle East.
- Locate the region called Mesopotamia.
- Locate the Tigris and Euphrates Rivers. Into what body of water do these rivers flow?

Mesopotamia in the Middle East

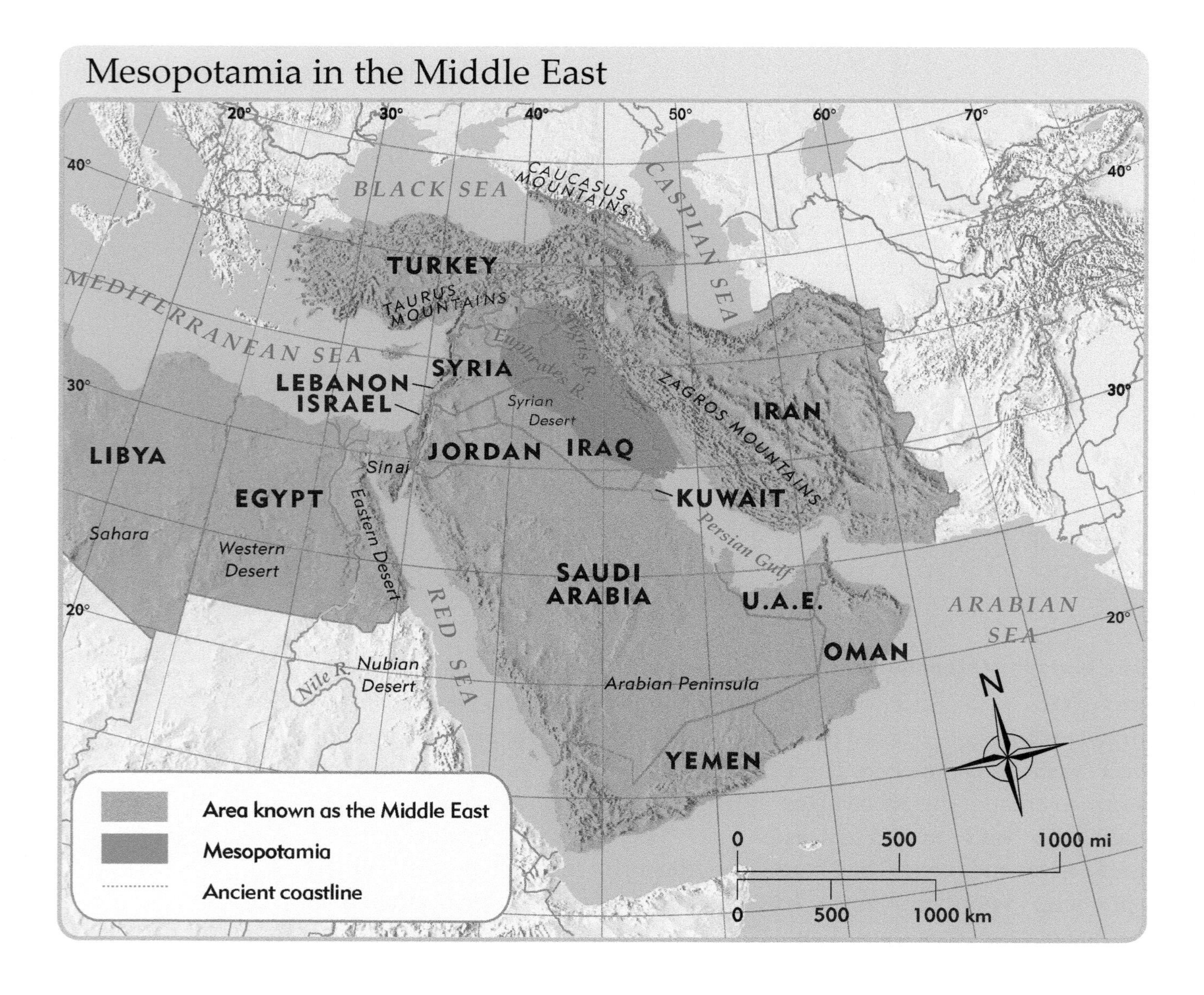

Northern Mesopotamia, with its mountains, hills, and fertile plateaus, was the life-giving part of the Middle East. The land and climate gave people many choices. The summers were long, hot, and dry, just as they are today. The winters were mild and rainy, just as they are today. The melting snow from the mountaintops kept rivers and streams flowing throughout the year. Wild grasses, such as wheat and barley, grew in the spring, and then dried up under the hot summer sun. In the winter, however, rains brought them back to life. Trees grew among the grasses and along the riverbanks. Oak, pine, and cedar covered the sides of the hills and low mountains.

By 10,000 B.C., people were leaving the desert region south of the Mediterranean Sea in search of better lands. Some of these people moved north and west, into the forest region. Others moved into northern Mesopotamia. There, along the banks of the Tigris and the Euphrates Rivers, human beings learned, little by little, to control their physical environment. They learned they did not have to be constantly on the move. They could plant wild grasses and harvest the grain. They could tame wild animals and use their herds for meat. How did these huge changes come about?

The First Farmers

Great changes seldom take place all at once. Human beings were not hunters and gatherers one day, then farmers and herders the next. That change took place very slowly and almost always near river valleys, where the first producers of food had a helping hand from Mother Nature.

The earliest human settlements were usually located in river valleys.

The first people to produce food were probably women. Well before 6500 B.C. in the Middle East, women learned to cut the wheat and barley grasses growing wild along the hillsides. Next, the women made an important discovery. They learned that if they let some of the ripe grain seeds drop to the ground, more grasses would grow in that place the next year. Eventually, the women learned that they could sow those seeds in fields where such grasses did not usually grow. Using sharp-

Mesopotamia Today

Mesopotamia, the ancient hub of civilization, straddles three modern nations—southeastern Turkey, eastern Syria, and a large part of Iraq. What made it one region? The Euphrates and Tigris Rivers. They flow south from mountains in Turkey, through Syria, to the plains of Iraq.

pointed digging sticks, they could break the ground and plant the seeds. With plentiful water and good luck, they could harvest the life-giving grain to make bread or porridge at season's end.

This new endeavor—deliberately planting seeds—was the beginning of farming or agriculture. Some scholars have called this giant step forward an *agricultural revolution.* Agriculture was a very important change indeed. It meant that human beings were beginning to control their physical environment.

People turned out to be very good at that, and soon they tried to improve the way they farmed, expanding the areas in which they could plant. In hilly country between rivers, trees shaded the ground. Few grasses would grow in the shade. That meant the farmers did not have to cut through many tough grass roots. The soil was fairly loose and easy to dig.

In this Mesopotamian stone relief, a man tends a small plant next to the trunk of a palm tree. The relief dates from about 3000 B.C., when many people around the world had learned to grow crops.

These early farmers had seen animals eating the bark of trees. The trees died soon afterwards. The early farmers learned from what they saw. They chose a small area and slashed the bark of all the trees that were growing there. They also dug the ground between the trees and planted seeds for grains. They knew that soon the trees would die and their leaves would fall off. The soil around the dead trees would get more sunlight. Then the grains would grow better than ever before.

The farmers also learned that fire could be a great help in growing more grain. They often burned the bushes and grass under the dead trees. Then they scattered the ashes, which were rich in nutrients, over the soil. That kind of farming is called *slash-and-burn agriculture.* It helped early people keep the soil fertile.

By about 3000 B.C., agriculture was common in many parts of the world. There were farmers in Europe. There were farmers along the northern coast of Africa. There were farmers in India and China, too. Nearly all these farmers planted along the banks of flooding rivers. We'll find out why soon.

- On a globe or map of the world, find those regions where early farming spread—Europe, the northern coast of Africa, India, and China.

The First Herders

With the development of agriculture, the human population grew. Plentiful harvests of wheat and barley provided more food. Fewer people starved.

But the area around the grain fields was not good for wild animals. When people cleared a piece of land, the gazelles, red deer, wild boar, and goats that once roamed these lands lost much of their natural food supply, and so they moved on. As time passed, hunters found fewer and fewer animals to hunt. Hunting had always required great skill. Now hunters needed even greater skill if they wanted to eat meat.

Some men chose to remain hunters, and they followed the animals into different regions. Other men, however, began to share in the work of agriculture. Certainly it was a safer and surer way to get food than hunting. Still others began to catch some of the wild animals that had stayed behind. Instead of killing them, they *domesticated* them—that is, they tamed the animals and kept them in herds. Like agriculture, domestication was another very important change. Keeping a small herd of goats, sheep, or cattle meant that people could be sure of having meat close at hand.

The herders watched the tame goats and cattle feed their young with milk. They thought, "Why don't we milk the goats and cattle for our own food? Why don't we use the sheep's woolly skin for our clothing?" Over the centuries, thoughts like these led many people to become herders. Keeping herds was another way for human beings to gain control over the physical environment.

All over the world, in river valleys and rain-watered lands, herders and farmers were changing the way human beings lived. They no longer had to keep moving from one place to another. They could raise their own food and gather in villages. By 4000 B.C., herders and farmers in Mesopotamia were opening the way for an even bigger and better change.

A young herdsman from modern-day Syria carries a baby goat from his family's flock. People in Mesopotamia began domesticating goats and sheep as early as 9000 B.C.

Herding and Farming in Mesopotamia

What was it like to live in northern Mesopotamia about 4000 B.C.? We don't know many details. We do know that some men and women were living in villages. They tilled the land nearby. Probably they kept a few animals, too. Other men and women lived outside the villages, and kept herds of animals. These herders, however, did not stay in any one place long enough to farm. They kept moving back and forth to find food and water for their animals. In the summer they moved to the hills. In the winter they returned to the low grasslands.

Herding became more important in the grassland areas. There, the

Man's Best and Oldest Friend

"Man's best friend" is also his oldest. Descended from wild wolves, dogs may have been tamed as early as 15,000 years ago, in East Asia. Records from Mesopotamia show that ancient people of that region hunted with a kind of mastiff. Animals domesticated for meat, milk, hides, and fleece were also descended from wild ancestors and tamed in the late Stone Age. Sheep and goats came first, perhaps around 9000 B.C., followed by pigs and cattle.

tough grass roots made digging difficult for the farmers. In other areas, where the soil could be dug up easily, farming became more important. In northern Mesopotamia, herding and farming had become the two important ways of life. People who got all their food by hunting had almost disappeared from the region, following the game animals into other lands.

The herders and farmers discovered that they could help each other. The herders could supply meat to the farmers. In their travels, they could also find things that the farmers needed, like stone for tools. In return, the farmers could supply grain to the herders. They could also give them grain stalks left over from the harvest. The stalks made excellent food for the herds of goats, cattle, and sheep.

More Discoveries

The early farmers had invented a simple spade and hoe. That made their work a little easier than digging with a pointed stick. After a time, farmers also invented a foot plow. This plow had a long curved handle. Just above the blade, it had a small peg. The farmer would put his foot on the peg, and then use his weight to push the blade into the ground. The foot plow was a better tool than the digging stick, the spade, or the hoe. Later, one man pulled the plow with a rope. Another man guided and pushed it.

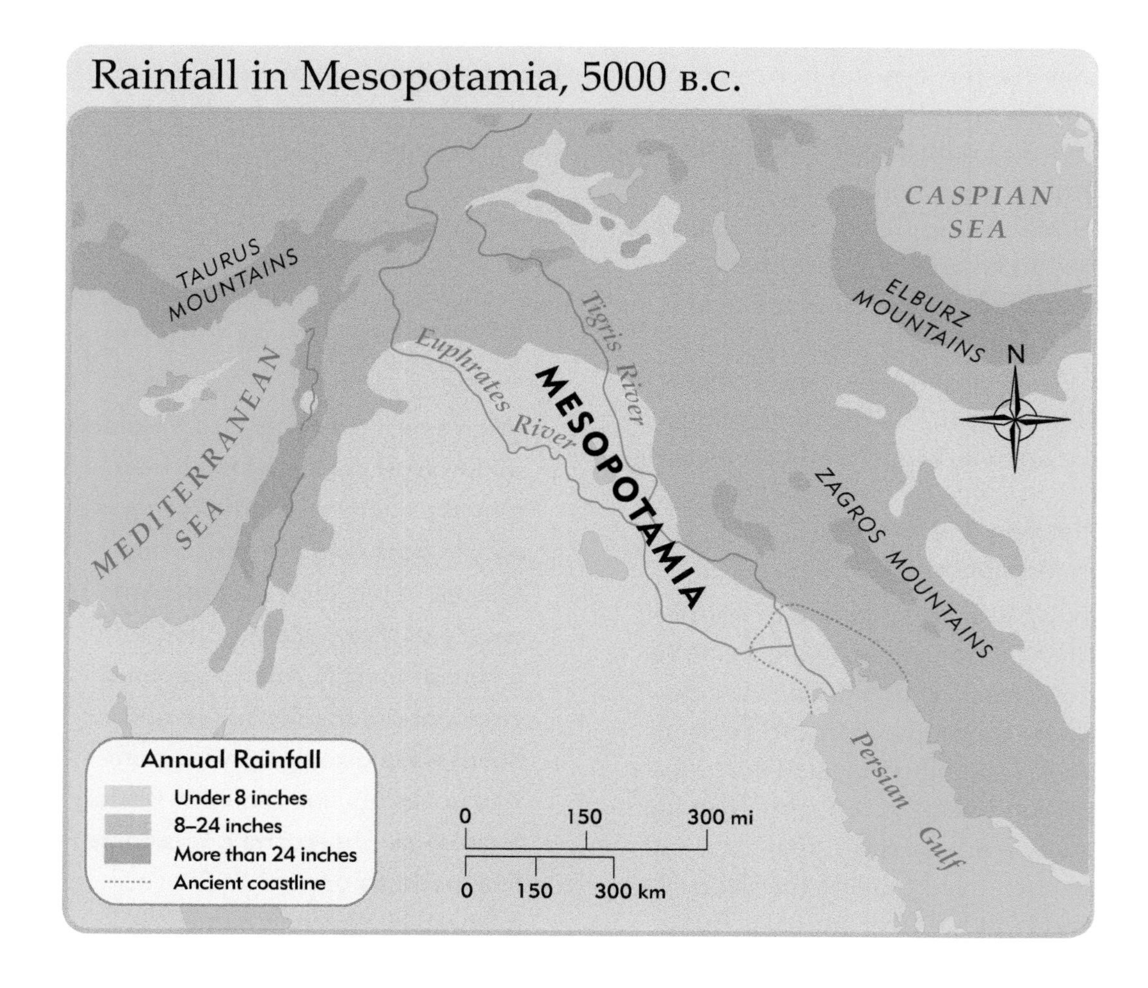

Centuries after the first plow was invented, someone got a bright idea. Instead of a man pulling the plow, why not hitch it to an animal instead? Suddenly there was an easier way to plow the ground. Human beings had learned that by using their minds, they would not have to use their muscles so often.

The Move to Sumer

The population in northern Mesopotamia was growing. As it grew, there was less land for each farming family. After a few years, the soil seemed to be worn out. It would no longer grow good crops. So the farmers cleared more land for new fields by using slash-and-burn agriculture.

To find new land, both farmers and herders began to move out of northern Mesopotamia. They went in every direction. The Tigris and Euphrates Rivers were the "roads" leading to the south. Many farmers followed these roads, setting up new villages in river valleys toward the south.

What was the new land like? The land between the rivers was a floodplain. Every year in the spring, as snows in the Zagros (ZA-grus) Mountains melted, the rivers flooded. After the floodwaters receded, the land was covered by a layer of rich soil. This soil was free of stones and tough roots, and excellent for planting. Since some of the low-lying land was swampy, many kinds of waterfowl and fish lived there. That made for good hunting. And as if to offer dessert and snacks, date palm trees grew wild along the riverbanks.

To better farm the land, Mesopotamian farmers used plows like this one, which is pulled by a team of oxen.

With such abundance, the population in the river valleys kept growing. Once again, growing population meant a growing need for land. Some people pushed even farther south, toward the mouth of the two rivers. There, in southern Mesopotamia, the climate was even hotter and drier.

- Look at the map on page 26. About how much rain fell in southern Mesopotamia in a year?
- How does this rainfall compare to the rainfall in northern Mesopotamia?

In ancient times, the land of southern Mesopotamia was known as Sumer (SOO-mur). To us, arid Sumer with its blistering summers and unpredictable rivers may not seem like a very good place for people to live. Yet Sumer was the land where, for the first time, people really learned to control their physical environment. Let's see how.

Harnessing the River and Irrigating the Land

The people in Sumer had rich soil and wanted to grow crops, but they needed more water. They learned that if they planted wheat and barley in the fall, winter rains would help, but even those rains were not always sufficient. Could human beings invent a way to water their fields? People watched for clues and found them.

Every spring, as you know, the rivers flooded. As the floodwaters receded, they left silt along the riverbanks. Silt is made of sand and soil carried along by the river waters. Year after year, this silt built up until it formed natural levees (LEH-veez), or banks of soil. These levees gave observant men and women the clue they needed to solve their water problem.

Let's exercise our imaginations and travel back in time. We'll spend an afternoon with three farmers in Mesopotamia as they figure out how to make the river work for them.

Taming the River

Imagining the Past

The rush of water sounded friendly, as it sometimes did in Sumer in late spring. Namtar was sure the river would soon subside. But then, Namtar was an optimistic fellow, perhaps because he was the youngest of the three men now sitting on his floor. His older brother, Kur, took a different view.

"That rush will soon turn to a roar," Kur said. He hung his head.

"Cheer up!" said Shullat, Kur's brother-in-law. "Maybe the gods will hold back the flood tide."

As if to disagree, the thunderous rush grew louder. The men stopped to listen. They had planted barley and wheat in the fall, and now the crops were ready to be harvested. If this rising river burst its banks, the plants could drown in a flash flood.

Thinking to distract Kur, Namtar passed him a bowl of sweet, chewy dates.

Kur ignored the offer. He paced and listened as water rushed outside and a light rain sprinkled the hard clay roof.

Shullat, nervous at the sound of rain, reached for the dates.

Kur spoke sharply. "Shullat, you have eaten your share."

"It was my sister Aya who gathered them!"

"And your sister is my wife," Kur replied.

"Then I am sorry my sister married such a greedy man."

"Stop, both of you," pleaded Namtar. "We share the same roof, plow, and field. We are brothers and must try to get along."

"Ah, Namtar," Kur said sadly. "It is just that I worry about Aya and Ubara."

Aya was Kur's wife, and Ubara was their six-year-old son. Last year, after a flood swept away the crops, food was scarce. The little boy grew frail. Somehow the entire family had made it through the winter, but this year's crop was crucial. Without it, Ubara and many others might not survive.

"Why is this land such a cruel master?" Kur cried. "In the hot summer, we roast in the sun, like sheep on the spit. Then comes winter with its thunderous storms. We are careful to plant before the rains begin, but we never know if the crops will be washed away by the spring's flood…." Kur's voice trailed off in despair.

"Surely the gods will be good to us this year," Namtar reassured him. "Surely they will make the river stay within its banks."

But to himself Namtar fretted, *The river, the river—it rules all of us year-round.*

Like Namtar and his brothers, every family in the village planted an acre of land in the fall near the river. They needed the river's precious water for their crops. The villagers knew the river would rise each spring. If the river was kind, it stayed within its banks—banks of soil the river itself built. The water brought the soil downstream and left it at the river's edge. Each year it left behind a little more soil, gradually building earthen banks that helped keep the river in place. As long as the river stayed behind those banks, all would be well. But if the river decided to rush over the banks and across their fields…. Namtar could not bear to think about it.

For another hour, the men listened to the torrent, as the rushing waters rose slowly but steadily higher. At noon, Kur's wife, Aya, entered from the side room and whispered in Kur's ear.

"Would the child have a taste for dates?" Kur answered, reaching for the bowl.

"He has eaten so many that they sicken him," Aya said. She was thinner than grass, as much from a mother's worry as from hunger. "But I will try."

Just then, the shower outside stopped. The sun returned and spread a peach glow across the broad blue sky. Without a word, the three men went outside. As they headed toward their field, other families left their doorways, too, all thinking one thought: Would the river stay in its banks?

"Look, Kur," Namtar said, pointing ahead. "I see puddles of water, but the crops are still there."

"For now," Kur replied. "But has the river peaked?"

The men trod a path past the field, their leather sandals sinking into the black muck. Kur took the lead. Shullat followed next. Twice, he sank and stumbled in the mud. Each time, Namtar helped him catch his balance.

"Slow down," Shullat called, but the anxious Kur moved ahead.

Kur was first to reach the riverbank. Namtar arrived next. Panting with effort, Shullat came last and looked over his brothers' shoulders.

Silently, they stared across the broad river. Agate-colored water raced by. Shullat pointed down to a clump of reeds growing from the bank. "Watch it closely," he said. "If the water level drops below it, we are safe."

"But if the water devours the reeds—" Kur muttered.

Shallat dug his toe in the mud. "If only the river had built its banks higher," he sighed.

"Yes, if only the banks were higher," Namtar said thoughtfully.

Namtar stood on the bank looking north and south along the river, studying its angry water. He studied the bank at his feet, which rose only a few inches above the rushing water. He looked at the field on the other side of the bank, and then back at his brothers.

"I have a plan," he said. "Shullat, go along the riverbank and ask the other families to gather here. Kur, run back to the house. Fetch the cart and all the shovels we use in the field."

Shullat set off, happy to leave the angry river for a while. Kur looked doubtful, but Namtar often had good ideas. Perhaps it was best to trust his brother now.

Soon, 20 families were standing in front of Namtar. He read panic in all of their faces.

"Namtar," one man asked, "why do you call us here?"

"The river rules us," Namtar answered, "but we can rule the river."

"Why say such things?" a widow called. "You will only anger the gods." The villagers muttered in agreement.

"We work together," said Namtar, "or we all starve." Just then, Kur arrived, pushing a two-wheeled cart loaded with shovels. Namtar grabbed a shovel, scooped up some wet earth, and threw it on top of the riverbank. He scooped up another shovel-full, then another, then another. Each one he threw on the riverbank.

"Do you see?" he asked.

The crowd was silent. Like many good ideas, it seemed too simple to work.

Finally one farmer said, "You are right! We can make the banks along the river stronger and higher!"

"But we don't have much time," Namtar said. "We must protect the northern field first."

"That would be mine," the widow said.

"Yes, otherwise it will flood the fields to the south. So, we'll all get our carts and our shovels and take them to your field. We'll build up the bank there first. If the river rises, at least we will have saved the widow's field. Those crops we can share at harvest time."

"And after the river goes down," Shullat said, "we will have all summer to work on each other's banks. With no flooding, our fields should bring a good yield—perhaps enough to set aside for the future."

Kur shook his head, thinking of his child, Ubara, weak and hungry. Namtar seemed to read his brother's troubled mind. He put his hand on Kur's shoulder. "At worst, next winter might be lean, Kur. Still, we will have enough food, I am sure of it. At best, we can store the extra food, and Ubara need not be hungry again."

Kur seemed unconvinced. "How can you be so sure of any of this?"

Namtar glanced at the spot on the bank where he had thrown a bit of earth. It barely seemed any higher, but if they all worked together, there was hope. And what was a man without hope?

"Our dams will work," Namtar said confidently. "The crops will grow. I am sure of it!"

In this story, Namtar, Kur, and Shullat built up the natural levees. They worked with their neighbors to make the levees higher and stronger to protect the fields from severe spring floods.

In time the people of Mesopotamia learned to use the levees in another way. When crops needed additional water in the winter, farmers could poke holes in the levees. The water would come pouring out. People could dig little channels to carry the water to their crops. As the years passed, hardworking men and women of Sumer made these little channels bigger. Eventually the channels became canals that ran for miles and miles, bringing water from the levees to the crops. This way of watering the land is called *irrigation*. Because of irrigation, the Sumerians (soo-MEHR-ee-uhns) did not have to depend entirely on rain to water their crops. Human beings were taking more and more control over their physical environment.

As his ancestors have done for millennia, this farmer uses irrigation ditches—and the Euphrates River—to water his dry fields.

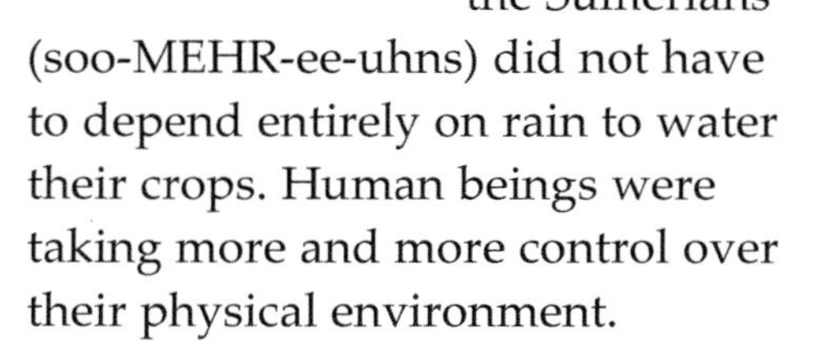

Creating a Surplus

The farmers of Sumer had fertile soil. Thanks to the floods, the soil stayed rich. It produced good crops. Thanks to irrigation, the crops grew even in dry weather. The farmers of Sumer had animals to pull their plows. All these things helped the Sumerians reap bigger harvests and do more work than human beings had ever done before.

As a result, the farmers grew more wheat and barley than their families needed to eat. When you have more than you need, you have a *surplus.* Year in and year out, the Sumerians grew surplus crops. *This surplus of food was an important part of humanity's great leap forward.*

Dividing the Labor

Think about it—why does it make such a difference to have a surplus of food?

If you don't have enough food, then almost everyone has to work to get enough food—hunting or gathering or growing—just to survive. But in Mesopotamia, when there was a surplus of food, some men and women were free to do other jobs. They no longer had to till the soil or tend herds.

Some people repaired the levees. Some dug the canals. Some became pottery makers and jewelers. Some made dried bricks of mud and used them to build houses. Others became priests. Still others took charge of groups of workers and showed them how to work together more efficiently.

Human beings were beginning to divide up the work. Everyone did something important, but not everyone had to do the same thing. *The division of labor was another important part of humanity's great leap forward.*

Building Cities

The people of Sumer also began to live closer together. They embarked on big projects like farming, irrigating, and building houses.

All these big projects were hard work. They required planning and the organization of many people, each doing a special job. These jobs meant that thousands and thousands of people could settle down permanently. The people no longer had to move on to find rich soil. Men and women, their children and grandchildren, could all stay in the same area.

And so it became possible for human beings to build cities. Sumerians seem to have been the first people to build cities. You'll be learning a lot more about Sumerian cities with their solid walls, fine temples, and monumental gates. *Cities were another important part of humanity's great leap forward. With the building of cities, we can truly say that "civilization" had begun.*

Sumer: Cradle of Civilization

What do we mean by civilization? The English word *civilization* comes from the Latin *civitas,* which means "city."

In 4000 B.C., human beings in many parts of the world still hunted their prey, gathered nuts and berries, grew wheat or rice, tended sheep, and lived in caves, huts, or tents. They painted and drew. They had language and song. They had family groups and their own customs. But did they have civilizations? No.

When we talk about *civilization,* we will be talking about many people living together in one area.

Three things must be true about these people:

1. They must have a *surplus of food.*
2. They must have *division of labor.*
3. They must have built *cities.*

Top: By the fourth millennium B.C., the people of Mesopotamia were living in cities. This aerial view shows the remains of the great urban center of Ur.

Above: An archaeologist's model of a typical Sumerian home.

"Civilization" exists only if all three of these things are true about a group of people.

What was the first civilization? Historians think it was probably Sumer. In the land between two rivers, people first learned how to control floodwaters and plant more food than they needed to survive. They began to divide their tasks and build cities. For these reasons, historians often call Sumer the world's first "cradle of civilization."

How do we know about the Sumerians' achievements? For a long time, we didn't. Sumer was a great civilization in its time, but it lay buried and forgotten for centuries. Its rediscovery was one of the great finds of history. We'll learn about that next.

This magnificent bull's head is made of hammered gold and lapis lazuli. It was unearthed in the Sumerian city of Ur and dates from about 2500 B.C.

Unearthing Sumer

The people who study our human odyssey, who try to understand what happened in the past and why, are called historians. History is the story of change over time. It's full of puzzles waiting to be solved and secrets waiting to be unearthed. In order to be a good historian, you have to be part detective, ready to hunt down all kinds of clues that may have been hiding for thousands of years. You have to dig up the evidence.

You have to act a bit like a scientist, too. You need to make sharp observations, come up with logical theories, and then test your ideas. Do those ideas explain what we know about the past? Do they help us understand the evidence we have about ancient times? It's tricky, because you can't set up a nice, neat experiment in a laboratory—the past is much more slippery than that!

A good historian also has to be something of a storyteller, ready to use imagination to recount the past. But history is not fiction. In history, you study real characters, settings, and events. What inspired these people? What made them think as they did? Why did they build this temple, or bury that ship, or paint those figures on the cave walls?

Above all, historians are always ready to follow a trail of questions. You often start out with one question and start digging to find an answer. You might be literally digging up old ruins, or doing research as you dig through books and papers. Pretty soon you run across interesting clues, and those clues raise more questions. Suddenly you realize that you've asked the wrong question to begin with, or that your new questions are

In this chapter you'll learn about the region called Mesopotamia, birthplace of the world's earliest civilization.

Top: This delicate ostrich eggshell vase was—remarkably—found intact in a Sumerian tomb.

Above: Archaeologists search for clues to the past at a dig in Syria.

a lot more interesting. And off you go, digging to find more answers and questions.

So if you like following trails, piecing together puzzles, and discovering tales of high adventure, you've come to the right place.

Let's spend a little time looking at how the mysteries of history get solved. To do that, we're going to go back more than 5,000 years to southern Mesopotamia—to Sumer—which was probably the first civilization on Earth.

The Sumerians accomplished all kinds of marvelous things. But, over time, they were forgotten. Just 150 years ago, no one even knew their name or that such people had ever lived. Even when Sumer was finally rediscovered, it was found by accident. Let's see how this first civilization was unearthed.

The Forgotten People

Today we know many things about the once-forgotten Sumerians. We know something about their cities and ideas, their temples and gods, how they looked and lived. We know about the food they ate, the songs they sang, and the language they spoke. We know all this because historians and archaeologists (ahr-kee-AH-luh-jists) kept digging into the past.

What's the difference between a historian and an archaeologist? They both solve mysteries of ages past and they both use evidence, clues from the past. But they focus on different kinds of clues.

Historians learn about the past in three ways:

- By studying written records, such as old letters, diaries, and books
- By looking at objects from the past, such as weapons, paintings, or tools
- And, in more recent days, by listening to "oral histories," spoken accounts from people who lived at the time

Archaeologists, on the other hand, are the diggers. They burrow into the Earth's surface and scientifically study artifacts. Artifacts are objects that people made and left behind, such as tools, pots, jewelry, musical instruments, and the remains of ancient buildings. Artifacts can tell us a lot about ancient societies that left no written record.

The discovery of Sumer is the story of how historians and archaeologists put together many clues to solve a great mystery. It's a story with many twists and turns. In fact, the people who discovered Sumer started by looking for traces of *other* ancient civilizations. But they kept running into clues that pointed back to an even older culture. They followed the trail of questions and clues further into the past, and eventually it led to Sumer.

Where's the Evidence?

Historians and archaeologists use logic and imagination to reach their conclusions, but their conclusions have to be based on hard evidence. The word *evidence* comes from Latin words that mean "what has been seen." Written accounts, objects, buildings, and even people's memories of their experiences are some of the evidence that guides students of the past.

Babylon was the heart of a powerful Mesopotamian empire during the seventh century B.C. *This picture shows how an artist imagined what the city looked like, filled with palaces and gardens.*

The First Clues: Old Stories

The first clues to the mystery of Sumer were written ones. They were old stories about ancient peoples. But these clues did not lead straight back to the Sumerians. They described other civilizations that flourished in Mesopotamia, civilizations that, as we now know, came *after* the Sumerians. Some of the stories were about an ancient people known as the Babylonians (ba-buh-LOH-nee-uhns).

The Babylonians were named for Babylon (BA-buh-lahn), their greatest city, which they built beside the Euphrates River. The stories told about a time when Babylon was ruled by mighty kings who sent great armies out from the city to conquer other lands. As they grew ever more wealthy and powerful, these kings filled the city with wonderful palaces and grand temples. In the countryside, meanwhile, Babylonian farmers cultivated fields of grain to feed the king, his armies, and the many citizens.

- Find Babylon on the map on pages 38–39. In what part of Mesopotamia was it?

Before we get back to Sumer, let's read two very old accounts of Babylon. Remember, for thousands of years, these accounts and some other stories were all that people knew about this ancient civilization. They had only these written accounts, but no hard evidence of the people and places described in the writings.

Our first account of ancient Babylon comes from Herodotus (hih-RAHD-uh-tus), a great Greek historian of the ancient world.

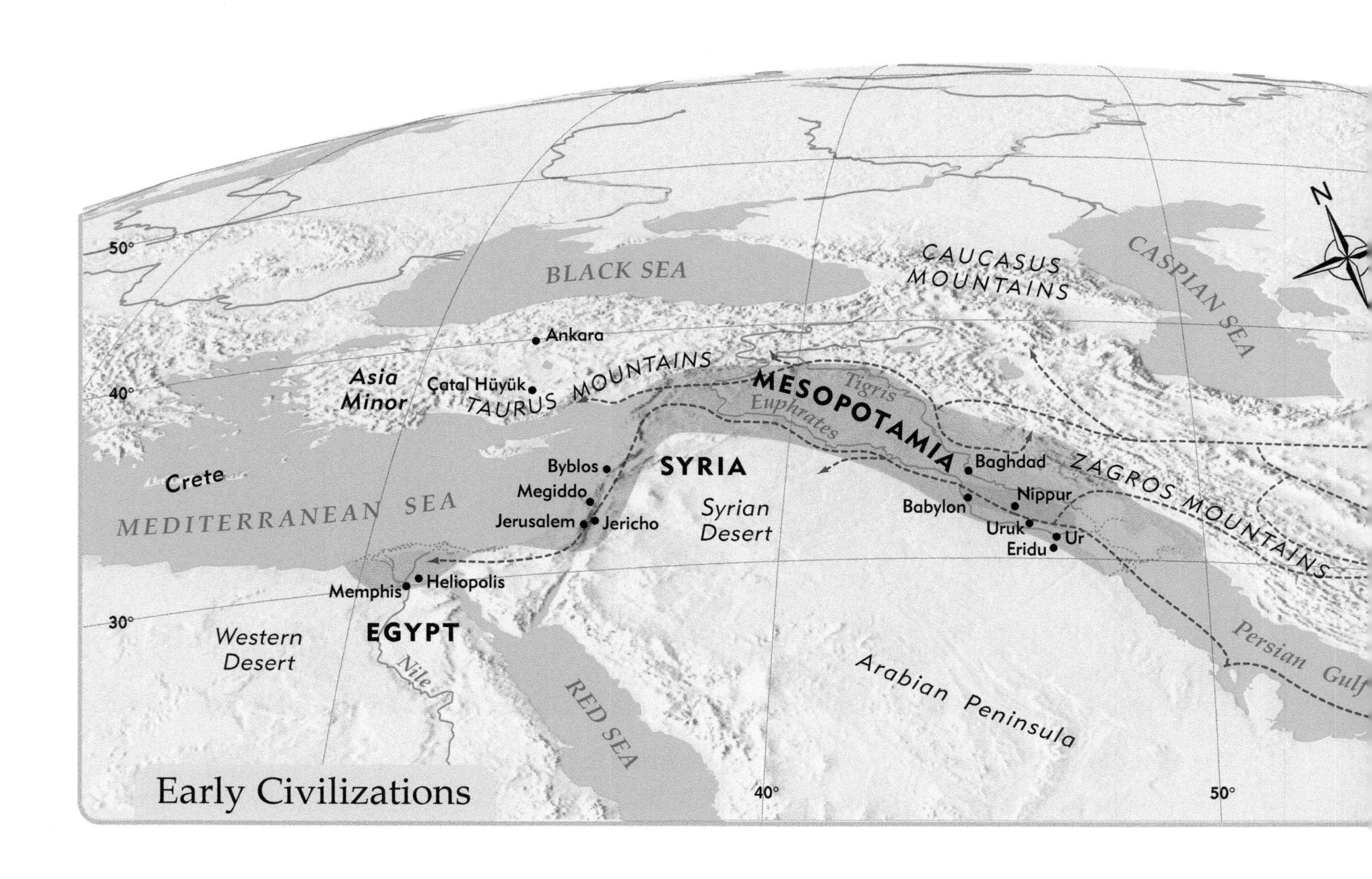

How Herodotus Saw Babylon

Very little rain falls in Babylon. There is just enough rain to make the grain begin to grow. After that, the plants must be irrigated with water from the Euphrates River. The waters of the Euphrates do not flood the grain fields naturally, but must be spread across the land by canals, buckets, and hard work. The hard work produces wonderful results. Of all the countries that I have seen, no other produces so much grain.

The most wonderful thing of all, next to the city itself, is that the vessels sailing down the river to Babylon are circular, and made of hides. They build them out of the branches of willows growing in the region above Babylon, which they then cover with hides. They line these round boats with straw, load them with merchandise, and float them down the river.

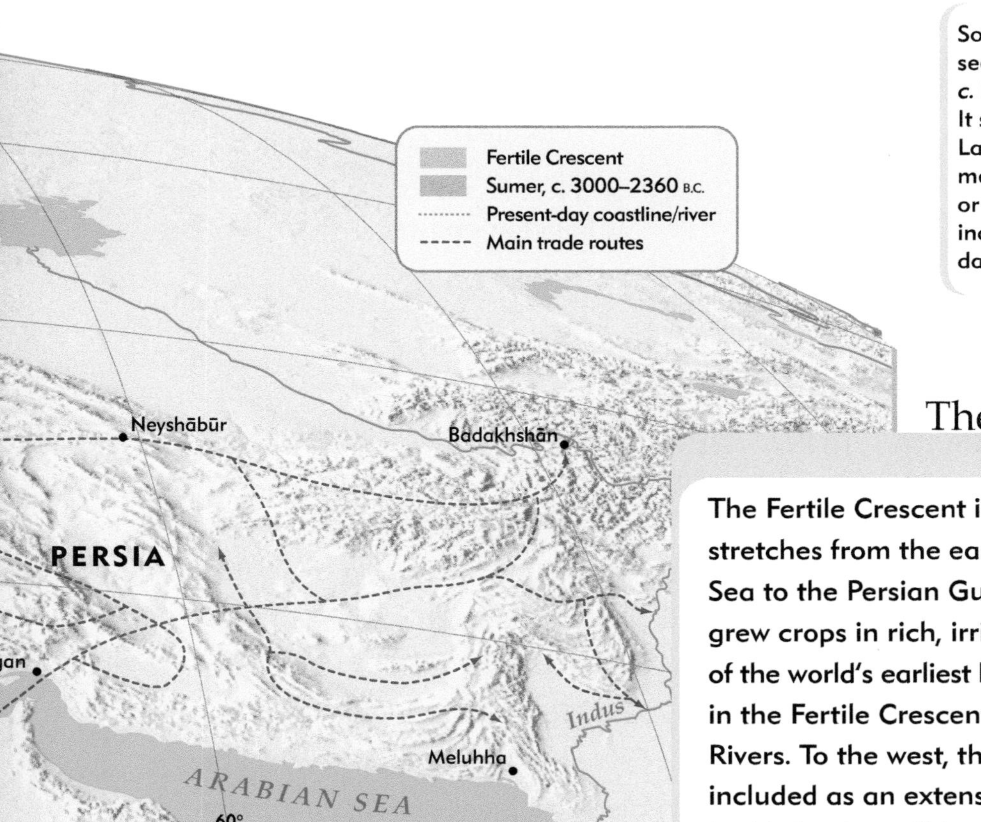

Sometimes you will see the abbreviation *c.* before dates. It stands for the Latin word *circa*, meaning "about" or "around," and indicates that a date is approximate.

The Fertile Crescent

The Fertile Crescent is a crescent-shaped region that stretches from the eastern shores of the Mediterranean Sea to the Persian Gulf. In this region, ancient peoples grew crops in rich, irrigated farmlands, and built some of the world's earliest known civilizations. Sumer emerged in the Fertile Crescent along the Tigris and Euphrates Rivers. To the west, the Nile River Valley of Egypt is often included as an extension of the Fertile Crescent. Later in this book you'll learn about the civilization built by the ancient Egyptians along the Nile. Locate the Fertile Crescent on the map.

The boats mainly carry casks of wine. Each vessel is steered by two paddles, held by two men standing upright. Some vessels are very large, some small; the largest carry a cargo of about 14 tons. Each vessel has a live donkey aboard. The larger ones have more. After they reach Babylon, they sell their cargo, auction off the boats' frames and straw, pile the hides on the donkeys, and go home by land. The swift current in the river makes floating upstream impossible. For that reason they make their boats of hides instead of wood, and when they get home they construct more vessels.

Other stories about the Babylonians are found in the Bible. For example, the second book of Kings tells about armies that marched out of Babylon to conquer the city of Jerusalem. The mighty Babylonian king at the time was called Nebuchadnezzar (neb-yuh-kud-NEH-zur).

- Find the city of Jerusalem on the map on pages 38–39. Is it in Mesopotamia? Where is it located?

Here is part of a biblical account of Babylon's power.

An Attack on Jerusalem

In those days the servants of Nebuchadnezzar came up to Jerusalem and besieged the city. And Nebuchadnezzar, the king of Babylon, came to the city while his servants were attacking it. And the king of Jerusalem gave himself up to the king of Babylon. He gave up himself and his mother, and his servants, and his princes, and his palace officials. The king of Babylon took him prisoner in the eighth year of his reign. He also carried off all the treasures of the king's house and cut in pieces all the vessels of gold in the house of the Lord. He carried away captive all of Jerusalem. He carried away all the princes and all the brave warriors, 10,000 captives, and all the craftsmen. And none were left, except the poorest people of the land. Thus he carried away the king to Babylon and the king's mother, the king's wives, his officials, and the chief men of the land. And he took them all into captivity from Jerusalem to Babylon.

Through the centuries, many people remembered the stories of ancient times, but they didn't remember much about the ancient peoples themselves. People lost track of the long-ago civilizations. The great cities, the magnificent palaces and temples, the lush gardens and rich fields of grain—all disappeared. Now the land was dry, dusty, and brown. It was a poor land. All that was left of the greatness of Babylon and Mesopotamia was a handful of old stories.

The Second Clues: Mysterious Marks

About 400 years ago, an Italian scholar named Pietro della Valle (PYEH-troh DAYL-lah VAHL-lay) went to southern Mesopotamia looking for proof that the old stories were true. When he arrived, he saw that the land was very flat. Yet, here and there, he saw great mounds that

rose up to break the flatness. The people who lived in Mesopotamia called these mounds *tels*.

Della Valle wondered what the tels could be, and he began to poke around. Near one of them, he found some square objects covered with strange marks. Looking closer, he realized that the objects were bricks. The marks on the bricks looked like the footprints of birds walking over wet sand.

When Della Valle went home to Italy, he took some of the bricks with him. There, other scholars studied the strange marks and concluded they were a form of writing made by an ancient people. They called this writing *cuneiform* (kyou-NEE-uh-form) because each of the marks was shaped like a wedge. Cuneiform comes from the Latin word *cuneus*, which means "wedge."

The bricks were an exciting discovery. They showed that people had once lived in southern Mesopotamia. Could these inscribed bricks be from ancient Babylon? No one understood what the marks meant, but the scholars hoped that someday someone would figure out how to read them. Then they could learn much more about the people who had left behind this strange form of writing.

The Third Clues: Tels and Tablets

Years passed. People found more and more bricks with the strange writing on them. They found them in different parts of Mesopotamia, usually near tels. Naturally, scholars became more and more interested in the tels. They scratched their heads and asked themselves what the mounds were, and how they got there.

The archaeologists starting digging, and before long they made a startling discovery. Every tel was a cross section of life through the ages. As they dug deeper, archaeologists realized that each tel held the ruins of a city rebuilt in a single place time and again. The deepest layers showed the earliest constructions. These ancient mounds were scattered all around southern Mesopotamia. They had been covered up for centuries.

The tels were composed of broken clay pottery, mud brick, dirt, and sand. There were few stones

Above: A clay tablet covered in cuneiform script.

Below: The remains of Ur rise above the sands of modern-day Iraq.

inside them because rock was scarce in southern Mesopotamia. To build their homes, the ancient people had to use materials they had at hand. For the most part, they worked with bricks made of river mud and clay.

The ancient peoples built their homes on high ground for protection from floods. When it rained, mud and clay from the bricks in their homes washed into the street. Little by little, over many, many years, the street level got higher. Meanwhile, the houses gradually wore down. It was easier to build new houses than to repair the old ones, so the old houses were leveled, and people put up new buildings where the old had stood. Over the years, the tels grew higher and higher.

All sorts of objects ended up being buried in the old houses—dishes, toys, jewelry, tools, and clay tablets. As time passed, most of them were broken, so usually just fragments were left behind.

Life was often hard for the archaeologists digging into the tels in Mesopotamia. Many grew sick, and some even died. At times sandstorms would cover up weeks and weeks of work. Sometimes the archaeologists didn't have enough money to stay in Mesopotamia for very long. The early archaeologists were sometimes able to dig through only the top layer of the tels.

But through hard work and persistence, the archaeologists did overcome many of their problems. They found the remains of old buildings, temples, statues, and tools. They also found clay tablets. Clay is a curious material. Out in the open, the rains will wear it away quickly. Yet clay that has been baked and buried under the earth can last for a very long time. The tablets that the archaeologists found were thousands of years old and covered with strange marks—the very same kind of writing that Della Valle, the Italian scholar, had found on the bricks. The archaeologists began to realize that the clay tablets might be the books of the ancient world!

The archaeologists still did not know about the Sumerians. They were still looking for the ancient civilizations, such as Babylon, described in the old accounts from Herodotus, the Bible, and other writings. But since no one could read the cuneiform, the clay tablets held onto their secrets.

These two luxury items were found beneath the Mesopotamian sands. The stunning multicolored necklace sparkles with gold, carnelian, malachite, and lapis lazuli. The 20-square board game is made of shell, lapis lazuli, and red limestone.

The Fourth Clue: A Key to the Strange Writing

The cuneiform writing was different from anything else historians and archaeologists had seen before. No one knew how to *begin* to read it. The scholars would need another clue to decipher all the strange symbols. It came not from the tels, or even from Mesopotamia itself. The key to cuneiform writing turned up in another part of the Middle East, in Persia (PUR-zhuh).

- Find Persia on the map on pages 38–39. What once was Persia is now the country called Iran. Locate Iran on an up-to-date map or globe.

At the foot of the Zagros Mountains of Persia, a huge cliff held a secret. In ancient times, Darius (duh-RIY-us) the Great, a Persian king, carved a message on this rock face. He wanted to make sure that everyone knew he was a great king, so he had the message carved in three languages. All three languages were written in cuneiform.

The writing stood about 300 feet above the ground, so the first challenge archaeologists faced was getting close enough to study it. Three hundred feet is about as tall as a 30-story building, so it was no easy task to get a good look at the writing on this sheer cliff. With a little ingenuity and a good dose of courage, an Englishman named Henry Creswicke Rawlinson rigged a system using long ladders, cables, and hooks. Then, dangling from the end of a rope, Rawlinson copied the writing.

The toughest work still lay ahead. Scholars had to figure out what the writing said. Rawlinson had a bright idea. He knew that many writings of Persian kings began like this: "So-and-So, the great king, the king of kings, the son of So-and-So…" Maybe the cuneiform writing also began with these words, the scholar suggested. So he went to work studying the cuneiform to test his idea.

The order of the marks told him that he was right. Now that they had a key, other scholars could figure out one of the messages. It described the king's victories in battle and how he had gained his throne. Perhaps they could use that message as a key to translate the other two messages. One of those two messages was written in the language of ancient Babylon. Scholars compared the Babylonian message with the writing on the tablets from southern Mesopotamia. They matched!

Scholars used proper nouns and their knowledge of the first inscription to help them decipher what the second Babylonian cuneiform text said. They suspected, though, that cuneiform was not designed for writing in Babylonian, because in some cases there was an awkward fit between signs and pronunciation. That made them wonder if the Babylonians had "borrowed" their writing from an earlier and separate people—a people who used the third language on the mountain. Can you guess whose writing the Babylonians "borrowed"?

The cliff where Darius the Great had his legend carved in cuneiform, in three different languages.

Step by step, the scholars had managed to find the earliest writings of all. Years later they would decipher these writings. Once they learned how to read them, a whole new world opened up for them. The clay tablets gave up their secrets, leading the archaeologists back past the Babylonians to the people who had invented cuneiform writing—the Sumerians. The mystery of Sumer was almost solved.

The Fifth Clue: Digging Deeper

Archaeologists finally put together the last pieces of the puzzle. As they dug into the tels of southern Mesopotamia, they unearthed the ancient cities of Babylon, and then older and older artifacts. At last they came to the cities of Sumer.

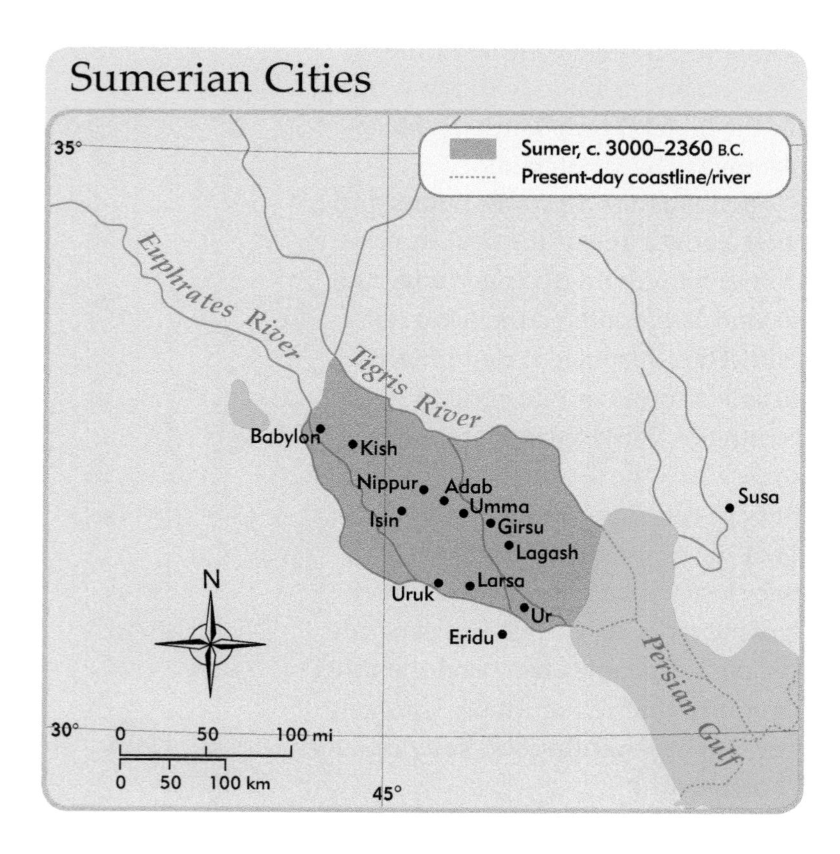

The archaeologists went to work studying the Sumerian artifacts and were astounded to find that many were made before 3000 B.C. People all over the world were amazed. Civilization in Mesopotamia was older than anyone had dreamed. The archaeologists had discovered remains from the earliest known civilization on Earth.

Often, the archaeologists could not figure out exactly what they had found. The artifacts had been buried for thousands of years, and many had been crushed by the weight of the soil on top of them. The pieces were mixed with dirt and clay. Archaeologists tried to remove their discoveries without breaking them into even smaller pieces. Sometimes it took hours to remove a tiny piece of a single object.

The teams of archaeologists working in southern Mesopotamia found all sorts of Sumerian treasures—helmets and gold crowns, gold drinking cups, daggers, harps, and silver jewelry. These artifacts show that the Sumerians had developed many skills and talents. And yet, for thousands of years, all this evidence of a thriving civilization lay buried and forgotten beneath the sand and dust of ages.

What Happened Here?

Sir Leonard Woolley was a British archaeologist who spent 12 years, from 1922 to 1934, excavating the Sumerian city of Ur (uhr). The map of Sumerian cities on this page shows where Ur was located.

Woolley made a discovery that excited the whole world. Deep in the ruins of Ur, he found 16 pits, which he called "the royal tombs." At the bottom of each lay the skeletons of many men and women. The pits were grave pits.

Woolley came upon surprise after surprise in the pits. He found the remains of soldiers with copper helmets on their heads and spears at their sides. He found lyres and harps and the musicians who had played them, their songs silenced forever. There were wagons with the bones of their drivers in them, and the bones of oxen lying in front.

In one tomb, the body of a woman was set apart from the others. She wore a fantastic headdress of gold and large crescent gold earrings. Her body was covered with beads of gold, silver, and lapis lazuli. Woolley had discovered the remains of a famous queen known as Queen Puabi (poo-AH-bee). The bodies of five men with copper daggers guarded the entrance to her grave, and her ladies-in-waiting slept near her in neat, orderly rows.

Woolley found no signs of struggle or violence, so all the men and women in the grave pit must have died peacefully. What did it mean? Woolley studied the clues to find out. One clue seemed especially important. Next to each body was a little cup. After studying all the clues, Woolley concluded that first a large, deep hole was dug in the ground, with a dirt ramp leading down into it. Queen Puabi's body was placed in a stone tomb in the grave pit. Then all the queen's servants went down the ramp, almost certainly knowing as they descended that they were going to die, and perhaps believing they would serve their queen in the world beyond. When they were all in the pit, each one drank from a cup that probably held some kind of drug that put them to sleep. While they were asleep, the pit was filled with dirt. Then the funeral was over.

We may never know for sure if Woolley's explanation was right. We do know that the grave pits were dug about 4,500 years ago, and that their treasures can still be seen today.

A Mystery Is Solved

Archaeologists and historians want to know much more about the life of the ancient Sumerians. Perhaps in time they will discover a civilization that developed even earlier than Sumer. But at least one great mystery has been solved. Sumerian civilization—forgotten for centuries—has been unearthed.

Three golden treasures discovered by Sir Leonard Woolley in the royal tombs of Ur—a queen's headdress, a goblet, and a warrior's helmet, all from around 2500 B.C.

Ancient Sumer lies in the modern-day nation of Iraq. In the late twentieth and early twenty-first centuries, Iraq was ravaged by tyranny and war. Excavations of Sumer stopped in 1991 after the Persian Gulf War. Archaeologists hope to go back to Iraq and resume their work as soon as they can.

This bronze figure depicts a Sumerian king of the third millennium B.C. *He holds aloft a basket of earth for making bricks, representing his role as the restorer and builder of temples to the gods.*

Working, Trading, and Building in Sumer

We've seen how historians go about the business of piecing together the past. They follow a trail of questions, always seeking evidence to answer those questions. Sometimes a question leads in unexpected directions.

You've seen, for example, how historians and archaeologists started out asking questions about Babylon and stumbled onto Sumer! Now let's take a closer look at mysterious Sumer, the place where civilization began.

We'll have to do some more detective work. After all, to reach back 5,000 years, we need to ask some probing questions. How did the Sumerians use the land? What did they produce? What kinds of jobs did they do? Did the Sumerians believe in one god or many? Could they read and write? Who governed them? Did they have laws? These are the sorts of questions we'll be asking to discover more about Sumerian culture.

Culture, Culture Everywhere

Every society has a culture of its own. A *culture* is a people's whole way of life. Their culture includes the things they do and the ideas that guide them. It includes their habits and customs, their religion and education, their art and music.

Our own society has a unique culture. The books you read, the music you hear on the radio, and the shows you see on TV are all part of our culture. So are the laws we have, and our ideas about right and wrong, and the lessons taught by schools and churches. The language we speak and the ways we communicate with each other—from using telephones and the Internet to magazines and

A society's culture includes its artwork, such as this Sumerian shell plaque of two goats.

Questions to Ask About a Culture

1. Geography
What is the land like? How have people used the land? Where do people live?

2. Economy
What goods are produced? How are goods produced? How are goods exchanged or traded? Who benefits from trade? Is money used? How is wealth distributed?

3. Religion and Philosophy
What do the people believe about God or the gods? What do they believe about the meaning of life? What do they believe about right and wrong? How do their beliefs affect their lives?

4. Knowledge, Education, and the Arts
Have the people developed any new knowledge? What kind of knowledge do they think is important? What can we learn about them from their painting, sculpture, building, music, or writing? How do they communicate with each other? Can people read? Are there schools?

5. Government and Laws
How are the people governed? Do they have laws? Who holds power and how is power distributed?

6. Society
Do the people live in groups such as families or clans? Are there rich people and poor people? Are there many in the middle? Are there slaves?

7. Technology
What major inventions or innovations have been made? For what purposes? How have these inventions and innovations changed life in this society?

8. History
Is there much change in the society? In what ways is society changing? Is the society changing slowly or quickly?

advertising—are all part of our culture today. Since a culture is a people's whole way of life, it includes many different things.

The chart on this page lists important questions that can be used to study any culture. In this chapter, we'll ask some basic questions about geography and economy to take a closer look at ancient Sumer. In later chapters, we'll ask more questions that guide us in our study of past cultures. So take a moment to read over the chart and make sure you understand all the key words.

Now we're ready to begin our detective work. We know what questions to ask about the Sumerians. Let's see if we can find some answers.

Putting the Land and Water to Work

The Sumerians learned to do something quite amazing for their times. They figured out how to control the yearly flooding of the Tigris and the Euphrates Rivers. They built thick earth walls, or levees, to hold back the waters of the spring floods. They also dug canals to carry water to the fields in fall and winter. With this system, they had just enough water for their crops.

It surely wasn't an easy task. It must have taken years and years of backbreaking labor under the blazing sun to build all the levees and canals. They managed to do it only by learning to work together. By helping one another, they were able to put the land to good use and take advantage of their physical environment. Only by dividing the labor could Sumerians have created the world's first civilization.

Even people who lived long before the Sumerians knew that the division of labor was a good idea. The early hunter-gatherers divided the work: Women looked after the children and searched for wild grains, fruits, and nuts, while the men hunted and fished.

But the Sumerians went much further than the hunter-gatherers. They carried the division of labor further than any group had before.

We can tell from the levees, canals, and fields the Sumerians left behind that they worked hard to use the resources around them. Large teams of workers cultivated the land, irrigated the fields, and harvested the crops. The results were wonderful. The Sumerians grew plenty of wheat and barley in the irrigated soil. For the first time in history, people produced a surplus of food, more food than people could consume at one time.

The surplus of grain kept increasing, and that profoundly affected life in Sumer. For one thing, it meant that not every Sumerian had to be a farmer. Some of the people were able to grow enough food for everyone, so the rest of the Sumerians were free to work at other jobs. Some became skilled craftsmen, such as carpenters, metal-workers, or potters. Some made cloth. Some tended sheep or raised cattle. Some became priests, soldiers, or doctors. Some became merchants, boatmen, or writers.

All these people were able to eat by doing their own special type of work in exchange for food. Soon more and more people were gathering in villages and towns to sell their wares, store their grain, and bargain for food. Villages and towns became cities.

**The Urban Edge:
Cities Make It Simpler**

These first ancient cities, with mysterious names such as Ur, Uruk, Kish, Lagash, and Umma, became energetic centers of life. They brought several advantages, too. With thousands of people together in a single place, more people could work together to accomplish bigger tasks. More people could do more and produce more. In an "urban" or city environment, many people had a place to store their grain, sell their pots and baskets, fashion their jewelry, and worship their gods.

Division of labor allowed the Sumerians to focus on particular tasks, such as weaving.

Right: This artifact highlights two examples of Sumerian ingenuity. The upper panel shows use of the wheel, which was invented in Sumer. The lower panel depicts soldiers wearing what may have been the world's first body armor.

Below: Like the two merchants in this relief, the Sumerians spent much time trading goods. Their surpluses of food and cloth allowed them to trade for metals and other rare items.

Sumerians proved to be excellent city-builders. By 3500 B.C., they lived in city-states. Each city-state was made of a city and the land around it. Each had its own ruler or king. Sumerian kings were ambitious. They surrounded their cities with high protective walls. Safe from attack by outsiders, they built large granaries and beautiful temples.

These ancient city-states teemed with activity. Sumerian poems tell of "lofty gates" and wide boulevards that were filled with parades and feasts at special times of the year. In the best part of town stood colorfully decorated temples and a few grand homes with flowering gardens and columned courtyards.

The archaeological evidence tells us, however, that most of the streets in Sumerian cities were narrow, winding, and unpaved. Little one-story, flat-roofed houses stood next to two-story buildings. The houses were made of mud brick, which kept the residents cooler in the hot, dry land of Sumer. Craftsmen and merchants sold their wares from open booths that lined the narrow lanes.

Outside the large walled cities lay smaller villages and settlements, along with the rich fields of wheat and barley laced with canals. In the fields, efficient farmers produced food for themselves and the city folk.

Reaching Beyond Their Borders

The land of Sumer had rich soil, water for irrigation, and a long, hot growing season. However, it lacked some important resources. For example, there were no metals and no tall trees, and there was not much stone in Sumer. The Sumerians needed these things, and slowly they learned they could get them through trade.

The Sumerians had a surplus of grain and cloth. So they began to trade some of their grain and cloth for the timber, stone, metals, and other things they lacked.

It took many centuries for trade to develop between the Sumerians and other peoples. During that time, the Sumerians learned how to transport goods over long distances. They invented the wheel, which meant they could use carts and wagons. They discovered how to make sailboats, too, which meant they could transport goods on the rivers and sea.

Sumerian merchants began bringing stone and wood down the Tigris and Euphrates Rivers from the northern mountains. Cedar wood came from the area that is now the country of Lebanon. Gold came from east of the country now called Iran, and possibly from Asia Minor. Silver, copper, and tin came from faraway lands. The beautiful blue stone known as lapis lazuli came from what is now the country of Afghanistan. In later centuries, some Sumerian merchants may have traveled as far as the Indus Valley, where they could buy spices, dyes, and jewels.

With the materials they acquired through trade, the Sumerians did marvelous things. Some craftsmen learned how to make beautiful vases and lamps out of copper and bronze, while others learned how to carve wood or stone. The Sumerians made statues and tools out of their new materials. They made weapons and armor, jewelry and furniture. Archaeologists have uncovered many of the things they made. Take some time to examine the pictures of Sumerian artifacts in this book.

The First Money

Barter was the earliest form of trading. When people barter, they trade without using money. For example, a farmer might give some sacks of grain to a carpenter in exchange for a couple of chairs. Or a doctor might agree to take care of a patient in return for three sheep.

Sometimes barter is still used in today's modern economy. In general, however, we use money to conduct business because it's much more convenient than trading things like sheep or sacks of grain. Money is a medium of exchange. That is, it's something that anyone can take in exchange for goods or work, and then use to buy something else.

As their civilization expanded, the ancient Sumerians needed a medium of exchange, too. For a time they used barley, which is a grain. They learned that almost everyone

A much-desired Sumerian trade item—lapis lazuli.

Producing a Surplus: Tips for Sumerian Farmers

Advice assembled from numerous fragments of Sumerian clay tablets:

1. **Before you begin cultivating your field, watch carefully the opening of the dikes, ditches, and mounts so that you will not flood the field with too much water.**
2. **After draining the water from your field, let shodden oxen trample it for you to loosen the weeds and level the ground.**
3. **While your field is drying, prepare the tools you will need.**
4. **When your field is ready for planting, add an extra ox to the plow ox. When one ox is harnessed to a second ox, the plow is larger.**
5. **After your field has been harrowed and raked three times and the ground pulverized fine with a hammer, tolerate no idleness in your field laborers. If necessary stand over them with a whip and allow no interruptions. Furthermore, do not expect your field workers to serve you. Since they must work day and night for ten days, their strength should be saved for the planting.**
6. **After the grain has begun to sprout, pray to the goddess Ninkilim, and shoo away the flying birds.**

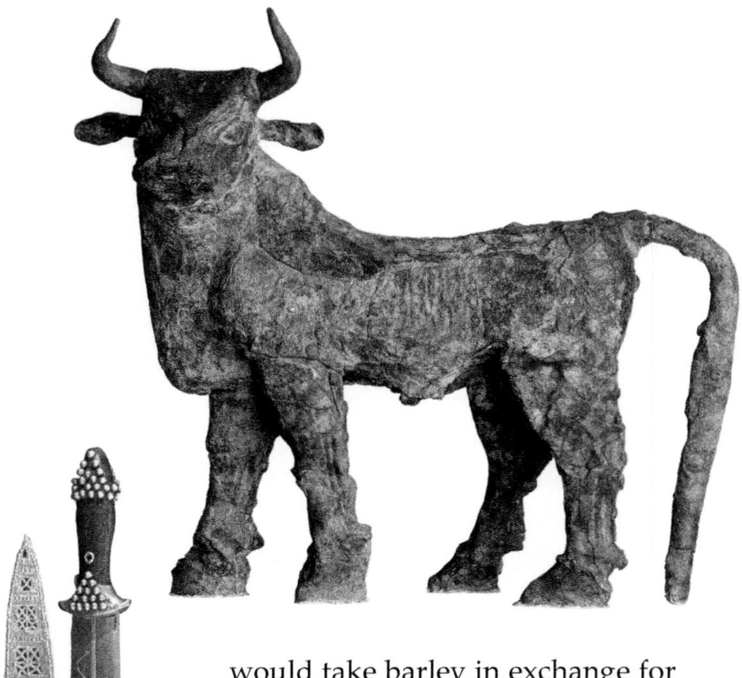

Out of the metals they imported from other lands, Sumerian craftsmen made extraordinary items, such as this copper bull and gold dagger and sheath.*

would take barley in exchange for goods. Sumerians paid their workers in barley. They baked their bread and brewed their beer from barley. The merchants used surplus barley to trade for things they wanted.

Barley, however, was not a very convenient medium of exchange. Large amounts of it were heavy. If the barley were not carefully stored, it could spoil. It was hard to handle and transport over long distances. So after a while, the Sumerians started looking around for something else they could use. Sumerian merchants found that silver would be accepted almost everywhere. As a medium of exchange, it was much better than barley. It was easier to use, easier to carry, and did not spoil. It didn't take up as much room, either.

Silver was valuable because it was a precious metal. It was precious because it was scarce. Sumerians weighed out the silver as they needed it. Later, they began using small bars of silver. They also wore silver coils like bracelets around their arms. They could snap off bits of a coil and use the pieces to buy things. Those silver bars and bits of coil may well have been the first pieces of metal money in history.

A Tiny Few at the Top

As we've seen, the Sumerians had more than enough food, and they used their surplus to trade. That made them a wealthy civilization.

But not *all* Sumerians were wealthy. In fact, most of them weren't. In Sumer there were some rich people, but there were far more poor people.

Out of every 100 men and women in Sumer, the vast majority were agricultural workers. Some of those workers were slaves. Both slaves and free workers spent long, hard days digging all those canals and bending over the crops in the fields. They plowed the land and planted and watered. It was their sweat and labor that produced the food surplus necessary for civilization to develop. Yet most had just enough food to stay alive. They enjoyed few of the beautiful things that civilization brought some Sumerians, such as the golden jewelry and copper vases that archaeologists dig up today.

Who, then, were the wealthy Sumerians? Who were the tiny few at the top who held most of the power and gained most from the trade and surplus of food?

In ancient Sumer, almighty governors and kings held much of the wealth and made many decisions about how things should be done. They told everyone else when to plant the fields, where to dig the canals, and how to water the crops.

Priests and scribes were powerful, too. The people held priests in high regard because they believed priests could communicate with the gods. Scribes were the knowledgeable class. They could read and write. Even the kings and priests couldn't do that.

In the next chapter, we'll learn more about the Sumerians' ideas about society. In the meantime, take a moment to learn about work, trade, and building in Sumer by reading the story of a beautiful bead.

The Beautiful Bead

Imagining the Past

It is a curious truth that people generally prize what they do not have more than what they have in abundance.

Sumer, as you must know, is rich in barley and wheat, but it possesses little timber, few precious stones, and no gold.

Thus, what is it that the kings and queens of Sumerian city-states desire most? Well, timber, yes, but that is not what warms their hearts. After all, these Mesopotamian rulers think they are related to gods and goddesses. Within their cities, they build grand palaces and temples. They wear elaborate headdresses and swathe themselves in costly stones and gold. Oh, yes, they adore gold—though it is nowhere to be found in their own lands.

For that reason, ships laden with Sumerian grain routinely set forth, manned by traders who travel to and from an island on the southern sea. There, all manner of goods are bought and sold—copper from the south, blue stones and red stones from the east. And gold—great quantities of dazzling gold.

So it was that a gold trader from the city of Ur headed to the harbor one morning. He boarded a large wooden ship that made its way down the river, then southward through the sea. For many days, the sailors pulled the oars with their mighty muscled arms. When the ship docked at the island, the trader bartered sacks of wheat for a bag of gold beads. After a brief stay, the vessel headed back to Sumer.

The trader kept his gold beads in a pouch around his neck. On board the ship, the trader found a place to sit. He spread a cloth in his lap, took the pouch from around his neck, and poured the precious contents onto the cloth. One by one, he picked up the beads and rolled them between his fingers, now smiling at the bright luster of one, now frowning at the somber dullness of another.

As he picked up one bead, he involuntarily gasped, for it stood out from the rest—so dazzling, smooth, alluring. Over and over he rolled it between his fingers, enjoying the very feel of it, until he heard approaching footsteps. Quickly he poured the gold beads back into the pouch, which he then draped around his neck.

He turned and saw one of the crew, a burly sailor, standing and watching him with an air of curiosity. The trader, as though he had not a care in the world, addressed the sailor in an idle tone.

"We seem to be making good speed," he remarked. "May the gods favor our voyage. I am eager to be back on land. How much farther?"

"We reach Ur tomorrow," the sailor answered, grunting as he lowered a heavy sack to the deck. "After we unload, I will set out for home."

"And where is home?" asked the trader.

"Uruk," said the sailor, "to the north."

"You should stay in Ur for a while," the trader advised. "There is no more wonderful city in all of Sumer!"

The sailor gave a skeptical grunt. "Well," he replied, "you may say what you want of Ur, but it's clear that you haven't seen the White Temple at Uruk. It is dedicated to the sky god, Anu, and is almost as big as the city itself!"

"How very nice," smiled the trader, "though I have heard that, as cities go, Uruk is not all that large. I tell you," he continued, "in Ur, our temple to the moon god, Nanna, has three huge stairways leading to the shrine at the top. And the walls surrounding Ur are so high that no invader would dare scale them. Why, thirty thousand people live inside those walls."

"The walls of Uruk make those of Ur look like fences!" the sailor retorted. "You know, of course, that the great Gilgamesh himself built our walls!"

The trader refused to be outdone. "Ah, but have you ever set eyes on Puabi, our queen? She shines with a radiance that dims the sun. Her person alone is bedecked with fabulous jewelry worth more than the wealth of whole kingdoms! Look here," said the trader, carried away with his own enthusiasm, "I will show you gold beads that will become a necklace for her—yes, for Queen Puabi herself!"

The trader pulled the pouch from around his neck, and poured dozens of shining beads into the palm of his outstretched hand.

"Splendid, are they not?" the trader beamed.

The sailor was impressed by the gold, but he only scowled and bent down to pick up his sack. As he tossed the sack over his shoulder and began to walk off, he grunted, "Well, those are pretty little beads"—he placed a special stress on *little*—"but come see the temple to the sky god in Uruk. Then, my friend, you'll know what splendid is."

The trader smiled, satisfied that he had proven the superiority of Ur. Then he poured the beads back into the pouch, secured it around his neck, and went to seek a resting place for the night.

The next morning, shortly after sunrise, the ship pulled into the harbor at Ur. "Home at last," the trader sighed as he left the vessel.

Meanwhile, the sailor prepared to begin unloading the ship's cargo. As he lifted the hatch to the ship's hold, a shaft of sunlight pierced the darkness below. Out of the corner of his eye, the sailor spied something gleaming, reflecting the sunlight. He bent, reached down, and plucked out a bead—the beautiful golden bead that had caused the trader to gasp in amazement, and which, the evening before, had slipped from the trader's hand as he poured his beads back into the pouch.

"Well, well, my glittery bead," said the sailor. "So, the braggart dropped you, did he?"

The sailor rolled the bead in his rough, weathered fingers. Then he wrapped it in a scrap of cloth, carefully stuffed it into a pouch, and set to work with the other sailors to unload the ship's cargo.

When the ship was at last unloaded, the sailor eagerly made his way from the harbor to the city of Ur. Indeed, the trader's boasts were true. The walls of the city were very high, and the gate was formidable. As the sailor passed through the gate, he could see thousands of flat-roofed houses that lined a vast maze of streets. Ur was indeed a marvelous city.

The sailor wound his way through the twisted streets of the city, surrounded by noisy crowds and the hum, buzz, and clatter of people buying, selling, working. One moment he heard the spinning of a potter's wheel, next the clang of a blacksmith's hammer, then the tapping of a sculptor's chisel.

After a time, the sailor found what he was looking for. As he entered the jeweler's shop, the pungent smell of heated gold stung his nostrils. The sailor took out his pouch and roughly shook the bead into his palm.

"How much for this gold bead?" he asked.

The jeweler took the bead between his fingers and inspected it carefully. His face showed no emotion, though he knew that he was holding a rare and outstanding specimen.

After a moment, the jeweler said, "For this bead, one sack of barley."

"One sack of barley!" barked the sailor. "What do you take me for? I know the value of this bead. Why it's—it's—" and then the word the trader had used came back to him—"it's splendid!"

The jeweler smiled. "Indeed," he acknowledged, "this is no ordinary golden bead. I will offer you three sacks of barley."

This satisfied the sailor. But he asked, "Have you no silver ingots? I prefer money to grain."

"If you insist," said the jeweler, "but only because this is such an outstanding specimen."

And so the sailor left with his silver, while the jeweler placed the beautiful bead in a special tray on his worktable. "I am not sure how I will use you, my little beauty," the jeweler said to the bead, "but when the time comes, I know I will use you well."

The jeweler turned to his other tasks. His craftsmanship was impressive. He gathered a tray of blue lapis lazuli stones. For hours, he chipped and smoothed their rough edges. Then he shaped them into beads and drilled holes through them.

The next morning, the jeweler was stringing various beads on a fine cotton thread—beads of gold, then red carnelian, silver, lapis, and agate. By the end of the day, he had strung almost fifty separate strands, each twenty inches long. As he prepared the last strand, he paused. Then his hand reached for the beautiful golden bead. He threaded it so that it rested in the very center of the top strand.

"Yes," he said quietly, "you have found your rightful place, my beautiful bead."

The next day, the jeweler tied the top of each strand to one long thread. The strands, threaded together, had become a curtain of shimmering stones, with the beautiful golden bead gleaming at the top.

"Now, my fine beauties," said the jeweler, "you are a cape fit for Queen Puabi!" Carefully, the jeweler draped the valuable cape over his arm and covered it with linen cloth. Off he went through the streets, to the queen's palace.

A few evenings later, a great banquet was held in the palace. Attendants strummed melodious lyres, while the appetites of the royal visitors were piqued by thoughts of the savory beef and foamy beer to come.

In the banquet hall, a sudden silence fell as Queen Puabi entered. Her subjects bowed low to the ground. When they were allowed to rise, they saw their lovely queen festooned with rings, bracelets, earrings, and a marvelous golden crown. All those, however, seemed but trinkets compared to the magnificent cape draped from the front of her neck to her waist—a cape that seemed a waterfall of droplets of fire, sea, earth, and sky. And there, at the top, dazzling the eyes of all viewers, rested a small glowing sun—the beautiful golden bead.

The ancient Sumerians worshipped gods they believed controlled the natural world, such as the god of vegetation represented by this statue.

Honoring the Gods: Religion in Ancient Sumer

Sumerians learned to farm the land and take advantage of their natural environment. With levees and canals they harnessed the rivers to grow rich fields of wheat and barley. With sailboats they caught the winds and carried some of that grain by sea. They traded for timber, stone, and metals, and then shaped these resources into things they needed or wanted—furniture, jewelry, tools, and more.

Still, there were many things Sumerians did not understand and could not control. Imagine for a moment that you are a farmer in ancient Sumer. One morning, as you walk down to the field to begin the day's work, you notice the river is covering a part of the land it has never touched before. By afternoon it has swallowed half the field and is racing toward your mud brick hut. By nightfall the flood has swept away levees, canals, and your entire village.

Or perhaps one year the river begins to shrink. Soon, along the edges where water once flowed, there is only mud, which slowly turns to hard, cracked earth. The canals dry up, and the grain in the field turns yellow and sickly. The river falls further, the crops turn to dust, and the smell of death is in the air.

The Sumerians had little understanding of such forces of nature. They did not know why rain fell, or why storms struck, or why the sun rose and set. They did not understand why diseases sometimes ravaged their villages, or why famine might visit their land. They knew only that they had no control over these things. An ancient Sumerian poem expresses the feeling of helplessness: "Mere man—his days are numbered; whatever he may do, he is but wind."

Headwaters of the Euphrates River, the waterway that made civilization possible in Mesopotamia.

Gods of Moon, Sun, and Rain

The Sumerians had no scientific answers to such mysteries, so they explained them in their own way. They decided that all the forces of nature were alive. A clap of thunder was alive. The moon and sun were alive. So were the rain and the winds. In fact, to ancient Sumerians, most of the world around them—trees, rivers, sky, earth, and just about everything else—seemed to be alive with mysterious powers.

The Sumerians began to worship many of the forces of nature. They worshipped a god of the sun and a god of the moon. They worshipped a god who ordered the rain to fall, which filled the Tigris and Euphrates Rivers. They worshipped a goddess who was the source of fertile soil. Their whole world was filled with gods, as well as with countless demons, spirits, and ghosts. All these supernatural beings, the Sumerians believed, caused things to happen in the world around them.

Let's read a Sumerian story that will help us understand what these ancient people thought about the power of the deities. (Deities are gods and goddesses.)

The Sumerian Story of the Great Flood

In those long-ago days there were many, many people living long and fruitful lives. But they made so much noise that the gods could not sleep. So the gods became irritated and decided to destroy all of humanity by sending a flood to cover the Earth.

One god, named Enki (EN-kee), pitied the humans, and decided to warn one good man named Utnapishtim (ut-nuh-PISH-tim) that the flood was coming. Enki told Utnapishtim to tear down his house and build a boat. The good man listened to the words of the god. He built a boat, and into it he loaded all of his possessions along with his family, all his relatives, and all the craftsmen. He loaded all the animals of the fields, both wild and tame.

Then a black cloud arose in the sky, and all that was bright turned into darkness. The rains came and the winds blew. Even the gods were frightened by what they had done. For six days and six nights, the flood marched over the Earth and waged war like an army. Then, on the seventh day, the sea grew calm and the flood was stilled.

Utnapishtim looked out at the world from his boat. All was silent. He could see no land, only water. All mankind had turned to mud! He sat down and cried.

Then a mountain appeared in the distance. The boat moved toward the mountain, became grounded on it, and would not budge. Utnapishtim set loose a dove that flew away, but found no resting place because the waters had not receded. So the dove returned. Later the man set loose a swallow, and it flew away but found no resting place. It, too, returned. Finally the man set loose a crow. The crow saw that the waters had gone down. It ate and flew around and cawed, and it did not return.

Utnapishtim gave thanks that he was alive. He sacrificed a sheep and made offerings to the gods. Because the man was so good, the gods gave him eternal life. But the rest of humanity was not so lucky. The deities decided human beings should live shorter lives. So from then on people died younger. Fewer people, less ruckus!

The Great Flood

Stories about a catastrophic flood appear in the traditions of many peoples. One famous account, which occurs in the Book of Genesis in the Bible, tells how Noah built a huge ark to escape the flood. Many scholars have concluded that the Sumerian and biblical accounts of a great flood are related.

The Sumerians believed that powerful, unpredictable gods controlled everything. If the gods were happy, human beings would be happy. If the gods were angry, the whole world might be destroyed. The gods could easily change their minds and their moods. One moment they might be satisfied with people, but the next moment they might be very angry. Anything the gods wanted to do, they did, as you'll see in this next story, which tells what the Sumerians believed about how the world was created.

Found at the temple of the goddess Ishtar, this stone worshipper with clasped hands reverently gazes heavenward.

The Sumerian Story of the Creation of the World

Once there was only endless sea, and from this sea a mountain grew. The mountain was heaven and earth joined together. The god of heaven and the goddess of the earth gave birth to a son. His name was Enlil (EN-lil), and he was god of the air. Enlil separated heaven and earth. Heaven became the sky and the "great above." Earth became the land and the "great below." They were separated by air.

But the world was still in darkness. Enlil was caught in the darkness and did not like it, so he and his wife gave birth to the moon. The moon-god sailed across the sky in a boat bringing light to the dark blue firmament. Around the moon the "little ones" (the stars) were scattered like grain. Around the moon the "big ones" (the planets) walked like wild oxen.

Still it was dark during the day. So the moon-god and his wife gave birth to a second deity, the sun-god. The sun-god rose in the mountain of the east and set in the mountain of the west. The world was bright.

These stories—some of them terrifying, others charming—helped the Sumerians explain the world around them. Sumerians thought they should honor their gods. So they carved statues of their powerful deities from stone, and from those statues we can see what they thought the gods looked like. Many looked like the statues the Sumerians made of themselves!

Human Beings: Slaves of the Gods?

In the minds of the Sumerians, their gods looked like humans—and they acted like humans. They liked good food and fine clothing. They got married and had children. Sometimes they were kind, and sometimes they were cruel. Either way, the Sumerians believed they had no control over what the gods did. Rather, the Sumerians believed that humans were slaves of the gods. The next story tells why.

The Sumerian Story of the Creation of Man

The gods had always toiled for a living. But when the goddesses were created, the gods had to work even harder to keep them happy. Producing enough bread to eat and enough clothing to wear was now a great chore. They decided that they needed servants who would take care of their needs.

So they took some clay from the moist ground. They shaped the clay until arms and legs appeared, and then they gave the clay life. Thus was man made from river mud and given life by the gods. Men were placed on Earth as servants of the gods. They gave food, clothing, and shelter to the gods. They set the gods free from ever having to work again.

As this story shows, the Sumerians believed that humans were created to be slaves of the gods. They were fated to spend their lives working hard in order to free the gods from toil.

Being the slaves of the gods wasn't easy. The Sumerians lived in fear of the gods' anger and tried to keep them happy by building temples and worshipping them. Religious ceremonies became a very important part of people's lives. They were a way to convince the gods that humans were serving them as they should. Wealthy Sumerians even paid artists to make statues of themselves carved in prayer that could be placed in temples to show the gods their devotion.

Since the greatest gods were busy with many important undertakings, each Sumerian believed he or she had a minor god as a personal god. The Sumerians pleaded with their personal gods to put in a good word for them with the more powerful gods. Through worship and blind obedience to the whims of their gods, the Sumerians hoped to gain protection from disasters such as floods, droughts, diseases, and famine.

But how did people know what would please the gods? They didn't—or at least most of them didn't. Only the priests and seers could fathom such mysteries. The priests, it was said, could talk to the gods and learn what would make them happy. Seers could read omens from sheep's livers and oil patterns. They could also tell a person whether he or she had displeased the gods and what rituals should be performed to remove the disfavor. Priests and seers were believed to be the gods' representatives on Earth. And that, as you can imagine, made the priests well respected and powerful.

A World Alive with Gods and Goddesses

An (ahn) was the Sumerian god of the sky, the "Father of the Gods" who presided over the heavenly assembly. Eventually the god Enlil took An's place as chief god.

Ninhursag (nin-HUR-sahg) was "Mother Earth," the source of fertile soil. She was the mother of the gods and all living things. Ninhursag helped create man from clay so the gods would not have to work for their food.

Enlil was "Lord Wind," the god of the air. Son of An the sky and Ninhursag the earth, he became ruler over the world. He possessed a Tablet of Destiny on which he could read men's fate. Kings in Sumer claimed they received their power to rule from Enlil.

Enki, whose name meant "Lord Earth," was the master of all beneath the ground. His realm supplied the earth with fresh water from springs and wells, and filled the Tigris and Euphrates Rivers. He placed fish in the rivers and reeds in the marshes, and ordered the rain to fall. Enki saved humankind from the flood, and gave kings their wisdom and craftsmen their skill.

Nanna (NAH-nah) was the moon-god, the son of Enlil and his wife Ninlil. Since the Sumerians based their calendar on the cycles of the moon, Nanna was the master of the months and seasons.

Shamash (SHAH-mahsh) was the sun-god who returned every day to chase away the darkness. Because he spread light and warmth, he was also the god of justice among humans.

Inanna (ih-NAH-nah) or **Ishtar** (ISH-tahr) was the goddess of love and war. Daughter of Nanna, the moon-god, she was the most powerful and fearsome of Sumerian goddesses. Later she was identified with the planet Venus, and an eight-pointed star became her symbol. As Ishtar, she was the patroness of the city of Uruk and was later revered in Babylon.

Utnapishtim was a mortal favored by Enki. His name means "He has found life." He survived the great flood and was given eternal life by the gods.

Ziggurats: Temples to the Gods

Each Sumerian city had its own special god or goddess. That deity was believed to provide protection and prosperity. The temple was the home of the city's god, so naturally it had to be the largest, highest, and most important building in town.

From the earliest days of Sumer, each city's temple was built on a high platform to keep it safe from unpredictable floods. As the city's wealth grew, the people built platforms on top of platforms to make the stair-stepped temple even higher, rising above the other buildings like a hill. This hill temple was called a ziggurat (ZIH-guh-rat). *Ziggurat* is an impressive word, but historians still don't know how to translate it. In the Sumerian language, it may have meant "high place," but no one is sure.

Ziggurats in the most powerful cities were high, terraced pyramids with each story smaller than the one below. Three long staircases led to the temple at the very top. Since they did not have much stone or timber, early Sumerians used sun-dried mud bricks for the core and baked brick for the exterior. Each level of a ziggurat was painted a different color—black, white, orange, blue, red, silver, and gold, from bottom to top. Perhaps gems were used to decorate the ziggurats as well. A Sumerian poem tells of one king threatening to destroy a city in Persia if its people did not send him gold, silver, and precious stones to decorate his temples.

Inside every Sumerian temple was a place for the god's statue. Before it stood a mud-brick table for

Ziggurats, like this one in Ur, were at the heart of Sumerian religious life.

offerings to the god. The priests brought the god sacrifices and gifts, including meals of the finest food—fish, mutton, honey, beer, and cake. In this same place, the Sumerians believed, the deity communicated his wishes to the priests. Only the most important priests could enter the room where the god lived.

Much life in a Sumerian city centered on the ziggurat, and yet the activities taking place on the towering hill temple were a mystery to most of the people. Farm workers, merchants, and craftsmen saw the priests climbing the stairs in solemn processions. They saw precious gifts being carried inside. They saw the priests emerging from secret rooms after communicating with the gods. All of these rituals must have created a sense of wonder and awe.

In a world in which almighty, whimsical gods controlled everything, there was much the people did not understand. In a time when humans thought of themselves as slaves of the gods, there was surely much they feared. But, they thought, as long as they honored the gods, prayed to them, built temples for them, and brought them gifts, perhaps the gods would show mercy. As long as they worked hard to please the gods, perhaps the all-powerful deities would protect them from harm. Even as they had learned to control much of their environment, and thus built a great civilization, the Sumerians turned to their gods in their attempts to explain or understand all that they could not control.

The mighty Sumerian hero Gilgamesh, shown here taming a lion.

Passing It On: The Written Word in Ancient Sumer

Whether building ziggurats, planning next year's harvest, or preparing a temple ceremony, Sumerians found they needed efficient ways to communicate with each other. Everything could proceed much more smoothly if people could leave a written record of their ideas.

Long before the time of the Sumerians, humans had learned to scratch pictures onto rocks and paint images on cave walls. It's one thing to paint pictures on cave walls, but it's quite another to put together written symbols to transmit ideas. Yet over time, that's just what the Sumerians did. They developed what archaeologists think is the world's first form of writing.

By 3500 B.C., Sumerian people—at least, those few who could write—could leave a lasting record of their thoughts. They developed an incredibly powerful tool for organizing their ideas and expressing themselves. The ability to write and read opened civilization to all kinds of new knowledge. Let's see how the Sumerians did it.

Numbers Came First

The rulers and priests of Sumer had to keep track of many important things. How much land was being farmed? How much surplus grain was in the temple? How much grain should go to the workers? How should important rituals take place?

The merchants of Sumer also had to keep track of their business affairs. How much grain had they sold? How much stone or copper could they buy? How much cargo did their ships hold?

Words on an ancient Sumerian tablet describe the excavation of a canal.

As civilization grew, rulers, priests, and merchants needed some place to keep all those facts and figures besides their own heads. So Sumerians invented symbols to represent numbers. And with those written symbols they developed a system of arithmetic. The diagram on this page shows a few of their numerals.

The Sumerians based their number system on two numerals—10 and 60. It's easy to see why they used 10 in their numerical notation. Most people learned to count by using the 10 fingers on their two hands. Today, thousands of years after Sumerian civilization, we still rely on the number 10. We use 10 as a base for calculations when we work mathematical equations and write decimals. Because we use 10 as a base, ours is called a "decimal system" (from the Latin *decem,* which means "ten").

But the Sumerians chose to use 60 as their base for calculations. They had a "sexagesimal" system! They probably chose 60 because it's a number that can be divided evenly many different ways, which makes many calculations quite simple. Base 60 also helped in their measurement of time and circles, and in astronomy.

Today, even though our system of arithmetic is different from the Sumerians', we still use some of their ideas. For example, when we measure a circle we divide its circumference into 360 degrees (6 × 60). When measuring time, we divide hours into 60 minutes and minutes into 60 seconds.

This clay tablet shows the dimensions of a piece of land.

Value	Early	Late
1		
2		
3		
4		
5		
10		
60		
600		

Over time, the symbols for Sumerian numbers became wedge-shaped.

How do we know Sumerians thought about these things? Multiplication tables and square root tables etched in clay still survive. Archaeologists have even found clay tablets explaining how to solve complex mathematical equations.

The Written Word

The rulers, priests, and merchants of Sumer needed to do more than keep track of what they bought or sold. They also needed to know which fields had been planted, who had paid tribute to the gods, and where ships were going. To meet these and other needs, they developed the world's first system of writing.

But it's not as though a scribe sat down one day and said, "Today I'm going to invent a way to write." The Sumerian system evolved much more slowly than that. It took many hundreds of years to develop.

Picture writing was the first step. Sumerian scribes began to write by drawing pictures or symbols for objects such as cows, hands, feet, and stars. As time went on, some of the pictures and symbols began to stand for more than one thing. A picture of a foot might also mean "stand," "walk," or "run." A picture of a star might mean "the sky," "the heavens," or "a god."

This way of writing was confusing since the same picture could mean many different things. It was also clumsy when it came to expressing certain words and ideas. For example, what pictures could the priests use to stand for "truth," "justice," or "courage"?

Over the centuries, Sumerian writing changed. Signs began to stand for words rather than objects. Pictures changed into wedge-shaped marks. The Sumerians were able to put the wedge-shaped marks together in a series, which allowed them to write sentences as well as words. As you've learned, scholars call this wedge-shaped Sumerian writing *cuneiform*.

One more change took place in Sumerian writing. Some of the wedge-shaped marks began to stand for sounds instead of ideas or objects. A special mark stood for each sound in the Sumerian language, so each time someone needed to write a word with a certain sound, he used the corresponding mark. This was huge progress. Now Sumerians could convey in writing whatever they could convey by speaking.

Objects	Early Picture Writing	Later Cuneiform Signs
Plow		
Boat		
Chisel		
Axe		

Sumerian writing evolved from picture-symbols to cuneiform.

The cuneiform on this clay tablet records a transaction—the transfer of a house and a slave—that took place more than 4,500 years ago.

You'll recall that cuneiform means *wedge-shaped*. Why were the marks left by Sumerian writers shaped that way? The answer lies in the "pens" the Sumerians used. They wrote by pressing reeds that were hard, sharp, and pointed into a tablet of soft clay. Each time they pressed a reed into the clay, it left a triangular, wedge-shaped mark. When they finished writing, they baked the tablet in the hot sun or in an oven so it would harden.

The written word is so much a part of our lives today we almost take it for granted, which makes it hard to grasp the Sumerians' achievement in inventing a system of writing. But writing allowed rulers to make decrees and priests to record the exploits of the gods. It allowed merchants to keep track of business, make contracts, write orders, and inquire about new trade.

It also made it much easier to pass knowledge along from one generation to the next. Much of what we know about Sumerian life and beliefs comes from the cuneiform records they left behind. Few other inventions have done as much to propel civilization forward.

Knowledge Is Power: The Scribes

It was so difficult to read and write cuneiform that very few Sumerians could do it. Not even kings and priests could read and write. In fact, literacy was confined to just one class, a special group known as scribes. Scribes began life as boys in wealthy families. These chosen few went to school and learned the complex writing system with its hundreds of characters.

School was tough. It went from sunup to sundown. Scribes spent long hours learning arithmetic and cuneiform, solving mathematical problems, and copying lines of text over and over. Scribes didn't just study mathematics and writing. They learned the official names of plants, animals, stones, and minerals. They memorized their civilization's great poems and copied them for future generations.

Scribes became indispensable members of every palace and temple. They were the ones who kept all the records and deciphered messages from other rulers or priests. Sometimes scribes were friends and spoke frankly in their writing because they knew only other scribes would understand what they said. They wrote about their time in school together. When they sent a decree or record to another scribe, they sometimes slipped in a word or two about their ruler's mood or attitude.

Tablets and Cylinder Seals

No matter how complex the system, writing was too important an invention for Sumerians to keep to themselves. As their trade grew, they sent more than products out of their country. They sent contracts, too. Sumerian writing spread to many parts of the Middle East.

Every big business deal had to be put in writing. Then the writing had to be signed by the people who were making the deal. So the Sumerians invented the cylinder seal, a device people could use to sign their names even if they did not know how to write.

Cylinder seals were usually made of stone and about an inch long. As the name implies, these seals were shaped like cylinders and had a hole running through the middle so they could be worn on a pin or on a string around the neck. Every important Sumerian had his own cylinder seal carved with a particular design. When a person had to sign his name on a tablet, he rolled his cylinder over the wet clay, leaving behind an impression. That impression became his signature.

Sumerian cylinder seals made all kinds of designs when rolled across clay—from pictures of heroes and animals to prayers to the gods. Often the Sumerians used cylinder seals to stamp clay seals on storage jars and storeroom locks. That way they'd know if anyone had opened them.

Archaeologists have found thousands of Sumerian clay tablets. Most of them deal with business matters, and they've given scholars a wealth of information about the economic life of the ancient Sumerians. They give us an idea of just how busy these people stayed, planting, building, and trading.

A few of the tablets also contain Sumerian laws. These precious records give us insight into Sumerian ideas of justice and how they organized their society.

Of Biting Noses, Slapping Faces, and Paying Silver: Written Laws in Sumer

The Sumerians may have been the first people in history to record their laws. Of course they didn't do it all at once. It took centuries to develop a set of written laws. Like the invention of writing, the development of laws was a huge step forward in the progress of civilization. Laws signified that people had shared understand-

The cylinder seal at far left is made of lapis lazuli. The design it made on the clay tablet below shows human-headed bulls and other fantastic creatures.

ings of the community in which they lived. People knew what was expected of them and what would happen to them if they didn't meet their obligations. A written code of laws also made it harder for dishonest rulers to twist laws to their own ends and take advantage of others. Written laws were a great step toward fairness and justice in society.

The laws of Sumer show that people were already thinking about power and how to protect the weakest among them. Some laws were intended to help those who could not always take care of themselves. Here are some examples from the later years of Sumerian civilization:

- A father had to support his children and the mother of his children.
- Slavery was legal, but slaves had certain rights. Slaves could own land. They could carry on business. They could even buy their freedom. Still, slaves were the property of their owner. They could be bought and sold. They could sometimes be severely punished at the whim of their masters. Free men could be made slaves if they failed to pay their debts.

Sumerian laws set down crimes for which people could be punished. They also named the punishment. By 2000 B.C., the Sumerians had laws that were less harsh than the laws of some of the people who lived long after them. Many ancient societies that came after the Sumerians demanded cruel physical punishment for crimes. In Sumer, however, people could sometimes pay a fine rather than face physical punishment. Here is one such law:

- If a man bites the nose of another man and harms it, he shall pay a certain amount of silver. If he harms the eye of another man, he shall pay a certain amount of silver. For a tooth, he shall pay $\frac{1}{2}$ that amount of silver. For an ear, he shall pay $\frac{1}{2}$ the amount of silver. If he slaps another man in the face, he shall pay $\frac{1}{10}$ the amount of silver.

This sculpture may represent two bull-like creatures helping Sumer's King Gilgamesh hold up the sun.

From this written record of Sumer's laws, we can figure out a few things about Sumerian society. For one thing, the people of Sumer seem to have had a problem with nose-biting! But on the serious side, we see that in the formation of their laws, the Sumerians were dealing with difficult ideas of justice and punishment.

An Ancient Tale of Heroes and Virtues

Cuneiform writing made it easier for rulers to rule, merchants to trade, and all people to live their lives. But perhaps the greatest gift of writing is and remains literature—the many stories that take people beyond their day-to-day lives. Did Sumerians have such stories? Yes, indeed. Like so many other things, their stories were a first.

In the late nineteenth century, scholars discovered broken cuneiform tablets recounting an ancient tale of heroic men and willful gods. Known as *The Epic of Gilgamesh* (GIL-guh-mesh), the long poem is one of the world's oldest pieces of literature. The earliest version was composed well before 2000 B.C.

The epic tells the story of Gilgamesh, a powerful king in ancient Sumer who begins his reign as a cruel, ruthless ruler. The oppressed people of his kingdom pray for help, and the gods create a champion named Enkidu (EN-kee-doo). Enkidu and Gilgamesh meet, fight, and come to respect each other, eventually becoming good friends. They share many adventures, and their friendship helps Gilgamesh learn to be a good king.

Let's read a brief retelling of episodes from the story of Gilgamesh to see what kind of heroes and virtues the Sumerians admired.

The Epic of Gilgamesh

Behold Gilgamesh, a man of strength, but restless and arrogant, too. He traveled to every country but never met anyone who could match his power. He ruled over the city of Uruk, where men wept and women sighed, for he was like a bull that must always show its might. The people cried to the gods, "Gilgamesh is no shepherd of the city. Send an equal to challenge him."

When the goddess of creation heard these pleas, she shaped a piece of clay and created Enkidu. He was a wild man with matted hair and a rough body. He ate with the gazelles and drank at their watering hole. He was so like an animal that one day a young hunter saw him and was fearful. The hunter ran home, crying, "Father, I have seen a wild man-beast. I dare not approach him."

"Go to Uruk," ordered the father. "Ask Gilgamesh to send a young woman to befriend this wild man." The son did as his father said. He returned with a young woman, who spent one week with Enkidu. She took his hand, speaking soft words, and he put behind him the life of an animal.

"Return with me to Uruk," the woman urged. "There lives Gilgamesh, who rules his people with the roar of a bull."

"I will challenge him," cried Enkidu, "for I am the strongest!"

So Enkidu traveled to Uruk and defied Gilgamesh. The men fought as if they were bulls. With bended knee and one foot planted on the ground, Gilgamesh finally overpowered Enkidu. "You are stronger than all men," Enkidu admitted.

Instantly Gilgamesh lost his anger. He offered his hand, saying, "Let us be brothers."

Enkidu replied, "Only if you do not abuse your power over the people." When Gilgamesh agreed, the two became fast friends.

One day, the restless Gilgamesh began to worry about his fame. "I am known here, but not elsewhere," he complained to his friend Enkidu. "We will go to the Land of the Cedars and destroy the evil Watchman, and I will raise a monument with my name on it."

"That land is a forest, surrounded by a giant ravine," warned Enkidu. "The Watchman guards it from a house made of strong cedar."

"We will travel together," argued Gilgamesh. "Shamash, god of the sun, will protect us. We will also protect each other, and if we fall in battle, our names will be known forever."

So the men set out with heavy weapons. For days they journeyed, until they came to the Green Mountain where cedars spread their shade. Gilgamesh took hold of his axe and felled a towering tree. When the Watchman heard the noise from far away, he came roaring out of his house. "Who has trespassed these woods?" he bellowed.

Through miles of trees he crashed, and when he came to the place where the cedar was felled, he cast an evil eye upon Gilgamesh.

"Oh, Shamash," Gilgamesh prayed, "how will we escape?"

The god of the sun then sent thirteen winds—an ice wind, a sandstorm, a south wind, a north wind, and many more—to cover the eyes of the Watchman. Unable to see, the evil one fell under Enkidu's blows. The mountains shook, and all the trees of the forest quivered. Gilgamesh cut down the trees of the forest, while Enkidu followed behind to clear the roots. The men turned toward Uruk, victorious.

Ishtar, the goddess of love and war, watched these events with great interest. After Gilgamesh returned and put on his royal robes, she said, "One such as you must be my husband." But Gilgamesh refused, knowing full well that a goddess could never love any man forever. Ishtar was enraged. She asked the god of the sky to send the Bull of Heaven to Uruk.

When the Bull reached the gates of the city, it snorted once, twice, three times. The earth split and hundreds of men fell to their deaths. On hearing the earth crack, Enkidu and Gilgamesh hurried to the gates, swords in hand. Enkidu seized the bull by the horns, and Gilgamesh grabbed it by its tail, plunging his sword deep between the horns.

Again, Ishtar was infuriated. She strode the great wall of Uruk, fuming. "Gilgamesh has scorned me twice and deserves only misery. He must lose what he treasures most."

That night, Enkidu had a dream foretelling the future. He lay down in tears before Gilgamesh. "The goddess has cursed us. One of us must die."

For eight, nine, ten days, Enkidu grew weak. On the twelfth day, his heart did not beat, and his eyes did not lift. With the loss of his friend, Gilgamesh raged like a lion. He tore out his hair and threw off his royal robes. "Oh, Enkidu," he cried. "I cannot accept this sleep that has taken you." Weeping, Gilgamesh wandered over the plains. "Enkidu has died," he grieved, "and one day I will die, too. I must find Faraway Man, Utnapishtim, whom the gods have given immortal life. He will help me understand the mystery of life and death."

...Enkidu grew weak. On the twelfth day, his heart did not beat, and his eyes did not lift.

So Gilgamesh set out on another difficult journey. He passed through the great mountain that guards the rising and setting of the sun. From there he went through the garden of the gods and to the edge of the ocean. A ferryman then carried him across the rushing waters of death. At last Gilgamesh found Faraway Man, resting at the mouth of two rivers.

"What business have you here?" Faraway Man said, surprised that a mortal man could make this dangerous trip.

"My friend whom I loved deeply died, and now I am afraid," answered the weary Gilgamesh. "How have you gained eternal life? How do I find eternal life?"

So Faraway Man, Utnapishtim, told Gilgamesh his tale of the flood and of his rescue, of his great boat, and of the power of the gods. He stopped his tale and looked at Gilgamesh. "Here is the secret, my friend. The gods gave eternal life only to my wife and me. In the world of ordinary man, no house can stand forever; no promise lasts for all time. But there is one gift you can take back to Uruk."

...he went through the garden of the gods and to the edge of the ocean.

Faraway Man proceeded to tell Gilgamesh of a plant called The-Old-Made-Young. "It grows deep in a pool. Hold it in your hands, eat it, and your youth will return for a time."

So the ferryman took Gilgamesh back the way he had come. When they stopped for the night, Gilgamesh went to a pool to cleanse himself. There he saw the plant floating in the clear water. "I cannot have eternal life," he rejoiced, "but tomorrow I shall enjoy my youth one more time!"

Gilgamesh plucked the plant and set off on a day's journey, intending to eat the plant the next day. But that evening when he went for a swim, and while he enjoyed the cool of the water, a snake approached, stole the plant, and sloughed off its skin as it slithered away. Tears ran down the cheeks of Gilgamesh. "I have gained nothing," he lamented. "I have lost everything.

"Let us leave," he told the ferryman, and after many days of travel, they reached the high walls of Uruk.

...a snake approached, stole the plant, and sloughed off its skin as it slithered away.

Gilgamesh gazed upon the city he had built. "These walls are strong,"

Gilgamesh observed. "Here is a place of well-built houses, of pleasurable gardens, and fertile fields. Here is a palace and a high temple for the gods. Long after I die," he thought, "here my deeds will live on."

Thus, Gilgamesh, the mighty king, had grown wise. He had traveled far and come to understand secret things, and he knew the tale of the days before the great flood. Upon a stone monument he engraved his story so that all might know it, and he lived as a great hero for the rest of his days.

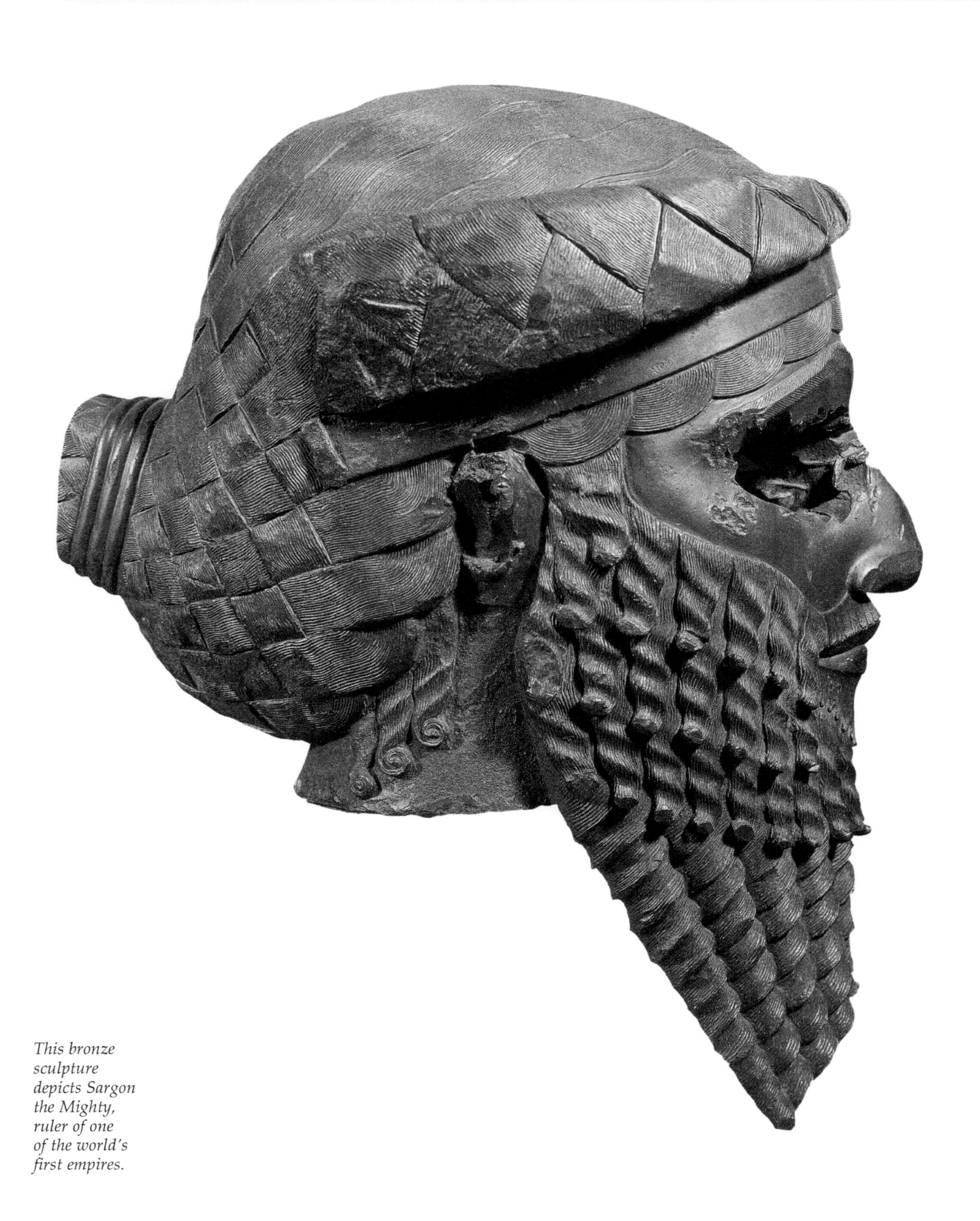

This bronze sculpture depicts Sargon the Mighty, ruler of one of the world's first empires.

The Sun Sets on Sumer

Sumerian civilization reached its "golden age" during the third millennium B.C., and then glowed like a burning ember for another thousand years. During that time, from 2500 to 1500 B.C., many changes took place in Sumer.

By 1700 B.C., the civilization that existed in Mesopotamia could no longer be called Sumerian. Let's see how this great change came about.

Big Changes in Sumer: The Beginning of the End

Geographic change played a key part in the decline of Sumer. Over the years the Sumerians kept irrigating their fields, and though they didn't know it, they were slowly poisoning their own land.

"Salinization" is the scientific name for their problem. The water Sumerians used for irrigation contained salt. The land they cultivated was very flat and had poor drainage. So the salt water stayed on the land a long time, and salt remained in the soil, making it less and less fertile. Crops no longer grew well in what had once been a fertile plain. The problem became serious between 2400 and 1700 B.C., and in later centuries harmed agriculture throughout the Middle East.

Sumer faced another problem. It grew too fast for its own good. When Sumer was young, its cities were small and separated by stretches of swampland or desert. Rulers from different cities often met to share ideas. But over the years the population grew, and so did the cities. Ur, Uruk, Kish, Lagash, and Umma (UH-muh) each began to cover more and more land. People drained swamps and irrigated deserts to grow crops. The cities became city-states. A city-state was made up of the city itself plus the land around it. Both the city and surrounding lands were under the same political control.

Soon the grain fields of one city-state bordered those of another. The rulers of the various city-states became rivals for territory, and the Sumerians fought with each other over boundaries and water rights. Some city-states even built canals that brought water away from the fields of other city-states into their own. That led to more fighting. Each city-state wanted to be the most important of all. First one and then another claimed power over all of Sumer. Wars broke out to see who was the strongest.

Wars between the city-states were often long, hard, and brutal. The armies used foot soldiers as well as troops who fought from donkey-drawn carts. Soldiers clad in copper helmets and leather kilts brandished swords, spears, and shields. After a battle with another city-state, the winning army would often kill all its prisoners. The king of one city-state boasted that in just one battle he killed 3,000 of the enemy.

A Sumerian soldier rides into battle aboard a war chariot pulled by four donkeys.

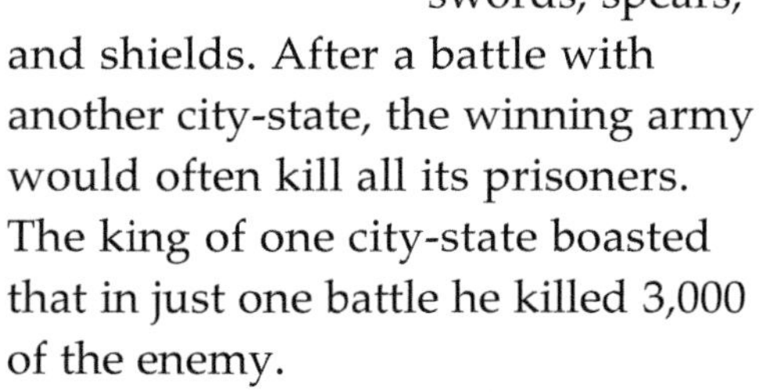

Sometimes the victors sold prisoners as slaves or held them for ransom. Sometimes they pillaged and destroyed the captured city. The victorious troops would knock its temple to the ground—the worst thing that could happen to a city-state, because the destruction of the temple meant that its god had gone down in defeat.

Over the years, kings of stronger city-states managed to dominate weaker ones. In the late twenty-fourth century B.C., the king of the city-state called Umma brought most of the other Sumerian city-states under his control. That marked the beginning of the world's first empire. It did not last long, however, for fighting soon broke out again among the city-states. War, or the threat of war, was a constant fact of life—hardly a healthy state of affairs for the long-term survival of Sumer.

A Threat from the Outside

Wars *among* the city-states plagued the Sumerians. But their culture faced another big threat—one that came from without.

Around the edges of Sumer lived many people who were jealous of Sumerian wealth and ease. They were nomads and herdsmen, not city-dwellers. These people had a culture and a way of life of their own, but they had not built civilizations. They liked what they saw in Sumer, however, and wanted a share in some of the good things that civilization brought. Unfortunately for the Sumerians, these people sometimes helped themselves by attacking and robbing Sumerian cities.

It wasn't hard for bands of warriors to sweep out of the frontier and strike the Sumerians. Because Sumer was located on the low-lying floodplain of the Tigris and Euphrates Rivers, it had few natural defenses and was open to attack on all sides.

The map on pages 82–83 shows these "cradles of civilization" in Sumer, Egypt, the Indus Valley, and China. Each began independently and apart from the others. Yet ideas spread easily, even in ancient times. People carrying goods from one region to another would tell others about new ways of growing crops, making things, and living together. As those ideas spread, more and more people learned that it was possible to settle down in one place, build cities, and find a better way of life.

Left: Merchants, like this one holding scales, helped spread Sumerian ways beyond the borders of Sumer.

Below: Laborers unload from a ship a product that was rare and highly prized in Sumer—timber.

The wars between Sumer's city-states made attacks even easier, since a divided, quarreling people are usually easy prey. As the fields of Sumer grew saltier, the harvests less bountiful, and food supplies smaller, the Sumerians may have had a harder time putting up a good fight. As the nomadic peoples kept attacking, Sumerian power began to slip away.

The Idea of Civilization Spreads

We've seen how, during the third millennium B.C., various geographic and political changes led to the decline of Sumer. Still, even though Sumerian civilization was getting weaker, the basic ideas behind civilization—such as the division of labor and city-building—were strong and were appearing beyond Sumer.

By 3100 B.C., in the valley of the Nile River, the Egyptians began to build one of the world's earliest civilizations. By 2500 B.C., people living in the valley of the Indus River had also built a civilization. And far away in what we now know as China, civilization was flourishing by about 2000 B.C.

As the Sumerian, Egyptian, and Indus River Valley civilizations developed, their people came in contact with each other. They traded ideas and skills. Each civilization borrowed new ways from the others. Each civilization, in turn, could act as a center from which the idea of civilization would spread.

While trade led to peaceful contact between peoples, ideas about civilization also spread through war. Let's learn about how war changed civilization throughout the Middle East.

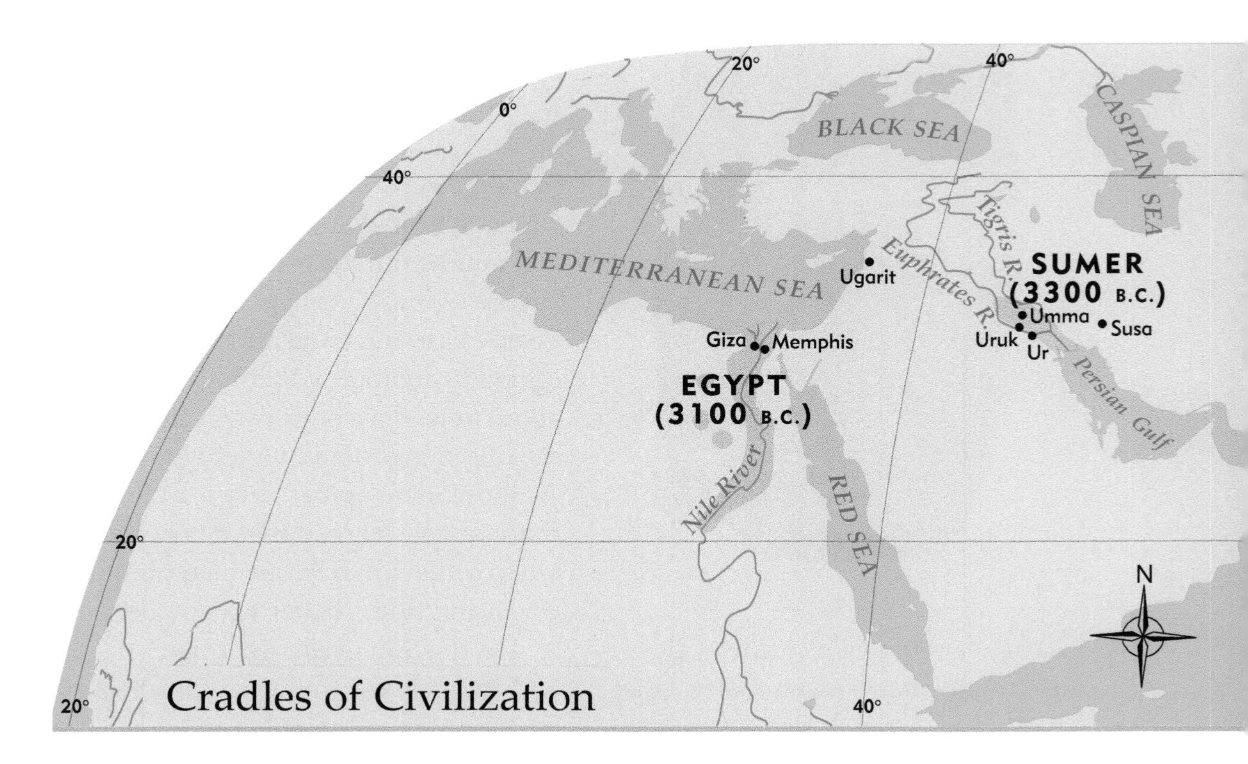

Cradles of Civilization

Sargon the Mighty

To the north of Sumer lay the land of Akkad (AK-ad). The Akkadians (uh-KAY-dee-uhns) had for many years lived side by side with the Sumerians. Over time they began to copy many of the Sumerian ways. From the Akkadians came a ruler destined to conquer Sumer and build one of the world's first great empires—Sargon the Mighty.

There are many legends about Sargon. One says that he was a man of humble origins, brought up by a gardener who found him as a baby floating in a reed basket on the Euphrates River. Another story says that he grew up as a servant in the royal palace of Kish. He became the trusted cupbearer who at every meal poured wine for the king, and then became king himself.

Such are the stories. We don't have much reliable evidence about Sargon's personal life. But we know a good bit about his career as a ruler, and we know that he was one of the world's first great empire builders.

Sargon organized the Akkadians into a strong fighting force and became their military king. This is how he described himself: "Sargon the mighty, King of Akkad, am I." He was indeed mighty. About 2300 B.C., he moved his army south. One by one he conquered the cities of Sumer, and for the first time Sumer fell under foreign rule. Sargon began to call himself King of Sumer and Akkad. The kings of the city-states were forced to pay money and goods to Sargon, the conqueror.

Everyday life in Akkad and Sumer did not change all at once. The work of irrigating and producing food went on as before. Gradually, however, Sargon's reign brought important changes. For example, the language of the Akkadians became the language of government. The Akkadians, however, adopted the cuneiform writing of the Sumerians.

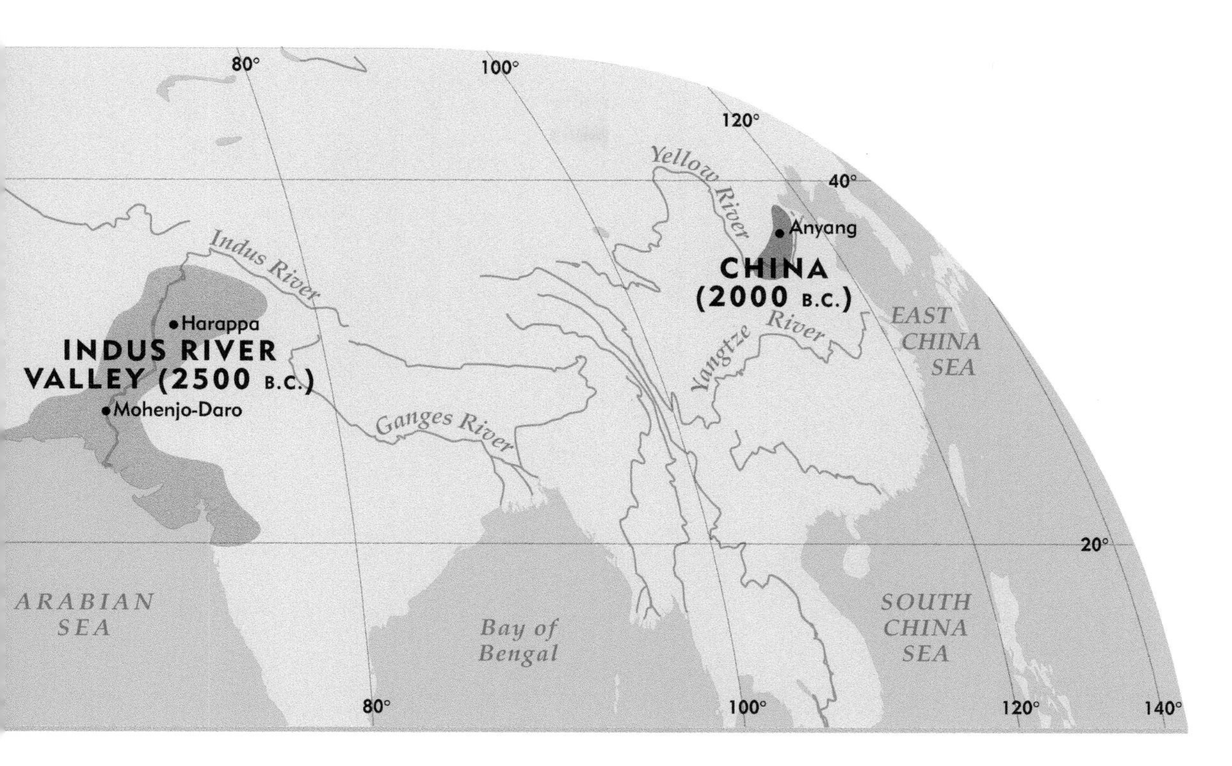

They used it to put their own language into written form. So now a second language was written in cuneiform. The Akkadians also began to worship Sumerian gods. As the years passed, the two cultures borrowed from each other, blended, and gradually produced something new.

Sargon united all the Sumerian city-states and Akkad into an empire, and then added other lands until he controlled all of Mesopotamia. The map on page 84 shows how far his empire eventually stretched. He must have made raids with his army over long distances. He may even have reached the coasts of the Black Sea and the Mediterranean. As his armies traveled and his empire expanded, Sargon spread civilization over a wider area.

Sargon the Mighty turned out to be not only a strong general but a wise ruler who reigned for 56 years. He built a magnificent capital city named Agade (uh-GAH-day) to be the center of his empire. He was one of the first kings to keep a permanent army to help control his realm, and one of the first to appoint governors to help rule over conquered cities.

An ancient stone relief shows King Sargon flanked by two of his courtiers.

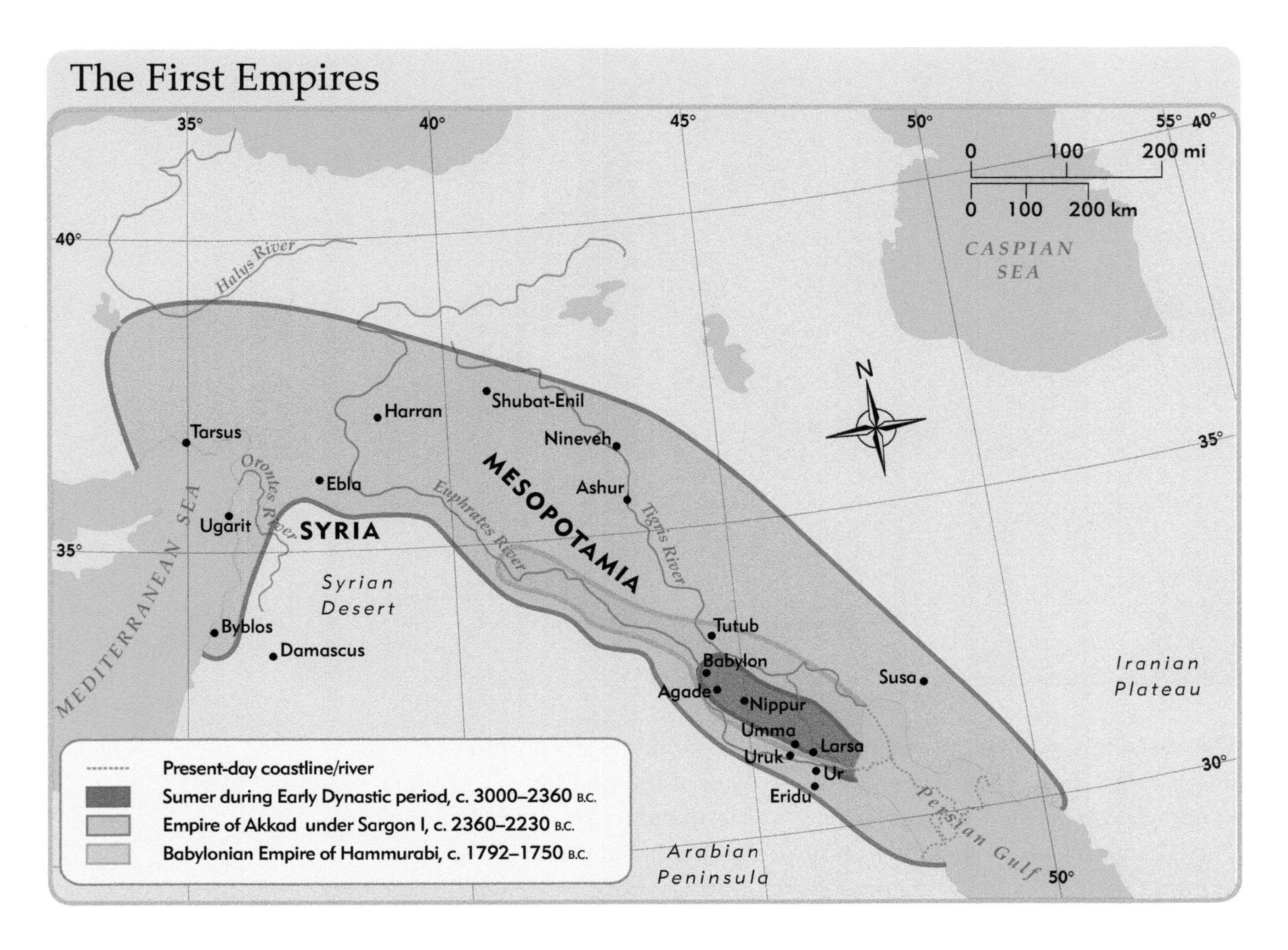

As Sargon's empire grew, so did his fame. One legend tells of merchants in a distant city who heard of his wisdom and begged him to come settle a quarrel. When Sargon finally showed up to see them, the sight of him alone was all that was needed to settle the dispute.

Yet Sargon did not have an easy time ruling his vast empire. He set a pattern of rule that continued throughout much of the Middle East's history. His armies did not settle down with the people they conquered. Instead, they simply made their new subjects give them food or other goods.

Of course the Sumerians did not like this treatment. Sumerian city-states often tried to revolt. They wanted a bigger share in the good things civilization brought.

Not only did Sargon have trouble with rebellious city-states, but he also had to deal with the nomads living on the frontiers, who were always waiting to attack. In the end, his empire became too large for him to control easily.

In his lifetime, Sargon fought more than 30 wars, trying to keep his empire all in one piece. His grandson, in his turn, pushed the boundaries of the empire beyond Mesopotamia. When Sargon's grandson died, however, invaders overran the land. The empire of Sargon the Mighty—one of the first great empires in all of history—came to an end.

Hammurabi and His Code

After the fall of Sargon's empire, confusion reigned as wars broke out among city-states. Nomads sometimes attacked, created new empires, and in time they too were attacked by other invaders.

In the eighteenth century B.C., a man named Hammurabi (ha-muh-RAH-bee) became king of the city-state of Babylon. At that time Babylon, on the banks of the Euphrates River, was one of the smaller city-states of Mesopotamia. But Hammurabi set out to make it great. An ambitious, determined man, he became the ruler of a great new empire. The map on page 84 shows how large an area he conquered and ruled. Babylonians, who were the descendants of the Sumerians and Akkadians, became the greatest political power in this vast region.

Hammurabi ruled between 1792 and 1750 B.C., and proved to be a great leader and wise man. He was the kind of ruler who took a genuine interest in the day-to-day affairs of the empire. He sent his soldiers to live among the people in conquered city-states. He assigned officials to rule for him throughout the empire, and he appointed tax collectors to get money for his government and projects. For years he devoted himself to building temples and canals. His most famous achievement, though, is a set of laws he left behind—the Code of Hammurabi.

Above: This 7½-inch bronze statue with gold foil is thought by some to depict Hammurabi, the mighty king of Babylon remembered for his code of laws.

Below: A subject seeks justice before the throne of Hammurabi.

The cuneiform writing on this tablet recounts some of the 282 laws of Hammurabi.

How do we know about the code? In the winter of A.D. 1901–1902, in the southwest corner of what is now the country of Iran, a French archaeologist unearthed some long stone slabs covered with cuneiform. The slabs lay far from ancient Babylonia, so at some time a victorious king must have hauled them away as war trophies. When scholars translated the cuneiform, they realized it was a very complete set of laws from the end of Hammurabi's reign. These 282 legal decisions regulated life in a large empire. Engraved on stone pillars for all to see, the code addressed everything from theft and murder to marriage and divorce.

This code was important not just because Hammurabi made many laws, but because he applied a single, organized set of laws over a vast realm. Hammurabi based his code of laws on even older Sumerian and Akkadian laws, which he adapted and integrated for his empire. He defined the purpose of his laws as "to cause justice to prevail in the land, to destroy the wicked and the evil, that the strong may not oppress the weak."

The Code of Hammurabi begins with an introduction praising the emperor's military victories. Hammurabi pledges to treat conquered people fairly and proclaims that he honors their gods. He then sets forth for his empire a body of laws covering a wide variety of matters such as prices, contracts, stealing, kidnapping, debt, and slavery. Here are some examples from Hammurabi's code:

- If a citizen has been accused falsely of a murder, the false accuser shall be put to death.
- A citizen who steals property from the temple or crown shall be put to death. Whoever receives his stolen property shall die.
- A son who strikes his father shall have his hand cut off.
- A citizen who puts out the eye of another citizen shall have his eye destroyed.
- A man who destroys the eye or breaks the bone of a slave shall pay in compensation one half of the slave's value.
- If a citizen cannot pay his debts and has sold for money his wife or son or daughter, they shall work for three years in the house of their purchaser and shall receive their freedom in the fourth year.
- If a citizen's wife suffers from attacks of intermittent fever, he may take another wife. However, he shall support his first wife for life.

Some of Hammurabi's laws seem harsh to us today. "An eye for an eye," for example, sounds like a bloodthirsty punishment. But in ancient times, it was a step toward controlling violence. In

Hammurabi's day, if a man in one tribe injured a man in another tribe, then *all* the members of the injured man's tribe might seek vengeance against *all* the members of the other tribe—often by trying to kill them. Terrible blood feuds resulted. Hammurabi's code tried to ensure that only those who committed crimes were punished, and that the punishment fit the crime. Seen in the light of history, "an eye for an eye" may be a harsh law, but it was a law meant to help people live together more peacefully.

Just *organizing* a set of laws for people to live by throughout an empire was in itself a great accomplishment. Hammurabi's code helped everyone know the rules. In a world that was often chaotic and brutal, and in a time when conquering kings could change laws to suit their whims, Hammurabi's code must have brought a sense of fairness to many people. It gave some order to society and helped people view the world as a more stable, predictable place.

We should also remember that in an age when might often made right, the Code of Hammurabi at least attempted to protect people without much power. "The strong shall not oppress the weak" was a main principle of the code. That was an important step forward in law and a sign of just how far civilization was advancing.

By the time of Hammurabi's code, Sumer was no longer a great political power. But its culture was still flourishing. Sumerian literature, science, and learning were preserved in schools. They continued to be taught for another 1,500 years. Sumer's cuneiform and deities, its ziggurats and city-states survived under new names and in new forms. Sumerian power had slipped away, but Sumerian achievements would influence the progress of civilization for centuries to come.

Two figures are shown atop this seven-foot pillar, or stele, *which bears the entire Code of Hammurabi. One is Hammurabi himself. The other is the enthroned Shamash, Sumerian god of justice.*

This picture shows how one artist imagined city leaders planning the future growth of Babylon during its golden age. Here they consider the capital's crowning glory—the Tower of Babel.

Nebuchadnezzar's Babylon

We began our study of history by learning about a jumble of clues that made archaeologists scratch their heads. The clues pointed toward an ancient civilization. At first the archaeologists believed this ancient civilization was the fabled city of Babylon, a place known to modern man through legends and the pages of the Bible.

The closer the scholars looked, the more they realized those clues were actually pointing back in time to a civilization even *older* than Babylon. That trail led them to ancient Sumer.

But as we've learned, the city-state of Babylon came to dominate Mesopotamia in the centuries after Sumerian culture faded. Under the rule of Hammurabi in the eighteenth century B.C., Babylon became a great center of government and trade.

Now we're going to zoom forward about a thousand years from the time of Hammurabi. Even after so many centuries, Babylon was still around—in fact, not only was it still there, it was grander than ever. By about 600 B.C., Babylon had risen to its greatest glory. The Babylonians built on the achievements of Sargon, Hammurabi, and the civilizations that preceded them to create a glorious city and sprawling empire, with grand palaces, a towering ziggurat, lush gardens, and mammoth walls with splendid gates. Even today, the name *Babylon* fires the imagination with visions of ancient grandeur.

In this chapter, you'll learn about the mighty Babylonian empire.

Babylon: Gate of the Gods

To weary travelers making their way across the parched land of

The Euphrates River made Babylon a bustling commercial center.

Mesopotamia, the great city of Babylon was an impressive sight. The ancient Greek historian Herodotus was suitably impressed. After visiting Babylon he declared, "It surpasses in splendor any other city of the known world."

The splendor of Babylon came from its great trading wealth. That wealth was based on the city's favorable location, sitting as it did astride important trade routes. Like spokes on a wheel, trade routes stretched out from Babylon to the other great commercial centers of the ancient world—down to the Persian Gulf, across to the ports of the Mediterranean, deep into the interior of Asia Minor.

Babylon stood on the banks of the Euphrates River. Every day, cargo-bearing ships sailed down the river to dock at the city's bustling harbor. The busy waterside and the markets of the city buzzed with the languages of people from all over the Middle East.

The Euphrates not only brought trade, it also brought life to the parched land. The Babylonians—like the Sumerians centuries before them—channeled the water of the river in canals and used it to irrigate their grain fields. And like the Sumerians, the people of Babylon used the mud of the riverbanks to build. Toiling in what was probably the ancient world's greatest brick-making industry, gangs of workers packed thousands of molds with mud that dried into bricks in the hot sun. From these mud bricks, the city was built.

For good reason, then, the Babylonians revered the Euphrates. Some even regarded it as a deity. But as you probably suspect by now, this was a city of many deities. In fact, *Babylon* means "gate of the gods." And to worship them, the city was filled with temples, each dedicated to one of the various gods of the Babylonian people.

Babylon was also an imperial capital. Its huge royal palaces proclaimed that this was a city at the heart of a powerful empire. It had been the capital of Hammurabi's empire during the second millennium B.C.

Herodotus: The Father of History

Herodotus, who lived in the fifth century B.C., was the first Greek historian. As a young man he traveled in Greece, the Middle East, and North Africa. Everywhere he went, he asked people about their customs, their beliefs, and their past. He wrote down much of what he learned in books, which are considered the world's oldest known volumes of history. Today Herodotus is often called "the father of history." You'll meet him again when you study the ancient Greeks.

Little survives of Hammurabi's capital city, however, as his empire declined shortly after his death. But 12 centuries after Hammurabi, a new king rebuilt Babylon as the capital of a new Babylonian empire. His name may be familiar from the pages of the Bible: Nebuchadnezzar II.

Nebuchadnezzar the Conqueror and Builder

Nebuchadnezzar was a warrior king. During his 43-year reign (which lasted from about 605 to about 562 B.C.), he was often at war with his neighbors, defeating their armies, sacking their cities, and increasing the size of his empire.

His first target was Egyptian armies in Syria. You'll study the rise of Egypt in the next chapter, but suffice it to say that at this time Egypt was powerful. Like Babylonian kings before him, Nebuchadnezzar thought of all Mesopotamia as his backyard. So when the Egyptians marched an army into the area around the upper Euphrates, Nebuchadnezzar attacked the Egyptians

Like their ancestors in ancient times, brick makers in twenty-first-century Iraq still shape clay into bricks and set them to dry in the hot sun.

Babylonian Empire Under Nebuchadnezzar II

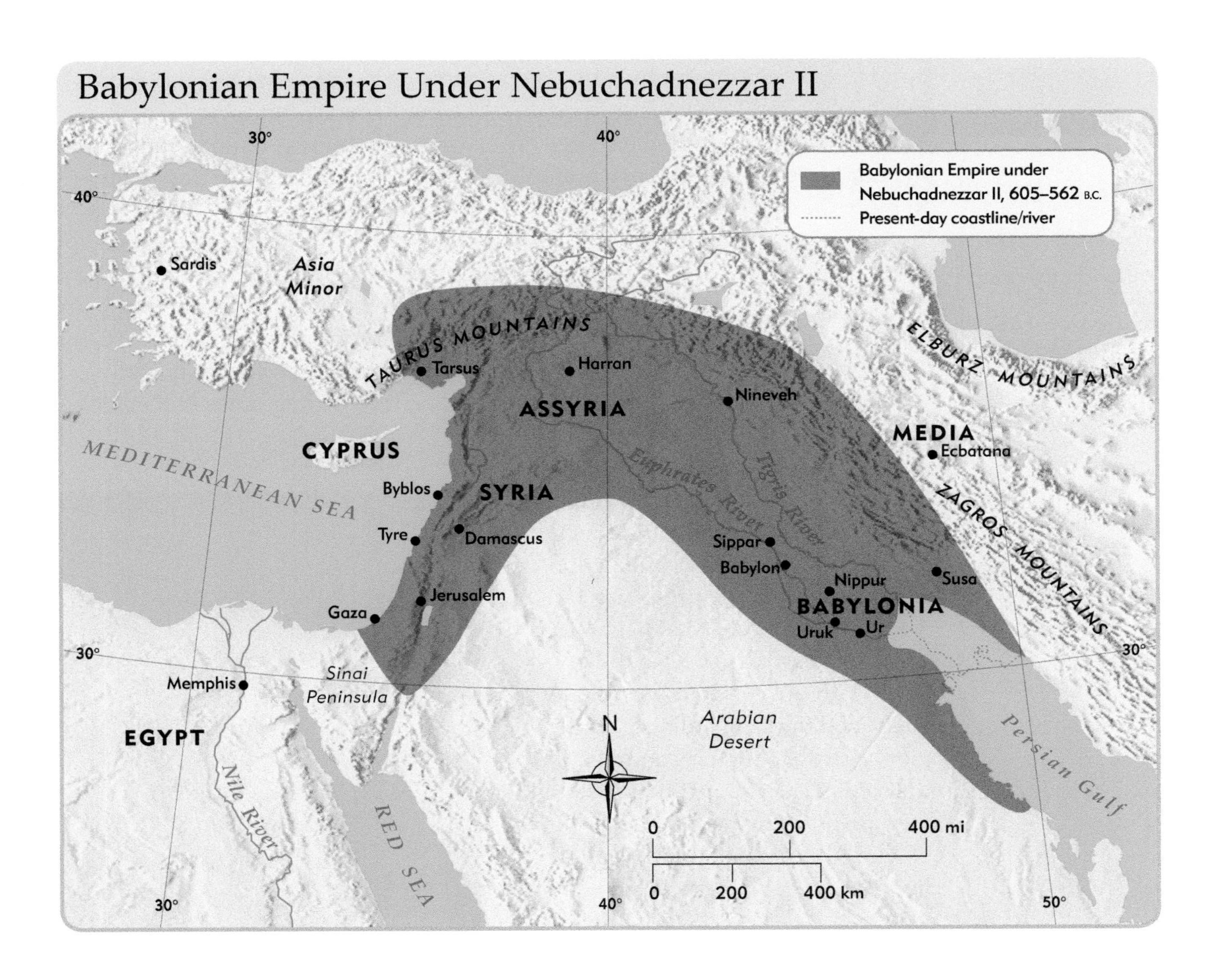

and sent them scurrying back toward their own river—the Nile.

Nebuchadnezzar then set out to conquer Syria and make it part of the growing Babylonian empire. His empire stretched from the borders of Egypt to the Persian Gulf and along the Mediterranean coast of what is now Lebanon. A determined and ruthless warrior, he let nothing stand in his way. When the Mediterranean port of Tyre (tiyr) refused to surrender to him, he laid siege to the city—a siege that lasted 13 years.

Above: Laborers at work on one of King Nebuchadnezzar's many building projects.

Right: The imposing Ishtar Gate has been reconstructed. It was one of nine entrances in Babylon's defensive walls.

Nebuchadnezzar could be ruthless in battle, but he did more than vanquish his enemies. He was a builder, too, and during his rule Babylon shone like a polished gem. The new capital rose by the shores of the Euphrates, a majestic city home to more than 200,000 people.

- Locate Babylon and the Euphrates River on the map of Nebuchadnezzar's empire on page 91.

Nebuchadnezzar was proud of his role as builder, but humble about his service to the gods. He left inscriptions on thousands and thousands of bricks, such as "Palace of Nebuchadnezzar, King of Babylon, who lives under the protection of Nabu and Marduk (MAHR-douk); son of Nabopolassar, King of Babylon." With great enthusiasm, he set about making Babylon surpass the glory days of King Hammurabi. Ever the soldier, he realized that first and foremost the city had to be secure. Nebuchadnezzar's Babylon would be the most solidly protected city of its day.

During his military campaigns, Nebuchadnezzar had spent much time trying to destroy his enemies' defenses. So he understood the importance of strong city walls. He fortified the sturdy double wall that encircled Babylon and built an outer wall beyond that. The outer wall was said to be so wide that two charots could be driven past each other along the top. Rising from some of these walls were defensive towers which served as battle stations. When the city was under attack, archers would climb into the towers and rain arrows on the enemy.

Still Nebuchadnezzar wanted more. Around the city's outer wall he built a moat. But unless it had water, a moat was nothing more than a ditch. Where could he find water in the desert? Again, the Euphrates provided the answer, flooding the moat with its prcious water. Bridges spanned the moat, allowing people to cross back and forth to the city. However, the bridges could be quickly dismantled during times of danger.

Nine gates led through the walls into the great city. Each was named for one of Babylon's gods. Nebuchadnezzar fortified these entranceways with massive cedar doors plated with bronze. Grandest of all the gates was the Gate of Ishtar (ISH-tahr).

You may recall Ishtar from the Epic of Gilgamesh. Ishtar was the Babylonian goddess of love and war. And the magnificent Ishtar Gate reflected her importance. Nebuchadnezzar rebuilt it three times, each time on a grander scale. The gate was decorated with tiles in a variety of brilliant colors. Across its walls marched images of strutting bulls and strange dragonlike creatures with a serpent head, feline front legs, and eagle talons on the back legs.

Passing through the Ishtar Gate, visitors entered the Processional Way. This great thoroughfare led through the heart of Nebuchadnezzar's city. On its walls strode 120 enameled lions, the animal that represented the goddess Ishtar.

Traveling along the Processional Way, visitors could see the glories of the city all around them. Great brick temples and the king's luxurious palaces dazzled the eye.

Nebuchadnezzar restored many of the city's temples, adorning them with precious metals, polished woods, and valuable gems. He paid special attention to the temple of Marduk, Babylon's patron god. Marduk was "the great lord of heaven and earth," the chief god of the Babylonians who was worshipped for his wisdom.

Inside Marduk's temple Nebuchadnezzar built a chamber fit for the deity, painted with dazzling colors. "I made its walls gleam like the sun, with shining gold," declared the king. "With lapis lazuli and alabaster I clothed the inside of the temple." A tall statue of the god presided within, covered with gold and dressed in the finest clothes and most ornate jewels.

Babylon's seven-story ziggurat also received improvements. This great landmark could be seen for miles around, a symbol of the city that seemed to reach to the very heavens. Some believe that this was the Tower of Babel referred to in the Bible.

Left: One of the carved dragons that adorned the walls of the Ishtar Gate. The dragon was associated with Babylon's patron god Marduk.

Below: This fanciful sixteenth-century painting depicts the Tower of Babel as a multistory ziggurat. The tower's upper stories seem to reach to the very heavens.

Nebuchadnezzar also restored the city's palaces. These were places of luxury and symbols of royal power. He filled them with beautiful fabrics, silver vessels, gold ornaments, and the best wines—all the treasures of a mighty empire. Slaves stood ready, awaiting his every command.

The king's favorite dwelling in the city was the great Southern Palace. There his immense throne room faced north onto the largest courtyard. This provided the monarch with as much shade as possible from the blistering Mesopotamian sun. "The seat of my kingdom," Nebuchadnezzar called his beloved palace, "the dwelling-place of joy and gladness."

Yet still another marvel stood close by. In a city filled with wonders, this one was perhaps the most wonderful of all—the Hanging Gardens of Babylon.

Nebuchadnezzar's Hanging Gardens

King Nebuchadnezzar achieved many great things in his life. He conquered neighboring lands, forged a mighty empire, and rebuilt Babylon into a splendid capital city.

But one marvel stood above them all—the Hanging Gardens of Babylon. These were elegantly terraced gardens, watered by the Euphrates—an ascending stair-step to the sky. Why did Nebuchadnezzar build them? According to legend, one thing worried the invincible king, one problem he had been unable to solve—the unhappiness of his young wife, Amyitis (AM-i-tis). Read the legend of his dilemma and his still-famous solution.

A Garden Fit for a Queen

Imagining the Past

The king loved Queen Amyitis. True, he had married her to create an alliance with her father, the king of Media (MEE-dee-uh). But this was more than just a marriage of convenience, a way to make peace between Media and Babylon. Nebuchadnezzar adored his wife, a beautiful princess who had grown up in the lush Zagros Mountains to the east. But those very mountains were now the cause of his worries.

"Why are you so unhappy?" he asked Amyitis one morning.

Amyitis made no reply. She stood on the palace balcony, her eyes gazing toward the east.

"Haven't I given you everything you could possibly want?" Nebuchadnezzar asked.

He moved beside her and she turned her face to him, a sad smile on her lips.

"Of course you have, my dear," she replied.

"Don't you have the most elegant of clothes, the most precious of jewels?"

Amyitis nodded.

"And don't you have servants waiting on you night and day? Your palaces are the envy of the world. You have the best food and drink my empire can provide. Why are you sad? What can I do to make you happy?"

Amyitis turned her eyes again to the east. The hot sun beat down on the throbbing capital. But the young woman saw none of the city's temples, palaces, or houses. She gazed out across the dusty plain toward the horizon—toward the land of Media. Toward her home.

"My husband," she began, laying a gentle hand on his arm, "you have given me everything a queen could want, even your love. But there is one thing you cannot give me." A tear rolled down her cheek. "You cannot give me the land of my birth."

The homeland of Amyitis was very different from the flat, sun-baked terrain of Mesopotamia. Media was green and lush, filled with meadows and creased with rugged mountains. It was a land that Amyitis loved, a land she could not seem to forget.

I wish I could do something about my wife's homesickness, Nebuchadnezzar thought. She cannot go back to the land of her birth; she belongs here with me.

And then Nebuchadnezzar, the great conqueror and builder, had an idea: I cannot take her back to her homeland, but perhaps I can bring her homeland to her!

He called for his best architects and craftsmen. Then he made plans to recreate the homeland of Amyitis—right in the middle of Babylon. Along the banks of the Euphrates, he would build an artificial mountain covered in the abundant greenery of Media. The gardens would be the most beautiful the world had ever seen.

Soon the work began. Hundreds of laborers started to construct a step-pyramid mountain from earth. Terrace upon terrace climbed upward, supported by pillars and walls, and sitting on a foundation of stone. On each terrace the men piled layers of rich soil. When watered and warmed by the sun, the soil would burst with life. Every variety of flowering trees and shrubs would be brought from the most distant corners of the empire.

The sun was certain to shine on the greenery. But where was the water to come from? Any plant would perish if it had to depend on the rare showers of rain that fell on Babylon. Once more, the sacred Euphrates was the source. At the base of the mountain, pumps operated by teams of slaves lifted the precious water up to the top. From there it flowed down through the terraces, watering the gardens at each level and keeping the vegetation green.

Finally, the mountain and its gardens were finished. Shade trees, exotic shrubs, and colorful flowerbeds flourished on all the terraces. The aroma of flowers filled the air, and drooping vines hung over the terrace walls. Life-giving water gurgled in fountains, pools, and miniature waterfalls, keeping the gardens cool.

On a clear spring morning, Nebuchadnezzar led his queen to the terrace of their palace home. She looked out in hushed wonder.

"Amyitis, my dear," announced the pleased king, "Media has come to you."

This, then, is the legend of Nebuchadnezzar's amazing gift to his homesick wife. In a way it was a gift to the world. The king created a botanical wonder, a magnificent feat of engineering that conquered nature itself. For this reason, the Hanging Gardens of Babylon were hailed as one of the Seven Wonders of the Ancient World.

It would be wonderful to cast our own eyes on these magnificent gardens, but they have long since vanished. How, then, do we know about them? From the writings of the Greek historian, Herodotus, who visited Babylon. To him we owe thanks for the descriptions of Nebuchadnezzar's startling efforts to defy nature, all, it is said, for the love of his wife.

And Queen Amyitis? Was she as impressed with her husband's efforts as Herodotus would later be? Did she fall in love with the gardens and with her adopted home? Or did she continue to long for the land of her birth, suffering a homesickness that even Nebuchadnezzar, mighty king of Babylon, was unable to conquer? Unfortunately, Herodotus did not tell us, and so we may never know.

The Seven Wonders

Long ago, some of the earliest historians celebrated the greatest buildings and monuments created by man as the Seven Wonders of the Ancient World. Nebuchadnezzar's Hanging Gardens of Babylon were one of these Seven Wonders. Today only one of the ancient wonders still stands—the great pyramids in Egypt. You will learn about the pyramids when you study the Egyptians.

The Pyramids at Giza—grandest of all the monuments of Egypt and one of the Seven Wonders of the Ancient World.

The Spread of Civilization: Egypt

While Sumerians built the first ziggurats along the Euphrates River, Egyptians were building a civilization of their own on the banks of the Nile River in northeast Africa. Ruled by kings who claimed to be gods, the Egyptians accomplished astonishing feats. They built gigantic pyramids that dazzle us still. They recorded their lives in elaborate picture-writing. They pondered life after death, preserving the bodies of their dead as mummies and preparing them to journey into the afterlife.

The Egyptians were the second of the great ancient civilizations. Their culture flourished for more than 3,000 years, making it one of the longest-lived civilizations in all of history.

The Gift of the Nile

In ancient Egypt everything began and ended with the mighty Nile, the longest river in the world. Look at a map and you'll see it spilling out of central Africa and heading north for 4,000 miles to the Mediterranean Sea. For the last 600 miles, it runs through the flat plains that were once ancient Egypt. At its mouth it breaks into several channels and gives birth to a broad, marshy *delta,* where the river flows into the sea.

Almost all of Egypt is desert—a dry, brown-red land where life struggles for a foothold. The Egyptians themselves called the forbidding desert *Deshret,* which meant "Red Land." But if you could fly over those barren stretches of desert in an airplane and look down at Egypt, you would see what looks like a thin green ribbon lying on a red-brown paper package. That green ribbon is the Nile River Valley.

This chapter explores ancient Egypt, a civilization that flourished in the northeast corner of Africa.

The life-giving waters of the Nile River.

In some places it is 10 or 12 miles wide. In a few places it shrinks to almost nothing. On that thin stretch of land alongside the river, ancient Egypt flourished.

Every year by late July, a month after the rainy season began in central Africa, huge amounts of water coursed down the Nile. As rains swelled the river, the Nile began to overflow its banks, flooding the parched length of land. This was usually a gentle rise—not as violent as the flooding along the Tigris and Euphrates Rivers. For several weeks the Nile would cover the land with muddy water. When the river receded again in September, it left behind a strip of rich, black soil several miles wide on either side.

The Egyptians called their country *Kemet,* which meant "Black Land," after this dark, silty soil. Here on this long strip of land hugging the Nile, they learned to till the land with a hoe, and to plant and harvest crops. Like the Sumerians, the Egyptians learned to take advantage of their river home. Since there was almost no rainfall in their land, they had to find a way to use the Nile's life-giving waters. Over the centuries, Egyptians harnessed the floodwaters of the Nile for irrigation. They learned to channel the precious waters to holes called "catchment basins," rationing it to their fields when needed. They also used the ox-drawn plow, which helped them till their fields.

A River Delta

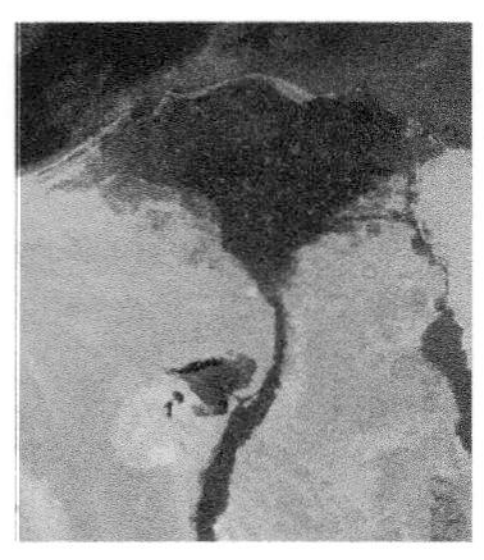

Satellite image.

A delta is a triangular piece of land at the mouth of a river. It's usually laden with rich deposits of alluvial soil (that is, soil deposited by flowing water). The term *delta* comes from the fourth letter of the Greek alphabet, which looks like this: Δ.

In the rich, black soil, the Egyptians grew wheat for their bread and barley for their beer. Cattle, sheep, and goats fed on the cereal chaff. All kinds of crops flourished—onions, beans, lentils, dates, figs, grapes, pomegranates, and flax to make linen. Over time, farmers began to produce the surplus of food needed for civilization. And along the Nile's banks grew reeds which—as we'll soon see—the Egyptians used to make into their version of paper.

The Nile was also a roadway the Egyptians used for travel and trade between the villages that sprang up along the river banks. Eventually, all kinds of boats and barges plied the river, from small skiffs made of reeds to large wooden boats powered by many oars. By 3200 B.C., the Egyptians had learned to make sailboats and began to send trading vessels across the Mediterranean and the Red Sea.

As time passed, a few villages grew into cities. Early on, Memphis, the Egyptian capital, became a major center of trade. Egypt had many of the same trading partners as ancient Sumer. There were few trees for timber in Egypt, so ships brought cedar and juniper from what is today Lebanon. The Egyptians imported silver and, later, horses from Syria. They loved jewelry and were partial to the richly veined, deep blue stone called lapis lazuli. This stone came from a land far to the east, an area now known as Afghanistan. From lands to the south in Africa, the river trade brought ebony, copper, cattle, gold, ivory, incense, and ostrich feathers. Surplus grain,

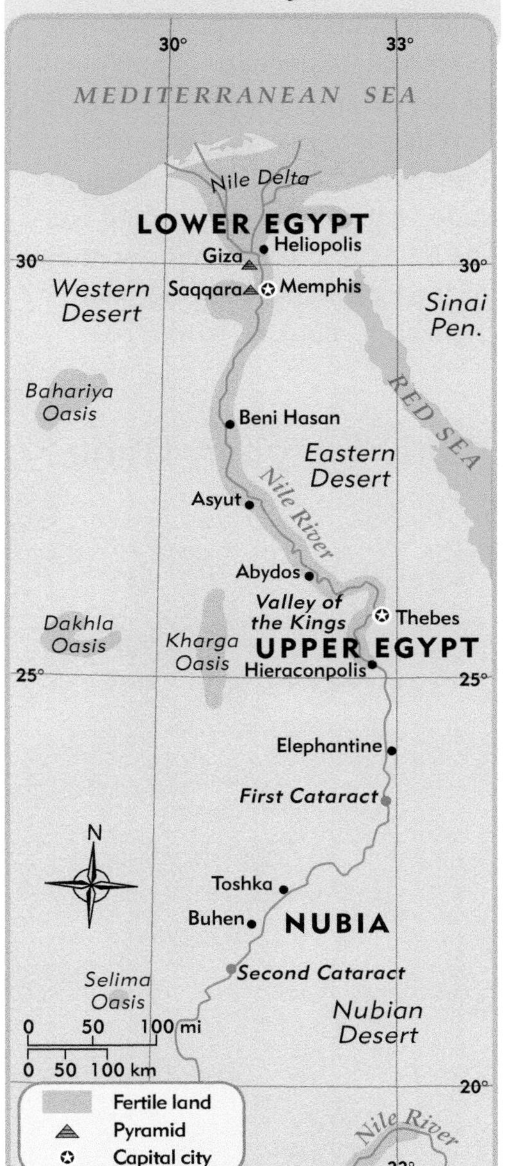

Upper and Lower

Look at the map and you'll see that Lower Egypt is *up* near the Nile Delta. Why is that? Because the part of a river nearest the sea is called the "lower" part of the river. The sources of the Nile River, where the river begins, are in the mountains of Central and East Africa—that's the "Upper Nile." Then it flows north, through Egypt, and empties into the Mediterranean Sea. That's the "Lower Nile," the part nearest the sea.

What's a Cataract?

A cataract is a large waterfall. Although the Nile is more than 4,000 miles long, it has six cataracts, so only the last 650 miles are easily navigable.

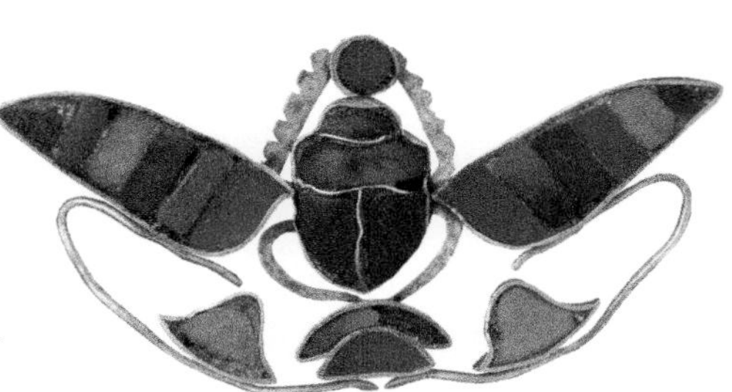

Top left: Wooden model of an ox-drawn plow.

Above: Scarab pendant decorated with lapis lazuli.

stone for building, copper for tools, semiprecious stones for jewelry—all moved up and down the Nile.

Life-giving water. Fertile soil. A surplus of food. An avenue for trade. A home for villages and cities. The Nile provided all of these things for the Egyptians who built their civilization along its banks. No wonder the ancient Greek historian Herodotus called Egypt "the gift of the Nile."

Worshiping Many Gods

Like the Sumerians, the Egyptians owed their harvests to a flooding river and the bounty of nature. Also like the Sumerians, the

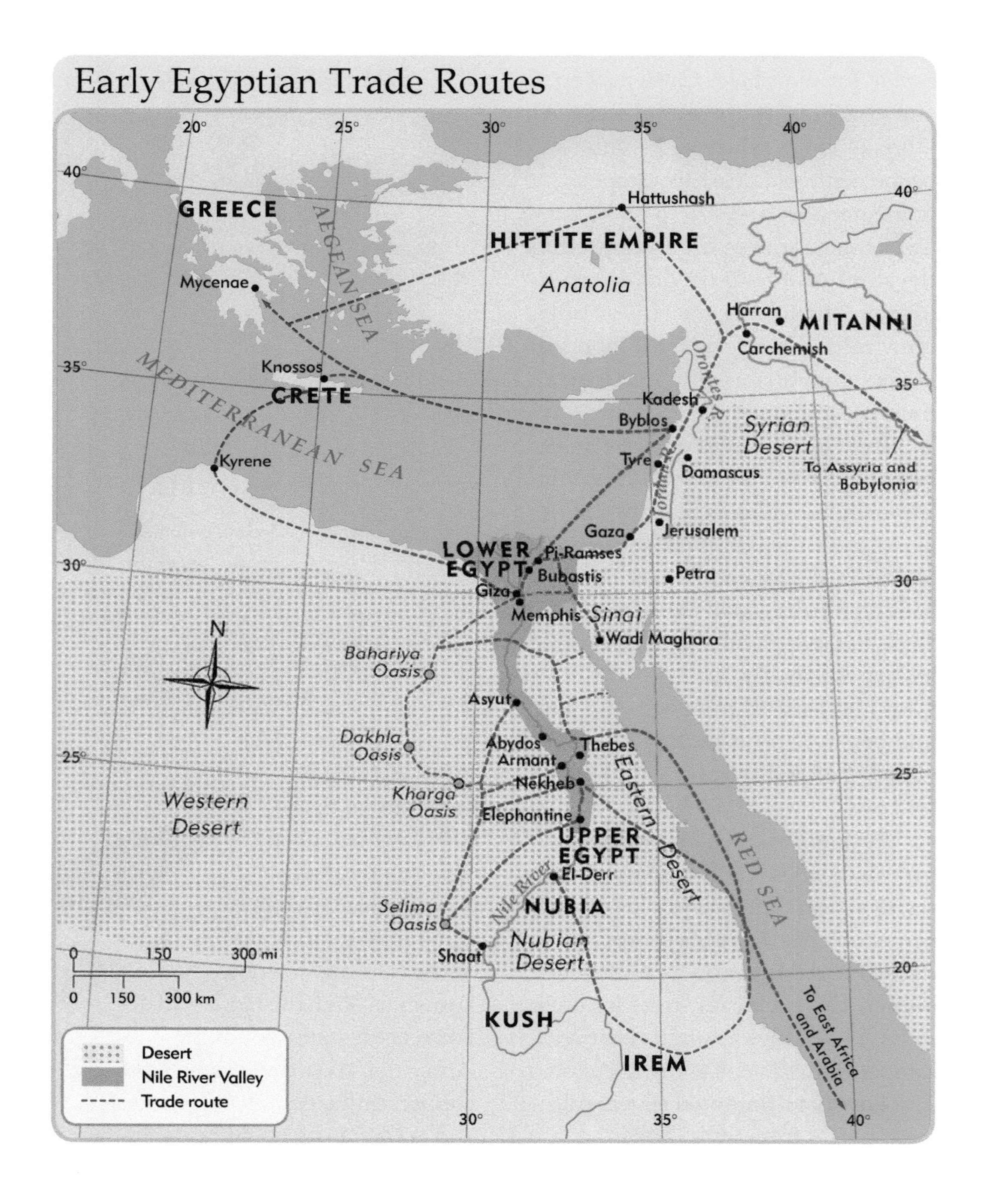

Egyptians worshipped many nature gods—in fact, more than 1,500 gods and goddesses.

There was Re (ray), the god of the blazing sun that fills the Egyptian sky nearly every day of the year. Pictured with a falcon head crowned by a solar orb, Re was the most important of all deities. His light and heat ensured good harvests. He was believed to be the father of the Egyptian ruler.

Osiris (oh-SIY-rus) was the powerful ruler of the dead, and his sister Isis (IY-sus) was a mother-goddess. Egyptians prayed to Isis for the healing of their children. Both gods were greatly loved and said to help humans in many ways.

Horus (HOR-us) was the son of Osiris and Isis. This falcon-headed god was at first god of the sky, pictured with the sun as one eye and the moon as another. He became the patron deity for the king. The king even claimed to be the living Horus.

Nut was worshipped as sky goddess. She was often shown with wings outstretched protecting the vault of the heavens.

Thoth (thohth) was the god of knowledge and wisdom. Shown with the long, curved beak of an ibis, Thoth dug for knowledge the way birds used their bills to dig for food.

The Egyptians worshipped these gods and many more. They prayed to them for good fortune and protection, and explained the mysteries of nature by their actions.

When Pharaoh Speaks

Archaeologists have found the remains of Nile River villages dating back more than 5,000 years. Over time the villages became part of two long kingdoms stretching along the river. Egyptians living in the Nile Delta were part of the Lower Kingdom—so-called because the Nile flows south to north, and their villages lay downstream. Villages upstream, or south of the delta, were part of the Upper Kingdom, or the land closer to the source of the Nile.

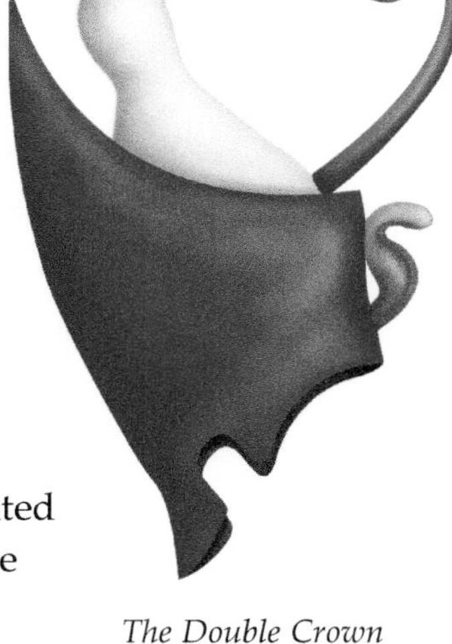

The Double Crown of Egypt.

Tradition has it that by 3100 B.C., the ruler of the Upper Kingdom—a king named Narmer—united the two kingdoms and founded the city of Memphis as his capital. To show his power in uniting the kingdom, he fashioned the Double Crown of Egypt. It was made of a white crown, once worn by the king of the Upper Kingdom, and a red crown, symbolic of the Lower Kingdom.

Narmer was the first in a centuries-long line of powerful kings who each ruled Egypt as the head of government, general of the army, chief of the priests—and even as a god. The Egyptians came to believe that each of their kings was the god Horus come to rule on Earth.

Left: Horus, the falcon-headed god of the sky.

Right: The mother-goddess Isis.

They revered their god-king so much that they thought it was disrespectful to speak directly about him. So in time, instead of mentioning the ruler himself, they spoke of "the palace" as having done this or that. The word *pharaoh* (FAIR-oh) meant "palace" or "great house," and people began to call their king *pharaoh* by the sixteenth century B.C.

As it has for millennia, the Great Sphinx keeps watch over the pyramids at Giza.

When the pharaoh sat on his throne, he sometimes held a symbolic shepherd's crook and a flail to show the care and power he held over his people. The pharaoh owned a lot of the land in Egypt and could do whatever he pleased with it. He often had several wives at once, and it was not unusual for his chief wife to be a sister or half-sister, perhaps to keep power in the family. When a pharaoh died, Egyptians thought he became one with Osiris, god of the dead. Then kingship usually passed to the eldest son of his chief wife.

The pharaohs of Egypt were powerful rulers—among the most powerful of the ancient world. Most were determined to leave their mark. They did so with great pyramids, imposing temples, and stupendous statues.

Building for the Next Life

For centuries, people have marveled at Egypt's great pyramids—the oldest and largest stone structures in the world. A king named Zoser (ZHOH-suhr) built the first pyramid at Saqqara (suh-KAHR-uh) around 2650 B.C.—about 500 years after Narmer lived. It was a tourist attraction in the ancient world. But the most famous pyramids stand not far from the modern city of Cairo (KIY-roh) at a place called Giza (GHEE-zuh). They were built by a pharaoh named Khufu (KOO-foo), his son Khafre (KAF-ray), and another pharaoh named Menkaure (men-KOW-ray). Preserved by the desert climate for 4,500 years, these

The Great Sphinx

The Great Sphinx is a huge stone statue with the head of a man and body of a lion. It measures 240 feet long, 66 feet high, and has stood in the desert for 4,500 years. It has the face of Khafre, one of the pharaohs who built the pyramids of Giza.

Why does the mysterious Sphinx have the body of a lion? Surely in part to remind onlookers of the pharaoh's great strength and power. The lion, the most powerful predator, was a symbol of the king. The Egyptians built sphinxes to stand guard over temples and tombs—including the magnificent pyramids.

pyramids are one of the Seven Wonders of the Ancient World.

It's still hard to believe that ancient people constructed these grand monuments without modern machinery, iron tools, explosives, or even workhorses. The Egyptians built the largest pyramid, the Great Pyramid at Giza, with more than two million stone blocks, weighing an average of two and a half tons each. Its giant base covers 13 acres, and it towers 450 feet into the air.

Why did the Egyptians build these giant monuments? To answer that question, we need to understand their religious beliefs.

The Egyptians believed that death was not the end of everything, but the beginning of eternal life—that is, the beginning *if* you had the right help getting to the next world. They built pyramids as tombs for kings, queens, and other royalty, and as homes for the next life.

Inside a pharaoh's pyramid, secret passageways led to a burial chamber where the ruler's body lay hidden and protected for eternal life. The pyramid was more than just a tomb. It was a place that guarded the dead, helped the soul on its journey to the next world, and made sure it lived well forever. It was a home for eternity.

The Egyptians believed that people would use their bodies in the afterlife. So they went through an elaborate ritual to prepare the body as a mummy before placing it in a tomb. A mummy is a body that has been dried and treated to protect it from decay. After a body was mummified, it was wrapped in layer after layer of linen strips. Lucky charms called amulets were tucked in its folds. Then the mummy was placed in a coffin, and the coffin was placed in a stone sarcophagus (sahr-KAH-fuh-gus) in the pyramid.

Top: The 3,000-year-old mummified remains of Pharaoh Ramses II.

Above: Jars that once held a pharaoh's internal organs.

Left: A highly decorated Egyptian coffin.

Of course the tombs of common folk weren't so grand. Most common burials were in simple pits in the desert. Mummies of the very poor were simply wrapped in coarse cloth, placed in a pit, and covered with sand.

When it came to the afterlife, Egyptians believed you *could* take it with you. They filled their tombs with food, clothes, furniture, games, and other things to make life in the next

Small statue of a butcher, from an Egyptian tomb.

world more comfortable. In the case of a pharaoh or wealthy Egyptian, the burial chamber was also filled with gold, jewels, spices, and other treasures. That's why the burial chambers were hidden in secret places inside the pyramids—to hide the treasure from thieves!

Of course, it would be hard to squeeze everything you'd need for all eternity into a burial chamber. So rich Egyptians filled their tombs with paintings and sometimes with small models showing scenes from everyday life, such as people making food. The tombs also held statues of servants for the next world. The

How Did They Build the Great Pyramid?

The ancient Egyptians built the Great Pyramid of Giza without benefit of modern machines or even iron tools. How did they manage it?

They started by using wooden hammers, copper chisels, stone mauls, and saws to cut huge limestone blocks from quarries. Next the Egyptians had to haul the blocks to the building site. Sometimes they brought them by boat on the Nile River, and then gangs of men dragged them by sled across the desert. Workers dug canals so boats could bring the stone as close as possible to the pyramid site.

There, stonemasons smoothed the sides and squared the corners of the mammoth blocks before other gangs pushed them into place. After they got the bottom layer of stones set, they built long ramps of earth and brick, and sled crews dragged more stones up the ramps to make the next layer. As they finished each layer, they built the ramps higher and longer so they could keep building up.

After they fitted all the layers in place, the Egyptians sometimes covered their pyramids with white stones so that from a distance the sides gleamed in the desert sun. Most of those covering stones are gone now, so the sides look like giant steps.

Scholars aren't sure how long it took to build the Great Pyramid, but it was probably about 20 to 30 years. It surely took tens of thousands of men. The laborers were probably poor farmers who worked on the giant tombs for three or four months a year while the Nile floods covered their fields.

Why build the pyramids so big? Pharaoh and his architects knew that if they wanted a monument to stand out in the vast emptiness of the Sahara, it had to be big!

Above: In this illustration from The Book of the Dead, *jackal-headed Anubis (far left) balances the heart of a dead person against the Feather of Truth.*

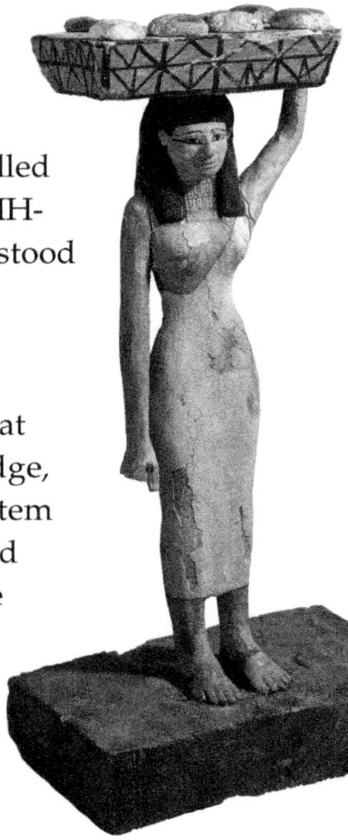

Below: The ancient Egyptians believed that statues of servants would come to life and attend them in the afterlife.

Egyptians believed that if the priests said the right prayers, these pictures and statues would come to life and forever supply the dead person with all his or her needs.

We have a good idea of what the Egyptians expected in the next world. A dead person would journey across a river to the kingdom of Osiris, ruler of the dead. There were many obstacles on the way, but the Egyptians had all kinds of prayers, hymns, and spells to guide them. This information was sometimes carved on tomb walls. By 1550 B.C., it was written down and placed in tombs. Known as *The Book of the Dead,* it gave a route to follow, chants for protection, and answers to questions the dead might be asked.

Finally, the dead person reached the Judgment Hall and was greeted by Horus, the son of Osiris. Anubis (uh-NOO-bus), the jackal-headed guardian of the dead, weighed the dead person's heart against the Feather of Truth. If a heart was heavy with sin and outweighed the feather, a horrible fate lay ahead. A light heart, however, meant that the owner had lived with virtue. He could then pass on to a happy, eternal life.

Writing It Down

Like the Sumerians, ancient Egyptians looked for some way to communicate commands from their kings, stories of the gods, and instructions for trade and building. Whereas Sumerians developed a wedge-shaped script called cuneiform, Egyptians invented a form of picture-writing called hieroglyphics (hiy-ruh-GLIH-fiks). The picture-symbols stood for ideas and sounds.

The word *hieroglyphics* means "sacred carving." The Egyptians believed that Thoth, the god of knowledge, invented this precious system that combined pictures and sounds. Hieroglyphs were carved mostly on temple walls, tombs, and monuments, sometimes to record the exploits of the pharaohs.

Above: Egyptian picture-writing, or hieroglyphs, from a pharaoh's tomb.

Below: A painted limestone statue of a scribe, sitting in typical cross-legged style. Scribes were important members of Egyptian society.

Egyptian scribes used a quicker system—a sort of hieroglyphic shorthand—to keep all kinds of official records for the pharaoh, from reports about harvests to plans for building temples.

Sometimes the Egyptians used animal symbols in their hieroglyphs, and these words show us how imaginative the Egyptians were. For example, there's a fearsome crocodile hiding in the word *trouble* and a tall, far-seeing giraffe in the word *predict*. There's a merrily leaping kid goat in the word *imagine*. A long-billed ibis digging deep for his food is paired with a wise owl in the word *discover*.

The Egyptians didn't just carve their symbols on stone. They also invented a paper-like writing material called papyrus (puh-PIY-rus), which they made by pressing together thin strips cut from the stalks of papyrus plants that grew in the marshes along the Nile. The scribes could roll their writing paper into cylinders for storage when they weren't using them. Eventually the busy Egyptians filled many libraries with their writings. A famous library in the city of Alexandria had more than 700,000 papyrus scrolls about history, astronomy, geography, and many other subjects.

The Rosetta Stone

Egyptians used hieroglyphs for more than three thousand years, but once their civilization came to an end, people forgot how to read the beautiful picture-symbols. Then in A.D. 1799, some French soldiers unearthed a black stone near Rosetta, a city in Egypt. The stone was divided into three sections. Greek writing covered one part. The other two parts were covered with ancient Egyptian symbols.

The Greek was easy enough to translate. It was a decree issued in 196 B.C., honoring a pharaoh of Egypt. Scholars soon realized that the other two sections probably said the same thing in Egyptian writing. Here at last was a chance to unlock the secrets of hieroglyphs!

It wasn't an easy task, partly because much of the Rosetta Stone's Egyptian hieroglyphic writing was missing. The first breakthrough came when scholars noticed the hieroglyphic section had five ovals containing identical symbols. The Greek text, meanwhile, mentioned the pharaoh's name five times. Beginning with those five matches, the scholars began the painstaking task of translating the hieroglyphs.

For more than 20 years they toiled away. Then in 1822 a brilliant young French scholar named Jean François Champollion (zhahn frahn-swah shahn-pohl-yawn), who had been studying the hieroglyphs of ancient Egypt since his youth, announced that he had finally deciphered the Egyptian writing system.

Scholars were able to produce dictionaries to help translate hieroglyphs on ancient papyrus scrolls, monuments, and pyramid walls. The Rosetta Stone helped reveal the stories, beliefs, and history of ancient Egypt.

Enjoying the Here and Now

With all this emphasis on death, tombs, and mummies, you might think Egyptians were gloomy people. Actually, nothing could be further from the truth. Since they left the walls of their temples and tombs covered with scenes of daily life, we have a glimpse of how the Egyptians lived. They worked hard, and they enjoyed the here and now, too.

Suppose for just a minute that you live in ancient Egypt, and you had the good luck to be born into a well-to-do family. Today is a holiday. How do you think you might spend it?

Maybe you'll go on a family outing. How about a sail on the Nile? You can have a floating picnic, and then swim in the river. But watch out for the crocodiles! While you're there, maybe you'll see a water tournament—two teams of boats filled with men holding long poles, all trying to knock each other into the river.

The Rosetta Stone—the key to unlocking a lost language.

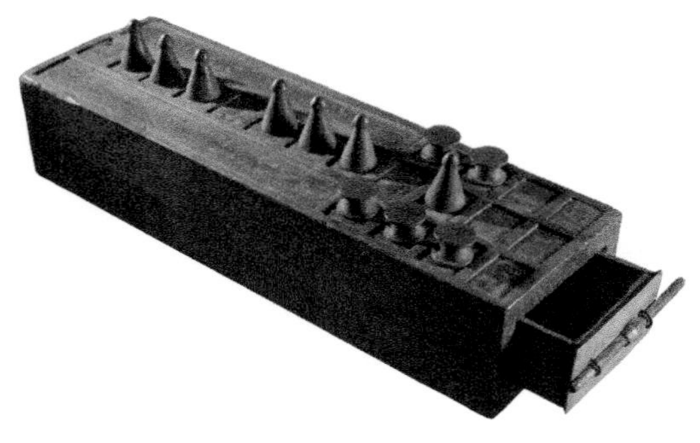

Right: Senet, an ancient Egyptian board game carved out of wood.

Above: Hunters in a light skiff try to spear two underwater prey—a hippopotamus and a crocodile.

Feeling more adventurous? You might hunt waterfowl with boomerangs, or fish with spears. Or if you're feeling courageous, grab your bow and arrows and your spear, and join a hunt for crocodiles, lions, or hippopotamuses.

Want something a little quieter? You can choose from all sorts of board games, including one called *senet* that was a lot like backgammon. Or you might play with some dolls, tops, or leather balls. Maybe you'd like to hang out with one of your pets for a while—your greyhound dog or your tabby cat.

Since it's a holiday, there's probably a banquet to attend. Hmm, what will you wear? Egyptians usually dress in white linen garments. The men wear skirts or robes, while the women often wear dresses. At the banquet you'll probably see people with their hair all done up in plaits or curls. The wealthy Egyptians even don elaborate wigs.

Both men and women like to outline their eyes with paint and wear lots of jewelry—gold, silver, copper, shells, and semiprecious stones. And Egyptians love perfume. They import the finest from their many trading partners. At banquets people often put cones of perfumed grease on top of their wigs. As the grease melts and runs down your face, it cools you and makes you smell good to your neighbors.

All of your friends and family love music, so there will certainly be some musicians playing harps and lutes to entertain you. Someone may sing a love song or two. You'll eat with your fingers until you

Right: The temple of Hatshepsut rises against the dramatic backdrop of desert cliffs. Hatshepsut was one of four female pharaohs of ancient Egypt.

get full—perhaps some antelope and gazelle meat, along with some fancy cakes, and fine wine made from grapes.

Well, you've had quite an enjoyable day! Of course, not everyone had such good times in ancient Egypt. Most people didn't have very much, and life could be very hard. For the well-to-do, however, Egyptian civilization meant a good life. No wonder they wanted to take it all with them into the next world!

A Pharaoh Leaves Her Mark on History

Most of the rulers of ancient Egypt were men, but not all. There were four female pharaohs. One of them was named Hatshepsut (hat-SHEP-soot). She ruled Egypt for 15 years, from 1473 to 1458 B.C. She was a powerful, energetic queen who liked to tackle big projects. She knew well that the many pharaohs before her had left their mark on the face of Egypt—Zoser with his Step Pyramid at Saqqara, Khufu with his great pyramid at Giza. As you'll see, Queen Hatshepsut was not one to be left behind. She found a first-rate architect named Senmut (sen-MOOT) and put him to work in her capital city of Thebes.

Here is a story about how Hatshepsut left her mark on history.

Queen Hatshepsut had herself depicted as a bearded pharaoh on one of the sphinxes that guarded her temple.

Hatshepsut Builds a Temple

Imagining the Past

That first glimpse always left her breathless. Queen Hatshepsut stood before the limestone cliff, gazing at her temple. It shimmered like a mirage. Three wide and graceful terraces rose from the sand, supported by hundreds of columns, their pale yellow stones mirroring Egypt's desert sands.

"It might have grown there on its own," she murmured.

"But, your majesty—!"

She turned. Behind her on the path stood Senmut with a look of shock spread across his face. He flushed under her steady gaze, his eyes dropping to his leather sandals.

Hatshepsut smiled. "Dear Senmut," she said. "I did not mean that literally. Surely you cannot imagine I've forgotten your superb work as architect and overseer." She looked pointedly at the many gold necklaces draped over his fine linen tunic, signs of her royal favor.

Wordlessly, Senmut bowed.

"Nor do I forget the labors of the common people." A faint shout echoed up. Down in the valley, dozens of men strained together at the ropes of a sled carrying a single giant block of stone.

Her gaze moved eastward, toward the river Nile, in the midst of its yearly flood. She frowned. "I only hope they will complete their work before the Nile recedes, when they must return to their fields."

"You are pharaoh, god on earth. The people live only to serve you."

"Then they must eat to live, so they may go on serving me." But she was smiling again. "Come, let us see how the building progresses."

Senmut followed the queen down the path. At the foot of the temple stood recently planted rows of small, prickly trees. Hatshepsut paused to inhale their spicy scent. "Someday my priests will burn incense made from the sap of these trees."

"The gods will be pleased."

"*I* will be pleased. No longer will the gold of Egypt pass into the hands of foreign traders," said Hatshepsut. "And all will remember it was I who brought the precious trees here from the far-off land of Punt." She glanced at Senmut. "How is that carving coming along?"

He bowed again, sweeping his arm toward the temple. "If your majesty wishes...."

They found a team of skilled masons hard at work chiseling pictures and hieroglyphs into the white stone walls. As the queen approached, the craftsmen dropped their tools and fell to their knees, pressing their noses to the ground.

Hatshepsut motioned them to rise. Curiously, she scanned the walls. "Ah, yes. This shows my fleet ready to sail from Thebes, with 30 brave and hardy sailors on each ship." She ran a finger across a raised carving of a very fat woman standing next to a donkey. "And here is the Queen of Punt! Twice my size and half my ability. Ah, but what a kingdom she has." She laughed, smoothing her tunic over her own slim hips.

"A glorious expedition," agreed Senmut. "To send Egyptian ships hundreds of miles south, to the very ends of the earth, perhaps never to return...."

But they did return, and it had been the greatest moment of her reign. Never would she forget the cheers of the crowd as the triumphant sailors paraded through the streets of Thebes with their exotic treasures—ebony and ivory, gold, incense trees, leopard skins, and—.

"Apes!"

Where Was Punt?

No one knows for sure where the kingdom of Punt was located. Some historians believe it was in modern-day Eritrea. Wherever its exact location, historians agree that Punt must have been on or near the coast of the Red Sea.

The architect looked puzzled. "Your majesty?"

"Apes," she repeated. "Be sure the stonemasons do not forget the apes and monkeys. I adore the funny creatures."

A small gesture from Senmut brought a servant scurrying to his side with papyrus, pigment pot, and brush. *Apes*, he scribbled in hieratic script, the squiggly symbols used for writing quickly. Later a lesser scribe would translate his notes into proper hieroglyphs for the carvers to copy.

Hatshepsut moved on, and Senmut followed.

Above their heads, a sculptor knelt on scaffolding, carving an enormous stone image of the queen.

"Lovely," said Senmut. "Nearly as lovely as the original." With her jeweled collar, red-tinted lips, and glittery gray-rimmed eyelids, she was indeed beautiful, the envy of all the ladies of the court.

But Hatshepsut was shaking her head. "Something is missing."

"I haven't painted the eyes in yet," the sculptor said.

"No...." She crossed her arms and stared up at the statue. "The beard! You must show me with the false beard and crown. Otherwise, future generations might doubt I was truly god-king of all Egypt." She sighed. It was a constant battle, making people understand a woman was pharaoh.

"Of course!" Senmut said hastily. "I am to blame. I should have ordered it so."

Hatshepsut went on as if she hadn't heard him. "And you must carve my royal name in hieroglyphs deep into the stone, so it can never be erased. If my name should ever be forgotten, then my soul will die and I will not be able to enjoy the afterlife."

The sculptor nodded. Everyone hoped for a joyous afterlife. There, even poor farmers could relax and play a game of *senet* while their crops grew tall and healthy in the field. How much more, then, must the rich and powerful anticipate eternal luxury and joy!

Their inspection over, the queen and Senmut passed down the steps and found themselves outside. Hatshepsut turned to regard her temple once again.

"Spectacular," she said. "Entirely original."

Senmut could not help but agree. Still, he knew better than to take credit himself for the design.

"Under your rule, Egypt has basked in prosperity and peace," he said instead. "Your majesty is wise to build this greatest of all monuments, so future generations may never forget your glorious reign."

Hatshepsut lifted a kohl-darkened eyebrow. "Greatest of all monuments?" she teased. "Greater than Khufu's pyramid at Giza? That took a hundred thousand men 25 years to build, or so I'm told."

"I—I didn't mean—" Senmut stammered. Surely she didn't think that he would dare to criticize a pharaoh, even one who had died over a thousand years before.

But Hatshepsut had already turned her attention elsewhere. Giza. That reminded her....

Ancient Egyptian Makeup

As we can tell from many surviving portraits from ancient Egypt, both men and women took special care to decorate their eyes. They used *kohl*, made from a dark metallic substance, to darken their eyelashes and eyebrows, and to paint outlines that gave the eyes a desired almond shape. The kohl also cut down the glare from the blazing desert sun. In the tombs of both rich and poor, archaeologists have found small containers, called kohl pots, used to store the eye makeup.

A fourteenth-century B.C. *bust of Nefertiti—its left eye missing—shows the cosmetics the queen may have used in real life.*

"Sphinxes," she said.

"I want sphinxes. Lots of them, to guard the road all the way from the west bank of the Nile to the temple."

Relieved, Senmut nodded.

The two stood side by side, admiring the temple in the light of the setting sun.

Pharaoh is pleased, thought Senmut. I wonder if she would agree to have my own image carved near hers within the temple? Or, perhaps…might she even allow me to be buried here?

He glanced sideways. Hatshepsut appeared lost in thought. Possibly even now she was considering how to reward her loyal servant?

Actually, she had forgotten Senmut entirely.

In her mind an image was taking shape—two great shafts of red granite, each a hundred feet high, their tops carved into a pyramid shape, then coated with pure gold and silver to reflect the rays of the sun for miles around. She would dedicate this pair of obelisks to the god of sun and sky.

Yes. Another monument. What better use for the abundant wealth of the royal treasury?

She turned to Senmut, noticing for the first time his eager look. Ah, excellent Senmut. He deserved to be rewarded for his help building her temple, and she did not mean to disappoint him.

No, indeed. Hatshepsut would grant her architect the highest honor she could think of. She would allow him to work on her next project….

In the end Hatshepsut honored Senmut by authorizing the placement of his tomb under the forecourt of her temple.

Amenhotep IV, the pharaoh who forbade worship of the old gods of Egypt.

Three Pharaohs of the New Kingdom

Ancient Egyptian civilization lasted for more than 3,000 years—so long that historians break it into different periods. Three of ancient Egypt's main periods are the Old Kingdom (2686–2181 B.C.), the Middle Kingdom (1991–1786 B.C.), and the New Kingdom (1554–1070 B.C.).

During the Old Kingdom, Khufu's Great Pyramid and other pyramids at Giza were built. During the Middle Kingdom, Egyptians greatly expanded their reach. They conquered territory to the south and traded with lands as distant as Syria. It was during the New Kingdom that Hatshepsut ruled.

Now we're going to find out more about the New Kingdom, the most glorious of Egypt's golden ages. We'll learn about three pharaohs who ruled during that five-hundred-year stretch. One brought change and confusion to ancient Egypt. Another was just a boy who died in his teenage years. He has come to be known as "King Tut." The third was Ramses II, a ruler who lived into his nineties. All three have fascinating stories to tell.

A Disruptive Pharaoh

We learned in the last chapter how important the many gods were to the Egyptian people. That's a lesson that at least one of the pharaohs did not seem to learn. During the mid-1300s B.C., Amenhotep IV (ahm-uhn-HOH-tep) became one of the most disruptive rulers Egypt had ever seen. He got that reputation not by destroying buildings (which he did), nor by attacking his enemies (which he did as well), but by dismantling a religion.

A sandstone bust of Pharaoh Amenhotep IV.

Amenhotep outlawed the worship of the many gods of ancient Egypt. He did not end the practice of religion. Instead, Amenhotep established a new religion, one that replaced the old gods with one new, all-powerful sun-god. A radiating sun disk represented this single god, called Aten (AH-tn). Aten alone was to be worshiped. Amenhotep declared, "There is none other than he."

To make his point, the new pharaoh decided to change his own name. He had been named after his father, Amenhotep III, whose name meant "Amen (AH-men) is pleased." Amen was one of the most important gods of ancient Egypt. The new pharaoh didn't want a name that recalled an old god. So he changed his name to Akhenaten (ahk-NAH-tn), or "the spirit of Aten."

Amenhotep makes an offering to the sun-god Aten, which he established as Egypt's only deity. To further honor his new god, the pharaoh changed his own name to Akhenaten.

Akhenaten's revolution in religion shook the land to its sandy foundations. The pharaoh's subjects were horrified at the changes. The priests of the old gods watched their power and prestige vanish. Akhenaten forced the people to worship a god they knew little about. Gone was Re, the old god of the sun, provider of bountiful harvests. Gone was Thoth, the god of knowledge and wisdom. Banished too, were the much-loved Osiris, his sister Isis, and their son, the falcon-headed Horus, god of the sky.

In their place was Aten, "the disk of the sun." Here was a god that seemed to have no personality and no history among the Egyptian people. Still, pharaoh would tolerate no resistance. Akhenaten wanted to wipe out the memory of the old gods of Egypt. He ordered squads of workers to use hammers and chisels to chip the gods' names off walls. They defaced the images of the gods that had adorned old temples.

Akhenaten then set about building a new capital, a place devoted to his god, about 250 miles downriver from the old capital of Thebes. There he could worship Aten in new temples without roofs, sacred buildings open to the life-giving rays of the sun.

A Boy-King Restores the Gods

As Akhenaten worked his will, one young member of the royal family watched it all. Some say he was Akhenaten's son; others say he was the pharaoh's youngest brother. Few noticed the boy, who seemed to occupy himself with childish pursuits—his shiny silver trumpet, his models of ships and animals. But the boy saw everything.

We do not know exactly what the child Tutankhaten (too-tahng-KAHT-uhn) was thinking. But priests at the time wondered if the old Egyptian gods were angry with their people. Without the help of the old gods, would Egypt be ruined? Later records show Egyptians denouncing Akhenaten as a "scoundrel," "rebel," and "criminal."

When Akhenaten died 17 years after he came to power, young Tutankhaten became king. This nine-year-old ruler and his eager advisors wasted little time returning Egypt to its traditional deities. Just as Akhenaten had removed images of the old gods, so the young king, guided by priests, got rid of all images of Akhenaten! Workers removed depictions of the old pharaoh from their monuments. The capital he had built was left to ruin, its temples and palace swallowed by the desert sands. The Egyptians moved their capital back to Thebes.

That took care of the past. But Egyptians had their future to worry about. When the new boy-king ascended the throne of Egypt, he immediately set about restoring the traditional gods of Egypt. He made the future clear by changing *his* name. The name he chose acknowledged the old god, Amen. He called himself "Tutankhamen" (too-tahng-KAH-muhn).

Tutankhamen ruled for just about 10 years. In addition to encouraging worship of the old gods, he restored defaced sandstone temples to their former glory. He used his short reign to build temples to the traditional deities, such as Amen, Re, and Osiris. "King Tut," as we have come to know the young pharaoh, returned Egypt to its familiar path. His death at around age 18 remains a mystery. Some people believe that he died during a hunting accident. Some say he was murdered. We may never know.

Whatever the reason, Tut was buried in a small tomb in the Valley of the Kings, the final resting place of pharaohs who had gone before him. The young king was largely forgotten. He lay for more than three millennia in the Valley of the Kings, until the year 1922. That was when a British archaeologist named Howard Carter found the boy-king's burial place. It was one of the greatest archaeological finds of all time. For the first time, an archaeologist unearthed a royal Egyptian tomb in excellent condition. At the end of this chapter, you can read the story of this amazing discovery.

Top: Ceramic statue of the boy-king Tutankhamen.

Above: Howard Carter and his assistants open King Tut's tomb.

Right: Ramses II rides his war chariot into battle against the Hittites at the battle of Kadesh.

Ramses the Second, Ramses the Great

After Tutankhamen's death, a series of pharaohs came to the throne. These rulers spent much of their time trying to strengthen Egypt's empire. The greatest of them was a ruler who would have *great* in his title—Ramses II (RAM-seez), or Ramses the Great. He ruled from 1290 to 1224 B.C.

A mighty warrior, Ramses donned his leopard skin cloak, mounted his chariot, and prowled the borders of his kingdom. With his highly trained army of charioteers, archers, and foot soldiers, the pharaoh put down revolts and fended off invaders who threatened Egypt's vast realm. His best-known campaign came against the Hittite (HIH-tiyt) empire in the north.

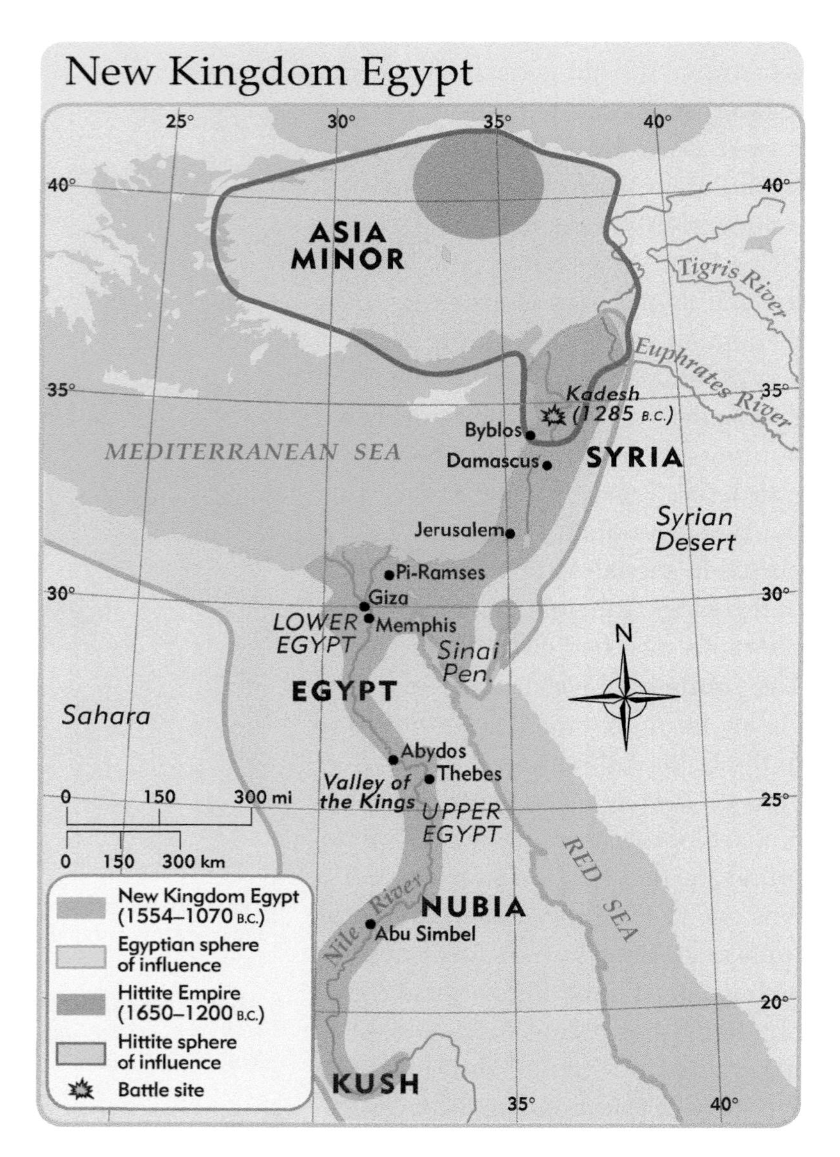

The Hittites were at that time the rising power of the ancient world. Their home was in the tableland of central Asia Minor, but their power reached south into Syria and over to the eastern edge of the Mediterranean—the very lands that Ramses wanted to retain for Egypt. It was inevitable that the two sides would clash. In 1285 B.C., they did.

The Hittites were formidable foes. Equipped with sturdy war chariots that carried a three-man crew, their army was a battering ram that smashed through the battle lines of any enemy—any, that is, except the ranks of Ramses the Great. For the Egyptians were skilled charioteers, too. And their war chariots were lighter and swifter than those of their foes. Ramses himself was a skilled charioteer. When he led his army north, said his scribes, "all the foreign lands trembled before him."

When the two sides clashed at Kadesh (KAY-desh), the Hittites did not tremble as much as Ramses would have liked. They drew the Egyptians into an ambush. Both sides fought hard, but neither could win. Ramses barely escaped with his life, while the Hittites failed to conquer the Egyptian lands. History has judged the battle of Kadesh a tie.

Ramses proved a more skilled statesman than a warrior. After the stalemate at Kadesh, he signed a treaty with the Hittites that gave the Egyptians control of southern Syria.

Ramses II was more than a warrior. Like many pharaohs before him, he was a builder. This pharaoh who loved to do everything on a grand scale launched a building spree the likes of which Egypt had never seen before.

A Capital Builder

At Karnak, in the capital city of Thebes, Ramses II completed a great pillared hall that was about the size of a modern-day football field—probably the biggest temple the Egyptians ever built. About 250 miles south of Thebes, in the splendid isolation of Abu Simbel (ah-boo SIM-bull), he raised a huge new temple hewn from a cliff face overlooking the Upper Nile. Four colossal statues of Ramses, measuring 66 feet from head to toe, sat watch at the entrance to the temple, whose interior penetrated about 180 feet into the rock face.

This was a pharaoh who took extra measures to be sure that he would be remembered. Inside the

Though eroded over the ages, four huge seated statues of Ramses continue to sit in regal splendor outside the temple of Abu Simbel. The smaller figures represent members of the royal family.

temple's great hall he had his builders raise eight massive statues of himself, each of them 30 feet tall. On the walls in between them, the pharaoh had his masons carve battle scenes that celebrated his victories in warfare.

The temple was designed with astonishing precision and accuracy. The skill of the Egyptian builders was especially evident on two particular days each year, one in mid-October, the other in mid-February. On those two days, which may have marked the pharaoh's coronation and birthday, sunlight poured through the temple's entrance into its deepest recesses. There the light fell on the faces of two smaller statues. One was that of—who else?—Ramses wearing a crown. The other was that of the god Amen—the god Akhenaten tried to dethrone and Tutankhamen had worked so hard to restore.

Never tiring of his own image, Ramses raised many statues of himself.

Ramses built more monuments to himself than any other pharaoh. He even "stole" many from his ancestors by chiseling their names from the monuments and writing in his own. And like Akhenaten, he built himself a new capital. The city was located far from Thebes, deep in the pharaoh's ancestral homeland in the Nile Delta, about 400 miles to the north. It was known as Pi-Ramses, and its full name meant "Domain of Ramses Great of Victories."

Ancient texts praised the new capital as "beauteous of balconies, dazzling with halls of lapis and turquoise." Government buildings, mansions for important officials, warehouses bursting with grain, and temples for Egypt's gods rose from the Delta's floodplain.

Ramses died about 1224 B.C., after reigning more than 60 years, almost twice as long as most Egyptians lived. He was buried at Thebes, where thieves who cared little for his greatness discovered his tomb. Determined to make off with the riches of this magnificent ruler, they stripped his mummy and tomb. His home for the afterlife was pilfered as thoroughly as those of all other pharaohs. All, that is, except those of the boy-king Tutankhamen.

Egypt's New Kingdom came to an end around 1070 B.C. when, weakened by internal struggles, Egypt itself became prey to its neighbors. The kingdom suffered invasion and rule by a series of foreign dynasties. Over the years Egyptians adopted some of these outsiders' ways. The conquerors, meanwhile, began to follow some Egyptian customs. The foreign rulers happily took the title "pharaoh" and even adopted the Egyptian religion. With all these changes and the passing of time, the ways of ancient Egypt gradually faded. But the treasures the Egyptians left behind in the dry desert climate—pyramids, sphinxes, hieroglyphs, mummies—still tell of the glory of the land of the pharaohs.

Before we say goodbye to ancient Egypt, let's find out how a British archaeologist named Howard Carter found King Tut's burial place. Our story takes place in the year 1922. It begins far away from Egypt—in England, where Howard Carter has just heard some bad news from Lord Carnarvon, the wealthy man who provided funds for Carter's explorations.

Discovering the Tomb of Tutankhamen

Imagining the Past

"You've been digging for five years," said Lord Carnarvon. "I'm afraid I simply can't afford to finance any further excavation."

"But we can't stop now!" protested Howard Carter. Carter's insides went hollow. The expense of an archaeological dig was huge. How would he ever manage to pay hundreds of workers? Not to mention the expense of tools, supplies....

Quietly, he said, "Discovering an intact royal tomb would repay all our efforts."

Lord Carnarvon sighed. "How many archaeologists have combed the Valley of the Kings in the last century? Every tomb has been unearthed—"

"Except the tomb of the boy pharaoh, Tutankhamen."

"—And every one," the lord went on, ignoring the interruption, "has been emptied thousands of years ago."

It was true. No one had ever found an intact royal tomb. The fabulous treasures meant to follow each pharaoh into the underworld had instead been carted off by ancient tomb robbers. But one tomb remained undiscovered, at least by modern-day archaeologists. And there was still one spot where Carter and his team had not yet searched. It was too soon to give up.

"With your permission, my lord," said Carter, "I will continue our work"—he paused—"at my own expense."

Carnarvon studied him for a long moment. At last, he smiled. "All right. I will pay for one more season." The smile faded slightly. "*One.*"

Carter arrived early at the site, whistling softly to hide his anxiety. A few days ago the digging had begun. Energy and hope had been replaced by growing doubt. Would months of backbreaking labor end yet again in disappointment?

He slid off his donkey's back and called out to the crew, "Good morning!"

No one replied. No one even moved. The workers stood staring at him silently. Oh, no. Had there been an accident?

Finally, the foreman spoke. A discovery had been made, and by the smallest, youngest, least important member of the crew—the water boy. Digging in the sand to make a place to set his water jars out of the sun, the boy had struck something hard. Cleared off, it turned out to be a step cut in the rock.

A step! Could it be true? As the men set to work, Carter struggled to control his excitement. A proper excavation must be done slowly and carefully. To hurry could mean to destroy priceless archaeological evidence.

By the next afternoon, there could be no doubt: It was the beginning of a staircase that led straight down, deep into the earth. They were looking at the entrance to a hidden tomb.

Be realistic, Carter told himself. The tomb might be unfinished—started, then abandoned—or complete, but never used. He'd seen that before. And even if a pharaoh had been buried there, what were the chances of it having remained safe from thieves? One in a million, maybe. Maybe less.

Workers continued to clear the steps. Three steps…five steps…eight steps…ten.

The sun was sinking by the time they uncovered step number twelve. And there, facing the staircase, stood the upper portion of a door.

It was a door of stone, covered in layers of plaster stamped with ancient seals. Heart pounding, Carter scanned the hieroglyphs. The seals were blurred. He could not make out a royal name, but looking more closely, Carter saw it. A resting jackal, ears alert; nine enemy captives, tied up with arms behind their backs. It was the royal seal. The jackal-headed god, Anubis, symbolized the king. But which king?

At the top of the doorway, Carter made a tiny hole. He held his flashlight up and peered inside. The passage was completely filled with rubble. Clearly, someone had tried very hard to keep trespassers out. Was he on the verge of discovering an untouched tomb?

Carter longed to see what was in the tomb, but he knew the discovery was important and that it did not belong to him alone. Lord Carnarvon—who, after all, had paid for the expedition—must be here to share that moment. Reluctantly, with the help of his crew, he reburied the steps, then posted men to guard the site.

Early the next morning, Carter sent a telegram to England:

AT LAST HAVE MADE WONDERFUL DISCOVERY IN VALLEY: A MAGNIFICENT TOMB WITH SEALS INTACT. RE-COVERED SAME FOR YOUR ARRIVAL. CONGRATULATIONS.

Two and a half weeks later—an eternity to Carter—Lord Carnarvon and his 20-year-old daughter Evelyn arrived. At Carter's request, a British engineer named Arthur Callender joined them as well.

This time, the door was cleared all the way to the bottom. And there Carter read the name upon the seals and his heart seemed to stop—*Tutankhamen*.

He noticed something else as well. The plaster had been torn apart and patched—twice. This damage could only mean that robbers had broken into the tomb. But would the royal priests have bothered to reseal the door so carefully if everything were gone?

Basket by basket, the workers dug out the long passageway. It led to another door just like the first.

Once again, Carter made a tiny hole. He held a candle to the hole, testing the air. Then, the others waiting anxiously behind him, he peered in.

Moments passed. Finally, unable to bear the suspense, Lord Carnarvon burst out, "Can you see anything?"

Carter could hardly find his voice. "Yes, wonderful things!"

Shapes were emerging from the cloak of darkness—two ebony-black images of the king, gold-sandaled, holding his staff; gilded couches crowned with lion heads or the head of Hathor; strange animals. And gold—everywhere he could see the glimmer and the glint of gold.

"Surely never before in the whole history of excavation," Carter wrote years later, "had such an amazing sight been seen as the light of our torch revealed to us."

A seated King Tut is anointed with oil by his wife.

Carefully, Carter enlarged the hole. Lady Evelyn, the smallest of the group, wriggled through first. With some difficulty, the men followed.

The room was packed with treasures, any one of which would have been ample reward for their search. A golden throne; vases of creamy alabaster;

boxes intricately painted to show scenes of royal life; great gilded couches in the form of animals, heads carved to look like a lion, a cow, or a crocodile crossed with a hippopotamus.

To Howard Carter, it felt as if the chamber had been filled not 3,000 years ago, but yesterday. A blackened lamp sat as if someone had just set it down; a bouquet of dried flowers, perfectly preserved, lay by the door. They even spotted the print left by a dirty bare foot.

Robbers had been here, but they had only taken what they could carry—jewelry, and vessels of precious metals. Larger items they had tossed aside. In one corner lay a heap of golden chariots, in pieces. Against the wall, two imposing life-sized black and gold statues faced each other—a young man in the headdress of a king, the sacred cobra rearing up above his forehead—Tutankhamen.

As the archaeologists explored, they found a hole leading into a second chamber. Smaller than the first, it was stuffed with even more objects—two thousand in all, piled six-feet high and jumbled all together. Here were many of the everyday objects the ancient Egyptians believed their king might find

Howard Carter helps raise a tray of artifacts from the tomb of Tutankhamen.

useful in the afterlife—sandals, a fan, bows and arrows, baskets of food and jugs of wine, even a board game made of ebony and ivory.

Carter could hardly believe what he was seeing. And a glance at Lord Carnarvon told him that his partner felt the same. It was more than the reward for all their work, more than the fulfillment of their wildest dreams.

But the most spectacular discovery was still to come. The section of wall between the two statues of the king was not a wall at all. It was a doorway. And through that doorway was the burial chamber.

A richly decorated gilded shrine filled nearly the whole room. Inside it was a second, smaller shrine, gilded as well; inside that, there was a third. In the fourth shrine was a stone sarcophagus, a vault where the pharaoh lay buried. Carter and Carnarvon caught their breath.

Before the sarcophagus could be opened, the shrines had to be taken apart piece by piece, and every item in the room recorded. Also, an elaborate pulley system was needed to lift the heavy stone lid.

Almost three years passed before the team was ready. In the meantime, Lord Carnarvon died. (Some said it was his punishment for intruding into the tomb—"the mummy's curse"—though he'd been in poor health for years.) On the big day, Carter stood alone before a crowd of curious onlookers.

The lid of the sarcophagus was raised. Carefully, Carter pushed aside the ancient linen. A fantastic coffin revealed itself, glittering with gold, fashioned in the shape of the dead king. In the days that followed, the team uncovered two more golden coffins, equally elaborate, nested within. Inside the third solid gold coffin lay the mummy. Over its face had been placed a magnificent object. The solid gold death mask of the boy king, Tutankhamen, stared up into the astonished eyes of Howard Carter.

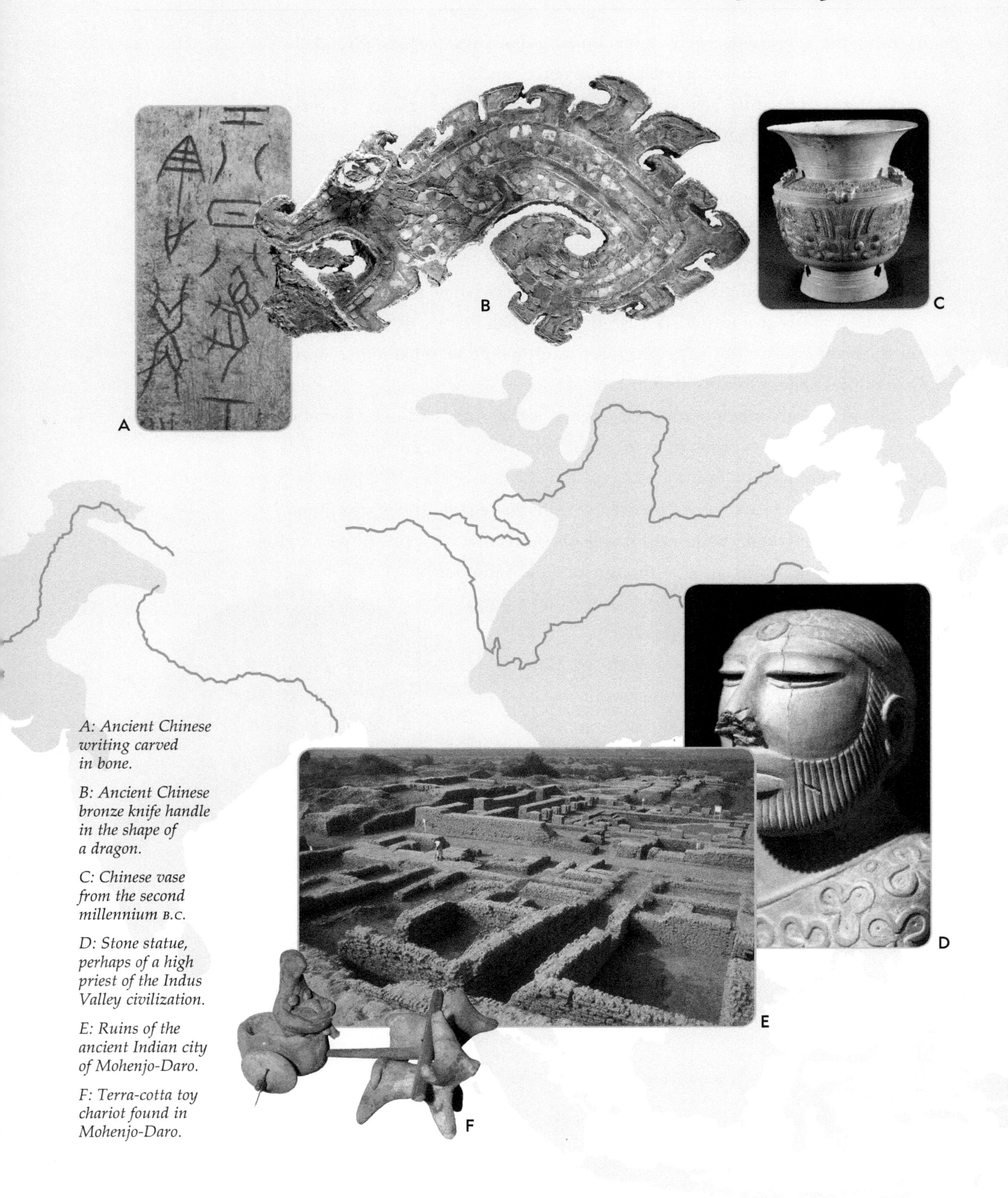

A: Ancient Chinese writing carved in bone.

B: Ancient Chinese bronze knife handle in the shape of a dragon.

C: Chinese vase from the second millennium B.C.

D: Stone statue, perhaps of a high priest of the Indus Valley civilization.

E: Ruins of the ancient Indian city of Mohenjo-Daro.

F: Terra-cotta toy chariot found in Mohenjo-Daro.

The Spread of Civilization: India and China

Sumer and Egypt are the two earliest civilizations known to us. By 3000 B.C., both were thriving along the banks of flooding rivers, building impressive cities, and even trading with each other. The Tigris and Euphrates Rivers in Mesopotamia, and the Nile in Egypt had been generous in their gifts of rich soil. The enterprising inhabitants of the river valleys figured out how to harness floodwaters and use the soil to grow abundant crops.

Sumer and Egypt were human firsts, but they were not the only river valleys where civilization emerged. In other parts of the world, other peoples followed a similar pattern. Along the banks of the Indus River, city-builders were at work by 2500 B.C. Thousands of miles away in China, another great civilization took root—one that has evolved through the millennia to this very day. The river valleys of India and China, like those in Egypt and Mesopotamia, became cradles of human civilization.

On the Banks of the Indus

Let's turn first to the valley of the Indus River. We know little about this civilization, but what we do know makes us eager to know more.

The early inhabitants of the Indus Valley planned cities with grid-like streets, developed sophisticated water systems, and built large buildings. They invented a complex system of writing, which scholars have yet to understand. By 2500 B.C., this Indus Valley civilization was flourishing. By 1500 B.C., it had declined, and the Indus Valley people themselves began mixing with others in the region.

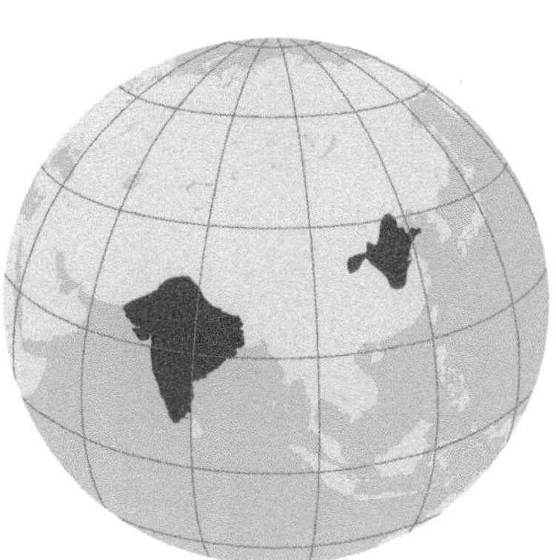

This chapter focuses on ancient Asian civilizations in India and China.

Headwaters of the Indus River, high in the snowcapped Himalaya. From here the river flows to the floodplains farther south.

The Indus River lies at the edge of a huge peninsula jutting from the southern part of Asia. We call this giant peninsula the "Indian subcontinent." Today it contains the countries of India, Pakistan, Bangladesh, Nepal, and Bhutan. The Indian subcontinent is home to nearly one and a half billion people—more than one out of every five people living on Earth.

The Indian subcontinent has the shape of a diamond. At the top of the diamond are the Himalaya, majestic snowcapped mountains that slope from the subcontinent's northern point to its eastern point. This mountain range, the highest in the world, separates the subcontinent from the rest of Asia.

The southern tip of the diamond stretches into the Indian Ocean. At the diamond's eastern point, the Ganges River flows into the Bay of Bengal, in the modern-day nation of Bangladesh. And on the western point of the diamond, in the modern-day nation of Pakistan, the mighty Indus River runs to the Arabian Sea. It is this waterway, the Indus, that gave India its name.

- On the map of India on this page, locate the Himalaya, Ganges River, Bay of Bengal, Indian Ocean, Arabian Sea, and Indus River.

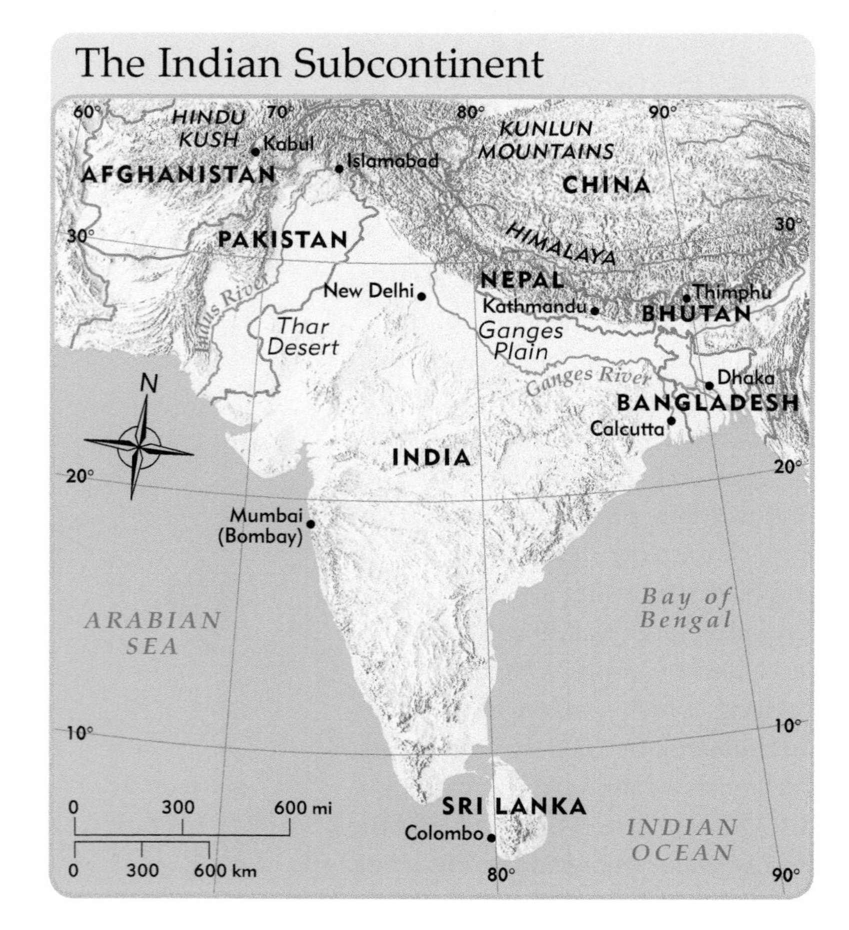

Much of the subcontinent's early history ebbs and flows with the waters of the Indus. The river begins high in the snowy valleys of the Himalaya. Each year, when the warm spring sun melts the snows, water tumbles through the mountain passes. The river swells and flows toward the sea, repeating the familiar pattern of the three rivers you already know, the Euphrates, the Tigris, and the Nile. As the Indus overflows its banks, it deposits alluvial soil—dark, rich silt—and turns the floodplain into fertile fields.

By the third millennium B.C., this rich soil made it possible for Indus Valley farmers to grow wheat, barley, and a variety of fruits. Using simple irrigation canals, the farmers reaped even greater harvests. Bountiful harvests, in turn, brought the two big rewards that made civilization possible—a surplus of food and division of labor.

The people of the Indus, like the people of Mesopotamia, domesticated animals, many of them unique to the region. Have you ever seen a zebu? It's a kind of humpbacked oxen found mainly in Asia, a strong creature when put to the plow. Indus Valley farmers used zebu, cattle, pigs, sheep, goats, water buffalo, and perhaps elephants as well.

For the first time in history, some of those who tilled the Indus Valley soil grew cotton and mastered the art of weaving its lightweight, sturdy fibers. The people of the Indus came to produce a tough, light cloth that would be in demand throughout the ancient world.

More than 300 cities and towns sprang up in the valley of the Indus River. Two of them stand out. One was called Harappa (huh-RA-puh). The other city, 400 miles downriver, is Mohenjo-Daro (moh-HEN-joh DAHR-oh). Much of what we know about this civilization comes from these urban sites.

- On the map on page 132, locate Harappa and Mohenjo-Daro.

The Cities of the Indus Valley

Picture this. Seated cross-legged, arms and hands outstretched to touch his knees, a strong man closes his eyes in meditation. A tiger, rhinoceros, water buffalo, elephant, and other animals look on. Now the scene changes. Incense swirls in a cloud about a single-horned beast. Change again. A man offers gifts to a tiger.

These unusual scenes, carved in soapstone squares in about 2500 B.C., are part of the mystery of the Indus Valley civilization. Who was the seated man? A god? Or a priest? What does the animal in a cloud of incense mean? Were tigers sacred? The answers to these questions remain a mystery to this very day.

Here's what we do know. A thoughtful people planned and lived in Mohenjo-Daro and the other Indus cities. Archaeologists have dug deep in these ancient sites and found that their broad main streets were straight and regular, forming nearly perfect grids. These neatly planned city blocks ran north and south, east and west. Narrow side streets wound between them, lined with solidly built brick houses of two stories or more. Standardized systems of

Above: Soapstone square showing a cross-legged figure. The writing above him has never been deciphered.

Below: An Indian humpbacked ox, or zebu.

weights and other measures existed in the cities, including quite uniform brick sizes.

Some of the early city-dwellers enjoyed indoor baths. The residents of the Indus cities even had toilets connected by a system of drains and water chutes running beneath the streets—an amazing achievement in urban planning for 2500 B.C. While the people of Sumer invented the wheel, and the people of Egypt gave us the sail, it seems that the people of the Indus were the first to have indoor plumbing!

Rising above the heart of Mohenjo-Daro was a large circular mound topped by a five-story building. This was perhaps the center of government or religion. It boasted a granary for surplus wheat and barley, an assembly hall, and a large public bath—39 feet long, 23 feet wide, and 8 feet deep. Was this enormous brick-lined bath used for religious or social purposes? Did people bathe there to purify themselves or to meet and discuss politics or business? Did cross-legged holy men or merchants sit

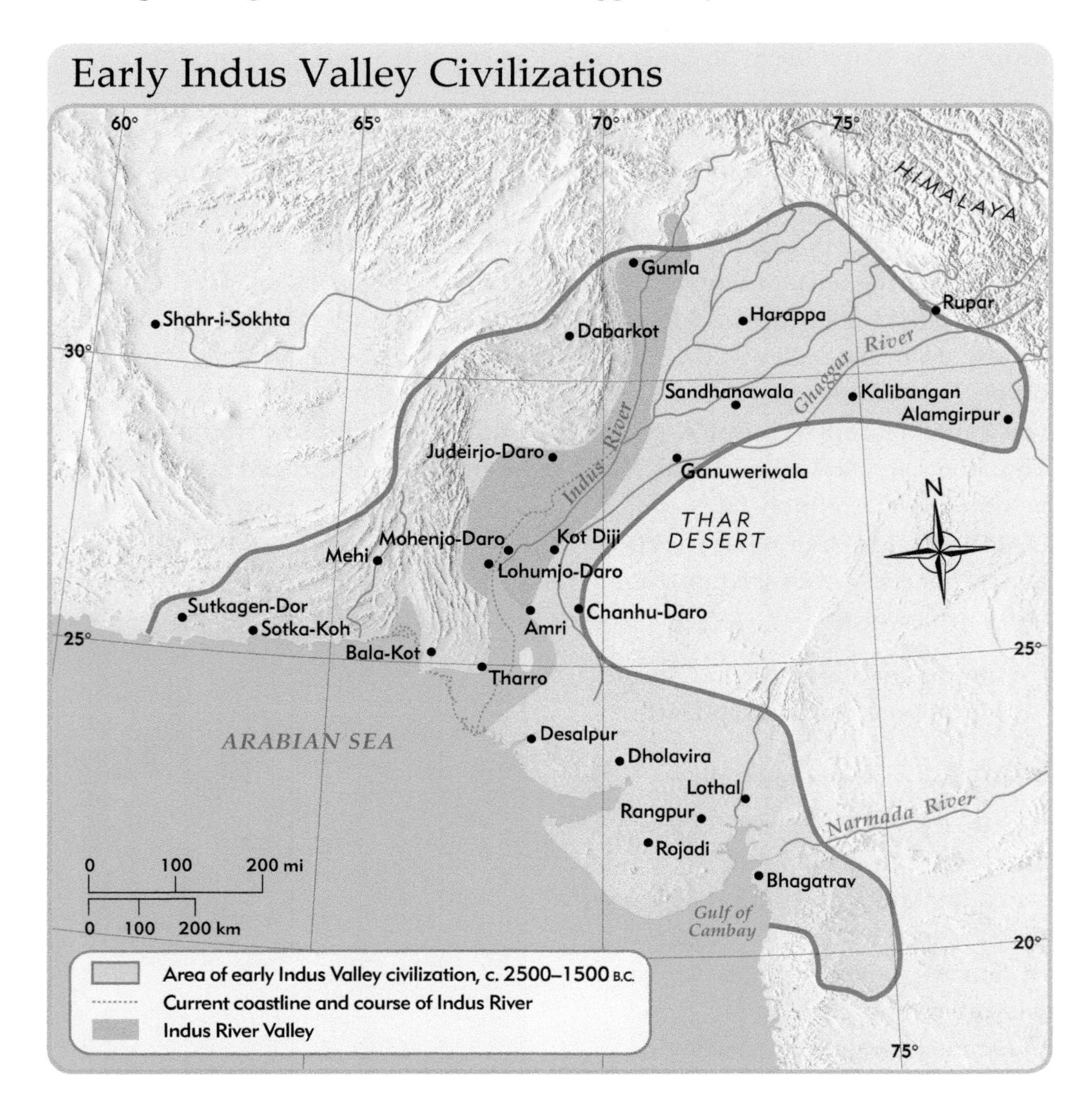

here? Scholars still speculate about the possible uses for these impressive works.

In the ruins of the Indus Valley cities, archaeologists are still unearthing clues that provide hints about this early people. They've found small terra-cotta statues showing how people dressed and perhaps what their gods looked like. They've found tools, mirrors, pots, pans, and even children's toys. They've uncovered a tantalizing amount of jewelry. It's clear that craftsmen from the Indus cities used gold, silver, copper, gemstones, and ivory to fashion ornaments and jewelry.

Indus Valley traders carried on business far and wide. They imported lapis lazuli, turquoise, and carnelian from lands to the west. They had the stones made into exquisite beads and ornaments, and then sent the finished jewelry on to Mesopotamia, Iran, and Central Asia. From ports on the Arabian Sea, Indus Valley merchants sailed through the Persian Gulf to Sumer, carrying cotton textiles, timber, ivory, gold—and chickens!

Merchants probably owned those carved soapstone squares with the unusual scenes. They were stamp seals or signature seals about the size of today's postage stamps. Like the cylinder seals used in Sumer, these seals were designed to leave an imprint in wet clay. Each merchant or official probably had his own seal and may have used it to identify ownership of bales of cotton or bags of grain. Beautifully carved depictions adorn the seals—a bull pulling a cart, a rhinoceros or elephant standing proud. The seals attest to the abundance of animal life on the Indus—zebu, garbed elephants, rhinoceros, antelopes, tigers, and buffalo abound.

The thousands of surviving seals also bear some form of writing, but so far scholars have not figured out how to read it. As you know, archaeologists found keys to help them translate the cuneiform of Sumer and hieroglyphics of Egypt. But they have not yet found a "Rosetta stone" to serve as a key to the unique script of the Indus Valley civilization.

Since we don't understand their writing, there is much we don't know about these people. We know they worshipped deities, but we don't know the names they gave their gods. We can tell the Indus Valley people were good at planning and had some government, but we can't identify their leaders and don't know how they were organized. We see that they loved to depict the world about them, but we don't know any of their great poems or myths. The door to much of this past will probably remain closed until more samples of the script turn up, and someone cracks the mystery of the Indus writing.

Above: An Indus Valley bull seal.

Below: Mohenjo-Daro's Great Bath.

Why Did the Indus Valley Civilization Decline?

The ruins of Mohenjo-Daro and other Indus cities hint at a great civilization that flourished for seven or eight hundred years. Though these people didn't build giant ziggurats or imposing pyramids, their cities bustled with activity. But by about 1500 B.C., their civilization had largely faded away, and trade fell off. Why?

It was partly because the Indus River and its tributaries changed course, causing huge floods, and disrupting agriculture and the economy. Indus Valley residents may have deforested their land to plant more fields, or to get firewood to bake vast numbers of bricks for building. Or perhaps irrigation gradually made the soil salty and unfit for agriculture, as in ancient Sumer. Or did disease bring about the ancient civilization's demise? In Mohenjo-Daro, archaeologists found a few skeletons lying in the street, as though the last people there died with no one to bury them. All of these explanations are possibilities.

The people of the Indus apparently abandoned their cities and began to live in simple villages. They also seem to have mixed with other peoples who were gradually migrating into their area from central Asia. Many Indus Valley people probably moved to more fertile regions of the subcontinent.

Sand and dirt blanketed the old citadels, until no one recalled the enterprising people who had lived there. Even though they were forgotten, parts of their culture have lived on. The current languages of South India are probably related to the language originally spoken by the Indus people. The cross-legged holy man on the soapstone seal looks a lot like those who engage in the modern practice of yoga. Some of the gods on the seals seem to resemble deities worshipped today by people in that part of the world. But what was the connection? There is much we simply do not know.

Two Indus artifacts—a game board (above) and a necklace with gold and other beads (right).

Investigating the Indus

About 200 years ago, British scholars heard reports of old artifacts buried in huge earth mounds near the Indus River. By 1921, Sir John Marshall, a British archaeologist, and his Indian colleague R.D. Banerjea were digging into those mounds. They discovered the remains of an entire civilization that had been lost for thousands of years—the one we now call the Indus civilization.

Since that time, archaeologists and historians have been poring over soapstone seals and other artifacts, trying to learn more about the Indus Valley people. Will we ever find a key to unlock the mystery of their writing? Will we ever know stories of the Indus Valley gods and leaders? Will we figure out exactly why a once-great civilization declined?

In the Valleys of Two Chinese Rivers

We've seen ancient civilizations rise along the banks of the Tigris and Euphrates Rivers in Sumer, the Nile River in Egypt, and the Indus River on the Indian subcontinent. Now we're going to travel farther east to China, where yet another ancient civilization was born.

Take a look at the modern-day country of China on a map or globe. You may already know that China is the most populous country in the world. About 1.3 *billion* people live there. But did you know that China is also the world's oldest living civilization?

True, civilization in China began a little later than in Sumer, Egypt, and India. But the civilizations that built Sumer's ziggurats, Egypt's pyramids, and ancient India's citadels, or fortresses, all came to an end. China is a different story. People in China today can trace their writing, history, art, and philosophy further back in time than people in any other modern nation. Civilization took root there more than 3,000 years ago, and it has been evolving nonstop ever since. That's why historians call it the world's oldest living civilization.

Twin Cradles of Civilization: The Yellow and Yangtze Rivers

Although civilization in China began a little later than in Sumer, Egypt, and India, as far as we know it began without contact with those three places. People in ancient China were cut off from the rest of the world by geographic features. To the north stretched the Gobi, a vast desert. In the west rose the jagged Himalaya and other mountainous lands. To the south and east lay the South China Sea, the East China Sea, and the Yellow Sea. These barriers would keep the people of China somewhat isolated for thousands of years.

- On the map below, locate the Gobi, Himalaya, Yellow Sea, East China Sea, and South China Sea.

By now you won't be surprised to learn that Chinese civilization got its start near a river—near *two* major rivers, in fact. The first was the Yellow River, which begins in the western highlands of China, flows north, makes an abrupt hairpin turn to the south, and then continues to the sea.

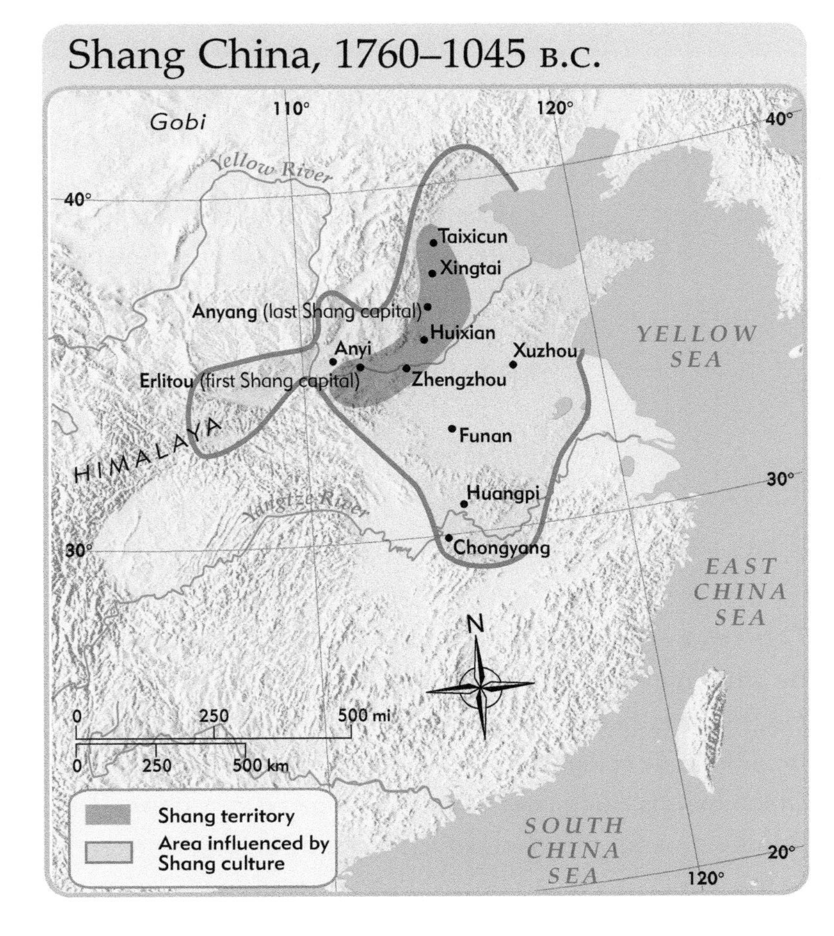

Top: Upper course of the Yellow River.

Above: A deep gorge along the Yangtze River.

The Yellow River is actually mud-colored. So why is it called *yellow*? Because it leaves a yellowish soil behind when the river's floodwaters recede. This soil is as fine as flour and good for growing millet, a kind of grain the Chinese people made into cereal.

Farther south, the Yangtze (YANG-see) River gave a second home to Chinese civilization. The climate there is warmer than in the north, the land green and lush. People discovered it was the perfect place to grow rice. Every spring, melting snow from the mountains turned to water and fattened the Yangtze River and its many tributaries. Farmers leveled land to make fields in the many well-watered valleys. The warm southern climate made possible two growing seasons every year, sometimes even three. So it wasn't long before the busy Chinese farmers had a surplus of food on their hands.

With that surplus, people were free do to other jobs besides farming—weaving baskets, making cloth, or fashioning pots to store grain. They began building simple wooden homes along the rivers and fields. Before long, villages and then cities were sprouting up. Civilization was beginning to bloom in ancient China.

- On the map on page 135, locate the Yellow River and the Yangtze River.

"Silk People"

The process of building a civilization in China sounds familiar, doesn't it? People who lived near rivers grew a surplus of food, divided the labor, and built villages and cities. But the Chinese did several things that set them apart from others. For one thing, they learned a secret they would jealously guard from the rest of the world for centuries—how to produce silk.

There's an old legend of how the Chinese first stumbled onto the

The Huang He and Chang Jiang

The Yellow River and the Yangtze River are also known by other names. The Yellow River is called the Huang He (hwahng huh). *Huang* means "yellow." The Yangtze is sometimes called Chang Jiang (chahng jee-yahng), which means "long river." Chang Jiang is a very appropriate name for this river, which is the third longest river in the world.

secret of silk. An empress, it is said, was having tea in her garden one day when a cocoon fell into her cup. The warm tea released a shiny white thread from the cocoon. She was not the squeamish sort, so she pulled the thread, and the cocoon slowly unraveled into a long glistening strand. The empress wondered if the delicate thread might be woven into cloth. Indeed it could.

That's the legend. We know it's not true because the Chinese didn't drink tea until much later. Yet it is true that as early as 2700 B.C., about the same time that Sumerians were building ziggurats and Egyptians were building pyramids, the Chinese likely used the silkworm to produce silk.

The silkworm feeds on the leaves of mulberry trees, so the Chinese planted mulberry groves. After the silkworms grew fat on the leaves and spun their cocoons, women would do the work of making silk. They had to boil each cocoon, carefully pull out a long single strand, and then twist the strands together to make thread. From that thread, they could weave the finest, softest cloth in the world. The women often embroidered dragons and tigers onto the cloth with a needle and thread. Or sometimes they painted the cloth with images of leopards, crows, and toads.

The Chinese loved their silk. Archaeologists have found royal tombs dating to 2000 B.C. with the occupants garbed in richly patterned silk clothes. And as we'll see later in our human odyssey, Chinese silk would eventually become the envy of the world. In the centuries to come, people from other civilizations would pay almost anything to get hold of the wondrous cloth. Silk became so valuable that a pound of it was worth a pound of gold. It became so famous that people who lived in China were known as the "silk people."

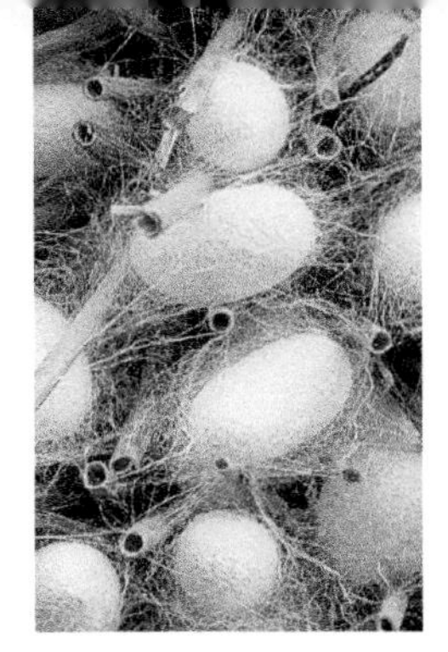

Cocoons spun by silkworms.

Writing and Religion

Like the Sumerians, Egyptians, and Indus River people, the Chinese developed a system of writing. We know about their writing because one of the materials they wrote on—bone—has survived in tombs. These bones were used to ask questions of the gods. By 1500 B.C., priests would heat bones of oxen or shells of turtles, and then watch as they cracked. They would ask the gods questions such as whether a battle would succeed or what was causing the king's toothache. They believed that the direction of the crack revealed the answer. Occasionally they wrote the question and answer on the bone using an early form of Chinese writing.

As in Sumer, Egypt, and India, the people of ancient China worshipped many nature gods. They believed the rivers, mountains, and forests were alive with spirits.

Above: Part of a bone covered with ancient Chinese writing and cracks that were used to foretell the future.

Left: A seventeenth-century Chinese painting of how silk was made.

Carving of a fierce dragon that adorned the wall of an imperial palace.

And then there was the dragon. To the Chinese, the dragon was an all-powerful and kind god who looked out for humans by showering rain on the parched earth and ensuring a good harvest. Dragons loomed large in Chinese culture—in ancient stories, in artwork, even on silk clothing. The dragon became a symbol of power. Chinese emperors wore dragons embroidered on their silk robes, and the people believed that as long as their emperor ruled wisely, the dragon would help protect them.

Chinese Calligraphy

Eventually the Chinese created a system of writing known as calligraphy, which means "beautiful writing." They made ink from flowers and plants, dipped pointed brushes into the ink, and painted delicate symbols onto bamboo or silk. Each character stood for a different word, so to read or write someone would have to learn hundreds if not thousands of characters. Few people mastered the difficult art of calligraphy, and their skill gave them a place of importance in Chinese society.

The Chinese looked as well to their ancestors for help and protection. They believed that their ancestors lived in heaven after death and took a great interest in the affairs of their children and grandchildren. People honored their ancestors by offering them food and drink, and by praying to them. Important events were announced out loud at the ancestral altar so ancestors would know about them.

Chinese rulers claimed that their ancestors were very powerful. The Chinese believed that when rulers died, they went to join their ancestors in heaven. Like the Egyptians, the Chinese seem to have had ideas about taking worldly things with them to the next life. Archaeologists have found royal grave pits filled with bronze vessels, precious ornaments, weapons, chariots, and even servants who were buried along with their ruler as a sacrifice. War captives, too, would often be sacrificed and buried in royal tombs.

The Mighty Shang

We learned that in ancient Egypt, when a pharaoh died his son usually became the new pharaoh, so that power stayed in the family and passed from generation to generation. The same sort of thing happened in China. When a Chinese emperor died, power usually passed to someone else in the family, sometimes a brother, but usually a son. So the history of China is marked by the rule of several dynasties. A *dynasty* is a single family that rules for many years.

China's first dynasty was called the Shang dynasty. It began about 1760 B.C. and lasted hundreds of years. It was probably during the Shang dynasty that the Chinese invented their system of writing.

The Shang emperors were busy rulers who liked to take on big projects that demanded thousands of workers. They were great city-builders. As Egypt had its pyramids and Sumer had its ziggurats, China had cities with huge walls—walls so big it's amazing to think that people of that time, without the help of any of our modern machines, could have built them. The walls of one Shang city rose 30 feet high, stretched 4 miles long, and measured 60 feet wide. Workers built them by pouring layer after layer of dirt into wooden frames, and stamping on each layer until it was hard as cement. Historians believe such defensive walls may have taken up to 20 years to build, with 10,000 laborers moving and ramming the earth.

Shang emperors also kept hundreds of workers busy making bronze goblets, cups, and bowls. Laborers crouched on hands and knees to drag sleds loaded with ore through cramped mine tunnels. Then skilled craftsmen turned the ore into bronze, and cast it into brilliant art. In the ruins of Shang cities and grave pits, archaeologists have found thousands of bronze vessels, often covered with images of animals and human faces, or spectacular geometric designs.

The huge city walls and fine bronze vessels tell us that Shang emperors were powerful rulers, able to command armies of workers to do their bidding. They must have been great organizers. They possessed a talent for directing the efforts of many people toward large public projects. Many of these people were slaves, captured in war, while others were farmers drafted to do public works.

The Shang dynasty ruled for several hundred years, until about 1045 B.C. Other dynasties would follow, and Chinese civilization would flower and grow in the many centuries to come.

A bronze wine vessel from the Shang dynasty. The elephant's trunk served as a spout.

Artifacts of ancient civilizations:

A: Egyptian scarab beetle ornament.

B: Dragon-shaped jade ornament from ancient China.

C: Chinese jade carving of a monster's face.

D: Alabaster portrait of Pharaoh Tutankhamen.

E: Carving of a Sumerian priestess.

F: Seal from the Indus Valley depicting a multiheaded beast.

A Look Back and a Leap Forward

We've barely begun our human odyssey, and already we've trekked across thousands of years and miles. Let's catch our breath and think about our journey so far.

A Quick Look Back Over a Very Long Time

We started this journey in the time we call prehistory—that long period before human beings could write. Prehistoric times lasted for many thousands of years, perhaps more than a million. People had to get by in harsh conditions. They lived in caves, cliffs, tents, or other crude shelters. They shared a dangerous world with all sorts of wild animals—bison, mammoths, giant deer, lions, bears, saber-toothed tigers. They fashioned crude tools out of a variety of materials, especially stone. That's why we call this long-ago era the Stone Age.

For the most part, Stone Age people were nomads, wandering from place to place in search of food. The men hunted wooly mammoths, deer, horses, and other animals. The women and children often gathered berries, roots, or nuts. Over time, bands of hunter-gatherers began to organize their wanderings according to seasonal patterns. They learned when fish were most plentiful in rivers, or when fruits would ripen in different areas. The rhythms of nature drew them to certain locations at the same time every year.

Then in the centuries before 6500 B.C., a huge change slowly began to take place. Humans learned, little by little, to control their physical environment. They learned they didn't have to be always on the move. If they used sharp-pointed digging sticks, they could break

This pear-shaped hand ax was probably used for chopping and pounding food. Such prehistoric stone tools gave an era its name—the Stone Age.

the ground and plant seeds. If they channeled water and had good luck, they could harvest life-giving grain at season's end. An agricultural revolution was underway.

As groups of people began to settle down to grow food, they discovered that they could tame some wild animals and keep them in herds. Domestication of animals increased people's odds of survival a bit more. By keeping a small herd of goats, sheep, or cattle, people could be sure of having meat close at hand.

Stone Age pottery from the Middle East gives clues about life in ancient times. The ram served as a beast of burden.

Civilization at Last

With people settling down and producing their own food, the stage was set for one of the most important changes in all of history—the development of civilization. As we learned, civilization existed only when three things were true about many people living together in one area:

> *They had a surplus of food.* People gradually got better at planting and growing crops. They invented plows, spades, and hoes to improve agriculture. With such advances, farmers could grow more food than their own families could eat.
>
> *They had division of labor.* Because there was a surplus of food, some men and women were free to do other special jobs. They could dig canals, make pots, or build houses. Everyone did something important, but not everyone had to do the same thing.
>
> *They built cities.* With more and more people living closer together—to be near crops or herds of animals—first villages and then cities began to appear. And with the building of cities, we can truly say that "civilization" had begun. (Remember, the English word *civilization* comes from the Latin *civitas*, which means "city.")

We saw that civilization emerged in four scattered river valleys:

- Sumer came first, more than 5,000 years ago, along the banks of the Tigris and Euphrates Rivers in the region known as Mesopotamia.
- In Egypt, civilization developed along the Nile River.
- The Indus Valley civilization grew along the Indus River.
- In China, civilization prospered along the Yellow and Yangtze Rivers.

Why were those areas such good places for the first civilizations to begin? A big part of the answer lies with the rivers. Their annual flooding brought water and rich soil that people could use to grow their crops. Farmers used the floods for irrigation

Right: Archaeologist's model of a house from the earliest days of civilization.

by building canals, levees, or catchment basins. Irrigation increased the surplus of food.

The rivers provided drinking water for both people and domesticated animals. And in time, the rivers became excellent avenues of trade. So, it makes sense that the first cities grew near these life-giving rivers.

But could civilization develop in lands without rivers that flooded once a year? Could it spread from those four river cradles to other parts of the world? That's the next leap forward in our human odyssey.

An Egyptian laborer irrigates a garden with water from the Nile River. The first civilizations flourished along the banks of rivers in Mesopotamia, Egypt, India, and China.

Civilization on the Move: Spreading to Rain-Watered Lands

Even before civilizations developed in the river valleys of Mesopotamia, Egypt, India, and China, people were growing crops in other areas. Most early agriculture took place in rain-watered lands—that is, lands that had enough regular rainfall to grow crops without the use of irrigation.

Rain-watered agriculture, like irrigated agriculture, could produce a surplus necessary for civilization to develop. Yet civilization did not emerge first in rain-watered lands. That's because producing food with irrigation was more dependable than simply relying on rain. People of the river valleys could usually count on their rivers to flood. They could count on the yearly deposits of rich soil, and they could store water for use during the hot, dry seasons. People who depended on rain falling from the sky had less certain harvests.

Cities were more likely to flourish in river valleys, too, since people gathered along the rivers. In rain-watered lands, people were more spread out. That made it harder to divide the labor, and more difficult to take on building projects that required lots of people.

Still, we know that by the end of the third millennium B.C., civilization was slowly spreading from the river valleys of Mesopotamia, Egypt, India, and China into rain-watered lands. How did this happen?

Civilization spread partly through trade and travel. As merchants and traders journeyed through different lands, they carried ideas from place to place. They carried building techniques and systems of writing.

Warfare played an important role, too. The use of the horse and the horse-drawn chariot spread through warfare. By the end of the third millennium B.C., conquerors began using armies to take over peoples in rain-watered lands. The new rulers often forced farmers to produce a surplus, which could be used to feed other workers. The

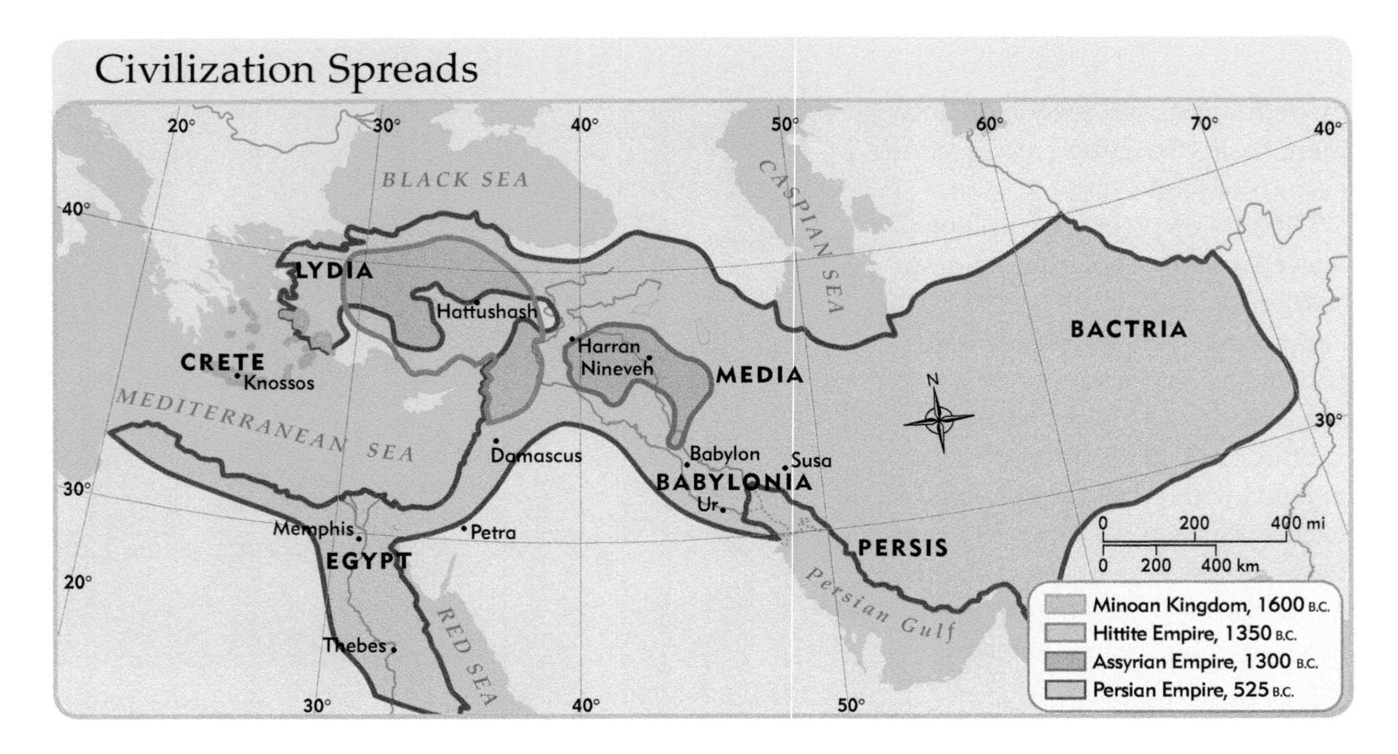

rulers then ordered those workers to build cities and tackle other big projects.

Through trade, travel, and warfare, the fruits of civilization slowly spread. And as the centuries passed, whole new empires rose and fell. A people called the Minoans (mih-NOH-uhns) developed a civilization on the island of Crete in what is now southern Greece. Minoan civilization reached its peak around 1600 B.C. By 1350 B.C., the Hittites had built a civilization in Asia Minor. They controlled most of the land between the Mediterranean and Black Seas. By about 1300 B.C., the Assyrians (uh-SIHR-ee-uhns) had built yet another empire in northern Mesopotamia. And still later, a people called the Persians (PUHR-zhuhns) managed to put together a mighty empire that stretched across the Middle East and into Asia. By then it was 525 B.C.

An aerial view of part of the ziggurat of Ur, a great stepped temple of ancient Sumer.

And so it went. Civilization had come a long way in 3,000 years, from its beginnings along a few river valleys. In time, it would take new forms and spread much farther still.

The Many Forms and Fruits of Civilization

We've seen that early civilizations took different forms and bore different fruits. In ancient Sumer, people built the huge temples called ziggurats, while in Egypt they erected monumental pyramids. In India farmers cultivated cotton, while the Chinese unraveled the secret of silk.

Each civilization had its own distinct culture, but they usually shared some important characteristics. Each developed some form of writing—cuneiform in Sumer, hieroglyphics in Egypt, characters in China, and the mysterious picture-symbols of the Indus Valley that scholars have yet to decipher. Each developed noteworthy architecture, whether ziggurats, pyramids, or walled cities. And each developed religious beliefs tied to nature. For the people of these early civilizations, the world was filled with gods, goddesses, and spirits both good and evil. People looked to their gods for explanations and protection.

Government was another fruit of the first civilizations. Powerful kings organized workers, divided the labor, and directed big projects. They told the workers when to plant or harvest, and where to dig canals. The rulers, priests, and scribes oversaw the building of Egyptian pyramids, the planting of Chinese mulberry groves, and the construction of the streets and sewer system in Mohenjo-Daro.

Each civilization had its own set of laws, such as the famous Code of Hammurabi. Sometimes ancient laws were harsh, but they were nonetheless important steps forward. As cities grew and empires spread, more and more people were coming into contact with each other. The rulers and their governments used laws to control and protect those people. They used armies to enforce their laws and their will.

Rulers also held onto power by appealing to religious beliefs. They often claimed special knowledge of the gods, or to be the gods' representatives on Earth. Sometimes they even claimed to be descended from the gods, or to be part god themselves. These claims caused people to respect and fear their rulers.

As time went on and the fruits of civilization became more plentiful, people had more time to think about their gods, religion, and the meaning of life. They thought about right and wrong, about people's actions, and the way they should live.

Ideas are among of the most important fruits of any civilization. In the next part of this book, we'll follow the human odyssey further and see the emergence of ideas that have guided the lives of billions of people from ancient times to this very day.

Top: Chinese workers gather the mulberry leaves essential for the production of silk.

Above: Hieroglyphic inscription from the tomb of an Egyptian pharaoh.

Time Line (10,000–500 B.C.)

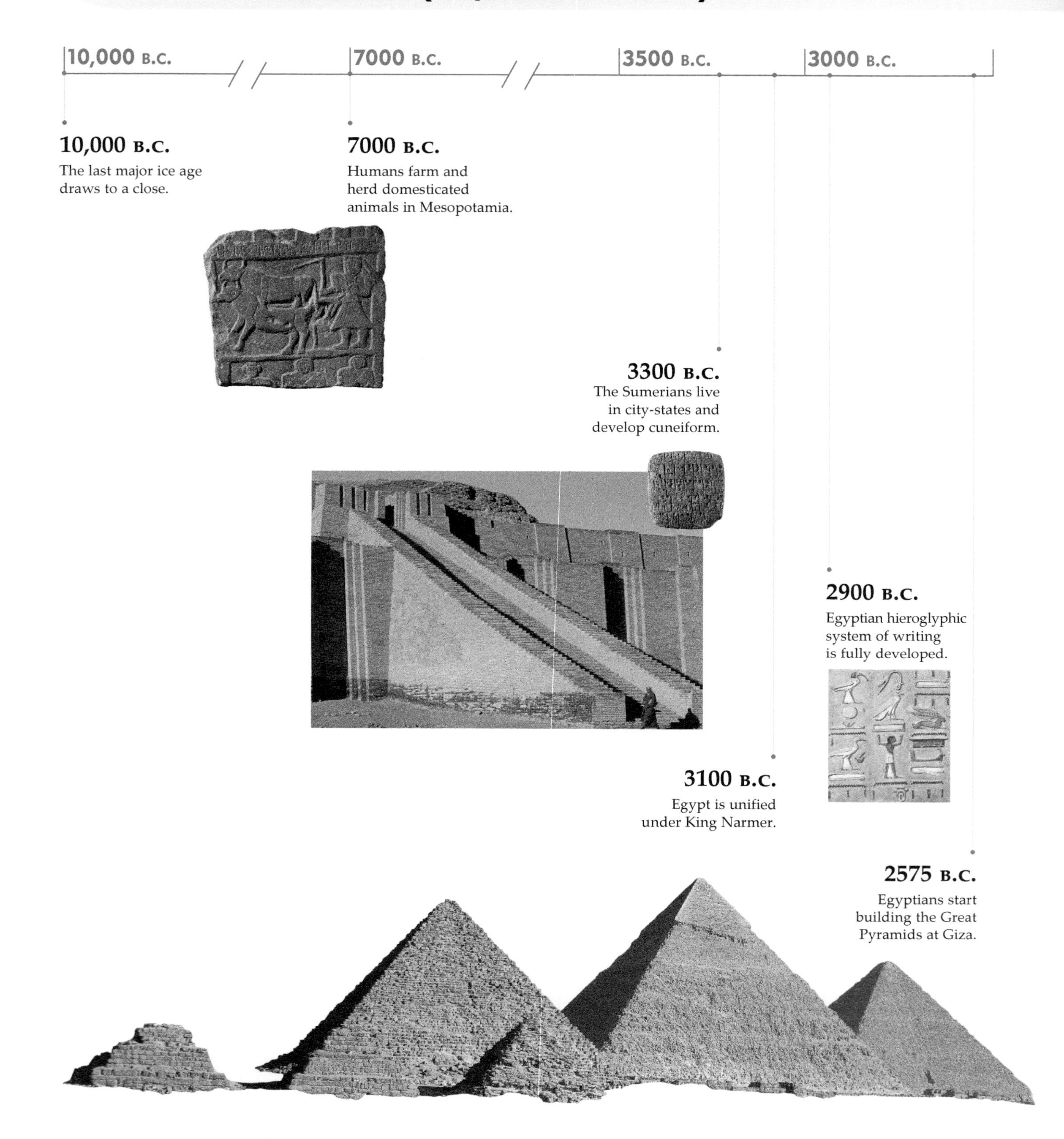

10,000 B.C.
The last major ice age draws to a close.

7000 B.C.
Humans farm and herd domesticated animals in Mesopotamia.

3300 B.C.
The Sumerians live in city-states and develop cuneiform.

3100 B.C.
Egypt is unified under King Narmer.

2900 B.C.
Egyptian hieroglyphic system of writing is fully developed.

2575 B.C.
Egyptians start building the Great Pyramids at Giza.

2500 B.C.	2000 B.C.	1500	1000 B.C.	500 B.C.

2300 B.C.
Sargon and Akkadians conquer Sumer.

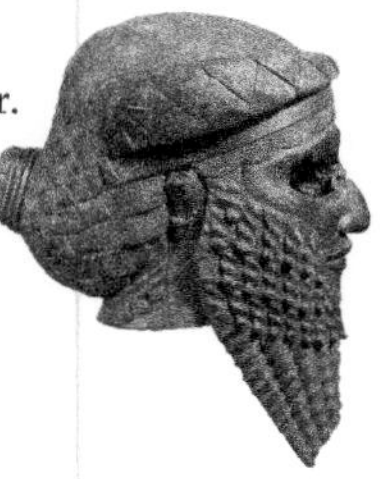

2500 B.C.
The Indus Valley civilization features planned cities (2500–1500 B.C.).

2000 B.C.
Chinese civilization develops along Yellow and Yangtze Rivers.

1780 B.C.
King Hammurabi of Babylon assembles code of laws (ruled 1792–1750 B.C.).

1700 B.C.
The Shang dynasty rules in China (1760–1045 B.C.).

1470 B.C.
Queen Hatshepsut builds her temple at Thebes (ruled 1473–1458 B.C.).

1360 B.C.
Tukankhamen restores traditional deities in Egypt (ruled 1361–1352 B.C.).

1250 B.C.
Ramses the Great builds temples at Abu Simbel (ruled 1290–1224 B.C.).

580 B.C.
Babylon reaches its height of power under King Nebuchadnezzar (ruled 605–562 B.C.).

Part 2, Introduction

A

B

C

D

A: Shiva, the Hindu god of destruction, dances in a ring of fire.

B: Bust of the Greek philosopher Epicurus.

C: Statue of the Chinese philosopher Confucius.

D: A Hindu prays in the sacred waters of the Ganges River.

E: A golden Jewish menorah.

E

What Were They Thinking?

We've been learning about ancient civilization—how it started, where it began, what things were common to all civilizations, what aspects were unique to each culture. Already many big patterns are emerging. We've seen that the first civilizations began in river valleys where farmers learned to grow grain. In time the farmers grew so much extra wheat or barley that not everyone had to be a farmer. People could specialize and do different tasks. Some could herd animals or work metal or weave cloth. That division of labor made it possible for many amazing things to happen. Whole cities could be built, huge pyramids and temples constructed, elegant palaces and gardens created. Scribes could write things down, from accounts to laws to epic tales. Artists could turn plain stone walls into intricate and colorful murals.

The Great Wall of China was one of the world's most massive building projects. The wall was begun in ancient times, but most of it was constructed during later centuries.

Human beings have always been creative. Around the globe in every time and place, people have always had the next project on their minds—something new, something never tried before. Even as people in different lands and civilizations set their sights on new goals, they seem to choose paths surprisingly consistent with their past as well.

What gives human beings ideas about what to do next? What encourages people to choose one path over another? Why did the Egyptians build pyramids instead of public baths like those near the Indus? Why did the Sumerians create ziggurats instead of mummies? Why did the Chinese revere their ancestors? Why would people build temples to many gods rather than one God?

Different peoples at different times and places have cherished different things. They've had different ideas about what's important. Sometimes, when people make choices you don't understand, you might exclaim, *"What were they thinking?"* To understand their choices, you have to make a leap of imagination; you have to try to get inside their heads.

In this part of our human odyssey, we're going to do just that. We'll try to get inside the heads of people who lived around the globe many years ago. We'll be looking at key ideas and beliefs that developed between 1800 and 400 B.C. That seems long ago, but this period saw the rise of ideas with long-lasting effects, ideas still with us today. Have you heard of Confucianism, Hinduism, Buddhism, or Judaism? All these "-isms" have developed over time, and are still with us today, but they are rooted in the period we're about to study.

First we'll examine key ideas and beliefs that developed in two eastern civilizations, in China and India. Then we'll move to western cultures, from the shores of the eastern Mediterranean Sea to the rocky hills of Greece, and learn about important thoughts and people there. Our study will help us figure out what different people value, why they value it, and why they made the choices they've made.

Human beings are full of surprises. People don't always live and act according to the beliefs and values of the past. But often what we value depends on ideas passed on by those who came before us.

Perhaps we can see this best in a story. Let's make an imaginative leap to China in the year A.D. 200. We'll meet a boy named Ren Li (rehn LEE). He's making paper—and some very interesting choices.

The Paper Maker's Son

Sweat trickled down Ren Li's forehead. His eyes stung. Impatiently, he rubbed them against his shoulder, careful not to loosen his grip on the long stirring rod. The great vat of boiling hemp fibers bubbled and steamed.

Imagining the Past

Later he would help his father dip the bamboo screens into the mushy pulp. Then they would press the water out and leave the screens to dry. After that came Li's favorite part—peeling off the clean new paper and rolling it into a neat scroll.

Li imagined a long-bearded scholar holding a freshly inked brush over his paper. What important knowledge would the man record? History? Medicine? Mathematics? Swiftly, the brush came down, making a bold, dark stroke—

"Li!"

Ren Zu (rehn TSOO) leaned against the doorway of the shop, arms crossed. How long had he been standing there?

"F-f-father!" stammered Li. "I was just—"

The paper maker shook his head. "My son, the dreamer." But the look in his eyes was less stern than his voice. "I have been dreaming, too," he said, "about a bowl of vegetables and millet. Do you think my dream will come true?"

The noon meal! Li nodded eagerly. These days, he seemed to be always hungry.

A few minutes later, he was dashing through the city streets, basket slung over a bamboo pole resting on his thin shoulder. As he approached the market, the streets grew narrower and more crowded. Tempting aromas teased his nose—roasted meat, noodles with bean curd, the sweet smell of steamed buns.

The gray-haired market vendor filled his bowl with millet, topped with a few vegetables for flavor.

Li thanked her with a polite bow. He knew he should run straight home with the hot food. But his duties at the shop did not allow him to explore the city every day. Surely staying out just a bit longer wouldn't hurt…

His feet carried him away from the market, toward the broader streets and fine, big houses surrounding the palace walls, finally stopping just outside a familiar open window.

Through the window Li could see the glossy black heads bent over their work. Were they studying the classics of the sage Confucius (kuhn-FYOO-shus)? He was China's wisest man. He had lived hundreds of years ago. Of course, like anyone, Li knew many of his sayings by heart. But, oh, to read the great words for himself!

Suddenly, he heard a clattering, and a sharp, high-pitched cry rang out. Li flattened himself against the wall.

"Teacher, I dropped my ink stone," said an apologetic voice.

A calligraphy lesson! Li peeked through the window again.

At the front of the room stood a tall old man with a long beard, the very image of the scholar Li had seen in his daydreams as he stirred the boiling vat. The man wore a blue silk robe, the luxurious material a sign of his high rank. Li tugged at the hem of his own rough hemp tunic.

The man moved among his students, stopping to look over the shoulder of a chubby boy holding a costly lacquered brush. The boy smiled, but his teacher frowned.

"Sloppy," he said. "Such careless work will not impress the officials selecting men to serve in government. You must be more diligent in your studies. How can you rule others when you have not learned to rule yourself?"

He took the boy's brush and dipped it into the black ink. A few quick strokes across the paper, and a graceful character appeared.

"Diligence," said the teacher. "Now you try."

The boy bowed his head.

Li set down his basket. With his bamboo pole, he traced the character into the dirt. Diligence. He copied it a second time, and then a third.

Absorbed, he did not notice the teacher moving toward the open window. Too late, he glanced up to find the teacher gazing down at him. Their eyes met.

For an instant, Li stood frozen. Then he snatched up his basket and ran.

Stupid, stupid, stupid! How could he have been so foolish? Never again would Li go near that school.

Panting, he rounded the final corner and stumbled into the shop. As his eyes adjusted to the dark inside, he saw the paper maker bent over his screens.

Li took the lunch bowl from his basket and handed it to his father. Please let it still be warm, he prayed. But from the look on Ren Zu's face, he knew his prayer had not been answered.

"The food is cold, and I have had to work alone." His father sounded angry. "Where have you been?"

A thousand excuses swirled through Li's mind. But his tongue refused to shape the words. Bad enough that he had been a disobedient and thoughtless son. At least he would not be so disrespectful as to tell lies.

"I was listening outside the school," he admitted.

His father looked at him. When he spoke at last, his voice was gentle.

"Li," he said. "You know we are not rich. If I could send you to the school, I would. Nothing would make me happier than to see you spend your days in study."

Li nodded, blinking back the tears.

Ren Zu went on, "Being an honest craftsman is no shame. Without our paper, how would knowledge be preserved? It is my duty to make the finest paper possible, and to teach my son our craft. And it is your duty to work hard and learn."

Together they ate their lunch in silence. Every now and then, Li sneaked a glance at his father. He did not look angry anymore. He looked sad and worried.

Li thought of a famous story about Confucius. A young man once asked the sage what it meant to be a good son. Confucius replied, "Let your parents' only worry be that you may fall sick."

I will be a better son, Li silently vowed. Never again will my father have to worry about me.

In the days that followed, he worked harder than ever. Without being asked, he swept the shop and dusted the rolls of pale yellow paper. He returned from errands so quickly his father did not even realize he had left. He did not even daydream anymore.

Late one afternoon, Li was working alone when he heard the shop door open. Out of the corner of his eye, he caught a flash of blue silk.

It was the teacher.

How had he found Li? Was he angry that Li had eavesdropped during the lesson? But the man looked just as surprised to see Li. He stared at him a moment. Then he spoke.

"Ah, yes. I remember. The young scholar scratching like a chicken in the dirt."

Li blushed, but said nothing.

"Why do you stand outside the window of my school?" the teacher pressed on. "Do you hope to learn enough to become an official? To become something better than a paper maker?"

The words burst from Li's mouth: "My father is a paper maker, and there is no one in the world better than my father!"

From the back of the shop, Ren Zu emerged. "What is this shouting?" When he saw the teacher in his long beard and silk robe, he turned pale. "Li, have you gone mad? An honored guest! A scholar! And an elder!" He bowed deeply. "Please forgive my disrespectful son."

Li's heart overflowed with shame. He bowed, too, grateful for this opportunity to hide his face.

At first he did not even recognize the sound, it was so unexpected. The teacher was laughing!

"Paper maker," he said, "do not scold the boy. Courtesy is a great treasure, but even greater is loyalty. A son loyal to his father will become a subject loyal to his ruler."

Ren Zu stammered, "An ignorant boy, if you will please forgive..."

"Ignorance can be cured," the teacher said. "My school is full of boys with the same disease, who care far less for their medicine."

Ren Zu bowed again. "You do us too much honor. It is true, Li has a great desire to learn. But he lacks the wisdom to accept his station in life. An education in the classics is impossible for such as us."

The teacher stroked his beard. "Did not Confucius say a gentleman is known by his behavior rather than his family?" He was silent for a moment. "I would like to find out what this boy can learn."

Li's heart rose. Was the old man offering to teach him?

"I cannot pay," said Li's father.

"There is no need—"

"And we do not deserve such generosity."

The teacher did not reply. He gazed around the small, dark shop. "Generosity?" he said. "My school needs two materials: clean paper and willing students. Give me some of both, and you will be the generous one."

Li held his breath. At last, his father slowly nodded.

"Excellent." The teacher turned to Li. "My servant waits outside. Bring him many scrolls of paper, and help him carry them to the school."

Li rushed to do his bidding.

"And hurry back, young chicken-scratching scholar. You are needed in the shop. Remember, you are still your father's son!"

The Shaping Power of Ideas

Li was fortunate. He got the chance to follow his hopes and dreams. Li admired knowledge and learning. He dreamed of becoming a scholar. He tried to realize that hope by listening to instruction and by diligently practicing, in whatever moments he could seize, the art of writing.

These ideas—the importance of knowledge, learning, and diligence—are part of Li, rooted in his mind and heart. But they, and much else, were deeply rooted in the culture of ancient China.

Li wishes to study the works of a man named Confucius. Already, he knows some of the great Chinese philosopher's sayings, and tries to live up to Confucian goals. Do you remember what goal Confucius had for the behavior of sons toward their parents? Li remembers that his father's only worry should be that his son might fall ill. Li tries to improve his behavior to make his father happy.

In the story we see that Li is a boy with a mind of his own. He doesn't rush right home after buying the millet, though he knows he should.

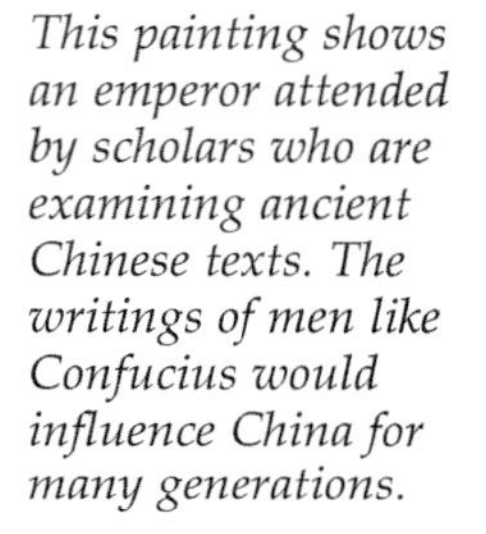

This painting shows an emperor attended by scholars who are examining ancient Chinese texts. The writings of men like Confucius would influence China for many generations.

Far left: Detail from an ancient Greek vase showing a woman reading to her companions.

Left: A Buddhist monk at prayer next to the fingers of a giant statue of the Buddha.

He doesn't hold his tongue when the scholar insults his father, though perhaps he ought to. Li has his own ideas and his own temperament. But many of his ideas and hopes, much of what he treasures, come from people who lived in China long before him.

This is true of people in all times and places around the world. We are each of us uniquely who we are, with our own individual ideas and character. At the same time, we are shaped by the ideas and values of those who came before us.

The period we are about to study was rich with important ideas. In China, the scholar Confucius, through his writings and teachings, influenced Chinese civilization for centuries to come. In India, the great religions of Hinduism and Buddhism emerged. These faiths are followed by more than a billion people today.

In the Middle East, the ancient Hebrews broke with tradition and started to follow not many gods but one God. They left the world of unpredictable nature gods behind. In Greece, people developed a new appreciation for the human person, human reason, and human dignity.

We are about to embark on a part of our human odyssey that is mostly an exploration of ideas, a journey to ancient civilizations in an attempt to find out, *"What were they thinking?"*

Above: Two Hindu deities on the belly of a many-headed serpent.

The great Chinese philosopher Confucius, who lived from 551 to 479 B.C.

The Life and Ideas of Confucius

In our story, Li was a Chinese boy who dreamed of becoming a scholar. He revered a wise man named Confucius, who had lived long before Li's own time. Who was this famous sage?

Imagine for a minute that you're visiting a bustling city in ancient China. The year is 497 B.C. The marketplace is filled with people laughing, talking, and shopping at stalls lining the streets. Merchants hurry back and forth. Vendors shout to come closer and inspect their wares. Nearby a juggler tosses eggs over his head while two acrobats turn somersaults in the air. Everywhere there are people, people, people.

In a quiet courtyard not far from all this activity, a group of young men sits on the ground, talking intently with a kind-looking teacher. One of the students nibbles at a bear paw as he listens. Another snacks on honey-fried bees. Their teacher is a giant of a man with a wispy beard, warts on his nose, and two buck teeth. He speaks with a gentle but firm voice, and the students hang on his every word. Nudging one of the young men on the shoulder, you ask in a whisper the name of the fellow holding everyone's attention. "Ah, that is Confucius," comes the reply. "If you want to learn how to live a good life, come join the discussion."

We're going to find out more about the life and ideas of this philosopher. But first, let's catch up on what has happened in China since the Shang dynasty.

This chapter focuses on the land where Confucius lived and taught—ancient China.

A buffalo-shaped bronze wine vessel from the Shang dynasty.

From Unity to Warring States

China's first dynasty, the Shang dynasty, ruled for more than 600 years. The ambitious Shang rulers united the early Chinese people. They kept thousands of workers busy building cities with huge stamped-earth walls. In the cities hundreds of skilled craftsmen cast bronze goblets, cups, and bowls. Meanwhile, scribes perfected a beautiful system of writing. Under the Shang, Chinese civilization flourished and spread.

Around the year 1050 B.C., a second family of rulers, called the Zhou (djoh) dynasty, came to power. For a while China remained a unified, peaceful land. But then the Zhou empire began to break down as rival lords vied for power. China splintered into an unruly collection of warring states. Each state was like a separate little country inclined to go its own way.

A king of China still sat on the throne, but he had little power. The real power belonged to the rulers of each state, who fought one another nearly all the time. The countryside was filled with rich lords who kept their own armies and acted like tyrants. They attacked each other and taxed the people to pay for their wars and fine houses. Leaders in China at this time were often cruel and indifferent. Rulers cared little about the common people, and justice was almost nowhere to be found.

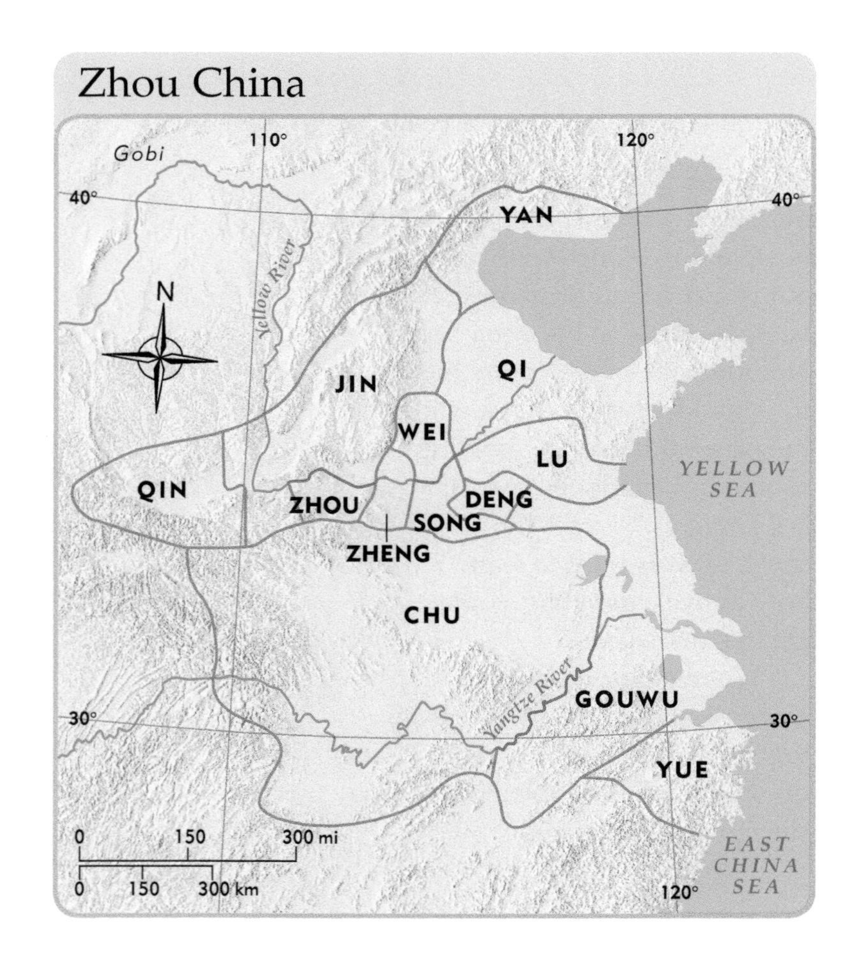

Confucius: The Great Teacher

Into this time of turmoil Confucius was born, around the year 551 B.C. On the map of China you'll see his home state, called Lu. According to tradition, Confucius' father was an old retired soldier and his mother a young peasant woman. When he was just three years old his father died. So Confucius started life in humble conditions.

Nevertheless, at an early age Confucius made up his mind to become a scholar. "At fifteen, I set my heart on learning," he said. He studied all the ancient writings he could get his hands on. He spent time absorbing the history of China's glorious past, and he traveled from state to state. In time, he gained a reputation as a learned man, and a group of young men began gathering around him to discuss ideas and listen to what he had to say. Everyone agreed that he was a good and wise teacher.

Confucius welcomed all students who came to learn, even those so poor they had nothing to offer as payment except a package of dried meat. He had only one requirement—a pupil had to show an eagerness to learn.

"I teach only those who burst with enthusiasm. I guide only those who are struggling to learn themselves," he said. "If I explain one corner of a subject, I expect the student to discover the other three for himself." The only kind of pupil he did not like was the lazy one. He would not teach anyone who did not try to think.

Confucius had some important ideas he wanted to pass on to others. He taught that the secret to a peaceful land and a good life was good character. Confucius taught that to live well, a person must be a "gentleman" or what we might now call "an exemplary person." According to Confucius, the gentleman was not one who was born rich or in high position. The gentleman was one who fulfilled his duties and thought of others. He was loyal to friends. He brought rest and comfort to old people, and was kind and loving toward the young.

Picture Confucius sitting under an apricot tree with his circle of students around him, all engaged in lively discussion about how to be an exemplary person. Confucius encouraged his pupils to disagree with him if they thought he was wrong, and he was never afraid to admit when he made a mistake.

Beneath the shade of an apricot tree, Confucius teaches his students—rich and poor alike—how to be exemplary people.

This great teacher set high standards for his own behavior. He said he often failed to meet his goals, but always worked to improve himself. Right behavior, he said, led to a good life, and every person must try to lead a good life, for only then would all people be happy.

In Search of an Enlightened Ruler

Confucius looked at all the warfare and injustice in the China of his day and longed to do something about it. If only, he thought, we could bring back the days of the early Zhou kings. To Confucius, that seemed a golden age when rulers acted with virtue and the common people treated each other fairly. He had some ideas about how to put things right, and what he

Right: Angered by Confucius' message, a local governor orders his men to pull down a tree where the great scholar taught.

Below: During his life, Confucius traveled throughout China. Here, in the company of two followers, he meditates by the side of a river.

wanted most was to take a role in government so he could try out his reforms. The problem was finding a ruler who would give him a chance.

From time to time Confucius was asked to work at different jobs in the government. For a while, he was made police commissioner of Lu. It is said that he did his job so well that crime virtually disappeared on his watch. Lost objects were always returned to their rightful owners, people had no fear of leaving their doors unlocked, and merchants treated their customers fairly.

Confucius was very honest in his work, but apparently he was a little too honest for most rulers. The high and mighty wanted to hear how great they were. Instead, Confucius bluntly pointed out their shortcomings. He told one noble, "If you weren't such a thief yourself, sir, no one would be trying to steal from you." He urged rulers to work harder to bring good government to the people. Reform yourself if you want your kingdom to reform, he told them.

It wasn't a message they wanted to hear. Corrupt officials feared that if Confucius' ideas of virtuous leaders took hold, they would soon be out of their jobs. Nobles didn't want to be

bothered with having to live up to high standards, so they usually ignored Confucius' advice. No ruler would put real power into his hands, and the jobs he did get didn't last very long. He was always hoping that the right opportunity to play an important role in government would come along, but it never did. So he spent most of his life as a teacher.

Sometimes Confucius taught in his own state of Lu. Sometimes he traveled through distant states, with his pupils following along. Confucius wanted his students to learn many things, but above all he wanted them to learn how to live good lives, to be exemplary men. He taught them to "hear much, choose what is good, and follow it; to see and read much and remember." That way, they would learn the right ways to think and act.

He taught as many students as he could, rich and poor, so that every young man might someday have a chance to be a leader. Even though no ruler would let Confucius try his ideas, he hoped that some day his students would follow his advice.

Confucius or Kongfuzi

Confucius' real name was Kong Qiu (KAWNG choo). In China he came to be known by the title Kongfuzi (KAWNG FOO-dzuh), which meant "Great Master Kong." Most people in the West know the great philosopher by the name Confucius, which is the Latin form of Kongfuzi.

He taught his students to be the kind of people he wanted to govern China. He went on traveling and spreading the truth as he saw it, shaping young people into leaders who one day might be good statesmen.

The Family and Good Government

Confucius thought and thought about how China could have a better government. He began by asking himself some questions. How do families keep order? What makes people feel happy and at home in their family? How are children taught what is right? How do they learn to behave well? Confucius believed that families, his country's littlest communities, could be an example for the larger community of China.

From the early years of Chinese civilization, the family had been very important. Sometimes hundreds of family members lived close together in one village. They farmed the land together and took care of one another. Those who had died were remembered and honored. People even offered prayers and sacrifices to their ancestors. In the same way, young people were raised to respect older relatives. This helped keep order and harmony in a family.

Confucius placed great importance on family obligations. It is within the family, he said, that people learn respect, cooperation, and the good habits that help them deal fairly with others. He often reminded his students that young people should honor and obey their elders, and that in return older generations should give young people the guidance and love they deserve.

Confucius regarded concern for others as the key to good behavior and good government. He did not see laws as the basis for a good, orderly society. Good conduct, instead, was most important. Good conduct inspired others to be good. When people treated each other fairly and with respect—beginning with family members treating each other well—society as a whole would grow more harmonious. Confucius himself quoted an old Chinese text: "Simply by being a good son and friendly to his brothers, a man can exert an influence upon government."

Confucius believed that well-ordered families set a good example for Chinese society as a whole.

The Five Relationships

Confucius said there are five different kinds of relationships between people. In each of these relationships, he said, there is a proper way to behave. His plan for an orderly society with a good government was based on these relationships.

The relationship between parent and child is the most important of all, Confucius said. That's because during childhood, children learn the proper way to live from their parents. According to Confucius, a person becomes a good man by first learning to be a good son, and then remaining good as he grows up. Confucius taught that a good son obeys his parents, shows a loving respect for them, and tries to learn from them. (Confucius certainly believed that his teaching applied to girls, too, but he focused on boys since his students were young men, and men ruled China.)

A father embraces his son and daughter, symbolizing the importance of the relationship between parent and child.

One of Confucius' pupils once asked him how he could show loving respect to his parents. Confucius' answer (which you've heard before) was, "Let your parents' only worry be that you may fall sick." By respecting parents and learning the right way to live from them, said Confucius, children gradually become good members of society. And parents, in turn, take responsibility for the care and behavior of their children.

Confucius said that three other relationships are like that between parent and child—the relationship between an elder brother and a younger brother, between husband and wife, and between ruler and subject. The younger child owed respect to the elder child. The wife owed respect to the husband. (In Confucius' day, the wife was considered subordinate to the husband in the family.) And a subject owed respect to the king. At the same time, the elder child, husband, and king all had to act in a way that made them worthy of respect.

The fifth relationship, according to Confucius, is between friends. He believed that true friends are equals. They owe respect to each other, and each must be worthy of the other's respect.

Confucius believed that a successful society depends on people taking their proper roles in each of these relationships. If people followed rules of good conduct and were honest, sincere, and respectful toward each other in these five relationships, then the entire world would be at peace.

A Golden Rule and the Way of Heaven

Confucius tried to encourage harmony between individuals. He wanted people to respect each other. To do this, he taught the earliest known form of the Golden Rule. "Do not do to others what you do not want them to do to you," he said. Each person should decide how he wants other people to treat him. Then he should treat other people the same way. Each person should remember his duties to others. Why? Because he would not want others to forget their obligations to him.

To Confucius, learning how to live with other people was the most important thing in life, more important even than making offerings to gods. He carefully instructed his students about how they should think and act toward one another. "Wherever you go in the world," he said, "you should treat all those whom you meet as if you are receiving a highly honored guest." Confucius said that a wise man is one who knows and understands others. A good man is one who loves others.

Confucius didn't talk about religion and gods. He spoke of "heaven," but he didn't say what heaven was. He didn't think it could be explained in words. He seemed to think of it as a great spirit of wisdom and goodness. People should try to follow the Way of Heaven in their thoughts and actions, he said. The Way of Heaven was the spirit of wisdom and goodness that prompted people to consider the needs of others and act as gentlemen. If people were open to that spirit of goodness and followed the Way of Heaven, they would lead a good life and find happiness.

Confucius taught that people should work hard to think better and act better. Everyone should always be asking himself, "What is the right thing to do?" Confucius thought that everyone can improve himself. He believed that people are basically good, and that anyone who tries can learn the right thoughts and behavior.

Top: Confucius encouraged people to treat each other with respect.

Above: An emperor receives his due—the reverence and honor of his subjects.

The King and Good Government

Confucius spent much of his career thinking and talking about good government. He believed that if government is bad, people can find it hard to lead good lives. There's an old story that illustrates his belief.

> One day Confucius saw a woman weeping by a tomb. He said to her, "You weep as though you are very sad."
>
> "So I am," replied the woman. "In this place, my husband's father was killed by a tiger. My husband also was killed by a tiger, and now my son has been killed, too."
>
> "If this is so, why do you not leave this terrible place?" asked Confucius.

The woman replied, "Here there are tigers, but at least the government is not bad."

"My pupils," Confucius taught, "hear and remember. Bad government is worse than a fierce tiger!"

From the *Analects of Confucius*

After Confucius died, his students wrote down what they remembered from their conversations with the great teacher. Their own students continued the process, as did later generations. So the book we know as the *Analects* (or the "sayings") *of Confucius* is actually the work of perhaps three centuries of scholarship. Here are some sayings from the *Analects*.

"First put yourself in order. Then be sure you act justly and sincerely toward others, and you will be a happy man."

To those working in government, Confucius said: "Go before the people with your own good example and work hard for their sake."

"An exemplary person helps bring out what is beautiful in other people and discourages what is ugly in them. A petty person does just the opposite."

"Let the ruler be as a ruler ought to be. Let the official be as an official ought to be. Let the father be as a father ought to be. Let the son be as a son ought to be. Then there will be good life and good government."

"It is the wiser person who gives rather than takes."

"He who studies but does not think is lost; he who thinks but does not study is dangerous."

"Is it not pleasant to learn with a constant perseverance and application?"

"He who wishes to secure the good of others has already secured his own."

Confucius taught that the people should treat the king like a father and follow his orders. A person who came before the king had to kneel, bow deeply, and touch his head to the floor three times. Such a way of bowing was called the *kowtow*, and it was meant to show great respect.

The king had duties, too. Confucius said that a ruler had to deserve his people's respect. He must be "upright," or wise and good. Then the people would honor him because he set a good example. They would be willing to follow him because they trusted him. They would want to obey, and would not have to be forced to follow the king's orders. Confucius thought that a good king would not need to punish people to make them obey.

Confucius taught that while the king was above the people, heaven was above the king—thus the king owed respect to the heavenly spirit of wisdom and goodness. He was expected to follow the Way of Heaven by ruling wisely and well. A king who did so would have happy people, and heaven would bless his rule. If a ruler departed from that path, heaven would allow the people to overthrow him.

Confucius told a ruler, "If you are good and want only what is good, then the people will be good. The ruler is like the wind. The people are like the grass. The grass must bend in the direction the wind blows."

Confucius said that the king must work hard to create good government. He did not believe that ordinary people should share in government.

Still, he thought that the ruler should listen to complaints from the people so he would know what they needed. Confucius did not say how a government should be organized or explain what rules the government should follow. He thought such matters should be left to the king and his advisors to decide. But Confucius believed firmly that an upright ruler would establish good government. It made no difference how much power the ruler had—as long as he was a good man, the government would be good. That idea would be challenged in years to come, but it was revolutionary for its time.

Confucius lived at a time when the power to rule was passed from generation to generation. Being born into a ruling family wasn't enough to be an upright ruler, Confucius insisted. An upright ruler must have good character. He must work hard to master the rules of good behavior and good government. He had to set a good example. "An exemplary person helps bring out what is beautiful in other people and discourages what is ugly in them," Confucius said. A king might gain power by inheriting it or conquering others, but he was justified in ruling only by following the Way of Heaven, thus bringing prosperity, safety, and harmony to his realm.

"I wish to speak no more."

Tradition says that one morning in 479 B.C., when he was 72, Confucius woke, spent some time walking in his courtyard, and then suddenly announced, "I wish to speak no more." He went back to his bedroom, lay down, and remained there day after day without saying a word.

Today a temple stands near the burial place of the great Chinese philosopher Confucius.

A hushed crowd waited in the street outside his house, knowing the end had come. On the seventh day, Confucius passed away. His students buried him on a riverbank in a grave that today attracts admirers from all over the world.

Confucius died believing he had failed. But he did not fail. After his death, his pupils wrote down his teachings and sayings in a book that has come to be known as the *Analects of Confucius*. The ideas in this slim volume were so alive with wisdom that they inspired all who came across them. Confucius' students went their separate ways and traveled through China as teachers, government officials, and court advisors, putting what they had learned to work.

And so Confucius' ideas spread across the land he loved until they were known by millions of people. Confucianism—all the teachings of Confucius together—became the single most important force in Chinese life. It was a set of ideas that would influence China for centuries to come.

A group of young men take a government entrance examination. Government officials were important and powerful figures in imperial China.

The Confucian Legacy

Confucius passed away without finding the upright ruler he sought—a wise ruler who followed the Way of Heaven and set a good example for people to follow. Would his dream of good government ever be realized?

Would an upright ruler finally appear? What would the legacy of Confucius be?

The Tiger of China

Confucius lived during troubled times, and he died just as China was entering a time of even greater turmoil. This era was known as the "Period of Warring States." Feuding between rival kingdoms would continue for more than 200 years, from about 450 to 220 B.C.

By the year 221 B.C., a powerful warrior-prince emerged in the western state of Qin (chin). Ambitious and ruthless, he defeated neighboring warlords and seized control of all the warring Chinese states. The man took the title Qin Shi Huangdi (chin shur hwahng-dee), which means "First Emperor of the Qin Dynasty." The old title, "king," was not grand enough for him.

Was the First Emperor the upright ruler Confucius had hoped for? As we'll see, he succeeded in uniting China, and he did bring order to the land. But this emperor had very little regard for the teachings of Confucius. According to those teachings, the people owed respect and obedience to their ruler. At the same time, the ruler had to act in a way that made him worthy of respect. A good ruler would not need to punish people to make them obey him. But this was not the way of the man whose harsh rule and mighty feats earned him the title "Tiger of China."

Qin Shi Huangdi, the "First Emperor."

Strengthening the Trunk

The First Emperor ruled a land that stretched from the East China Sea to the foothills of the Himalaya, north to the edges of Mongolia, and south to present-day Vietnam.

- On the map on page 174, find the territory ruled by Qin Shi Huangdi.

Like a tiger on the prowl, the First Emperor set about changing the face of China. "I must make this great realm into a single empire," he told his advisors. "People all over China must think of themselves as one people under a single lord. They must not owe loyalty to separate states. All of the local nobles must be subject to me!"

One of the bronze coins of the newly unified China, with its distinctive center hole.

The nobles, however, remained powerful, and Qin Shi Huangdi knew that they posed a threat to his supreme rule. So he forced them to leave their states and move to the imperial capital, where he could keep a close watch on them. To take their place, he appointed 36 governors who would report directly to him. The districts they governed were now parts of a unified empire.

Qin Shi Huangdi succeeded in setting up a centralized government for China, that is, a government in which most of the power lay in the hands of the emperor and his court. With officials in the outlying districts reporting to a central government in the capital city, Qin Shi Huangdi had more control over his realm. The Chinese had a saying for what the First Emperor had done. They called it "strengthening the trunk and weakening the branches."

The emperor liked nothing better than touring his realm. As he did so, he discovered other problems. He saw that his subjects used many different units to weigh and measure things. He saw that people in different places used different forms of writing.

The emperor realized how confusing this all was. A bag of rice weighed in one village might be given a different weight in another village. Reports written in one part of the empire could not be read in another.

Currencies were different, too. The coins of the old states were still in use—and they were all different. Cast in bronze, they had various shapes. One was the shape of a spade. Another looked like a knife. One even had the shape of a cowrie shell. Money earned in one region could not be spent in another.

Qin Shi Huangdi ordered that everyone in the empire should use the same weights, measures, and writing. To motivate people to change from their old habits, he declared that anyone who clung to the old ways would be guilty of treason. He also

The First Emperor: An Upright Ruler?

The First Emperor was born Prince Zheng in the state of Qin in 259 B.C. His name actually meant "upright," but those who served him disagreed. "He is merciless, with the heart of a tiger or a wolf," wrote a courtier. He devours his enemies "as a silkworm devours a mulberry leaf."

imposed a unified currency. The new imperial coins were round with a hole in the middle so they could be strung together and suspended from belts.

The emperor even made a standard width for carts. Everybody would now roll along in the same ruts, packing them into hard smooth tracks. And they would do so on the new roads that the emperor was beginning to build.

A Great Wall and a Great Tomb

The First Emperor was a great builder. He constructed roads and canals all across China. These, he believed, would knit together the distant corners of his realm and bring all under his control.

At last, China was starting to look like an empire. But as the First Emperor's cold eyes surveyed his domain, he knew that he still faced one large problem. And this one came not from within his empire, but from without.

For centuries, nomadic northern invaders had attacked the Chinese. Riding swift horses, these fierce raiders from the area we now call Mongolia thundered into Chinese villages, killing and stealing at will.

From Characters to Calligraphy

When Qin Shi Huangdi came to power, the Chinese had been writing for more than a millennium. Their system of writing used thousands of characters, or written symbols. These characters varied from region to region. Qin Shi Huangdi wanted to unite his empire, so he told his officials to standardize all the characters. This meant that everyone, no matter where they lived, would use the same characters to mean the same things. The Qin dynasty developed a new system of writing that survives in large part to this day. This script had more than 3,000 characters.

Later, during the Han (hahn) dynasty, the Chinese created a writing system known as calligraphy, which means "beautiful writing." They made ink from flowers and plants, dipped pointed brushes into the ink, and painted the delicate characters onto bamboo or silk. Highly skilled calligraphers had to hold their brushes straight up, as their hands and elbows were never supposed to touch the silk or paper.

Calligraphers also had to memorize the thousands of characters used in Chinese writing. With each passing year there were more symbols to remember. One famous Chinese dictionary from A.D. 100 lists more than 9,000 characters. Each represented a different object or idea. Many resembled the object they were communicating. For example, *big* looked like a stick figure of a big person standing with arms outstretched. The character for *water* resembled several streams running into one river. And *mountain* contained three lines rising like mountain peaks.

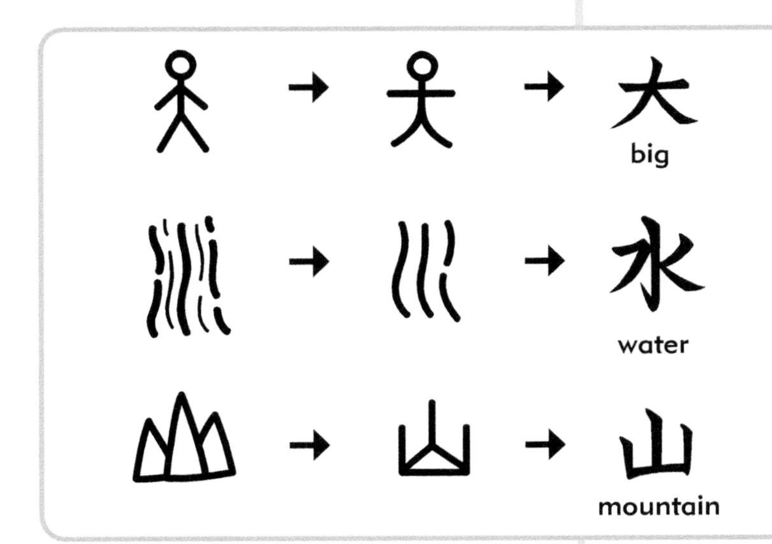

The Great Wall of China was a huge stone barrier against nomadic raiders from the north. Only a few sections of Qin Shi Huangdi's wall remain. The section above was rebuilt during a later dynasty.

At times these nomadic peoples threatened to invade all of China.

"I must make my land safe," the First Emperor told his advisors. "I have to protect it from these invaders from the north. I will build a strong barrier to keep them out."

With his usual energy, the emperor set about building a wall across China. But this wall was to be like no other. Qin Shi Huangdi forced more than a million workers to toil day and night on the project. They worked high in the mountains through seven bitter winters and as many blistering summers. Hunger, exhaustion, and overwork killed many. For this reason, the wall has been called "the longest cemetery in the world."

Generations of Chinese workers labored at building the Great Wall. Eventually it snaked some 4,500 miles across deserts, mountains, valleys, and hills. In some places it was six horses wide and five men high. Forty-foot towers rose every few hundred yards, the distance said to be that of two arrow shots. This meant that any enemy attacking the wall would be within range of a deadly arrow shot by archers in each tower. For centuries the wall protected China from invasion. In later centuries it sometimes fell into ruin, and sometimes was rebuilt. It still stands today, the longest man-made structure ever built.

- On the map on page 174, locate the Great Wall of China.

How Long Is the Great Wall?

It depends on how many of its loops and branches you include. The main part of the wall spans about 2,000 miles. But if you were to walk alongside the entire wall and all its branches, you would hike about 4,500 miles. Aerial photos have revealed buried portions of the wall that would make it even longer than that. The Great Wall is so long, no one is sure exactly how long it is!

The First Emperor's reign over all of China was short, just 11 years. As his tomb shows, his plans for the afterlife were as great as his ambitions on earth.

Other great leaders had built monumental tombs. The First Emperor did not know about the pyramids raised by the pharaohs of Egypt a millennium earlier. But the Chinese emperor's efforts were similarly grand. His army had served him well in this life. He would take another "army" to protect him in the afterlife.

The many chambers of the emperor's tomb were spread over 22 square miles. Inside several of these chambers he placed about 7,500 life-sized, terra-cotta statues to guard him in death. Some of these clay soldiers stood at attention. Others knelt at the ready with bows and arrows. Still others rode on horseback. This emperor clearly believed he would be a powerful ruler in the world to come.

The soldiers buried at the First Emperor's tomb were not discovered until 1974, when two farmers digging a well in a field unearthed part of his silent army. The steadfast soldiers had been on guard for their long-dead emperor for more than 2,000 years.

Like many rulers in ancient times, Qin Shi Huangdi possessed a colossal ego. He spared no trouble glorifying himself. But he also displayed an impressive ability to organize huge numbers of workers for massive projects. Qin Shi Huangdi set an example that other Chinese emperors would follow for centuries to come. Throughout China's history, powerful rulers would not hesitate to use armies of workers to tackle enormous public projects, from constructing walls and laying roads to digging canals and building dams.

The Han Dynasty and the Legacy of Confucius

When the First Emperor died in 210 B.C., he left an empire exhausted and ready for change. Qin Shi Huangdi thought he had founded a dynasty that would last for 10,000 generations. But only four years after his death, his dynasty fell in a bloody civil war. The victors in that war founded a dynasty called Han. This dynasty lasted more than 400 years.

For guidance, the Han rulers began turning to the teachings of Confucius. The old sage had taught that the role of rulers is to bring happiness to their subjects—a lesson that

As they have for more than two millennia, these terra-cotta soldiers continue to stand guard at the tomb of Qin Shi Huangdi.

the Tiger of China, Qin Shi Huangdi, apparently had not cared to learn. During the Han dynasty, the *Analects of Confucius* and the great teacher's ideas set the tone for public life. Some emperors lived relatively simple lives. They sought the advice of scholars as they governed their empire. The Han emperors did not reject everything from the previous dynasty. For one thing, they valued the centralized government that Qin had established. Indeed, they built on what the First Emperor had achieved, and made it even better.

Under the Han, the officials of the civil service became the elite of China. These were the men who ran the empire, some in the imperial capital, some in the outlying districts. But the Han made one important break with the past. They thought the conduct of these powerful officials should be guided by the ideas of Confucius.

The Han emperors sought smart, virtuous men to help administer the government. No longer would family ties be qualification enough. A rich uncle would not be able to get a

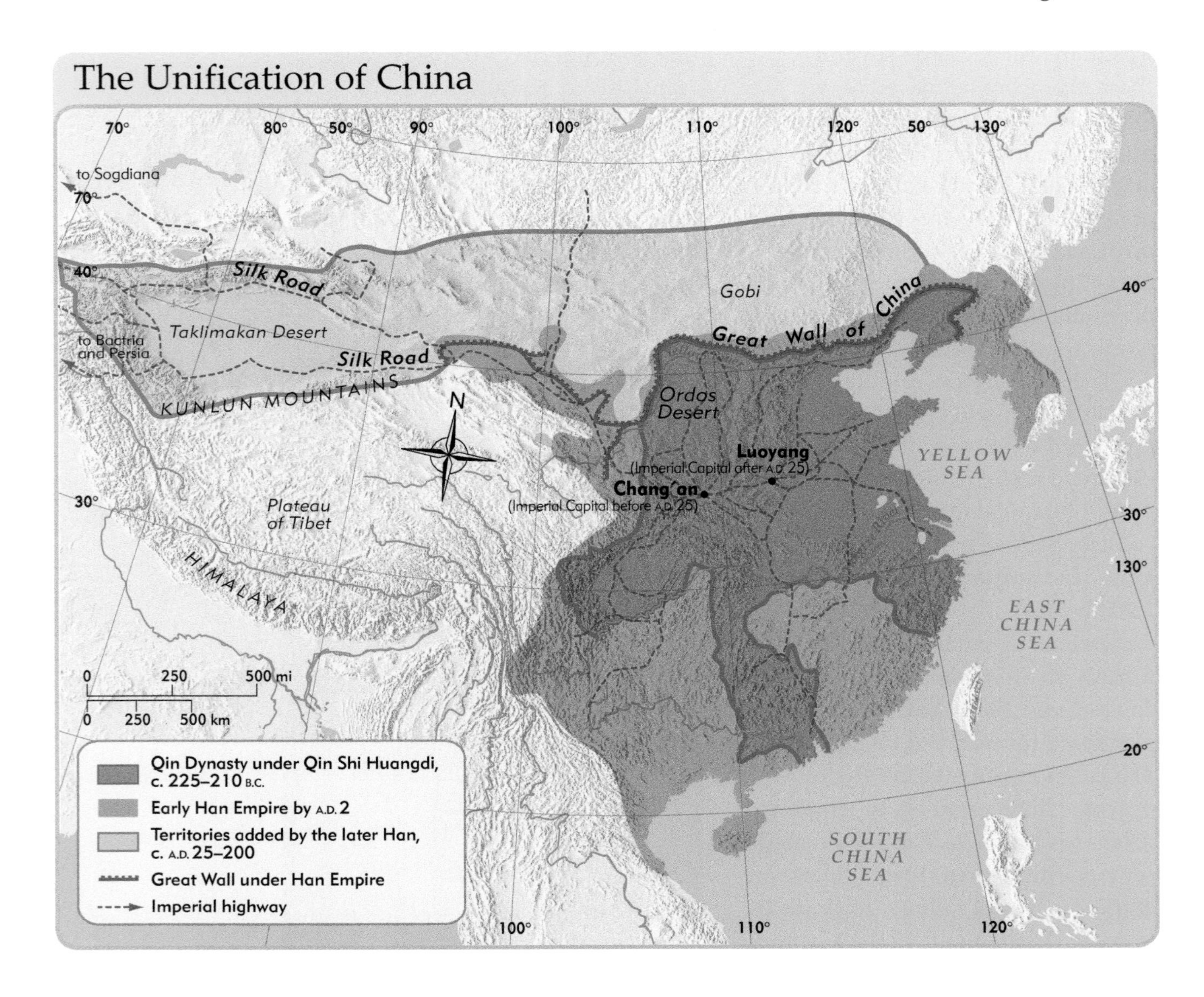

nephew a job in the government. Those who served the state should do so on merit—on the basis of their intelligence and skills.

To find these gifted men, the Han emperors established a system of recommendations. All over China, local officials nominated promising young men of virtue and talent. These young men went to the central government to be interviewed. To be selected, they had to show the Confucian virtues of honesty, sincerity, and respect for their elders. Of course they also had to be able to read and write, since government work involved a lot of paperwork. Ambitious young men sought out Confucian teachers in the hope that they would gain a reputation for the Confucian virtues.

All this was very different from the days of Qin Shi Huangdi. Qin had come to power through military might, and he used the same might to stay in power. To pay for his building projects, he had taxed the people heavily, and he used force to make the people toil for him. But, as one Confucian saying put it, "An empire can be conquered on horseback, but not governed from a horse." In other words, good government depends on the support of the people, rather than power exercised in battle. For all his power, the support of the people was one thing the First Emperor never had.

For the most part, the Han emperors tried to govern fairly and justly, in ways favored by Confucius. In 124 B.C., they set up the Imperial University to teach the Confucian classics to future government officials. Later, the Confucian classics were carved in stone in the capital city. Scholars journeyed from the empire's distant provinces to make copies of them.

Part of the Imperial University set up by the Han emperors to promote the teachings of Confucius.

Setting Out on the Silk Road

The Han dynasty did not wish to give up any territory gained by the Tiger. They extended China's realm into the lands that are now Vietnam and Korea. They also extended the empire west toward Central Asia. And their influence would extend much farther to the west, thanks not to the march of imperial armies but to the enterprise of Chinese merchants who traveled what has come to be called the Silk Road.

Today's Han

So glorious were the achievements of the Han dynasty that today most Chinese still refer to themselves as "the people of Han." Numbering more than a billion, the Han are not only China's largest ethnic group, but the largest in the world.

As his ancestors did before him, a young Chinese boy leads a small camel caravan along the Silk Road.

The Silk Road was the most famous overland trade route of ancient times. Stretching across western China and Central Asia, it linked for the first time the land of Confucius with the West. By 100 B.C., trade caravans loaded with precious silk began to clatter along the road toward Persia. Under constant threat from bandits, the caravans crossed lofty mountains, windswept plateaus, and deserts that were searingly hot by day and bitterly cold by night. But the high prices paid for silk made it all worthwhile. In Persia the silk was traded to merchants who carried it to the ports of the Mediterranean coast. By the first century B.C., Chinese silks were for sale in Rome.

Silk was the most prized of Chinese exports. But the merchants' caravans also carried spices, ivory, jade, and fine-quality ceramics. On the return journey they brought back a variety of products, including glass, wine, perfumes, linen, woolen goods, horses, and camels. Camels were the major beasts of burden along the Silk Road. Hardy and surefooted, they could withstand the extreme heat and cold of the long journey across Asia.

- On the map on page 174, locate the Silk Road.

One Hump or Two?

The camels that plodded along the Silk Road were the two-humped variety—Bactrians. Named after a part of Afghanistan once known as Bactria, these great "ships of the desert" were ideally suited to the arduous conditions they faced. While the single-humped dromedaries are fleeter of foot, Bactrian camels can endure temperatures as low as 40 degrees below zero.

The Gift of Paper

Silk was one great Chinese innovation made available to the rest of the world during the Han dynasty. Chinese inventiveness would provide another. Its value is impossible to estimate. You're looking at it right now—paper.

Do you remember our friend Li? His father was a paper maker. Papermaking was perfected in China in

Left: The work of government scribes—here copying documents for the emperor—required vast amounts of paper.

Below: A worker dips a screen into watery pulp, one of the steps in papermaking.

A.D. 105. By that time, Chinese paper makers used a variety of fibrous plants to make paper, such as hemp, bark, or bamboo. They softened the fibers by soaking them in water, before boiling and pounding them into a pulp. To make a sheet of paper, they dipped a fine screen into the pulp to gather a thin layer of fibers. Next, the paper makers pressed the screen to remove the water, then left it to dry on a heated wall. When dry, the finished sheet of paper was peeled off the screen. After it was coated with salt and glue to make sure that ink applied to it would not run, the paper was ready to use.

The Han civil service had a huge appetite for paper, as did the country's many scholars. Scribes wrote books on rolls of paper, among them the classics of Confucius, now preserved for the ages. With the increase in books came the growth of literacy in China. Scholarship increased. Ideas flourished. It was a development that would have made the great philosopher proud.

Paper Replaces Papyrus

While the Egyptians had been writing on papyrus since ancient times, the Chinese invented paper as we know it. Papyrus was a mat of reeds, pressed into a hard, thin sheet. When the Arabs brought Chinese papermaking to Egypt in the eighth or ninth century A.D., paper quickly replaced papyrus, the material after which it was named.

Sandstone carving of the Hindu god Vishnu, preserver of the world.

The Birth of Hinduism

The Chinese weren't the only people thinking about how to live a good and moral life. Such questions have occupied the minds of people throughout history. Confucius came up with important answers to those questions, and Confucianism became a philosophy that has influenced the Chinese for generations. But Confucianism was just that—a philosophy, not a religion. Confucius tried to answer questions about how people should treat each other, and how they should live honorably and peacefully. He did not try to answer questions about who made the world or which gods to honor.

Other people did ask such questions. West of China, some important ideas had been developing for a very long time. You remember that on the Indian subcontinent, on the banks of the Indus River, a civilization rose in the third millennium B.C. and declined seven or eight hundred years later. The Indus River peoples left thousands of soapstone seals that showed not just zebus and elephants, but a cross-legged man apparently meditating. No one knows exactly what happened to the people of the cities of Mohenjo-Daro and Harappa, but the modern religion of Hinduism (HIN-doo-ih-zuhm) may have been born there.

Hinduism is one of the world's oldest living religions. Nowadays it has perhaps 800 million to 900 million followers, most of them in India. Hinduism incorporates a very wide range of beliefs—a belief in many gods, as well as in one universal essence. Hindus have written great works of literature and built ornately carved

This chapter explores the Indian subcontinent, the birthplace of Hinduism.

The Indus River rises in the steep valleys of the Himalaya.

temples. Their ideas have profoundly influenced people in Asia and around the globe.

The tradition of Hinduism emerged out of the mixing of peoples and cultures of the Indus Valley with those of Aryan-language speakers who gradually migrated into India from central Asia and settled on the Ganges plain.

Aryan Settlers on the Indian Subcontinent, 1200 B.C.

- Look at the map on this page. Find the Hindu Kush Mountains in what is now Afghanistan. Now locate the Indus and Ganges Rivers.

Aryan Settlers

About 1500 B.C., after the ancient Indus River Valley civilization had already declined, many groups of nomadic horsemen and herders crossed the banks of the Indus into northern India. These tribesmen from central Asia had no fear of war. They called themselves "Aryas" (AHR-yus). Their language came from an old language at the root of many modern languages, including Persian, most European languages, and English. Deftly riding their chestnut horses through mountain passes, and driving their cattle before them, they moved out of the foothills of what is now Afghanistan onto the fertile plains of northwestern India.

As the Aryan herders came out of the mountains, they must have been delighted at the lush grasslands that met their gaze. They were cattlemen, and those pastures seemed to guarantee a future for their herds. That was worth fighting for. Aryans were skilled with the bow and arrow and masters of the horse-drawn chariot. On light spoke-wheeled chariots, they charged into battle.

Those in their path seemed powerless to stop the newcomers. Some of the early settlers along the Indus fled south. Others remained, living alongside the Aryans, exchanging grain for their cattle, goats, and sheep. At night they listened to the hard-drinking men tell stories of their steed-taming gods. These people settled in the north Indian plains and, in time, spread as far east as the Ganges River.

By 1200 B.C., Aryan-dominated cultures had overspread the top of the diamond that is the Indian subcontinent. They brought a new language, Sanskrit (SAN-skrit). They also brought ideas about society and religion that would last a very long time.

The Emerging Caste System

What sort of ideas did the Aryans bring? Led by warrior chiefs, these wandering people settled in villages and established Sanskrit as the dominant tongue. Once settled in their new land, they turned for leadership less and less to the warrior chieftains who had led them in combat and more and more to their priests, called *Brahmans* (BRAH-muhns).

The Aryans gradually developed a system of social classes that came to be known as the *caste* system. Aryans believed themselves superior to those they conquered. As the name *Arya* (which means "of noble birth") tells us, these central Asians looked down on the other peoples and cultures of northern India. They considered themselves a higher caste, or social class. The Sanskrit word for caste, *varna*, actually meant "color." It's possible that the fairer-skinned Aryans believed themselves superior to the darker-skinned aboriginal people of the Indus. But the castes or varnas didn't have to do mainly with skin color. They were religious and social groupings, and over time, each caste kept more and more separate from the others.

Aryan religious leaders said people were divided into four main classes, or castes. At the top were the Brahmans. They were the religious leaders and keepers of the sacred books. They were greatly honored and conducted all holy rites.

Beneath Brahmans came the warriors, or nobility, known as

Above: Deep in thought, a Brahman studies a Hindu holy text. Brahmans are members of Hinduism's priestly caste, or highest social group.

Below left: A tablet from northern India inscribed with Sanskrit, the language of the Aryan invaders.

Indra, the Aryan god of storms and war, depicted as a four-armed man wielding daggers and riding a white elephant.

Kshatriya (KSHA-tree-ah). Then beneath the warrior class came the merchants and farmers, or *Vaishyas* (VIYSH-yuhs).

Finally, there were servants and ordinary workers, known as *Shudras* (SHOO-druhs). Many of the original Indus peoples seem to have been included in this lowest caste.

These were the four major castes. In time a fifth large group was added to the bottom of this pyramid—the "untouchables," also known as *outcastes*. Untouchables had the lowliest jobs, such as sweeping the streets, and were excluded by Brahmans from the rest of society. They could not drink from the same wells or live in the same neighborhoods as people in higher castes. Most high caste people would not touch a member of this lowest group. Some felt contaminated even by the shadow of an untouchable.

Within the four major castes, thousands of subcastes developed, known as *jatis* (JAH-thees), from the term *birth*. For example, within the Shudra caste there were carpenters, potters, weavers. There were also subcastes among the Brahmans, Kshatriyas, and Vaishyas. Each subcaste had its own rules of behavior. Social contact between people of different castes was very limited. Marriage between castes was forbidden.

This system of castes and subcastes formed the basic structure of the new society that emerged on the Ganges plain as an Aryan-dominated culture moved east. The caste system also came to play a central role in the emerging religion of Hinduism.

Hinduism and Reincarnation

Although the roots of Hinduism may go back as far as the Indus Valley civilization, the religion's major gods can also be traced to the Aryan newcomers. They had many nature gods: for example, Indra, the thunder-armed god of storms and war; Agni, the hungry fire god and god of the hearth; Varuna, the four-headed god of the skies and controller of rivers and seas. More than thirty deities are honored in the early Sanskrit hymns. Some of the gods were stern and vengeful, others were good-natured and high-spirited.

Early Aryan poets wrote hymns to their gods. The bulk of the *Vedas* (VAY-duhs), the oldest Hindu texts, were composed between 1400 and 800 B.C. They sing the praises of these gods and are the first sacred writings of Hinduism.

As the Aryans moved east and settled among people in the plains near the Ganges River, they also began to worship more local gods. They absorbed many deities from the local peoples already living there. In new sacred writings, such as the *Upanishads* (oo-PAH-nih-shahds), the Aryan settlers added ideas about the castes and how to reach spiritual perfection.

What did these Hindu ideas teach? Hinduism taught that the essential self of a living being, called *Atman* (AHT-muhn), never dies. Hinduism also taught *reincarnation*—the idea that when the body dies, the self is reborn, either as a human or an animal. All life, Hindus said, is an endless cycle of death and rebirth. What one did in this life determined one's caste or position in the next life. The self was believed to have as many lives as necessary to reach spiritual perfection.

How did this work? The self could be born as a prince or a worker or a cow. But by fulfilling one's duties and being faithful to one's obligations, no matter what one's caste, the self could grow and go on to a higher caste in the next life. If people were not faithful to their duty and failed to live nobly, they would be reborn in a lower caste or as an animal.

By 1000 B.C., the caste system had become deeply intertwined with Hindu religious beliefs. If a person were born into a lower caste, his only hope was to work hard, fulfill the duties of his caste, and pave the way for betterment in the next life and eventually toward spiritual perfection. For example, an untouchable who led a good and honest life would not necessarily stay an outcaste forever. His faithfulness might ensure a higher caste in his next life. But just as a good life might lead to reincarnation as a Brahman, a selfish or ignoble life might lead to rebirth as a cat or a dog, perhaps even as a worm. These religious beliefs helped convince people at the bottom of society to accept their present condition and the authority of those above them.

Agni, the god of fire, was said to be Indra's twin. He had seven arms, seven tongues, and two faces. Here he sits astride a ram.

A Path to Release: Yoga

Ancient Hinduism taught ways to improve the chances for release from the cycle of death and rebirth. Adherence to duty was one way. Yoga was another. Yoga, a set of mental and physical disciplines, emphasized meditation to transcend dependence on the body. People performed yoga by putting the body in positions not unlike those found on the ancient Indus seals. The goal was to unite the self with the the universal essence.

Gods on the Ganges

As time went on, more sacred texts were composed and the number of Hindu deities grew. While Hindus worshipped many gods, three main gods became popular over the first millennium B.C.: Brahma (BRAH-muh), Vishnu (VISH-noo), and Shiva (SHIH-vuh).

Brahma was a four-headed creator god. Vishnu was the blue-skinned preserver of the world. Shiva, the god of destruction, was often pictured dancing in a ring of fire.

As more Aryans peopled the plains near the great Ganges, they came to consider the river sacred. From its headwaters in the Himalaya, the mighty waterway flows 1,500 miles to empty into the Bay of Bengal. But according to tradition, the Ganges River has a divine source—it flows down from the god Shiva's hair.

The Sacred Ganges

Many Hindus believe that by bathing in the Ganges they can cleanse themselves of sin. The sick and the injured sometimes dip into the holy waters in hopes of healing. Others go there to die. Toward the end of their lives, some Hindu pilgrims flock to a particular holy site along the banks of the river. It is said to be a gateway to heaven.

Great stone steps allow the faithful to get close to the waters of the Ganges. Some Hindus have their ashes scattered on the river's surface. To Hindus, death here is a final act of purification. The cycle of death and rebirth, they believe, may now be at an end.

Hindus believe that worshippers can be purified by bathing in the waters of the Ganges.

In addition to Brahma, Vishnu, and Shiva, Hinduism came to include thousands of other gods and goddesses. Each of these many Hindu deities had its own personality, and each had a different role. They included the monkey god, Hanuman (HUN-oo-mahn), and the beloved elephant-headed god, Ganesha (guh-NAY-shuh).

Ganesha is the remover of obstacles, who helps people get started in new enterprises. His fat belly symbolizes the prosperity he brings to those who worship him. According to Hindu teaching, Ganesha was created by the goddess Parvati (PAHR-vuh-tee), wife of Shiva. One day, while her husband was away from home, the goddess made a baby boy out of clay and named it Ganesha. She dried it in the sun, and Ganesha came to life.

When Shiva returned, he found a small boy guarding his house, refusing to let him in. Shiva grew angry. In a rage, he chopped off Ganesha's head. Parvati was very upset. She made Shiva promise to replace the head with the head of the first creature he could find. Because this was an elephant, Ganesha got an elephant's head, and he has had it ever since.

Hindus retell countless such legends about their gods. Do they worship one god or many? Some would say that the many gods they worship are all representations of a single universal essence. But each individual deity could be a teacher.

Early Hindus came to believe their gods could take human form

Ganesha was the elephant-headed god of wealth and wisdom. His fat belly symbolized the prosperity he was said to bring to his followers.

and provide valuable lessons for mankind. The lessons of the gods nearly always stress the virtue of adherence to duty. The most famous example is in the *Ramayana* (rah-muh-YAH-nuh), a very long epic poem. The *Ramayana* tells the story of virtuous Prince Rama (RAH-muh). He is said to be a form of the preserver god, Vishnu, so Rama is often pictured as having blue skin like Vishnu. The prince's heroic adventures illustrate the triumph of good over evil. They also show human beings how to live a life faithful to duty by caste and gender. Around the third century B.C., Hindus in ancient India were listening to the *Ramayana*. Here's a short retelling of this ancient story.

The Ramayana

Old King Dasaratha (dah-shah-rah-dah) stood on his palace balcony, looking down on the peaceful, shady streets of Ayodhya (ah-YOH-dyah). Below, his subjects went about their business. Brahman, soldier, merchant, farmer—each knew his place, and each performed his duty. Surely, thought the king, nowhere could there be a kingdom so happy and prosperous.

"I've been a good king," he said aloud. "I am ready to retire."

Dasaratha had four sons. All four were everything princes should be—brave, strong, clever, honest, loyal, and devoted to doing what was right. But there could be no doubt which son the gods had chosen to rule his kingdom—Prince Rama.

Rama was no ordinary prince. When he was only sixteen, he had protected a holy man from hideous demons who came to torment him. On his way home from this adventure, Rama stopped in a neighboring kingdom to see the great bow of Shiva. The king had promised his daughter, Sita (SEE-tuh), to the man who could string the bow. Many powerful warriors had tried, but a dozen straining all together could not even pry the weapon from the ground.

Beautiful and kind, the princess Sita instantly won Rama's heart. He lifted the bow as if it weighed no more than a toothpick, and bent it back with such vigor that the bow broke like a dry twig.

The prince and his new bride returned to a joyous welcome in Ayodhya. Among the happy crowd, it was even said that Rama was really the god Vishnu, preserver of the universe, born into human form to destroy evil in the world.

Yes, indeed, thought Dasaratha. Rama must be made king. With Sita beside him, Rama would rule the land with justice, compassion, and wisdom.

When the old king announced his choice, everyone was pleased. Everyone, that is, except Rama's stepmother. She was determined to see her own son, Bharata (BAH-rah-tah), on the throne.

"My king," she said, "long ago, you promised to grant me two wishes. Do you remember?"

"Of course, my dear," said Dasaratha. "Anything. What would you like?"

The queen smiled. "I would like you to crown our son Bharata king. And I would like you to exile Rama to the forest for fourteen years."

The old king wept and raged, but she refused to take back her requests. What could he do? He had given his promise.

Rama's favorite brother, Lakshmana (lahk-SHMAH-nah), turned pale with anger when he heard the news. "You are the rightful king," he said to Rama. "Anyone who tries to take your place will feel the edge of my sword."

"No!" said Rama. "You know it is our sacred duty to obey our father in all things. I will leave Ayodhya with a willing heart."

"Then I go with you," said Lakshmana.

"And I," said a quiet voice. It was Sita. "For *my* duty, beloved Rama, is to be always by your side."

Leaving their royal chariot behind, the three companions set out together on foot. They had only walked a few days when they heard behind them the pounding of hoof beats.

Bharata swung himself down from his horse. Tears streamed down his face.

"Our father has passed away," he said. "Sending you away broke his heart. Rama, I never wanted to be king. Please come back and take your throne."

Rama embraced his brother. "Dead or alive," he said, "my father's wish is law. I must not return for fourteen years."

"Then give me your sandals," said Bharata. "I will place them on the throne. And as long as you are gone, I will rule only in your name."

Bharata returned to the palace, while Rama and his loyal companions pressed on into the deep, dark woods, where demons ruled the night. Around them, the wind howled; even the dry branches of the trees trembled and groaned.

Rama had no fear. With the help of Lakshmana, he attacked the demons, killing all who crossed their path. Rama and Sita brought spring back to the forest. Birds sang in the trees, and flowers of every color bloomed beneath their feet. Holy men who lived as hermits in the forest praised their names.

But there was one to whom the name of Rama brought no joy—Ravana (RAH-vuh-nh), ruler of the demons.

Ravana drove a magic chariot that flew a thousand times faster than any eagle. He could flatten an entire village with a single sweep of any of his twenty arms. A scowl on the face of one of his ten heads would bring a storm to destroy a whole season's crops. His tremendous power was exceeded only by his pride.

"So Rama thinks he can attack my demons with impunity," snarled Ravana. "Well, we shall see."

While Ravana plotted, Rama and Lakshmana built a small hut in the woods. Every morning Sita gathered delicious wild fruits for them to share. In the evening, they sat around the fire, warming their hands and telling stories. They lived simply but happily.

One day, Sita saw a beautiful golden deer prancing through the forest.

"Rama!" she cried. "Come and see. It is the loveliest creature I have ever seen."

"Then I will capture it for you," her husband promised. He told Lakshmana to remain behind with Sita, then set off in pursuit of the deer. Soon, deer and man had disappeared into the woods.

A moment later, Sita and Lakshmana heard a cry.

"Help! Help me!"

Wide-eyed, Sita turned to Lakshmana. "Rama is in trouble. You must go to him."

"But he told me to stay here."

"He is your brother," Sita said. "How can you ignore his cries?"

Lakshmana ran off toward the sound of Rama's voice.

No sooner was he gone, however, than a wandering hermit appeared before Sita. She offered him food. As she approached him, he revealed himself as the demon Ravana. He seized her, and carried her off in his flying chariot.

Lakshmana found Rama unharmed but the deer had been a servant of the evil Ravana in disguise. Quickly, Rama returned to the hut, but Sita was gone.

Grief-stricken, Rama set out at once in search of his lost wife. On and on the two brothers plodded, but they found no sign of Sita. At last, they came to the land of the monkeys. There they met the monkey Hanuman, and they told him their sad story.

"I am the son of the wind," said Hanuman. "I will find her for you."

After much searching, Hanuman realized where she must be—on Lanka, the legendary island to the south, surrounded by sea monsters, home of the demon ruler Ravana.

With a single great leap, the monkey soared high above the ocean. He landed on the island. There, in a tree overlooking a high-walled garden, he spied a beautiful woman weeping.

"Why do you weep?" asked Hanuman.

"I am the princess Sita," she replied. "Ravana wants me to be his bride, and he has threatened me with dreadful punishments if I continue to refuse. But I will never betray my husband Rama."

"Have courage," said the monkey. "Rama is on his way to rescue you. I have brought you his ring as a pledge." And with another extraordinary bound, he flew across the ocean once again, back to the waiting brothers.

The monkey soldiers spent five days and nights breaking boulders from rocky cliffs and throwing them into the sea. They built a long bridge of stones that spanned the water to the island. Then, with Rama, Hanuman, and Lakshmana at their head, they swarmed across to lay siege to the demon stronghold.

The battle raged, fierce and bloody. Invisible enemies attacked Hanuman and his army from all sides; giants and snakes and poisoned arrows slew the brave monkeys by the thousands.

But Rama was not just a man, not just a prince, not just a great warrior. He was Vishnu, reborn on earth. He had the power of the gods.

Rama faced Ravana. Weapons gleamed from each of the demon's twenty hands—flaming arrows, daggers sharp enough to fell a tree, battle axes bigger than a man. But Rama did not flinch from this awful sight. Calmly, he raised his bow and aimed the arrow at Ravana's heart.

The demon ruler fell.

Sita joyously ran forward to greet her victorious husband. He took her hand and, followed by the faithful Lakshmana and Hanuman, led her to the magic chariot of the dead Ravana. Together they flew back over the ocean, all the way to Ayodhya.

When they arrived home, they discovered that the fourteen years of Rama's exile had passed. Bharata welcomed the travelers with feasts and celebrations. Then he removed his brother's sandals from the throne, and Rama, courageous and dutiful, took his rightful place at last.

The face of the Buddha is a picture of serenity in this sandstone carving.

The Life of the Buddha

In the fifth century B.C., while Confucius was teaching in China and people were listening to tales from the *Ramayana* in India, another wise teacher attracted followers in India. This young man started by asking some of the same questions that Confucius and many Hindus were asking. What is man's place in the world? How can people live good lives? How should we behave? How can we find peace and happiness? He asked the same questions, but he found different answers.

This teacher began life with the name Siddhartha Gautama (sid-DAHR-tuh GOW-tuh-muh), but he is known to the world as the Buddha (BOO-duh), which means "The Enlightened One." His ideas and the path he set forth are known as Buddhism (BOO-dih-zuhm).

Buddhism began in India at a time when most people there practiced early forms of Hinduism, and the two faiths share some important beliefs. Most Buddhists, like most Hindus, believe in the idea of repeated rebirth, or reincarnation. They believe that after a person dies, his self is born again in another body. He might be reborn as a person. He might be reborn as an animal, or even as an insect. Most Buddhists and Hindus believe this chain of reincarnations goes on and on.

Buddhism is a religion and a way of life for many people in Asia and elsewhere. There are more than 360 million Buddhists in the world today.

- On the map on page 192, note the countries where Buddhism is frequently practiced, and those in which Buddhism has strongly influenced the culture.

The Buddha sits in meditation under the leaves of a bodhi tree, a tree now regarded as sacred by Buddhists.

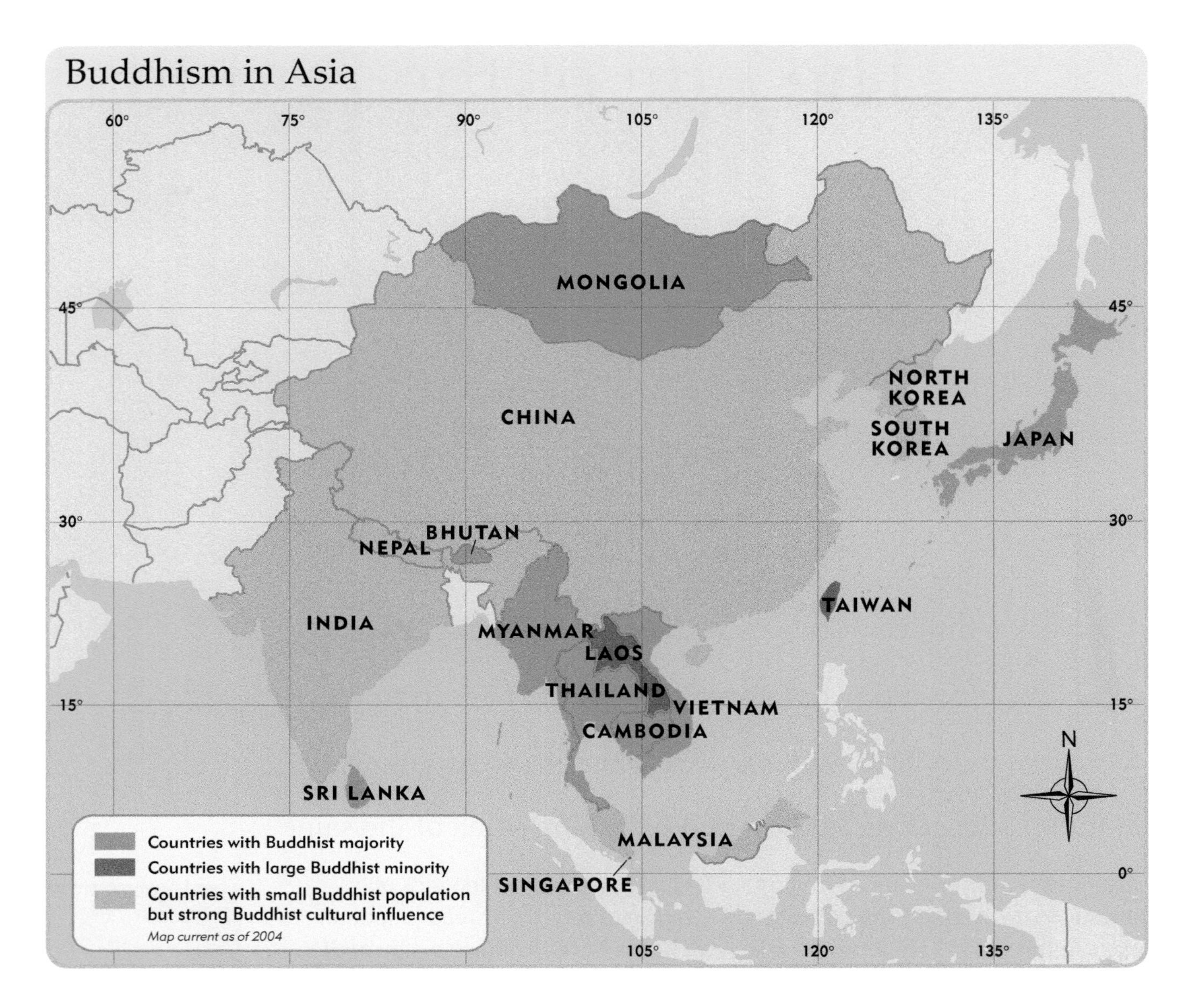

Birth of Siddhartha Gautama, who would later be known as the Buddha. One story says that as soon as he was born he took seven steps, and that lotus flowers blossomed at each step.

The Story of the Buddha

The story of Buddhism begins in the foothills of the Himalaya around 500 B.C. Near the sacred Ganges River in a tiny kingdom in northern India, a young prince was born. The child was named Siddhartha Gautama. Siddhartha was no ordinary boy. He was a Hindu and a member of the noble or warrior caste. He was also the son of a king. Many stories have been told about his early life. Here is one that Buddhists tell about Siddhartha Gautama's birth.

A Prophecy of Things to Come

In one of his many previous lives, Siddhartha Gautama had been a holy man. His name had been Kasappa (kah-SYAH-pah). When Kasappa lay dying, he made a promise. He would be reborn, he said, as a great teacher.

After his death, one of his servants decided to find the reborn Kasappa. He traveled all over, looking at newborn babies. At last he saw an infant who was only two days old. The baby raised a hand to bless the servant, and the servant knew in his heart that this was Kasappa, reborn as Prince Siddhartha Gautama.

Then the faithful servant spoke to Siddhartha's mother and father, the king and the queen. "If your son remains always in the palace," he said, "then he will grow to become a great and powerful prince. But," he continued, "if your son leaves the palace, he will become a holy man and a great teacher. He will give up all his power and wealth, and travel to seek the truth about life. Men will remember his name forever."

Siddhartha's father, the king, grew very worried when he heard this prophecy. He wanted his son to rule his kingdom someday. How could his son give up wealth and power?

The king ordered that no one should ever tell Siddhartha what the servant had said. Gautama would learn to be a prince, not a holy man or teacher. He would have everything he wanted. No sick people or poor people would be allowed to come near the palace, and Siddhartha would never see anything unpleasant or unhappy.

And so to the palace the king brought the finest musicians to play their most beautiful music day and night. Prince Siddhartha had the softest silks to sleep on, the tastiest foods to eat. Everywhere he walked around the palace grounds, there were lush gardens, full of sweet-smelling, brightly colored flowers and wide, clear pools. But around the gardens, around the entire palace, there was a thick, high wall. The king built the wall so that his son would never see the pain, sickness, or suffering that happens to all other people. And for many years Siddhartha never looked over the wall or left the palace.

If the king had his way, Siddhartha Gautama would never want to give up his luxurious life in the palace.

Siddhartha's Early Life

Prince Siddhartha Gautama led a comfortable life in his father's palace. He had many servants and everything he wanted. Of course, Siddhartha had to go through some hard training. He studied languages, poetry, science, and math, and excelled at all that he undertook. He had to learn to ride, drive a chariot, and use a bow. After all, the son of a king had to be a skilled warrior. He also had to learn to rule a kingdom.

At that time, most Indians were Hindus and worshipped Brahma, Vishnu, and Shiva, among other gods. Siddhartha Gautama was raised as a Hindu. He was taught that every living thing had an eternal self. Even animals and insects had selves, just as men did, so a person had to be kind to every living thing.

Siddhartha also was taught that all men belonged to one of the four main caste groups, or to the pool of "outcastes." As a boy, Siddhartha never had to wonder what he would be when he grew up. His destiny was clear—he would become king. As a member of the Kshatriya, the noble caste, he would marry a Kshatriya girl, and their children would be Kshatriyas raised in the palace.

Siddhartha learned how to be a good prince and follow the rules of his caste. If he followed them, he might be re-born as a Brahman in his next life.

Like everyone else, Siddhartha learned to respect the Brahmans. Everyone was supposed to serve and obey them. Only the Brahmans knew how to perform Sanskrit rituals for the high gods and how to bless the fields and flocks. If a man wanted a good harvest, he might pay a Brahman to say the right prayers. If the river flooded, a Brahman could appeal to the gods to stop the flood.

As you can imagine, the Brahmans became very powerful. Meanwhile, people in the lower castes often lived very hard lives. They could only hope that if they obeyed the Brahmans, they might someday be reborn into a higher caste.

These things didn't trouble young Siddhartha because he didn't know how the poor lived and suffered. His father had filled his childhood only with pleasant things. When the prince grew up and married and had his own son, he still enjoyed an easy life.

Suddenly something happened to change the young prince's life forever. While there are different stories of what happened, here follows one of the often-told accounts that Buddhists relate about the great change in Siddhartha Gautama's life.

Siddhartha lived the life of a wealthy prince. Here he rides forth in the company of one of his courtiers.

Siddhartha Gautama Begins His Search

In the comfortable palace of his father the king, Prince Siddhartha Gautama had grown up sheltered from all illness, poverty, and pain. He had never heard the old servant's prophecy that he would someday be a great teacher. He did not remember his past lives. In the twenty-nine years of his life so far, he had never once seen suffering or death.

Prince Siddhartha grew up an intelligent, kind, and generous young man, but he was troubled in his heart. He loved his father, enjoyed his friends, and had everything his heart desired. At times, however, as he wandered alone through the beautiful palace gardens, he felt care descend like a weight upon his heart. In these moments, he knew that though he should be happy, he was not. And as he pondered why this should be, he felt still more troubled.

More and more, his mind wandered to the world outside the high palace walls. One day he asked his father, "What is outside the palace walls?"

"There's nothing for you to see out there," his father answered. "Stay here in the palace. Love your wife and son. Eat the good food and ride your fine horses. Enjoy the music and the poetry!"

But Prince Siddhartha kept asking, and finally, the king agreed to let him go out and see the city. First, however, the king secretly went to Siddhartha's chariot driver and told him to stay only in the streets near the palace. The king ordered all of those streets swept, and the fronts of the buildings cleaned and decorated. He told his subjects to hide all the sick people and old people so that Siddhartha Gautama would not see them. Then, finally, he allowed his son to go out.

As Siddhartha Gautama rode forth in the chariot, he was at first delighted. "The city is as beautiful as my palace!" he exclaimed. "How wonderful it must be to live here! How happy these people are!"

But as his chariot turned a corner, Siddhartha Gautama saw an old, old man with long gray hair, wearing torn, dirty rags. His skin was wrinkled, his eyes were dripping, and he had no teeth. Slowly, the old man dragged himself along the road with the help of two sticks.

"What is that?" Prince Siddhartha asked his chariot driver. "That cannot be a man! Why is he all wrinkled? Why is his hair gray instead of black like mine? What is wrong with his eyes? Why doesn't he have any teeth? Tell me, what is this that I see?"

"My prince," said the chariot driver, "that is a poor, old man. He was once young, strong, and handsome like you. But now the sight grows dim in his eyes, his legs grow brittle, and his arms grow weak. He eats only the food he can beg from people passing by—from those who are kind enough to throw him a scrap rather than an insult. O my prince, everyone will grow old and feeble in time—even you."

Siddhartha Gautama, who had never before seen an old person, was shocked. But a few minutes later, he was even more shocked when they passed a man sitting on the sidewalk, bent over in pain and moaning loudly.

"What is wrong with that man?" he asked.

"He is sick," the chariot driver said. "His body has failed him. His groans tell of the pain that twists him from within. Soon, death will take him."

"What is death?" Siddhartha Gautama asked.

Just then, they passed a funeral procession. A man's body, placed in a coffin and wrapped all in white, was being carried through the streets. The man's family and friends followed, weeping bitterly. Siddhartha was astonished. He looked at the chariot driver with wide, questioning eyes.

"That is death," said the chariot driver. "Death is the end of life. We will all die—even you, my prince."

Siddhartha gasped, and then lapsed into a troubled silence. As they drove on, they left the city and came to the countryside. There, sitting under a tree, was a man dressed in a ragged robe, thin and pale, but with a serene expression on his face.

"Who is that man?" asked Siddhartha Gautama. "Why does he look so peaceful? Does he not know about sickness, old age, suffering, and death?"

"Yes, he knows," replied the chariot driver. "And because he knows, he has given up all of his money and fine things; he has left the world behind to seek answers. He is thinking very hard; he is searching for the truth."

"What truth?" asked Siddhartha Gautama.

"The truth about why people suffer. He is trying to find a way for people to be peaceful and content even in a world in which all must suffer and die."

Later, when he returned to the palace, Siddhartha Gautama's mind was troubled by many difficult questions. Must all men suffer? Why are people so unhappy? What can they do about it? The teachings of Hinduism did not answer his questions. Where could he turn for the truth?

Siddhartha Gautama could enjoy his princely life no longer. He felt that he could not live in such luxury and ease while others suffered.

The prince wanted to solve the problem of suffering, but how could he when he didn't even know what suffering felt like? After much thought, Siddhartha Gautama decided to give up his wealth and family. He resolved to leave the palace. So he took off his fine clothes, dressed in poor rags, and went out into the world to find the truth.

Siddhartha Gautama soon met some holy men who were also looking for truth. They said that he should stop thinking of the needs of his body. Hunger, thirst, rest, comfort, pleasure—all of these, said the holy men, must be given no thought or care. Instead, they said, Siddhartha Gautama must think only of his mind and spirit. That, they said, was the way to find truth.

Siddhartha Gautama joined these holy men, who were *ascetics* (uh-SEH-tiks)—men who practiced self-denial in order to find a spiritual truth. For six years, he wandered with the ascetics, wearing only rough clothing made of bark cloth. Some days they ate only a little rice. Other days they ate nothing at all. They lived in the forest or in caves, and they slept on the ground.

Siddhartha Gautama tried asceticism (uh-SEH-tuh-sih-zuhm)—he denied the needs of his body. He tried to think about truth and goodness, but he did not feel any closer to the answer. This way of finding truth didn't seem to be working. When he was cold and weak with hunger, he couldn't think clearly. Surely, he thought, there must be another way to find truth.

So Siddhartha Gautama left the ascetics and wandered off alone. Finding a quiet place under a tree, he sat down. He made up his mind to sit there until he found the answer. For days he thought about good and evil, and about life and death. Finally something happened. He felt his mind open up, and at last he understood the truth about life.

His new knowledge was like a great light. Siddhartha Gautama felt free from pain and suffering. Because of this experience, he was later called the Buddha, meaning "The Enlightened One."

The Buddha Goes Forth

After his experience of enlightenment, the Buddha went forth to teach his message. Neither the life of extreme pleasure nor the life of extreme asceticism leads to truth, he said. As the Buddha explained it, since suffering is caused by desire, we must learn to overcome desire. People suffer because they desire worldly things such as wealth or power. But no matter how much they get, they will always want more. They will even hurt other people to get more. Then great unhappiness and ever-increasing desires will follow.

The way to free oneself from desire, said the Buddha, is through meditation and compassion. Meditation and compassion, he said, would reveal that the universe and all that is in it is impermanent, passing away like a wisp of smoke or the ripples on the surface of a pond. Once people understood this truth, he said, then they would be free of desire, and thus free from suffering.

As you can imagine, the Buddha's followers did not immediately understand his words. They were hard to grasp. But the Buddha taught his followers patiently.

To help his followers understand his ideas, he used simple stories that emphasized self-restraint and compassion. Some of these tales have been collected and are called Jataka (JAH-tuh-kuh) tales, literally meaning "accounts of the Buddha's past births." They all tell lessons about how to live a good life based on the Buddha's own deeds and advice in his past lives.

Let's read what the Buddha had to say about suffering and death in a Jataka tale called "The Mustard Seed." In this story Shakyamuni (SHAH-kyah-moo-nee), a physician, is the Buddha in a past life.

The Mustard Seed

A wise and faithful woman named Kisa Guatami (KEE-suh GOW-tah-mee) had an only son, and he died. In her grief she carried the dead child to all her neighbors, asking them for medicine. Her neighbors shook their heads and said to one another, "She has lost her senses. The boy is dead."

At length Kisa Guatami met a man who gave her some hope. "I cannot give you medicine for your child," he said, "but I know a physician who can."

"Pray tell me, sir, who is it?" the woman begged.

The man replied, "Go to Shakyamuni."

Kisa Guatami went to Shakyamuni and cried, "Lord and Master, give me the medicine that will cure my boy."

The physician answered, "You must bring me a handful of mustard seed." And when the woman in her joy promised to procure it, Shakyamuni said:

"The mustard seed must be taken from a house where no one has lost a child, husband, parent, or friend."

Poor Kisa Guatami now went from house to house. Everywhere she went, people pitied her and offered her mustard seed. But then she would ask, "Has a son or daughter, a father or mother, died in your family?"

They answered her, "Alas, the living are few, but the dead are many. Do not remind us of our deepest grief." In every house, someone beloved had died.

Kisa Guatami grew weary and hopeless. She sat down at the wayside, watching the lights of the city as they flickered up and were extinguished again. At last the darkness of the night reigned everywhere. And she considered the fate of all human beings, that their lives flicker up and are extinguished. And she thought to herself, "How selfish am I in my grief! Death is common to all. Yet in this valley of desolation there is a path to immortality for those who have surrendered all selfishness."

Kisa Guatami had the body of her son buried in the forest. Returning to the physician, she took refuge in him and found comfort in his teaching. Shakyamuni said: "The life of mortals in this world is troubled and brief and combined with pain. All who are born must eventually die. Such is the nature of living beings. As all earthen vessels made by the potter end in being broken, so is the life of mortals. Both young and adult, both those who are fools and those who are wise, all fall into the power of death.

"Not from weeping nor from grieving will anyone obtain peace of mind. On the contrary, his pain will be the greater and his body will suffer. People pass away, and their fate after death will be according to their deeds. If a man lives a hundred years, or even more, he will at last be separated from the company of his relatives, and leave the life of this world. He who seeks peace should pull out the arrow of grief and complaint. He who has drawn out the arrow and has become composed will obtain peace of mind. He who has overcome all sorrow will become free from sorrow, and be blessed."

And Kisa Guatami found this teaching a balm to soothe the pain in her troubled heart.

A monk at prayer outside a Buddhist shrine.

The Buddha's Teaching and Legacy

The Buddha's quest for understanding began with the question of suffering. Why is there suffering? How can human beings become free from suffering? After his experience of enlightenment, the Buddha gave a name to freedom from suffering. He called it Nirvana (nir-VAH-nuh). *Nirvana* means "blowing out the flame," or putting out what the Buddha said were inner fires of greed, hatred, and ignorance.

The Buddha said that Nirvana is the highest goal for human beings who seek to end the cycle of birth, death, and rebirth. When a person reaches Nirvana, he no longer knows suffering. Pain cannot touch him. He is free.

What about reincarnation? The Buddha taught that a person could escape from the cycle of birth, death, and rebirth when he reaches Nirvana. A person could live many times without reaching Nirvana, since reaching it had nothing to do with caste. A Shudra worker might reach Nirvana in just one lifetime. A learned Brahman priest might never reach it. It all depended on how a man or woman acted.

This idea that people's actions—not their caste—determined their fate was new to the people of India. It provided hope. "By deeds a person is a Brahman; by deeds a person is an outcaste," said the Buddha. Good deeds and thoughts help a person reach Nirvana, and each must reach Nirvana through his own efforts. No priest or offering to the gods could help. In fact, the Buddha said, people did not need the Brahman priests. They could find the truth themselves.

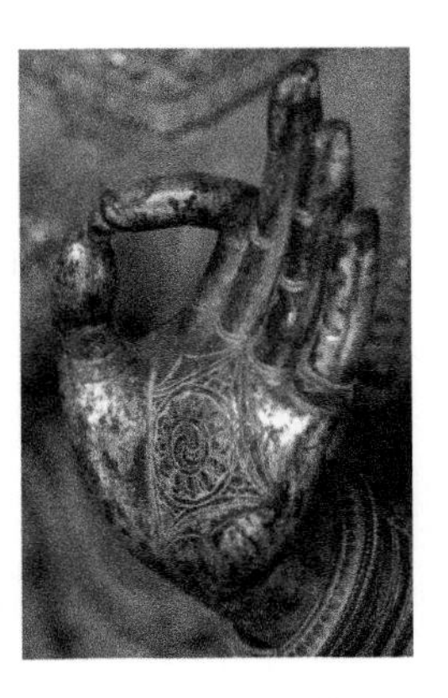

Hand of the Buddha in a gesture that symbolizes teaching.

Pursuing the Path to Nirvana

According to the Buddha, all life is a great wheel of suffering. The Buddha taught that people suffer because they want worldly things such as wealth or power, and no matter how much they get, they always want more. Great unhappiness follows upon desire, and desire leads to ever-increasing desire, and so the wheel of suffering goes round and round without end.

If life is a great wheel of suffering, is there any escape? Yes, said the Buddha. To begin, it is necessary to understand what the Buddha taught as the Four Noble Truths. First, all life is suffering. Second, suffering is caused by our desires and greed. Third, there can be an end to suffering and desires. Fourth, there is a path to Nirvana.

How could people find that path to Nirvana? The Buddha said that people should follow the Middle Way. This means that they should not desire great pleasures, such as strong drink, rich foods, or great luxury. At the same time, they should not impose great hardships on themselves, such as fasting or other forms of self-denial. They should live between these extremes.

The Buddha also preached an Eightfold Noble Path to live a good life and to reach Nirvana. That path was:

- Right understanding: seeking knowledge of the truth
- Right effort: trying to resist evil
- Right speech: saying nothing untrue or hurtful about others
- Right action: acting virtuously
- Right livelihood: doing work that does not harm others
- Right mindfulness: striving to have no evil thoughts
- Right thought: controlling feelings and ideas
- Right concentration: training thoughts through meditation

Living the Eightfold Noble Path

The Buddha said people progress toward Nirvana by pursuing this Eightfold Noble Path. They grow in compassion and love for all living beings—even animals and insects. This meant, among other things, that people should not kill an animal for meat. They should not get rid of insects that are eating crops. They should treat animals with kindness and respect. Such creatures, the Buddha taught, also have selves. Indeed, they might once have been human beings in a previous life.

The Wheel of Dhamma

Buddhists believe all life is a great wheel of suffering. They have a wheel as their symbol. The Buddhist symbol is the wheel of dhamma (DHUH-muh). *Dhamma* is the teaching that Buddhists believe turns the self onto the path to Nirvana.

Once a student asked the Buddha, "How can I advance toward Nirvana?" The Buddha gave this advice: "Speak the truth. Do not give in to anger. Give generously to those who ask."

The Buddha said that each person has to find Nirvana alone. A person cannot learn this from a teacher. The teacher can only point the way. But, said the Buddha, "The man or woman who has reached Nirvana is like a great rock. The wind does not make the rock tremble. So pain and praise do not make the man or woman tremble." Nirvana, he said, frees people from fear and pain. It also frees them from the cycle of rebirth.

The Buddha as a Teacher and Model

For the rest of his life, the Buddha went from place to place, teaching all who would listen. He and his students traveled along the Ganges River Valley, visiting many towns and villages. Wherever they went, people admired his joy and peacefulness. Some of the men and women who heard him became monks and nuns, men and women who devoted their lives to his teachings.

After the Buddha's death, his followers wanted to remember his teachings. For a long time they passed on what they had learned by word of mouth. Finally, four centuries after the Buddha's death, his talks and stories were collected in books of writings. Many Buddhists throughout the world still study these writings today. People also began making statues of the Buddha. The statues helped them remember his life and teachings.

The Buddha thought of himself as a teacher. He didn't want to be regarded as a god. In fact, he didn't want people to depend on any gods at all. Each person has to find truth for himself, he said. Nevertheless,

Above: A stone statue of the Buddha, meditating in typical cross-legged pose.

Below: A modern-day monk instructs a young novice in Buddhist teachings.

some people began to think of the Buddha as a deity. They believed that he had come to save men and women from pain and unhappiness, and that the Buddha could help them if they prayed to him. Today some Buddhists think of the Buddha as a man and teacher. Others think of him as a god and a focus for prayer.

A young Thai boy preparing to become a Buddhist monk dons a flower headpiece and takes part in a festival.

The ideas of the Buddha have lasted for more than two and a half millennia and spread to many countries. As they spread, people in different areas transformed some of those ideas. They gave to Buddhism the characteristics of their own cultures.

On a certain day in Thailand, for example, children celebrate the Buddha's birthday by decorating little boats with flowers and candles. At sunset they set the boats afloat in the river. In Tibet, men chant Buddhist prayers in a temple built in their own national style. In Japan, a housewife offers a bowl of rice before a statue of the Buddha. All these people speak different languages. They all have different customs. But they have one thing in common—they are all Buddhists.

How did Buddhism spread to these different lands? In the third century B.C., eager monks set out from India to spread the teachings of the Buddha. Those first missionaries, however, got help from an unlikely source—a warrior king.

Asoka Follows the Buddha

Two centuries after the Buddha's death, there rose in India a powerful ruler who would spread this new Buddhist faith across Asia. His name was Asoka (uh-SOH-kuh). As we'll see, he was an unlikely person to accept the peaceful ideas of the Buddha.

Asoka was a member of the Maurya (MOW-uhr-yuh) dynasty, the family that ruled most of northern India. The Maurya were ruthless and successful warriors. And Asoka

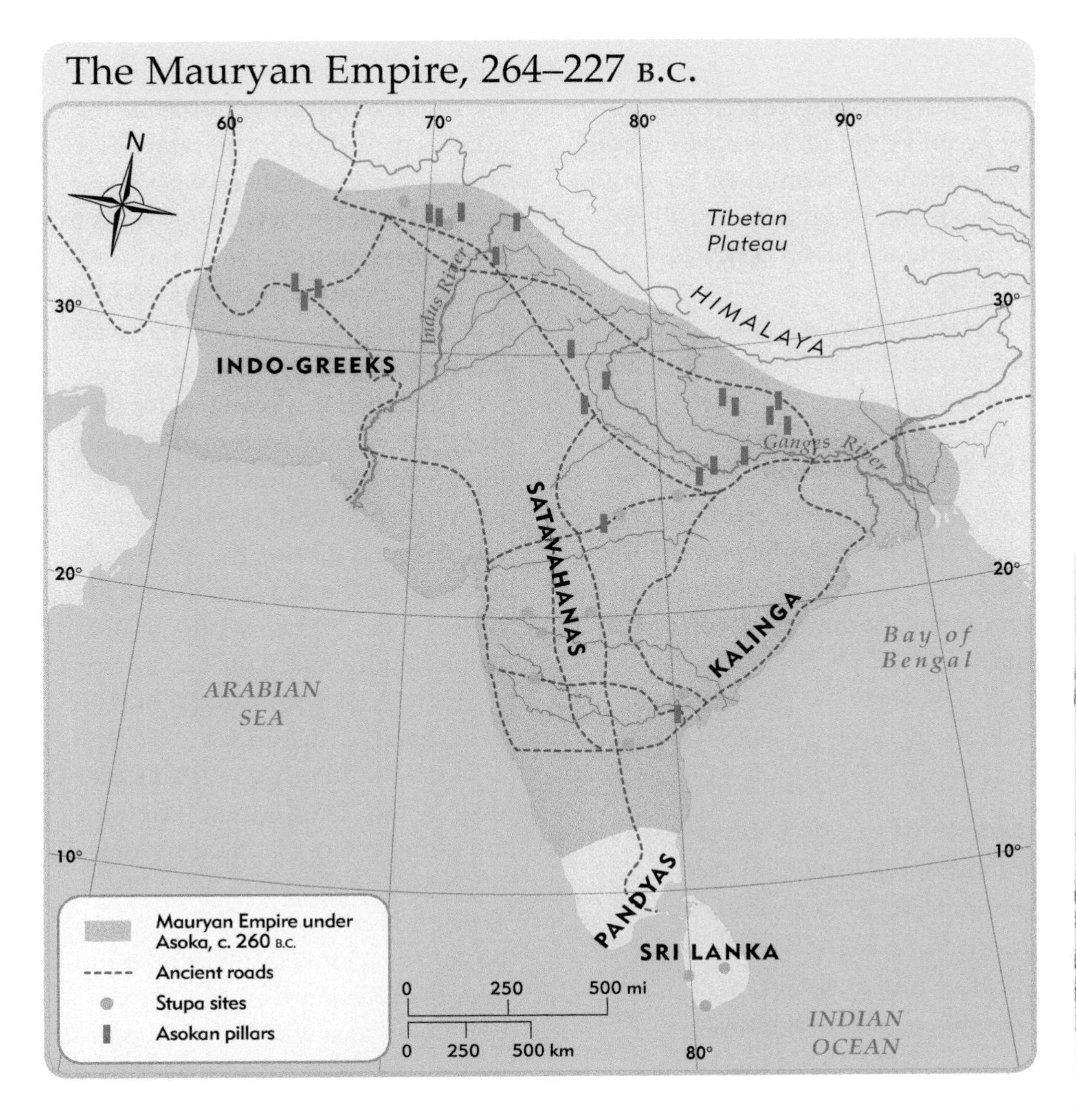

was no exception. According to some accounts, he was one of eight brothers who fought a four-year civil war among themselves after their father died. Around 269 B.C., Asoka emerged as the victor, slaying his brothers in the struggle.

During Asoka's reign, he used the same brutality to expand the Mauryan empire. Shortly after becoming emperor, he conquered the independent kingdom of Kalinga (kuh-LING-guh) on India's east coast. The conquest was bloody and merciless. His inscriptions claim that some 100,000 soldiers died in the fighting. Another 150,000 were taken prisoner and enslaved.

Was this really the man who would spread the gentle Buddha's ideas of compassion and harmony? Surprisingly, it was.

After so much violence, Asoka's heart filled with remorse. He felt terrible sorrow for such loss of life. It changed him forever. He sought wisdom and understanding from Buddhist monks and decided to become a Buddhist.

For the rest of his life, Asoka vowed to rule with righteousness. He preached goodness, compassion,

Converted to Buddhism, the one-time warrior king Asoka sits in the cross-legged style of the Buddha.

Carved lions stand watch from atop one of the stone columns built by Asoka. The polished sides of the columns were inscribed with Buddhist teachings and royal edicts.

and mercy to all living creatures. He would fight no more and would spare the lives of animals. He would eat no meat. From now on, all his conquests would be conquests of faith.

Having changed his own life, Asoka set about changing the lives of his subjects.

The Emperor of India

Asoka now spoke of all Indians as "my children," and he wanted for them "every kind of welfare and happiness, both in this world and the next."

The emperor built hospitals for animals as well as for humans. His subjects could use these without charge. He constructed fine roads to improve communications and trade. For the comfort of travelers, shade trees flanked the roads. Water wells and lodgings dotted the route.

Asoka had a special use for these roads. He wanted to spread the Buddhist religion, so he sent monks to teach throughout the land. In addition, Asoka built *stupas* (STOO-puhs), Buddhist places of worship said to contain relics of the Buddha or of a famous Buddhist leader. According to tradition, Asoka built 84,000 of these great domed structures.

Asoka built other religious monuments, too. Throughout his realm and along his roads, he built magnificent stone columns rising 40 to 50 feet in the air. Carved lions atop the columns looked toward the four corners of his large empire. Below each lion was a wheel that stood for the teaching of the Buddha. The polished sides of the pillars were inscribed with Buddhist lessons that Asoka had learned. One said:

> Asoka, the conqueror of the Kalingas, has felt deep sorrow because the conquest of the people involved slaughter, death, and captivity. Asoka now teaches you to respect the value and sacredness of life, to abstain from killing of animals and from cruelty to living things.

A World Religion

Today the Buddhist wheel appears on the flag of India, and the four lions

The Buddha in Art Around the World

As Buddhist ideas spread, artists in different countries made statues and paintings of the Buddha. Often sculptors around the world depicted him with long earlobes stretched by princely jewels, as well as a topknot representing wisdom and enlightenment. Sometimes they pictured him as one of their own people. The Japanese, for example, carved Japanese-looking Buddhas.

Statues sometimes show the Buddha standing or reclining, but most often he is sitting. Each position in which he sits means something. Many times he is shown sitting cross-legged with his eyes half-closed. This shows that the Buddha is deep in meditation, detached from the world around him. He often sits on a lotus flower, a beautiful flower with its roots deep in the mud below the surface of the water. The lovely flower with its roots in the mud stands for the idea that a human being can transcend this world of desires and reach a higher, purer truth.

have become the official symbol of the modern Republic of India. But the religion these symbols represent did not take deep root in the country where it was born. Following the death of Asoka, Hinduism—not Buddhism—grew stronger among many of India's peoples.

Buddhism, however, began to thrive elsewhere. Asoka had sent his missionaries forth, and each generation of missionary monks carried the Buddhist teachings farther east—across the Bay of Bengal to Burma (now called Myanmar) and Thailand, and on to Sumatra, Cambodia, Vietnam, and Borneo. Other missionaries traveled overland, and hundreds of years later still others traveled to central Asia and to China. From there the faith spread to Korea and Japan. Because of the efforts of Asoka and many others who followed him, Buddhism became one of the world's great religions.

Asoka's own son became a Buddhist monk and missionary known as the great Mahinda (muh-HEEN-duh). He took the teachings of the Buddha to the island of Sri Lanka (sree LAHNG-kuh) off the coast of India. We don't know the exact circumstances surrounding Mahinda's arrival on the island, but we know that a home was not ready for him, and that he was said to have slept in a cave while a mud "palace" dried. Let's travel back in time and picture how it might have happened.

- Find the island of Sri Lanka on the map on page 205. In the time of Asoka, the island was known as Lanka.

The Great Mahinda

Imagining the Past

"Pick up that palm branch!" Senerath (say-NAY-ruhth) shouted to a boy on the beach. "Do you want the great Mahinda to think we don't take care of our island?"

The boy walked right past the palm branch, without picking it up. Maybe he hadn't heard Senerath shouting over the sound of the waves. More likely, Senerath thought, he hadn't *wanted* to hear.

Frowning, Senerath walked out on the beach and picked up the offending branch himself. As if he didn't have enough things to do!

Senerath had been especially busy ever since the king put him in charge of getting the island of Lanka ready for a visit from Arhat Mahinda. Mahinda was the favorite son of the great Emperor Asoka of India, and Senerath wanted everything to be perfect for his visit.

Senerath had found the finest cooks to roast deer for a feast honoring the great Mahinda, and he had found the perfect spot—a beautiful mountaintop—

for the official welcoming ceremony. But he still hadn't found a place for the great Mahinda to stay.

Most of the people on the island lived in small mud huts, which could be built quickly. But Senerath knew a mud hut would not be large enough for the great Mahinda and all of the servants he would surely bring. A larger structure made of mud would take weeks to dry, even in the hot sun of Lanka, and Mahinda was expected any day.

Senerath worried about this problem all day. Then, in the middle of the night when everyone else on the island was asleep, he figured out how to build a large structure—a mud *palace,* really—that would dry quickly. He would heat the mud with fire from torches.

When the men of Lanka heard about Senerath's plan the next day, they didn't want to build such a large structure or dry it with their torches.

"This sounds like too much work!" one man said.

"And it sounds too hot!" said another.

"The king has put me in charge of preparations for the prince's visit," Senerath reminded them. "So you have to do what I say!"

Grumbling, the men began hauling dirt and water to the spot Senerath had selected. By the end of the day, the mud was taking the shape of a building. But it was very wet.

The next morning a king's messenger told Senerath that the great Mahinda was expected today.

"Oh no!" Senerath said. "We're not ready!"

He told the men to light their torches and hold them up to bake the mud.

"Hold the flames closer!" Senerath shouted.

The men moved closer, but the mud was still wet.

"Closer!" Senerath shouted.

The men moved closer, and their faces blistered from the heat. When he saw the mud was beginning to dry, Senerath hurried off to help the cooks put a skinned deer on a spit over the fire. Then he chose palm wines for the feast and rushed to find boys who could carry the great Mahinda to the ceremony on the mountain.

Soon Senerath returned to the mud construction and found the men resting.

"Pick up those torches!" Senerath shouted. "Get back to work!"

"What are they doing?" asked a strange voice behind him.

Senerath turned to see a bald man in a dust-covered robe.

"They're building a palace for a prince," Senerath said proudly. "I designed it."

"A prince?" the stranger said. "A prince is coming here?"

"The emperor of India is sending his son, the great Mahinda, to visit our island," Senerath said. "I am in charge of preparations."

"Ah." The stranger smiled. Then he went to a nearby well, filled a large bowl with water, and took it to one of the men, who stopped working long enough to drink the water.

"What are you doing?" Senerath shouted.

The stranger did not answer, but took water to another man.

"Go away!" Senerath shouted. "These men have work to do!"

The stranger went back to the well and took more water to another man.

"Didn't you hear me?" Senerath shouted. "I'm in charge here!"

The stranger offered Senerath a small smile, but kept carrying water between the well and the men. Senerath opened his mouth to shout again, but something in the stranger's smile silenced him. Besides, Senerath noticed that the men worked faster after drinking the water.

After the last man drank his water, the stranger made one more trip to the well. He brought back a bowl of water for Senerath.

"You must be thirsty, too," the stranger said. "So much shouting. In your next life, you may be a silent turtle."

Senerath refused the water. "I am very busy right now, getting ready for the great Mahinda," he said.

"You should take care of yourself and your men," the stranger said. "Mahinda can sleep in a cave."

The great Mahinda in a cave! Senerath laughed. Then he looked into the stranger's eyes and saw he wasn't joking. This foolish stranger's eyes glowed with such peace that, for a moment, Senerath thought how pleasant it would be if he weren't such an important man and if he didn't have so much important work to do.

Out of the corner of his own eye, Senerath saw some of the men watching him talk with the stranger. "Get back to work!" he shouted. "Hold those torches closer!"

When he turned back, the stranger was gone.

A short time later, a messenger came and said the king wanted to see Senerath right away.

Senerath hurried to the king. He was surprised to find the king sitting on the ground, next to the bald stranger, still in his dusty robe.

"We can begin the celebration," the king said. "The great Mahinda is here." He nodded toward the bald stranger.

This stranger was the great Mahinda? Where were his fine robes? And his servants?

The stranger smiled at Senerath. "I am the son of Emperor Asoka," he explained, "but I left the palace to become a monk."

Senerath wasn't sure what a monk was, but he knew it couldn't compare with being a prince. Surely this man had to be joking. Then Senerath looked into his eyes and saw the same peace he had seen before.

"I follow the teachings of the Buddha," Mahinda said. "The Buddha told us to live simple lives. He told us not to grow attached to the things of this world. When monks travel, he said we should carry only eight items: a robe, a belt, a razor, a needle and thread, a walking stick, a water strainer, a toothpick, and"—he held up the bowl he had used earlier to carry water from the well—"an alms bowl."

An alms bowl? The son of the great Emperor Asoka *begged* for his food?

Mahinda seemed to know what Senerath was thinking. "We accept—but never beg for—offerings from our followers."

"We will offer you plenty of food tonight," the king said. "Is that not true, Senerath?"

Senerath nodded. "The deer is on the spit, and our finest wines are ready."

"It grieves me to know that a deer was killed for me," Mahinda said. "The Buddha said we should not kill animals or drink anything that clouds the mind."

"I see we have much to learn about this Buddha," the king said.

"The Buddha was a wise and gentle man who lived in India many years ago," Mahinda said. "He taught mercy and compassion for all living things."

Senerath thought of Mahinda's kindness in carrying water to the men. Then he remembered how he had shouted at Mahinda. Embarrassed, Senerath looked down at his feet.

"We all must learn," Mahinda said gently. "My father, the great Asoka, waged war and killed many people before he learned. Now he is sorry for the suffering he caused, and he wants to spread the peaceful teachings of the Buddha throughout the world."

"He wants to begin here in Lanka," the king said proudly.

"I will spend my life teaching the people of Lanka about the Buddha," said Mahinda.

"Senerath will help you," the king said. "He is very organized and knows how to get things done."

Mahinda hesitated, and Senerath knew he was remembering all of the shouting. "Senerath can help me for a time," Mahinda said. "But he must learn the teachings of the Buddha, and he must overcome his inner fires. But I believe he can do it. He might even become a monk himself someday and take the teachings of the Buddha to other lands."

Senerath looked up. "Might I go to India?"

"Farther than India," Mahinda said. "Farther east. But first, you must learn the teachings of the Buddha."

"No," the king said. "The first thing Senerath must do is finish your house."

"It will take a few more days," Senerath said. "The mud is not yet dry."

"Please, do not trouble yourself," Mahinda said. "I told you—Mahinda can sleep in a cave."

Abraham leads the Hebrews into the land of Canaan.

A Chosen People

In many times and places, people in ancient civilizations worshipped many different gods. The Sumerians offered prayers to An, Enlil, and Enki. The Egyptians looked to Re, Osiris, and Isis. The Babylonians, Chinese, and Indus Valley people had their various deities. People in ancient times believed their gods ruled the forces of nature. These gods gave people ways to explain events they marveled at or could not understand, from the swelling of life-giving rivers to lightning that split the sky.

The belief in many gods is called *polytheism* (PAH-lee-THEE-ih-zuhm). The word comes from the ancient Greek language—*poly* (meaning "many") and *theos* ("god"). For millennia, polytheism characterized the ancient world. Some gods were believed to be kindly and honest. Others were ruthless and greedy. Some had animal heads. Others had human faces. But each was believed to control some important part of life.

Slowly, however, another belief emerged. Remember Akhenaten? He was the Egyptian pharaoh who angered his subjects when he decreed they could no longer build temples to their traditional deities. He replaced the old gods with one new, all-powerful sun-god. Many Egyptians, including the boy pharaoh, Tutankhamen, didn't like this. They did not want a single, faraway, impersonal deity. They wanted gods who could help them with daily concerns such as a good harvest, healthy children, or victory in war. So "King Tut" restored the old gods in Egypt.

In most ancient civilizations, polytheism—the belief in many

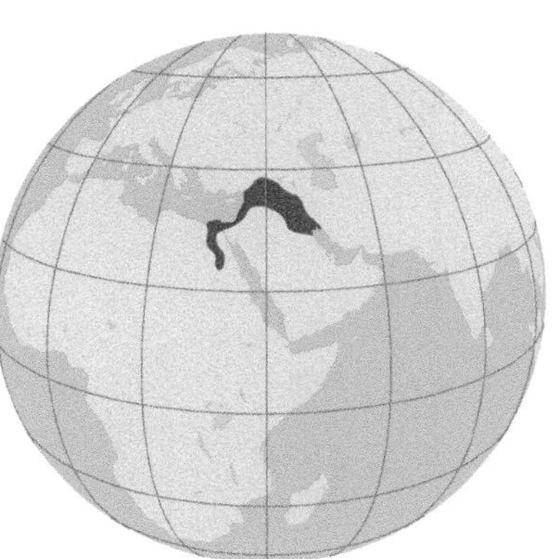

This chapter focuses on the experiences of the Hebrew people in the ancient Middle East.

gods—was the rule. But one Middle Eastern people had another idea—the idea of *monotheism* (MAH-nuh-THEE-ih-zuhm). Monotheism means belief in one god. Like the word *polytheism,* it comes from putting together two Greek words: *mono* (meaning "one") and *theos* ("god"). The ancient Hebrews, who began like the Sumerians on the banks of the Euphrates River, would develop and spread an idea with big consequences.

The Ancient Hebrews

The ancient Hebrews were one of the first peoples to worship one God. Around the year 2000 B.C., they were living along the banks of the Euphrates

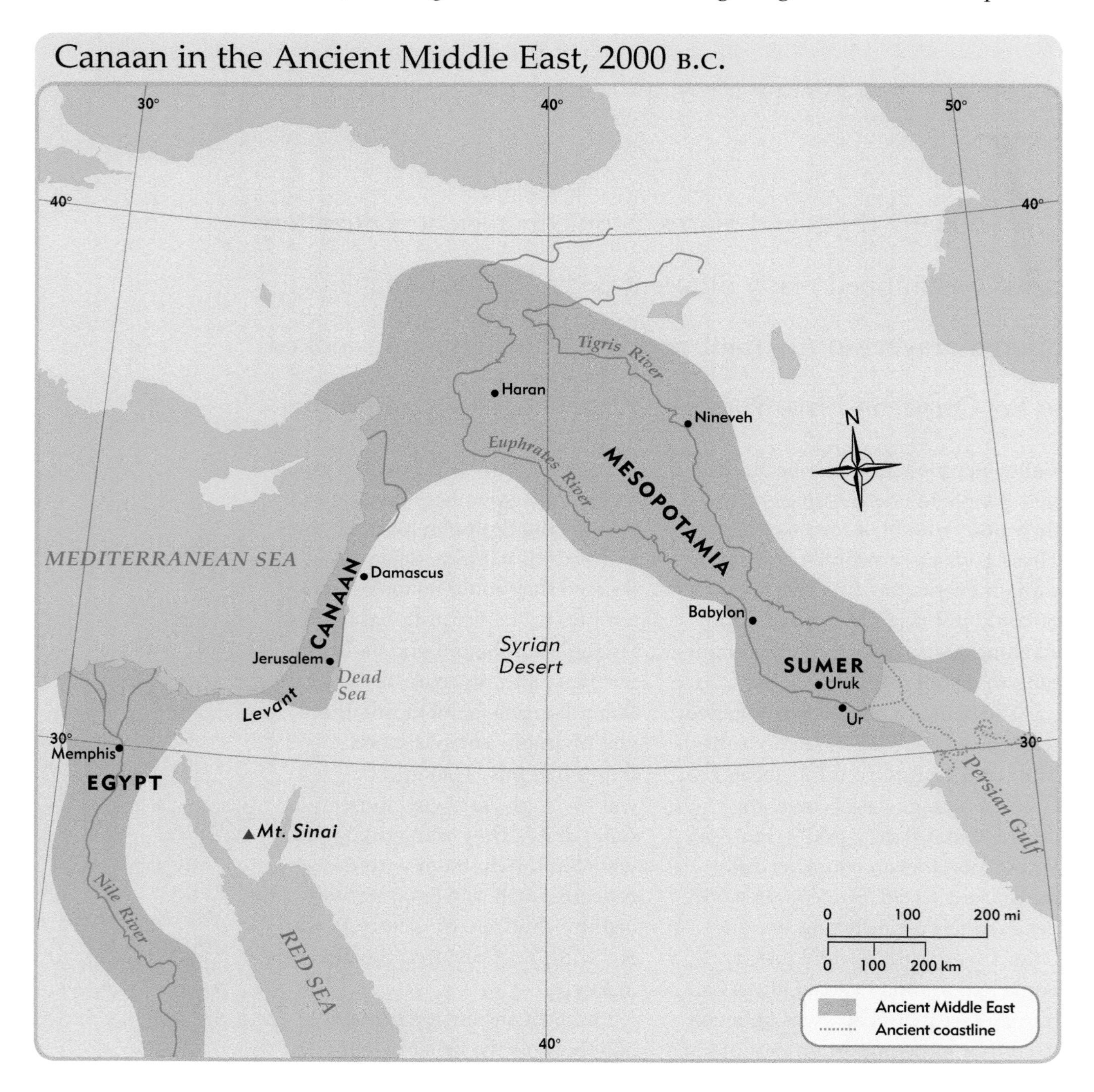

Far left: The Hebrew caravan enters Canaan.

Left: A scroll of the Torah, the holy book of the Hebrew people.

River in Sumer. Then they began to move west on a long journey that would take them to a land on the eastern edge of the Mediterranean called Canaan (KAY-nuhn). That journey—and the ideas that came out of it—would have profound effects on the development of civilization for centuries to come.

- On the map on page 214, locate Sumer, the Euphrates River, and Canaan.

Compared with other peoples of the ancient Middle East, the Hebrews weren't particularly wealthy or powerful. Yet they gave the world a rich legacy of ideas. The Hebrews carried the idea of monotheism farther than any people had before. They placed their trust in one God and wanted to discover what he expected them to do. They came to see themselves as a people chosen by the one God in whom they placed their faith.

The religion of the ancient Hebrews is known today as Judaism (JOO-dee-ih-zuhm or JOO-duh-ih-zuhm), and the followers of Judaism are known as Jews. The Hebrews wrote many books about what they learned from their history and what they understood of God. These sacred writings are known as the Torah (TOHR-uh). The Torah tells us much about the history of the Hebrews, their beliefs in God, and their laws. Most of the information we have about the early history of Judaism comes from the Torah itself.

The Torah

The word *Torah* can be used in different ways. The narrowest meaning is the Pentateuch (pen-tuh-TOOK), the first five books of the Hebrew Bible. These books are Genesis, Exodus, Leviticus, Numbers, and Deuteronomy. The word *Torah* can also refer to the whole Hebrew Bible, what Christians call the Old Testament. Finally, in its broadest sense, *Torah* signifies the entire body of wisdom and teachings contained in Jewish sacred literature, as well as in oral tradition.

Abraham, known as the "father of the Hebrews."

The Father of the Hebrews

In many ways, the history of the Jewish people begins with Abraham, whom the Torah says was the first great Hebrew leader and the first to believe in one God. Even today, Abraham is remembered as the "father of the Hebrews."

Abraham: What's in a Name?

The father of the Hebrews, known to history as Abraham, was called Abram during the early part of his life. According to the Torah, God changed his name. The Hebrew holy book says that God promised Abram many descendants and then changed his name to Abraham, which means "father of many nations."

Many scholars believe that Abraham was born in the city of Ur in Mesopotamia some time around 1800 B.C. The great ziggurat of Ur was probably a familiar sight to him as he grew up. His family, like all people of Mesopotamia, believed in many gods. Legend has it that Abraham's father was a maker of clay idols worshipped by the people of Sumer.

The history of the Hebrews tells us that Abraham's father decided to leave southern Mesopotamia and move his family northwest to a place called Haran (huh-RAHN). Beyond this, the Torah is silent about Abraham's early life. This suggests that, to the Hebrews, the details of Abraham's youth were less important than the central idea of his worship of just one God.

- On the map on page 214, locate the cities of Ur and Haran.

Abraham didn't spend the rest of his days in Haran. Suddenly he left, never to return. Why did he leave so suddenly? The Torah gives this answer:

> Now the Lord said to Abraham, "Go from your country and your father's house to the land that I will show you. And I will make of you a great nation, and I will bless you, and make your name great, so that you will be a blessing. I will bless those who bless you, and curse those who curse you. And through you will all the families of the earth be blessed."

The Torah says that Abraham obeyed God's command. He took his family and all his possessions, and set forth from Haran to a new land.

Abraham Moves to a New Land

Abraham's "family" didn't include just a wife and children. In fact Abraham had no children when he left Haran. His family was probably a small tribe of herdsmen and shepherds, and may have numbered several hundred people, including relatives and servants.

Let's imagine what this family looked like as it set out. Flocks of sheep and herds of oxen ambled along. The family's goods were loaded on donkeys or men's backs. The people and animals together must have looked like a small town on the move. Of course this group could not travel very fast. Sometimes they had to rest and let the animals graze. And frequently they would have to halt to prepare meals and make clothing. It took Abraham's family years to reach the land they believed God had chosen for them.

That land was Canaan, and it was the home of a people called the Canaanites (KAY-nuh-niyts). This strip of land along the sea lay between two great civilizations—Egypt to the southwest and Mesopotamia to the northeast.

Study a map of that part of the world, and you'll quickly see why Canaan has often been called a "land bridge." To the west lay the Mediterranean Sea. To the east was stony desert. The people who traveled between Egypt and Mesopotamia usually went through Canaan, as it was the easiest route. The area became an important link between these two great civilizations. Traders, goods, and ideas constantly moved through this land bridge between Egypt and Mesopotamia.

- On the map on page 214, locate Canaan, the Mediterranean Sea, the Syrian Desert, Egypt, and Mesopotamia.

It was to Canaan that Abraham brought his family. The Hebrews believed a second great event took place there. The Torah says that God made an agreement with Abraham, an agreement known as the Covenant (KUH-vuh-nuhnt). God said he would choose Abraham's family as his special people. If they would worship him and him alone, God would give them the land of Canaan and make them into a mighty nation, and Abraham's descendants would be more numerous than the stars. The Torah says that Abraham accepted the Covenant from God. He declared that he and his family would worship one God.

A *covenant* is a solemn, binding agreement or promise.

The Hebrew View of History

The Hebrews believed that God's will could be seen in history. More specifically, they believed that God had revealed himself in the Hebrew's own history. Looking back, they could point to different events and leaders in the past and say, "Here God made an agreement with us," or, "Here God gave us strength to win this battle. This shows us how mighty God is."

By looking at their history, the Hebrews believed they could learn what God had done for them, and what he expected of them. So the Hebrews kept careful historical records. They wrote many books about what they learned from their history and what they understood of God. The Torah, their holy book, is one such account of how the Hebrews saw God's will at work in their history.

A limestone relief shows the Canaanite god Baal holding a thunderbolt above his head.

The Hebrews in the New Land

The Hebrews' worship of one God was still a very new idea. As yet, they did not have a long history to look back on, since it went back only as far as the life of Abraham. But they had come to believe one important thing about their God—he expected the Hebrews to worship him and him alone.

The people surrounding the Hebrews—the Egyptians, the Sumerians, and the Canaanites—were still polytheists. They worshipped many gods with names such as Baal (BAY-uhl), whom they said made crops grow, and Asherah (ASH-uh-ruh), a goddess of love. The Hebrews believed it was all right for these other people to worship their gods while they worshipped their own "God of Abraham."

The Torah tells us that Abraham's descendants wandered through Canaan for many years. They slept in tents and kept herds of cattle, sheep, and goats. To find grazing land and water, they had to move from place to place. When the animals had eaten all the grasses in one place, the Hebrews moved on to another spot.

Not all the Hebrews lived like nomads. Some traded in Canaanite cities, while others settled down and farmed the land. Some of these Hebrews began to live as the Canaanites did. They wore Canaanite clothing and followed Canaanite customs. Sometimes they even took up the religion of the Canaanites and forgot about the God of Abraham. They worshipped Baal and Asherah.

The Hebrew nomads, the family of Abraham, didn't forget to worship one God. Since they kept to themselves, it was probably easier for them to hold on to their beliefs. The Torah says that Abraham had a son named Isaac (IY-zuhk), and Isaac's family kept alive the worship of one God. Isaac and his wife had a son named Jacob, also called Israel, and he too kept alive that idea. The chil-

Where Does the Word *Israel* Come From?

Abraham had a son named Isaac, and Isaac had a son named Jacob. In Jewish scripture, Jacob is also called "Israel." His twelve sons became fathers of the Twelve Tribes of Israel. Thus in the Torah (as well as in the Old Testament), you often will see the ancient Hebrews referred to as "Israelites." The modern nation of Israel, founded in 1948 as a homeland for Jews, draws its name from these Biblical origins.

dren of Israel carried from place to place the idea of a single God, who had chosen them as his special people. Finally, they carried the idea into Egypt.

How did they get to Egypt? The Torah says this surprising journey began with the treachery of eleven jealous brothers. Here is a retelling of that famous story.

Abraham's son Isaac lays hands of blessing on one of his own sons, Jacob.

Joseph and His Brothers

Long ago, in the land of Canaan, there lived a wealthy man named Jacob. He had hundreds of sheep and cattle. He had droves of camels and donkeys. But what made him truly rich were his twelve strong sons.

While Jacob loved all his sons, he loved the one called Joseph best. To show his pride in the boy, Jacob gave Joseph a coat of many colors. When Joseph's older brothers saw that he was their father's favorite, they grew jealous of him.

One day Joseph had a dream. He told it to his brothers.

"Behold," he said, "we were binding sheaves in the field. My sheaf arose and stood upright. And your sheaves stood round about, and bowed to my sheaf."

Joseph's brothers saw a meaning in the dream. "Do you think you will rule over us someday, little brother?" they said angrily.

Soon after this Joseph's brothers went to find new pastures for their flocks some miles away from their home. Jacob sent Joseph to see how his brothers were getting along.

When Joseph's brothers saw him coming, they made up their minds to kill him. "Behold, here comes the dreamer," they said to one another. "Let us slay him and cast him into a pit, and say some evil beast devoured him."

When Joseph drew near, they grabbed him, pulled off his coat of many colors, and threw him into a deep, empty pit. Then the heartless brothers sat down to eat their meal, ignoring Joseph's cries.

While they ate, a caravan approached. It was a band of merchants on their way to Egypt, their camels laden with spices and myrrh.

The brother named Judah asked, "What good does it do us to kill our brother? Instead, let us sell him to these merchants."

This plan satisfied them all. So they drew Joseph out of the pit and sold him to the merchants for twenty pieces of silver. Then they killed a goat and dipped Joseph's coat in its blood. They took the coat to their father and said, "This have we found."

The poor father cried, "It is my son's coat. An evil beast has devoured him. Joseph was surely torn to pieces." Jacob wept. He tore his clothes, put on rough mourning robes of sackcloth, and would not be comforted.

But Joseph was alive. Day by day, he trudged along beside the camels of the caravan under the hot, cloudless sky. At last the palm trees that border the river Nile came into sight. Joseph had come to the land of Egypt.

Egypt at that time—more than four thousand years ago—was a great and rich country. There the merchants sold Joseph as a slave to the captain of the royal guard of Pharaoh.

Even though he was now a slave in a strange land, Joseph did not lose heart. He made up his mind to do his best, no matter what might happen to him.

As the years passed and he grew into manhood, he proved himself to be so honest and wise that his master trusted him with everything he had. He made Joseph the manager of all his lands, houses, and goods.

But the time came when misfortune again befell Joseph. The wife of Joseph's master was a thoughtless, wicked woman. She accused Joseph of things of which he was not guilty, and had him thrown into Pharaoh's prison.

Even then Joseph did not lose hope. He was so wise and trustworthy that the jailer soon made him his chief helper.

One morning, Joseph noticed that some of the other prisoners looked troubled.

"Why do you look so sad today?" he asked.

They told him, "We have each dreamed a strange dream, but there is no one to tell us what it means."

With the Lord's help, Joseph told them the meaning of their dreams.

Then it happened that Pharaoh had a strange dream. He dreamed that while he stood on the banks of the Nile, out of the river came seven fat cattle to feed in a meadow. And after them came seven poor, lean cattle. And the seven lean cattle ate the seven fat cattle. But though the seven lean cattle had eaten the fat cattle, they remained as lean as before.

Next, Pharaoh dreamed that he saw seven ears of corn upon one stalk, full and good, and after them seven ears withered and thin. And the seven thin ears devoured the seven good ears.

Pharaoh thought a great deal about his strange dreams. He sent for all the wise men of Egypt, but none could explain it.

Then Pharaoh's chief butler told him of a Hebrew prisoner who was skilled at interpreting dreams. Pharaoh called Joseph to the palace and said, "I have had two strange dreams. I am told that you understand such things."

"The answer is not in me," said Joseph, "but God shall give Pharaoh an answer."

Pharaoh told Joseph about his dreams. Joseph said, "Both dreams mean the same thing. The God of my father has sent them to you so that you might know the things that are about to happen in Egypt. The seven fat cattle and the seven full ears of corn mean that there will be seven years of plenty. And the seven lean cattle and the seven thin ears mean seven years of famine."

Joseph advised the king to store food during the seven years of plenty to use during the seven years of famine. He also advised him to find a wise, honest man to be in charge.

Pharaoh took this advice. He appointed Joseph himself to fill the office. He gave Joseph fine clothes and put a gold chain about his neck. He took the ring from his hand and put it on Joseph's. He made Joseph governor over all the land of Egypt. Only Pharaoh himself had more power than Joseph. The years of plenty came. Joseph gathered grain as the sand of the sea. Then the seven years of famine began, and the people cried out to Pharaoh for bread. Pharaoh told them to go to Joseph. So Joseph opened all the storehouses and sold grain to the Egyptians.

The famine spread beyond Egypt. All around, the people knew terrible hunger, especially in Joseph's old home, the land of Canaan, where his father Jacob and his brothers still lived.

Jacob heard that grain could be bought in Egypt. So he told his sons to go down into that country and buy a supply. Ten of Jacob's sons set out for Egypt. But his youngest son, Benjamin, he loved dearly. So he kept the boy at home.

Since Joseph was now the governor of Egypt, all who wished to buy grain had to go to him. The ten sons of Jacob bowed before him, but they did not recognize him. How could they? They had not seen him since he was a boy. Now they found a man of great power, dressed in royal garments.

Joseph knew his brothers at once. His heart yearned for his own people, but he wished to test his brothers, so he spoke to them roughly. He accused them of being spies. "You say you have a younger brother at home," he sneered. "Bring him here so that I may see if you speak truly."

The brothers knew that their father would grieve if Benjamin were called away. So they refused. Joseph threw them into prison for three days. Then he called them before him again.

He heard his brothers speaking tenderly of their father and of Benjamin. He heard them admit how cruel they had been to him in selling him into slavery. He heard them agree that this punishment had come to them justly for their cruelty.

All this time it was hard for Joseph to keep back his feelings. His brothers did not think that the governor of the land understood what they were saying, for he spoke to them through an interpreter. But Joseph understood it all, and he turned his face from them and wept.

Finally the brothers agreed to bring the boy, Benjamin, into Egypt. Then Joseph filled their sacks with corn, and they trudged home to Canaan.

A hard task was now before the brothers. They had to tell their father that the governor of Egypt had ordered them to return and bring Benjamin with them. This came near breaking the old father's heart. Joseph dead! And now Benjamin was to be taken away! He felt that he could not let him go.

But the famine still lasted. Soon the store of food the brothers had brought from Egypt was gone. They must either starve or go back for more. So Jacob had to let them go and take with them the child of his old age, the little Benjamin.

All eleven of Joseph's brothers stood before him and bowed to the earth. Joseph ordered a great feast set for them. When he saw Benjamin, it was even harder for him to keep back his feelings. He had to hasten away into his own chamber and weep.

Then Joseph gave orders to the steward of his house. "Fill the men's sacks with food," he said, "as much as they can carry. And put my cup, the silver cup, in the sack of the youngest son."

At dawn the next morning the brothers set out for home. But they had not gone far when they were stopped by Joseph's steward.

The steward said, "Why have you returned evil for good? You have taken my lord's drinking cup!"

Each brother took down his sack and opened it. Of course, when the steward emptied Benjamin's sack, there glittered the silver cup.

The brothers cried out in terrible distress and hurried back to the city. They threw themselves at Joseph's feet and begged him to let the boy go free.

Judah said, "Please, my lord, our father loves him best of us all. Losing the boy would send him to his grave. Please, sir, let me be your servant in my brother's place."

Then Joseph knew that his brothers' hearts were no more filled with selfishness. He cried out to them, "I am Joseph, your brother whom you sold into Egypt. But do not be grieved or angry with yourselves that you sold me, for God sent me before you to save your lives."

He fell upon his brother Benjamin's neck and wept, and Benjamin wept on his neck. Then the brothers, twelve now, talked together for a long time. At last, Joseph said, "Go, fetch our father and all your families down from Canaan. The best part of Egypt's land shall be yours."

Joseph's family did as he commanded. They journeyed down into Egypt and made their homes there. Then, at last, Jacob held Joseph's children in his arms and blessed them. And there was great happiness between them for the rest of their days.

As for Joseph, he held his high office during all his long life. He was the true king, for he was Pharaoh's wise guide, and made the people happy.

This story added more to the Hebrews' ideas about God. First, it was proof to them that God could see the future as well as the present and the past. As the Hebrews interpreted their history, years before the famine God had sent Joseph to Egypt so the people of Israel could be saved.

Second, they said, this event showed that if God's people were faithful to him, he would be just and fair to them. Joseph suffered through hard times as a slave, but he remained faithful—and so, the Hebrews believed, God helped Joseph become an important man in Egypt. The Hebrews believed the same would be true of other men. When they were in need, God would step into their lives to help them. In return, men should be like Joseph—faithful to God and good to other men, as Joseph was good to his brothers.

The Captivity in Egypt

After the famine was over, the Israelites did not return to Canaan. They settled down in Egypt and turned to farming or herding. Like the Canaanites, the Egyptians were polytheists, still worshipping Osiris, Isis, Horus, and other gods.

We've seen that in Canaan, many Hebrew farmers took up the polytheistic religion of their neighbors. There was danger of the same thing happening in Egypt. As the Hebrews settled there, it would have been easy for them to adopt Egyptian ways. But, as the Torah reports, something happened to keep them from doing that.

In Egypt the Israelites continued to work hard. They were used to the tough life of nomads. They remained loyal to their tribes and families. Years passed. Joseph and his brothers passed away. The pharaoh who elevated Joseph passed away. But Hebrew descendants remained in Egypt, and their families grew larger and larger.

Eventually the Egyptians noticed that the number of Hebrews was growing exceedingly fast. This alarmed the Egyptians. What if the Israelites became too strong? What if they sided with Egypt's enemies? A new pharaoh decided to take some harsh steps to head off such possibilities.

The Torah says that the pharaoh made slaves of the Israelites. He put them to work building Egyptian cities and temples. The Hebrews now found themselves in captivity.

Even in captivity, though, the Israelites grew in number, which made the pharaoh even more uneasy. If these people kept growing, they might turn against their Egyptian masters. So, the Torah says, the pharaoh issued a heartless decree. He ordered his soldiers to kill all the Hebrew's baby boys. "Every boy born to the Hebrews, you must throw into the Nile," he declared.

The Hebrew slaves were forced to live apart from the Egyptian people. The forced separation helped keep them from turning to polytheism. Back in Canaan, the Hebrew farmers couldn't see much difference between their own lives and the lives of the Canaanites. In Egypt, however, the Hebrew slaves could see how different they were from the Egyptians. The Egyptians were free and they were not. In spite of their hardships, the people of Israel kept their faith in the God of Abraham.

Moses Leads the Escape from Egypt

The Torah says that the Hebrews remained slaves in Egypt for many years. Had their God forgotten them? Was he unable to help them

Pharaoh's daughter rescues a Hebrew baby from the Nile River and names him Moses.

outside of Canaan? No, they said—their God had not forgotten them. He was, they believed, able to help them in Egypt as well as Canaan. They had faith that he saw their plight and would answer their pleas.

The Torah tells of a baby boy born into a Hebrew family. Since the pharaoh had ordered all Hebrew sons killed, the infant's mother hid him by setting him afloat in a basket of reeds on the Nile River. One of the pharaoh's own daughters found the baby and named him Moses, which meant "drawn from the water." The child grew up among the Egyptians, yet in time he would prove faithful to his own people.

The Torah says that God spoke to Moses and told him it was his task to free the Hebrews from the Egyptians. Moses was frightened, but God told him he would give him the right words to say. Moses had reason to be frightened. A very powerful pharaoh was on the throne, probably Ramses II. Ramses, as you recall, was a great conqueror and prolific builder. He always had another project in mind and was not likely to let the Hebrews go. So when Moses went to the pharaoh and demanded that his people be allowed to leave Egypt, the pharaoh refused.

Then, the Torah says, a series of plagues fell on Egypt. Cattle died of disease. Insects ate the crops. Storms ruined the harvest. In all this the Hebrews saw the hand of God. They believed he was punishing the Egyptians in order to free his chosen people. But the pharaoh's heart was hardened, and Ramses would not let the Israelites go.

Finally, the Torah reports, Moses warned of a last plague, one that would be the most deadly of all. If the pharaoh wished to spare his own people, he must free the Israelites from bondage, Moses said. The pharaoh refused.

The Torah says that in this last plague, the firstborn child of every Egyptian, from the lowliest worker to the pharaoh himself, would die, while the angel of death would pass over the houses of the Hebrews as long as they marked their doorposts with the blood of a lamb. When this last plague was to come, the Israelites should be ready to flee, eating a ceremonial meal of roasted lamb and unleavened bread.

According to the Torah, death came to the Egyptian firstborns. The pharaoh, overcome with sorrow, gave the Hebrews permission to leave his land. Moses led them on the Exodus (EK-suh-dus), or journey out of Egypt.

The pharaoh soon changed his mind and sent his army after the Hebrews. In their chariots, the Egyptian soldiers pursued the Israelites to the shore of the Red Sea. The Torah says that God told Moses to stretch out his hand over the sea; the waters parted, and the Hebrews walked across dry land. When Moses lowered his hand, the waters returned and swallowed up the Egyptians in their chariots.

To the Hebrews the Exodus was a crucial event in their history. It revealed more about their God and his power. Their God was not weak, they said. He had the power to save a whole nation. He was, they said, more powerful than the pharaoh's army and all the gods of Egypt.

In thinking about the Exodus, the Hebrews also remembered God's Covenant with Abraham. They believed that when God freed the children of Israel, he was keeping his Covenant. He was showing the Israelites that they were his chosen people. He was taking them back to the land of Canaan, their promised land. And so the Exodus added to the Jewish understanding of their God as just and ever faithful to his chosen people.

In this sixteenth-century painting, the Hebrews watch as the pharaoh's army drowns in the Red Sea.

The Feast of Passover

Every year Jews celebrate Passover. They eat a ceremonial meal similar to one described in the Torah. It commemorates the angel of death "passing over" the houses of the Hebrews, sparing their children, and preparing them to leave bondage in Egypt.

In the early sixteenth century, the great Italian artist Michelangelo sculpted this statue of Moses. Some scholars think the bumps on the statue's head symbolize rays of light.

The People of the Law

The Torah tells us that the Israelites wandered through the desert from Egypt to Canaan for 40 years. They traveled like nomads, moving from waterhole to waterhole. During all that time they were in a wilderness, and their life was very hard. Many of them thought their God had forgotten them. Often, when they were without food or water, they turned against Moses, their leader. But, the Torah says, Moses told them that the God who had freed them from bondage would not let them perish in the wilderness, as long as they continued to believe in God and obey him.

From this part of their history the Hebrews came to believe that God sometimes sent trials and trouble to strengthen them. When Jews in later ages faced perils, this idea helped them survive many hardships. Wars, disease, and exile did not destroy their faith. They believed God led them out of Egypt and stayed with them through the desert. They believed that God would remember them—if they continued to obey him.

During this time, the Israelites developed another important idea. It was this: Not only did they serve just one god, the God of Abraham and Moses, but there *was* only one God. And that God cared not just about how people worshipped him, but how they treated each other. God wasn't interested only in burnt offerings or sacrifices. As the Hebrews understood it, God cared more about people as ethical beings—about how they behaved, what they thought, and how they treated others.

The ancient Hebrew idea of God's ethical expectations of humanity was a new idea in the history of religion.

An artist's depiction of the Ten Commandments, which the ancient Hebrews believed were laws from God.

The Hebrews believed that God delivered the Ten Commandments to Moses on top of Mount Sinai.

Later religions, such as Christianity and Islam, took up this idea as well. It encouraged people in all these religions to think about how they should treat others. Let's see how this idea developed.

The Ten Commandments

The Torah says that once, during the 40 years in the wilderness, Moses left his people for 40 days and climbed to the top of a mountain peak called Mount Sinai (SIY-niy) to talk with God. When he came down, he brought two stone tablets containing a list of ten laws that every Hebrew must obey. These laws have come to be known as the Ten Commandments. The Torah says that God himself gave these laws to the Israelites, and that the stone tablets were written with the finger of God.

The Ten Commandments told the Hebrews to worship only the one God. They were not to carve idols or statues of gods. They were not to misuse God's name. They were not to kill or steal. They were not to lie when under oath to tell the truth. They were to honor their parents. The Torah says that all of the Hebrews swore to obey the Ten Commandments. They believed that if they followed these laws, God would lead them out of the wilderness and give them the land of Canaan. Once again he would make them prosperous and happy.

Ethical Monotheism

Modern-day philosophers have a name for the ancient Hebrew idea that only one God exists and that God cares about how people treat each other. They call it "ethical monotheism." *Ethics* is the study of morals in human conduct. *Ethical monotheism* is an idea that came to influence other world religions.

Once again the Covenant of Abraham was renewed. The God of Abraham, Isaac, and Jacob promised to be the God of the Hebrews, and the Hebrews promised to be his people.

The Ten Commandments marked an important change in the relation between the Hebrew people and their God. Until then, the Hebrews believed that God spoke only to the leaders, who then told everyone else what God wanted. The Ten Commandments, however, showed that God had shared the Covenant with the entire Hebrew people. He had set down rules that every Hebrew man and woman must obey. Rich or poor, young or old—every Hebrew, even the leaders, had exactly the same duty to God. Each person mattered equally in the eyes of God.

The Unchanging Law and a New Understanding of God

The Torah says that Moses told the Hebrews about many other laws besides the Ten Commandments. These other laws were also God's laws, Moses said, and they would help the Hebrews know how to act in their day-to-day lives. There were laws about land and animals. There were laws about debts and payments. In fact, there were laws covering just about every kind of human activity, from punishing criminals to what people could eat and not eat. All these laws gave the Hebrews a clearer understanding of their God.

Some laws told the Hebrews how to behave toward God, but many of the laws told the people how God expected them to treat each other. In other words, the laws also concerned people's behavior, duties, and moral values.

This was quite a change from the polytheistic religions around them. The Sumerians and Egyptians believed that their gods were selfish and cared mainly about the offerings that people made to them, not about how people treated each other. The Hebrews came to believe their God was different. Their God, they said, was not like the gods of their neighbors and enemies, who cared mostly about tributes and animal sacrifices. God, said the Torah, wanted his people to "cease to do evil, learn to do good, search for justice, help the oppressed, be just to the orphan, plead for the widow."

The Ten Commandments

I am the Lord thy God, who brought thee out of the land of Egypt, out of the house of bondage. Thou shalt have no other gods before me.

Thou shalt not make unto thee any graven image.

Thou shalt not take the name of the Lord thy God in vain.

Remember the Sabbath day, to keep it holy.

Honor thy father and thy mother.

Thou shalt not kill.

Thou shalt not commit adultery.

Thou shalt not steal.

Thou shalt not bear false witness against thy neighbor.

Thou shalt not covet anything that is thy neighbor's.

(Based on Exodus 20:2–17)

This idea that God had ethical expectations of people was an important change. The Hebrews saw their God as one who cared about them, and expected them to care for each other. So he gave them special rules about caring for the poor and sick, and treating each other fairly and kindly. The laws revealed a God who wanted them to be charitable and show mercy toward one another.

To the Hebrews, all these rules about how to live were God's law. They believed no one could change God's law to suit his own whim, for they saw it as the law for all time. This, too, was a great change from the polytheistic religions around them. While the Egyptian gods, for example, were always changing their minds, the God of the Hebrews gave his laws once and for all. God's law—the Ten Commandments and other laws of how to live—became the most important guide in the lives of the Hebrews.

The Land of Milk and Honey

The Israelites believed that Canaan was the land God had promised them. They often called it the Promised Land. To them it was "a land of milk and honey" where life would be good. Still, Canaan turned out not to be an empty land just waiting for new settlers. Many people already lived there, and the Hebrews knew they would have to fight for it.

According to the Torah, Moses died before the Israelites entered Canaan, and a new leader named Joshua took charge. Joshua was very different from Moses. He had

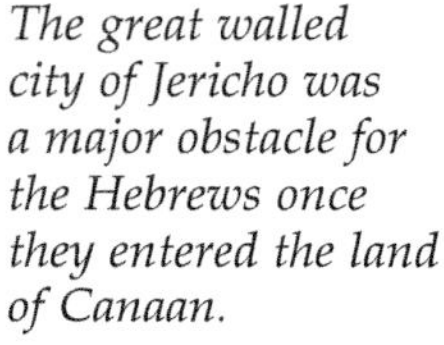

The great walled city of Jericho was a major obstacle for the Hebrews once they entered the land of Canaan.

a different job to do, for now the Hebrews needed a brave soldier and general to lead them.

Looking back on their history, they remembered Egypt and their escape from the pharaoh's army. They believed their God had been stronger than the soldiers of the pharaoh. Now they believed their God would help them conquer new enemies, that he would lead them into battle and help them defeat the people who did not believe in him.

Joshua led the Israelites in their conquest of Canaan. They marched to the walled city of Jericho, besieged the city, and prayed. The Torah says when Joshua blew his horn, the walls of Jericho collapsed, and the Israelites won the city. In the next two centuries the Israelites won all of Canaan.

The Israelites Choose a King

In the eleventh century B.C., the Hebrews faced a new and serious danger. A powerful, nomadic people called the Philistines (FIH-luh-steens) came from across the Mediterranean Sea and settled on the coast. Soon they were moving inland and threatening Canaan, the region the Hebrews considered their Promised Land.

The Israelites needed protection against the fierce Philistines, the Torah says, and some suggested that the tribes join under one king. A single king, they argued, could organize and govern all the Hebrew tribes, making them stronger against the Philistine threat. Other Hebrews countered that such a move would be wrong. They thought, "God himself rules us. We do not need a king."

Blowing horns and carrying aloft the symbols of their faith in God, the Hebrews march around Jericho's stone walls.

Finally, however, the Israelites decided to unite under one ruler. They were eager to choose one who would please God. They took their ideas of government from their religion. They saw a good government as one that obeyed God's laws. This was especially important if a king was at the head of the government. They believed their king must obey all of God's laws, for if he didn't, God would punish him and the whole nation, too. The most important thing to the Hebrews was to have a good and just king. They chose a young man named Saul.

At first Saul seemed to be a good choice. But then quarrels broke out.

What a Philistine!

The Philistines were a sea people who in time of turmoil fled the Aegean and settled on the coast of Canaan. They challenged the Israelites for possession of Canaan. The Philistines were not great artists or poets, but they knew how to smelt iron and make excellent weapons. Nowadays, if someone is called a "philistine," it's meant as an insult. It means that person has no appreciation of the arts or is uncultured.

The war with the Philistines went badly. The kingdom was falling apart. The Israelites believed that Saul must have angered God in some way.

The City of David

If the Israelites had continued to quarrel among themselves, the Philistines probably would have conquered them. But Saul was killed in battle around the year 1000 B.C., and a new leader stepped forward to replace him. The Israelites' second king was named David.

David was already a popular hero, well known for his bravery and devotion to God. Hebrew scriptures say that as a young man, he had killed a huge Philistine warrior called Goliath (guh-LIY-uhth). The fight was one whose fame lives to this day. As the Torah tells the story, young David, armed with only a sling, his courage, and his faith in God, hurled a stone at the towering Goliath and struck him dead. In later wars against the Philistines, David's soldiers also fought bravely.

Hebrew scriptures say that the young shepherd-boy David killed the Philistine giant Goliath with a slingshot.

Under David, the Israelites drove back the Philistines. The Hebrew army captured the city of Jerusalem, and David made it the capital of his kingdom. The Israelites called Jerusalem "the city of David."

- On the map on page 235, locate Jerusalem.

David ruled for about 40 years, and under his reign Israel became a wealthier and stronger kingdom that remained united against its enemies. A man who loved music, David wrote many psalms, or hymns, to God, and he tried to obey God's law. Though he sometimes failed, the Hebrews considered him a great king. They believed that God must be with him.

When David became an old man, he gave up the throne, and his son Solomon became king. Famous for his wisdom, Solomon constructed a great temple and palace in Jerusalem. Solomon ruled with skill and diplomacy, working to keep peace, dispense justice, and encourage trade with other peoples. He is said to have written many songs and proverbs that eventually found their way into the Torah.

The Israelites came to believe that the temple that Solomon built in Jerusalem was the only temple they could have. They had only one God, so they could have only one temple, and there they offered sacrifices of animals, fruit, or grain to honor God. The temple in Jerusalem became the center of Hebrew worship.

The Fall of Jerusalem

Solomon's reign was not without its troubles. The Hebrew tribes still sometimes quarreled with each other, and after Solomon's death around 930 B.C., the kingdom split in two. The tribes in the south formed the kingdom of Judah (JOO-duh). The north became the kingdom of Israel.

Arms outstretched toward heaven, the Hebrew king Solomon dedicates his temple to God.

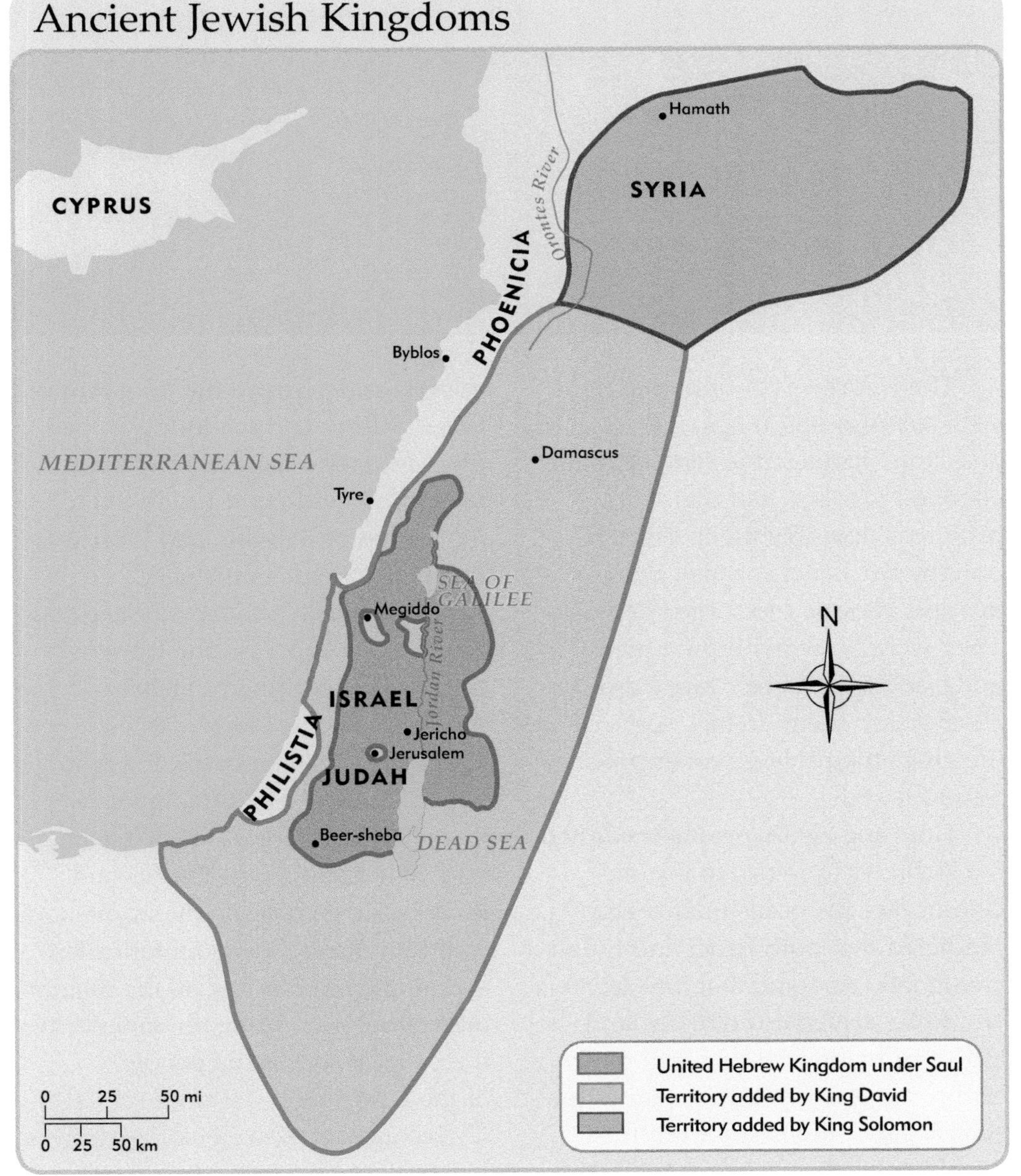

As imagined by an artist many centuries after the event, King Nebuchadnezzar's army attacks the Hebrew capital of Jerusalem.

The Hebrews continued to fight with surrounding tribes. Both Judah and Israel managed to fend off their enemies, yet they had many other problems to worry them. The old polytheistic beliefs of the Canaanites still appealed to some Hebrews. They went on worshipping many gods, and the Hebrew kings did not always stop them. In fact, some of the kings themselves worshipped different gods.

Time and again, prophets warned the Hebrews to return to the one God or face his punishment. They predicted that both Israel and Judah would fall apart, and that the Hebrews would be driven out of their land, killed, or made into slaves in return for breaking God's law. Around the year 720 B.C., the first part of their prophecy seemed to come true. The Assyrians destroyed the kingdom of Israel, killing and scattering its people. More than one hundred years later, the kingdom of Judah fell to the armies of Babylon and their warrior king, Nebuchadnezzar.

You may recall Nebuchadnezzar as the king who built the Hanging Gardens. According to Hebrew scripture, Nebuchadnezzar also attacked Jerusalem twice. He first seized it in 597 B.C., forcing more than 10,000 of Jerusalem's citizens into exile in Babylon. The Second Book of Kings records the event: "And he carried away all Jerusalem and all the princes, and all the mighty men of valor.... None remained, save the poorest sort of the people of the land."

Nebuchadnezzar took his captives to Babylon, hoping to discourage future defiance in Israel. But it didn't work. Only a decade later the remaining Hebrews in Jerusalem rebelled. Nebuchadnezzar was furious. He sent his army against the city again. He meant to take care of this trouble spot once and for all.

After a long siege, Jerusalem fell. The Babylonians plundered the city. What they couldn't carry off, they put to the torch. Nebuchadnezzar's soldiers destroyed the city's great temple, built by King Solomon himself. They led the rest of the Israelites to Babylon as slaves.

- On the map on page 214 in Chapter 6, locate Babylon.

The Babylonian Captivity

The time the Hebrews spent in Babylon is known as the Babylonian Captivity, and it was a dark period for them. They would remain in captivity, homesick and sorrowful, for the next 70 years. One of the psalms in the Torah laments this time of exile from Jerusalem (called "Zion" in the psalm):

> *By the rivers of Babylon, there we*
> *sat down, yea, we wept,*
> *when we remembered Zion...*
>
> *How shall we sing the Lord's song*
> *in a strange land?*

Yet the exiled Hebrews did not lose heart completely. Once again they looked back to their past. The whole nation was being punished, they thought, because so many of them had been unfaithful to God. If they returned to their faith, perhaps God would forgive them. He had brought them out of slavery in Egypt. Surely he would bring them out of slavery in Babylon.

The words of the prophets gave the Hebrews much to think about in exile, and even some hope. Two of the greatest prophets were Jeremiah (jehr-uh-MIY-uh) and Ezekiel (ih-ZEEK-yuhl). Their teachings helped hold the Hebrews together. Ezekiel reminded them of their responsibility to the law, and said that he had heard the word of God: "If the wicked will turn from all the sins he has committed, and keep all my statutes, and do that which is lawful and right, he shall surely live, he shall not die." And Jeremiah told the Hebrews that God had not deserted them: "For I will restore health to you, and your wounds I will heal, says the Lord."

These prophets taught that God was pleased when men and women were faithful and just. They could still be faithful and just even though they were no longer in the Promised Land, even though their temple in Jerusalem had been destroyed. They could still worship God because he

For decades the Hebrews endured captivity in Babylon.

Always carried with great reverence, the Torah is the sacred record of the Hebrew people.

wasn't tied to one place—to one temple. He was, the prophets said, wherever his people were. The prophets preached that God was with the Hebrews, even in Babylon.

These teachings had a profound effect on the Hebrews' ideas. They no longer believed that God had to be worshipped in the temple in Jerusalem. Because they believed he was everywhere, he could be worshipped in any place.

The First Synagogues

In exile the Hebrews began a new form of worship. Wherever a group of them gathered, they would worship God together. These groups formed the first synagogues (SIH-nuh-gahgs). A synagogue was not a temple, but rather simply a place where people gathered to worship God.

The Israelites did not offer sacrifices in the synagogues. That ritual was still reserved for a temple. But they chanted the old hymns they had learned, and they talked about their past. In a way, the synagogues served as schools. There the Hebrew children learned about their history and God, so that they would not forget God's law or what their ancestors had done. The synagogues helped them keep their religion.

Without a temple the Hebrews could not offer sacrifice, and so they turned more and more to prayer. They came to believe that each man could talk directly to God, and God would hear his people. This belief gave the Israelites comfort. They felt that God wasn't fooled by rich offerings, for he could see into a person's heart and tell if that person were good or not.

The Hebrews gathered all the writings from their early history. Scholars and scribes arranged and copied them, and then they were read aloud to the people to make sure all the Israelites knew their history. Never again would they forget the teachings of their ancestors. All Hebrews would know the laws.

The Return from Babylon

Although the Hebrews didn't worship the Babylonian gods while they were in exile, they did learn many things from the Babylonians, who had built a prosperous civilization. For example, they grew to love and respect written books.

Around the year 539 B.C., the Persians invaded Mesopotamia and captured Babylon. Cyrus (SIY-rus), Emperor of Persia, freed the Hebrews. Some of them returned to Judah and took their new ideas with them. They began to rebuild Jerusalem and its temple, as well as Hebrew society. They wanted to keep the new ideas alive, yet they also wanted to keep their old beliefs strong.

One idea the exiles brought back with them was the idea of synagogues. Their synagogues became houses of learning as well as places of worship. In the synagogues laws could be read, and all Hebrews could study them.

The new laws and ideas worked well. The Hebrews were no longer attracted to polytheism. They were determined that never again would they turn away from their God. To the Israelites it seemed as though God had again renewed his Covenant. First, he had renewed it during the 40 long years they had wandered in the wilderness after the Exodus from Egypt. Now he had renewed it again, after 70 years of exile in Babylon. He had, they believed, brought them back home.

Ideas That Have Lived On

The ancient Hebrews developed ideas about God that became important for other faiths. These ideas were: There is one God who made all things and rules all things. He is invisible, but present everywhere. God reveals his will through events in people's lives and in human history. God expects people to obey his laws. Most of all he expects them to obey the Ten Commandments. God values good behavior more than offerings or ceremonies, and therefore people must behave well. They must respect and aid others. Each man and woman is important to God, and each has dignity. Each can worship God for himself.

These basic beliefs of the ancient Hebrews were new in the ancient world, but they've had a long life. They are still the basic beliefs of millions of people in the world today. They are the beliefs of the Jews, who follow the religion of the ancient Israelites. They are a vital part of the later faiths of Christianity and Islam. Twenty-five hundred years after the Babylonian Captivity, these beliefs have not only survived, they have had an enormous influence on the course of the human odyssey.

Modern-day Jews continue to pray at the Western Wall of Solomon's temple.

The ruins of a temple dedicated to the sea god Poseidon stand on a rugged hill by the waters of the Aegean Sea.

The Greeks and Their View of Nature

In the next two chapters, we'll get to know another great civilization—ancient Greece. Greek ideas about human abilities and the workings of nature mark a big turning point in the human odyssey. In fact, the ideas that came out of Greek civilization are the basis for some of our most important ideas today.

In the United States and other nations, we have learned much from the ancient Greeks. Our form of government, many of the words we use, some of the literature we read, the images and themes in our art, our ideas about freedom and the value of the individual, the way we think about the world around us—all of these have been deeply influenced by the ancient Greeks. If it had not been for the Greeks, we would not be who we are today. In a way, as the English poet Percy Bysshe Shelley once said, "We are all Greeks."

Who Were the Greeks?

Jutting into the Mediterranean Sea is the rugged peninsula that in ancient times made up mainland Greece. A thin strip of land connects the northern section of the peninsula with the southern section. The southern section is known as the Peloponnese (PEH-luh-puh-nees), and is sometimes called the Peloponnesian (peh-luh-puh-NEE-zhuhn) peninsula. About one third of the size of Italy, this mountainous land is flanked by the Aegean (ih-JEE-uhn) Sea to the east and the Ionian (iy-OH-nee-uhn) Sea to the west. Hundreds of islands dot these seas.

This chapter explores ancient Greece, a land in the eastern Mediterranean.

Southeast of the Peloponnesian peninsula lies a large island called Crete.

- Look at the map below. Locate the Peloponnesian peninsula, Crete, the Mediterranean Sea, the Aegean Sea, and the Ionian Sea.

As early as 3000 B.C., civilization was flourishing on the island of Crete. Historians call it the Minoan (mih-NOH-uhn) civilization after the legendary King Minos (MIY-nus). You may have read stories about Minos. According to ancient myths, he built a labyrinth (LA-buh-rinth)—a complicated maze—on Crete to house a monster called the Minotaur (MIH-nuh-tor), which had the body of a man and the head of a bull. The Minoans constructed beautiful palaces with grand courtyards. They made pottery and jewelry, sailed the Mediterranean, and developed a system of writing.

Adorned with the tentacles of a great octopus, this 3,500-year-old vase testifies to the grandeur of Minoan civilization.

People had settled on the stony islands and craggy shores of the Peloponnesian peninsula as well, but civilization was slower to develop there. Why? Because farming this rocky land was difficult. There were no predictable flooding rivers, no broad fertile plains. It took a while for early inhabitants to cultivate more food than they needed.

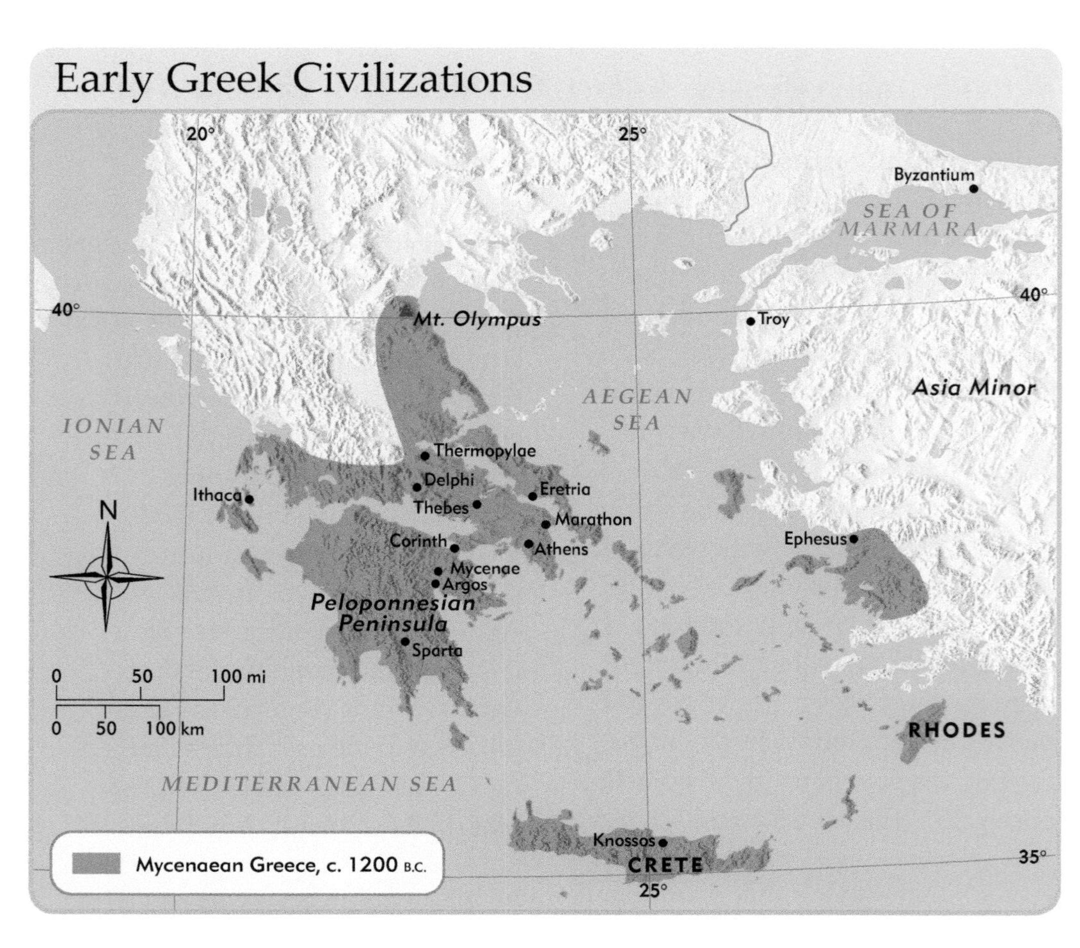

(Can you explain how a surplus of food is related to the development of civilization?)

Even though there was no flooding river on the Peloponnesian peninsula, there were springs that fed small valleys. The people began to farm in these spring-fed regions. Fertile coastal areas also caught the eye of determined settlers, and Greek farmers began sowing wheat and barley on their meager plots. In time, those scant resources were made to yield a surplus.

The first civilization to develop on the mainland of Greece is called Mycenaean (miy-suh-NEE-uhn). By 1600 B.C., the Mycenaeans built fortified towns around central palaces. They had kings and priests. They dominated the region, and probably traded with the Egyptians and the Hittites. They buried their rulers in long shaft-graves, along with treasures of bronze, silver, and gold. They had writing, too.

Historians think that around 1200 B.C. the Mycenaeans won a war against the city of Troy in Asia Minor. The conflict is known as the Trojan War, after the inhabitants of the city of Troy, who were called Trojans. Eventually people began to tell wonderful legends about that war. You may have read some tales about the Trojan War from a long poem called the *Iliad* (IL-ee-uhd), by the Greek poet Homer.

Because of war, invasion, and internal strife, Mycenaean civilization passed away. Their system of writing was lost. Some Mycenaeans fled to Asia Minor. Others returned to life in isolated villages. It was a dark age, and memories of past glory lived on only in the poems people recited and songs they sang.

By 750 B.C., however, small city-states were flourishing with names such as Athens, Sparta, Corinth, and Ithaca. Some of these city-states were on the mainland, while others were on islands in the Mediterranean Sea. Each was separate and ruled itself. Each was surrounded by fields for crops and herds. The people who lived in these city-states did not think of themselves as one nation. They were citizens of Athens or Sparta or Corinth.

Over time, however, the people in these separate city-states did come to think of themselves as one people. They called themselves the Hellenes (HEL-eenz). We call them the Greeks. They were one people because they shared the same language and beliefs, worshipped the same gods, and had the same stories and heroes. They had the same culture—a culture that was unique in some remarkable ways.

- Locate the city-states of Athens and Sparta on the map on page 242. Athens and Sparta are in rocky, mountainous areas.

These stone fortifications date from the thirteenth century B.C., when Mycenaean civilization flourished in mainland Greece.

Several cities and towns in the United States are named after ancient Greek city-states, including Athens, Georgia; Corinth, Mississippi; Sparta, Wisconsin; Syracuse, New York; and Ithaca, New York. Are there any towns with Greek names in your state?

Right: Much of the Greek landscape is rugged and difficult to cross. For this reason, its people have often taken to the seas for travel.

Below: Flanked by dolphins, a Greek sailor plies the sea.

The Sea and the Climate

As you can tell from looking at the map, the land of the Greeks was different from other lands we've studied. It had few large rivers. In fact, many rivers in Greece dry up in summer for want of rain.

What ancient Greece lacked in rivers, it made up for in sea. The sea was Greece's great waterway, linking the mainland and hundreds of islands. Long arms of the sea stretched into the coasts, around many peninsulas. The Aegean, Ionian, and Mediterranean Seas became all-important highways for trade and travel. Fishermen, merchants, sailors—even pirates—went to sea for a living. Small ships carried goods and ideas back and forth.

For half the year, sailing could be hard in this region of the Mediterranean. From November to April, high winds and heavy rains often kept Greek ships at home. But for the other half of the year, the climate was warm and dry. There were few storms or high waves to trouble the sailors, and they could get on with the business of fishing, trading, and colonizing—that is, setting up new homes far away.

The Greeks were fascinated by the blue sea surrounding their home. On a sunny day, the water sparkles like sapphire. On cloudy days, or at sunset, it appears dark purple. Perhaps that's why the Greeks often called it the "wine-dark sea."

One of the Greeks' earliest and greatest poems, Homer's *Odyssey* (AH-duh-see), tells of the hero Odysseus (oh-DIH-see-us) and his long homeward journey over the sea after the Trojan War. The adventures of Odysseus in storms and shipwrecks were favorite Greek stories. It

The Origins of the *Iliad* and the *Odyssey*

The poet of the *Iliad* and the *Odyssey* is generally identified as Homer. According to tradition, long ago in Greece, a blind poet, Homer, wandered from city to city and earned his living by reciting poems, including the *Iliad* and the *Odyssey*. Many scholars agree that a real poet named Homer did indeed live in the eighth century B.C., and that he composed these great poems, basing them on old legends. Others say that the *Iliad* and the *Odyssey* belong to the time long before written history, when the stories of heroes' deeds were sung and recited, and so passed down by word of mouth from one generation to another. In this way, they believe, these great poems grew, being added to and gradually shaped through many years.

took Odysseus ten years to get home. He might have reached home more quickly by land, but no Greek would walk when he could sail.

Let's read two descriptions of the sea from the *Odyssey*. In this first selection, Homer describes the sea as a friend. He begins with a poetic comparison to describe how the sea urges a ship along on its voyage, and then he goes on to describe a calm harbor.

The Sea as Friend (*from Book XIII of the* Odyssey)

And even as on a plain a yoke of four stallions comes springing all together beneath the lash, leaping high and speedily accomplishing the way, so leaped the stern of that ship. The dark waves of the sounding sea rushed mightily in the wake, and she ran ever surely on her way. Not even a circling hawk, the swiftest of winged things, could keep pace with her. Even thus she lightly sped and cleft the waves of the sea....

So when the star came up, the brightest of all, heralding the light of early Dawn, even then did the seafaring ship draw nigh the island. There, in the land of Ithaca, is a certain harbor, with two headlands of sheer cliff that slope to the sea and break the mighty wave that ill winds roll without; but within, the ships ride unmoored when once they have reached the place of anchorage. At the harbor's head is a long-leaved olive tree, and close by is a cave, pleasant and shadowy, where the honeybees hive.... And there are great looms of stone, on which the nymphs weave cloth dyed the deep purple of the sea.

Trading ships enter a bustling island port.

Both the *Iliad* and the *Odyssey* have been translated from Greek into many languages, including many different English translations. The selections here are adapted from a late nineteenth-century translation by Samuel Henry Butcher and Andrew Lang.

The Sea as Enemy (*from Book V of the* Odyssey)

In the following selection, Homer describes how the sea can be an enemy. Here, the god of the sea, Poseidon (puh-SIY-dn), takes out his anger against Odysseus.

Poseidon, god of the sea, shaker of the earth, gathered the clouds and troubled the waters of the deep. Grasping his trident in his hands, he roused all storms and shrouded in clouds the land and sea—and down sped night from heaven. The East Wind and the South Wind clashed, and the stormy West and the North, born in the bright air, rolling onward a great wave.

The wave crashed down upon Odysseus, driving him on with terrible might. The raft reeled, and far from it he fell, and lost the helm from his hand; and the fierce blast of the jostling winds broke his mast in the midst, and sail and yardarm fell far into the deep. Long the water kept him under, nor could he rise from beneath the rush of the mighty wave. But at last he came up, and spat forth from his mouth the bitter salt water, which ran down in streams from his head.

As the *Odyssey* shows, the sea could be a friend to the Greeks, a smooth highway and a link to others. The sea could also be an enemy and a source of chaos. It could endanger its passengers and forever sever a man from his fellow men. But it was not the sea alone that challenged most ancient Greeks.

One of the few bountiful products of the thin Greek soil—olives.

Living on the Land

The land itself defied the Greeks. Most of it was stony and hilly. Its rugged mountains and steep slopes made it hard to eke out a living. Even today there are few plains where wheat and barley can grow or cattle can graze. In winter, harsh rains wash the soil from the hillsides, which makes those slopes poor places for growing crops.

But the ancient Greeks were determined. They discovered that two plants would flourish there—grapevines and olive trees. These didn't seem to mind the higher slopes and thin, stony soil. In fact, their roots helped hold the soil in place. On lower lands, meanwhile, Greek farmers grew what grain they could.

The ancient Greeks raised goats because the sure-footed animals could graze the rocky hillsides.

The Greeks came to depend on these three crops—grain, grapes, and olives. In September and October they harvested the grapes, and then pressed them to make wine. After this harvesting, it was time to plant grain. The growing season for grain lasted until May or June. But the damp winter was not a time of rest. They picked olives from December through February and pressed them for oil.

The hillsides made good grazing land for sturdy sheep and goats. These animals, in turn, provided wool for clothing as well as milk and cheese, though not much meat. The Greeks also raised pigs for food, and hunted duck, wild boar, deer, and hare. For other foods they turned to the sea. Many men who lived along the coasts and on the islands fished for a living.

Greece has a Mediterranean climate, with mild, wet winters and hot, dry summers. That climate allowed the Greeks to venture onto the sea in the warm, pleasant months. And it blessed Greece with summer skies of a deep, vibrant blue.

In the dry season, to a shepherd tending his flocks on the hillside, or to a sailor skimming from island to island across the wine-dark seas, the clear blue sky must have seemed like an open view to the heavens. Perhaps these clear skies, with their infinite vista of blue, lifted the thoughts of the ancient Greeks and inspired them to be a curious, creative people. It's a fanciful notion—but great ideas they surely had, as we're about to see.

Who Were the Gods? Who Was Man?

The Greeks loved to tell stories. The *Iliad* and the *Odyssey* were some of the first tales. These great poems, told by the poet Homer, show the Greeks in the heat of battle, and then finding their way home. In these stories, human beings are often tested by willful gods and pitted against each other. They can rely only on their resourcefulness and sometimes on the aid of a friendly god.

Greek myths about their mighty gods and valiant heroes still fill us with wonder today. Let's read one of those myths. It holds some important clues about the ideas of the Greeks.

Prometheus and the Gift of Fire

Long ago, there was a giant named Prometheus (pruh-MEE-thee-us). Prometheus did not care to live among the clouds high on Mount Olympus with the gods and goddesses who spent their time drinking nectar and eating ambrosia. So he went among men to live with them and help them, for his heart was filled with sadness when he found that they were not happy. They were the most miserable of all living creatures, hunted by wild beasts and by one another. They were poor and wretched, living in caves and holes in the earth, dying of starvation and shivering with cold, because there was no fire.

"If only they had fire," said Prometheus to himself, "they could at least warm themselves and cook their food. And after a while, they could learn to make tools and build themselves houses. Without fire, they are worse off than the beasts."

Then he went boldly to Zeus (zoos), the king of the gods, and begged him to give fire to men, so that they might have at least a little comfort in the cold and darkness.

But Zeus replied, "I will not give them even a spark. No, indeed! Why, if men had fire they might become strong and wise like ourselves, and after a while they would drive us out of our kingdom. Let them shiver with cold and live like the beasts. It is best for them to be poor and ignorant, so that we Mighty Ones may thrive and be happy."

Prometheus made no answer. He had set his heart on helping mankind, and he would not give up. He turned away, and left Zeus and his mighty company forever.

As he was walking by the shore of the sea he found a reed growing. When he had broken it off, he saw that its hollow center was filled with a dry, soft substance that would burn slowly and keep burning a long time. He took the long stalk in his hands and started with it toward the dwelling of the sun far to the east.

"Mankind shall have fire in spite of the tyrant who sits on the mountaintop," he said.

He reached the place of the sun in the early morning just as the glowing, golden orb was rising from the earth and beginning his daily journey through the sky. He touched the end of the long reed to the flames, and it caught on fire, burning slowly. Then he turned and hastened back to his own land, carrying with him the precious spark hidden in the plant.

He called some of the shivering men from their caves and built a fire for them, and showed them how to warm themselves by it and how to build other fires from the coals. Soon there was a cheerful blaze in every home, and men and women were warm and happy, and thankful to Prometheus for the wonderful gift he had brought to them.

It was not long until they learned to cook their food and so to eat like men instead of like beasts. They began at once to leave off their wild and savage habits, and instead of lurking in the dark places of the world they came out into the open air and the bright sunlight.

In time, Prometheus taught them a thousand more ways to improve their lives. He showed them how to build houses of wood and stone, and how to tame the sheep and cattle and make them useful, and how to plant and sow and reap, and how to protect themselves from the storms of winter and the beasts of the woods. Then he showed them how to dig in the earth for copper and iron, and how to melt the ore, and how to hammer it into shape and fashion from it the tools and weapons they needed in peace and war.

Things might have gone on very happily indeed, had it not been for Zeus. One day, when he chanced to look down upon the earth, he saw the fires burning, and the people living in houses, and the flocks feeding on the hills, and the grain ripening in the fields. This made him very angry.

"Who has done all this?" he thundered.

And someone answered, "Prometheus!"

"That insolent giant!" he cried. "I will punish him!"

He commanded two of his servants, whose names were Strength and Force, to seize Prometheus and carry him to the topmost peak of the Caucasus (KAW-kuh-sus) Mountains. Then he sent Hephaestus (hih-FES-tus), the blacksmith of the gods, to bind Prometheus with iron chains and fetter him to the rocks so that he could not move hand or foot.

Hephaestus did not like to do this, for he was a friend of Prometheus. Yet he did not dare to disobey. So the great friend of men, who had given them fire and lifted them out of their wretchedness and showed them how to live, was chained to a mountain peak. There he hung, with the storm winds whistling always around him and the pitiless hail beating in his face, and fierce eagles shrieking in his ears and tearing his body with their cruel claws. Yet he bore all his sufferings without a groan, and never would he beg for mercy or say that he was sorry for what he had done.

Another Greek myth tells us that, in time, a great hero defied Zeus and set Prometheus free. You might have heard of this hero—he was called Hercules.

Armed with Reason

The myth of Prometheus was a favorite among the Greeks. Prometheus, the giant who brought the gift of fire—and with it warmth and light and progress—was a great hero. But human beings, in the resourceful ways they used fire, were victors as well.

Surely, the Greeks thought, men were not as great as gods. Humans had to honor the gods with temples and statues and special offerings. If human beings presumed that they were as great as gods, then, said the Greeks, they were guilty of *hubris*, or unacceptable pride. But the myth of Prometheus showed that human beings did have a very special gift—a gift symbolized by fire.

Just what does fire stand for in the myth of Prometheus? What was this special gift that separated man from all other creatures? The Greeks believed that *man's special gift was his mind.*

The Greeks saw human beings as thinkers and problem solvers. Their minds, like fire, lit the way. With thought and reason, they could take the gift of fire and set it to work for them. They could look at the world around them and figure out how it worked and how to make good use of its treasures.

This was perhaps the most important Greek idea—that when people use their minds and reason, they can understand much about the world around them. Unlike many other ancient peoples, the Greeks rejected the notion that humans are nothing but slaves to the gods. The Greeks came to believe that there were three important things they could understand with their minds: the workings of nature, human nature itself, and the best ways for human beings to live together in communities.

Wondering About Their World

Armed with such confidence, the early Greeks began to look around them. They were full of questions about their world and they were proud to ask them. Perhaps that's why they called man "the only animal who asks questions." What is lightning?

Greek Gods and Goddesses

The early Greeks believed their gods dwelt in splendor on the craggy peaks of Mount Olympus in northern Greece. There they feasted on ambrosia and nectar, quarreled, laughed, and got involved in the affairs of men. The Greeks believed that the gods and goddesses sometimes came down from Mount Olympus to walk among people on earth, helping those they favored, and punishing the wicked. Their help might come in the form of a gift, such as strong armor and a sturdy shield, or a solution to a problem. Punishment might mean turning a person into an animal to teach him a lesson, or causing a storm at sea to drive a hero's ship off its course. In the Greek myths, a god or goddess could be a powerful ally or a terrible foe.

- Zeus (zoos) was king of the Olympian gods and the god of justice. He marshaled the thunderheads and hurled his bolts to earth below.
- Hera (HAIR-uh) was goddess of marriage. She was Zeus's beautiful, scheming, and willful wife.
- Poseidon (puh-SIY-dn), god of the seas, was the broad-chested brother of Zeus. He stirred the seas with his trident and made the earth tremble.
- Athena (uh-THEE-nuh) was the gray-eyed goddess of wisdom. The beloved daughter of Zeus, she had sprung full grown from the head of her father.
- Artemis (AHR-tuh-mus), goddess of wildlife, the moon, and the hunt, was also the daughter of Zeus.
- Apollo (uh-PAH-loh), god of light and of music, law, and reason, was the shining twin of Artemis.
- Ares (AIR-eez) was the violent god of war.
- Hephaestus (hih-FES-tus), the crippled blacksmith, was the god of fire and metalwork. The son of Hera and Zeus, he was lamed when he was thrown to earth in one of their quarrels.
- Aphrodite (a-fruh-DIY-tee) was the goddess of beauty and love. She was born from the foam of the sea and became the wife of Hephaestus.
- Demeter (dih-MEE-tur), the goddess of grain and fertility, helped crops grow plentiful and fruitful.
- Hestia (HES-tee-uh) was the goddess of home and hearth.
- Dionysus (diy-uh-NIY-sus) was the son of Zeus and the god of wine. It was said he introduced the grapevine to Greece.
- Hades (HAY-deez) was the god of the underworld.

Zeus

Hera

Athena

they wondered. What causes earthquakes? What is the sun, and why does it move across the sky?

Their first answers were simple ones. They looked at the forces of nature and explained them with myths of nature gods. Lightning, they said, was the spear of the god Zeus flashing through the air. Earthquakes were caused when the sea-god Poseidon stamped his foot. The rising and setting sun was the god Helios traveling his daily course across the sky in his glowing chariot. These gods, said the Greeks, caused the storms and floods and earthquakes that man could not understand.

Above: The Greeks thought that the sun rose and set as the god Helios drove across the sky in his great chariot.

Below: A Greek astronomer of the second century B.C. *makes detailed observations of the heavens.*

As we've learned, other early peoples had asked these same questions and found similar answers. For example, the Egyptians worshipped Re as their sun-god. Likewise, the Sumerians had their god Shamash, who returned every day to chase away the darkness and spread warmth and light.

Some of these ancient peoples went on to add much practical, useful knowledge to their beliefs. The Egyptians practiced medicine. The Sumerians worked out a system of mathematics. The Babylonians learned something about astronomy. The Greeks learned from these peoples. But they went one step further.

The Greeks never grew tired of asking why and how things happened. The more they asked, the less they liked the old answers. Could humans learn more about lightning than the myth about Zeus told them? Could they come up with a better explanation for earthquakes than a sea-god stamping his foot? Yes!

The Greeks were certain that by using their minds and carefully observing the universe, they could figure out the "why" and "how." They began to wonder: What if there are explanations for the workings of nature that have nothing to do with gods? What if nature is not so unpredictable after all? What if things happen in the natural world according to certain rules or laws?

Figuring Out the Laws of Nature

People have always been aware of some order in nature. Even early humans saw that the seasons always come in the same order. They saw that the sun always rises in the east and sets in the west. How did they explain what they saw? They said the gods had made things that way.

But the Greeks began to look at the sun in a different way. Perhaps the gods *had* made the sun. Still, what was it made of? Was it burning air? Was it a flame? Where does the sun go when it sets? How big is it? How far away is it?

When the Greeks asked such questions, they didn't stop believing in their gods. Yet they did not expect their gods to answer the questions. The Greeks were confident that human beings themselves could figure out the answers. After all, the gods had given minds to mortals. It was up to human beings to use their minds and figure out what was what.

The Greeks observed the orderly world and wondered if perhaps there were laws in nature. They looked for unchanging laws—ones that were always the same and always at work. Such "natural laws," they believed, could help them explain the patterns they witnessed in the universe, and even the changes in those patterns. This was a whole new approach to learning. It assumed the world was not chaotic and uncontrollable, but orderly in a way that humans could understand.

Exploring nature became a passion for the Greeks. Their word for nature was *physis* (FIY-sis). Our word *physics* comes from it. In fact, many of our ideas of scientific study are Greek. Rather than using myths to explain the world, we look for explanations in the workings of nature itself. We still ask the same questions the Greeks asked: What are the laws of nature? How do they work?

The Greeks began to explore nature by observing it very closely so that they could describe it. Then they used their reason to explain it. They felt that their explanations had to be logical—they had to make sense. The Greeks believed that by using the mind's power to reason, they could discover the laws of nature.

Modern-day scientists still follow the Greek example, but they go one step further. They try to test and apply what they know. Modern scientists try to use their findings to change nature and control it. The Greeks didn't consider it so important to experiment or apply their thoughts to everyday problems. Usually they were satisfied if they discovered laws of nature that seemed to make sense.

Today we use the word *science* to mean the organized study of the universe and laws of nature. The Greeks used a different word. They called it philosophy. The word *philosophy* comes from putting together two Greek words—*philo,* meaning "love," and *sophia,* meaning "wisdom." So philosophy literally means the "love of wisdom."

Today the word *philosophy* also means thinking about the meaning of life and man's place in it. People who study philosophy are called philosophers. To the Greeks, studying the laws of nature, thinking about man's place in the world, and loving wisdom were all one and the same. The Greeks were among history's earliest scientists *and* philosophers.

That is one reason our culture today owes so much to the ancient Greeks. The idea that the world is orderly and that humans can understand much about their universe is one of the Greeks' great gifts to us. Our firm belief in the power of the human mind to solve problems and unlock mysteries around us—to use reason to grasp the laws of nature—first took hold millennia ago under those boundless Greek skies.

A young student displays the Greek "love of wisdom."

In a later chapter, you will meet three ancient Greek philosophers regarded as some of the greatest thinkers of all times—Socrates, Plato, and Aristotle.

Part 2, Chapter 9

An Athenian athlete prepares to hurl his discus into the air. The ancient Greeks considered the human body a thing of beauty and their athletes as noble as their philosophers.

The Greek Celebration of Man

"There are many wonders in the world, but none is more wonderful than man." That's how one ancient Greek writer summed up the Greek fascination with human beings, their abilities, and their works. The Greeks were intrigued by nature, but they were even more fascinated by human beings. We see this celebration of human potential in their stories, games, art, histories, and politics.

Homer's *Iliad* and *Odyssey*: Epics for All Time

In the last chapter, you read two passages from the *Odyssey* by Homer. While we have no definite knowledge of Homer, many scholars think that he lived around 750 B.C. In the *Odyssey*, there is a passage that describes a blind poet reciting verses that bring tears to the eyes of the hero, Odysseus. This has given rise to the traditional belief that Homer was himself blind. Certainly he had an ear for language and a gift for verse.

Imagine the scene. In the evening firelight, the chill night air silent with anticipation, the blind poet rises, and in a voice deep and rhythmic holds a crowd spellbound with his poetic tales of fierce battles, impassioned heroes, and willful gods.

The stories themselves had been recounted for centuries. But they are more than simple stories, they are epics—long poems that set forth in a grand manner the deeds of great heroes. They told of a war that took place centuries before between the Greeks and the Trojans—the people of Troy in Asia Minor. Historians do not know for sure if the Trojan Wars were real or mythical, but Homer told the stories better than all who came before or any who have come since.

Bow at the ready, a graceful archer adorns this plate from sixth-century B.C. Athens.

Homer's *Iliad* and *Odyssey* are the two most famous epic poems in western literature. The *Iliad* tells the story of the last year of the Trojan War. The title, *Iliad,* comes from the word *Ilium,* which is the Greek name for "Troy."

According to legend, the Trojan Wars began when Helen, the beautiful wife of King Menelaus (meh-nl-AY-us) of Sparta, was kidnapped by Paris, son of the king of Troy. Legend had it that Troy became the site of a ten-year war as the Greeks banded together to win back Helen for Menelaus and avenge the honor of Sparta's king. In the tenth year of the war—so the story goes—the Greeks, led by Odysseus, succeeded by hiding many soldiers in a large wooden horse they offered as a gift to Priam, the Trojan king. Once the Trojans dragged the horse within the walls of their city, the Greek warriors emerged and sacked Troy.

Greek warriors emerge from their hiding place inside the great wooden horse to sack the city of Troy.

In the *Iliad,* Homer celebrates the determined Greeks who must wage war to win Helen back, and the embattled Trojans who fight nobly to fend off the invaders. At the center of the epic stand two great warriors—the wrathful Achilles (uh-KIH-leez), bravest and strongest of the Greeks, and Hector, the bravest of Troy's defenders, who fell at last by the hand of his heroic foe.

The *Odyssey* tells the story of the Greek hero, Odysseus. After the fighting at Troy ends, Odysseus sets sail for home. In his journey, he faces dangers, monsters, and wrathful gods, but his quick wit and ingenuity ultimately bring him back to his faithful wife and son. You can read a tale from the *Odyssey* at the end of this chapter.

The *Odyssey* is a celebration of human ability in the face of grave dangers. As early as 750 B.C., the poet Homer seems to have been assuring Greeks that human efforts mattered. Not all was up to fate. To live life nobly was the greatest calling.

Were the Trojan Wars Real?

Many historians believe the Trojan Wars were real and took place during the Mycenaean civilization around the year 1200 B.C. In 1870, a German archaeologist named Heinrich Schliemann (HIYN-rik SHLEE-mahn) began to excavate for the ancient city of Troy in northwestern Turkey. He and his team uncovered ruins of what would prove to be nine cities, one on top of the next. Modern archaeologists speculate that one of those cities is ancient Troy.

Let the Games Begin

We've learned that the ancient Greeks admired the human mind and powers of reason. They also considered the human body an object of beauty. A healthy male body was thought praiseworthy and glorious. So Greek men and boys exercised often to keep strong and fit. Athletics, as much as eating and sleeping, became part of everyday life. Running, jumping, wrestling, and boxing were all part of a young boy's education. The Greeks admired their athletes as much as their statesmen or philosophers.

In ancient Greece, athletic games became a way of honoring the gods. At the foot of Mount Olympus, believed to be the home of the gods, the Greeks began hosting athletic games to honor mighty Zeus, king of the gods. The earliest records of contests go back to 776 B.C., but the games probably originated hundreds of years before that. They were held every four years for more than a thousand years.

The contests became so important to the Greeks that they even stopped wars between city-states to hold the competition. The Greeks even measured time in terms of Olympiads, or four-year periods between the games.

What were the games like? The finest male athletes from each city-state arrived on the western part of the peninsula to test their strength, speed, and courage. Up to forty thousand eager spectators crowded the stands. Dedicated to Zeus, the manliest of gods, the contests celebrated male physical excellence. No women competed on the field or sat in the stands. Still, the games were awaited and celebrated by all.

The side of this ancient vase is decorated with runners in a footrace, the oldest and most popular of all Olympic sports.

The first Olympics were simply running events, but in time the contests grew. Athletes competed in running, wrestling, and the long-jump. They tossed the javelin (a long spear), and threw the discus (a stone or metal disc). They faced off in boxing and chariot races.

Evidence of Ancient Olympics

The ancient Greeks left an abundance of evidence about what happened during their Olympic games. These records survive in many different forms. The Greeks depicted athletes and sporting events on their pottery, on their coins, and in their statues. They wrote poems about the competitors and compiled lists of victors' names. They inscribed the most glorious achievements on gravestones, stone slabs, and bronze plaques.

Archaeologists have spent much time examining ruins at Olympia, the site of the ancient games. Thanks to their work, we can see the very arena in which Milo of Kroton, Leonidas of Rhodes, and Greece's other great athletes won fame that has endured for centuries.

Huge feasts and celebrations awaited the victors, who were crowned with wreaths made of olive branches. Their images were sculpted in marble. These early Olympics even created some ancient superstars. Milo of Kroton won the wrestling competition five times between 532 and 516 B.C. Leonidas of Rhodes swept the running events between 164 and 152 B.C.

The Human Form as Art

We can see the Greek admiration for humanity not just in their games but also in the works of art they left behind. Early Greek artists chose to picture animals or abstract designs, but as time went on, Greek artists turned their attention to humanity. They wanted to show the human form in all its glory.

Thousands of colorfully painted pots and vases remain from ancient Greece. Most were used as jars or vats for storing grain, wine, and oil. The Greeks wanted such objects to be more than useful; they also wanted them to be beautiful. So they made vessels both strong and graceful, and artists adorned them with human figures that seem to leap to life. Artists painted heroes battling, runners racing, ordinary people picking olives or meeting friends—any scene that focused on the lives of human beings and their doings.

Greek artists were lucky to have good materials on hand. There was plenty of red clay for potters to shape into durable vases. Even more important, white marble lay in the earth in Greece. With that marble sculptors made statues unmatched in the ancient world, statues that seem to do everything but sing.

Today's Olympic Games

Today's Olympic Games are an inheritance from ancient times. The original Olympics were held from 776 B.C. to A.D. 394. Then they faded into a distant past. In the 1870s the past came back to life. A group of German archaeologists began to excavate the temple and stadium at Olympia. People began to think about reviving the games, this time as an international competition.

Olympic games resumed in Athens in 1896 with participants from Greece, France, the United States, Britain, and many other lands. The games now reflect our modern world, as both men and women compete in many events. They give athletes from all over the globe a chance to prove what the human body and spirit can accomplish—an idea the ancient Greeks would have applauded.

Athletes from many nations parade at a recent Olympic Games.

Sculptors chiseled perfectly shaped athletes, powerful heroes, and beautiful women. The famous "Kritios Boy," for example, shows how well Greek sculptors understood the structure of the human body by the fifth century B.C.

In time, Greek craftsmen created sculptures in bronze, too. Casting freestanding statues in bronze had advantages over chiseling marble. Bronze resisted exposure to wind and rain better than marble. And with bronze, sculptors could more fully capture the human body in action. A sculptor didn't risk having an extended marble limb collapse under its own weight. Few bronze sculptures have survived, however. Most were melted down and used for other purposes. We know the famous sculpture "Discus Thrower" by Myron (see page 254) only by later Roman copies. This statue of an athlete in action still breathes life.

One of the most famous surviving bronze statues was found in a shipwreck 140 feet beneath the surface of the Aegean Sea—a majestic statue of the god Poseidon, or possibly Zeus. Almost seven feet tall, the god is cast as a powerful athlete. His dramatic pose, with arms fully outstretched, perhaps grasping a trident or about to hurl a thunderbolt, was only possible for sculptors working in bronze rather than stone. Not surprisingly, the Greek artist fashioned the god to look like a perfectly formed human being—a shining example of how, through their art, the Greeks expressed their admiration for the human form.

Human Endeavors as Memorable

It wasn't just the human form that interested the ancient Greeks. It was human actions, accomplishments, and past deeds. By the fifth century B.C., Greeks were looking back at the human past in a careful way, trying to record it, wondering what they could learn from human activity long ago. The Chinese had some chronicles of the past, but the Greeks were the first civilization to study history in an organized manner.

Above: The beautifully sculpted statue known as the "Kritios Boy."

Below: A bronze casting of a powerful Greek god—either Poseidon or Zeus.

Their fascination with the past began with the work of the man known as "the father of history"—Herodotus (hih-RAHD-uh-tus).

Herodotus was fascinated by the past and by the lessons it taught. He had no written histories to consult, so he decided to write his own. His approach was simple. He traveled far and wide—throughout Greece, across the Middle East, down into North Africa. As he traveled, he asked questions of the people he met. He asked about their customs and manners, about their religions and beliefs, about what they knew of their past. Herodotus wrote down what he learned in a book—the world's earliest surviving volume of history.

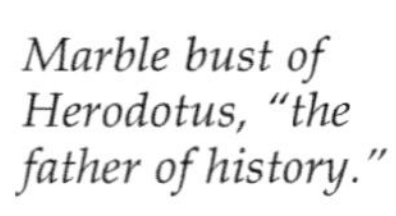

Marble bust of Herodotus, "the father of history."

Because Herodotus probably read his *Histories* to the public, he knew the importance of a good story and filled his writings with lively tales. Some were true. Others were not. Herodotus included them anyway, wanting to hold his readers' interest and hoping that they would learn from an embellished human past.

Our English word *history* comes from the ancient Greek word *historeo*, which means "learn by inquiry." The Greeks knew that to understand the past they had to inquire into it and find solid evidence of what had happened.

Another young Greek historian of the fifth century B.C. built on the work of Herodotus. His name was Thucydides (thoo-SID-uh-deez). Like Herodotus, he believed people could learn from history. But rather than writing about a distant past, Thucydides chronicled the events of his own day, especially the wars between the Greek city-states. He wrote in great detail and with painstaking care. He spent no time on fanciful stories or fantastic tales.

What did Thucydides think of Herodotus? Did he believe his own writings "better history" than those of his predecessor? Perhaps. According to tradition, though, when Herodotus was reciting his work one day, a young boy was so moved by the narrative that he started to cry. In a twist that is worthy of Herodotus, the boy turned out to be none other than the future historian Thucydides himself.

With Herodotus and Thucydides, we have the beginnings of the discipline of history. These men were among the first to study the past in an organized way and write a record of human actions and accomplishments. The beginnings of written history in ancient Greece provide yet further testimony to the Greeks' great interest in humanity.

The Greek "Citizen-States"

Herodotus and Thucydides were interested in stories of past times partly because they were very attached to the city-states in which they lived. Sometimes those communities made war on each other. We've learned that the ancient Greeks didn't unite under one king ruling the entire mainland and islands. Instead they lived in small city-states such as Athens, Sparta, Corinth, or Thebes.

Geography helped determine this political landscape. The mountains and sea divided the land, forming natural barriers between city-states. But another reason the Greeks lived in city-states was that they preferred it that way. They believed the individual state—the *polis* (PAH-lus), as they called it—gave them a better way of life. They believed it gave them a better way to exercise the freedom that, as the myth told it, had been so hard won for them by Prometheus.

The Greek word *polis* is often translated as "city-state," but it wasn't just "a city and its surroundings." The better translation for polis is "citizen-state." Each polis was a small state run not by a mighty monarch with unlimited powers but by citizens who often wrote constitutions and used some forms of elected government.

The Greeks knew all about great empires like Egypt and Persia. In an empire, one powerful ruler governed all the people. He was often considered a god-king. His word was law and nobody challenged it. People who lived hundreds of miles away from him had to obey. The Greeks,

Much like the Greek cities of old, a modern-day hilltop village perches between mountains and sea.

however, did not believe any mortal ruler could be a god or should act as a god. They thought living under such a king or emperor would be no better than slavery.

The Greeks both admired human potential and doubted the wisdom of kingly rule. They asked themselves: How could a king living in one city know what the people in another city need? Why should so many people obey just one man? How could they be sure that he would be a good ruler? Aren't free and learned people capable of making their own laws?

The Greeks believed that because each city-state knew its own needs, each should make its own rules, have its own form of government, and keep its own army. Each city-state should even be free to decide what gods it would worship.

A citizen of a polis, or city-state, addresses an assembly of his fellow citizens.

Our words *politics, political,* and *metropolis* all come from the Greek word *polis.* They remind us that the ancient Greeks have deeply influenced our ideas about how to govern ourselves.

Citizens could share in making their city greater or better. They could help to make laws. They could share in governing. They could feel proud and free.

The Polis as School

For citizens of ancient Greece, the city-state, or polis, represented everything good about Greek life. It was not just a kind of government, but a sort of school. A citizen from ancient Greece might have put it this way: "We serve on juries for the polis. This teaches us to be just. We fight to defend the polis. This teaches us to be brave. We make laws to protect the polis. This teaches us to be unselfish. Our statesmen set examples from which we can learn. Our laws teach us to behave properly. Our temples teach us to honor the gods. Our polis shows us how to lead a good life."

To the ancient Greek, the polis wasn't just a place; it was the people as well. Gradually the Greeks developed the idea that the polis should serve the will of all its citizens. The citizens, in turn, should be devoted to the polis and be directly involved in its government.

In the city-state of Athens, men becoming citizens took an oath that shows the affection and sense of responsibility the Greeks held for the polis. The young men were 17 to 19 years of age, about the same as an American college freshman today.

Here follows a modern version of the oath, which has been widely adapted by schools and institutions around the world.

Part of the city of Athens and nearby countryside as it would have looked in ancient times.

The Athenian Oath

> We will never bring disgrace on this our city by an act of dishonesty or cowardice.
>
> We will fight for the ideals and sacred things of the city, both alone and with many.
>
> We will revere and obey the city's laws, and will do our best to incite a like reverence and respect in those above us who are prone to annul them or set them at naught.
>
> We will strive increasingly to quicken the public's sense of civic duty.
>
> Thus in all these ways we will transmit this city, not only not less, but greater and more beautiful than it was transmitted to us.

The citizens of Athens were proud to pledge this oath.

But Who's a Citizen?

Citizens of a polis had the honor and duty of sharing in governance. But not all the people in a city-state were citizens. In fact, the vast majority were not. Women, for example, were not citizens. They did not participate in politics or attend schools. In some city-states, women were very important at the numerous religious events. But in others they rarely appeared at public events. In all city-states, women had great responsibility for managing the household, raising children, and keeping the accounts of the home's goods and expenses. In some city-states they could own property.

Foreigners generally were not given citizenship. Sometimes even the sons and grandsons of foreigners could not be citizens. There were often many free workingmen living in a polis—merchants, craftsmen, doctors, teachers—who came from other places. Their skills were respected, and they could even earn riches in their trades, but because they were not born in the polis, they were not considered citizens.

At the bottom of the ladder in the life of the polis were slaves. Many of these slaves were people who had been captured in wars or pirate raids. Most were non-Greeks. They did everything from laboring in fields and mines to working in shops to teaching children. Slaves did much of the heavy work and often helped to keep trade and manufacturing going. While the ancient Greeks prized freedom, their liberty often came at the expense of others. Does this mean the Greeks were hypocrites? They said they valued human ability and loved freedom, but most people were not citizens, and thus did not get the chance to exercise that freedom fully. To understand this contradiction, we need to think about the Greeks in the context of their time.

Female dancers and musicians celebrate the god Dionysus. Though not citizens, women often performed important ritual functions, as shown on this dish. They also managed households, sometimes owned property, and figured prominently in Greek drama.

Greek civilization emerged in a world of kings and empires. It emerged at a time when many people elsewhere in the world were ruled by tyrannical kings who claimed to be gods. The Greeks said this was wrong. They would not tolerate being ruled by a so-called god-king.

In Greek assemblies, courts, schools, and juries, more people were taking part in civic life as free citizens than ever before in history. The Greeks even called this system *democracy*, which means "rule of the people." In fact, as we've seen, not all the people ruled. Nevertheless, the Greek citizens' rule of the polis was, in these ancient times, an important new way of thinking about how people should be governed. The Greeks were trailblazers. In time, as their ideas spread, the course that started as a narrow, rocky path would become a wide avenue of freedom.

Celebrating Human Possibilities

The Greeks weren't the only early people to ask what good government is. Confucius, for example, thought that virtuous rulers created good governments. They could inspire their citizens to be virtuous. The Hebrews thought that good governments were those that obeyed God's laws and inspired their people to do the same. But the Greeks set themselves apart by trying to understand government in a more scientific way.

Greek thinkers didn't believe a single person could rule wisely over large numbers of men. Sooner or later, they said, one all-powerful ruler would end up interfering with men's freedom. They didn't agree with the Hebrews about government, partly because they had such different ideas about God or the gods. Most Greeks were polytheists. They didn't look to their gods to show them right laws or ways of acting. They felt that man would be able to figure out these things for himself. Man, they said, should use his mind and past experience to choose the kind of government that would work best.

The importance of human beings was foremost in the Greek mind. As the symbolic meaning of the myth of Prometheus suggests, from the moment Prometheus stole fire for the frightened creatures in caves, human beings had proven they could think for themselves. They had been given the gift of reason, and combined that with the will to strive toward excellence.

Admiration for human ability and potential revealed itself in Greek literature and athletics, in their art and histories. It showed itself in their "citizen states," which prized freedom. As we'll see, Greek faith in the power to think and reason would help steer the course of the human odyssey for centuries to come.

A Tale from the *Odyssey*

Human daring, resourcefulness, and ingenuity—qualities greatly admired by the ancient Greeks—are brought to life in the figure of Odysseus, the hero of Homer's *Odyssey*. You're about to read a selection from that famous epic.

To remind you of the background: After leaving Troy, Odysseus wanders for many years, prevented by dangers and wrathful gods from returning to his home in Ithaca, where he is awaited by his faithful wife, Penelope, and his son, Telemachus (tuh-LEM-uh-kus). In the following selection, as the action begins, Odysseus—shipwrecked, exhausted, and alone—has washed up on the island of the Phaeacians (fee-AY-shuhns). The kind king and his people take Odysseus in and care for him. Here, after a feast, Odysseus tells the Phaeacians the story of one of his great adventures.

Odysseus and the Cyclops

Adapted from The Children's Homer *by Padraic Colum.*

"First of all I will declare to you my name and my country. I am Odysseus, son of Laertes, and my land is Ithaca. And now I will tell you, king, and tell the princes and captains and councilors of the Phaeacians, the tale of my wanderings.

"The wind bore my ships from the coast of Troy, with our white sails hoisted. We should soon have come to our own country, all unhurt, but the north wind came and swept us from our course and drove us wandering…

"Later we came to the land of the Cyclopes (siy-KLOH-peez), a giant people. There is an empty island outside the harbor of their land, and on it there is a well of bright water that has poplars growing round it. We came to that empty island, and we beached our ships and took down our sails.

"As soon as the dawn came we went through the island, starting the wild goats that were there in flocks, and shooting them with our arrows. We killed so many wild goats there that we had nine for each ship. Afterwards we looked across to the land of the Cyclopes, and we heard the sound of voices and saw the smoke of fires and heard the bleating of flocks of sheep and goats.

"I called my companions together and I said, 'It would be well for some of us to go to that other island. With my own ship and the men on it, I shall go there. The rest of you abide here. I will find out what manner of men live there, and whether they will treat us kindly and give us gifts that are due to strangers—gifts of provisions for our voyage.'

"We embarked and we came to the land. There was a cave near the sea, and round the cave there were mighty flocks of sheep and goats. I took twelve men with me and I left the rest to guard the ship. We went into the cave and found no man there. There were baskets filled with cheeses, and vessels of whey, and pails and bowls of milk. My men wanted me to take some of the cheeses and drive off some of the lambs and kids and come away. But this I would not do, for I would rather that he who owned the stores would give us of his own free will the offerings due to strangers.

"While we were in the cave, he whose dwelling it was returned to it. He carried on his shoulder a great pile of wood for his fire. Never in our lives did we see a creature so frightful as this Cyclops (SIY-klahps) was. He was a giant, and, what made him terrible to behold, he had but one eye, and that single eye was in his forehead. He cast down on the ground the pile of wood that he carried, making such a din that we fled in terror into the corners and recesses of the cave. Next he drove his flocks into the cave and began to milk his ewes and goats. And when he had the flocks within, he took up a stone that not all our strengths could move, and set it as a door to the mouth of the cave.

"The Cyclops kindled his fire, and when it blazed up he saw us in the corners and recesses. He spoke to us. Our hearts were shaken with terror at the sound of his deep voice.

Agamemnon was the leader of the Greeks in the Trojan war. _Priam_ was king of the Trojans.

"I spoke to him saying that we were Agamemnon's men on our way home from the taking of Priam's city, and I begged him to deal with us kindly, for the sake of Zeus who is ever in the company of strangers and suppliants. But he answered me saying, 'We Cyclopes pay no heed to Zeus, nor to any of your gods. In our strength and our power we deem that we are mightier than they. I will not spare you, neither will I give you aught for the sake of Zeus, but only as my own spirit bids me. And first I would have you tell me how you came to our land.'

"I knew it would be better not to let the Cyclops know that my ship and my companions were at the harbor of the island. Therefore I spoke to him guilefully, telling him that my ship had been broken on the rocks, and that I and the men with me were the only ones who had escaped utter doom.

"I begged again that he would deal with us as just men deal with strangers and suppliants, but he, without saying a word, laid hands upon two of my men, and swinging them by the legs, dashed their brains out on the earth. He cut them to pieces and ate them before our very eyes. We wept and we prayed to Zeus as we witnessed a deed so terrible.

"Next the Cyclops stretched himself among his sheep and went to sleep beside the fire. Then I debated whether I should take my sharp sword in my hand, and feeling where his heart was, stab him there. But second thoughts held me back from doing this. I might be able to kill him as he slept, but not even with my companions could I roll away the great stone that closed the mouth of the cave.

"Dawn came, and the Cyclops awakened, kindled his fire, and milked his flocks. Then he seized two others of my men and made ready for his mid-day meal. And now he rolled away the great stone and drove his flocks out of the cave.

"I had pondered on a way of escape, and I had thought of something that might be done to baffle the Cyclops. I had with me a great skin of sweet wine, and I thought that if I could make him drunk with wine, I and my companions might overcome him. But there were other preparations to be made first. On the floor of the cave there was a great beam of olive wood which the Cyclops had cut to make a club. It was yet green. I and my companions went and cut off a fathom's length of the wood, and sharpened it to a point and took it to the fire and hardened it in the glow. Then I hid the beam in a recess of the cave.

"The Cyclops came back in the evening, and opening up the cave drove in his flocks. Then he closed the cave again with the stone and went and milked his ewes and his goats. Again he seized two of my companions. I went to the terrible creature with a bowl of wine in my hands. He took it and drank it and cried out, 'Give me another bowl of this, and tell me your name that I may give you gifts for bringing me this honey-tasting drink.'

"Again I spoke to him guilefully and said, 'Noman is my name. Noman my father and my mother call me.'

"'Give me more of the drink, Noman,' he shouted. 'And the gift that I shall give is that I shall make you the last of your fellows to be eaten.'

"I gave him wine again, and when he had taken the third bowl he sank backwards with his face upturned, and sleep came upon him. Then I, with four companions, took that beam of olive wood, now made into a hard and pointed stake, and thrust it into the ashes of the fire. When the pointed end began to glow we drew it out of the flame. Then I and my companions laid hold on the great stake and, dashing at the Cyclops, thrust it into his eye. He raised a terrible cry that made the rocks ring and we dashed away into the recesses of the cave.

"His cries brought other Cyclopes to the mouth of the cave, and they, naming him as Polyphemus (pah-luh-FEE-mus), called out and asked him what ailed him. 'Noman,' he shrieked out, 'Noman is slaying me by guile.' They answered him saying, 'If no man is slaying you, there is nothing we can do for you, Polyphemus.' Saying this, they went away from the mouth of the cave without attempting to move away the stone.

"Polyphemus then, groaning with pain, rolled away the stone and sat before the mouth of the cave with his hands outstretched, thinking that he would catch us as we dashed out. I showed my companions how we might pass by him. I laid hands on certain rams of the flock and I lashed three of them together. Then on the middle ram I put a man of my company. Thus every three rams carried a man. As soon as the dawn had come the rams hastened out to the pasture, and, as they passed, Polyphemus laid hands on the first and the third of each three that went by. They passed out and Polyphemus did not guess that the ram he did not touch carried out a man.

"For myself, I took a ram that was the strongest and fleeciest of the whole flock and I placed myself under him, clinging to the wool of his belly. As this ram, the best of all his flock, went by, Polyphemus, laying his hands upon him, said, 'Would that you, the best of my flock, were endowed with speech, so that you might tell me where Noman, who has blinded me, has hidden himself.' The ram went by him, and when he had gone a little way from the cave I loosed myself from him and went and set my companions free.

"We gathered together many of Polyphemus's sheep and we drove them down to our ship. The men we had left behind would have wept when they heard what had happened to six of their companions. But I bade them take on board the sheep we had brought and pull the ship away from that land. Then when we had drawn a certain distance from the shore I could not forbear to shout my taunts into the cave of Polyphemus. 'Cyclops,' I cried, 'you thought that you had the company of a fool and a weakling to eat. But your evil deeds have been punished.'

"So I shouted, and Polyphemus came to the mouth of the cave with great anger in his heart. He took up rocks and cast them at the ship and they fell before the prow. The men bent to the oars and pulled the ship away or it would have been broken by the rocks he cast. And when we were farther away I shouted to him, 'Cyclops, if any man should ask who set his mark upon you, say it was Odysseus, the son of Laertes.'"

Part 2, Conclusion

A

B

A: The Hebrews believed that Abraham, here depicted with three heavenly visitors, accepted a covenant between God and his people.

B: Students of the Chinese philosopher Confucius engage in discussion under the shade of riverside trees.

C: The god Vishnu, whom Hindus revere as the preserver of the universe.

D: A statue of the Buddha, sitting cross-legged in silent meditation.

C

D

The Power of Ancient Ideas

How powerful ideas are! They motivate many of our actions. They help us decide how to live. People fight and sometimes die for them. We've been studying some important thoughts and beliefs of people who lived between 1800 and 400 B.C. From Abraham to Confucius to Buddha to the thinkers of ancient Greece, we've been looking at philosophy and religion—the most important ideas about God or the gods, about good and evil, about the meaning of human life, and about the nature of the world. Those ancient ideas influence us still.

The following questions will help you review some of the ground we've covered. As you read them the first time, ask yourself: How would a Sumerian answer this? Then go through them again and ask yourself: How would a student of Confucius reply? What would a Buddhist think? What would an ancient Israelite say? And finally: How would a citizen of a Greek polis respond?

- Is there a godlike power over human life? What is it? Does it get involved in the affairs of human beings?
- Are there "laws of nature"? Can human beings hope to understand them? Can we learn to control the forces of nature?
- How can men and women live the best life…
  By thinking and reasoning?
  By knowing their place in society?
  By doing their duty?
  By overcoming selfish desires?
  By respecting their elders?
  By obeying God or the gods?

Testimony to the importance of religion in ancient Greece, this temple to the sea-god Poseidon once looked down upon sailors voyaging to and from Athens.

Above: The ideas of Confucius have not only been important to scholars like those depicted in this drawing from sixteenth-century China; they have also helped form the foundations of Eastern civilization.

Below: A stained-glass window depicts Moses during the Israelites' wandering in the wilderness. The Ten Commandments, which the Hebrews believed God delivered to Moses, are one of the foundations of Western civilization.

- Do human beings live many times on Earth?
- Is the human body important? Why or why not?
- Should ordinary people share in the business of government?
- Should people choose their own form of government?
- Does good government matter? What *is* good government? Whom should one obey?

Some of these questions are easy to answer, and others hard. We can't always find good answers, nor do people always agree on the best answer.

Eastern and Western Civilizations

So far in our human odyssey, as we've sailed through the waters of centuries and moved from east to west, we've studied some of the important ideas and beliefs of different peoples. In the second part of this book, we've made stops in China, India, the Middle East, and Greece. In the east—China and India—we learned about Confucianism, Hinduism, and Buddhism. Farther west, we studied the rise of Judaism, as well as Greek ideas about nature and human beings. These important philosophies and religions are sometimes seen as the root of what are called "Eastern civilization" and "Western civilization."

What distinguishes East from West?

Geographers say one thing; historians say another. Geographers say that if you look at a globe, the continents of Europe, Asia, Africa, and Australia are all in the east. That's "the Eastern Hemisphere." The "Western Hemisphere," they tell us, is made up of a lot of ocean plus North and South America.

For historians, there's a different way to think about East and West. They consider China, India, and Japan

to be part of "Eastern civilization." But even though Europe is in the Eastern Hemisphere, historians consider most European nations part of "Western civilization." Why is that?

For historians, what distinguishes East from West is not just the Ural mountain range separating Asia from Europe, but instead some of the very ideas we've been studying. The ideas that came out of China and India long ago have been foundations for Eastern civilization. The ideas of the ancient Hebrews and Greeks are the root ideas of Western civilization. Those ideas—the ideas of the ancient Hebrews and Greeks—ended up being most influential in Europe. And later, Europeans took those ideas to the Americas when they colonized those continents.

As Western civilization developed, it would incorporate other ideas. But in general, the big body of ideas and beliefs that we think of as "Western civilization" has its roots in the ancient civilizations of the Jewish and Greek peoples. Western civilization echoes the Jewish belief in one God, as well as the emphasis on the importance of law. From the ancient Greeks, Western civilization has inherited convictions about the ability of human reason to figure out the workings of nature, the dignity and worth of human beings, the importance of individuals, and the potential of human beings to shape their own destiny.

If we think of Western civilization as the civilization of Europe and (eventually) the Americas, then Eastern civilization is generally the civilization of the various peoples of Asia. The historic roots of Eastern civilization lie not simply east of the Urals, but in the soil of Confucianism, Hinduism, Buddhism, and other beliefs we have not yet studied. The followers of Confucianism prized reverence for elders, duty to family and country, diligent study, putting one's own desires last, and service to a larger whole. Both Hinduism and Buddhism have valued fulfillment of duty, honorable conduct, contemplation, and detachment from the things of this world. They have regarded each human life as but one in a possible series of lives, a long trial that must be endured in order to find Nirvana, or peace.

One of the oldest religions in the world, Hinduism remains the dominant faith in India. These Indian women sing songs and throw colored dust in the air as part of a Hindu festival.

Of course when we refer to "Western civilization" and "Eastern civilization," we are speaking in the broadest and most general terms. Within the West, you can easily see many cultural differences in the ways that people think and live. City dwellers in Paris, France, obviously lead lives very different from the lives of the inhabitants of an isolated Mexican village. Similarly, in the East, local cultures and ways of life vary greatly. The experiences of a fisherman on a small Japanese island are not likely to resemble the experiences of a factory worker in Malaysia.

And yet, despite local differences, you will find that Westerners in general share certain ideas and beliefs, and that Easterners in general share other ideas and beliefs. It is these ideas and beliefs—such as the Western belief in the importance of individuals, or the Eastern belief in reverence for elders—that make up, on one hand, Western civilization, and, on the other hand, Eastern civilization. Shared ideas bind together the various peoples in each civilization.

There is an old saying: "East is East and West is West, and never the twain shall meet." You have seen some differences between Eastern and Western beliefs and ideas. Still, are there only *differences* between East and West? Of course not. There are many ideas that a Confucian, a Buddhist, an ancient Israelite, and a Greek citizen might agree on. What might those ideas be? Consider how thinkers from both East and West might answer these questions:

- Should parents be responsible for their children?
- Should children respect their parents?
- Should human beings keep their promises?
- Should people obey the laws of their society?

Some Concluding Thoughts

We began by asking, *"What were they thinking?"* We've seen that, unlike a piece of ancient pottery—which might crumble and blow away as dust—many ideas and beliefs of the

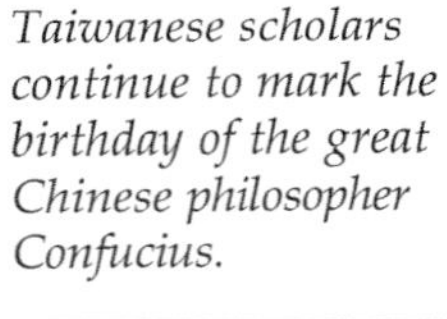

Taiwanese scholars continue to mark the birthday of the great Chinese philosopher Confucius.

ancient civilizations remain with us still. Indeed, some of the most important ideas and beliefs continue to form the foundations of Western and Eastern civilizations.

Over time, the ideas that characterize Western and Eastern civilizations have evolved. But as we move forward in the study of history, you'll see just how influential these frameworks of thought have been. They have influenced the governments nations have chosen, the laws they have passed, the art and architecture they have created, and much more.

Do you remember peeking in on Ren Li, the Chinese paper maker's son who wanted to be a scholar? His greatest desire was to seek knowledge and study Confucian writings. His hope was to please his parents and serve his people, perhaps as a government official. His plan was to work diligently and master his own weaknesses. Li is an imaginary boy, a character in a story. Yet many of his thoughts and hopes could be shared by people around the world, by children in all civilizations. On the other hand, many people might have thoughts and hopes very different from Li's. How we judge events, what we think is important, how we understand what we see—all are very much influenced by the past, and in Li's case, by growing up in a culture with Confucian roots.

Ideas and beliefs shape who we are. By studying ideas, we can learn to see the roots of some of our own thinking. And we might learn to understand people better, especially people whose ideas differ from our own.

In the next part of our study, we'll continue to focus on the ancient Greeks. Then we'll meet another noteworthy civilization, also brimming with important ideas—the Romans. We'll get to know two religions, Christianity and Islam, whose ideas—like those of Hinduism, Buddhism, and Judaism—are still followed by millions of people today. Many great stories and big ideas await us in the next phase of our human odyssey.

A Buddhist temple in modern-day Japan.

Time Line (1800–200 B.C.)

1800 B.C.
Abraham goes to Canaan.

1200 B.C.
Probable time of the Trojan War, pitting Greeks against Trojans.

1400 B.C.
The first of the *Vedas*, oldest Hindu texts, are written.

1500 B.C.
Aryans migrate to India.

1250 B.C.
Moses leads the Hebrews out of Egypt.

1000 B.C. | 800 B.C. | 600 B.C. | 400 B.C. | 200 B.C.

550 B.C.
The Hebrews are held captive in Babylon.

206 B.C.
Han dynasty begins in China (206 B.C.–A.D. 220).

250 B.C.
Asoka reigns in India (269–232 B.C.).

450 B.C.
Herodotus writes his *Histories* (lived 484–425 B.C.).

220 B.C.
Qin Shi Huangdi, the First Emperor, rules China (221–210 B.C.).

1000 B.C.
Saul, David, and Solomon rule the Hebrews (1029–931 B.C.).

500 B.C.
The Buddha teaches in India (lived 563–483 B.C.).

750 B.C.
Homer composes the *Iliad* and *Odyssey*.

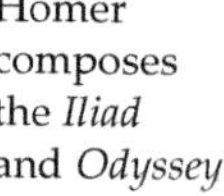

500 B.C.
Confucius teaches in China (lived 551–479 B.C.).

776 B.C.
First recorded Olympic Games take place in Greece.

Part 3, Introduction

A

D

A: Bust of Democritus, one of the Greek thinkers who carefully examined the natural world.

B: Ruins of a Greek temple.

C: The Cyclops, a giant from Homer's Odyssey.

D: The Trojan Horse from Homer's Iliad.

C

What's So "Classic" About the Classical World?

B

"I love that book—it's a classic." What do we mean when we say that a work of literature is a "classic"? We mean it has lasting value. We mean that the writing is so superb, or the story so compelling, or the themes so universal—or all of those at once—that the book will merit attention for generations. The *Iliad* and the *Odyssey*, for example, are classics. So are works by Shakespeare, Jane Austen, and Mark Twain. In literature, a classic captures the imagination of people past, present, and (very likely) future—in other words, it is timeless.

In history, however, we mean something different when we use the terms "classic" or "classical." In history, those terms refer to a particular time and place. "Classical civilization" refers to the civilizations of ancient Greece and Rome between about 500 B.C. and A.D. 500. These two Mediterranean civilizations stretched thousands of miles and flourished for nearly a thousand years.

Classical civilization is also "classic" in the sense of "timeless." Ideas and institutions from ancient Greece and Rome have continued to influence people for more than two thousand years, especially in the West. Let's take a look at some traces of classical Greece and Rome around us.

Classical Roots of Modern Language

Every day, people in English-speaking cultures use words that have roots in the ancient Greek and Roman languages. The word *history* comes from the Greek *histor*, meaning "learned." When you say, "I've got to make a telephone call," you are using a term that comes from two Greek words—*tele* ("far off") and *phone* ("voice" or "sound"). When you say, "I'm going to listen to some music," you're using a word that descends from *mousike*, the Greek term for any art inspired by the goddesses known as the Muses.

Latin, the language of the ancient Romans, is the foundation for French, Italian, and Spanish, among other modern tongues. They are known as "Romance languages," not because they are good ways to communicate when people are in love, but because they developed from the Roman language. The English language uses thousands of words that come from Latin. Here are a few:

agriculture	*agricola* (farmer)
aquatic	*aqua* (water)
fortune	*fortuna* (chance)
library	*liber* (book)
literature	*littera* (letter)
nature	*natura* (nature)
student	*studere* (to study)
terrain	*terra* (land)

The Parthenon (far right in this picture) in Athens is perhaps the most famous classical building in the world. Its design has influenced architecture for thousands of years.

The Drama of It All

Stories passed down from the ancient Greeks and Romans are among the greatest tales ever told: Hercules performing impossible labors, Pandora opening the mysterious box, the Trojans pulling the great wooden horse inside the walls of their city. The title of this series, *The Human Odyssey*, comes from the ancient Greek poem featuring the hero Odysseus.

The Greeks also gave the world drama, the art of storytelling on stage. The word "theater" comes from the Greek *theatron*, which means "viewing place." Modern-day artists, poets, authors, and movie directors often turn to Greek myths and plays for inspiration.

As you've learned, the Greeks crafted marble and bronze sculptures that celebrated the human form. Those works still influence ideals of human beauty. Classical notions of beauty also live in today's buildings. If you go to Washington, D.C., and want to see the United States Constitution, you must visit the National Archives building. That huge columned structure was built to resemble a Greek temple. Just up the street, the U.S. Capitol building, with its giant dome, is inspired by both Greek and Roman architecture.

The Romans were among history's greatest builders. Whenever you see a building with a rounded arch, you're looking at a design the Romans perfected. The famous Arc de Triomphe (ahrk duh tree-AWNF) in Paris is an architectural tribute to the Roman arch. The Romans invented concrete, which allowed them to build massive structures. Today's engineers and architects still study Roman roads, bridges, and buildings.

Science and Mathematics

The ancient Greeks viewed the world as an orderly place that operates according to natural laws. They believed that human beings could, through study and reason, come to

Below: The classically inspired facade of the National Archives building in Washington, D.C., resembles a Greek temple.

Bottom: The Arc de Triomphe in Paris was built in the style of a Roman arch.

Right: This sixteenth-century painting shows the Greek mathematician Pythagoras formulating the famous theorem that bears his name.

Below: This is an English version of the Hippocratic Oath, a pledge by doctors to treat patients to the best of their abilities. It is named after Hippocrates, a physician from ancient Greece.

understand the laws of nature. Greek thinkers made careful observations of nature. Several branches of science—such as biology, zoology, astronomy, and ecology—take their names from Greek words.

The philosopher Democritus (dih-MAHK-raht-us) was one of the first to argue that everything in the world is made of invisible and indivisible particles. He called such a particle *atamos*, which means "uncuttable." From Democritus we get the word *atom*. The ancient Greek physician Hippocrates (hip-AHK-ruh-teez) is sometimes called the father of medicine. Today many doctors take a pledge called the Hippocratic Oath,

in which they promise to treat patients to the best of their abilities.

THE OATH

I SWEAR by Apollo the physician and Æsculapius & Health & All-heal & all the gods & goddesses that according to my ability & judgement I WILL KEEP THIS OATH & this stipulation—to reckon him who taught me this Art equally dear to me as my parents to share my substance with him & relieve his necessities if required; to look upon his offspring in the same footing as my own brothers & to teach them this Art, if they shall wish to learn it WITHOUT FEE OR STIPULATION & that by precept lecture & every other mode of instruction I will impart a knowledge of the Art to my own sons & those of my teachers & to disciples bound by a stipulation & oath ACCORDING TO THE LAW OF MEDICINE but to none others. I will follow the system of regimen which according to my ability & judgement I consider FOR THE BENEFIT OF MY PATIENTS & abstain from whatever is deleterious & mischievous. I will give no deadly medicine to any one if asked nor suggest any such counsel & in like manner I will not give to a woman a pessary to produce abortion. WITH PURITY & WITH HOLINESS I WILL PASS MY LIFE & PRACTICE MY ART. I will not cut persons laboring under the stone, but will leave this to be done by men who are practitioners of this work. Into whatever houses I enter, I will go into them for the benefit of the sick & will abstain from every voluntary act of mischief & corruption AND FURTHER from the seduction of females or males of freemen & slaves. Whatever in connection with my professional practice or not in connection with it, I see or hear in the life of men which ought not to be spoken of abroad, I WILL NOT DIVULGE as reckoning that all such should be kept secret. While I continue to keep this Oath unviolated, may it be granted to me to enjoy life & the practice of the Art respected by all men in all times! But should I trespass & violate this Oath, may the reverse be my lot!

ΙΠΠΟΚΡΑΤΗΣ

To the Greeks, no subject was more important than mathematics. At a famous school in Athens, an inscription over the door read: "Let no one enter here who is ignorant of geometry." Perhaps you have studied the Pythagorean Theorem, a famous formula about right triangles (any triangle with a 90° angle), named after the Greek mathematician Pythagoras (puh-THAG-uh-rus). It is one of many important mathematical concepts the Greeks gave us.

The Romans also left their mark on science and mathematics. For example, scientists still use Latin names to classify plants and animals. Most of the planets in our solar system, from Mercury to Pluto, are named for gods of the ancient Romans.

Civics and Government

Many governments around the world reflect the legacy of classical times. Modern democracies have inherited many Greek ideas, including government by the people, trial by jury, and equality before the law. Democracies also owe much to the Romans, who, as you will learn, had a genius for making and administering laws.

The men who wrote the United States Constitution studied the history of classical times. They looked to ancient Greece and Rome to learn how to set up a government. When they designed a legislature for the United States, they called one house the Senate. As you'll learn, the Romans also had a Senate. Many ideas about a balanced government—a government divided into different parts so that no one part grows too powerful—have roots in Roman times.

When the American Founders chose a motto for the young United States, it was no accident that they used the language of the Romans—*E pluribus unum,* which is Latin for "Out of many, one." Classical ideas and symbols abound in the American system of government. Whether you're heading into a voting booth or standing next to the Jefferson Memorial in Washington, D.C., you are enjoying some modern fruits of Greece and Rome.

In this section of our book, we'll explore the classical civilizations of ancient Greece and Rome. The Greeks came first. You've already had an introduction to some important ideas the Greeks developed by 500 B.C. Now we'll take a closer look at the classical world during an amazing two-hundred-year period.

Top: Words in Latin, the language of ancient Rome, adorn the Great Seal of the United States. They read E pluribus unum*—"Out of many, one."*

Above: The right to vote in elections is another legacy of ancient Greece and Rome.

An aerial view of the acropolis of Athens and its crowning glory, the great temple known as the Parthenon.

Two Greek City-States

The Greek world of ancient times was much larger than the present-day country called Greece. It consisted of a rugged, mountainous peninsula jutting into the Mediterranean Sea, numerous islands, and the west coast of Asia Minor.

The long rocky peninsula that made up the Greek mainland divided two branches of the Mediterranean—the Ionian Sea to the west and the Aegean Sea to the east. The Greeks had set up colonies all around the rim of the Aegean Sea and much of the Mediterranean. They were, said one of their philosophers, like "frogs around a pond."

By the eighth century B.C., the people of the Greek world held many things in common. They worshiped the same gods. They spoke a common language. They all delighted in the poetry of Homer, whose *Iliad* and *Odyssey* were filled with tales of adventure and heroism.

All of these things made them feel Greek. But it did not make them feel like a single country or nation. Instead, the Greeks owed loyalty to their own city-state, or polis. A polis consisted of a city and the lands around it. Most were less than a hundred square miles in area. Most were ruled by aristocratic families.

The fiercely independent city-states of Greece often went to war against each other. For this reason, most were built around an *acropolis* (uh-KRAH-puh-lus), a forfied hill where the people could take refuge in time of attack.

This chapter explores ancient Greece, a civilization located in the eastern Mediterranean.

Public buildings frame the Athenian agora, or marketplace. The acropolis rises in the background.

While the acropolis served its main purpose during wartime, the daily life of the city unfolded in the marketplace, or as the Greeks called it, the *agora* (A-guh-ruh). The agora was both a marketplace and a meeting place. Here, in the cool of the early morning, farmers from the surrounding countryside brought their animals and produce. Local craftsmen arrived to set up their stalls for the day's trade. And magistrates came to the law courts and government buildings surrounding the agora. Here, too, the men of the city gathered to settle business matters, discuss politics, or simply chat about the latest news.

Ancient Greece was made up of hundreds of city-states. Corinth was one of the richest, sitting astride an important trade route between central Greece and the Peloponnesian peninsula to the south. Thebes was cattle and horse country, its people shrewd in business. Ephesus (EH-fuh-suhs), across the sea in Asia Minor, was another center of wealth and commerce, and the home of a great temple and theater.

Each city-state had its own culture and way of life. We're going to take a closer look at the two most powerful, Sparta and Athens. These two city-states were just 150 miles from each other, but they developed societies that were worlds apart.

- On the map on page 287, locate the following: the Peloponnesian peninsula, Asia Minor, Mediterranean Sea, Ionian Sea, Aegean Sea, Sparta, and Athens.

The Warrior-State of Sparta

Located deep in the Peloponnese, the southern section of the Greek mainland, Sparta was the great warrior city-state of ancient Greece. Sparta was so strong that in its early days it did not need the defensive walls that surrounded most cities.

Spartans were a wary group. They disliked new ideas. They were suspicious of outsiders. And they punished by death anyone who dared to disagree with their rulers.

The Spartans built no great temples. They crafted no lasting works of art. They did not write literature.

But they did raise fierce warriors—the mightiest warriors of the Greek world.

For Spartan males, preparation for war began early, in fact at birth. By law, all boys born in Sparta were brought before government officials for examination. Only those who looked likely to grow into strong, healthy soldiers were allowed to live. The weak were of no use to this military state. They were abandoned to die on the slopes of a nearby mountain.

At seven, boys left their homes and mothers, and went to live in cold, uncomfortable military barracks with other boys their own age. There they began the harsh training that would build their strength and courage, and turn them into rugged fighters.

Under the watchful eye of an instructor, Spartan boys learn how to wrestle, an important part of their training as warriors.

The boys were often cold and hungry. They wore only a single tunic, winter and summer, and often went barefoot. Food rations were small and unappetizing. (The most famous Spartan dish was a broth made from blood and vinegar.) All of this had a purpose. It was designed

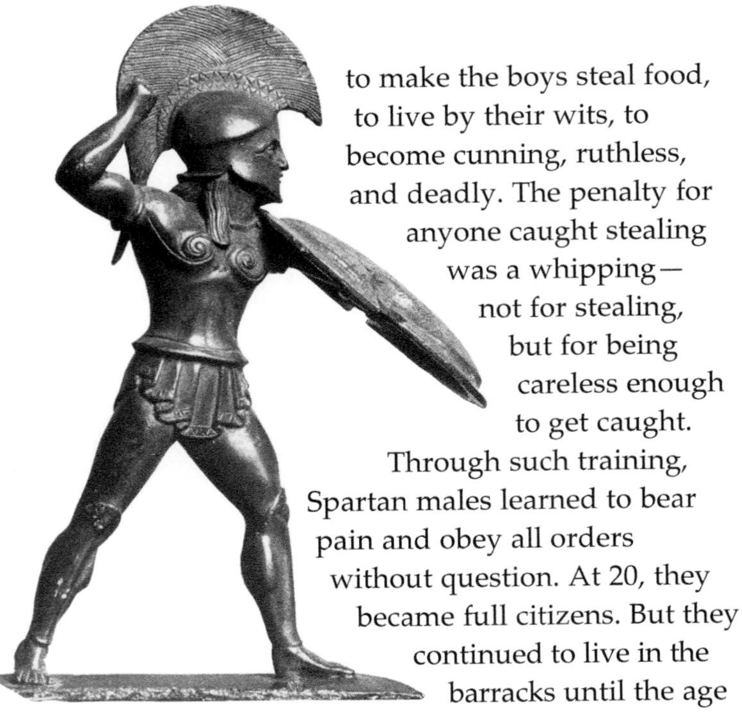

Above: This bronze statue shows a Greek warrior, possibly Spartan, as he prepares to attack. The statue once held a spear.

Below: Running Spartan girls—famous for their athletic skill—adorn the side of an ancient vase.

to make the boys steal food, to live by their wits, to become cunning, ruthless, and deadly. The penalty for anyone caught stealing was a whipping—not for stealing, but for being careless enough to get caught.

Through such training, Spartan males learned to bear pain and obey all orders without question. At 20, they became full citizens. But they continued to live in the barracks until the age of 30. Even when a young man married, he still slept and ate with his comrades and only saw his wife and children during visits home.

Spartans were direct in their manner. Their speech was brief and to the point, not wasting any words—what we would now call "laconic" (luh-KAH-nik). In fact, the Spartans gave us the term *laconic*, which describes a person of few words. It comes from *Laconia*, the name of the region of the Peloponnese where the Spartans lived.

Endurance of hardship. Contempt for luxury. Toughness of mind and body. The hardy Spartans prized all of these qualities. Today the term *spartan* means "sparse, basic, the bare minimum, with nothing to spare."

Spartan girls were tough, too. From an early age, they were trained to run and jump, and even to wrestle. While males were raised to fight, females were brought up to bear strong, healthy children. For the Spartans, all other female roles were of little importance. Once a Greek woman from another city-state visited Sparta and began to show off her weaving skills. A local mother was not impressed. She pointed to her four well-behaved sons. "These," she said proudly, "should be the occupation of a good and noble woman."

Like the men, Spartan women learned to be hard and unflinching. In this city-state, displays of affection were thought of as signs of weakness. "Return with your shield or upon it"—this was the traditional farewell of a Spartan woman to her son or husband as he marched off to war. In other words, come back in glory from battle, holding your shield proudly—or be carried back upon it, dead. A warrior who returned without his heavy round shield was one who had dropped it in his haste to run away from the enemy—and this would bring terrible shame on his family. A Spartan warrior never retreated, never took a step back in battle. He would rather die.

As every Spartan knew, it was the duty of warriors to battle the state's enemies. But they also had to protect Sparta from its large population of slaves, known as *helots*. Spartans had conquered the land they lived on and enslaved its inhabitants. These slaves tilled the land and did most of the hard work. They made

Lycurgus, the great legal reformer, delivers laws to the Spartan people.

up a majority of the population, but they had no political rights. Only the strength of the Spartan army kept them in their place and made sure they grabbed no share of political power. In fact, some historians think that Sparta became a military society mainly to control the helots, who vastly outnumbered the free citizens.

Sparta was what we call an *oligarchy* (AH-luh-gahr-kee). An oligarchy is a government in which a small group holds all the power. But in Sparta, it was an oligarchy regulated by laws. According to tradition, after a helot uprising Sparta turned to a great lawgiver named Lycurgus (liy-KUHR-gus). Lycurgus reformed the political system and provided the state with a new constitution.

By the seventh century B.C., Sparta had a mixed form of government. The state had two kings who led the armies in battle. A council of aristocratic elders wielded most of the day-to-day power. And an assembly represented the interests of the rest of the citizens. Sparta's warriors stood guard over the helots, ready to crush any demands for freedom or power.

While Sparta, like many other city-states in ancient Greece, used force to put down any popular unrest, one city-state stepped boldly in another direction. Sparta's neighbor to the east, Athens, gradually began turning power over to the people. Let's turn now to this city-state that gave the world some of its greatest innovations, thinkers, and works of art.

Athens: A Favored City

Girded by hills and perched on the edge of the blue Aegean, Athens enjoyed a prized location. Athenians were proud of their city-state and believed their polis was a favorite of the gods. They told stories of how Athens had become so glorious, of how her people came to show such genius. Here is the ancient legend of the founding of the great city.

Athena's City

The eagle wheeled far overhead, a white flash almost vanishing against the deep blue sky. It spread its wings and coasted in the rising air, turning, soaring lazily. Suddenly, swift and sharp as an arrow, the predator plunged to earth. An instant later, it again climbed aloft, its prize wriggling helpless in its talons.

Over the rugged peaks of Mount Olympus, a giant laugh boomed out, ringing with pride and pleasure.

"What a marvelous creature that bird is!"

Zeus, the king of the gods, stood, massive arms crossed, feet planted wide on the rocky slope, watching the eagle disappear into the blue.

"Such speed! Such grace! My own thunderbolt is not more deadly accurate." He shook his head admiringly. "To the other animals, the eagle is like Zeus himself—ruler of the sky, all-powerful, all-knowing, always watching from above..."

Nearby, Athena hid a smile. "But the eagle is content to exercise its power," she thought, "and not brag about it." As usual, her father's boasting pushed beyond the limits of the truth. Powerful he was, yes—more so than all the other gods together. But even the king of the gods could be tricked. Why, once his own brother, her uncle Poseidon, had—

Zeus, still talking, broke into her thoughts. "I wonder, daughter, how you satisfy yourself with *that*."

He jabbed a finger at the small brown clump of feathers on Athena's shoulder. The owl opened a sleepy eye and gazed at him reproachfully.

Athena smoothed the bird's ruffled plumage. "My little owl hunts at night," she said. "He is too wise to compete for prey with the all-powerful eagle."

Her father gave her a sharp look. Then he burst out laughing. "Wise indeed, oh yes, wise indeed."

Of all his children, Zeus had to admit that gray-eyed Athena was his favorite. Perhaps that was because only Athena had no mother. Her birth had not been of the ordinary sort. She had sprung from his head, full-grown and clad head to toe in armor. This unusual beginning made her his alone.

Zeus felt a rush of affection toward the young goddess. And affection always made him generous.

"Dear child," he said. "Loyal companion. You carry my shield and thunderbolt, yet never ask anything for yourself. Is there no favor I could grant you? No small wish I might indulge?"

Athena smiled. The morning's cloudless sky had told her Zeus was in a pleasant mood. She had joined him on his outing with the eagle, hoping for just such a moment.

Rather than answer right away, she said, "Let me show you something."

She pointed, and Zeus peered down. Far below, a grassy hilltop lay dotted with sheep. Among the sheep a solitary barefoot shepherd strolled.

Zeus frowned. "Has this mortal displeased you? Shall I send down my thunderbolt?"

He raised his arm, but Athena caught him before he could strike.

"No, Father. It is not the shepherd I wished you to see. It is the city."

"City?" The frown deepened. "I see no city."

"You see what *is*. I want you to see what *may be*." She shaded her father's eyes with her own hand. "Please look again."

Athena

He did. Sheep and shepherd had now disappeared. Through a shimmering mist he saw the grassy hilltop crowned with a magnificent marble temple, many-columned.

"A temple," Athena said. "To be built in my honor."

All around, a city was sprouting up. Men and women hurried about their business. A marketplace took shape, filled with fine crafts and lush produce from the surrounding farmland.

Beneath a tree, an old man sat, with younger men gathered eagerly around him.

"Who is that?" asked Zeus.

"A wise man, a teacher. They will call him 'father of philosophy.'" Athena's gray eyes shone. "My city will bring many gifts to the world: Democracy. Philosophy. Great drama, sculpture, architecture. Athens will be a beacon of civilization."

"Athens, eh? So you intend to name it after yourself?"

But before Athena could answer, there was a low rumble that grew into a deafening roar. The sea, which a moment before had lain tranquil and blue, now turned iron gray as great waves crashed against the cliffs. Just when Athena thought the noise would shatter the ground they stood on, the waters parted and a golden chariot burst to the surface. Instantly, the sea calmed.

Athena gazed down at the driver of the chariot. Seaweed streamed through his long beard, trailing over his massive chest and shoulders. The trident, his great three-pronged spear, was gripped in one enormous fist. It was Poseidon, brother of Zeus, ruler of the sea.

Athena's face was smooth, her noble brow untroubled. Only an angry screech from the owl perched on her shoulder gave away her feelings.

"Brother!" called Zeus. "Welcome! What business tears you away from the comforts of your splendid palace on the ocean floor?"

Poseidon

Poseidon came straight to the point. "I couldn't help but overhear you two talking about my city—"

"*Your* city!" cried Athena.

"Certainly. Does it not lie on the coast? To which god should its people turn but the lord of the sea?"

Athena appealed to her father. "It is my city. I have shown you a vision of its greatness."

"A great city needs a great protector," said Poseidon. "Only Zeus himself holds more power than I. And even that might have been otherwise."

Zeus sighed. Long ago, he and his two brothers had drawn lots to divide the universe. As a result, Poseidon ruled the sea. Hades, their brother, ruled the underworld. And Zeus, the winner, ruled the sky and all the gods.

Hades had been satisfied to stay in his dark realm and reign over the dead. But Poseidon seemed forever discontented, always wanting more.

Clouds gathered overhead as Zeus fingered his beard. How was he to weigh these two competing claims? How to choose between his brother and his daughter?

"I am older and wiser," Poseidon pushed on. "Athena is a mere girl. Give her a lesser city."

Mere girl! The owl bristled.

"I may be younger than you," Athena said calmly, "but do not forget I am the goddess of *wisdom,* and of civilization. Who better to watch over this most civilized of cities?"

Poseidon sneered. "One good tidal wave from me, and where would your civilized city be?"

Athena's gray eyes flashed. "Uncle, I was not born fully armed for nothing. I can be as warlike—"

"*Enough!*" A bolt of lightning split the coal-black sky.

Startled, Athena and Poseidon turned to Zeus.

"No more squabbling," he said. "We will decide this matter with a contest."

The sky began to lighten.

"Each of you must offer a gift to the people you wish to rule. The one whose gift I judge to be the best wins the city."

No sooner had Zeus finished speaking than Poseidon stepped boldly forward. In one strong, swift motion, he raised his trident over his head and brought it crashing down.

The earth trembled. Then, like a volcano, it exploded. Dirt and rock flew everywhere.

When it subsided, an amazing sight met their eyes. On the spot where the trident had struck stood a creature at once glorious and terrible. Muscles rippled along its gleaming sides. Hooves big enough to kill a man pawed restlessly at the rocky ground. Rearing, the animal tossed back its head.

"My gift," said Poseidon, "is the war horse. Imagine a mighty army led by horse-drawn chariots and soldiers on horseback, enemies falling in fear before them. With this gift, my city will rule the world."

He folded his arms and stepped back. As far as he was concerned, he'd already won.

Zeus eyed his daughter. "Well?"

Athena said, "He is right. A city that has such creatures will be a city of conquering warriors."

Poseidon smiled.

"But," she went on, "I wish something better for my people than a life of war. So…." She waved a graceful hand.

At first, nothing seemed to happen. No rumble or crash, no shaking of the ground greeted her gesture.

Then Zeus noticed the small green shoot beneath his feet. As he watched, it grew into a sapling, then a full-grown tree, its branches heavy with a small round fruit.

"It is the olive," said Athena. "In the summer, my people will gather underneath its shade to nourish their bodies with its fruit and their minds with shared ideas. When winter comes, its firewood will keep them warm. And with the oil, they may fill their lamps and shine a light into the darkness."

Zeus looked from his daughter to his brother.

"Your horse is superb," he told Poseidon. "Any city would be grateful to receive this gift."

Poseidon gave Athena a triumphant glance.

"But your gift," Zeus said, turning to Athena, "shows true wisdom. It is the gift of peace and plenty. The city—the city of *Athens*—is yours."

The Athenian Way

Athens became the largest and most populous of the Greek city-states, a great center of the arts, learning, and trade. Its people were known for their energy and zest for life.

Myth may have made Athens the city of Athena, but it still owed much to Poseidon, the lord of the sea. Sheltered from its rivals by mountains to the north, it was protected in the other directions by the waters of the Aegean. Yet the sea was also a channel of communication. Along with the trade that made the city prosper, the sea drew to Athens a constant flow of people and ideas.

Unlike the Spartans, the Athenians embraced new ways of thinking about the world. Free-speaking and freedom-loving, they enjoyed nothing better than debating ideas, declaring their views, and arguing politics. The *un*-laconic Athenians loved to tell anyone who would listen just what was on their minds.

Like other city-states, Athens was ruled by rich aristocratic landowners for much of its early history. But as overseas trade increased in the seventh century B.C., the new wealth often went to men who were outside the ruling classes. Not surprisingly, these rich merchants, craftsmen, and bankers wanted some political power for themselves.

The poor were discontent and restless as well. Struggling farmers who went into debt risked being sold into slavery. Riots often erupted. Powerful leaders rose up, challenging aristocratic rule.

The rulers of Athens knew that the pressure for change was too great to be ignored. So in 594 B.C., they charged one of their own, a wise aristocrat named Solon (SOH-luhn), with the task of reforming the government.

Solon set about weakening the aristocracy's stranglehold on power.

Unlike the Spartans, who used few words, the Athenians loved to debate. The figures below, deep in discussion, decorate an ancient drinking vessel.

Above: Bust of the statesman Solon, who helped plant the seeds of Athenian democracy.

Below: A seventeenth-century painting depicts the story of Solon visiting the fabulously wealthy Croesus.

He permitted the wealthy merchants of Athens to hold positions in government. He said all citizens were entitled to participate in a body to decide the laws. This governing body became known as the Assembly. Solon also set up people's courts, with juries. And to ease the plight of the poorest farmers, he ended the practice of enslaving debtors.

Solon was a great traveler. One day, according to the historian Herodotus, he appeared in the court of Croesus (KREE-sus), a king in Asia Minor. Croesus, it was said, was the richest man in the world.

"Now tell me," Croesus demanded, "you have journeyed far and seen much. Who is the most fortunate man you have ever met?"

Solon did not pause. "Why, Tellus of Athens," he replied.

Croesus was shocked. Who was this Tellus? Who could be more fortunate than Croesus himself, with all his great wealth and luxury? Solon explained: Tellus had been a free citizen of Athens. His sons were brave and honest, and they had given him many fine grandchildren. Then, after a long and happy life, Tellus had died heroically in battle. He had been fighting in defense of his fellow Athenians, who remembered him with honor and gratitude. What more could any man want?

Solon greatly reformed Athens, though problems still remained. For example, the aristocrats continued to own nearly all of the land. But thanks to this one great lawgiver, seeds of change had been planted. In the years ahead, they would send up strong shoots and flower in memorable ways.

Demos Has Its Day

Solon was a noble who thought power should not be in the hands of nobles alone. This wise aristocrat was a friend of the *demos*, the Greek word for "the common people." But Solon was not the only Athenian aristocrat to take such a stand. After several decades of turmoil following Solon's death, another Athenian statesman made important changes. His name was Cleisthenes (KLIYS-thuh-neez).

Cleisthenes, too, was of noble birth. But his family had experienced exile and hardship at the hands of other powerful aristocratic clans. Cleisthenes believed the secret to a better Athens was a less aristocratic Athens—fewer powerful families and more powerful citizens.

In the year 508 B.C., Cleisthenes designed for Athens its first democratic constitution. He wanted to ensure that all citizens were represented in the Assembly and other governing bodies of Athens. Cleisthenes is widely regarded as the founder of Athenian democracy. *Democracy* means "rule by the people." And for the Athenians, who loved talking and debating as much as the Spartans enjoyed fighting, this was a wonderful gift.

Now all Athenian citizens, rich and poor alike, could make a speech and vote at the Assembly. No longer restricted to gossiping in the agora, the citizens of Athens could attend the Assembly and freely give voice to their views and concerns. Should a law be changed? Should the state go to war? Was a particular leader gaining too much power? Any citizen who wished could stand up and say his piece. Politics had become the business of every man, not just the wealthy or the aristocrats, the privileged few.

Athens had given the world its first democracy. While Spartans relied on oligarchy and military might, the Athenians embraced the rule of the people. In the centuries ahead, this young democracy would inspire all who sought liberty.

But first, Athens had to face severe challenges. In the fifth century B.C., like a dark cloud over the waters of the Aegean, a new threat loomed over Athenian democracy. The armies of the powerful Persian Empire were moving west.

How Democratic Was Athenian Democracy?

By modern-day standards, Athenian democracy was limited. Women, slaves, and many foreigners were not citizens. They could not join the Assembly, vote, or hold public office. But by the standards of the ancient world, Athenian democracy was remarkable. Compared to other political systems of the time, it granted a voice and a vote not just to the rich or well born, but to ordinary men.

Athenian warriors going into battle against the Persians at Marathon.

Defending Greece: The Persian Wars

While Sparta, Athens, and other Greek city-states grew in strength along the shores of the Aegean, another civilization rose like a new sun to the east. In 500 B.C., the mighty Persian Empire sprawled across an enormous expanse. The Persians, who began their conquest along the banks of the Tigris and Euphrates Rivers, conquered Mesopotamia, Egypt, and even parts of India. Then they pressed west, overwhelming Asia Minor and meeting for the first time the fiercely independent citizens of the Greek city-states.

The conflicts between the Greeks and Persians would come to be known as the Persian Wars. With their outcome rested the fate of the Greek city-states—and the future of Athenian democracy. Would the Greeks retain their independence or fall subject to a faraway king?

Darius, the King of Kings

The map on page 300 shows the extent of the vast Persian Empire around 500 B.C. It included most of Asia Minor, where Greek colonists had founded some cities.

- On the map on page 300, locate Asia Minor and the three leading Greek cities there—Ephesus, Miletus, and Sardis. Locate Sparta and Athens as well.

King Darius I, ruler of the Persian Empire and enemy of Greece.

The ruler of the Persian Empire at this time, Darius, was so powerful that his people called him the "King of Kings." Darius' army was massive and well-armed. Whenever

Persian Empire

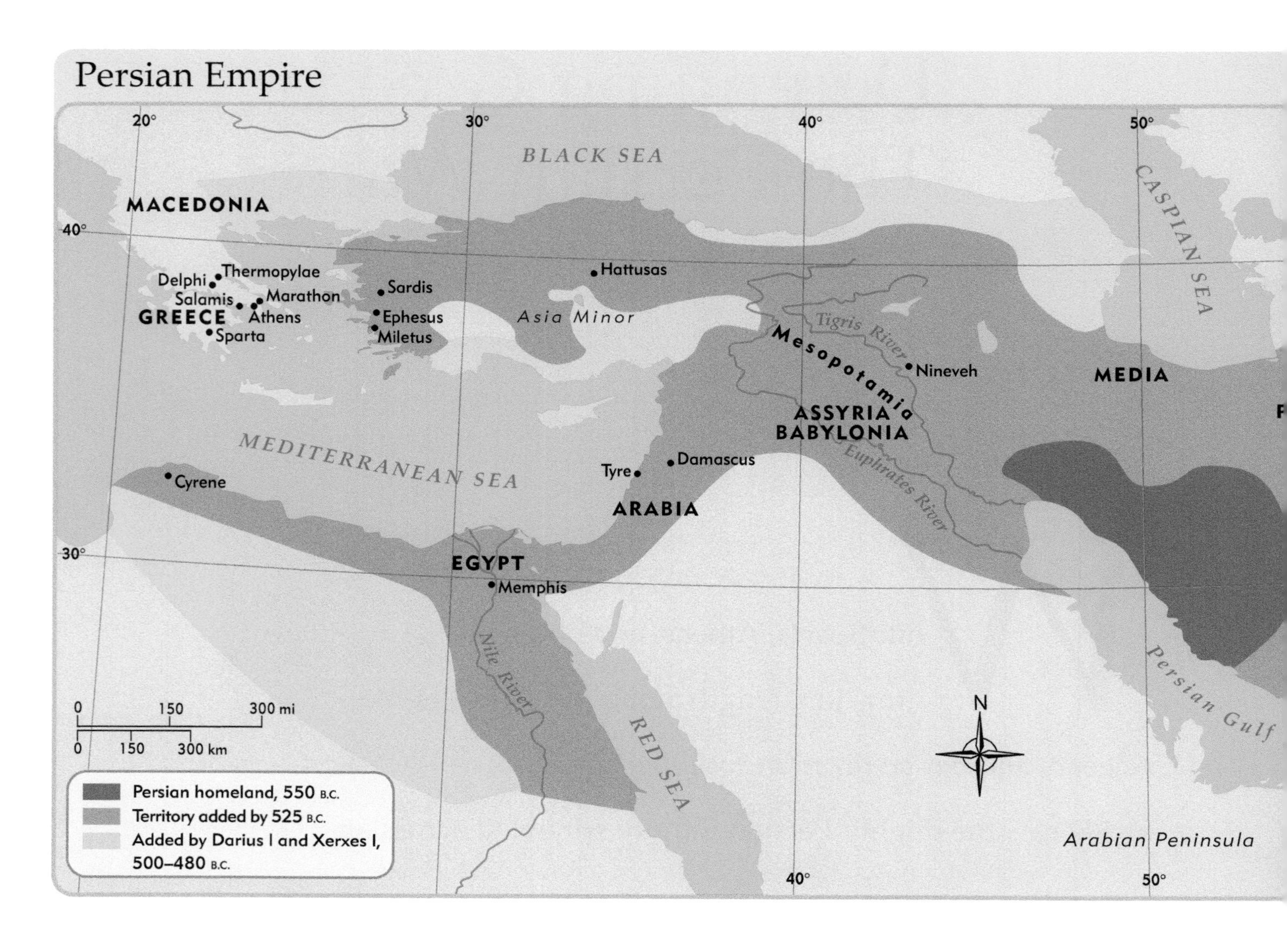

trouble brewed in his realm, the King of Kings dispatched armies to put down the unrest.

The Greeks, as you know, were proud of their city-states and proud to be free citizens. They strongly resisted the thought of living under an all-powerful ruler who reigned hundreds of miles away. So it won't surprise you to learn that Greek colonists in Asia Minor rebelled against Darius and called upon the city-states of mainland Greece for help. The Spartans did not lend a hand, but the freedom-loving Athenians answered the call by sending ships and soldiers to assist the uprising.

The rebels, with Athenian help, made a bold attack on the Persians and burned Sardis, one of the most important cities in Asia Minor. A shocked Darius demanded to know who had dared to help the rebels. "The Athenians," answered his men.

The Persian army soon crushed the Greek troublemakers in Asia Minor. But the victory did little to soothe Darius' anger. The King of Kings vowed never to forget that the Athenians had helped the Greek colonists. From that day on, a servant stood beside him while he ate. At each meal, the servant's task was the same. "Master," he repeated, "remember the Athenians."

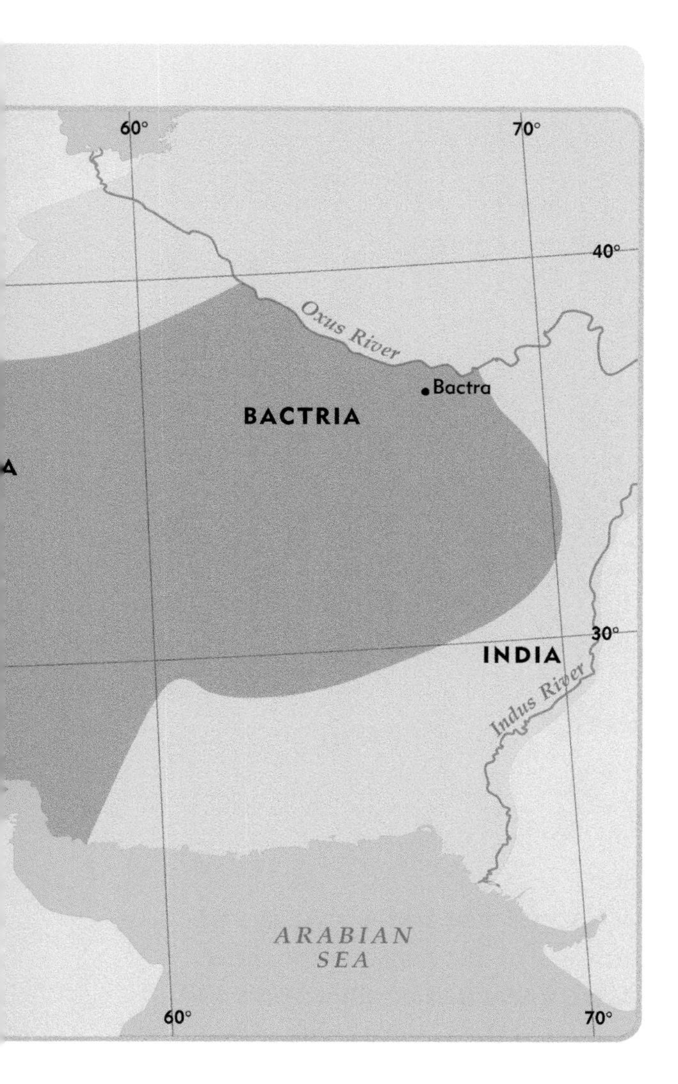

The Battle of Marathon

Darius bided his time, preparing his army and keeping an angry eye on the Greeks. After a while he sent messengers to Athens and Sparta.

"We come from the King of Kings," the messengers announced. "Darius intends to make this land part of his empire. There is no point in resisting. Give us some earth and water from your cities as a tribute. When we take it back to Darius, he will know that you recognize him as your emperor, and he will not attack."

The Athenians and Spartans were furious. They responded by grabbing the messengers and throwing them down a well. "You'll find plenty of earth and water for your emperor down there," they said.

When Darius heard the news, he was outraged. In 490 B.C., he dispatched the Persian army across the Aegean Sea. It landed on the Greek mainland just 24 miles north of Athens on the plain called Marathon. Frightened Athenians sent a runner to Sparta to ask for help. But the Spartans were not willing to battle the mighty Persians just then. They claimed they had to finish celebrating a religious festival and could not come until it was over. The Athenians would have to face the Persians on their own.

The prospects for Athens seemed grim. Its army was only half the size of the Persian force. Besides, the Persians were trained soldiers, while the Athenians were mostly farmers and shopkeepers. They had a weak

A Message from the King

Darius I, who ruled the Persian Empire from 521 to 486 B.C., wanted to make sure everyone knew he was a great king. He ordered a small army of workers to carve a message proclaiming his accomplishments onto a rock face in Persia, 300 feet above the ground. He had the message carved in three languages.

Centuries later, the writing helped archaeologists unlock one of the great secrets of the ancient world. One version of the messages was carved in the Persian language, another in the cuneiform of ancient Babylon. Archaeologists used these two messages to decipher the third. It turned out to be the writing of a civilization people had forgotten about for centuries. King Darius had led historians to the earliest known civilization on earth—ancient Sumer.

During the Battle of Marathon, the Greek forces (on the left as pictured above) fought in a densely packed formation known as a phalanx.

cavalry, and no bows and arrows. Yet the Athenians had three things in their favor. First, they were free men fighting invaders—they had the fierce motivation of those determined to defend their own land, homes, and families. Second, they had a fine general, a man by the name of Miltiades (mil-TIY-uh-deez). Third, they had a special Greek way of fighting that the Persians had not encountered before. They marched into battle in a densely packed formation called the phalanx (FAY-langks).

The illustration on this page gives you an idea of how effective a phalanx could be in battle. The phalanx usually attacked in a running trot, smashing into the lines of enemy soldiers. Looking over the plain at Marathon, Miltiades saw how he might win the battle. Most of his men had heavy shields and armor. The Persians, on the other hand, depended on their bows and arrows. If the Greeks could get through the storm of arrows that would be raining down on them, they might have a chance.

On the plain of Marathon, the two armies moved toward each other. When the Persians saw the Athenians coming at them without horses or archers, and so few in number, they thought they were madmen. But the Athenians kept close together and raised their shields to form a solid wall that saved them from the arrows. Then, at close range, they drew their swords and threw themselves at the Persians.

The Persians had put their strongest soldiers at the center of the line. Miltiades, however, had concentrated his strength on the ends of his line. Quickly his strongest soldiers beat the weaker Persian soldiers, then rushed in to help the Greek troops at the center. The Persians found themselves surrounded. They could not even retreat safely. Miltiades' plan won the battle. According to the historian Herodotus, 6,400 Persians died while the Greeks lost only 192 men.

To inform the Athenians of the great victory, the Greeks sent one of their soldiers, a strong runner, Pheidippides (fih-DIP-uh-deez), whose name meant "spare the horse." According to legend, Pheidippides ran more than two dozen miles from Marathon to Athens without stopping, over hills, rocks, and ditches. When he reached the city, he gasped, "Victory is ours!" and then dropped dead from exhaustion.

Prophecies of Woe

Soon after the Battle of Marathon, the Greeks discovered buried treasure. They found mines of rich silver ore near Athens. When the ore was mined, Athens would have great wealth. But what should Athens do with all that treasure?

Some Athenians thought the wealth should be divided: Let each citizen get a share, they said. Other citizens thought the riches should be used for building. Then Themistocles (thuh-MIS-tuh-kleez), a general who had fought at the Battle of Marathon, proposed a different idea. He thought Athens might not yet be safe, and the wealth should be spent to build ships.

Of course, as a port city and center of trade, Athens already had many merchant ships. But, Themistocles insisted, Athens desperately needed a fleet of warships, in case the Persians launched another invasion. The citizens agreed, and the Athenians used their new wealth to build 200 swift and slender wooden ships.

Miltiades, who led the Greeks in battle at Marathon.

Many Athenians wondered if their new warships would ever be put to the test in battle. When Athenians wanted to know what lay in store for them, they trekked high in the mountains to a place called Delphi (DEL-fiy).

- Locate Delphi on the map on page 300.

Modern-Day Marathons

The modern-day footrace known as a marathon is named for the legendary run made after the battle of Marathon. The official distance for a marathon race is just over 26 miles—about the same distance said to be covered by Pheidippides, the messenger who ran to Athens with news of victory over the Persians.

At Delphi, there stood a shrine to the god Apollo. The Greeks believed that Apollo spoke through a priestess called an oracle. This priestess was famous throughout Greece, for her prophesies always seemed to come true.

The Athenians sent representatives to consult the oracle at Delphi. Would the Persians attack again? Would there be war? If so, who would win it? According to the ancient Greek historian Herodotus, the priestess gave this terrible answer:

> Why do you sit here, doomed ones? Fly to the ends of the world! Leave your homes and the heights of your city. The head shall not remain in its place—nor the body, nor the feet beneath. All is ruined! Death is speeding in a chariot. Fire and the god of war will bring you low. The temples reel and tremble. Blood runs from their roofs. It streams in prophecies of woe. Go, flee from the sanctuary. Bow your hearts to grief!

Upon hearing this awful prophecy, the Athenians were terrified. The oracle was never wrong. Surely the Persians would destroy Athens and its people! But the Athenians prayed

Remains of the shrine to Apollo at Delphi, high in the mountains of Greece.

to their gods for mercy, and then they returned to Delphi and begged for another answer.

This time, the priestess delivered a very puzzling prophecy:

> All else shall be taken—even the gold of the holy mountain. But the all-seeing Zeus grants your prayers. The wooden wall alone shall not fall. It will shelter you and your children. But do not wait for the men on foot and horse from Asia. Turn your backs. Flee from the foe. A day will come when you will meet him. Divine Salamis (SA-luh-mus) will bring death to many women's sons!

This sounded a little more hopeful. Still, what did it mean? What was the "wooden wall"? Themistocles had the answer. The "wooden wall" meant the wooden warships of Athens. As for the oracle's advice, "Do not wait for the men on foot and horse," that meant that the Athenians should not fight on land. They should defend themselves by sea, in battle against the Persian navy. The meeting place would be near Salamis, an island close to Athens. To prepare, said Themistocles, the Athenians must build yet more ships!

Rowers and Rammers

Athens built the largest navy in ancient Greece. Most of their ships were called triremes (TRIY-reems). They usually had masts and sails, but the real power of a trireme came from its rowers.

The rowers sat in groups of three. Rowing was a dangerous job, because triremes sank other ships by ramming them. The Greeks built triremes with long, metal-tipped spikes that jutted from the bow just below the water line. At ramming speed, these spikes could rip a hole in another ship. Enemy ships also tried to ram the triremes, which put the rowers in great danger. The Athenian rowers were unarmed, and they were usually the first men killed in a naval battle.

Rowing a trireme was not only dangerous but also exhausting. The well-trained rowers had to work in perfect rhythm. That took strong discipline. They had to be able to follow orders quickly, for if they lost even a few seconds, disaster could follow.

The Persians used slaves to row their ships. The Athenian rowers, however, were free men. They were usually poor men, as well. Athenian foot soldiers had to have enough money to buy armor, but an Athenian rower didn't need to buy anything. All he needed was a strong back and strong arms, so even a poor man could help defend Athens by rowing.

Greek triremes often traveled under sail, but they relied on their oars during battle. Each warship had a metal-tipped spike to ram enemy vessels.

Persia's new king, Xerxes, reclines on his throne. Encouraged by his advisers, he planned a second Persian invasion of Greece.

Athenian rowers were proud of their skill and courage. They knew they played a vital role in defending their city-state. They served their polis well, they said, so why shouldn't they share in governing it? Why shouldn't they have the same rights as other Athenians? As time went on, and the Athenian navy grew more important, the rowers demanded more rights, and little by little they gained them. The growth of the navy not only gave the Athenians more confidence, it also helped Athens become more democratic.

Bearing Arms for Athens

In time of war, all citizens of Athens from about age 17 through 59 were required to serve as soldiers if needed. Armored foot soldiers called hoplites carried spears, short swords, and shields into battle. Hoplites had to pay for their own equipment, so they usually came from fairly wealthy families. A soldier whose father had been killed in battle, however, was armed by Athens at public expense.

The Brave Three Hundred

Ten years would pass before the Persians attempted another invasion of the Greek mainland. Darius died, and his son Xerxes (ZURK-seez) came to the Persian throne. If anything, Xerxes was more arrogant and ambitious than his father. He was determined to conquer the proud Greeks.

Xerxes amassed a military force staggering in its size—probably 200,000 soldiers or more, as well as several hundred ships. Surely now he would be able to take the prize his father had so desired. After all, the Greek city-states were small, and they weren't united. In fact, they were usually busy fighting one another. How could they stand up to mighty Persia?

The Greeks knew that no polis alone was strong enough to beat Persia. Their only hope was to work together. And so 30 city-states put aside their quarrels and formed a league of defense against the Persian threat. They agreed that Sparta, the warrior state, would be their leader.

In 480 B.C., the Persians attacked from the north. To reach Athens and Sparta, the Persian army would have to pour through a narrow pass in the mountains at a place called Thermopylae (thuhr-MAH-puh-lee). Thermopylae meant "hot gates" and was named for the hot springs that bubbled up from the earth nearby. King Leonidas (lee-AHN-ih-dus) of Sparta guarded the pass with only six or seven thousand Greek troops. They were vastly outnumbered, but they had positioned themselves in the narrowest part of the pass, where they hoped to hold off the Persians.

- Locate Thermopylae on the map on page 300.

King Leonidas' name meant "like a lion" in Greek, and if ever there was a man as proud and daring as a lion, it was he. As the Persians moved toward the pass, the Spartan scouts reported that there were so many troops, their arrows would darken the sun like a cloud. "All the better," Leonidas is said to have replied. "We shall fight them in the shade."

The Persians attacked again and again, but each time the Greeks drove them back. For two days Leonidas held the pass, but then fortune turned against him. Aided by Greek traitors, the Persians located trails around the pass and in the dark of night began to outflank the Greeks. Realizing doom was certain, Leonidas ordered most of his troops to retreat to the south. With his personal guard of 300 Spartans, he would hold the pass as long as possible.

Xerxes' army rushed forward. Leonidas and the brave Spartans stood fast for a day, but one by one they fell. When the sun went down, not one Spartan remained alive. Since that time, the Spartans at Thermopylae have been remembered as a great example of honor in battle and faithfulness to duty. Years later, the Greeks erected a monument at the pass that read:

> Pause, traveler, ere you go your way. Then tell
> How, Spartan to the last, we fought and fell.

A small force of Spartans battles the Persian army at the pass of Thermopylae.

Battle of Salamis

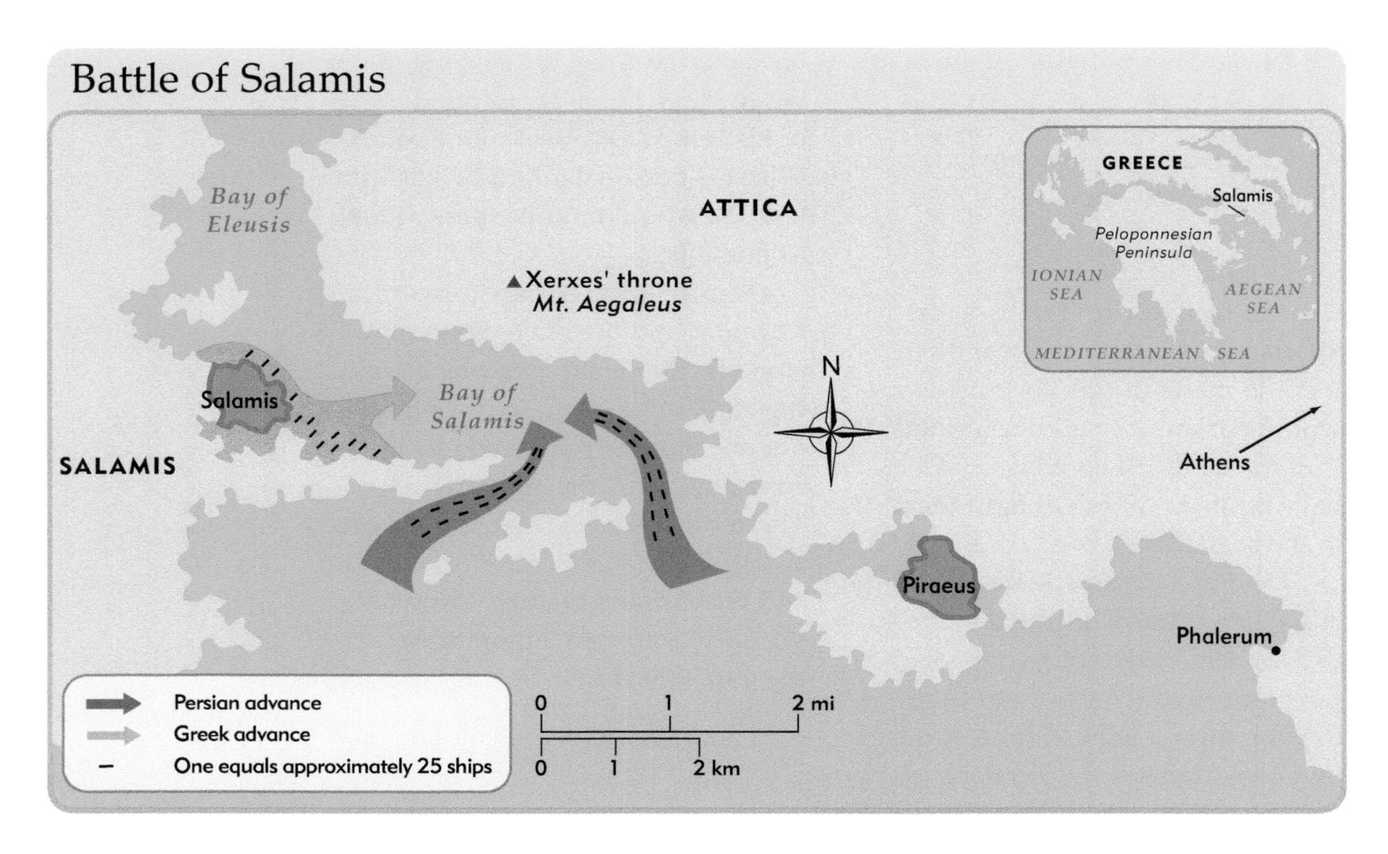

Xerxes had taken the pass, but at the cost of thousands of men and a delay of a few days. The time cost him dearly. He marched his army south from Thermopylae and found Athens empty. The Athenians had sent their families to safety on the island of Salamis. The Athenian army was waiting aboard ships nearby. The Greek soldiers could see Athens going up in flames.

How Long Were the Persian Wars?

The series of fights between Greece and Persia that came to be known as the Persian Wars lasted for half a century, from about 499 to 449 B.C. The most intense fighting came in the decade from 490 to 480 B.C., when the Persians launched invasions against the Greek mainland. The Persian Wars are sometimes called the Greco-Persian Wars.

Yet they did not try to stop the Persians. That was part of the plan. The Athenians had chosen to fight not on land, but on the sea.

The Tide Turns at Salamis

The cunning Themistocles, leader of the Greek navy, came up with a daring plan. Between Athens and Salamis lay a narrow strait, which the whole Persian fleet could not enter at once. The Greek fleet waited near one end, hoping to lure the Persian ships into the channel. That way the Greeks would have to fight only a few of the Persian ships at a time. (See the map on this page.)

The Persians took the bait. Xerxes, sure of victory, sat on a throne atop a cliff so he could watch his ships destroy the Greeks. The Persians rowed into the treacherous strait, thinking that they were moving in for the kill. Instead they found a well-trained navy waiting. Athenian triremes lurking nearby rushed forward to ram and attack.

Most of the Persians were foot soldiers unaccustomed to fighting at sea. The Persian rowers had to be whipped into battle. Worst of all, the Persians found themselves in strange waters. The Greeks, on the other hand, were good sailors and knew the waters of Salamis well. The Athenian rowers battled with the ferocity of men who were defending their own land, as indeed they were.

In the Battle of Salamis the Persians lost more than 200 ships. A horrified Xerxes watched his vessels sinking into the wine-dark sea. The mighty Persians proved to be no match for the little Greek city-states and the powerful Athenian navy. Xerxes felt lucky to escape with his men. Within a year he returned home. The Persian Wars eventually came to an end.

For the Greeks, the victory was enormous, and for the Athenians it was doubly glorious. After all, they managed to fight off one of the greatest armies in the ancient world. Greek poets, artists, and statesmen recounted again and again the stories of Marathon, Thermopylae, and Salamis. They would never forget that brave men had laid down their lives to keep Hellas free from a grasping foreign empire. The Athenians congratulated themselves on clear thinking and preparation.

Triumphant against the mighty Persians, confident in their institutions, and convinced of their own capabilities, the Athenians were on the verge of a time of greatness, a Golden Age perhaps unsurpassed in all of history. "The pillar of Greece, famed Athens, the divine city," as one Greek poet described it, would lead the way.

A Greek trireme—a huge eye painted on its bow—smashes through Persian ships in the waters off Salamis.

Statesman, general, democrat, and builder—Pericles was the leader of Athens during its golden age in the fifth century B.C.

The Age of Pericles

When the Athenians returned home after the Battle of Salamis, they faced a terrible sight. Persian troops had destroyed their shining city. Few homes were left standing. The city walls were in ruins. Even the temples had been burned to the ground.

Yet the Athenians felt far from ruined. After all, their navy had defeated the powerful Persians. And they felt sure that in a democracy, where free men ruled, great things were always possible.

So the proud Athenians began the task of rebuilding their city. They were determined to make it more glorious than ever. In the years following the Persian Wars, the Athenians filled their city with gleaming marble temples and finely sculpted works of art. Athens became the cultural center of Greece. It teemed with great playwrights and fine actors. Greek tragedies and comedies were performed in huge outdoor theaters. People also flocked to Athens to discuss exciting ideas and witness the city-state's lively democracy.

The Athenians accomplished so much following the Persian Wars that this time is often called the Golden Age of Athens. The period also goes by another name—the Age of Pericles (PER-uh-kleez). The age is named after a great statesman who led the Athenians for more than 30 years. His name is associated with the highest ideals and achievements of the ancient world.

One of Athens' outdoor theaters.

Pericles: The Man Who Gave His Name to an Age

Pericles led Athens during one of the most inventive and creative periods in history. He came from two of the oldest and noblest families of Athens.

His mother was a niece of the great lawgiver, Cleisthenes, who had given Athens its first democratic constitution. Pericles had been educated by some of the leading philosophers of his day. Yet despite his aristocratic background, his political sympathies lay with the *demos*, the common people of Athens. He was determined to continue the reforms of his great-uncle and serve his city-state by making it more democratic than ever. His belief that the people should rule themselves guided his career.

A sober, serious man, Pericles had a long pointed face that earned him the unflattering nickname "Onion Head." His critics accused him of being cold and conceited. They said that he allied himself with the people only to get power. To his admirers, however, Pericles was a brilliant man with a clear vision for the polis. He did not speak in public often, but when he did, the Athenians listened carefully. Almost every year, from 461 B.C. until his death in 429 B.C., they elected him to be one of their chief leaders.

A seated Pericles examines plans for the rebuilding of his beloved city after the destruction caused by the Persian Wars.

It was Pericles who inspired Athenians to rebuild their city after the devastating Persian Wars. Under his leadership, the Athenians continued to strengthen their navy. They built two long, stone walls protecting the route between the city and its harbor, Piraeus (piy-REE-us), so that even in wartime the city would be able to get food and supplies by sea. Pericles supported the work of Athenian writers, artists, architects, and thinkers. He wanted Athens to be a "school for Greece" where people could create great works of art and search for truth.

Perhaps most important, under Pericles more and more men gained rights and had a chance to share in government. After their stunning victory against the Persians, the city's rowers won the rights they sought. Pericles went further to guarantee common people their rights. Before the time of Pericles, public officials were never paid for their work. This made it hard for people without much money to serve in office. But Pericles established salaries for civic positions so that not just the rich could serve. He worked to change the laws so that the common people were allowed to serve in any public office.

Even under Pericles, democracy was not complete in Athens. For one thing, women and slaves could never become citizens, and thus weren't allowed to take part in the running of the polis. Still, in a time when many people in other lands were under the stern rule of a king or emperor, Athens stood out. Under the guidance of Pericles, Athens was the most advanced democracy the ancient world had known.

Athenian Democracy in Action

How did democracy work in ancient Athens? Let's imagine an Athenian citizen, Simon, and spend some time with him.

Simon isn't a wealthy man. He's a metalworker by trade, with a small shop in Athens. He isn't the best metalworker in Athens, but he has enough work to make a decent living. Simon is proud of his work, and he's even prouder of his polis.

Simon is a citizen of Athens—which means he is a free male age 18 or over, and was born to Athenian parents. He has served in the Athenian army, and like all citizens, he serves in the Assembly. The Assembly meets about 40 times a year. The meetings are held outdoors and begin very early in the morning. All citizens—especially those living in the city itself—are expected to be there.

Since Simon lives in the city, he can easily get to the meetings of the Assembly. It's not so easy, however, for citizens who live in the country. They may have to travel miles to get to the meetings, so they often miss them. And if they arrive late, they may not get in. The Athenian Assembly has only 6,000 seats and closes when it's full.

The Assembly is a powerful branch of the Athenian government—here, the people debate issues and make decisions. To be taken seriously at the Assembly, one must be a good public speaker. A speaker who can sway the opinions of the Assembly is a man to be reckoned with. Pericles, for example, commands much respect because he can state his views so eloquently.

In this ancient relief, a figure representing democracy crowns another symbolizing the Athenian people.

When a citizen addresses the Assembly, Simon and his friends are a feisty audience. When they don't like a speaker, they boo and hiss. They laugh at anyone who makes mistakes in speaking. If a speaker is really bad, the Assembly may even make him pay a fine. Who is *he* to waste their time?

When the time comes to vote on an issue, Simon votes by raising his hand. A majority of votes decides any question, and like all good Athenians, Simon obeys the decision of the majority. He obeys it even when he doesn't agree with it. At Assembly meetings, even though Simon is often loud and noisy, he takes the voting seriously, for he knows that it often decides the fate of Athens.

Simon usually enjoys the Assembly meetings. Politics is his favorite pastime. He talks about politics, he argues about politics, and sometimes he even fights about politics.

The Council of Athens is another body in which Simon can serve. Members of the Council are chosen by lot. Every year the names of 500 citizens are drawn from a large pot, and these 500 serve on the Council for a year. They carry on the day-to-day business of Athens, decide what things will be discussed at the next Assembly meeting, and write laws on which the Assembly will vote.

There are other ways in which Simon can serve Athens. The polis needs guards and market inspectors. It needs officials of all kinds. Someone must be in charge of the harbor, and someone must count the tax money. Someone must check the food supplies, and someone must run the warehouses. The officials who do these jobs are chosen from the Assembly by lots, and they perform their duties for one year.

It may seem strange that the Athenians were willing to fill so many important jobs by drawing lots. But the lottery system gave every citizen an equal chance to serve Athens in nearly every part of government. In that sense, it was a very democratic approach to running the city-state.

It may also strike us as strange that people who served in the Assembly, Council, and other roles did not need to have any experience. A street cleaner or barber might be chosen over a man with legal or scholarly knowledge. But this seemed perfectly reasonable to the Athenians. Pericles himself said that the simplest craftsman could understand the responsibilities of citizenship.

The Ten Generals

There are some jobs in Athenian government that are not left to chance. The chief officials of the city-state are called the Ten Generals. The Ten Generals command the army and navy. They are responsible for defending Athens. They plan strategy in times of conflict and lead the troops in battle.

The Ten Generals are more than military leaders. They are also in charge of carrying out the decisions of the Assembly and Council. They meet with foreign ambassadors and oversee the city-state's activities, such as the repair of ships and collection of taxes.

All this takes great skill and experience, which is why Athens doesn't choose generals the way it chooses Council members. Rather than drawing the names of the generals by chance, the Assembly elects them. Year after year, Simon and his fellow citizens elect Pericles as one of the Ten Generals.

Simon isn't afraid of the Ten Generals, because they hold their offices at the pleasure of the people. They must obey the Assembly. If the Assembly votes for war, the generals have to make war—even if they think the Assembly is wrong. In such matters, Simon's vote counts just as much as a general's vote. When a general loses too many battles, the Assembly votes on what to do. It may decide to fine the general or even send him into exile.

For the most part, Simon and the other citizens admire the Ten Generals. In the Assembly, they always give the generals a chance to speak and be heard. That's how Pericles leads Athens. He doesn't have any special powers. He can't order the citizens to obey him. But as one of the best speakers in the polis, he always makes a forceful case at Assembly meetings, telling the citizens what he thinks is best for Athens.

The Athenian Courts

From the early days of the polis, Athens had used juries to try cases. For many years citizens weren't paid to sit on juries, but Pericles suggested compensating them for their services. The citizens agreed with Pericles and made a law.

As part of his duty as a citizen, Simon sometimes serves on a jury in cases of murder, theft, and other crimes. Juries in Athens are huge. Most are made of 201 men. Some contain 501 men, and a few as many as 1,001! A jury for a trial is chosen by lots to prevent bribery. The Athenians have no full-time judges or lawyers, so jurors have a tremendous amount of power in deciding the fate of someone accused of a crime.

During the trial, someone makes a speech in favor of the accused man. Someone also speaks against him. Simon knows that a powerful speaker can sway the emotions of the jury, so he tries to listen carefully to both sides. When the speakers have finished, the jury votes whether the accused man is guilty or innocent. If guilty, each side suggests a punishment. Then the jury votes for the punishment it thinks is fair. The jury speaks for the people, and its decision is final.

Simon doesn't mind serving on a jury when called. In fact he welcomes it. Like most Athenians, he enjoys a good argument and well-spoken piece of rhetoric. But he also takes his jury duty seriously, for he knows that the right to a fair trial by one's fellow citizens is important in a democracy.

In our imagined character of Simon, you've seen just how deeply Athenian citizens were absorbed in the affairs of their polis. While Athenian democracy fell short of perfection—as you know, women and slaves were denied many rights, including the right to vote—still, those who qualified as citizens played an extraordinary role in running the polis and determining its future. Athenian citizens took great pride in their freedom, opportunity, and

Below: Athenian jurors used bronze ballots to cast their votes. Ballots with solid posts, like the lower pair, indicated a "not-guilty" vote; ballots with hollow posts, like the top one, indicated a "guilty" vote.

Bottom: Historians aren't exactly sure how this ancient allotment machine worked, but they do know that Greeks inserted tokens in the slots to help select government officials.

duties. Their ideal was that every citizen should have the experience, information, and interest to make wise decisions for the city-state.

Pericles and the Glory of Athens

The words of Pericles himself give us a good idea of the pride Athenians felt in their polis. In about the year 430 B.C., Pericles gave a speech remembered as one of the greatest in history. He gave it during a time of war with Sparta and some of the other Greek city-states. The purpose of his address was to honor Athenian soldiers who had died in the fighting. The speech is known as the Funeral Oration of Pericles.

How do we know what Pericles said so long ago? Fortunately, his words were reported by the ancient historian Thucydides, who wrote a history of the war with Sparta. Thucydides was a general himself and strove for accuracy in his writings, so it's likely that these words come close to what Pericles said.

The great orator Pericles honors Athenian warriors killed in a war against Sparta.

Here is part of Pericles' speech. Notice that he does not talk much about the dead soldiers. Instead, he talks about what they died for. He talks about Athens and why Athenians should be proud of their city.

I will not talk about the battles we have won. I will not talk about how our ancestors became great. Instead I will talk about our spirit and our way of life. I will talk about those things that have made us great.

Our government does not copy those of our neighbors. Instead, ours is a model for them. Ours is a democracy because power is in the hands not of a minority, but of the whole people. Everyone is equal before the law. We do not care what class a man belongs to. We care only about his ability. No one is kept from government because he is poor.

Our political life is free and open. So is our day-to-day life. We do not care if our neighbor enjoys himself in his own way. We are free and tolerant in our private lives. But in public affairs, we obey the laws. We especially obey the ones that protect the lowly.

Here is another point. When our work is done, we are in a position to enjoy all kinds of recreation for our spirits. There are ceremonies and contests all year. In our homes we find a beauty and good taste which delight us every day and drive away our cares. Our city brings us good things from all over the world.

And our city is open to the whole world. We never keep people out for fear they will spy on us. That is because we do not rely on secret weapons. We rely on our own real courage and loyalty. The Spartans, now, train hard from childhood on. We live without all their controls. But we are just as brave in facing danger as they are! Our love of beauty does not lead to weakness. Our love of mind does not make us soft.

Everyone here is interested in the polis. *We do not say a man who is not interested in politics is minding his own business. We say he has no business here at all!*

Looking at everything, I say Athens is a school for the whole of Greece. Future ages will wonder at us. The present age wonders at us now. Everywhere we have left memorials of our greatness.

I could tell you what we gain by defeating our enemies. Instead, I would rather have you gaze on the greatness of Athens every day. Then you would fall in love with her. You would realize her greatness.

Make up your minds to this. Our happiness depends on our freedom. And our freedom depends on our courage. Because of that, I will not mourn the dead. In their lives, happiness and death went hand in hand.

Architecture and Art in the Age of Pericles

The Athenians' pride in the polis showed not only in their politics but also in their architecture and art. After the Persians destroyed Athens, Pericles himself planned the new city. He wanted it to be the magnificent heart of a great and prosperous city-state. He wanted the Athenians to fall in love with their home. Pericles called the finest architects, artists, and sculptors of the day to Athens, and he persuaded the Assembly to provide money for building. The results were glorious.

The Athenians began with public buildings. High atop the Acropolis—the rocky hill rising 300 feet above the rest of the city—they planned a splendid group of temples and meeting places. The Greeks wanted their architecture, like all of their art, to reflect a sense of grace, balance, and perfection. Today, even though the buildings on the Acropolis lie in ruins, they still convey the Greek attachment to elegant proportion and simple lines.

On the Acropolis stands one of the grandest examples of Greek building—the Parthenon (PAHR-thuh-nahn), a huge temple to Athena, the patron goddess of Athens. Even in its ruined state, the temple is a dazzling reminder of the Greeks' ingenuity and achievement.

The Greeks constructed the Parthenon with 22,000 tons of pure white marble hauled to the Acropolis from mountain quarries 11 miles away. Massive columns surround the rectangular temple and help support its roof. Greek architects and sculptors carefully constructed the columns so that they swell slightly in the middle and then taper at the top. Instead of standing perfectly straight, they lean inward a little.

The Parthenon's majesty is still evident even in the ruins of the temple.

Up close, you might notice these slight irregularities. From a distance, however, the angles and measurements the Greeks chose make the columns look perfectly straight and even. If the ancient architects had not planned the gentle swelling and tapering, the columns might easily have looked heavy and clumsy. Seen from the city below, the great temple sitting high atop the Acropolis looks like an example of architectural perfection.

Behind the surrounding columns lay a huge enclosed space called a *cella* (SEL-uh), which was divided into two rooms. One room served as a treasury. The other contained a towering gold-and-ivory statue of Athena, carved by the most famous sculptor of the time, a man named Phidias (FID-ee-us). From her gleaming hilltop temple, the giant statue gazed down at the glory of Athens. You can imagine how the bright-eyed goddess might have smiled to hear a raucous meeting of the Assembly, or a noisy lawsuit being decided on the basis of eloquent speeches. Or she might have been moved by one of the dramas the Athenians loved to watch in their outdoor theaters. Or she could have thrilled to the voice of Pericles, urging Athenian citizens to think carefully about the decisions before them.

Phidias designed many of the statues and carvings that adorned the Parthenon. Sculptures on the east pediment (the triangular end of the roof) showed the birth of Athena. According to legend, she sprang fully armed from the forehead of her father Zeus. The west pediment showed the famous contest between Athena and Poseidon to see who would become the patron god of Athens. On the marble above the temple's columns, sculptors carved mythological battles between warriors, gods, giants, and the half-horse, half-man creatures called centaurs. Other carvings depicted the people of Athens, including priests, maidens, and men on horseback in a parade honoring Athena.

With its awe-inspiring proportions, rich carving, and heroic scenes, the Parthenon was meant to honor the gods. But it was also a tribute to Greek confidence in the talents of man. It was a monument to the glory of Athens itself. The Athenians wanted their city-state to be a showcase for Greek ideas and achievement. Pericles and his fellow citizens wanted visitors to gaze wide-eyed and exclaim, "Look what these Athenians can do!" They surely succeeded, because even today the ruins on the Acropolis boast of the grandeur of the Age of Pericles.

Greek Theater: Dramatically Different

The ancient Greeks gave the world a new form of storytelling—drama, or the play. Our word *drama,* in fact, comes from the Greek word meaning "action." The first Greek dramas took place during religious festivals honoring Dionysus, the Greek god of wine and fertility. As early as the 530s B.C., Athenians were holding contests for the best dramas. The winner of the first competition was a man named Thespis, the earliest known actor. Our word *thespian,* meaning "actor," comes from his name.

In this nineteenth-century depiction, a statue of the goddess Athena stands inside the Parthenon.

The Athenians built the Parthenon between the years 447 and 432 B.C., and they built it so well that it stood for 2,000 years. In 1687, some gunpowder stored inside exploded and wrecked much of the building.

Many of the Parthenon's famous sculptures were later taken to museums in Athens and London. In the British Museum in London, the sculptures from the Parthenon are known as the Elgin Marbles, named after Lord Elgin, the British diplomat who collected them and sent them there.

What's left of the Parthenon on the Acropolis is now being restored and preserved. The grand temple still inspires awe.

Elgin Marble

Greek drama reached its height during the Age of Pericles, when huge outdoor theaters were built across Greece. At these theaters, thousands of people gathered for drama festivals, which were partly religious ceremonies honoring the gods, partly civic celebrations of the city-states, and partly a chance for people to have a good time.

The most important festival in Athens took place in the springtime and lasted several days. At the Theater of Dionysus, on a hillside below the Acropolis, playwrights and actors competed for coveted prizes. Fourteen thousand people crowded into the rows of stone benches that curved around a circular acting area called the *orchestra.* Greek audiences were an enthusiastic, sometimes rowdy crowd. They spent whole days watching plays as they snacked on figs, sipped wine, cheered, hissed, and sometimes threw olive pits at the actors.

During the Age of Pericles, only a few actors performed in each drama—never more than three on stage at a time. All the actors were men, so they played both male and female parts. They wore big masks painted with exaggerated mouths to identify their characters and moods.

The rest of the performers—15 men or so—made up the chorus. During a play, as they sang or chanted, the chorus members would comment on the action, and sometimes take part in it.

Above: During performances, Greek actors wore life-sized terra-cotta masks with exaggerated expressions.

Below: Ruins of the great semicircular Theater of Dionysus in Athens.

Ancient Greece statues of masked comedians.

The Greek playwrights wrote both tragedies and comedies. The tragedies were usually about the relationships between human beings and the gods, and relationships between family members. They took their stories from old myths, the poems of Homer, or Greek history. Tragedies often dealt with human pride and ambition, and the punishments inflicted by the gods upon characters who showed excessive pride or arrogance. Tragedies often ended with the main character's death. The Greek tragedies are some of the greatest plays ever written. Even today, people read them and see them performed in theaters.

The Greek comedies poked fun at human foolishness and vanity. The Athenians felt free to laugh about almost anything. Sometimes they made fun of famous leaders.

From their plays, the Athenians learned about themselves. They could see how different people—great or weak, brave or foolish—faced life's challenges. The plays not only gave audiences a chance to enjoy themselves, they also helped the Athenians examine human nature and society. These wonderful dramas were yet another way for the Greeks to express themselves and explore their world.

The Great Greek Playwrights

The Greeks wrote hundreds of tragedies, but fewer than 35 survive. All but one of the existing tragedies were written by three playwrights.

Aeschylus

Aeschylus (ES-kuh-lus), the earliest of the great dramatists whose work survives, won at least 13 contests for tragedy. His plays were concerned with moral questions and sought reasons for the laws in the universe. One of his plays, *Prometheus Bound*, tells of the Titan who gave fire to humans.

Sophocles

Sophocles (SAHF-uh-kleez) was known to have written 123 plays, but only seven survive. He often explored man's ability to determine his destiny by using his mind and free will. His famous play *Oedipus* (ED-uh-pus) *Rex (Oedipus the King)* may be the greatest Greek tragedy.

Euripides

Euripides (yuh-RIP-uh-deez) wrote plays criticizing many Athenian customs, such as their treatment of women. He questioned the moral standards of his time and often portrayed the Greek gods as cruel beings. *The Trojan Women, Medea* (muh-DEE-uh), and *Electra* are three of his famous plays.

The Athenian playwright generally considered the greatest writer of comedies was Aristophanes (air-uh-STAHF-uh-neez), whose plays include *The Clouds, Lysistrata* (lih-sih-STRAH-tuh), and *The Frogs*. In *The Frogs*, Aristophanes made fun of the tragic dramatist Euripides.

A Day at the Theater

Imagining the Past

Dameon (DAY-mee-uhn) shivered. It wasn't the cold, although the predawn air still held a chill so early in the spring, especially on the windy side of the Acropolis. But rising before the sun was second nature to a country boy like him. At home, he'd be halfway through milking the goats by now.

No, this was a shiver not of cold but of excitement.

"You have the tokens to get us in, right?" he asked Timocrates (tih-MAHK-ruh-teez).

"Tokens?" His cousin stared at him. "I thought *you* had the tokens."

Dameon's heart plummeted. People from all over Greece had swarmed to Athens for the yearly festival honoring Dionysus, the god of fertility and wine. For the next few days, from dawn to dusk, the city's greatest playwrights would present their latest works, competing for the coveted crown of ivy.

No one wanted to miss the show. Without a token, Dionysus himself wouldn't get a seat in the enormous open-air theater that bore his name.

"You should see your face!" Timocrates laughed. "Such tragedy. What a fine model you would be for Poplio the mask-maker. A frown like yours could be seen from the last row of the theater."

He held out his hand, palm up. On it rested two bronze tokens, small and round, a single letter stamped on each.

Dameon was so relieved to see them that he almost didn't mind his cousin's teasing. It was all very well for Timocrates, who lived in Athens and had seen dozens of plays. He had even acted in the chorus under the direction of the celebrated playwright Sophocles, a fact he'd managed to mention at least ten times since Dameon arrived.

But for Dameon, this visit to the Theater of Dionysus was a lifelong dream. Once, many years ago, his father had traveled to Athens for the festival and seen Aeschylus stage his epic trilogy, the *Oresteia* (or-es-TIY-uh). The experience had proven unforgettable.

Growing up, Dameon never tired of hearing his father describe every detail, though he had heard the story many times before.

"Tell me again about the dead king," he'd beg.

"Bloodthirsty boy," said his father, but with a smile. "Oh, what a moment! All through the play, the queen was plotting, determined to take revenge on her husband, Agamemnon (a-guh-MEM-nahn), for sacrificing their daughter to the gods. And then…"

"And then…" Dameon echoed, knowing what came next.

"And then," his father continued, "a door opened in the *skene* (skay-NAY), the structure at the back of the stage. A platform on rollers was pushed out. On the platform lay the murdered king. And over him, frozen like a statue, stood the queen, holding—"

This was Dameon's favorite part. "A bloody axe!"

"The entire audience gasped in horror." His father shook his head. "Can you imagine? Fourteen thousand people, all at once, held their breath. Ah, Athens will never have a dramatic genius to equal Aeschylus," he sighed.

Now, remembering, Dameon sighed too. How he would have loved to see the *Oresteia*! But old Aeschylus had died not long after finishing his masterpiece. Today's contest would feature the work of a new generation of playwrights.

"I wonder who will win," Dameon said aloud. He shifted the cushion he carried under one arm. His cousin had warned him about sitting all day on a hard wooden step.

"Sophocles, of course," said Timocrates. "He always wins." Timocrates swung their well-stuffed picnic basket as he climbed.

Dameon couldn't resist the urge to needle his confident cousin. "I hear Euripides is very original in the way he retells the ancient myths."

"Euripides!" Timocrates snorted. "No one likes him. His heroes aren't heroic at all. They act just like ordinary people. Now, Sophocles—"

Just then, they topped the hill. His cousin went on speaking, but Dameon didn't hear another word.

The sun was coming up, and its golden-pink rays revealed a breathtaking scene below. Rows and rows and rows of steps, carved into the hillside and covered with wooden planks, descended in a giant horseshoe shape. It was bigger than anything Dameon could have imagined.

At the bottom, in the center of the horseshoe, was a round, flat area.

"The orchestra," said Timocrates, following his gaze. "Where the chorus members sing and dance and comment on the action. When I was in the chorus, I stood right there." He set down the basket and pointed, peering down as if expecting to recognize one of his own footprints.

Behind the orchestra was a raised stage, where Dameon knew the actors would perform. Before the time of Aeschylus, his father had told him, only one actor took the stage, and he had no one to speak to but the chorus. Aeschylus was the first to put two actors onstage together, where they could share news, discuss the situation, even argue. It made his plays much more dramatic.

Now Sophocles had added a third actor. Where would it end? Soon the stage would be as crowded with actors as the orchestra was with chorus members.

The wooden steps were quickly filling up. Timocrates said, "We'd better sit down."

The letter on their tokens told them which row they'd be sitting in. The two young men found their seats and set their cushions down between the markings on the wood that showed how much room they were supposed to take.

"In the old theater," said Timocrates, "the seats were wooden bleachers. Then one day the bleachers collapsed right in the middle of a performance." He glanced down at the center of the orchestra, where an altar sat garlanded with flowers for the occasion. "Maybe Dionysus didn't like the play."

Dameon shifted in his seat uneasily.

"Relax." His cousin clapped him on the shoulder. "The only way *these* seats could go would be if the entire Acropolis caved in. Anyway," he went on hastily, as if afraid the god might overhear and take him up on his suggestion, "today Sophocles presents his new play, *Oedipus the King*. Dionysus is sure to be pleased."

The sun had risen now, and the giant amphitheater was packed with excited spectators. To Dameon, every seat seemed full. The air tingled with anticipation. Sophocles was the reigning king of drama, and many were eager to see him triumph yet again. Others were rooting for one of his challengers to topple him from his throne.

Vendors hawking snacks added to the festive feeling. Dameon's stomach growled as the gleaming heaps of olives, figs, and nuts passed by. But when he saw the coins change hands, he was glad of their own picnic basket stuffed with bread and cheese.

Down near the orchestra, a sudden stir caught his attention. An older man in an elegantly draped wool cloak had just arrived. People moved aside for him respectfully. One of the judges, possibly? Or even Sophocles himself?

Timocrates leaned over. "That's Lasus," he said. "The backer of the play. I heard he spent three thousand drachmas (DRAK-muhs) on this performance."

Three thousand drachmas! Dameon could hardly imagine so many silver coins. His family could live for years on that much money.

The wealthy patron took his seat directly in front of the orchestra. "I wish we could sit so close," said Dameon. Their seats were far up and back, and he wondered how much they would see and hear.

"Don't worry," said Timocrates. "We won't miss a thing. The big masks make it easy to tell the characters apart. And the actors make their voices boom out to the farthest rows. The shape of the theater helps, too—"

He would have gone on, but the play was starting.

A masked actor walked out onto the stage, carrying a spear. On his head he wore a crown.

"Oedipus," whispered Timocrates.

As the doomed hero began to speak his verses, his deep voice flowing out to the waiting audience, once again Dameon shivered. He leaned forward, intent, breathless, no longer aware of his cousin next to him or the crowd around him. The world of Athens vanished as Dameon lost himself in the world of the play.

Alexander the Great's conquests spread Greek culture throughout the Mediterranean world and as far east as the Indus River.

A Fall, a Rise, and a Final Burst of Glory

The next one and a half centuries were a time of turmoil in the Greek world. In Athens, the city's vibrant democracy, timeless architecture, lifelike sculpture, and spell-binding drama all flourished. How long would that last?

The Athenians thought it would last *forever*. But Sparta was uneasy with the growing power of her rival. The tension between the two leading city-states of Greece would lead to a new outbreak of war and a humiliating defeat for once mighty Athens.

Even in defeat, Athens remained home to people of astonishing intellect and ability. Greek philosophy, which produced many of the greatest thinkers of Western civilization—Socrates, Plato, and Aristotle—shone most brightly after the fall of Athens. And another "great" had his moment in the sun as well. Even as the sun set on Athens, a young prince made plans to expand the power of Greece. Alexander the Great, as he became known, would try to make Greek culture everyone's culture.

Athens: Pride Before a Fall

In the decades after the Greek defeat of Persia, the confident Athenians, under the leadership of Pericles, cast their eyes abroad. They were now unrivaled masters of the sea. As their ships plied the waters of the Aegean, merchants traded the goods of Greece for products from distant lands. The Athenians began to forge a mighty empire.

At the close of the Persian Wars, Athens sought cooperation from other city-states on the shores of the Aegean. In 477 B.C., at Delos (DEE-lahs), Athens came together

After the Battle of Salamis, the Athenians were masters of the Aegean.

with the Greek city-states of Asia Minor and the Aegean islands. Together they established the Delian (DEL-lee-uhn) League.

The league's aim was to keep the Persians at bay. Each city-state gave ships and money to the league, which became powerful and rich. Athens gave more ships than any other city-state, so it was chosen to command the fleet and lead the league.

As the Persian threat declined, however, the league's member states grew uneasy with Athenian power and ambition. In 465 B.C., the island of Thásos (THAH-saws) tried to withdraw from the league. The Athenians took action. They sent their navy to blockade the island, forcing the polis to tear down its walls, surrender its fleet, and give up some of its territories.

The Athenians claimed such actions were necessary. The league, they said, must remain united. True, the league had brought prosperity to the region by securing the sea lanes and enforcing the peace. Trade flourished and industry expanded. The other Greek city-states, however, paid a heavy price for this prosperity.

Athenian officials began to meddle in the affairs of other city-states. Athenian courts stepped in to decide legal disputes among members. The Athenians made everyone else use their coins and system of weights and measures. By the time the league's treasury was moved from Delos to Athens in 454 B.C., the Delian League had in effect become a maritime empire under Athenian control.

***Maritime* means having to do with the sea, or with travel or trade on the sea.**

Greek Against Greek: The Peloponnesian War

One important city-state had never joined the Delian League—Sparta, the great warrior state ruled by a privileged oligarchy. From their citadel deep in the Peloponnese, the Spartans watched with alarm the growth of Athenian power. They had seen the Athenians intimidate their neighbors and roll over anyone who stood in their way.

The Spartans were not eager for war with the Athenians. The two city-states had a treaty. Sparta knew that a war with its eastern neighbor would be long and costly. Besides, the Spartans were land fighters; they had no interest in ruling the sea.

But when the Athenians began to bully one of Sparta's allies, the Spartans decided to take action. In 431 B.C., the war-toughened soldiers of Sparta once again donned their armor, grasped their shields, and prepared for battle—this time against Athens.

In the war to come, the many city-states of Greece took sides with either Sparta or Athens. Many of Sparta's allies came from the Peloponnese, the southern part of mainland Greece. That area gave the conflict its name—the Peloponnesian War.

The Athenian leader, Pericles, knew the power of the Spartan army. But he had faith in the walls of Athens—not just the stone walls that encircled the city like protective arms, but the "wooden walls" that were the city's ships.

The Athenian navy launched attacks on the Peloponnese, and the Spartans made raids near Athens.

But neither was able to deliver the decisive blow. For most of the war, the two sides were at a stalemate.

The Athenian attacks were bothersome, but they never really threatened Sparta. As for the raids of the fearsome Spartan army, Pericles had an answer. When the Spartans approached, he told the Athenian troops to take refuge inside the city. There they could live off the vital shipments of grain that continued to arrive aboard the Athenian ships.

Then catastrophe struck. A terrible plague broke out in the overcrowded city, perhaps carried by a ship from Egypt. People began to die by the hundreds, then the thousands. Lawlessness took hold of the city. The Athenians began to lose heart. By the time the plague was over, a quarter of the population was dead. Among the victims was Pericles himself.

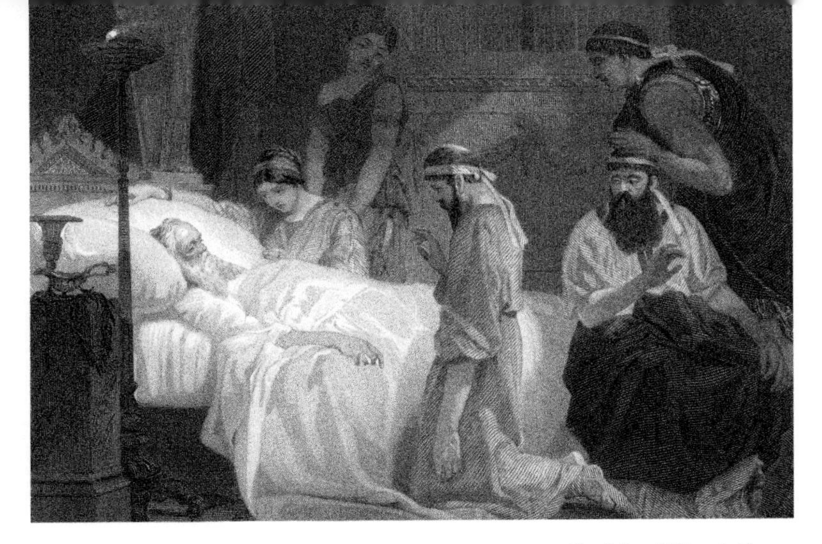

Pericles falls victim to a plague that struck Athens in 430 B.C.

The Fall of Athens

The plague-stricken Athenians were wearying of war. Desperate for victories, they launched a great expedition across the Mediterranean Sea to the city-state of Syracuse. Located on the

Peloponnesian War, 431–404 B.C.

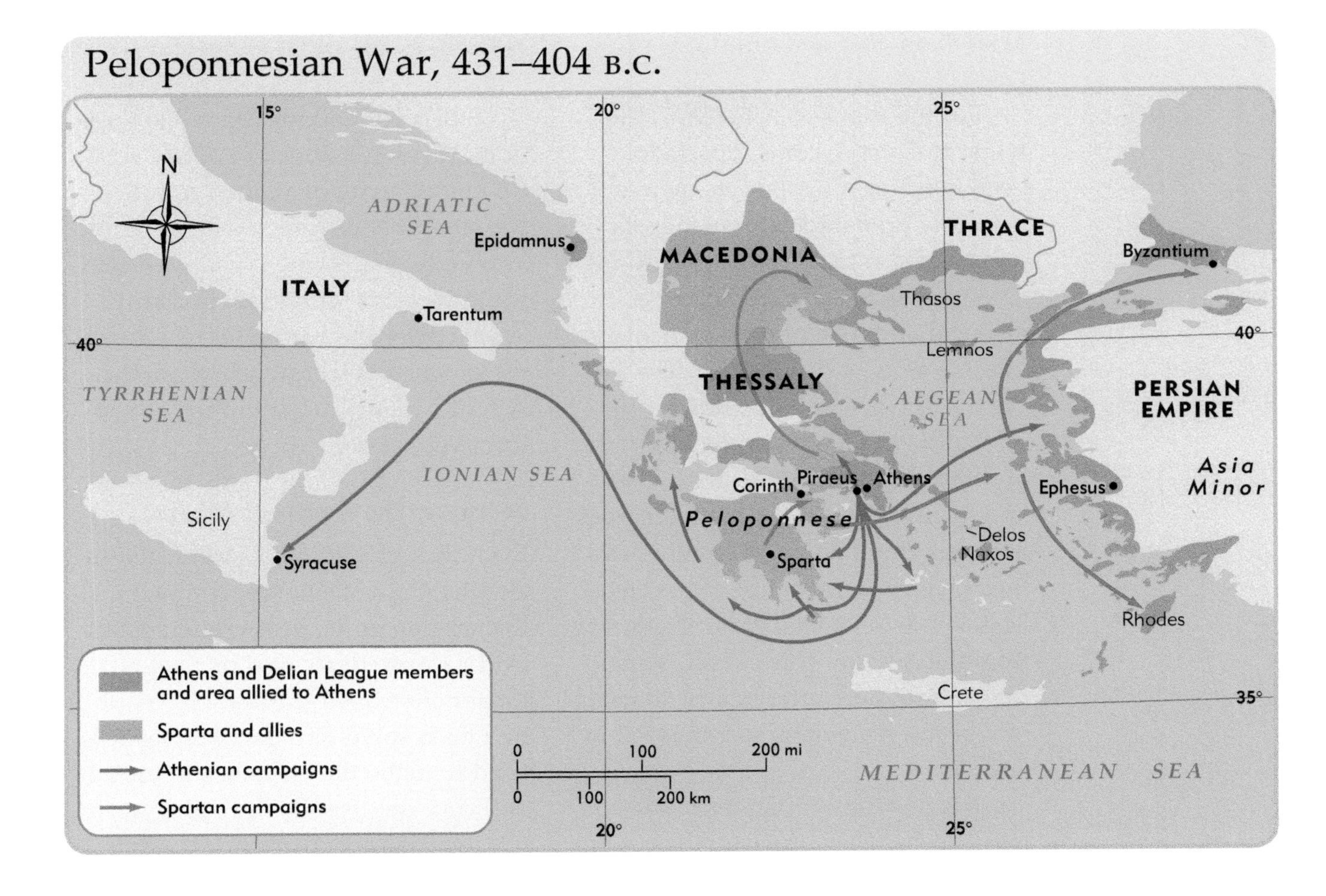

Already dominant on land, the Spartans eventually built a fleet capable of challenging Athens at sea. Here they attack Athenian ships off the coast of Corinth.

island of Sicily, Syracuse was rich and powerful, and a rival of Athens. A victory there would bring much-needed treasure to Athens. But the expedition was a disaster. Thousands of soldiers died and hundreds of warships were lost.

For the shocked Athenians, the worst was yet to come. Sparta had been building a navy of its own and was now prepared to challenge its enemy at sea. In 405 B.C., the unthinkable happened. The Spartan fleet attacked and defeated the Athenians in the waters of the Aegean. The people of Athens were devastated.

Following their naval victory, the Spartans blockaded the city by land and by sea. For a time, the Athenians held out. But many of their allies saw their chance to break free of the Delian leader. The city's vital grain shipments from the Aegean were cut off. Starved into submission, after nearly 30 years of war the Athenians surrendered in 404 B.C.

The victorious Spartans marched into Athens. They broke up the empire and cut the Athenian navy down to a small fleet. Some of the enemies of Athens demanded that the city be sacked and burned, and its citizens sold into slavery. But the Spartans refused, as a mark of respect for Athenian heroism against the Persians.

Still, the Spartans did try to wipe out Athenian democracy. They set up an oligarchy of 30 men to rule the city. The oligarchs, who became known as the Thirty Tyrants, treated the Athenians with great brutality. A year after the surrender of Athens, the people overthrew the oligarchs. A shaky democracy returned to the humbled city of Athena.

Socrates: The Gadfly of Athens

Even though democracy returned to Athens, the polis never regained its former power. Its best soldiers and leaders were dead, and its fleet no longer controlled the sea. Its wealth had been spent on war. New leaders tried to make the citizens feel proud and confident again, but Athenians felt their failures deeply.

During this dark time, when the glory of Athens seemed to be slipping away, a handful of great thinkers emerged—brilliant men who thought intensely about what had gone wrong and what is truly important in life. Some of the greatest philosophers in history lived and taught after these deadly wars, in the twilight of Athens.

Our word *philosophy* comes from the Greek word *philosophia*, meaning "love of wisdom." The Greek philosophers were truly lovers of wisdom. They were devoted to the quest for truth. What can we actually *know*? they asked. What can we be certain of? What is the universe made of? They were sure that by asking questions, thinking about things carefully, and using their powers of reason, they could find truth. Their faith in reasoned inquiry set Western civilization on a path that it follows to this day.

Greek thinkers had already been puzzling about truth and the workings of nature for more than a century when the man was born whom we now remember as the first great Greek philosopher. Socrates (SAHK-ruh-teez) was born around 470 B.C. He was an inquisitive Athenian who loved his city-state and its citizens. He served as a soldier in the Peloponnesian War and as a member of the Athenian Assembly. He wanted more than anything else for his fellow Athenians to think carefully about the best ways to live their lives.

Socrates put Greek philosophy on a new path. Earlier Greek philosophers had focused on nature and the universe. These earlier philosophers had asked: How does nature work? What are its laws? Socrates thought those were important questions, but even more important, he said, are questions such as: What is the right way to live? How can we know our true selves? What is the good? Socrates insisted: Pay attention to your soul and your character.

He led by example. As a young man and a soldier for Athens, Socrates received orders from the Thirty Tyrants to arrest an innocent citizen. The greedy oligarchs wanted the wealthy citizen's money. Socrates risked his own future by disobeying the orders. He even publicly challenged the tyrants. When they ordered several people executed for no reason, Socrates asked boldly if a good shepherd was one who got rid of his sheep. The tyrants warned him that *he* might be the next sheep to be slaughtered. Fortunately, the Thirty Tyrants were overthrown.

Still, Socrates kept asking uncomfortable questions. He wandered the streets of Athens, going wherever the

Socrates was the first great philosopher of ancient Greece. But his probing questions earned him many enemies among his fellow Athenians.

crowds were thickest, trying to get people to examine their beliefs about how to live a good life. He never accepted money for his efforts, so he was very poor. But that did not concern him. He cared about the soul, not the body. It is said that Socrates once stood in a single spot all day and night puzzling over a philosophical question.

Socrates taught not by giving speeches but by asking questions. "What is justice?" he would ask. "What is courage? What is beauty?" At first a man might respond confidently to these questions, but Socrates would then ask more questions. He claimed to be ignorant about the answers himself. The more he pressed his questions, the more he forced people to think hard about their own ideas. And gradually, they began to recognize their *own* ignorance. To Socrates, this—to acknowledge what one does not know—was the first step to wisdom.

Socrates believed that gaining knowledge, including knowledge of oneself, was the road to happiness. "The unexamined life," he said, "is not worth living." He urged his fellow Greeks to think deeply about right and wrong, about how they treated each other, about their religious beliefs, and about what was good for their souls.

Socrates called himself the gadfly of Athens. A gadfly is one who constantly questions or criticizes. Socrates kept pestering the Athenians to examine themselves and their society. Unfortunately, many people in Athens were in no mood for such persistent questioning. They were tired from war and defensive about their downfall. They didn't like someone constantly challenging their ideas and traditions. Some thought Socrates a dangerous man because he urged young people to question accepted ways of thinking.

In 399 B.C., resentful Athenians put Socrates on trial for his life. They accused him of being unfaithful to the gods and teaching dangerous ideas to the young. The great philosopher was condemned to death. While he was in prison, Socrates had the chance to escape, but he refused to break the law of his beloved Athens. On the day of his execution, his jailor brought him a cup of hemlock poison. Socrates took it from the weeping jailor's hands. Surrounded by family and friends, he calmly drank the hemlock and died.

The eighteenth-century French artist Jacques-Louis David (zhahk-lwee dah-VEED) painted this famous work called The Death of Socrates. *It shows Socrates, about to drink the poisonous hemlock, assuring his companions he has no fear of death.*

Socrates in Action

Here is an example of how Socrates questioned people to make them think about their own ideas. When the Athenians placed Socrates on trial, they accused him of teaching dangerous ideas to young people. Socrates defended himself by asking his chief accuser, Meletus (muh-LEE-tus), a series of questions. The account of the trial of Socrates was written by the philosopher Plato in a work called the Apology.

Socrates: Come here, Meletus, and let me ask a question. You think a great deal about the improvement of young people?

Meletus: Yes, I do.

Socrates: Tell the judges, then, who improves the young. For you must know, as you have taken pains to discover who corrupts them, and are accusing me. Speak up, friend, and tell us who their improver is.

Meletus: The laws.

Socrates: But that, my good sir, is not my meaning. I want to know who the person is who, in the first place, knows the laws.

Meletus: The judges, Socrates, who are present in court.

Socrates: What, all of the judges, or some only and not others?

Meletus: All of them.

Socrates: That is good news! There are plenty of improvers, then. And what do you say of the audience here—do they improve young people?

Meletus: Yes, they do.

Socrates: And the senators?

Meletus: Yes, the senators improve them.

Socrates: But perhaps the members of the citizen Assembly corrupt them? Or do they too improve them?

Meletus: They improve them.

Socrates: Then every Athenian improves and elevates the young, with the exception of me. I alone corrupt them? Is that what you affirm?

Meletus: That is what I stoutly affirm.

Socrates: I am very unfortunate if that is true. But suppose I ask you a question: Would you say that this also holds true in the case of horses? Does one man do them harm, and the rest of the world do them good? Is not the exact opposite true? One man—the horse trainer—is able to do them good, while others rather injure them. Is not that true, Meletus, of horses, or any other animals? Yes, certainly. Happy indeed would be the condition of youth if they had one corrupter only, and all the rest of the world were their improvers.

Above: Bust of Plato, the most famous follower of Socrates.

Below: Plato addresses a group of his students at the Academy, one of the world's first centers of higher learning.

Plato and the Philosopher-King

After the death of Socrates, many of the philosopher's students fled Athens. A dozen or so years later, one of them came back. His name was Plato (PLAY-toh), and he would prove that although the Athenians had killed Socrates, they could not kill his ideas.

Plato was born around the year 427 B.C. into one of the most distinguished Athenian families. His mother was related to the great lawmaker, Solon. At the age of 20, Plato joined the followers of Socrates and soon showed himself to be one of the most able students.

After Socrates died, Plato wrote accounts of his trial and death. Called the *Apology* and the *Crito*, these works describe the courtroom scene in Athens and praise Socrates' life, as well as the manner in which he faced death.

Saddened at his teacher's death and disillusioned with his fellow Athenians, Plato traveled abroad for several years. When he returned to Athens, he opened a school and taught there for 40 years. The school stood in a grove of trees said to belong to the Greek hero Academus, so it was called the Academy. At the Academy pupils studied subjects as diverse as astronomy, biology, mathematics, and government. Later generations and civilizations would build universities and colleges, but Plato's Academy was one of history's first centers of higher learning.

Socrates had left behind no writings, so most of what we know about him comes through the works of Plato. Fortunately for us, Plato was one of the most gifted writers of the Greek language. He composed a series of writings in which he recalled conversations between Socrates and his students. These writings are called the *Dialogues* because they portray groups of people discussing different things. The main speaker in each dialogue is always the revered master, Socrates. In these writings, Plato explored many of the questions Socrates had asked, such as "What is justice?" and "How do we live a good life?" After a while, Plato developed his own philosophy and put his own ideas into Socrates' mouth.

Plato was very interested in the best way to govern a polis. The death of Socrates made Plato think hard about Athenian democracy. In his view, the "mob" had sentenced his teacher to death, and he was convinced that uneducated, undisciplined masses could not make good decisions. He viewed democracy as a ship with an unruly crew but no captain, a ship that couldn't sail straight because the sailors were always fighting about who should steer.

In Plato's most famous dialogue, called the *Republic,* he turned his back on democracy. He argued that a polis needed to be directed by "philosopher-kings," educated people skilled in the art of governing. At his Academy, Plato tried to instruct the finest minds in Greece so that they might become such philosopher-kings.

Plato wrote about many different ideas in his dialogues—about art, what is best for the soul, how to be happy, and how humans must use reason to live good lives. His works are still read and discussed today. In the more than 2,000 years since he died, few philosophers have made us think so deeply about truth, beauty, and goodness.

Aristotle: Master of Those Who Know

Socrates had educated Plato, and Plato, in turn, schooled a brilliant young man who became the leading philosopher of ancient Greece. His name was Aristotle (AIR-uh-stah-tl). Born in 384 B.C. in a part of northern Greece called Macedonia (ma-suh-DOH-nee-uh), Aristotle was at home in royal settings. He was the son of the personal physician to the king of Macedonia.

Aristotle's intellect shone early on. He went to Athens and began attending Plato's Academy in 367 B.C., when he was just 17 years old. He studied there for 20 years. Aristotle was the Academy's brightest student. Plato called him "the intelligence of the school."

When Plato died, Aristotle left Athens. He spent time in Asia Minor and married a woman much younger than himself. Then he got a job offer. The king of Macedonia wanted this famous philosopher to tutor his bright young son, Alexander.

Aristotle worked hard to teach Alexander that the Greek culture was the most glorious that the world had seen, and the Greeks the most noble people. To inspire Alexander to be courageous and honorable, he told him the stories of the *Iliad.*

A relief shows Plato (right) and the most accomplished Academy student—Aristotle.

Eventually Aristotle returned to Athens where he founded his own school, called the Lyceum (liy-SEE-uhm). He became the most learned of the Greek philosophers. His curiosity was boundless, and he wrote on all kinds of subjects—botany, zoology, chemistry, astronomy, physics, politics, and drama. It seems that Aristotle thirsted to understand *everything.*

Like other Greeks, Aristotle was very interested in the ability of humans to reason. He did a lot of thinking about thinking. He was the first philosopher to analyze how people can use logic to reason well and be certain of their conclusions. Here is a simple example of the kind of Aristotelian logic called a syllogism (SIH-luh-jih-zuhm):

- Fact: All mammals are warm-blooded.
- Fact: A cat is a mammal.
- From those two facts, we can conclude that a cat is warm-blooded.

Here is another example of such logic:

- Fact: All men are mortal.
- Fact: Socrates was a man.
- Conclusion: Socrates was mortal.

For Aristotle, that kind of logic was just the beginning. His organized study of logic and its rules set Western thought on a path toward scientific understanding.

Like Plato, Aristotle also thought hard about the best way to govern a polis. Some people have called Aristotle "the father of political science." Aristotle defined three types of government, based on how many people rule. *Monarchy*, he explained, is rule by one person; *aristocracy* is rule by a few individuals; and *polity* or what we now call *democracy* is rule by many.

Aristotle argued that any of these forms of government could serve the people. Any of them, he thought, could be dedicated to the good of all. The problem was that each form could become corrupt. When monarchs abused their power, they became what Aristotle called "tyrants." When aristocrats abused their power, Aristotle called them "oligarchs." When the many of the democracy abused the few, then you had "mob rule" or "anarchy."

Aristotle had more faith in democracy than Plato, as long as people followed the law. In a successful democracy, he said, "the law ought to be supreme over all." Still, given the failure of democracy in Athens, he was wary of mob rule. He considered anarchy, or the absence of any law and order, to be the big failing of democracies.

Aristotle was widely admired in his time, yet he lived in an age when some people considered ideas dangerous. Like Socrates, Aristotle had his enemies. And eventually they charged him—like Socrates—with a lack of reverence for the gods. Remembering what had happened to Socrates, Aristotle decided to leave Athens. He died the following year, in 322 B.C.

Aristotle's Long-Lived Authority

When Aristotle died in 322 B.C., he left behind so many writings about so many things, it seemed as if his works contained the sum of all knowledge. He wrote so much that all of his works together are sometimes called "the world's first encyclopedia."

In later centuries, Aristotle would be called "master of those who know." Scholars cited him as a trusted authority: "Of course," they would say, "according to Aristotle...." Hardly a branch of science, philosophy, religion, or art grew without feeling his influence. His works on science were relied on for centuries. So great was Aristotle's authority that even when he was wrong—such as his view of the universe as a series of spheres—it proved difficult for people to accept new facts or evidence that contradicted him!

Alexander the Great

Even before Aristotle's death, power in Greece was shifting north toward Macedonia, the birthplace of the

great philosopher. After the Peloponnesian War, Greek city-states to the south had grown weaker. Yet their culture and ideas continued to spread far and wide. How did this come about?

In 359 B.C., an ambitious man named Philip II seized the throne of Macedonia. He united the tribes in that area, put together an army, and turned it against the city-states of Greece. The Macedonians quickly triumphed. Soon most of Greece lay under Philip's control.

- On the map on page 329, locate Macedonia.

Philip had a son named Alexander, and there was never any doubt that the boy would follow in his father's footsteps. It is said that as a child Alexander burst into tears because he was worried Philip wouldn't leave any lands for him to conquer.

It was this willful child that King Philip summoned Aristotle to teach. Alexander studied under the great philosopher for three years. While Aristotle taught Alexander to love Greek culture, he did not succeed in teaching the boy to control his desires.

Alexander was ambitious to a fault. He had his heart set on conquering as much of the world as he could. And he got his chance in 336 B.C. when Philip was murdered by one of his own officers. Alexander became king at the age of 20 and almost at once set out to conquer new territories.

For inspiration Alexander carried a copy of Homer's *Iliad* with him throughout his campaigns. Alexander liked to think of himself in terms of the old Greek heroes. In fact, his mother had assured him that the great hero Achilles was one of her ancestors. His father had told him that his side of the family was descended from Hercules. Distinguished ancestry indeed for a would-be conqueror!

We get a glimpse of Alexander's determination and pride in the famous story of the Gordian Knot. It is said that early in his career, Alexander came to a town in Asia Minor named

Above: A gold coin with the head of Philip II of Macedonia, father of the man history remembers as Alexander the Great.

Below: Arm outstretched to emphasize a point, Aristotle instructs the young Alexander in Greek culture and learning.

Gordium, and there he saw something quite strange—a huge, complicated knot of rope. An ancient prophecy said that whoever managed to unravel it would rule all of Asia. Alexander looked carefully at the knot, contemplated the task, then raised his sword and sliced through the knot. "Thus I cut all Gordian knots," the young king declared.

Above: Alexander the Great rides in triumph into the ancient city of Babylon.

Below: The Macedonian army wins a great victory over the Persians in Asia Minor. Eventually, Alexander would forge an empire that extended from the Adriatic into India.

Alexander proved to be a brilliant general, and soon his army was sweeping across Asia. He conquered the Persian Empire. He pressed into Mesopotamia. He took over Egypt. He marched over the Hindu Kush mountains to the banks of the Indus River, and didn't even flinch when confronting an army of war elephants. No wonder he became known as Alexander the Great. His conquests stretched over a million square miles—the largest empire the world had known.

- On the map on page 339, note the extent of Alexander's empire.

Alexander's ego seemed to expand with his conquests. Wherever he went, he founded cities, and tradition has it that he named more than 70 after himself. Alexandria in Egypt would become the most important of these cities.

Meanwhile, he alarmed his soldiers by adopting Eastern customs in his personal life. He fancied himself something of an Eastern monarch and dressed in long, flowing Persian robes. He married a Persian princess and arranged for 80 of his officers to marry Persian women at a huge wedding ceremony. He even adopted the Persian tradition of making his officers lie on the ground before him when they made requests. The action infuriated his own men. The freedom-loving Greeks, after all, had a long history of battling Persian emperors who had tried to lay them low.

Finally, after years of fighting, Alexander's weary men refused to go on. They would fight no more for the proud man who had started to think of himself as a god. Reluctantly, Alexander started back toward home. He never made it. In 323 B.C., after a night of heavy drinking, Alexander the Great contracted a fever and died in Babylon in a soldier's tent. He was 32 years old and had been king for 13 years.

The Hellenistic Age

Alexander's empire fell apart soon after his death. In the coming years, the military might of the Greeks became only a memory. But Alexander's conquests did much to change a large part of the world. Greek settlers immigrated to the cities Alexander founded, and Greek traders traveled far and wide. They took with them the Greek language and ideas. Greek laws, architecture, and art spread through Asia and North Africa. So did Greek science and philosophy.

At the same time, many Eastern ideas spread into Europe. Alexander's campaigns had opened the eyes of the Greeks to whole new worlds. Just as Alexander had mixed Greek and Persian customs in his personal life, the people of Greece, Asia, and North Africa began to absorb parts of each other's cultures.

Never before had ideas and traditions traveled so much. We call this time when Greek and Eastern cultures mixed the Hellenistic Age. It lasted for some 300 years after Alexander's death in 323 B.C. The term *Hellenistic* comes from the word *Hellenes*, the Greeks' own name for themselves.

During the Hellenistic Age, Greek civilization became the common bond throughout much of the world surrounding the Mediterranean Sea. As we'll see, the lofty ideas of the Greeks would deeply influence other empires and ages to come.

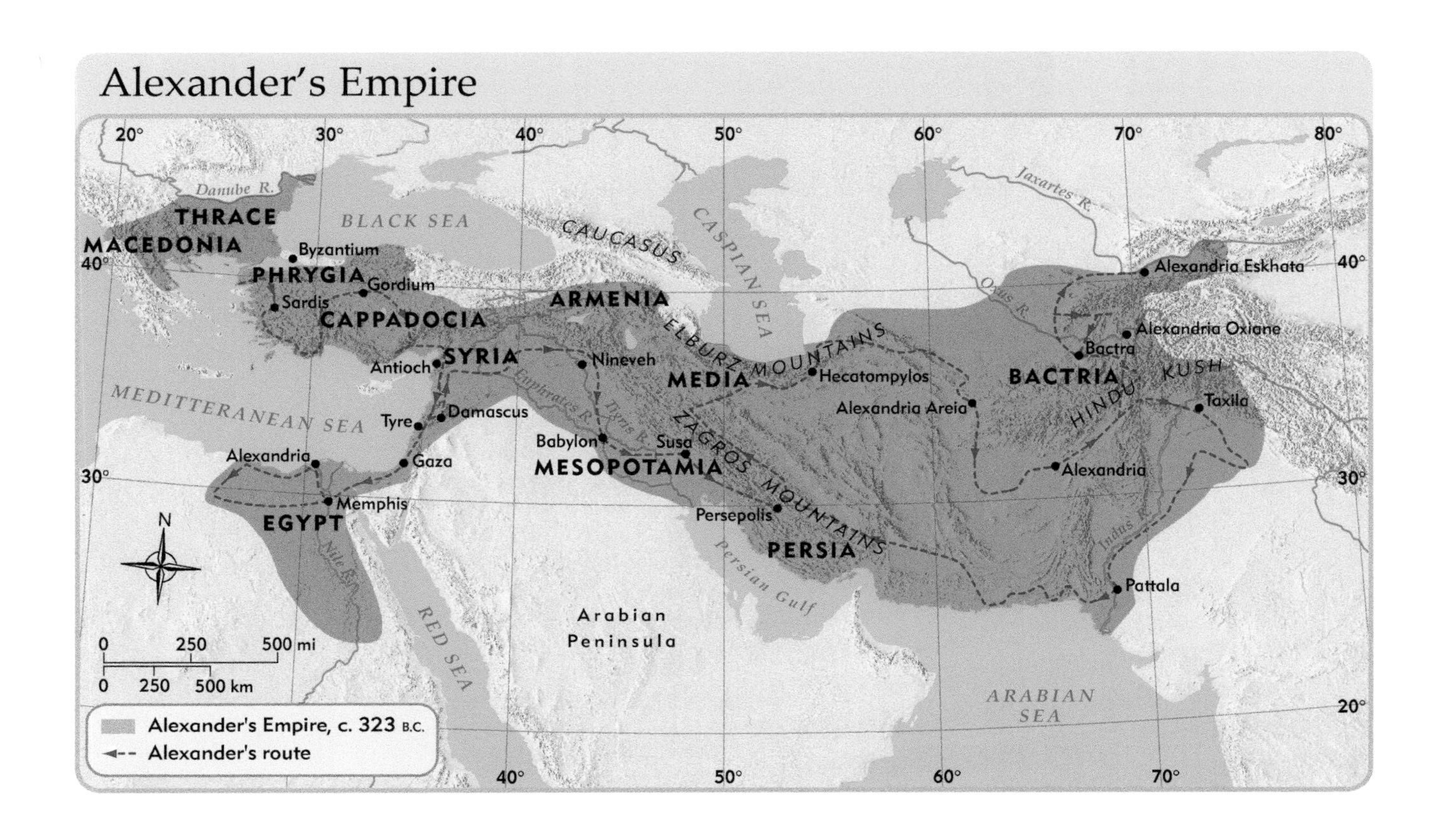

This temple on the banks of the Tiber River was dedicated to the Roman god of ports and harbors.

The Roman Republic

West of Greece, the boot-shaped Italian peninsula stretches south into the Mediterranean Sea. On a map, the boot looks as if it's marching west. That's a good symbol for what happened in the years following the decline of Athens and the breakup of Alexander's empire. In many ways, the center of power and culture in the Mediterranean world shifted west from Greece to Italy.

One city on the Italian peninsula was responsible for that westward shift—Rome. From a community of shepherds housed in mud huts, Rome became a vibrant city spreading over seven hills. It also became the center of the largest empire the world had yet known.

For more than a thousand years, the power of Rome grew. Its laws and language followed its soldiers over thousands of miles of land and sea. Its ideas and customs took root around the globe. Many of these ideas still help shape our culture.

What are these ideas and how did the Romans develop them? To find out, let's return to the very beginnings of Rome.

The Hills and Plains of Latium

Rome began as a tiny farming village in Latium, a fertile plain in central Italy south of the Tiber River. The first settlers of Latium were called "Latins" —that is, "people of Latium." One of many small tribes in ancient Italy, the Latins found lakes, springs, woods, and good pasture land in Latium. They also found a number of steep wooded hills rising from the plains. There, safe from enemy attacks, they built their early settlements.

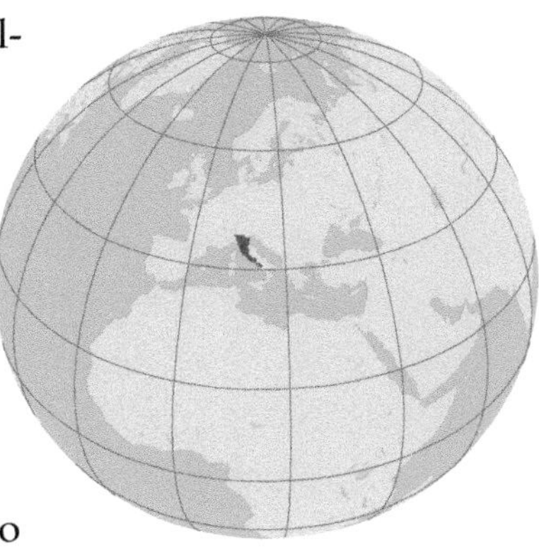

This chapter explores Rome, a city in the Mediterranean land of Italy that gave its name to an entire civilization.

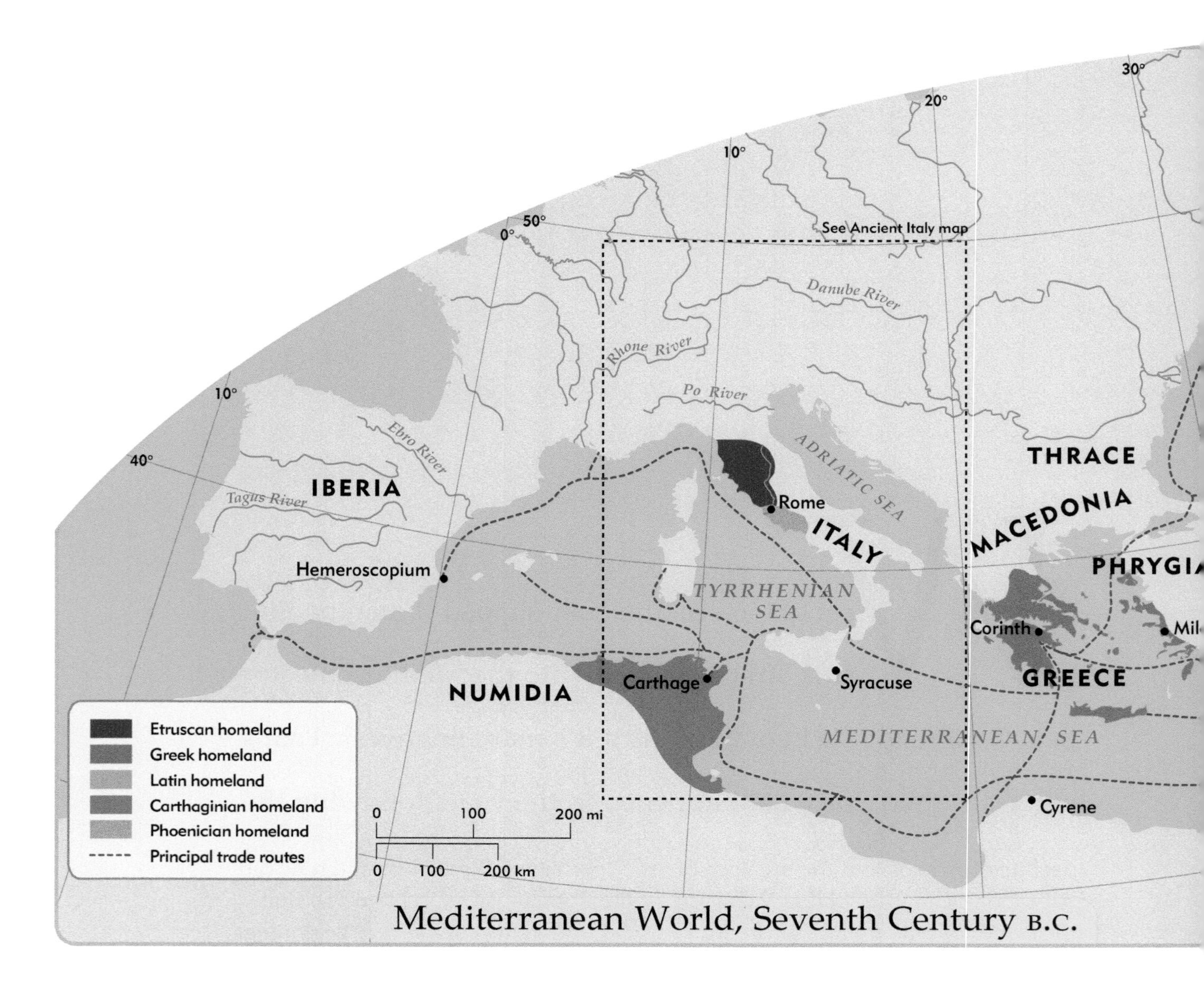

Mediterranean World, Seventh Century B.C.

The Latins enjoyed many other advantages in central Italy. Like much of Greece, Italy basks in a Mediterranean climate, with hot, sunny summers and mild, rainy winters. Wheat grew well there, and winter rains made the grass lush and long. The Latins kept oxen, goats, sheep, pigs, and chickens. This community of farmers and shepherds learned to plant fruit and olive trees. Like the Greeks, the Latins found olive oil valuable for trade.

- On the map directly above, locate the following: the Mediterranean Sea, Asia Minor, Italy, Greece and Macedonia, Rome, Egypt, Adriatic Sea, and Tyrrhenian Sea.
- On the map of Ancient Italy on page 343, locate the following: the Tiber River, Latium, Arno River, Rome, Po River, Adriatic Sea, and Tyrrhenian Sea.

Rome itself began on the Palatine, (PA-luh-tiyn) one of the steep hills settled by the Latins. This wooded hill was close to a small island in the Tiber River. The island was a fine place to cross the Tiber, and the Palatine was a very good place for

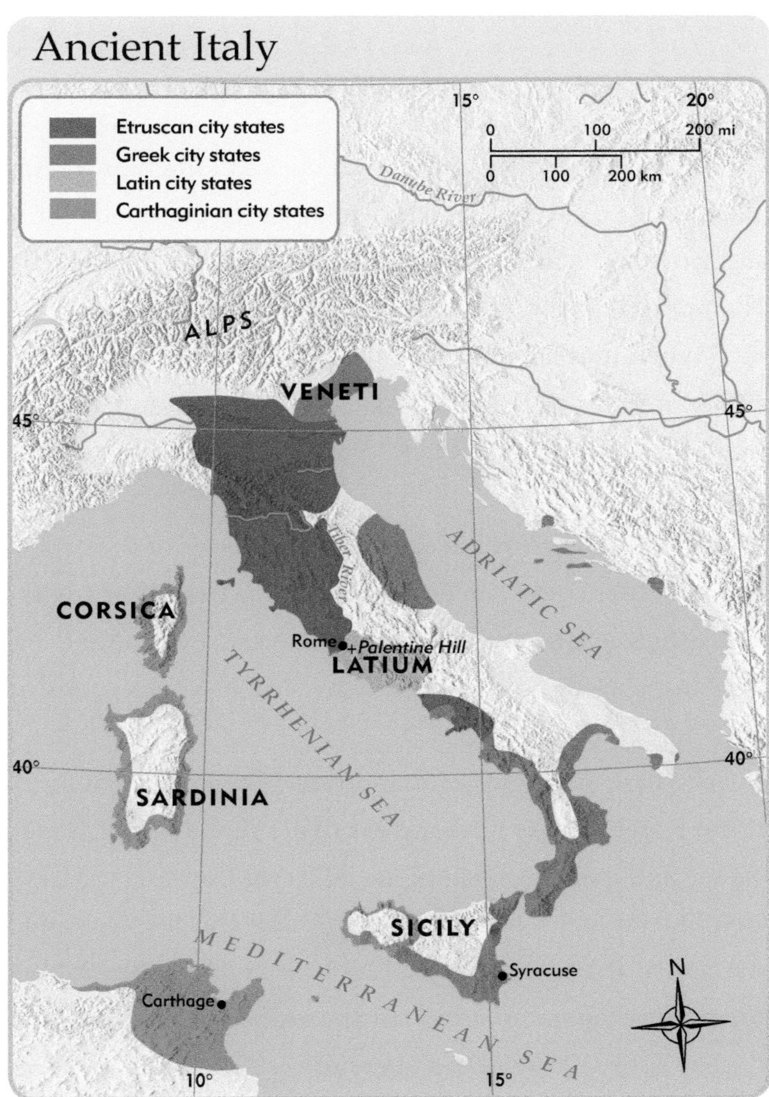

The ruins of ancient buildings rise from the Palatine, one of the seven hills where the city of Rome began.

controlling the island. So whoever controlled the Palatine controlled both the river and the plain.

The Palatine had two other advantages. First, it was surrounded by six other hills, which made it easy to defend. Second, the settlers could use the nearby Tiber River for passage to the Mediterranean Sea.

No one really knows when Rome was first built, not even the Romans themselves. They chose April 21, 753 B.C., as a starting date for their history. They told a famous legend about how the city was founded.

The Legend of Romulus and Remus

Long ago in Italy there lived a wicked king named Amulius (uh-MYOO-lee-us). One day he heard some news that made him pace the floor and frown. His niece, he had learned, had just given birth to twin baby boys. The father was the Roman god of war, Mars.

"When these children grow up," Amulius fretted, "one of them might try to take my throne." So he issued a terrible order. He told a servant to carry the babies to the Tiber River. "Fling them into the water," he said, "and make sure they drown."

The servant drew his cloak over the faces of the crying infants and hurried away. But when he reached the river, his heart filled with pity. "I cannot bear to see these babes drown before my eyes," he thought. So he wrapped the boys in the cloak, put them side by side in a basket, and pushed the basket onto the river.

The basket drifted until nightfall, when it caught in the roots of a fig tree at the water's edge. It happened that a mother wolf was roaming the Tiber's banks, and, hearing feeble cries, she crept up to the basket. The babies didn't look like her cubs, but they were young and helpless and hungry. With a tug she pulled the basket out of the water and dragged it back to her cave. There she nursed them and cared for the twins as if they were her own.

Not long afterwards, a shepherd looking for a lost lamb passed the cave and heard happy cries from within. Creeping inside, he spotted two plump

baby boys. The shepherd took them home, and he and his wife brought them up as their own sons. The couple named the boys Romulus (RAHM-yuh-lus) and Remus (REE-mus).

Years passed, and Romulus and Remus grew up to be strong young men. One day they were hunting in a forest beside the Tiber, and as they looked around they noticed seven hills.

"That would be a safe place for a city," said Remus.

"True," Romulus agreed. "A city on seven hills would be easy to defend."

So they asked every shepherd they knew to help them build a city. Using sharpened stakes and wooden spades, the men began the work. They built a few huts of mud and straw. Romulus and Remus built the best house for themselves, constructing it of stone and clay.

Then trouble began. Who would rule the new city? Both Romulus and Remus claimed the right. They agreed to let the gods decide.

All night long, Remus sat alone on the summit of a hill called the Aventine (A-vuhn-tiyn). Romulus sat alone on the Palatine. At last dawn appeared, feeble and gray on the hilltops. Remus, watching from his lonely post, saw six vultures winging their way overhead.

"Look, a sign!" he called. "The gods have chosen me!"

But a few minutes later, the deep-toned voice of Romulus rang out.

"The victory belongs to me! I see twelve vultures flying over the Palatine!"

Romulus decided to name the city after himself—Rome. At once he began to lay the boundaries of his little town. Remus, meanwhile, skulked and complained.

"We must have a strong wall around our city," Romulus declared.

The shepherds began the work. Soon a wall of earth and loose stones was rising around the new city. It was only waist high and looked crooked, so it was little wonder that Remus laughed at it.

"What a fine, strong wall it is!" he sneered, and running forward he leaped over it with a bound.

His feet had barely touched the ground when a furious Romulus struck him with a jagged rock. "You will not laugh at Rome!" the angry brother shouted. Remus fell, speechless and bleeding, to the ground. A few minutes later, he was dead.

"Thus perish all who attempt to pass the walls of Rome!" Romulus declared.

According to legend, that is how Rome began. Nowadays, if you visit Rome, you'll see bronze statues of two boys playing beneath a she-wolf, trying to get her milk. Romulus and Remus are still celebrated as the city's founders.

It is said that at the time Romulus killed Remus, people began to prophesy. "Twelve vultures flew over Romulus," they said. "Each vulture stands for 100 years in the life of his city. That means the power of Rome will last for 1,200 years." How close did they come to being right? According to tradition, Rome began in 753 B.C. The last emperor to live in Italy gave up his throne in A.D. 476. Figure it out!

Marcus Agricola, a Boy of Early Rome

We can learn about life in early Rome by spending a little time with a 10-year-old Roman boy. We'll call him Marcus Agricola (uh-GRIK-uh-luh). Marcus was born in 460 B.C. He isn't very tall, but he is wiry and strong.

A Roman plowman urges on a pair of oxen while another man sows seeds from his basket.

Life isn't easy for Marcus and his family. They have a mud-brick home inside the city walls. They spend most of their time outside the city, because that's where their farm is. Farming is hard work for the entire family. It takes great strength to handle the wooden plow. Marcus isn't strong enough to help with plowing, but he can help hoe and dig. He can also help trim the trees in the orchard. Marcus and his older brothers all have their share of chores.

When Marcus isn't working, he loves to wander around the countryside. Often he goes out to hunt small animals such as rabbits. His catches are always welcome at meal time. Marcus and his friends may go swimming in the river, even on cold days. Roman boys are raised to be tough. They can stand all kinds of hardships, including the cold.

Sometimes Marcus and his friends fight with wooden swords. As boys, they're only playing, but when they grow up they'll fight for real. A Roman must always be ready to drop his plow and grab his sword to defend his city. There is always danger that another tribe will attack the Roman fields.

Marcus has a sister named Claudia. A hard worker, she helps her mother grind wheat into flour and cook the meals. The two spin thread and weave cloth. Claudia helps make clothes for Marcus and the rest of the family. Making clothes and preparing food take up much of the women's time. Claudia's mother is usually very busy because it's her job to oversee the management of the household.

Claudia and Marcus know what their lives will be like when they grow up. Claudia will be a Roman wife and mother. Marcus will have a bit of land to farm. He'll become a Roman citizen. Already he knows that he will have to understand several things very clearly. The most important of these are the values of *authority* and *discipline.* Let's see what these words mean to Marcus and his family.

The Paterfamilias in Early Rome

Discipline means several things to Marcus. It means behaving well in front of other people. It means not complaining when there is not enough to eat. It means obeying his elders. Marcus wants to be very disciplined because he knows Romans admire that virtue. He also knows that it takes hard work to make a living in Rome, and that hard work demands discipline.

When Marcus thinks of authority, he thinks of his family. There are twelve people in his family. First there are his grandparents. They have two sons and an unmarried daughter. Each of their sons has a wife. Between them, the sons and their wives have five children, including Marcus. Marcus' grandfather is the *paterfamilias* (pa-tuhr-fuh-MIH-lee-us), or "father of the family."

The paterfamilias is the oldest living male in a family, and by Roman law he is the absolute ruler of the household. He owns everything the family has—even the people in it. In Marcus' family, his grandfather is the paterfamilias. He has the power of life and death over everyone else in the family. He has the legal right to disown, sell into slavery, or even kill family members who displease him.

The paterfamilias has the right to decide whether to keep newborn babies or not. When a baby is born in Rome, it is placed on the ground. If the paterfamilias picks it up, the baby is formally accepted into the family. But if the baby is sickly, or if the family cannot support another child, the paterfamilias can order that the child be placed outside in a place where passersby will see it. That way someone will pick the child up and raise it as a slave.

Marcus' grandfather has never placed a baby outside or sold a family member into slavery, even though he has the right to. Actually, Marcus' grandfather loves his family very much. He's proud of having fine sons and grandsons. He feels responsible for their well-being and does his best to be a wise paterfamilias. Everyone in the family depends on him. He must decide what is best for the whole family and set a good example. No family can be strong if its paterfamilias is weak or foolish. That's why Marcus' grandfather often seems so stern. After all, being the paterfamilias is serious business.

Marcus' grandfather makes offerings to the gods for the family. He must be respectful of the gods, because if he isn't, the whole family might suffer. To Marcus, the gods do not seem faraway and frightening. They are familiar, everyday gods. One god watches over the hearth fire. Another watches over the cooking utensils. Another watches over the plow and ox. Still others watch over the weaving, sewing, and planting. "They do their share by guarding us," says Marcus' grandfather. "But they won't do the work for us. That is our share."

Everyone in the family must do his share. Marcus realizes that the family is more important than any one member of it. If one member doesn't pull his weight, the rest will suffer. That's why discipline and hard work are so important, and why Marcus tries hard to be a good grandson.

Who Rules? Early Roman Government

Long before Marcus' time, Rome was ruled by kings. An early Roman king was very much like the paterfamilias of a large family, holding the same type of authority and commanding the same respect. All the Roman people made up his "family." The Roman king was also the chief priest of the Romans, making offerings for all the people. He directed the Romans' work. No one questioned his orders, for that would be like disobeying the paterfamilias. There was no written law. The king's word was law.

The *fasces* (FAS-eez) was the symbol of the Roman king. It was a bundle of rods tied tightly together, with an axe in the center. The rods were a sign that the king could beat or punish the people, while the axe was a sign that the king could sentence people to death. When the king appeared in public, attendants carried fasces to remind people of how much power the king had.

Some of the early kings were wise rulers. They wanted the Romans to be safe and prosperous, so they treated them fairly. Other early kings were cruel and selfish. When a king was bad, there was no way to control his power. *Rex* is the Latin word for "king." Under bad kings, *rex* became the most hated word in Rome.

Birth of the Roman Republic

By the sixth century B.C., the Romans were growing unhappy with kings. One group was especially unhappy—the patricians (puh-TRIH-shuhns). Patricians were the aristocrats of early Rome, the wealthy families,

A Roman carries the fasces, a bundle of rods tied around an axe—the symbol of royal power.

proud of their renowned ancestors. They had grown weary of obeying all the king's orders and wanted a greater share in the government. A king named Tarquinius (tahr-KWIN-ee-us) paid no attention to their complaints. Finally the patricians revolted, and around 509 B.C. they forced Tarquinius to flee.

Now the Romans had to form a new government. They no longer trusted one-man rule and wanted a government that would give more rights to citizens. They did not form a pure democracy, like the Athenians, but instead a republic.

A republic is a government in which citizens elect their leaders. The leaders have the authority to make important decisions on behalf of the people. The real power still belongs to the citizens, however, for in a republic the people can vote to replace their leaders if they don't approve of the job they're doing.

Our word *republic* comes from the Latin words *res publica* (rays POO-blih-kah). These two words mean the "public thing" or "public good." A *res publica* is a government for the good of everyone.

The Roman Republic was hardly set up before it was tested. Tarquinius and his followers asked a powerful neighboring people called the Etruscans (ih-TRUHS-kuhns) for help. The Etruscans agreed to help Tarquinius regain Rome.

- On the map of Ancient Italy on page 343, note the location of the Etruscan tribes.

Rome's neighbors to the north, the Etruscans, were the republic's traditional enemies. This tomb drawing illustrates the fighting abilities of Etruscan warriors.

To rid themselves of the Etruscan threat, the Romans would need loyalty and discipline. Could a republic expect such virtues from its citizens? If men were free, would they obey their commanders? Would citizens fight well without a king to rule them? These were important questions for the Roman Republic. To see how the people responded, let's read an ancient Roman legend.

Horatius at the Bridge

The city of Rome had never been in such danger. Porsena (PAWR-suh-nuh), leader of a powerful Etruscan city, had raised a great army. Rumors flew through the streets of Rome that even now he was marching toward the Tiber River. The Romans knew they did not have enough men to face the Etruscans in open battle, so they kept inside their city walls and placed sentries to watch over the dirt roads.

One morning the sentries spotted Porsena's army marching relentlessly over the hills from the north. "What shall we do?" the people asked themselves. "If they gain the bridge, we can't stop them from crossing the river, and then all hope will be lost."

Among the guards at the bridge was a brave soldier named Horatius (huh-RAY-shus). He was on the far side of the river, and when he saw the Etruscans approaching, he called out to the Romans behind him.

"Cut down the bridge as fast as you can!" he yelled. "I'll take two men and hold the enemy at bay!"

With their shields before them and long spears in their hands, the three brave men stood at the far end of the bridge and launched volley after volley against Porsena's soldiers.

Behind Horatius, the Romans hacked away at the beams and posts. Their axes rang and the chips flew. Soon the bridge trembled and was ready to fall.

"Fall back!" they called to Horatius and the two with him. "Fall back and save your lives!"

But just then Porsena's men made another rush for the bridge.

"Run for your lives!" Horatius told his two companions. "I'll stand and keep the road."

His comrades turned and ran across the bridge. They had hardly reached the other side when a crashing of timbers thundered in their ears. The bridge toppled to one side and fell with a roar into the water.

When Horatius heard the sound, he knew the city was safe. Slowly he moved down the river's bank.

A spear thrown by one of Porsena's men grazed his face, and the Etruscans shouted with joy to see the red blood flow. But still Horatius did not falter. He cast his spear at the enemy, then turned and dove into the Tiber.

Spears whistled through the air and splashed into the water all around him. But Horatius was one of the best swimmers in Rome, and before long he had reached the other side. His friends were waiting to pull him to safety.

Shout after shout greeted Horatius as he climbed the bank. The Romans welcomed him as a hero, for they knew he had saved their city. They called him Horatius Cocles (KAWK-leez), which meant "One-eyed Horatius," because he had lost an eye defending Rome. They raised a statue in his honor and gave him as much land as he could plow around in a day. And for hundreds of years afterward, Romans told and retold the story of Horatius at the bridge.

A Matter of Class: Plebeians vs. Patricians

The legend of Horatius shows that the Romans were loyal to their new republic and willing to fight to defend it. After Porsena's attempt to capture Rome, the city continued to fight frequent wars with neighboring cities and tribes, but Rome did not fall.

While the Romans eventually succeeded in getting rid of tyrannical kings, the young republic faced more challenges. One challenge rose from the common people. Even though no king held absolute power over them, they did not at first share much of the power or privileges of the new republic.

Most of Rome's common people were farmers who tilled the land. A few were wealthy and had large estates, but most were poor commoners who worked hard to survive. They didn't have as many rights as the patricians enjoyed. They could hold public office, but few did. They weren't allowed to marry patricians. Being poor, they often found themselves in debt to moneylenders, and the moneylenders were usually patricians.

Roman laws about debt were quite harsh. A commoner who could not repay what he owed could find his property seized and himself locked up in a patrician's private prison. He could be sold into slavery along with the rest of his family. He could even be put to death. The most common outcome, though, seems to have been "debt bondage," in which the debtor became a slave to the moneylender while he worked to pay off his debt.

Rome's frequent wars with its neighbors made the situation worse. Ordinary citizens were expected to serve as unpaid soldiers when necessary, and even supply their own equipment. Long campaigns placed harsh burdens on these families and drove them deeper into debt. Invading armies made life even more difficult as they destroyed farms and plundered harvests. Rome suffered economic decline throughout the fifth century B.C. Whenever possible, patricians expanded their estates at the expense of small landholders, turning the former owners into debt-bondsmen who had to work the land.

Year after year, the common people suffered in silence, until finally they could stand it no longer. One day, it is said, an old man suddenly appeared in Rome's marketplace. He was a pitiful sight, thin and sickly and dressed in rags. When asked how he had fallen so low, he bared his shoulders and revealed the marks of cruel blows. Then he pointed to even older scars on his breast, signs of honorable wounds he'd received in war.

Four plebeians, or commoners, go about their tasks in a kitchen that might have been owned by a wealthy patrician.

It turned out the old fellow had once fought bravely for Rome. When he returned from war to enjoy what he hoped would be the fruits of peace, he discovered that his fields had been burned and his cattle had been driven off. He fell deeper and deeper in debt. Finally his creditor made him a slave and whipped him savagely until he was near death.

The man's story infuriated the common people. They refused to fight in the army and in 494 B.C. threatened to build their own city. These angry citizens banded together and called themselves "plebeians" (plih-BEE-uns). In Latin the word *plebs* means "the common people." Rome's plebeians, or "plebs" for short, were made up of both poor and wealthy commoners. The poor were angered by their landlessness, the burden of military service, and debt bondage. Poor and wealthy plebeians alike demanded more political power.

Rome's patricians gradually realized they would have to change their ways. They grudgingly gave the plebeians a greater say in Rome's republic.

Patricians and Plebeians in the Roman Republic

Plebeians complained that there was no set of written laws applying to everybody. Instead, the patricians administered justice according to traditional rules known only by priests, who were patricians themselves.

In 450 B.C., the laws of Rome were finally written down and published as the Twelve Tables, which were posted for all to see. When the plebeians saw how many laws there were to follow, they weren't happy. Still, Rome was extremely proud of its Twelve Tables. Over the centuries, the Romans would go on to prove their genius for making laws.

One of the laws that made up the Twelve Tables decreed that Roman cemeteries, like the one above, had to be built outside the city limits.

Bit by bit, plebeians chipped away at patrician privileges and won more rights. In the fifth century B.C., they gained the right to marry patricians. In the fourth century, they won big changes. Debt bondage was much reduced. A Roman citizen could no longer be put into chains because he owed money.

Plebeians gained rights in government as well. Two officials, called consuls, were responsible for overseeing much of the government.

This carving shows a group of toga-clad Roman senators, members of the most powerful body in the Republic. The inset photo of a silver coin depicts a Roman citizen casting his vote.

In the fourth century B.C., Romans decided that one of the consuls must always be a plebeian. The consuls were powerful men, but there were limits to their authority. They were elected to serve just one-year terms, and either consul could forbid the actions of the other, so that no single man would hold too much power.

The two consuls shared power and executed laws approved by the Senate and the Assemblies. The Senate was the most powerful body in the government. Senators came from wealthy, landowning families, so the Senate often ignored the interests of the poor. Not all senators were patricians, but most were. Unlike the consuls, who served brief one-year terms, the senators served for life. In their long robes, called togas, edged in purple, they proposed laws and tried to figure out the best path for the republic.

For a long time the Senate ratified laws passed by Rome's Assemblies. Over time the republic developed two Assemblies—two bodies of citizens that helped make laws and run the republic. The Centuriate Assembly included all citizens, but patricians had the greatest influence on its decisions. The Tribal Assembly also included all citizens but was set up in such a way that the wealthiest could not determine its course.

During the fifth and fourth centuries B.C., despite social strife, the Romans succeeded in creating a government based on law in which many people had a voice.

Think about some of the successful features of the republic:

- Laws clearly spelled out
- Two annually elected leaders called consuls
- Two representative Assemblies, and one powerful Senate

The Roman Republic, while by no means perfect, was still a remarkable achievement for its time. The republic would last for about 500 years.

The Romans told many stories of heroes who risked their own fortunes and lives to save the republic. One of the most famous is the story of Cincinnatus. This fifth-century B.C. Roman was a real statesman and general who wanted Rome to remain a republic. Here is the legend of the great hero.

The Story of Cincinnatus

Lucius Quinctius Cincinnatus (LOO-shee-us KWINGK-shee-us sin-sih-NAT-us) was one of the most powerful men in the Senate that ruled ancient Rome. He was also one of the most honorable.

When his grown son became involved in a scandal, Cincinnatus did all he could to help the young man start over. But the devoted father lost all his wealth. Cincinnatus and his wife Racilia (ruh-SIL-ee-uh) moved to a small farm west of the Tiber, where the senator himself had to plow the fields and dig the ditches. Cincinnatus did not complain that he now spent more time in a simple tunic, working the earth, than in his senator's toga. Nor did the Romans lose sight of Cincinnatus' great worth.

One day, when the aging man was at the plow, covered with grime and sweat, he saw several men on horseback galloping toward him. They seemed worried and in a terrible rush.

"What is wrong?" Cincinnatus asked.

The men had been sent by the Senate. First, they asked a blessing for Cincinnatus and their country. Then they urged, "Put on your toga, Cincinnatus, and hear the words of the Roman Senate."

Cincinnatus called for his wife to bring him the toga. While she was getting it, he wiped the dirt and sweat from his arms and hands as best he could. Then he put on the toga. "Now tell me," he said.

The men told him the Roman army was in dire peril. The forces of Rome were surrounded by an enemy tribe on Mount Algidus (AL-jee-dus).

Five Roman horsemen had managed to escape and tell the Senate of impending doom.

In great excitement, the men before him said, "Oh, wise Cincinnatus, we come to tell you that the Senate has given you complete power to rule in this time of emergency. We greet you as our dictator. Come now, and lead us out of peril!"

"Dictator?" cried the astonished Cincinnatus.

"The senators beg you to come to Rome immediately," said one of the messengers. "They have named you dictator so you will have the power to act quickly and do whatever is necessary to save the republic."

Cincinnatus did not hesitate. He mounted a horse the men had brought with them, and they galloped away. He left his plow standing in the field. All the way to Rome, he worried that the army's defenses might already be failing.

As a ferry carried Cincinnatus across the Tiber, senators came out to greet him. So did his three sons, including the one who had caused Cincinnatus so much shame. All three wanted to fight for Rome, and they were ready to take orders.

Not everyone was happy to see Cincinnatus. By now most citizens of the republic had heard that the Senate had made him dictator. Many didn't like the idea of giving one man so much power. As Cincinnatus passed through the streets, they watched him suspiciously and wondered what he would do.

Cincinnatus posted men at the city walls to watch for the enemy, the Aequi (EE-kwiy). Then he went into his private rooms and mapped out a plan to save Rome.

By dawn he was ready. He suspended all public activity in the city. He ordered all shops to close and forbade the transaction of any kind of business. He ordered every man of military age to report for duty before sunset, equipped with weapons as well as food and water for five days. Cincinnatus said that old men, women, and children should help the new soldiers get ready.

Everyone in Rome spent the day fixing food, gathering wood, and preparing weapons. Even those who didn't like Cincinnatus followed his orders. They were afraid of what he might do if they disobeyed.

By sunset the new soldiers were ready. Most assumed they would rest that night and start out fresh the next morning to meet the enemy in battle. But Cincinnatus wanted to surprise the Aequi. He led his soldiers away that very night and attacked the Aequi while they were sleeping. The Aequi were so surprised that they soon surrendered and begged for mercy.

Cincinnatus knew that if the Aequi had won, they would have slaughtered the Roman soldiers. But he said he did not want the blood of the Aequi; all he wanted was their confession that they were beaten. He told them to admit their loss by marching under a Roman yoke made of three spears. The Aequi soldiers marched under the yoke and returned to their homes in the mountains.

Cincinnatus returned triumphantly to Rome. He led his soldiers, along with the army that had been trapped on Mount Algidus, through the city's streets. Everyone cheered because they knew Cincinnatus had saved Rome.

But now, what would Cincinnatus do? Some Romans feared that he might try to remain dictator, or maybe even make himself king, for the rest of his life. As dictator, he would certainly enjoy an easier life. He would not have to push a plow or dig a ditch or worry about rain for his crops. His meals would come to him on gilded trays, he would wear fine togas, and people would do what he told them to do.

But Cincinnatus did not believe Rome should be ruled by one man, for then it would cease to be a republic. Cincinnatus believed important public decisions should be made by many different people debating and working together, as they did in the Roman Senate.

So once again, Cincinnatus surprised everyone by resigning. He went home to his wife, Racilia, and his farm along the Tiber River. He picked up his plow just where he'd left it in the field, 16 days before.

In the centuries since, Cincinnatus has been remembered as the model citizen—willing to drop what he is doing to help when his country needs him, but just as willing to give up power when his help is no longer required.

The "American Cincinnatus"

George Washington followed the example of Cincinnatus when he resigned his commission as commander of the Continental Army that defeated the British in the American Revolutionary War. Washington was so popular right after the war that some wanted to make him king of America. Instead, he resigned his post, returned to his farm in Virginia, and became known as the "American Cincinnatus."

Roman citizens and soldiers unite in celebration after a victorious battle on the Mediterranean island of Sicily.

Rome Rising and the Republic Challenged

In its early years, the Roman Republic often found itself at war with other peoples in Italy. At first these wars were largely a matter of survival for Rome. It was a hostile world, and Romans had to be ready to defend against invading tribes and rival city-states.

The little republic began to win most of its wars. Filled with pride in their city-state, Roman soldiers fought with bravery. More and more people came under Roman rule. Often the Romans granted citizenship to their defeated enemies, in order to make the conquered peoples loyal to Rome.

By 265 B.C., Rome had conquered most of Italy south of the Po River. Roman ways and ideas spread throughout the Italian peninsula. Latin language and customs took root among conquered peoples. Roman law became the law of Rome's former enemies.

- On the map on page 360, identify the extent of Roman territories by 487 B.C., 300 B.C., and 265 B.C.

At first, as Roman power grew and its territories expanded, the lives of the Romans stayed pretty much the same. People still followed the "old ways" of discipline and hard work. Even senators took pride in being able to plow a field. Romans believed that their republic stayed strong because of the tough Roman character and their respect for law. And for many years, that remained true. But the continued growth of Roman power brought changes that strained the traditional way of life and the old virtues. Rome was on the rise, but, as you'll see in this chapter, that rise would test the republic.

Thanks to the military successes of its soldiers, Roman influence began to spread the length of Italy.

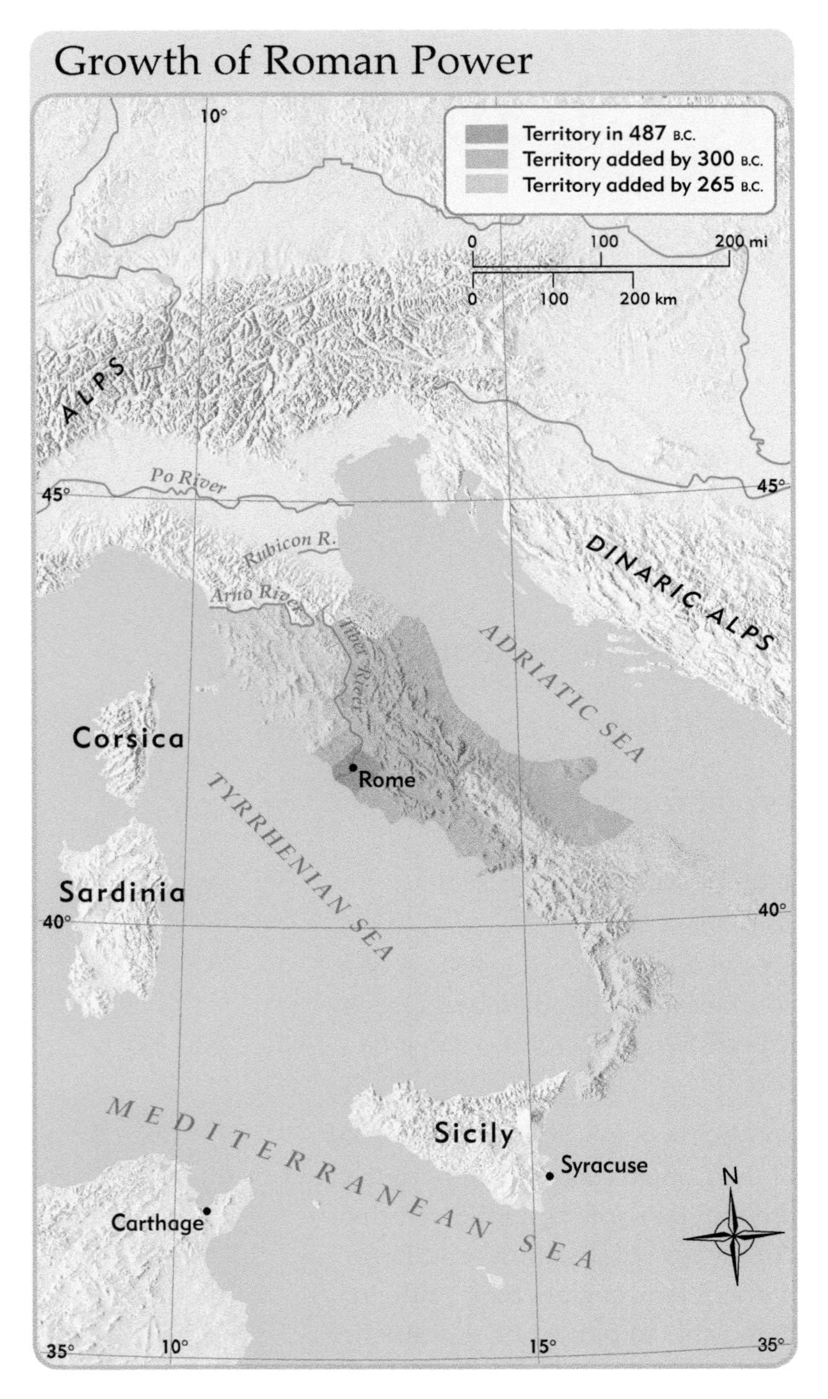

The First Punic War: Rome Takes to the Sea

Across the Mediterranean in North Africa lay another powerful city-state called Carthage (KAHR-thij). The Carthaginians (kahr-thuh-JIN-ee-uns) had grown rich from trade. Indeed, this wealthy trading center controlled much of North Africa's Mediterranean coast as well as the southern part of Spain, which at the time was called Hispania.

Carthage boasted a powerful navy, and its ships dominated the western Mediterranean Sea. This fleet allowed Carthage to control the islands of Corsica and Sardinia, as well as the western half of Sicily. Rome's navy, on the other hand, was weak and small. Roman ships could sail certain parts of the Mediterranean only with the permission of Carthage.

- On the map at left, locate Rome, Carthage, Corsica, Sardinia, and Sicily.
- On the map on page 362, locate the areas controlled by Rome and by Carthage about 264 B.C.

Eventually the Romans grew to resent Carthage's power. "We've conquered most of Italy," they said, "but these Carthaginians threaten us. They control the sea lanes along the coasts of North Africa and Hispania. And now they're in Sicily—right at our doorstep. They could extend their empire into Italy! At the very least, our own ships won't be able to come and go as they please as long as Carthage dominates the sea. Our foreign trade will be at the mercy of Carthage."

In 264 B.C., the Romans decided to stop Carthaginian advances in Sicily and seek the rich plunder that a war with Carthage might bring. After a few years of successful fighting, the Romans fixed on the goal of driving the Carthaginians out of Sicily altogether. That was the start of a long series of fights between Rome and Carthage known as the Punic (PYOO-nik) Wars.

We call them the Punic Wars because the Latin word for Carthaginian was *Punicus* (PYOO-nih-kus). There were three Punic Wars in all. They began as a quarrel over an island, and turned into a life and death struggle between the Romans and Carthaginians.

The First Punic War lasted from 264 to 241 B.C. Roman strength at that time was on land, in foot soldiers. The Romans had to find a way for their army to become a navy, so they could fight on the sea. They went to work building and gathering as many ships as they could. They rigged their ships with an ingenious device—a long, swinging gangplank with a sharp spike at the far end. The plank was wide enough for two men to walk side by side. During battle a Roman ship could pull beside an enemy vessel and drop the plank so that the spike would come crashing down on the other ship's deck. Then Roman foot soldiers could rush across the gangplank and overwhelm the enemy in hand-to-hand combat.

With their swinging gangplanks, the Roman fleet was a force to be reckoned with. After many battles on land and sea, and frequent changes of fortune, the Romans managed to drive the Carthaginians out of Sicily. The First Punic War ended with Roman victory. Roman pride and confidence soared. They had taken on a mighty foe and won. But the fighting between the two rival powers had only begun.

Newly built Roman warships ply the waters off Sicily during the First Punic War against Carthage. Rome's capture of the island brought the war to an end.

The Second Punic War: Hannibal Crosses the Alps

After the First Punic War, Rome's sea power grew rapidly. Roman ships used Sicily as a base for trading. At the same time, however, the Carthaginians were growing more powerful on land. Over the next several years, the Carthaginians built a powerful army. Although they had lost Sicily, Sardinia, and Corsica, they expanded their empire in Spain.

Among the Carthaginians, one man emerged as an extraordinary general. His name was Hannibal (HAN-uh-buhl). Hannibal had been raised to despise the Romans. It is said that when he was just nine years old, his father took him into a temple and made him swear that he would spend his life trying to destroy Rome. In 218 B.C., Hannibal set out to make good on his oath, and the Second Punic War began.

Hannibal, the great Carthaginian leader, launched the Second Punic War against Rome in 218 B.C.

Hannibal was a brilliant military leader. He realized that the Romans thought of Carthage as a naval power, and so would expect an invasion by sea. He knew the Romans would be ready to defend Italy's coast against an attacking Carthaginian fleet.

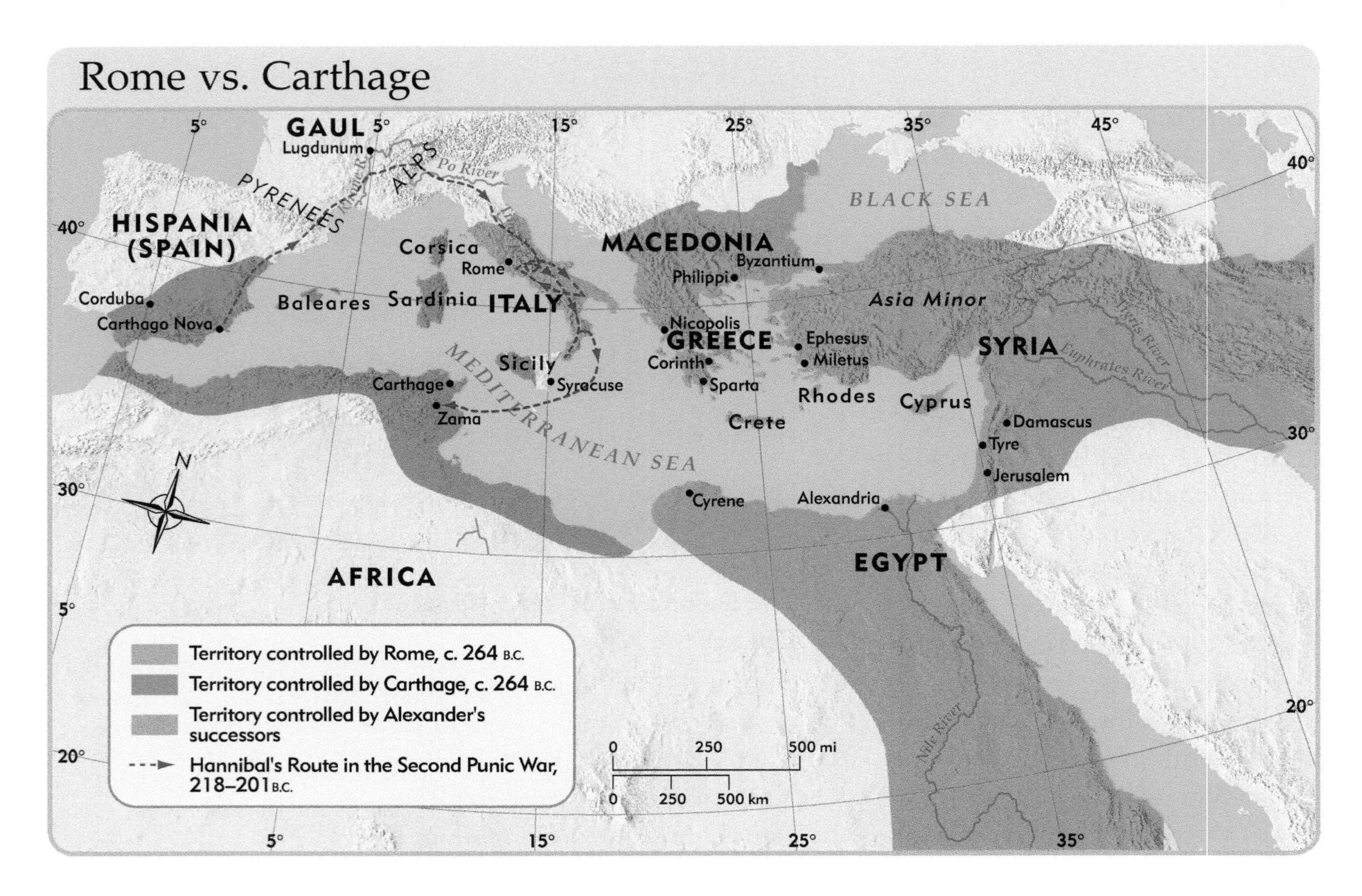

So, Hannibal cleverly decided on a different approach. He would attack Rome from the north, by land.

Starting out from the city of Carthago Nova, or New Carthage, in Spain—a city his father had founded—Hannibal led 50,000 troops and 9,000 horses across the Pyrenees Mountains and over the Rhone River. He also took with him 37 elephants from North Africa. These huge lumbering beasts could trample enemy lines like tanks. As summer turned to autumn, Hannibal's army approached Italy. But before they could march south along the peninsula, the Carthaginians would have to face one of the most forbidding natural barriers on earth—the stark, rugged peaks of the mountain range called the Alps.

Crossing the high, snowy Alps took two terrible weeks. Fierce tribesmen occupied the steep, narrow valleys and attacked at every opportunity. Often horses and pack animals lost their footing and slid headlong over cliffs. Many more froze to death. Soldiers perished by the thousands in the snow and ice of early winter. Hannibal's men finally stumbled out of the rocky highlands to find a land of green pastures and plains. But they had paid dearly for the chance to attack from the north. Almost half the army and most of the elephants had died along the way.

Hannibal was undeterred. He launched attack after attack against Roman forces, fighting with the ferocity of one who had sworn undying hatred for the enemy. The Romans suffered many bitter defeats at his hands. One battle was so disastrous that, it was said afterwards, every woman in Rome wept for a dead son, husband, father, or brother.

For 15 years Hannibal raided towns all over Italy. He wiped out crops and burned orchards, in an attempt to defeat Rome by destroying its agricultural resources. He left villages and whole towns in ruins. He aimed to shatter the Romans, both physically and in spirit.

The Romans, however, were not easily crushed. They now turned to attack Hannibal's homeland, Carthage. Hannibal had to rush home to defend it. In 202 B.C., at a town south of Carthage called Zama, a Roman army defeated the general who had so boldly led his troops across the Alps. A year later the Second Punic War came to an end with Rome once again victorious.

Hannibal himself lived several more years. At first he tried to rebuild Carthage under Roman rule, and later he stirred up trouble for his old enemy again. In 183 B.C., he died by his own hand. He took poison from a ring he carried about with him rather than surrender to the Romans one last time.

The Third Punic War: The Destruction of Carthage

For 50 years following the Second Punic War, Carthage and Rome were at peace. By 150 B.C., Carthage showed signs of growing rich and powerful again. Some Romans felt threatened. They felt they could not be secure as long as the rival city in North Africa survived. One Roman statesman, known as Cato the Censor, ended every speech he made, no matter what he was speaking about, with the cry, *Carthago delenda est*—"Carthage must be destroyed."

Riding atop a war elephant, Hannibal marches his army through Italy, determined to crush Roman power forever.

And so war broke out once more. The Third Punic War lasted from 149 to 146 B.C. Rome triumphed again, and the victors made sure there would be no fourth war. The Romans went from house to house, killing Carthaginians throughout the city. By the war's end, the city's population was reduced from 250,000 to 50,000. The unhappy survivors were sold into slavery. The Romans burned the city and cursed the site, decreeing that it should never be inhabited again. As word spread of what had happened to Carthage, the Romans came to be feared as brutal conquerors.

North Africa became a Roman province. Now Rome controlled all the western Mediterranean and most of Spain. Meanwhile, in the east, Rome had extended its domination over Greece and much of Asia Minor.

This lifelike Roman sculpture of a young girl demonstrates the influence that Greek culture began to have on Rome.

Rome was no longer a city-state fighting to fend off rivals and protect its trade routes. It was turning into a sprawling empire. More and more, the Romans began to gaze at foreign territories and think to themselves, "Why not seize those lands as well?" They had boundless confidence in themselves now. They had utterly destroyed the Carthaginians. It seemed that no one could stand in their way.

Learning from the Greeks

As Rome conquered new lands, it gained territories east of Italy, where the Greeks had built their great civilization. Beginning in 200 B.C., Roman soldiers began marching into Macedonia, Greece, and then Asia Minor. These areas lay at the heart of what had been the empire of Alexander the Great. Alexander had been

Left: The Romans built their own Greek-style theaters, like this one in territory they conquered in Hispania, a land now known as Spain.

Below: These Greek-style columns were part of a temple the Romans constructed in North Africa.

dead for more than a century, but the Hellenistic ideas he helped spread through much of the Mediterranean world were alive and well. While Italy had long traded with Greece, now the conquering Roman armies plundered Greek cities and towns, taking more and more Greek paintings, sculpture, and treasure back with them to Rome. The Romans also took educated Greek slaves to Rome to tutor young Romans. These slaves helped bring Greek literature, rhetoric, and philosophy to the growing empire.

The practical Romans, who were talented in governing and making war, also proved ingenious at taking traditions from conquered peoples and remodeling them to suit Roman needs. The more the Romans learned about Greek culture, the more intrigued they were. The Greek sense of the dignity of man and the worth of human endeavors appealed to them. They began adopting all kinds of Greek ideas.

The Romans were particularly fascinated by Greek arts, literature, and philosophy. They read Homer's *Iliad* and *Odyssey*, as well as the works of Plato and Aristotle. Many Roman families sent their sons to school in Athens or hired Greek tutors for their children. Greek craftsmen and teachers traveled to Rome. The Romans modeled their plays and theaters after the Greeks.

Roman artists admired Greek sculptures that depicted perfectly formed human beings. They copied Greek statues and created their own sculptures celebrating Roman accomplishments. The down-to-earth Romans often made their statues more realistic than the sculptures of the idealistic Greeks. For example, the Romans didn't hesitate to include wrinkles or warts on faces.

Roman engineers and builders borrowed Greek ideas. They built temples surrounded by columns and created amphitheaters to hold large audiences. The Romans built on a grander scale than the Greeks and used innovations of their own, such as arches and concrete.

Even in their ideas about the gods, Romans borrowed heavily from the Greeks. They adopted Greek deities and gave them Roman names. Zeus, king of the Greek gods, became Jupiter, king of the Roman gods. Aphrodite, the Greek goddess of love, became known as Venus. Ares, the Greek god of war, became the god Mars, who led Roman armies to victory.

Many Romans were attracted to Hellenistic ideas because they recognized that Rome had a new role to play in the world. It was no longer a small city-state of farmers, shepherds, and craftsmen. It was becoming the capital of a vast empire. Greek ideas seemed more advanced and sophisticated than the old, simple Roman views—more attractive to a people who were beginning to think of themselves as sophisticated. So Hellenistic ideas, which had already penetrated many lands east of the Mediterranean, now spread westward through Rome.

The Romans so admired Greek architecture that in time Rome came to resemble a Grecian city. This depiction of Rome's ruins was painted by an eighteenth-century Italian artist.

Roman Deities and Greek Origins

Ancient Romans worshipped some gods that were uniquely their own. The god Janus (JAY-nus)—who had two faces, one looking forward and one looking back—was the god of gateways and of beginnings. Our month of January is named after him. But Romans also saw many similarities between their own ancient deities and those of the Greeks. Eventually they began borrowing Greek myths and made them their own. They began to worship the same gods the Greeks worshipped, though the Romans gave these deities new Latin names.

Janus

Greek God	**Roman Name**	
Zeus	Jupiter	king of the gods
Hera	Juno (JOO-noh)	queen of the gods
Poseidon	Neptune	god of the sea
Hades	Pluto	god of the underworld
Athena	Minerva (muh-NUR-vuh)	goddess of wisdom
Aphrodite	Venus	goddess of love
Ares	Mars	god of war
Apollo	Apollo	god of light, music, and poetry
Artemis	Diana	goddess of the moon and hunting
Demeter	Ceres (SEER-eez)	goddess of agriculture
Hermes	Mercury	messenger of the gods
Hephaestus	Vulcan	blacksmith of the gods
Hestia	Vesta	goddess of the hearth
Dionysus	Bacchus (BA-kus)	god of wine

Minerva

Diana

Jupiter

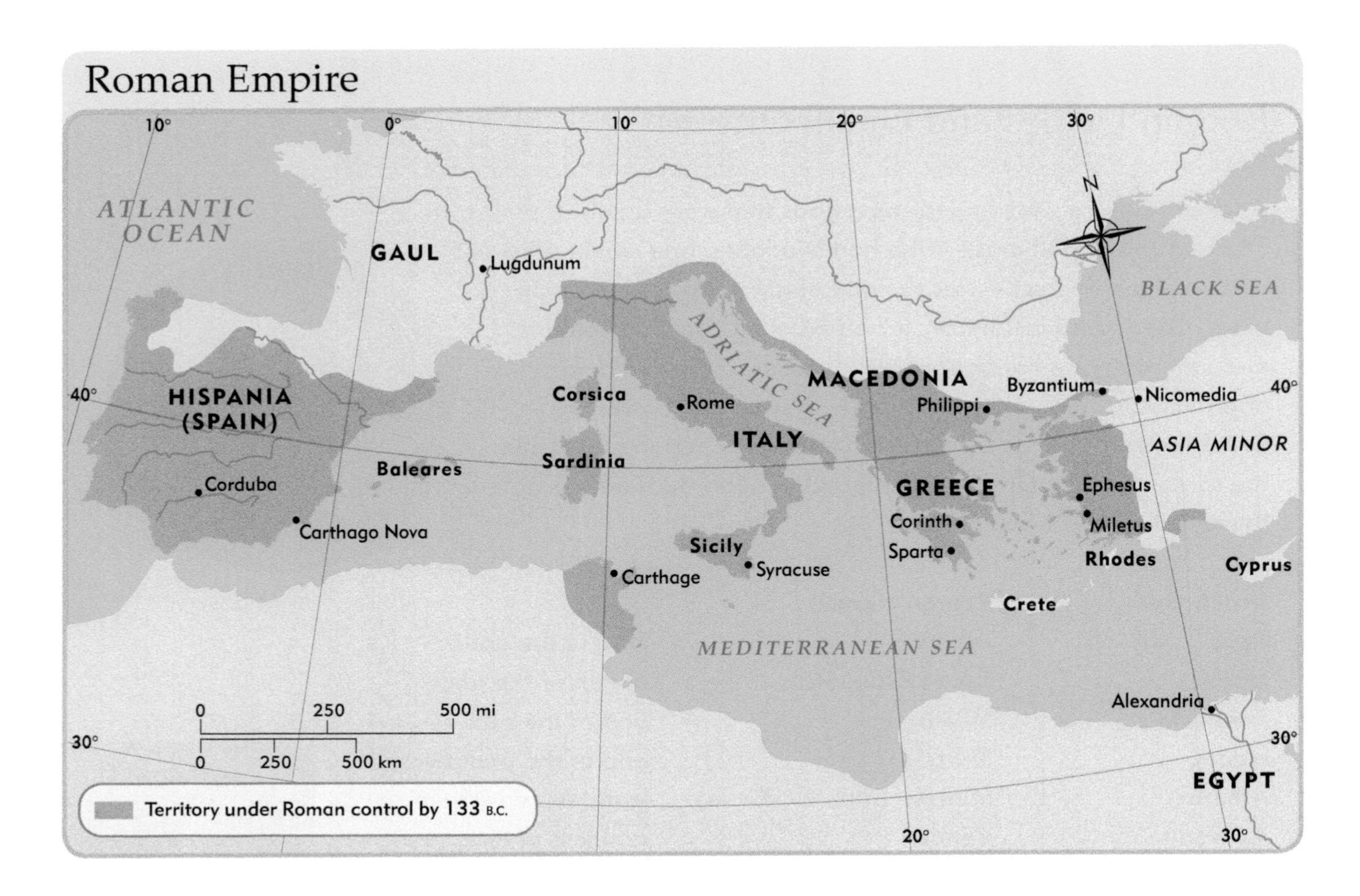

Roman Triumphs, Roman Troubles

By 146 B.C., at the end of the Third Punic War, Rome had gained a great empire. Greece and Macedonia lay under Roman control. Most of the land along the northern shores of the Mediterranean was Roman. Rome had won Spain from Carthage. The shores of the Adriatic Sea were Roman, as Asia Minor would be within a short time. Even Egypt found it wise to become an ally of Rome.

All this new territory brought new wealth for some Romans. Conquest, it turned out, provided a quick and easy way to riches. Romans could amass fortunes by taking from others in foreign lands rather than having to work in the field or orchard.

As money, luxuries, and slaves poured into Rome, many old ways of doing things began to change. As always in Roman history, the great majority of citizens continued to be manual laborers and small peasant farmers who worked the land. But a small, wealthy minority owned large estates and financed large-scale trade. Roman thinkers worried about the effects of so much new wealth on both classes of Roman people.

Superb artwork and fancy tableware from the east now adorned many Roman homes. Wealthy men could buy many luxuries that came from different parts of the world—silk from China and cotton from India. Some people worried that as the Roman ruling class led more luxurious lives and began to value riches and refinement, they would become soft and tyrannical. Others worried that the love of ease and luxury would corrupt the plebeians, tempting them away from the old values of hard work and discipline.

With no foreign enemies threatening Rome, people were freed from the fear that had kept them unified for so long. The old Roman virtues of self-sacrifice, austerity, self-control, duty, obedience, and respect for authority began to weaken. Many grew alarmed as they saw new riches tempting people away from traditional Roman values. "This is wrong," they said. "Go back to the old ways. Forget about foreign conquests and empires. Our fathers made Rome a republic. Let it stay that way!"

But newly wealthy Romans paid no attention. They were enjoying their luxuries. "Why be poor and simple when we can be rich and comfortable?" they asked. "Rome is strong and powerful. It is Rome's destiny to rule the world!"

Most of the new wealth went to noble families. The gap between rich people and poor people grew wider.

The Punic Wars had brought big changes to land ownership in the Roman Republic. Thousands of farmers had left their land to go fight against the Carthaginians. Hannibal's army had destroyed many small farms. When the fighting ended, wealthier men bought the empty farms and added them to the land they already owned.

The Punic Wars had also brought changes for workers in the republic. During the fighting, the Romans had taken many prisoners. Most of the captives became slaves, and often they were put to work on the estates of rich landowners. Some wealthy Romans now had hundreds of slaves working their lands. Who would pay a free man to do work when slaves could be used for nothing? As a result, thousands of free workers suffered. They were left without land, without work, and without money. What happened to them?

The slaves shown on this ancient mosaic were taken captive in North Africa and brought back to Rome.

Let's find out by spending some time with a free worker. His name is Firmus. He's a typical small farmer who has come to Rome.

Hard Times in the Roman Republic

Firmus admires the old Roman ways. He likes things to be orderly and simple. He works hard. He believes in discipline and duty. All he wants is an honorable family and his little farm. He was born on the family farm, and he expected to spend his whole life there. But things haven't turned out the way he planned.

Ever a loyal Roman, Firmus had marched off willingly to fight Hannibal. When he returned, he found his farm in ruins. The olive trees and vines were burned; his home and tools were in shambles. His family could hardly grow enough food to survive. Where could he get money for new tools? Firmus held on as long as he could, but finally he had no choice. He was forced to sell the little farm to a wealthy buyer.

Firmus took his family to the city of Rome, where he hoped they could find work. But things in Rome are no better. In fact, they are much worse. Firmus and his family have to share a dirty, crowded house with other families. Each family has to live in one room.

Firmus spends weeks looking for work. Finally, he finds a job as a helper to the neighborhood baker. He is luckier than many of his friends. They have to live on grain handed out by the government.

The baker isn't much better off than Firmus. He makes only cheap, coarse bread. That's all he can sell, because only poor men come into his shop. Rich men have their own slaves to bake for them.

Firmus and his family hate their crowded house and spend as little time there as possible. Like thousands of poor Romans, they spend much time in the streets and marketplace. They feel cheated. They are bored, restless, and unhappy. They look forward to the frequent holidays when they can see races and wrestling contests, as well as plays and parades. The government also arranges cruel, bloody fights to entertain the poor people. It's an unhappy way of life, one very different from life on the farm. Firmus has lost his independence. He no longer feels like a free Roman citizen.

This relief shows a Roman baker in his store, one arm extended toward a basket of bread. The availability and price of bread were always important matters for the poor of Rome.

The Forum is the great public meeting place of Rome. There, poor men like Firmus gather to hear the latest news. They exchange gossip and jokes, listen to politicians speak, and argue about this official or that. Mostly, though, they talk about their own problems.

"What we need is land," says Firmus. "Our fathers lived on the land. They led good, simple lives. They never had time to be bored."

"I agree with you," says Balbus, the butcher's helper. "But where can we get land? Can you afford to buy any? Can I? Can we find some rich man to sell us any? Half the men in Rome can't even buy bread! How can they buy land?"

Firmus frowns and scratches his head. "Well, all the same, that's what we need. Why can't we have land? I fought for Rome. So did you, Balbus. Is this how Rome pays us back? There are so many rich men in this city! They eat dates from Africa and their wives wear peacock-colored silk from China. Why can't I have just a piece of land and a little house? Who wants to live in this noisy city? I want to go back to the old ways."

The Republic in Crisis

Thousands of men like Firmus came to Rome, and year by year they grew more unhappy. Veterans who had fought in Rome's wars were especially bitter. They wanted some kind of reward—power or money—for having fought. They were proud men, and they were becoming more desperate.

Many Romans were losing faith in their government. Wealthy individuals owned or controlled most of the land. They expanded their large estates as victorious Roman armies captured more and more slaves and brought them back to Rome. Now landless peasants such as Firmus flocked to the city, but they were adrift. Some Roman statesmen said land ought to be redistributed to these former soldiers and citizens. They even called for laws to redistribute land. But powerful landowners, who dominated the Senate, refused to give up their land and agree to such laws.

Poor people felt increasingly hopeless. True, they had the Tribal Assembly, which had been formed in the fourth century B.C. and was composed mainly of plebeians. But it seemed to help little. While the republic was supposed to run according to written laws, the laws were only as strong as men's willingness to obey them.

Riots broke out more and more often. Rome had nearly a century of unrest and bloodshed. Military leaders began fighting each other for power. They promised soldiers land and money in exchange for their services. For the first time, Roman armies seemed to be more loyal to their commanders than to Rome itself. Sometimes a general would step forward and try to seize the reins of government. The republic couldn't cope with the strong men who wanted to rule Rome by force.

Roman soldiers conquered vast territories for the republic. In return, they began to demand land as payment for their services. Some of the army's generals even tried to take over the government.

In 88 B.C., Rome fell into a civil war that continued off and on until 82 B.C. Consuls backed by armies battled each other. Thousands died in the fighting, and thousands more were put to death. The Senate was no longer able to rule and keep order. Senators simply tried to back the strongest man. So did the Roman people. They followed one leader after another. The boast of Rome—its organized law and its working republican institutions—had broken down. The Roman Republic teetered on the edge of collapse.

Bust of Julius Caesar, the Roman general who declared himself "dictator for life"— though his life ended shortly after he took that title.

Days of Empire

As the Roman republic descended into chaos, a young aristocrat watched with interest. His name was Julius Caesar (JOOL-yus SEE-zuhr). Caesar was a spellbinding orator, a gifted writer, and a skilled politician.

He had studied Greek philosophy. He had served as an important government official in Spain. In the year 59 B.C., he was elected to the office of consul in Rome. But Julius Caesar could see that the people who held real power in Rome were now military leaders. The best way for ambitious men to win authority at home was to win battles abroad.

Single-minded and ruthless, Julius Caesar set out to do just that. He knew that he needed military victories, wealth, and the backing of an army to gain popularity and power in Rome. So when his one-year consulship was over, Caesar had himself appointed governor and head of the army in Gaul, in what is today France.

- On the map on page 376, locate Gaul.

In Gaul, Caesar proved himself a brilliant general. At that time, central and northern Gaul were wild lands, places where the rule of Rome did not reach. The Gauls were a tough, hard-fighting people. In 390 B.C., they had invaded and plundered the city of Rome itself. The Romans had not forgotten this centuries-old insult. In 58 B.C., Caesar set out to break their power and bring the land to heel.

It took eight years of hard fighting, during which Caesar proved himself both a brilliant and a brutal warrior. His conquests made the large, rich, and heavily populated land of Gaul a new province of Rome. He even

Roman soldiers lay siege to a settlement in Gaul, a land now known as France.

launched two expeditions against the people of Britain, whose tribes had helped the Gauls in their struggle.

During the years of battle, as Caesar the general led his troops, Caesar the writer kept the Roman public up to date on all of his victories. His accounts of the fighting thrilled people at home, and the fame and popularity of the daring young general grew. By 50 B.C., Caesar had built a loyal personal army of 10 legions. More than 50,000 battle-hardened troops stood ready to follow their general wherever he led.

A *legion* was a unit of the Roman army consisting of about 5,000 soldiers.

Meanwhile, Caesar had kept himself informed of events in Rome. He was appalled by what he heard. By 50 B.C., Rome was in chaos. Rival factions in the government plotted against each other. Rioting mobs roamed the streets. Law and order meant nothing.

Caesar's Rise to Power

While Caesar's success in Gaul made him popular with his troops and the ordinary people of Rome, it stirred jealousy in others. Caesar's rivals in the Senate quickly saw the threat posed by the conquering hero. They decided to take action. They ordered Caesar to resign his army command and return home.

Caesar, camped with his army near a bridge at the Rubicon (ROO-bih-kahn) River, pondered his future. If he resigned, he would be at the mercy of his enemies in Rome. If he led his men across the Rubicon, there would be no going back. He would be asking for war. The river marked the boundary that divided Italy from the provinces. And under Roman law, to cross the river with an army was an act of treason against the state.

- On the map on page 360 in Chapter 6, locate the Rubicon River.

Caesar hesitated only a moment. He marched his troops across the Rubicon—and plunged the Roman world into a new and disastrous civil war. To this day, the expression "to cross the Rubicon" means to take an action from which there is no turning back.

Once across the river, Caesar boldly led his soldiers on a march toward Rome. The general had launched his bid for power.

Caesar's enemies panicked. They fled the capital, taking what troops they could with them. Caesar set off in pursuit. He swept through Spain and Greece before heading off to Egypt and Asia Minor. One by one, he defeated his enemies. *"Veni, vidi, vici"* (WAY-nee, WEE-dee, WEE-kee), Caesar declared after one of his victories. "I came, I saw, I conquered."

After two years, he returned to Rome. There he declared himself

Sword raised, Caesar leads his all-conquering army across the Rubicon River into northern Italy. With this act, he signaled his intention of challenging the government in Rome.

Brutus and his fellow conspirators attack Julius Caesar in the Senate chamber.

dictator. In 44 B.C., his title became "dictator for life."

A Murder Foretold

Caesar did not abolish the Senate in Rome, and he did not declare the end of the republic. But as dictator for life, Caesar now had absolute power. Every day he transacted business on a golden throne. And with great satisfaction, he accepted religious honors and dedications that referred to him as a god.

Although Caesar ruled with a firm hand, he won the praises of the people. He celebrated parades and public holidays with great style. Dressed in the robes of Jupiter, borrowed from the god's temple, he rode through the streets of Rome. Tradition says that a slave walked behind Caesar, whispering over and over into his ear, "Remember, you are only mortal." But Caesar was deaf in one ear, and it was into this ear that the slave whispered.

With great energy, Caesar tackled a huge number of problems. He organized the administration of the provinces. He lowered taxes and gave land to the poor. He established a new calendar. With small changes, the calendar—named the Julian calendar, after Julius Caesar—is the one we still use today.

Once again, Caesar's actions alarmed his enemies. Under the rule of the dictator, the senators had seen their power evaporate. Many feared Caesar would soon declare himself king, a title most Romans despised. In fact, he was already ruling as a king, lacking only title and crown. A group of senators, led by Caesar's friend Marcus Brutus, began to plot the dictator's overthrow.

Caesar soon learned of the danger he faced. His friends warned him of the threat to his life. His wife had a dream in which she saw him viciously murdered, and she begged him not to leave the house. A soothsayer told him to take special care on March 15, the day the Romans called the Ides of March. Caesar ignored the warnings. On March 15, 44 B.C., he strode boldly into the Senate chamber.

Seeing Caesar arrive, the plotters seized their opportunity. They surrounded the dictator, pulled out daggers, and began to stab him. Twenty-three times they plunged their daggers into his defenseless body. One of the cuts came from Brutus.

As Caesar saw his friend ready to strike, he is said to have declared, *"Et tu, Brute?"* (et TOO, BROO-teh) The Latin words were a terrible condemnation: "You, too, Brutus?"

The great Julius Caesar was dead.

A Succession of Caesars

Caesar's murderers fled the Senate house, waving their bloody daggers in triumph. They thought that they had saved the republic. But they were too late.

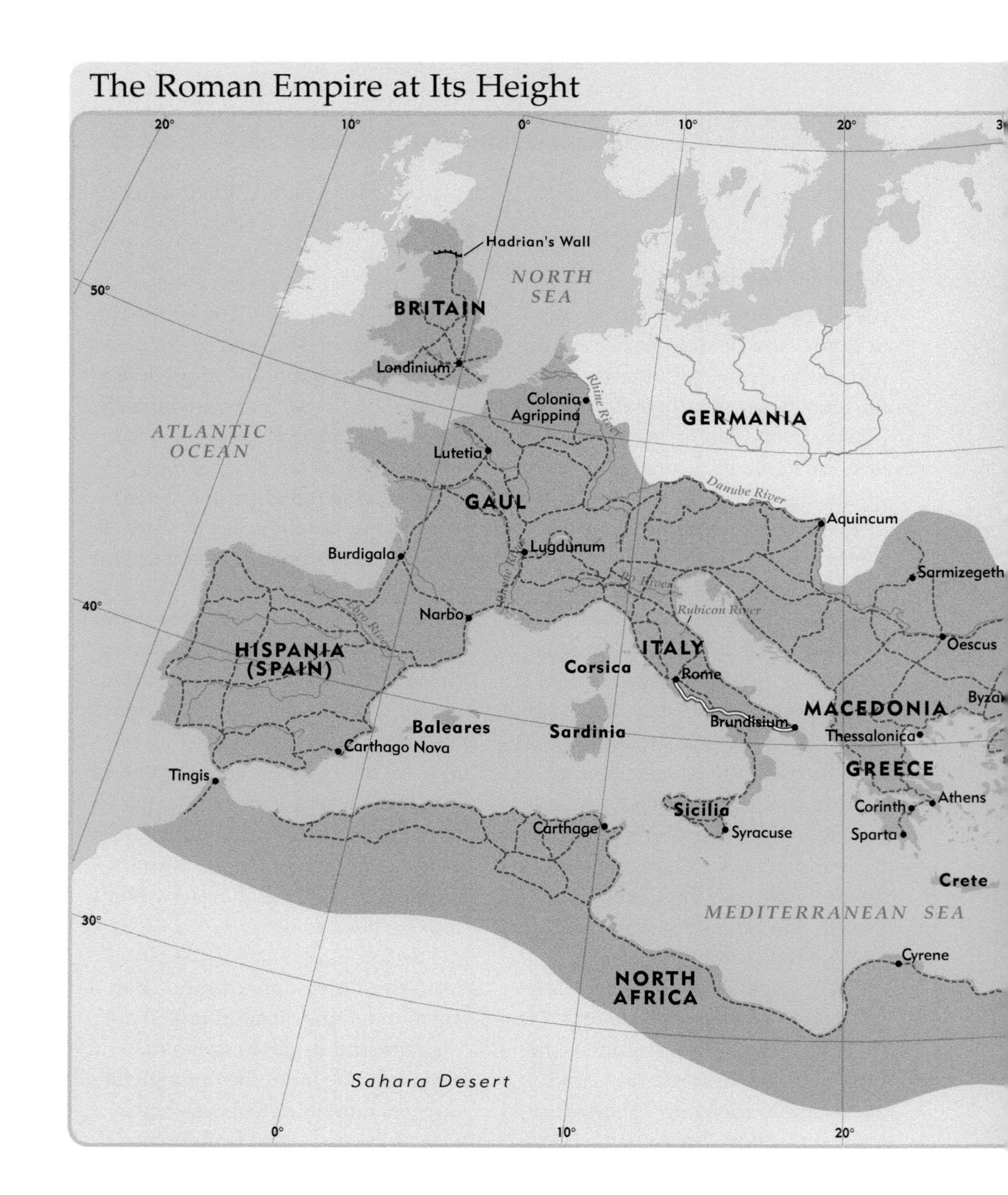

The Roman Empire at Its Height

Caesar's supporters went on the attack. The dead leader's great-nephew and adopted son, a young man named Octavian (ahk-TAY-vee-uhn), hunted down the killers and seized power for himself. The family of Julius Caesar once again controlled Rome.

In 27 B.C., the Senate voted that young Octavian be given the name Augustus, which means "exalted one." Caesar Augustus was the title Octavian used. The Senate gave him the right to rule over all of Rome's religious, military, and civil affairs. The Senate was reduced to giving advice.

Caesar Augustus established a new imperial order. The Roman republic was dead, and in its place stood a Roman empire ruled by an all-powerful emperor.

Caesar's great-nephew and adopted son, Octavian would take the title "Caesar Augustus" and launch Rome on the road to empire.

Augustus' main concern now was to restore peace and stability to Rome. The Romans were tired of constant civil war and eager for a strong ruler. But Augustus, recalling the fate of his uncle, knew he had to tread carefully. Even the most powerful emperor could not rule if the people turned against him.

The Pax Romana

The rule of Augustus ushered in a new period of peace and prosperity for the Roman Empire. The *Pax Romana* (paks roh-MAH-nuh)—the "Roman Peace"—extended over the whole Mediterranean world for about 200 years.

Hail Caesar!

Caesar was the family name of Julius Caesar. When Julius Caesar's great-nephew became emperor, he took his great-uncle's surname and became known as Caesar Augustus. In time *Caesar* became the title for all emperors who would rule Rome. In other times and nations, supreme rulers, such as the Russian czars (zhars) and German Kaisers (KIY-zurs) , liked to show their power by taking the title *Caesar*. *Czar* means Caesar in Russian. *Kaiser* means Caesar in German.

A statue of the great orator Cicero, who placed a high value on the laws of Rome.

During the Pax Romana, the empire continued to expand, and there were some wars on the frontiers. But never before had so many nations lived at peace with one another. At its height the empire stretched from Spain to Assyria and from North Africa to Hadrian's Wall in Britain. Across this vast realm there was one official language. There was one system of coinage, weights, and measures. There was one government administration, and one body of laws.

- On the map on pages 376–77, note the extent of the Roman Empire at its height. Locate the following territories along the empire's outer boundaries: Britain, Spain, North Africa, Egypt, and Assyria.

The Romans valued their law above all else. According to one of their great orators, a man named Cicero (SIS-uh-roh), a state without law was like a body without a mind.

The always-practical Romans tried to give their state an orderly mind. Called *jus gentium* (yoos GHEN-tee-uhm) or the "law of nations," Roman law applied to all people under Roman rule. This set of legal principles employed common-sense ideas about fairness, but also recognized local practices and rules. The best imperial governors enforced the law in the provinces while respecting as much as possible the customs of the people they governed. Roman law kept order in the empire.

What Was Hadrian's Wall?

Roman soldiers built this 80-mile stone wall across Britain during the reign of Emperor Hadrian (A.D. 117–138). Hadrian liked to travel his vast realm. In 122, he visited Britain and ordered the construction of a massive wall to act as a defensive barrier between Roman territory to the south and invaders to the north. The wall stretched from coast to coast and included towers, forts, and gates. Sections of this impressive structure can still be seen today.

To help keep the peace, Roman rulers also granted to loyal subjects—and sometimes to whole towns—the gift of Roman citizenship. It was a highly prized gift. "I am a Roman citizen. I appeal to Caesar." This was the cry of every citizen who believed his rights had been disregarded. He could demand to be tried by the emperor or one of his judges. Citizenship brought responsibilities as well. For example, citizens had to pay taxes and serve in the army. To most, such responsibilities seemed fair. After all, they helped finance and defend an empire that Roman citizens could call their own.

All Roads Lead to Rome

As their influence spread, the Romans built a system of roads to connect the different territories they controlled. They started building their first great road in 312 B.C. and called it the Appian (A-pee-uhn) Way, after Appius Claudius Caecus (SEE-kuhs), a Roman official who began its construction. Outside of Rome, the highway was lined on either side with magnificent tombs of wealthy Roman families. The Appian Way eventually ran from Rome to Brundisium (bruhn-DIH-zee-uhm), now the city of Brindisi (BREEN-dee-zee), on Italy's southeastern coast.

As time passed, more and more roads spread out from Rome like the spokes of a great wheel, linking the city to the farthest reaches of its empire. The Romans eventually built 50,000 miles of roads, from Britain to the edge of the Sahara in Africa,

The Appian Way was the main highway leading south out of Rome. It is paved with stones that were polished and then carefully fitted together.

from Spain to Asia Minor. Many were marked with milestones and supplied with inns where travelers could sleep and get fresh horses.

Roman engineers oversaw the construction of the highways, though soldiers often did the work between military campaigns. The roads were the best in the ancient world. They were built so well that they could last decades without needing repairs. Some portions of Roman roads are still used today.

The Romans valued their roads for several reasons. The highways allowed Roman armies to move swiftly throughout the empire. Good roads also increased travel and communication, so Rome could spread its culture over a wider area. Along the imperial highways creaked carts loaded with goods such as wool, timber, corn, and wheat. Luxury goods such as silk, jewels, and spices came from as far away as China and India. Merchants, messengers, soldiers, and travelers trekked to and from the empire's capital city. Romans could say with pride that "all roads lead to Rome."

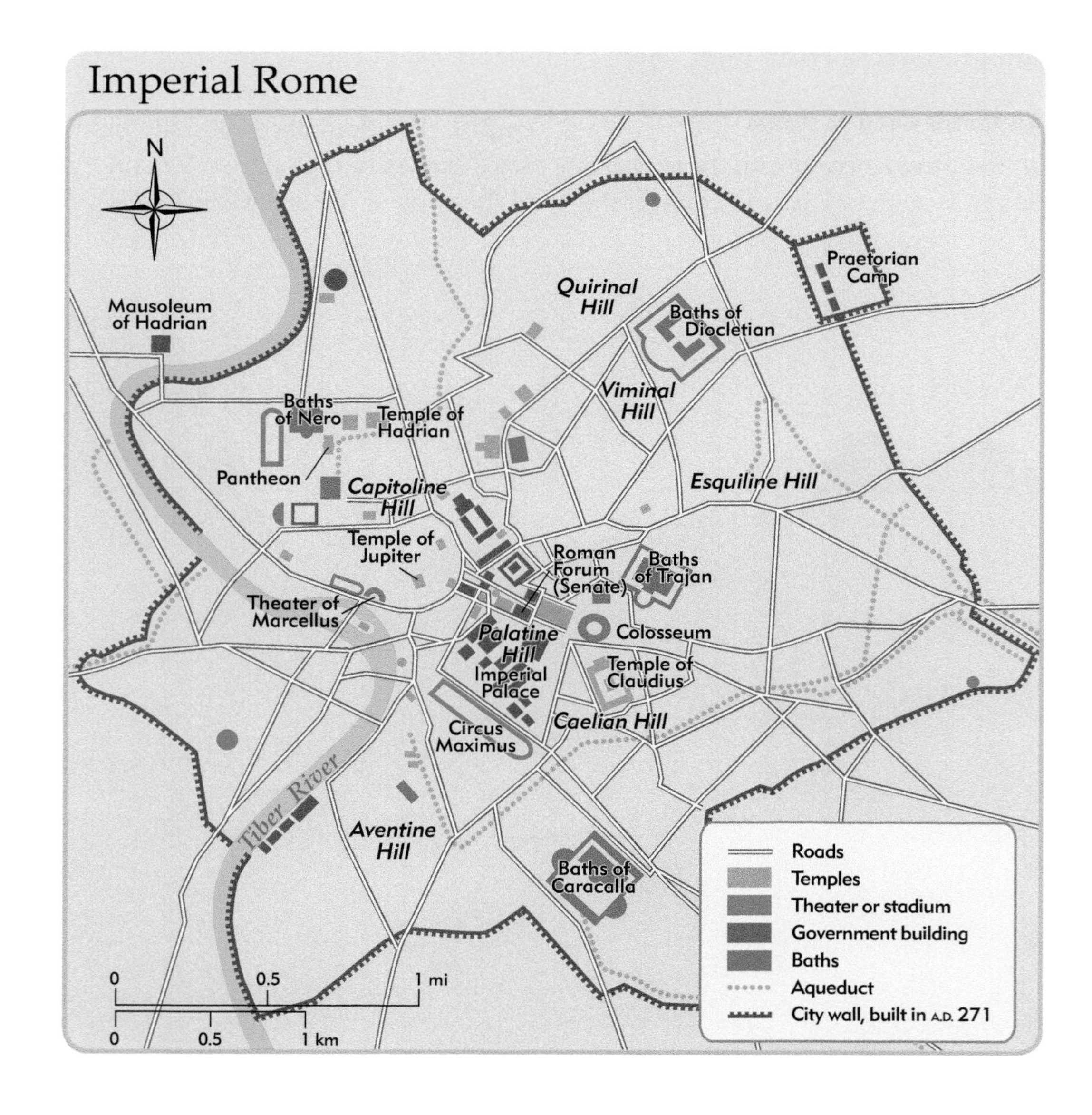

This huge oval-shaped amphitheater known as the Colosseum was the venue for many of Rome's games.

The Imperial Capital

The great capital city of Rome had become a huge commercial center. By the end of the second century A.D., its population had grown to about one million. Hundreds of warehouses were bursting with grain, oil, wine, salt, spices—everything needed to feed the hungry citizens of Rome.

Caesar Augustus spent vast sums of money and employed the best architects and sculptors to beautify Rome. He built new roads and bridges, and repaired the city's great temples and theaters. Augustus once declared, "I found Rome built of sun-dried bricks; I leave her covered in marble."

At the heart of it all was the Forum, a complex of great squares and temples, and miles of covered markets. The Forum was the main center of government, business, law, and religion in Rome. Here was the Temple of Romulus, the legendary founder of the city. Here, too, stood a column that marked the very center of the empire. The distances on every road that led to Rome were measured from it.

All around the Forum stood the public buildings of the city. To the east towered the huge amphitheater of the Colosseum (kah-luh-SEE-uhm). To the south lay the Circus Maximus (SUHR-kus MAK-suh-mus). And scattered about the city were the public baths—about 170 of them in all. It was in these places that the people of Rome found their entertainment.

"Bread and Circuses"

Augustus and the emperors that followed him knew they had to keep the people happy. If the many poor and unemployed people in the city became restless, they could riot and threaten the peace. To prevent them from becoming too restless, the emperors provided the people with all kinds of games, races, and spectacles, much of it bloody and cruel.

Many of the "games" in the city of Rome took place at the Colosseum, a gigantic stone oval three to four stories high, which had taken about 10 years to build. Some 50,000 spectators poured through 80 entrances and crammed into its tiered seats.

There they watched specially trained fighters known as gladiators. Some gladiators carried a heavy shield and short sword, while others wielded a trident, dagger, and net. Thus armed, they met in the arena and often battled each other to the death.

As the gladiators marched past the box where the emperor sat, they cried, "Hail, Caesar! *Morituri te salutant*—Those who are about to die salute you!" During big festivals, thousands of these fighters paired off for combat. When a gladiator fell to the ground, the victor looked to the emperor for a decision. If the emperor gave a sign for mercy, the fallen gladiator would be spared. But if the emperor gave a sign for death, the loser would be slain. The crowd roared their approval or dismay.

Top right: A man pits his skills against a leopard, a spectacle sure to thrill Roman crowds.

Above: Two Roman gladiators battle each other in a scene played out thousands of times in the Colosseum.

Below: Chariots thunder around the Circus Maximus, the largest of the racetracks of Rome.

Other violent spectacles took place for the amusement of the public. Wild animals from across the empire and beyond were brought to the Colosseum and set upon each other. An elephant might be sent out against a rhinoceros, or a bear turned loose among buffalo.

Sometimes man was pitted against beast, as armed hunters stalked their prey around the arena. Exotic animals—lions, tigers, leopards, elephants, even polar bears—were hunted to death in the Colosseum. Sometimes, the hunted became the hunter. Wild beasts were set upon unarmed criminals or slaves, who were torn apart and devoured for the sport of the watchers.

Most spectators of these events were not moved by compassion. The greater the slaughter, the more the people seemed to love it. They began to demand ever larger, more spectacular entertainments. Small armies sometimes reenacted military battles at the Colosseum. And naval combats—with real killing—took place on artificial lakes.

More popular still were the races at the Circus Maximus. The Circus Maximus was the largest of a half dozen circuses in and around Rome. These were nothing like the circuses we know today. They were U-shaped structures enclosing long racetracks where the empire's finest charioteers competed against each other in their four-horsed, two-wheeled chariots. Packed crowds of up to 250,000 attended races at the Circus Maximus, which boasted a track of more than 1,200 yards. At the drop of a white handkerchief, the race was on—a total of seven laps around the course. The crowds went wild, cheering their favorites and gasping with delight as a chariot lost a wheel, a driver tumbled to the ground, or a chariot crashed while taking a corner too fast.

Rome's rulers provided all these bloody and cruel public entertainments. They also provided monthly rations of free grain, oil, and wine. The leaders thought that a well-fed and entertained public would be a peaceful public. "These people want only two things—bread and circuses," a Roman writer complained. He could have added a third—holidays.

The Romans always had time for a holiday and a parade. At one point, there were nearly 200 public holidays a year, in honor of religious festivals, the emperor's birthday, and military victories. (The Romans, however, did not take weekends off from work, as we do.) Caesar's invasion of Britain was celebrated with 20 days of public holiday. The celebrations for the opening of the Colosseum went on for 100 consecutive days!

This magnificent Roman aqueduct rises in three tiers of arches above a river gorge. Water gurgled along a channel at the top, more than 160 feet above the river.

Water, Water Everywhere

Bread, circuses, and holidays—these seemed to keep the masses content. For the wealthy of Rome, of course, life was very different. Their homes often had fountains and a garden, as well as an atrium, a large, airy room inside the main entrance. Wealthy Romans adorned the interiors of their homes with all sorts of artwork. Walls were painted with mythological scenes, landscapes, or still lifes. Floors were decorated with mosaics (moh-ZAY-iks)—tiny pieces of colored tile arranged to form a picture or a design. Statues also graced the homes of the rich, many of them copies of earlier Greek works.

Some houses had indoor plumbing, with water pumped in so the rich could enjoy a bath in the privacy of their own home. Indeed, providing water to Rome was a major undertaking. Special stone channels known as aqueducts (AK-wuh-dukts) carried abundant supplies of water into the city from the surrounding hills. Sometimes these aqueducts ran along the ground, and sometimes they rose overhead, supported by brick arches.

Above: Roman steam rooms like this one were heated by a furnace that circulated hot air.

Below: This great public bath was fed by hot mineral springs.

The Romans were very proud of their aqueducts. They saw these magnificent structures as proof of the empire's greatness, and much more useful to humanity than the pyramids of Egypt.

The Romans had a point. Daily, somewhere between 50 and 200 gallons of water for every person in Rome surged through the city's 11 aqueducts, much of it making its way to the public fountains on each city block.

Of course the people didn't drink all that water. Most of it went to supply Rome's huge public baths. How huge? One of the public baths could hold 3,000 people.

The public baths of Rome were elaborate structures, their walls covered with marble and mosaics, their waters flowing from silver taps into marble basins. They became the center of social life, open to all for a tiny admission fee. At the baths, friends met to chat, to conduct business, to play dice games, and to go through a series of bathing rituals—in steam rooms, dry heat rooms, hot pools, and cold pools. They might also exercise in an adjoining gymnasium.

An Epic to Rival Homer: Virgil's *Aeneid*

The Romans were proud of their great capital and empire. Caesar Augustus wanted to encourage that pride. He decided it was time to celebrate Roman genius and splendor, just as the Greeks had celebrated theirs. In a new forum, Augustus built a splendid temple that recalled the magnificent Parthenon of Greece.

Then the emperor turned to Rome's finest poet, Virgil (VUR-juhl), to compose a new story about the founding of Rome. Caesar Augustus thought the ancient legend of Romulus and Remus suckled by a she-wolf was not grand enough for Rome. He wanted an epic poem to rival the *Iliad* and the *Odyssey*. He knew the quality of Virgil's work. Would Virgil do it?

Virgil, a shy man, hesitated at first, but at last he said yes. He knew this poem would be the work of a lifetime. It should be written in the style of the ancient Greeks, but emphasize the virtues of ancient Rome. The hero should exemplify all the old Roman virtues—duty, honor, and respect for paterfamilias.

For his hero, Virgil chose Aeneas (ih-NEE-us), a prince of Troy. Legend said that Aeneas was the son of the goddess Venus. After the Trojan War, Aeneas escaped from Troy and sailed west. After many adventures, he led the Trojan exiles to settle in Latium, where they became the ancestors of the Romans.

Virgil modeled his masterwork, called the *Aeneid* (uh-NEE-id), after the great Greek epic of the Trojan War, Homer's *Iliad*. Every educated Roman knew the story of the Trojan War. They knew that a Trojan prince, Paris, had seized the beautiful wife of the Greek king, Menelaus, and taken her to Troy. They knew that thousands of Greek soldiers had sailed to Troy for vengeance and to take back the lovely Helen.

A Golden Age for Speakers and Writers

During the reign of Caesar Augustus, Rome enjoyed a literary golden age. Some of the greatest poets and writers the world has ever known lived at that time. Chief among them was Virgil (70–19 B.C.), whose masterpiece was the *Aeneid*. Virgil, who had lived through the civil strife at the end of the republic, celebrated not just Roman greatness, but also the peace and stability that Augustus brought to Rome.

Virgil

The historian Livy (LIH-vee) (59 B.C.–A.D. 17) shared this viewpoint. He wrote 142 books on the history of Rome, from its founding to his own day. Throughout, Livy glorified the unique destiny of the Romans.

The great Roman orator Cicero (106–43 B.C.) excelled in the spoken word. Cicero was one of those called a "new man" because none of his ancestors had held office. But because of his brilliant public speaking, he became one of Rome's leading citizens.

Cicero

Cicero's tongue had many targets, among them the Roman games. "What pleasure can it give a person of taste," asked Cicero, "when a feeble human being is torn to pieces by an incredibly strong wild animal?"

In the *Aeneid*, Virgil describes how the war ends with the trickery of the Greek hero Odysseus, whom the Romans called Ulysses. It is Ulysses who devises the plan of the Trojan Horse. Greek soldiers are hiding inside a gigantic wooden horse, which the Trojans drag through the gates into their city. At night, under cover of darkness, the Greek warriors emerge from the horse and set fire to Troy.

When the Greeks attack, the sound of roaring flames awakens the Trojan hero Aeneas. A loyal son, he thinks first of his father, Anchises (an-KIY-seez). Anchises' home is sheltered among the trees, not far away. Aeneas climbs to the rooftop and sees that Troy is in flames.

Aeneas decides he must save Priam, the king of Troy, who is like a father to all Trojans. He hurries to the palace, where he hears women wailing, and the pitiful noise of groans and blows. Aeneas is horrified to see the king stabbed to death by a Greek.

It is at this point in the action that the following selection from the *Aeneid* begins.

The Escape of Aeneas

Adapted from *The Aeneid for Boys and Girls* by Alfred J. Church

Aeneas saw all these things, but he could give no help, being but one against many. The sight of old King Priam lying dead made him think of his own father, and of his wife Creusa (kree-OO-suh), and of his little son Ascanius (as-KAN-ee-us), and how he had left them at home alone and without defense.

And he thought, "Shall I not return to them, for here I can do nothing?" He turned his eyes and saw Helen in the temple of Vesta. She was sitting by the altar, hoping to be safe in a holy place. She was greatly afraid, fearing the Trojans, upon whom she had brought ruin, and her husband whom she had deceived.

When Aeneas saw her he was full of rage. "Shall this wicked woman go safe to Sparta?" he thought. "Shall she see again her home and her children, with women of Troy to be her handmaidens? Shall Troy be burnt and King Priam slain, and she, who is the cause of all this trouble, come to no harm? It shall not be; I myself will kill her. There is no glory in such a deed. Who can get honor from the death of a woman? Nevertheless, I would be taking vengeance for my kinsfolk and my countrymen."

But while he thought these things, there appeared to him his mother, Venus, in such a shape as he had never seen her before, not like a woman of the earth, but tall and fair, as the gods who dwell on Mount Olympus see her.

And Venus spoke to Aeneas, saying, "What means this rage, my son? Have you forgotten your old father Anchises, and your wife and little son? Surely the fire had burnt them long ago, if I had not cared for them and preserved them. And as for Helen, why are you angry with her? It is not she who has brought this great city of Troy to its ruin; it is the anger of the gods. See now; I will take away the mist that is over your eyes. Look there; see how Neptune, god of the sea, is tearing down the walls with his three-forked spear, and is rooting up the city from its foundations! See there, how Juno stands in the great gate of the city, with a spear in her hand, and great hosts of Greeks from the ships! See how Minerva sits upon the citadel, with a storm cloud round her, and her awful shield upon her arm! See how Father Jupiter stirs up the enemies of Troy! Fly, my son. I will be with you, and will not leave you till you reach your father's house." When she had so spoken, she vanished in the night.

Then Aeneas looked as his mother bade him, and saw the dreadful forms of gods, and how they were destroying the city, and as he looked, all seemed to be sinking down into fire. Just as an oak in the mountains, at which the woodmen cut with their axes, bows its head, with its branches shaking round about it, till at last, after bearing many blows, it falls at once, and crashes down the side of the mountain, so Troy seemed to fall.

When he had seen this, he turned to go to his home. His mother was by his side, though he could not see her, and he passed through the flames, and was not hurt, nor did the spear of the enemy wound him.

When he got to his home, he thought first of the old man, his father, and said to him, "Come now, let me carry you away from this city, to a safe place among the hills."

But Anchises would not go. He did not wish to live in some strange country when Troy had been destroyed. "No," he said. "You must go, for you are strong and have many days to live. I will stay. If the gods had wished me to live, they would have preserved this place for me. It is enough for me that already I have seen the city taken, and lived. Say good-bye to me, therefore, as you would say good-bye to a dying man. Already I have lived too long."

So Anchises spoke, nor could they persuade him to change his mind, though Aeneas, and his wife, and even their little child Ascanius begged him with many tears.

When Aeneas saw that he could not change the old man's purpose, he resolved to go back to the battle and die. But his wife Creusa threw herself on the ground and caught his feet. She held out to him the child Ascanius, and cried, "If you are going back into the battle that you may die there, then take your wife and child with you. For why should we live when you are dead? But if you have any hope that arms may help us, stay here, and guard your father and your wife and your son."

While she was speaking there happened a most wonderful thing. A fire glowed about the head of the child, Ascanius. It played round his long curls, and sparkled on his forehead. His father and his mother saw it, and were astonished. At first they thought that it was real fire, and would have fetched water to put it out. But when the old man Anchises, who was wise in such matters, saw it, he was glad, for he knew that this was no common fire, but a token that the child was dear to the gods. He looked up and cried, "O, Father Jupiter, if thou hearest prayer at all, hear me now, and give us a sign."

While he was speaking, a great clap of thunder resounded on the left hand, and a star shot through the skies, leaving a long trail of light behind it, passing over the city till it was hidden behind the woods of Ida. When the old man saw this, he bowed his head and said, "I will make no more delay. Lead on, and I will follow. O gods of my country, save my house, and my grandson. This sign came from you."

Then said Aeneas, for the fire was coming nearer, and the light growing brighter, and the heat more fierce, "Dear father, climb on my shoulders. I will carry you, nor shall I be tired by the weight. We will be saved, or we will perish together. Little Ascanius shall go with me, and my wife shall follow behind."

Then he turned to the servants and said, "Men of my house, listen to me. You know that as one goes out of the city, there is a temple of Ceres in a lonely place, with an old cypress tree close by. There we will meet. Go each by different ways, not all together, that we may not be seen by the enemy. And do you, my father, take in your hands the images of the household gods. My hands are red with blood, and I must not touch holy things till I have washed them in running water."

Then he put a lion's skin upon his shoulders and stooped down, and the old man Anchises climbed upon them. And the boy Ascanius laid hold of his hand, keeping pace with his father as best he could with his little steps. And Creusa followed behind.

So he went, with many fears. He had not been afraid of the swords and spears of the enemy, but now he was full of fear for his father and wife and child.

When he had nearly got to the gates of the city, a dreadful thing happened. They heard a sound of approaching feet in the darkness, and the old man cried, "Fly, my son, fly; they are coming. I see the flashing of the shields and swords." So Aeneas hurried on, but his wife was separated from him. Whether she lost her way, or whether she was tired and sat down to rest, no one knew. Aeneas never saw her again, nor did he know that she was lost till all the company met at the appointed place, and she alone was not among them.

It seemed a grievous thing to him, and he cried out against both gods and men. Then he told his companions that they must take care of the old man and of Ascanius, and that he would go and search for his wife. So he first went to his house, thinking that by some chance she might have gone back there. He found the house indeed, but the Greeks were there, and it was nearly burnt. After this he went to the citadel and to the palace of King Priam. He did not find her, but in the temple of Juno he saw two Greek warriors, Ulysses and Phoenix, keeping guard over the treasures from the temples, and over the long lines of women and children taken as prisoners. And still he looked for his wife, going through all the streets of the city, and calling her name aloud.

While he was doing this her image seemed to stand before him. It was she, and yet another, so tall and beautiful did she seem. And the spirit said, "Why are you troubled? These things have come about by the will of the gods. Jupiter himself has ordered that your Creusa should not sail across the sea with you. You have a long journey to make, and many seas to cross till you come to the place where the river Tiber flows softly through a fair and fertile land. There you shall have great prosperity. Weep not for your Creusa, for I shall not be carried away to be the slave of some Greek lady. And now farewell. Think sometimes of me, and love the child Ascanius, for he is your child and mine."

So spoke the spirit. But when Aeneas would have answered, it vanished out of his sight. Three times did he try to put his arms round her, and three times it seemed to slip away from him, being thin and light as air.

And now the night was far spent and the morning was about to break. So he went back to his comrades and found a great company of men and women, all ready to follow him, wherever he might lead them. And now the morning star, which goes before the sun, rose over Mount Ida, and Aeneas, seeing that the Greeks were in possession of Troy, and that there was no hope of help, again took his father on his shoulders, and went his way to the mountains, his people following him.

That summer Aeneas and his companions built ships for the voyage, dwelling meantime on Mount Ida. By the next summer the work was finished, and old Anchises commanded that they should wait no longer. So they sailed, taking their gods with them, and seeking a new home.

A nineteenth-century painting of ancient Jerusalem and the rugged terrain of Judea, birthplace of Christianity.

Judea and the Rise of Christianity

During the reign of Caesar Augustus, the Roman Empire covered more than half of Europe, most of North Africa, Asia Minor, and parts of the eastern Mediterranean and Mesopotamia. Historians estimate that the empire included from 50 to 70 million subjects. Most conquered peoples accepted Roman rule, even if grudgingly. Some became as Roman as the Romans themselves.

The Land of Judea and Its People

East of Rome, however, lay a province called Judea (joo-DEE-uh). Its people definitely did *not* accept the Roman way of doing things. Out of Judea came new ideas that would change the mighty Roman Empire. In fact, the beliefs that emerged in Judea would eventually sweep much of the world. For in this tiny, out-of-the-way Roman province, the religion of Christianity was born.

- On the map on page 396, locate the province of Judea.

The Jews of Judea inherited the traditions of their Hebrew forefathers. Their neighbors in the region believed in many gods, but the Jews placed their faith in only one God. They followed the laws and teachings of the Torah, the first five books of the Hebrew Bible.

Judea had been conquered several times in the centuries before the Roman Empire. First came the Assyrians, around 720 B.C. Then Nebuchadnezzar had forced the Hebrews to live in exile in Babylon. After that, the Persians had conquered Babylon

This chapter explores the land of Judea, a province of the Roman Empire located in the eastern Mediterranean.

and allowed the Hebrews to return home. Later, Alexander the Great defeated the Persian Empire, and the Jews became his subjects.

As you know, with the conquests of Alexander, Greek culture spread eastward as Greek traders and settlers moved into newly conquered lands. In most places, Greek culture blended easily with the old ways, creating a Hellenistic culture. In Judea, however, many Jews did not want to be "Hellenized." Let's see why.

Hebrews in a Hellenistic World

Judaism was more than just a set of beliefs. It was a whole way of life. The Jews considered the instructions in the Torah to be God's law for his chosen people. For the Jews, the Torah did not just speak of right and wrong. It also reminded them of their special covenant with God and told them specific ways to live out this covenant. It told them what to eat and what to wear. It told them when and how to work. The Torah became the most important guide in their lives.

By following the Torah, the Jews had been able to keep their own traditions even under foreign rule. Many Jews felt that changing their way of life and adopting "foreign ways" would mean losing their identity as God's chosen people. It would mean changing God's law.

With Alexander's conquest, however, came a steady flow of Greek people, ideas, and art into Judea. Some Jews admired the art and philosophy of the Greeks. They liked the wealth and comforts of Greek life. They decided they could enjoy these benefits without giving up Judaism. They began to imitate the Greeks and gradually became Hellenized.

Hellenistic culture spread very slowly in Judea—too slowly for the region's impatient rulers who reigned after Alexander's death. These foreign rulers tried to force the Jews to adopt Greek ways. They said the Jews could not practice their own religion, but must worship other gods. The Jews revolted and overthrew these heirs of Alexander.

For a short while, the Jews lived without foreign rule. It proved impossible, however, to wipe out the

The Origin of Hanukkah

Hanukkah (HAH-nuh-kuh), the Jewish Festival of Lights, comes from a time of Jewish triumph over foreign rule. In 165 B.C., Jews in Judea overthrew the tyrant Antiochus (an-TIY-uh-kus) IV, who had demanded that they worship Greek gods. A brave Jewish family, the Maccabees, led the revolt. After defeating their foreign foes, the Jews found the temple in Jerusalem in near ruin. They set about restoring it. They could find only one small flask of holy oil with which to light the temple's sacred lamp. It is said that the oil burned brightly for eight days—long enough to procure more oil. Jews commemorate this event each year by lighting a menorah, an eight-branched candelabrum with one candle for each day the oil burned.

influence of Hellenism. Two parties grew powerful in Judea. One party wanted to rid the region of Hellenistic ways. The other wanted to keep them. Civil war broke out, and the Hellenized Jews asked Rome for help. The Romans lost no time in coming to the aid of the Hellenized Jews. But when the civil war was over, Rome ruled Judea.

Roman Rule in Judea

Judea came under Roman rule in 63 B.C. Roman troops and officials tried to keep strict control of the region, but the proud Judeans (joo-DEE-uhns) seemed ready to revolt at any time. Most Jews regarded the Romans as cruel occupiers who looked down on conquered peoples.

The Romans couldn't understand Jewish attitudes. How could these Judeans possibly think that their own customs were best? Wasn't the Roman way the way of the world? Often, the Romans insulted the Jews and their religion without even realizing it. For example, Roman coins carried images of men and animals. The Jews found this offensive because the Torah forbade the use of "graven images." Why did these Romans have to drag their idols into Judea? Wasn't it bad enough, the Jews thought, that the Romans worshipped so many false gods, such as Jupiter and Mars? At times they even seemed to worship the emperor himself as a god!

One small group of Jews was especially opposed to Hellenism and Roman rule. This group, called the Zealots (ZEH-luhts), regarded rule by foreigners as an offense to God. "We bow to no one but our God," they cried. "The Romans must go!"

The Zealots reminded the Jews of a message from their prophets of old. The prophets had predicted the coming of the Messiah (meh-SIY-uh), God's chosen leader, a mighty king who would liberate the Jews and drive out the Romans. Some people even said the Messiah would be an angel-like being who would descend from the heavens on wings of fire. He would start a new kingdom—an all-powerful kingdom of God.

In A.D. 6, the Zealots led a rebellion against Rome. Some Jews tore down the Roman golden eagle, the symbol of the Empire, which stood at the gates of the Jewish temple in Jerusalem. The Romans arrested the troublemakers and condemned them to be burned alive. An angry mob stoned some Roman soldiers, and riots broke out. The Romans brutally crushed the uprising. They used a terrible punishment called crucifixion. They nailed the offenders to wooden crosses and left them to die. In this uprising, the Romans crucified 2,000 Jews and left their bodies hanging on crosses for days for all to see.

Roman rule grew harsher, and the harsher it grew, the more unrest it caused. Bands of Zealots hid in the mountains of Galilee (GA-luh-lee),

The heads on Roman coins—like this one of a female with an oak leaf crown—offended the Judeans. The Jewish Torah forbade the use of "graven images."

Hills overlooking the Sea of Galilee, to the north of Judea.

north of Judea. To most Jews, the Zealots were patriots and heroes. Eager followers were sure that one of them must be the Messiah, but many of the Zealots ended up dying on Roman crosses. Rome was determined to stamp out any further rebellion.

Some Jews were afraid of the Zealots. Perhaps they feared that the resistance of the Zealots would make Roman rule become even harsher. Perhaps they were enjoying the wealth that Roman rule had brought to some in Judea. In any case, they urged the Romans to catch the Zealots and punish them. The Romans needed no urging.

In A.D. 26, Pontius Pilate (PAHN-chuhs PIY-luht) became the Roman governor of Judea. Pilate handled trouble in a fairly simple way. He arrested anyone who might cause unrest. If a rebel claimed to be the promised savior who would overthrow Roman rule, the new governor quickly had him killed. Pilate had no intention of letting one of these so-called Messiahs incite rebellion under his rule.

In about A.D. 30, Pilate got word of still another Messiah. He came from the small, hilly province of Galilee.

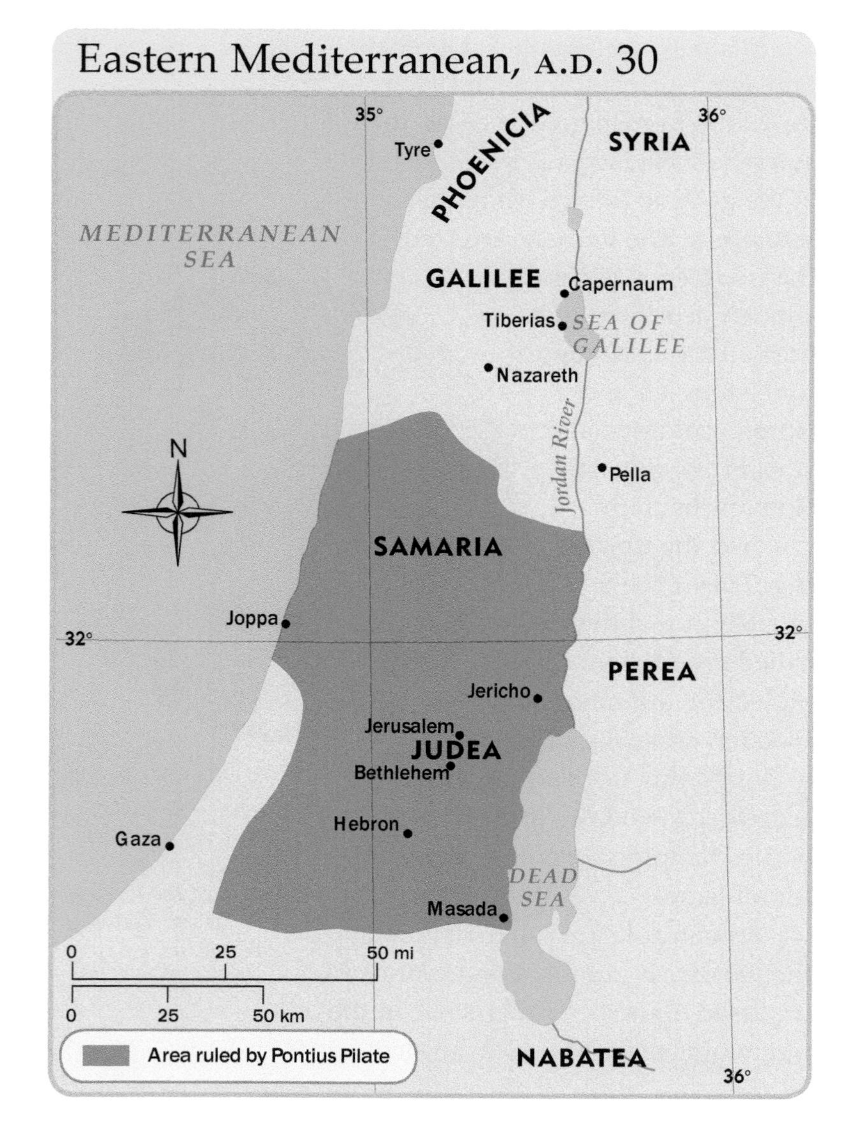

- On the map at left, find Jerusalem in the province of Judea. Find the province of Galilee, north of Judea.

The Early Life of Jesus

The man from Galilee was a Jewish carpenter named Jesus. His life would be short—only about thirty-three years. He spent only three of those years teaching. Yet he was certainly one of the most influential people who ever lived.

Years after Jesus died, some of his followers wrote down descriptions of

This seventeenth-century painting shows shepherds visiting Jesus in Bethlehem at the time of his birth.

his life and teachings. These writings, later collected and made part of the Christian Bible, are known as the Gospels. *Gospel* comes from two old English words meaning "good news."

According to the Gospels, Jesus had a humble birth in Bethlehem, a little town in Judea. He was raised, however, in the town of Nazareth, to the north in Galilee. The Gospels say little about Jesus' childhood, but he probably grew up helping his father with carpentry work. Like other Jewish children, he studied the Torah and learned about the history of the Jews. His family took him to the temple in Jerusalem, the holy city of the Jews, to observe Passover, the time when the Jews celebrated their ancestors' liberation from bondage in Egypt. Jesus learned the words of Moses and of the later prophets. He memorized the laws, prayers, psalms, and sayings of his people.

Nazareth was a small, out-of-the-way village. Still, there was unrest and trouble there. People grumbled about Roman rule and having to pay Roman taxes. They argued about what the Torah really meant, and what the kingdom of God would be like. Sometimes men passed through town preaching and making prophecies. Some said that Rome would fall. Others said that Judea would be destroyed. Still others kept urging people to watch for the Messiah. Looking around him, Jesus must have seen many men and women who seemed to live confused, unhappy lives.

When Did Jesus Live?

As you have learned, the calendar used by much of the world is based on a system that divides years into B.C. (before Christ) and A.D. (*anno Domini*, Latin for "in the year of our Lord"). This system, devised in the sixth century, designated the year of Jesus' birth as A.D. 1. Modern-day scholars believe that Jesus was actually born earlier than A.D. 1—perhaps in the year 4 B.C. He died around the year A.D. 29.

Right: Watched by an angel, John the Baptist baptizes his cousin Jesus in the waters of the River Jordan. This work was painted by an Italian artist around 1560.

Below: Jesus prays in the wilderness before beginning his teaching in Galilee.

When Jesus was about 30, he heard that his cousin John, known throughout Galilee as John the Baptist, was preaching and urging the Jews to prepare for the Messiah's coming. Those who listened and promised to reform their lives were immersed by John in the River Jordan. This ritual, called baptism, was a symbol of washing away old sins or offenses against God. Jesus asked John to baptize him. The Gospels say that when Jesus rose from the river's waters, he felt the spirit of God touching him. He believed the time was coming for him to bring God's message to the world.

The Gospels say that Jesus went to a lonely place in the wilderness to think, pray, and be alone. He needed to decide how to do his work. He wanted to be sure he was strong enough for his mission. When he came out of the wilderness, he was ready. "The time that was appointed has come, and the kingdom of God is here," he said. "Repent and believe the good news."

The Good News

Jesus went north to Capernaum (kuh-PUHR-nay-uhm) by the Sea of Galilee. He walked from village to village, across fields, down dusty roads, along the shores of lakes, spreading the "good news." He did not seek out wealthy, important citizens. His message was for everyone, including poor people who were troubled or ill, even those who were frightened because they had done wrong in the eyes of God and the law. He listened to their troubles. He comforted them with news of God's love. God loved them like a father, he said. He promised that with faith, people could begin new lives.

Jesus taught that the kingdom of God the Jews awaited was not an earthly kingdom like the Roman

Empire. It was not a kingdom of marble temples or gold and silver. Rather, it was a way of living. It was, Jesus said, about living a life ruled by God. To Jesus, the important thing about the kingdom of God was having faith in God and behaving toward others the way God wanted.

And how did God want people to behave? Jesus quoted words of Moses that were known to all Jews. "You shall love the Lord your God with all your heart, with all your soul, with all your mind.... And you shall love your neighbor as yourself." But Jesus said that the old law of Moses was not enough. A good man did not revenge himself. He did not hate his enemies. "Love your enemies," Jesus said. "Do good even to those who hate you." For those who had long suffered under the cruel rule of the Romans, these words must have been hard to accept.

The words of Jesus were not always gentle. He said that men often were liars and hypocrites, proud and self-satisfied. Jesus was especially critical of some religious leaders of the Jews called Pharisees (FAIR-uh-seez). The Pharisees insisted that Jews observe every detail of the Torah. They sometimes seemed smug because they believed they were being more faithful to God's law than most Jews. But Jesus said they "laid heavy burdens" upon the people. Rather than feeling superior to others, said Jesus, they should try to serve and help even the poorest. Love one another, Jesus urged. All people, he said, are precious to God and should treat one another justly and lovingly.

Jesus showed kindness to the lowliest people. The Gospels report that he spent time with ragged beggars and lepers. He promised forgiveness for criminals if they would repent and put their faith in God. He taught that people can show their love for God by doing good for others. They must feed the hungry, clothe the poor, and shelter the stranger. This, he said, was the way to find God's kingdom.

These words disappointed and shocked some Jews. They wanted a Messiah who would drive out the Romans and build a great kingdom. They didn't want to hear messages about feeding beggars and clothing the poor. Other Jews, however, heard Jesus eagerly. More and more people flocked to hear him.

Word spread that Jesus was a worker of miracles. The Gospels say that he cured lepers, that he gave

This painting, by a French artist of the 1600s, shows Jesus healing the blind of Jericho.

lame men the strength to walk, and that he fed a hungry crowd with just five loaves of bread and two small fishes.

Of the many who followed him, Jesus chose twelve men to be his close companions and go everywhere with him. They were not rich or powerful. Most of them earned their living in simple country trades. Some of them, including Peter, Andrew, James, and John, were fishermen. "Come with me, and I will make you fishers of men," Jesus said. So they left their nets to accompany him.

These twelve men were Jesus' first disciples (dih-SIY-puhls). *Disciple* comes from a Latin word meaning "pupil" or "learner." The twelve are also known as his *apostles* (uh-PAH-suhls). Jesus wanted these men to understand his message about God's kingdom. He wanted them to carry on his work after he was gone.

Teaching Through Parables

Jesus often told brief stories, called parables, to help people understand his message. Once, when he reminded some listeners that they should love their neighbors, an expert in the Jewish law stood up and asked, "Who is my neighbor?" Jesus responded by telling the parable of the Good Samaritan.

The phrase "Good Samaritan" would have seemed odd to Jews in Jesus' time. That's because often they did not get along with people from Samaria, a region that lay south of Galilee. In the parable Jesus told, the traveler who helps the wounded man is the last person the Jews would have expected to offer aid. Here, from chapter 10 of the Book of Luke in the Christian Bible, is the story Jesus told. In the parable, the "Levite" is a Hebrew who serves as an assistant to priests.

The Parable of the Good Samaritan

A man was going down from Jerusalem to Jericho, and he fell among robbers, who stripped him and beat him, and departed, leaving him half dead. Now by chance a priest was going down the road; and when he saw him he passed by on the other side. So likewise a Levite, when he came to the place and saw him, passed by on the other side.

But a Samaritan, as he journeyed, came to where he was; and when he saw him, he had compassion, and went to him and bound up his wounds, pouring on oil and wine; then he set him on his own beast and brought him to an inn, and took care of him. And the next day he took out two denarii [coins] and gave them to the innkeeper, saying, "Take care of him; and whatever more you spend, I will repay you when I come back."

Which of these three, do you think, proved neighbor to the man who fell among the robbers?

Jesus in Jerusalem

Jesus spent perhaps three years moving through the countryside, teaching in small towns and villages throughout Galilee. Then he went to Jerusalem for Passover. Jews had come from all over Judea for the holiday. Many had heard of Jesus and his teachings. They welcomed him eagerly, and some even greeted him as the Messiah.

The Jewish leaders watched Jesus carefully. In Jerusalem, he entered the temple and there he saw agents of the Pharisees selling offerings. Jews entering the temple were supposed to buy an offering to bring to the altar. The money, of course, went to the Pharisees. Jesus knotted a rope as a whip and sent the Pharisees' offerings flying, overturning their tables and saying, "My house shall be a house of prayer, but you have made it a den of thieves."

A fourteenth-century depiction of Jesus entering Jerusalem for Passover.

Many of the Jewish high priests and Pharisees grew alarmed. They were the same men who had been suspicious of the Zealots. They were suspicious of anyone who claimed to be the Messiah. In their minds, Jesus was undermining their leadership by proclaiming a new message from God, one that went beyond the old laws.

The Sermon on the Mount

In the Christian Bible, the book of Matthew recounts how Jesus sat down with some of his followers on a high place and taught them about the message he wanted them to spread. His words have come to be known as the Sermon on the Mount. Here is a part of the Sermon on the Mount.

> **Blessed are the poor in spirit, for theirs is the kingdom of heaven.**
> **Blessed are those who mourn, for they shall be comforted.**
> **Blessed are the meek, for they shall inherit the earth.**
> **Blessed are those who hunger and thirst for righteousness, for they shall be satisfied.**
> **Blessed are the merciful, for they shall obtain mercy.**
> **Blessed are the pure in heart, for they shall see God.**
> **Blessed are the peacemakers, for they shall be called sons of God.**
> **Blessed are those who are persecuted for righteousness' sake, for theirs is the kingdom of heaven.**

Who was this carpenter to tell them they were wrong? They worried that this rabble-rouser was becoming dangerously popular.

A small group of Jewish leaders began hatching a plot. On the eve of Passover, Jesus celebrated the traditional supper with his disciples in Jerusalem. According to the Gospels, he broke the bread and blessed the wine, and had a long, last talk with them. He warned them that something awful was about to happen, that he would suffer, but that something glorious would come of it, too.

The Gospels say that after supper Jesus went to a nearby garden to pray. Toward dawn a crowd of armed men sent by the chief priests appeared and seized him. They hauled him before Pontius Pilate, the Roman governor.

The chief priests accused Jesus of trying to break the old laws. They accused him of stirring up the people with his preaching. They said he claimed to be the new king of Judea, and that he preached revolt against Roman rule. They cried out that he must be punished.

According to the Gospels, the crowds shouted, "Crucify him! Crucify him!" Pilate handed over Jesus to be put to death. Roman soldiers mocked him, beat him, and spat on his head. Then they took him to a hill in Jerusalem, nailed him to a cross, and left him to die. The Gospels say that, even in death, Jesus showed a

A sixteenth-century painting shows Jesus surrounded by his 12 disciples at what is now known as the Last Supper.

love few people could understand: "Father, forgive them, for they know not what they do," he said.

That evening, Jesus was buried in a tomb cut in a rock. His disciples, terrified for their own lives, fled into hiding. But, according to the Gospels, two days after Jesus' crucifixion, some of his followers went to his tomb and found it empty. Soon afterward, the Gospels say, Jesus appeared to his disciples, talked with them, and told them to carry on his work. Word of his resurrection began to spread. "He is alive!" his followers joyously greeted each other. "Surely he is the Messiah!"

The Apostles Set to Work

Headed by Peter, the apostle Jesus had chosen to lead them, Jesus' most devout followers set out to carry on his work. Their success was surprising. They started to teach, and people started to listen.

Peter and the other disciples taught that Jesus was the Son of God. They said that he was indeed the Messiah—not one who wanted earthly power, but one who brought the message of God's love. The apostles and disciples told of miracles Jesus had performed. They spoke of his death on the cross, and said that on the third day he had risen from the dead. They predicted that some day he would come again to complete the work he had begun.

Some Jews believed the disciples' teachings, and the number of Christians began to grow. The early Jewish Christians came from many different backgrounds. Still, they all shared certain ideas. The most important was their belief in Jesus as the Son of God and the savior of mankind. They believed that by following the teachings of Jesus and living as he had taught, people could be saved and enter heaven. These ideas became the basis of the Christian faith.

And so in a small corner of the Roman Empire, Christianity took root. Over time, as we shall see, it spread far and wide.

The apostle Peter teaches about the life and message of Jesus Christ. This artwork was painted in Spain in the 1300s.

This fifteenth-century Italian painting shows the apostle Peter explaining the Christian message to a crowd.

The Spread of Christianity

Christianity began in a little corner of the Roman Empire but would grow to become an important world religion. It spread through the missionary work of the first apostles and the tireless efforts of a man history remembers as Paul of Tarsus. Some scholars think Christianity would never have become a world religion without the work of Paul.

As Christian communities sprang up in Judea, Syria, Greece, and finally in Rome itself, Romans started to take notice. By A.D. 64, the Roman government took action against the young religion. For the next two centuries, Christians in the Roman Empire were sometimes tolerated, and sometimes persecuted.

From Saul to Paul

As Peter and other disciples of Jesus preached in Jerusalem, the chief priests of the Jews worried. What did this new faith mean for Jews in Judea? Was this new message of Jesus consistent with old Jewish law? The followers of Jesus were stirring enthusiasm for a new "kingdom of God" that could only trouble the wary Romans. Would Rome intervene in Judea again?

Jesus himself had angered some of the Jewish high priests. They now resolved to take action against his followers. One young Pharisee stood ready to help resist the followers of Jesus. His name was Saul. We know about Saul from his own writings and from accounts about him in the Christian Bible.

As a young man Saul hated the followers of Jesus. Born in the port city of Tarsus (in what is today Turkey) sometime around the year A.D. 10, Saul grew up as a Jew in a

Artists often depict Paul carrying Christian scripture and the "sword of the spirit"—a symbol for the word of God.

Above: A Jerusalem mob stones Stephen to death. Stephen was the first Christian martyr. A martyr is someone who dies for his or her faith.

Right: Paul spreads the Gospel of Jesus Christ to the many peoples of the Roman world.

Hellenistic world. Tarsus was a busy city of seafarers and merchants. Although he spoke Greek and was raised amid Greek ideas, Saul was also steeped in his family's Jewish heritage. He studied the Torah and the Hebrew language. Saul's family was prosperous, and they had long enjoyed the privileges of Roman citizenship.

As a young Pharisee, Saul journeyed to Jerusalem for more formal studies of Jewish traditions. There he joined the group of Jews who condemned the followers of Jesus. He thought their new ideas violated Jewish law and threatened the religious understandings that Jews had lived by for centuries.

One day Saul looked on while an angry mob stoned to death a follower of Jesus named Stephen. Saul did not object. He thought the man deserved his fate.

Saul made up his mind to help stamp out Christianity. He set out from Jerusalem with orders to track down and arrest Christians in the city of Damascus and bring them to trial.

It seems that on the road to Damascus, Saul's life changed dramatically. One account in the Christian Bible says he was blinded by a great light, fell to the ground, and heard the voice of Jesus asking why Saul persecuted him. After that, the Bible says, Saul came to believe in Jesus. Saul himself said that God "had been pleased to reveal his Son to me in order that I might preach him among the gentiles." (*Gentile* is a biblical term for a person who is not Jewish.)

It is clear that Saul of Tarsus had an experience that made him a different person. He went from being one of Christianity's greatest enemies to one of its greatest teachers and disciples. To show that change, Saul stopped using the Hebrew form of his name, Saul, and began to use its Roman form, Paul.

For the next 20 years, Paul traveled throughout the lands of the eastern

Mediterranean, spreading the faith he had once tried to destroy. Never resting, he went from town to town and village to village, telling people about Jesus. When he moved to another town, he left behind a new group of Christians.

Paul Reaches Out to All

Paul wanted *everyone* to know Jesus' message, so he preached not only to Jews but also to gentiles. Since Paul spoke and wrote Greek, the common language of the Hellenistic world, he was a very effective messenger to the gentiles. Paul traveled far and wide—to Asia Minor, to Greece, and ultimately to Rome.

- On the map below, note the extent of Paul's travels.

More than any other disciple, it was Paul who insisted that Jesus' message was for all people, not just for the Jews. He said Jesus was the Messiah for all. The word *Messiah* in Greek is *Christos* (KREES-tohs), and it was through Paul that Jesus became known as "Jesus Christ."

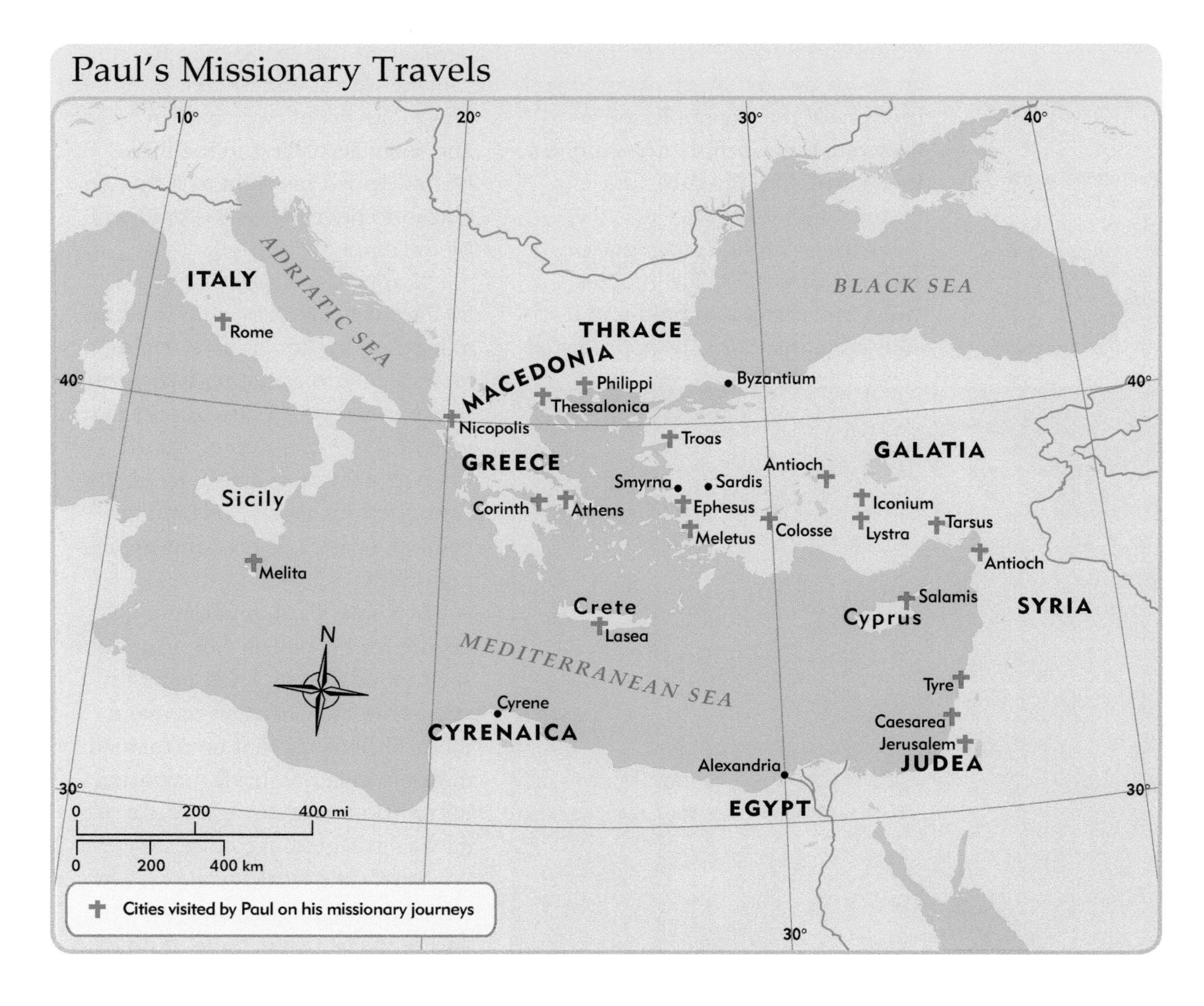

Sometimes Paul would write long letters, or epistles (ih-PIH-suhls), to the people he had converted, answering their questions and settling problems. The letters were full of vivid explanations of Jesus' message, as well as practical advice. In one letter he wrote, "Whatever is true, whatever is honorable, whatever is right, whatever is pure, whatever is lovely, whatever is of good repute, if there is any excellence and anything worthy of praise, let your mind dwell on these things." In another letter he said, "Love bears all things, believes all things, hopes all things, endures all things." He sent his letters to groups of Christians in towns throughout the Roman Empire—places such as Corinth, Thessalonica (theh-suh-LAH-nih-kuh), and Philippi (FIH-luh-piy).

Whether in the synagogue or speaking directly to the gentiles, Paul's preaching was bold and it angered many. Some Jews protested that he was turning people away from the Torah. Others thought he threatened Jewish customs by mixing Jews and gentiles together.

Paul writes a letter to one of the Christian groups that began to spring up in the Roman Empire. Such letters, or epistles, later became part of the Christian Bible.

Paul's life was filled with danger. Sometimes he had to flee quickly after preaching to people who did not accept his views. More than once he ended up in prison.

During a visit to Jerusalem, Paul faced an excited mob that probably would have beaten him to death if the Romans had not stepped in to keep the peace. Roman soldiers arrested Paul, at least in part for his own safety. Paul's enemies demanded that he be tried for causing unrest and breaking Jewish laws. Paul spent two years in prison and then, according to the Bible, he demanded his right as a Roman citizen to have his case considered by the emperor himself.

"I appeal to Caesar," he said. So Paul was taken by ship to Rome to be tried by Roman law. There he remained for another two years, living in a rented house under the watchful eye of a Roman guard. Even under house arrest, he gladly continued his work, welcoming visitors, writing letters, and preaching boldly.

In Rome, Paul apparently lost his life for his beliefs. Some accounts say that he first traveled to Spain, spreading the Christian message there. Others say that he remained in Rome awaiting trial. According to tradition, sometime after A.D. 60, he was executed in Rome.

But Paul's work survived. The letters he wrote eventually became part of the Christian Bible. With Paul,

This fourteenth-century painting shows Paul being arrested in Jerusalem. As a Roman citizen, he had the right to present his case before the emperor in Rome.

the message of Jesus spread from a handful of Jews in the area near Jerusalem to gentiles throughout the eastern Mediterranean and finally even to Rome itself.

The Romans Take Notice

Other Christians also tried to spread their faith in Rome. Tradition has it that Peter, one of Jesus' apostles, spread the faith up the Mediterranean coast, and then moved on to Rome where he too taught the message of Jesus.

Before becoming a disciple of Jesus, Peter had been a fisherman. He was not as well educated as Paul, nor as eloquent. But he was a man of fervor and determination. He made converts, and small Christian communities began to form in the Middle East and in Rome.

Up to this time, the Romans had paid little attention to these wandering men who talked of a Jew who had risen from the dead. After all, their vast empire was full of people who held beliefs in different gods. At first they saw no threat from this new faith called Christianity. But that was about to change.

In A.D. 64, a great fire swept through Rome, blazing unchecked for nearly a week. The city's ashes were still smoldering when the first rumors swept the city.

Right: A great fire rages through the city of Rome in the year A.D. 64.

Below: Bust of the emperor Nero, who blamed the fire on the Christians.

"Nero (NEE-roh) himself set fire to the city," said some.

"He watched it burn while strumming his lyre and singing of the destruction of ancient Troy," said others.

Nero was none other than the Roman emperor. No other emperor had been more brutal or ruthless. Nero had begun his reign by poisoning two of his main rivals to the throne. When his mother kept telling him what to do, he had her killed as well.

It is likely that Nero had nothing to do with the burning of Rome. But he needed a scapegoat, someone to take the blame. So he told the people of Rome that the Christians had set fire to the city.

Terrible persecution followed. Nero had Christians thrown to the lions. Others were burned alive. Some faced death as Jesus had, crucified on a cross.

Among the Christians to die in Nero's persecution may have been the two men who had done more than any others to spread the new faith—Peter and Paul. Tradition has it that both men died in Rome at this time.

Nero died shortly after his cruel acts. Many Romans had been appalled by their emperor's actions against the Christians and felt a new compassion for the followers of Jesus. For the next two centuries Christians in Rome enjoyed periods of tolerance, sometimes broken by renewed bouts of persecution. The persecutions seemed only to strengthen their determination.

Diocletian's Great Persecution

By the third century A.D., Rome was in turmoil. The empire by now was enormous, and it had become increasingly difficult for even the most capable of emperors to govern.

As the rule of law broke down, the capital itself was often in chaos. During one 16-year period (A.D. 244 to 260), 16 men claimed the title of emperor, and none of them died a natural death.

Enemies on the borders of the empire were constantly launching attacks. In the north, a Germanic people known as the Goths invaded Roman territory many times. In the east, the Persians overran Mesopotamia and Syria. Threats also sprang from Africa, Gaul, and Spain.

During these difficult times, Christians once again became targets of persecution in the Roman Empire. Fearful and suspicious Romans wondered: Why won't these Christians worship the gods of Rome? Why won't they bow down before the emperor? What place does this foreign cult have in Rome itself, the very heart of the empire?

In A.D. 284, a Roman general named Diocletian (diy-uh-KLEE-shun) became emperor. Diocletian took the reins of power firmly in hand. He set about restoring peace to Rome and setting up a new form of government. His efforts to establish order succeeded, but at a terrible cost to the Christians of Rome.

As a general, Diocletian was used to having his orders obeyed, quickly and unquestioningly. He also believed in the unity of the Roman state. In A.D. 302, he ordered all soldiers and administrators to sacrifice to Rome's traditional gods, and he expected it to happen. By this time, Christians were a large minority in Rome, and they refused to follow

Faith Underground: The Catacombs

Beneath the city of Rome is a network of underground passages and rooms known as the catacombs. Early Christians used the catacombs as burial places and occasionally as hideaways. Among the most famous catacombs are those carved by third- and fourth-century Christians in the soft rock. Here they buried their dead and held funerals.

The Christians decorated some of the corridors with symbols of the young religion. Scratched on a wall, a dove with an olive branch stood for the peace and happiness of the soul. An anchor represented hope. And most common of all, the fish stood for Christ. (The Greek word for *fish* was made of the initial letters of Jesus' name and title—"Jesus Christ, Son of God and Savior.")

Anchor and fish symbols

In the catacombs, Christian artists also produced wonderful wall frescoes, which they created by painting on wet plaster. Often they depicted scenes from biblical accounts of when God had delivered his servants from times of trouble—Noah surviving the flood, Moses leading the children of Israel through the wilderness, David going forth to meet Goliath, Daniel in the lions' den. The art reflected the Christians' faith that God would save them from their trials.

Fresco

The narrow, winding tunnels of the catacombs made good places to hide during times of persecution or invasions. The Christians sometimes used them for hideaways, though not as places of worship.

Catacomb

Above: Emperor Diocletian launched the Great Persecution, a time of terrible suffering for the Christians of Rome.

Below: A nineteenth-century depiction of the slaughter of Christians in the catacombs.

the command. Emperor Diocletian was on a collision course with the Christians. Between A.D. 303 and 305, a terrible persecution followed.

Roman soldiers began seizing Christian property, burning scripture, and arresting and executing Christian leaders. They burned an entire town in which everyone professed to be Christian, killing all the inhabitants. In other places they horribly tortured believers before putting them to death. The killing and torture of Christians during this time came to be known as the Great Persecution.

But the killing of believers did not stamp out Christianity. In fact, it had the opposite effect. Many people were drawn to the faith because of the bravery Christians showed in the face of death. Christians seemed to grow in strength and in numbers. Ultimately, imperial Rome would prove weaker than those who were prepared to die for their faith.

A *martyr* is someone who dies for the sake of his or her beliefs. According to tradition, one martyr who provided a powerful example of bravery in times of persecution was a Christian priest and physician named Valentine. There are many legends about the man known to history as Saint Valentine. Historians believe that around A.D. 269, the Emperor Claudius ordered the death of this Christian priest and Roman citizen. Here is one legend of the man for whom Valentine's Day is named.

The Legend of Saint Valentine

Imagining the Past

The pretty, dark-haired girl lifted the lid of the clay pot and brought her nose close to the opening. She sniffed once, cautiously, and then again, more deeply. She smiled.

"Nettles," she said. "To ease the pain of childbirth."

Valentine turned from the table, where he had been crushing dried leaves into a powder. He peered into the pot.

"Right again!" The physician shook his head in wonder. "How in the world do you do it?"

Carefully, the girl replaced the clay lid. "I may be blind, but my other senses are as sharp as anyone's. Maybe sharper. Father says it is the justice of the gods."

Justice! Gazing into the sightless eyes, Valentine felt a tear well up in his own. What justice would rob a child of sight from her day of birth? Bianca had never traced the free flight of a bird across the sky, never stared at a beautiful statue, never seen the love on her own father's face.

Valentine scanned his shelves, the neat rows of bowls and bottles filled with the herbs he'd worked so hard to gather. He sighed deeply. Not one of his salves or tinctures would do anything to make Bianca see.

As if reading his thoughts, she said, "Someday I'll be a healer like you. And then I will find a way to cure blindness."

"Of course. Of course you will."

But Valentine did not believe his own words. Such a cure did not belong to human powers. It would take a miracle.

Every night, he knew, Bianca and her father prayed for this very miracle. Sometimes they prayed to one god, sometimes another—from great Jupiter down to their family's own household gods.

Valentine prayed for Bianca, too. But Valentine did not pray to the Roman gods. For Valentine was not just a physician; he was also a Christian priest.

Other Romans didn't understand the Christians. How could this little group say their god was the only God? What people didn't understand, they didn't like. And often their dislike turned into something stronger. Many Christians in Rome had been taken off to jail, tortured, even killed.

"Valentine." The girl's voice brought him back. "Test me again?"

The doctor looked around the room, searching for a medicine Bianca wouldn't know. Then he saw the bowl of flowers on the windowsill, bright flames of orange gold. He had picked them just this morning.

He held the bowl up to her nose and watched her inhale the faint, delicate fragrance. Her face lit up with pleasure.

"Crocuses! The first flowers of the year."

A light knock at the door interrupted them. A patient needing treatment? Valentine hurried to answer. Before he could reach the door, the tapping stopped. Then, a moment later, it began again, a little louder.

The code!

Valentine paused, alarmed. Who would come to his door in broad daylight, using the code meant for their private gatherings of prayer? One of his fellow Christians must be in serious trouble.

He pulled open the door. A tall, broad-shouldered figure filled the doorway for an instant, then quickly ducked inside.

"Marius!" Valentine embraced his guest. "What brings you here? Are you hurt?"

The young man slumped into a chair. He tapped his chest. "Do you have medicine to cure a broken heart?"

"Don't tell me that Livia no longer returns your love."

Marius said indignantly, "She is as constant as the stars in the sky."

"Then what has happened?"

"We wish to be married," Marius cried, "but since I am a soldier, the emperor will not allow it!"

Valentine sighed. The Roman Empire had good laws and bad laws, but this was surely one of the worst. Roman soldiers were forbidden to marry. The empire was always in need of troops to defend its borders, and Roman emperors believed that if soldiers had no families, they would be more willing to leave home and fight for Rome.

"Listen to me, Marius," said Valentine. "Tomorrow night, you and Livia must come to me in secret. After all, I'm a priest as well as a physician. I will marry you."

A soft voice added, "And I will help."

Startled, the young man leapt to his feet. "Who's there?" He glanced at Valentine. "I thought we were alone."

"It's my assistant, Bianca."

"The jailer's blind daughter?" Marius peered into the dark corner. "Her father works for the emperor. She will betray us."

Valentine said, "She is my friend."

"I will not betray you," said Bianca. "I'll stand watch at your wedding."

The young man frowned. "How can you stand watch? You can't even see."

"Nor can you, in the dark of night," she replied. "But I can hear as well as anyone. I will listen for the footsteps of the soldiers."

Late the next night, the young couple arrived. True to her word, Bianca waited outside, a silent figure hidden in the shadows. Casting a nervous glance over his shoulder, Marius gave the secret knock. A moment later, the door cracked open and a hand drew them inside.

A single candle lit the room. Valentine faced the couple. In a voice no more than a whisper, he began the Christian marriage ceremony.

Just then, Bianca gave a cry of warning.

Quickly, Valentine led them to the back door. "Run!" he said. "The soldiers must not find you here."

"What about you?" said Marius.

"I cannot leave Bianca to face them alone."

Outside, dark shapes surrounded him. And then the darkness was complete.

Valentine woke on a cold stone floor. His bones ached. Above him, sunlight streamed through a tiny window. Outside his cell rested a small, familiar figure.

"Bianca!" He stretched his hand through the bars. "You escaped the soldiers."

The girl smiled sadly. "What could they do to me? I already live in a prison."

Did she mean this prison, where her father was the jailer? Or the dark prison of her blindness? Either way, Valentine thought, her words were true.

"Your warning saved Marius and Livia."

"But not you."

"I am alive," he said. "Thanks be to God."

Bianca's hands twisted together in her lap. "The emperor has said you must give up your strange Christian beliefs."

Valentine shook his head. "Never. It is impossible."

"Doctor, you must!" Tears welled up in her sightless eyes. "If you refuse, you will be executed. The date is set for the fourteenth of February."

February 14. Less than a week away.

The days passed. Through the tiny window of his cell, Valentine watched the parade of life go by. Crocuses bloomed. Birds billed and cooed, their mating season just begun. Giggling groups of girls sat underneath the trees, writing their names on folded slips of paper for the boys to draw out on the day of the ancient festival of love called Lupercalia.

Every day Bianca visited him in his cell. At first she begged him to give up his religion and save his life. But he would not be moved. "Jesus suffered and died," he said; "and if it must be so, then so will I." So she simply sat with him in silence, their fingers touching through the iron bars.

The night before his execution, Valentine lay awake. For the first time his heart was filled with doubt. Where was God now?

Then he heard a rustling outside his window. When he looked out, an extraordinary sight met his eyes.

Marius and Livia stood there together, a lit candle clasped in their joined hands. But they were not alone. Around them crowded many more young couples, each with a shared candle. Some Valentine recognized as Christians. Others were ordinary Romans, neighbors he had cared for in their childhood injuries and illnesses.

Bianca stepped forward. "They have come to be married by you." All doubt vanished. As he performed the marriage ceremony through the window, his heart was filled with joy.

The next morning, Valentine heard the approaching footsteps of the emperor's soldiers, who were coming to lead him to his execution. Bianca still sat by the window. "Oh, dear Valentine," she cried, "why must this happen?"

"God sometimes brings good from evil, my child," he said. Then he reached through the bars to grasp her hand one final time. As he did so, he placed a small paper package in the girl's hand.

As the soldiers led Valentine away, Bianca unfolded the paper. Inside was a single crocus. She felt the smooth petals. She smelled the gentle fragrance. And then, suddenly, there was something more—brilliant, flaming orange-gold—and she *saw* it.

Her fingers traced strange black marks on the paper. She did not know their meaning, but in time she would read them over and over again:

From your Valentine.

Such is the legend of Valentine, honored as a man of courage and patron of lovers. He was beheaded on February 14, 269. His remains were buried in the Roman catacombs and later a church was built on the site.

A headless statue stands amid the ruins of a Roman city in North Africa. By the fifth century A.D., the once-mighty Roman Empire was on the wane.

Rome on the Wane

By the third century A.D., Rome had forged the largest empire the world had ever known. It included territory in Europe, Africa, and Asia. Roman laws governed perhaps 70 million people. Roman citizens came from many lands.

But the very vastness of the empire caused problems. Rome's armies were numerous but spread over thousands of miles. The people were heavily taxed.

It was difficult and risky for any one man to try to run so vast an empire. Under a strong emperor, like Caesar Augustus, the empire might prosper. But it was bound to suffer under a weak or bad emperor, like Nero. From time to time, there was no emperor at all. Ambitious men raised armies and warred with each other over the throne. When they fought, law and order went by the wayside.

Meanwhile, troubles brewed on the empire's far edges. From the north and east, land-hungry tribes threatened the empire's borders. Under strong emperors, the army had a chance of holding these fierce tribesmen back. Under incompetent emperors, however, the army grew weak and these fierce invaders often stormed into Roman territory.

The larger the Roman Empire grew, the more difficult it proved to maintain. Rome was still spectacular. Its Colosseum and Circus Maximus still thundered with eager crowds. Its aqueducts still spanned the countryside. Its roads still led the world to its doorstep. But amid the grandeur, the seeds of the empire's destruction were taking root.

With capable leaders like Caesar Augustus at the helm, Rome prospered. But the sprawling empire faltered under incompetent rulers.

Abysmal Emperors at the Helm

The ancient Greeks had always been suspicious of rule by one man. After all, they asked, how can we be sure that a king or emperor will be a good ruler? What happens if an emperor turns out to be corrupt, depraved, or even insane?

The Romans found out. Sometimes their emperors were wise, but sometimes they were abysmal—as low as you can get.

Caligula (kuh-LIG-yuh-luh) was one of the worst. He was born with the name Gaius Caesar Augustus Germanicus (GAY-us SEE-zuhr aw-GUS-tus juhr-MAN-ih-kus), but as a child he wore military boots, so his father's soldiers called him *Caligula* ("little boot"). He became emperor in A.D. 37, and at first the people liked him. But soon it became apparent that the emperor was not entirely sane.

Above: Bust of Caligula, one of the worst Roman emperors.

Right: The emperor Nero shows his indifference to the burning of Rome.

Caligula wasted huge sums of money indulging his bizarre tastes and sense of humor. Once he had hundreds of boats tied together to make a temporary floating bridge so he could ride horseback across the Bay of Naples. He announced that he had become several gods at once and even ordered that a statue of himself be placed in the Temple of Jerusalem, which caused riots among the Jews there. He also declared that he had defeated the god Neptune and ordered Roman soldiers to march up and down the beach collecting sea shells as spoils of war.

For his horse, Incitatus (in-kee-TAH-toos), Caligula built a marble stall with an ivory manger. The horse wore purple blankets (purple was the color of Roman emperors) and a collar of gems. Caligula ordered silence in the entire neighborhood so Incitatus wouldn't be disturbed. The emperor was once overheard at a banquet telling his horse, whom he had invited to the feast, that he would make him consul.

Caligula ordered the murder of so many people that eventually his own soldiers got fed up. In A.D. 41, they assassinated the emperor.

You've already heard of Nero, the emperor who, according to legend, strummed his lyre as Rome burned. Fortunately, after Nero and a period of turmoil, Rome enjoyed five good emperors. The most famous was a thoughtful statesman named Marcus Aurelius (mahr-KUS aw-REEL-yus).

Commodus often dressed up as the mythical hero Hercules, wearing a lion skin and carrying a club.

But in A.D. 180 a terrible ruler named Commodus (KAHM-uh-dus) came to the throne. Commodus spent most of his reign seeking pleasure and trying to win glory for himself. He took to dressing like the mythical hero Hercules, wearing lion skins and carrying a club. He also announced that he was the new Romulus, and that Rome was now to be called *Commodiana* (kuh-MOH-dee-ah-nuh). He renamed the Roman legions *Commodianae*. The Senate became the Commodian Fortunate Senate. Not quite satisfied, he also renamed all the months and one day of the week after himself.

Commodus liked to pretend he was a gladiator and "fight" in public. This disgusted many Romans, but they had to cheer him on. He dressed in a purple robe and a cape with gold fringes, and on his head he wore a crown of gold set with jewels. As he entered the arena, the senators had to shout, "You are lord! You are first! You will be victor!" Commodus had

Some Thoughts from Marcus Aurelius

While Rome's emperors ranged from abysmal to excellent, from A.D. 98 to 180 Rome did enjoy five gifted rulers who worked hard at governing and protecting the empire. One of them, Marcus Aurelius, ruled Rome from A.D. 161 to 180. He came to power when the empire was beginning to face difficult problems, such as plague and invading tribes along the Danube River. Maybe these hard times inspired Marcus Aurelius to think about some of life's hardest questions. He turned out to be a good philosopher.

Marcus Aurelius wrote down many of his thoughts about life. These writings are known as the *Meditations*. Here are a few of his thoughts:

> Live each day as if it were your last—never worried, never idle, never arrogant. That is perfection of character.
>
> Desire only one thing: that your actions be those of a reasoning man.
>
> Can I be angry with my fellow man? He and I were born to work together, like a man's two hands. To hurt each other would be against nature's laws. For what is anger but a way of upsetting nature's laws?
>
> Do not waste time arguing what a good man should be. Be one.

no trouble winning all of his fights. The gladiators were under orders to let him win.

Rome was now facing serious problems, and Commodus did little to solve them. Angry Romans tried several times to assassinate the emperor, and finally, in A.D. 192, an assassin strangled Commodus in his bath. Then the generals set about fighting for power. The Pax Romana was coming to an end.

What Went Wrong

From the time their legendary hero Romulus built his city on the Palatine, with its commanding views in every direction, the Romans had been looking outward. They united the Italian peninsula. They defeated Carthage. They conquered Greece. They marched into Britain and Gaul. They overran Asia Minor and dominated Egypt. They pounded east to Mesopotamia and took on an empire called Parthia.

All that empire building came at a cost. The bigger the empire, the more troops were needed at the frontiers to protect it. One solution was to hire soldiers who lived on the frontier. But those soldiers had families and farms near their posts, and were not willing to go defend other parts of the empire. They also tended to support their local commander over leaders in Rome.

The once-invincible Roman army lost more and more battles by the late third century. This rock sculpture depicts a Roman emperor kneeling in defeat before a mounted Persian king.

Another solution was to enlist more Romans as soldiers to protect the frontiers. But sending more Romans overseas meant keeping less manpower near Rome itself. That meant fewer farmers in Italy, and fewer crops. People grew hungry. Taxes grew high. But that was not the worst of it.

One very high price Rome paid for its empire building was disease. In A.D. 165, Roman troops who had battled the Parthians in the east returned to Rome with a killer in their midst—the plague. This deadly disease from central Asia is believed to have killed 10 percent of the Roman population. And that epidemic was but the first. From A.D. 250 to 400, waves of smallpox and other forms of plague ravaged Rome.

The assault from disease came as neighboring tribes launched attacks against the empire. Rome had stretched its frontiers all the way to the Danube River. Now tribes along the Danube fought back. Marcus Aurelius himself died fighting on the Danube near the city now called Vienna. He was defending Roman borders and trying to expand them.

Germanic tribes on the Danube were not the only ones attacking Rome. Parthians waged war in the east, and North Africans pressed from

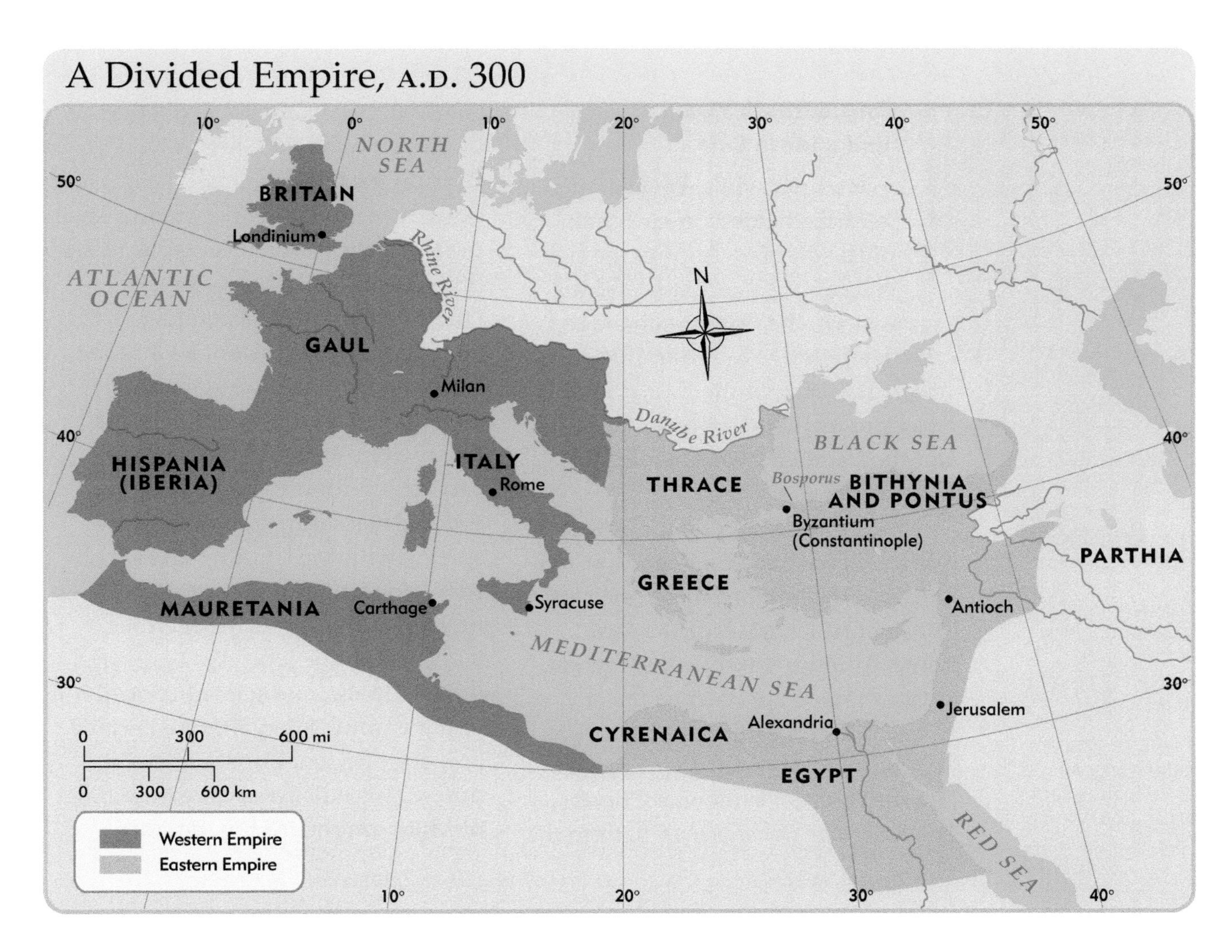

the south. Could an empire this large last? If so, how should it be governed?

Diocletian Divides the Empire

Diocletian—one of the emperors who persecuted Christians—realized that the Roman Empire had grown too large for even a good emperor to run smoothly. He tried to solve the problem by splitting the empire into two sections—eastern and western. There would be two emperors instead of one. One emperor would govern the western part of the empire, and the other would govern the eastern part. That division, he hoped, would bring stronger government. Each emperor had the same title, Augustus, and the same power. Each Augustus would have an assistant, called Caesar. When an Augustus died, the Caesar would become emperor in his place.

- On the map above, locate the Eastern Empire and Western Empire.

According to law, Rome was still one empire. As time went on, however, more and more there seemed to be two separate empires. The Western Empire had its own Augustus and Caesar. So did the Eastern Empire. Each empire had its own sets of problems and interests. The old Roman Empire that once embraced the Mediterranean world became ever more fractured and fragile.

The head of Emperor Diocletian adorns this gold coin.

Constantine's Vision and a Move East

For a brief while, Diocletian's reforms helped. In each half of the divided empire, the two rulers—the Augustus and his assistant, the Caesar—managed to keep things in order. But by A.D. 311, each of the four rulers was claiming to be the only Augustus, and they battled over who would rule the empire.

One of those battling for power was a brilliant leader named Constantine (KAHN-stuhn-teen). In one battle, Constantine led his army toward Rome. According to various legends, as Constantine approached the city, he had a vision. In the sky, he saw a flaming symbol—a blazing Chi Rho (kiy roh) cross, a symbol of Christ. The letters *chi* (X) and *rho* (P), from the Greek alphabet, are the first letters of the Greek word for Christ—XPICTOC. Beneath the flaming cross, the legends say, Constantine saw fiery letters spelling the Latin words *In hoc signo vinces* (in hohk SIG-noh WING-kays)—"In this sign you shall conquer."

Constantine was not a Christian, but he recognized the symbol of Christ. He had a new emblem made like the one in his vision, and he carried it with him into battle. He ordered his soldiers to mark their shields with the Chi Rho cross. Marching under this sign, Constantine hoped to defeat his enemies.

Constantine won this battle and others after it, and gained control of the empire. Soon after he became emperor, he sent out an edict, or order. This edict was called the Edict of Milan (muh-LAHN), because

Above: Bust of Constantine, one of four leaders struggling for control of the empire.

Right: In this painting by a seventeenth-century artist, Constantine (the figure with a wreath on his head) sees the Chi Rho cross before going into battle.

An ancient inscription showing the Chi Rho cross, symbol of Christ.

the emperor issued the edict after a meeting in Milan, Italy. The Edict of Milan said that all religions were free to exist in Rome. It mentioned Christianity in particular. No longer were Christians to be persecuted, said the edict, and any property that had been taken from them had to be returned.

Constantine's edict was a great turning point in the history of Christianity and the Roman Empire. For some 250 years, under persecuting emperors from Nero to Diocletian, people in the Roman Empire had risked their lives to follow the teachings of Jesus. But Constantine's edict made Christianity a legally recognized faith. Christians could enjoy the full rights of Roman citizens. They could hold offices in the government.

Once legal, Christianity began spreading faster than ever, especially in the cities where poor and humble folk were clustered. People liked this religion that offered comfort in troubled times and gave them hope for a better future—if not in this life, then in the next. The teachings of Jesus, including the call to love and help one's neighbor, seemed to give meaning to their hard lives.

Constantine made one other very important change in the empire. He moved the capital from Rome to a city farther east. For a long time, the Eastern Empire had been stronger and richer than the Western Empire. There was more trade and business in the East. The brightest future, it appeared, lay there. So Constantine decided to locate his new capital in the ancient Greek city of Byzantium (buh-ZAN-tee-um).

Byzantium lay on the Bosporus (BAHS-puh-rus), a strait connecting the Mediterranean and Black Seas. The city was a great center of trade between the two halves of the Roman Empire, so it was a logical place to create a glorious new capital.

- On the map on page 423, locate the city of Byzantium.

In time, Byzantium became known as Constantinople (kahn-stant-n-OH-puhl), meaning "the city of Constantine." Constantine wanted his capital to be a second Rome. He built theaters, baths, forums, circuses—and churches. Constantinople was a city dedicated to Christianity. It became the center of the Eastern branch of the Christian Church.

When Constantine died in A.D. 337, he left a busy capital in the East. He also left a rapidly expanding Christian Church. However, he himself did not convert to Christianity until the very end of his life. He was baptized on his deathbed and died the first Christian emperor of the Roman Empire. As we'll see in coming chapters, the Eastern Empire he left behind would flourish for more than a thousand years.

The Decline and Fall of the Western Empire

While the Eastern Empire was gaining strength, the Western Empire was growing weaker. A tangled knot of emperors, generals, and invading tribes fought over land. No one seemed to be in charge of the government. Roads and buildings fell into disrepair. War, famine, and disease took many lives.

In many ways, the most serious threat was the invading tribes, whom the Romans called "barbarians." Today people use the word *barbarian* to describe someone who is crude, coarse, or brutal. But in the study of history, the term refers to the tough, hard-fighting tribes perched along the Roman Empire's borders.

This carved stone relief shows a Roman soldier battling a fierce tribal warrior. In the 400s, Rome's army found it increasingly difficult—and finally impossible—to control barbarian tribes.

Among the tribes the Romans called barbarians were nomadic peoples such as the Visigoths, Vandals, and Huns, who had been living along the fringes of the empire for years. As authority in the Western Empire decayed, these tribes found it easier to overrun Roman lands and towns.

In the year 410, the Visigoths plundered and pillaged all the way to the city of Rome itself. When the

emperor of the Western Empire and his court heard they were coming, they packed all their belongings and fled the city.

For 800 years Rome's thick walls and mighty armies had kept the city safe from attack. But now the army was weak and frightened, and walls weren't enough to stop the fierce Visigoths. They swarmed into the city and took everything they could lay their hands on. They toppled Rome's beautiful golden statues and melted them down into 5,000 pounds of gold. They loaded their horses with bag after bag of Roman jewelry. They packed up 30,000 pounds of silver, 4,000 silk tunics, 3,000 animal skins, and 3,000 pounds of pepper. When they had finished sacking the city, they burned a few buildings and marched away.

In the years that followed, waves of Vandals, Visigoths, Huns, and other tribes swept back and forth across what were once Roman lands.

What's a "Barbarian"?

Like many words in the English language, the word *barbarian* comes from the Greeks. The ancient Greeks used the word *barbaros* to describe anyone whose language they couldn't understand. To Greek ears, such people were making a noise that sounded like "ba, ba, ba" when they spoke. The Romans later picked up the term and used the word *barbarus* to describe people who couldn't speak Greek or Latin.

Left: Mounted Visigoths sweep unopposed into the city of Rome.

Below: Romulus Augustulus, last emperor of the Western Empire.

The West went through emperor after emperor. Finally one Roman general decided to fix things once and for all. He announced that his son would take over as emperor of the Western Empire. There was only one problem. The general's son was just a child, perhaps as young as six.

The general put royal purple robes on the tiny fellow and ordered the army to obey him. Then he gave his small son a big name—Romulus Augustulus. The people were insulted when they heard such revered names from Roman history being so misused. They called the boy Momyllus (MAWM-ee-lus), which means "little disgrace."

The people didn't have to worry about the little disgrace for long. Ten months later, barbarians captured Romulus Augustulus and his father. They killed the father, but spared the son. In the year A.D. 476, they sent Romulus Augustulus to live in a big house on a high hill overlooking the city of Naples. The barbarians gave him a yearly allowance of 6,000 pieces of gold, perhaps as a sign of respect for Rome's former greatness. The last Roman emperor—who was just a little boy—was locked up far away from the throne. And that was the end of the Roman Empire in the West.

Civilization, however, did not die out in the West. The Christian Church began filling many roles the Roman government could no longer handle. More and more people turned to the Church and depended on it.

Still, an age had passed away. The light shining from the classical world—the glory of Greece and Rome—grew dimmer. With the fall of the old Roman Empire, that light went out in Western Europe.

A: Plato's Academy in Athens.

B: The classically inspired dome of the U.S. Capitol.

C: A triumphal procession in ancient Rome.

D: Jesus teaches about the kingdom of God.

E: Apollo, Greek god of light and patron of Roman emperors.

The Enduring Legacy of the Classical World

Twelve centuries—twelve hundred years. That's the expanse of time we've traveled so far in this part of our study of the human odyssey. A lot happened during that time. Let's pause and reflect on our journey.

The Legacy of Greece

We started around 750 B.C. in ancient Greece, a land of rugged mountains and busy city-states. We took a close look at two very different city-states, Sparta and Athens.

Sparta was famous for its tough warriors. "Return with your shield or upon it," Spartan mothers told their sons as they marched off to battle.

But Athens, the birthplace of democracy, was the real jewel of Greek civilization. In the boisterous Assembly, Athenian citizens could pass laws and direct the affairs of the *polis*. The rule of kings and nobles gave way to rule by citizens. Not everyone in Athens voted and not everyone was free, but Athenian democracy broke new ground. Never before had ordinary citizens exercised so much power.

In the fifth century B.C., Greek civilization faced a huge challenge when the Persians tried to make Greece part of their empire. The Greeks fought on the plains of Marathon, in the pass at Thermopylae, and on the sea at Salamis. Finally they turned back the Persian attackers. By the time the fighting was over, Athens, with its triumphant fleet, had emerged as the leading city-state of Greece.

Side view of the Parthenon, temple to the goddess Athena.

Greek culture flourished in the Age of Pericles, as we sometimes call that Golden Age of Athens following the Persian Wars. Under the wise and energetic leadership of Pericles, the Athenians turned their city into

High atop the Acropolis, the ruins of the Parthenon and other ancient temples still rise above the city of Athens.

the cultural center of Greece. They built the magnificent Parthenon and other shining marble temples high atop the Acropolis. Artists sculpted statues that looked as though they might spring to life. Writers such as Aeschylus, Sophocles, and Euripides wrote dramas performed before eager crowds in the Theater of Dionysus. Some of their plays are still studied and performed today.

The Athenians probably thought their city's timeless architecture and lifelike sculpture would last forever. But conflict with Sparta in the Peloponnesian War brought humiliating defeat for Athens. Even in defeat, Athens remained home to a people of great intellect and ability. Greek philosophy, which produced the brilliant Socrates, Plato, and Aristotle, shone brightest after the Golden Age of Athens had passed.

During the republic, Romans of different classes had a voice in government for the first time.

Aristotle's pupil, a young Macedonian prince known to history as Alexander the Great, expanded the power of Greece and established the largest empire the world had known to that time. The empire fell apart not long after his death. But through his conquests, Greek culture spread farther than ever before. In this Hellenistic Age, Greek civilization became the common bond throughout much of the Mediterranean world.

Roman Republic and Empire

After the break-up of Alexander's empire, our human odyssey took us to Rome. Legends tell how Rome got its start when Romulus founded a town on the Palatine, one of seven hills by the Tiber River in Italy.

The Romans were a sturdy, no-nonsense people. They valued hard work, discipline, and loyalty. They respected authority, and prized order and the rule of law. Around the year 500 B.C., they took another step forward in government. The Romans decided they wanted their government to be a republic, in which citizens elected their representatives and leaders.

The Roman Republic lasted nearly 500 years and had enduring consequences. In the republic, both plebeians and patricians had a voice in running the state. With its Senate, Assemblies, and consuls, Romans set an example for balancing power, one that would be studied and followed by later republics. The Romans conquered most of Italy, and they built the best roads in the ancient world to connect the territories they controlled. As their influence spread, they were quick to absorb the best of other civilizations. They especially admired the Greeks. The Romans absorbed Greek ideas about art, architecture, and the gods.

Between 264 and 146 B.C., Roman armies fought and won the three Punic Wars against the Carthaginians. When the wars were over, the Roman Republic found itself ruling most of the world surrounding the Mediterranean Sea.

But triumph was followed by trouble. As the spoils of war and wealth of nations poured into Rome, many of the old ways of doing things began to change. Regard for the old Roman virtues—such as self-control, hard work, and duty—seemed to erode. Luxury items such as silk, lapis lazuli, and gold poured into the prosperous republic. The gap between rich and poor widened. Many farmers lost their land and ended up in Rome, searching desperately for ways to keep their families alive. Respect for the law faded. Civil wars broke out. The Roman Republic plunged into crisis.

An ambitious young general named Julius Caesar saw his chance. He had been on a military campaign in Gaul. Now he returned home. He crossed the Rubicon with his army, defeated his rivals, and declared himself dictator for life.

But Caesar's enemies worried about his ambition. They stabbed him to death in the Senate chamber in 44 B.C. Some hoped to save the republic, but the republic was already dead. Caesar's nephew, Octavian, became Rome's first emperor. The Senate gave him the title Caesar Augustus.

This painting shows Julius Caesar dispatching soldiers to the North African province of Carthage.

Days of glory followed for the Roman Empire. During the next two hundred years, the Pax Romana brought new stability, order, and peace to the Mediterranean world. Roman laws, government, roads,

These architectural splendors from Asia Minor show how Greek and Roman influence spread throughout the Mediterranean region.

aqueducts, coins, and customs spread far and wide. Great temples, palaces, public baths, and markets filled Rome itself. Crowds jammed the Colosseum and Circus Maximus. Roman emperors commanded mighty legions. As one ancient historian exclaimed, "Great are their possessions, the people that won them are greater still!" Such glory, however, could not last forever.

The Rise of Christianity and the Fall of Rome

In a remote corner of the Roman Empire called Judea, something happened that would change the empire and, eventually, much of the world. A Jewish carpenter from the province of Galilee began to attract a following. Some said this new teacher was the long awaited "Messiah."

Many of the Jewish high priests and Pharisees grew alarmed. They worried that the teachings of Jesus went beyond the old laws of the Torah. They saw Jesus and his followers as a threat to Judaism. They convinced the Roman authorities that this Galilean was disturbing the Roman peace.

A nineteenth-century depiction of Jesus of Nazareth, whose life and teachings changed the course of history.

The Romans condemned Jesus to death and crucified him on a cross. But his followers didn't disappear. Inspired by their belief in Jesus' resurrection, Peter, Paul, and many others continued to spread his message. Their beliefs became the basis for a new religion, Christianity.

Slowly but surely Christianity spread through the Roman Empire, even to Rome itself. Helped by tireless missionaries such as the convert Paul, the new faith spread among gentiles as well as Jews.

Some Roman emperors saw Christianity as a threat. Christians refused to worship the emperor as a god. For some 250 years, beginning with the emperor Nero and ending with Diocletian, Christians suffered times of persecution. But Jesus' message refused to die. On the contrary, Christianity steadily gained followers.

The Roman Empire, meanwhile, was wrestling with serious problems. It had become too vast to govern well. Land-hungry tribes that the Romans called barbarians threatened the borders. Plague ravaged the cities. Bad emperors often made things even worse. One emperor, Diocletian, tried to make it easier to rule such a vast empire by splitting it into two sections, Eastern and Western, so that a different Augustus could rule each part. His solution didn't really help.

After various battles for power, Constantine triumphed. As emperor, Constantine realized the Eastern Empire was the stronger half. He moved his capital from Rome to Byzantium. He also legalized Christianity, which helped the religion spread even more. By A.D. 392, in a dramatic turnaround, Christianity had become the official religion of Rome.

In the year A.D. 410, the unthinkable happened. Barbarians sacked Rome. It was the beginning of the end. In A.D. 476, barbarian tribes overthrew the last emperor of the Western Empire. The old Roman Empire was dead. The new Christian Church, however, was still very much alive.

The Classical Contribution

Greece and Rome, the classical civilizations that dominated the Mediterranean for more than a millennium, left an enduring legacy—particularly in the Western world.

Think about some of the ideas and practices Greece and Rome introduced. The Greeks proposed the idea of fixed laws in nature. They said that there must be natural laws that can be observed, studied, and understood. Science, as we know it today, has important roots in the ancient Greek world.

In this fanciful sixteenth-century painting, the Italian artist Raphael has depicted all the great philosophers of ancient Greece in one setting. Plato and Aristotle stand in the middle.

To the Greeks, human beings were not merely worthless slaves of the gods. They were, rather, a marvel. The Greeks admired human intelligence and reason. They were proud that human beings could reflect on their lives, their responsibilities, and their duties. "The unexamined life is not worth living," said Socrates. Greek thinkers were convinced that human beings could use reason and intelligence to seek wisdom and live a good life. The Greeks invented the discipline of philosophy, a word that means "love of wisdom."

Socrates, Plato, and Aristotle taught not just the Greeks of their time, but other civilizations and generations to come. For centuries, educated Romans were schooled in the thinking of the Greeks. The Romans admired this thoughtful people, and the ideas and philosophy of Greece would strongly influence Rome.

Greek confidence in human ability and worth inspired new art, architecture, and politics. Greeks and Romans alike sculpted stunning, lifelike statues of men and women from marble. Sculptures such as *The Discus Thrower* and the statue of Athena at the Parthenon celebrated the glory of the human form. Even Greek and Roman buildings celebrated the logic of the human mind. The buildings were ordered, symmetrical, perfectly proportioned.

In politics, it is fitting that Greeks and Romans, with their confidence in human potential, started the first democracies and republics. For a time, these civilizations banished kings and princes in favor of governments that gave citizens a voice.

An engraving of the statue of Athena that once stood in the Parthenon.

Do you remember the difference between a democracy and a republic? The Athenian form of government, democracy, was rule by all citizens. Citizens voted on laws at regular meetings. That form of democracy was practical as long as the polis was small.

Romans, the practical innovators of the classical world, figured out a way to make popular government work over a larger territory. The idea of a republic, in which citizens elected representatives and leaders, was a bold innovation for the fifth century B.C.

Romans made even greater advances in law. From the time they set down their Twelve Tables in 450 B.C., to the time Julius Caesar drew up a code for the whole empire in the first century B.C., Romans showed a special talent for law. And they were very capable administrators. The Pax Romana provided

order and stability because Romans were very good at organizing and administering.

These were some of the lasting contributions of Greece and Rome—confidence in human ability and reason, conviction that the workings of nature could be understood, and serious thought about popular government and the responsibilities of citizens.

What Difference Did It Make?

Looking back, you may wonder: Did any of this really matter? In the end the Greeks fought among themselves. The warrior Spartans vanquished the democratic Athenians, and eventually Alexander the Great conquered them all. While Rome lived as a republic for more than four centuries, it then succumbed to the dictatorial rule of Julius Caesar and a string of all-powerful emperors after him. The Pax Romana ended with barbarian invaders pounding across Rome's overextended frontiers, and then sacking the city itself.

So, what difference did it all make?

A very great difference. The light of classical civilization dimmed in the period after the fall of Rome, but as you'll learn in later studies, Greek and Roman ideas eventually blazed forth again. They continue to cast a clarifying glow even in our own time. In art, architecture, philosophy, politics, literature, and more, the contributions of Greece and Rome shaped the thought and actions of Western civilization for many centuries. Indeed, the legacy of the classical age is an enduring body of ideas without which Western civilization as we know it is unimaginable.

Left: Cicero, one of Rome's most eloquent orators, delivers a speech before the Senate.

Below: The design of the Jefferson Memorial in Washington, D.C., reflects the architecture of ancient Greece and Rome.

Time Line (600 B.C.–A.D. 500)

600 B.C.	500 B.C.	400 B.C.	300 B.C.	200 B.C.	100 B.C.

508 B.C.
Cleisthenes designs Athens' first democractic constitution.

480 B.C.
Greeks defeat the Persians at Salamis during the Persian Wars.

450 B.C.
The Roman Republic publishes its laws as the Twelve Tables.

432 B.C.
Athenians finish building the Parthenon during the Age of Pericles.

367 B.C.
Aristotle begins studies at Plato's Academy in Athens.

323 B.C.
Alexander the Great dies after building a vast empire through conquest.

202 B.C.
Romans defeat Hannibal and the Carthaginians in the Second Punic War.

44 B.C.
Julius Caesar is assassinated in the Roman Senate, and civil war follows.

27 B.C.
Octavian takes the title Caesar Augustus, becoming the first Roman emperor; the 200-year-long Pax Romana begins.

A.D. 1 | A.D. 100 | A.D. 200 | A.D. 300 | A.D. 400 | A.D. 500

A.D. 80
Romans dedicate the Colosseum.

A.D. 330
Constantine makes Byzantium the capital of his empire.

A.D. 476
Barbarians overthrow the last emperor of the Western Roman Empire.

A.D. 50
Paul spreads the new religion of Christianity.

A.D. 313
Christianity becomes a legal religion in the Roman Empire.

C. A.D. 29
Jesus is crucified in Jerusalem.

Part 4, Introduction

A: An English castle of the fourteenth century.

B: A French medieval tapestry depicting the grape harvest.

C: A Chinese statue of the Buddha, made during the Middle Ages.

D: A fourteenth-century mosque in Timbuktu.

The Medieval World

B

In A.D. 476, when Rome fell, no bell tolled for the end of an era, and no trumpet heralded a new age. In many ways, nothing seemed so very different from what had been going on for years. For more than two centuries, the sprawling Roman Empire had been attacked by barbarian tribes. The city of Rome itself had been sacked decades before. And yet, in the late fifth century, something new had begun.

Today we refer to the period between approximately A.D. 500 and 1400 as the Middle Ages. No one at the time called it that. After all, people in those days did not think of themselves as being in the middle of different eras. But later thinkers coined the term *Middle Ages* as a way of describing what they saw as a nearly thousand-year bridge between the great classical civilizations of Greece and Rome and a new modern era.

The medieval knight has come to stand for the era in which he lived. The one at right is departing for the Crusades.

Sometimes we refer to this period from the late fifth century to the late fourteenth century as "medieval" times. The term *medieval* comes from the Latin words *medius* ("middle") and *aevum* ("age"). So medieval is simply an adjective that means "relating to the Middle Ages."

The medieval world was much more than a bridge between two periods. This age began in almost all parts of the world as a time of uncertainty and danger. Nomadic tribes were on the move, hungry for land and power. As time went on, events took place that had lasting influences on history. Many roots of our modern world lie deep in medieval times. Even in the twenty-first century, we can see evidence of the Middle Ages around us. Let's take a look at a few examples.

Language, Customs, and Institutions from the Middle Ages

A proud homeowner might call himself "the king of his castle." If, on a cold and rainy night, someone stops on the highway to help you fix a flat tire, you might call him "a knight in shining armor." Newspapers might refer to a politician who struggles to reform the medical system as "a real crusader."

Those expressions all hark back to medieval times, when people built castles to protect themselves, when knights in shining armor really did patrol the land, and when knights and peasants marched together on "crusades," wars over who would rule the Holy Land.

Have you heard the expression, "from here to Timbuktu" (tim-buhk-TOO)? The phrase means "from here to a location as distant as you can imagine." It refers to a great West African city that thrived in the Middle Ages. Timbuktu, which you'll soon explore, was famous as a center of wealth and learning. When Medieval Europeans heard of this fabulous city, it seemed to them as far away as one could imagine—thus the expression, "from here to Timbuktu."

The medieval era has given us more than a handful of familiar expressions. Many of our present-

This modern-day photo shows the West African city of Timbuktu. Built of sun-baked brick, the city was a great center of trade and learning during the Middle Ages.

day customs, including some of the holidays we celebrate, date back to the Middle Ages. In fact, the word *holiday* comes from medieval times, when work stopped for religious festivals on certain "holy days." In the United States, many people celebrate Halloween on October 31 because the medieval Christian Church chose November 1 as All Hallows' Day, a day to remember all saints. (*Hallow* meant "saint," or a holy person.) The day before All Hallows' Day became All Hallows' Eve, or Halloween.

Another custom with medieval roots is the practice of putting up a Christmas tree. The tradition probably got its start in medieval Germany, where people decorated evergreen trees with apples at the end of December.

The Middle Ages saw the beginnings of an institution that might have a great effect on your life in the near future. You'll likely go to a college or university someday. Universities first appeared during medieval times in Europe and the Middle East.

The first universities trained people to be priests, scholars, lawyers, and doctors. As time went on, students began to study subjects such as writing, speaking, logic, mathematics, astronomy, and music. In their final exams, students took part in public debate to demonstrate what they had learned. Today many universities still follow that custom. Students who wish to earn higher degrees take oral exams or explain their studies to panels of professors.

Early universities in the Middle East taught mathematics and astronomy. This thirteenth-century Arab painting of Aristotle teaching astronomy shows the high regard Muslim scholars had for Greek philosophers.

Right: An aerial view of Christ Church Cathedral in Oxford, England. Like many medieval churches, it is designed in the shape of a cross.

Below: A spectacular stained glass window at Chartres Cathedral, France.

An Age of Faith with Lasting Effects

The Middle Ages witnessed profound developments in religion. During this period the Christian faith grew and became an organized church that reached out to most of Europe. And during this time the eastern branch of the Christian Church split with the west—a separation that continues to this day.

Many ongoing Christian traditions date back to medieval times. For example, today many churches are built in the shape of a cross, following a practice common in the Middle Ages. Stained-glass windows were first used in medieval churches. Church steeples are echoes of medieval times, when builders decorated their churches with towers and spires that were meant to draw worshipers' thoughts toward heaven.

Another one of the world's major religions, Islam, was born in the Middle Ages. As you'll learn, Islam emerged in the Middle East and united the Arab world. It quickly spread throughout the Mediterranean region and became the basis for one of the largest empires in history. The religion of Islam now has more than a billion followers worldwide.

Christians and Muslims were not the only ones to spread their religion during the Middle Ages. Buddhist missionaries trekked east, introducing their faith to people in southeast Asia, China, and Japan. In various lands, enormous statues of the Buddha show the missionaries' lasting influence. Today Buddhism is the most widely practiced religion in many Asian countries.

We'll begin our exploration of the Middle Ages in a rising empire called the Byzantine (BIH-zn-teen) Empire. From there we'll move on to the Arabian Peninsula and into Africa, then to Western Europe, and finally end up in the Far East. You'll learn about individuals, civilizations, and ideas that shape our world today. You'll find out why knights served lords, and who Genghis Khan and Mansa Musa were. You'll see that the medieval era was both a child of the classical past and a parent of our modern times.

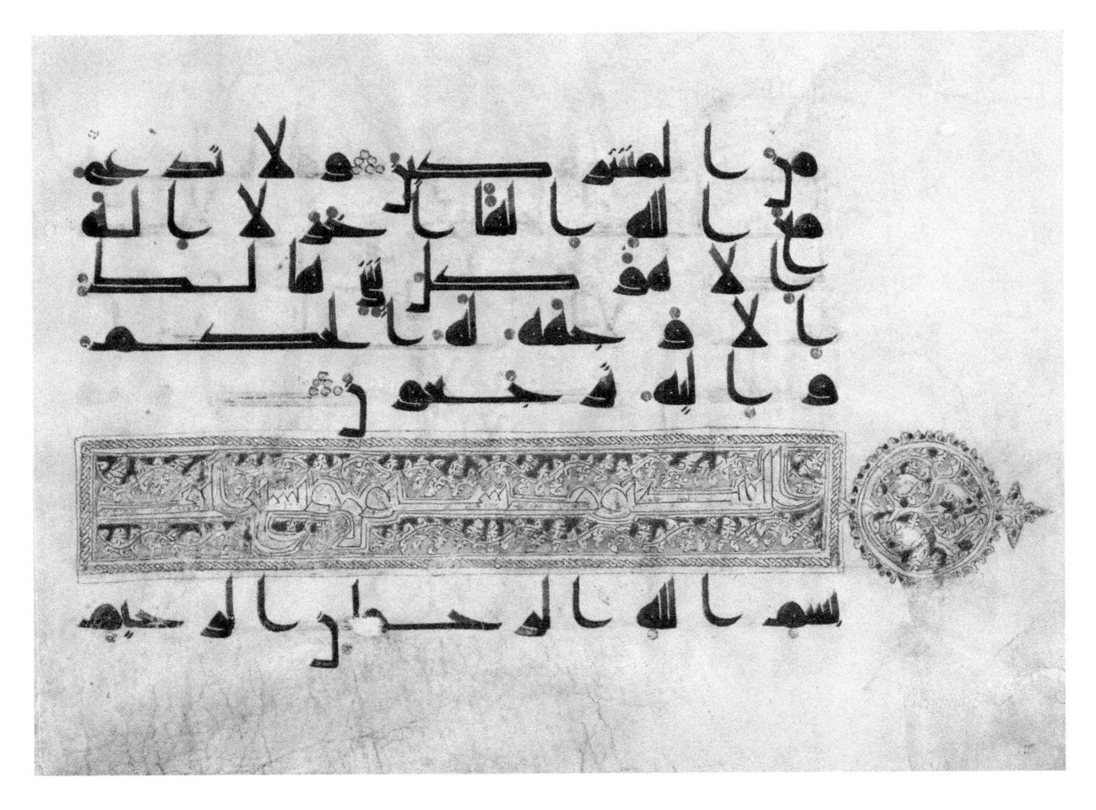

Arabic script adorns a page from the Qur'an, the holy book of Islam. This copy of the Qur'an is more than a thousand years old.

The great cathedral of Hagia Sophia was the crowning glory of the Byzantine capital of Constantinople. Some of the cathedral's features, such as the four towering structures called minarets, were added in later years.

Rome Moved East: The Byzantine Empire

In the fourth century, the emperor Constantine made two decisions that would influence the course of the human odyssey for the next millennium and beyond.

First, in A.D. 313, Constantine issued the Edict of Milan, which made Christianity an accepted religion within the Roman Empire. Constantine's decision to legalize Christianity was a pivotal moment in Western history. Christianity began to grow at an even faster rate than before. By A.D. 392, it would be the official religion of the Roman Empire, east and west.

Second, Constantine decided to move the imperial capital from Rome to a city in the Eastern Roman Empire called Byzantium. That city gave its name to an empire that would endure long after the Western Roman Empire was gone—the Byzantine Empire.

The City of Constantine

When Constantine decided to move the capital of his empire from Rome to a new city, he considered a number of sites. One possibility was the ancient city of Troy, where, as the poet Homer sang in the *Iliad*, great heroes such as Achilles and Hector had engaged in epic battles. Another possible site was the holy city of Jerusalem.

In the end, the emperor chose neither of these. He recognized that the cultural and economic heart of his empire was in the Greek-speaking East. Thus he settled on Byzantium, a little-known Greek city on the banks of the Bosporus, the narrow channel of water that divides southeastern Europe from Asia Minor.

Constantine set about transforming the city on the Bosporus into a new

This chapter focuses on the Byzantine Empire which, at its height, was the dominant power in the Mediterranean region.

Rome. He built defensive walls, a palace complex, public squares, theaters, baths, aqueducts, forums, and circuses. All were constructed with the same engineering skills that had made the old Rome great.

But Constantine built something new. Unlike the emperors before him, Constantine built churches. In this new capital, the very buildings would proclaim the new strength of the Christian faith.

By the time Constantine died in A.D. 337, he left a busy, thriving capital in the East. It had a new name, too. In his honor it was renamed Constantinople—"the city of Constantine."

- On the map of the Byzantine Empire at right, locate Constantinople (formerly called Byzantium).

The emperor's choice was indeed an inspired one. Perched on the edge of Europe, the new capital was the beating heart of a vast commercial region. From Constantinople, trade routes linked three continents in a network of caravan tracks, rivers, seaways, and paved imperial highways. It had been said that all roads led to Rome; now, however, they seemed to lead to Constantinople.

From Russia and the north came ships laden with furs, gold, salt, and honey. From the granaries of Egypt to the south came wheat and barley. From India, China, and points east came ivory and porcelain, silks and spices. To the west of Constantinople lay fertile farmland where grapes and grains grew in abundance.

Constantinople grew rich. Within its walls there accumulated more wealth than the world had ever seen. It grew big, too. Like iron filings to a magnet, people from all over the world were attracted to the city. In time the population swelled to about a million.

In its streets and bazaars, its docks and marketplaces, Greeks mingled with Africans, and Jews with Syrians. There were merchants from Italy, Britain, and Gaul, diplomats from Russia and Arabia, sailors from all points of the compass. Constantinople was the great melting pot.

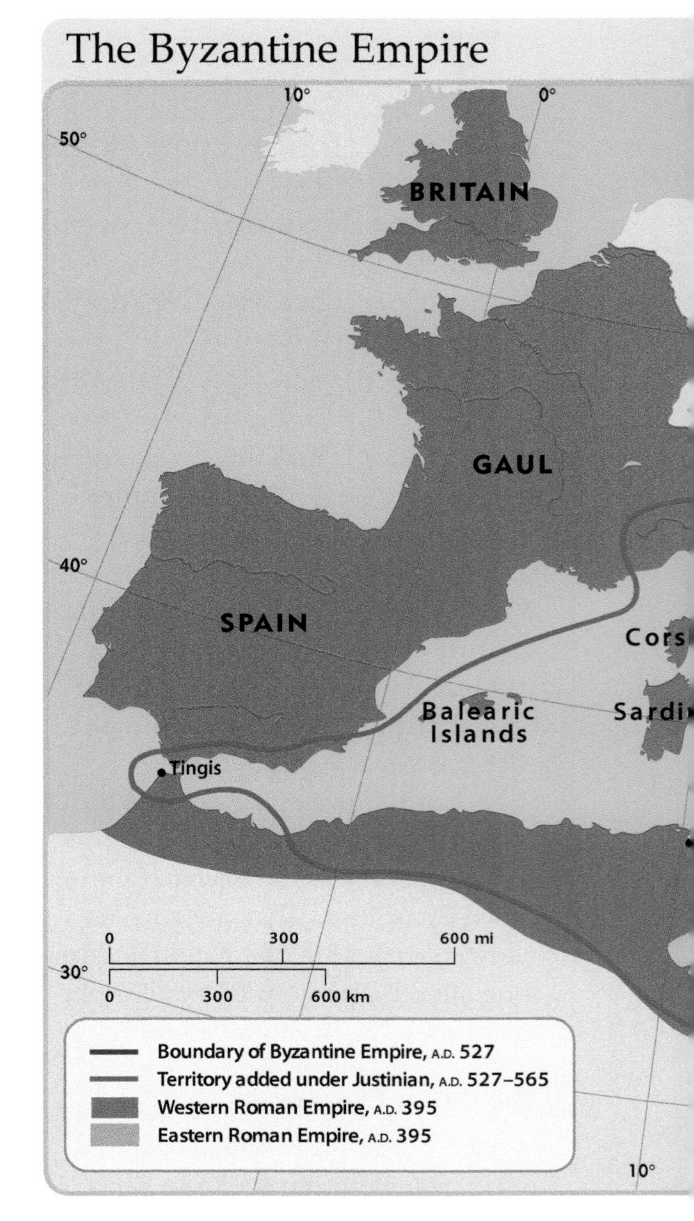

Much of Constantinople's daily life unfolded in its bazaars, the city's busy street markets.

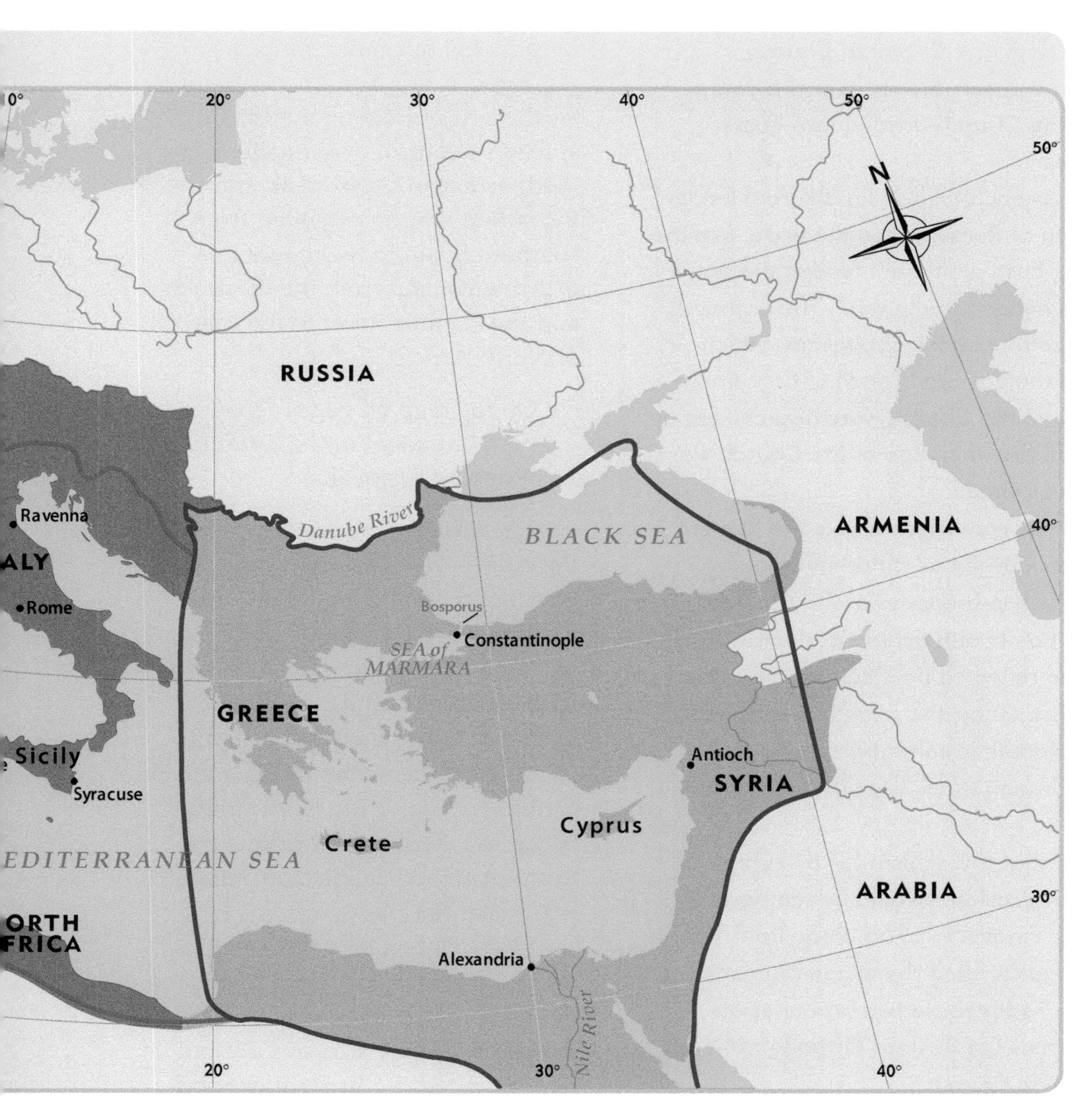

After Constantine's death, rule of the Roman Empire was divided between his sons and nephews. Eventually the empire split into two parts—the Eastern Empire, ruled from Constantinople, and the Western Empire, ruled from Rome.

An East-West Split in the Church

You know that the Roman Empire was divided into East and West. Over time, the Christian Church experienced a similar division. Slowly over the course of the Middle Ages, the Church divided into Eastern and Western branches.

These two branches each followed a different leader. In the West, the bishop of Rome, called the pope, was the spiritual leader. In the East, a different leader, the patriarch (PAY-tree-ahrk), headed the faithful. The patriarch was located in Constantinople, the capital city, which became the center of the Eastern branch of Christianity.

The two branches of the Church were also divided by language. In the West, the language of the Church was Latin. In the East, it was Greek.

As decades and then centuries passed, the Eastern and Western Churches developed different religious practices. By 1054, the two branches of the Church disagreed on several points of teaching or doctrine. These differences also reflected political disagreements between East and West. Once, the pope in Rome and patriarch in Constantinople excommunicated each other—that is, each branch threw the other out of the Christian Church!

Everyone thought that this schism (SKIH-zuhm)—which means a split or division—would be temporary. But the schism lasted. Finally, in 1965, Pope Paul VI and the Patriarch Athanagoras lifted the excommunications. But the split remains. Today these two branches of Christianity are known as the Eastern Orthodox Church and the Roman Catholic Church.

The fate of the empire's two branches would prove the wisdom in Constantine's choice of a capital. As you learned, in the fifth century the Western Empire fell to invaders from northern Europe. But the Eastern Empire—the Byzantine Empire—would rise to great heights of glory and remain intact for more than a thousand years.

The Spread of Byzantine Culture

After the fall of the Western Roman Empire, the Byzantine Empire remained strong and grew stronger. As the heir of Rome, for a time it spread its control over much of the Mediterranean. At its peak, the Byzantine Empire extended from southern Spain to the mountains of Armenia, and from the Black Sea and the Danube River to the coast of North Africa.

- On the map on pages 446–47, note the extent of the Byzantine Empire at its peak.

The Eastern Empire preserved the glories of Greek and Roman culture. Eager to maintain their links with the past, the people of Constantinople adorned their public buildings with classical statues. As the old influences from the West began to blend with others from the East, a new culture—a unique *Byzantine* culture—began to take shape. Striking new forms of art and architecture emerged in Constantinople.

The dazzling new works of art and architecture were largely inspired by the Church. For above all, the Byzantine Empire was, as Constantine had intended, a Christian empire.

To display their faith, the Byzantines developed an enduring style of religious art and architecture marked by bold, vibrant colors, precise geometric designs, and elaborate ornamentation.

Art to Dazzle the World

Constantinople's best architects and builders raised magnificent new churches. These great domed cathedrals became treasure troves of Byzantine art.

Some Byzantine artists specialized in frescoes. Fresco painting required masterful technique, because painters had to apply their pigments directly to plaster while it was still wet on the walls.

Other artists spent painstaking hours painting on wood to create religious works of art known as icons. Icons depicted holy people and events, such as the birth of Jesus.

The most spectacular works of Byzantine art were mosaics (moh-ZAY-iks). *Mosaics* were elaborate murals in which small pieces of glass or stone were used to form intricate pictures. On a surface of rough wet plaster, gifted craftsmen carefully pressed into place small stones and glass pieces of different hues— whites and pinks, grays and greens, reds and browns, glittering golds, each placed at a slight angle to the plane of the wall, to heighten the reflection of light.

Adorning the vaults, walls, and domes of churches, these mosaics were breathtakingly beautiful. Most mosaics represented Christian themes.

Below: A Byzantine fresco shows Jesus and his disciples on the night before his arrest.

Bottom: The mosaic-covered ceiling of a Byzantine church.

In the bright sunshine of midday or the candlelight of evening, Byzantine churches glowed with the reflected light of mosaics.

Byzantine craftsmen handed down their techniques and traditions as carefully as precious heirlooms. The new styles spread from Constantinople and, like an incoming tide, lapped at the shores of the Mediterranean world. Greece, the Balkans, Italy, Syria, and Egypt—all were influenced by Byzantine art. It is a legacy that draws admiration and wonder to this day.

The Emperor Who Never Slept

After Constantine, emperor followed emperor, and the Byzantine Empire increased in splendor and power. It would reach its peak in the sixth century under the emperor Justinian (juh-STIH-nee-uhn).

Justinian was a man of boundless energy and determination. Always busy, he ate little and, so it was said, never slept. It was a good thing. The emperor had much to do. It was during his reign that the Byzantines regained many territories once ruled by Rome.

The emperor Justinian extended his empire and united it with a common set of laws.

Justinian was determined to extend Byzantine power across the Mediterranean. He saw it as his divine mission. He thought that God would help him take back the lands of the old Roman Empire, which, in his view, had been lost through carelessness.

By 534, Justinian's armies had captured former Roman provinces in North Africa. A year later they occupied the island of Sicily. In 536 they marched into Rome. Eventually Justinian's troops drove the Germanic tribes out of Italy. They seized control of Corsica, Sardinia, and the Balearic Islands. And they established a foothold in southern Spain. During his reign, Justinian doubled the size of his empire until the "new Rome" of Constantinople ruled much of the Mediterranean world.

- On the map on pages 446–47, note the territories that Justinian added to the Byzantine Empire.

Justinian's Code

Like their Western Roman ancestors, the Eastern Romans took great pride in their laws. Over the centuries, however, the laws of the empire had become outdated. Sometimes one law repeated another. And sometimes two laws might say opposite things.

Justinian found the whole situation confusing. He told his advisors that a single empire needed a single set of laws. He wanted all his subjects to obey the same laws, no matter where they lived. The laws should be easy to understand and, he insisted, they should not contradict each other.

Shortly after he became emperor, Justinian set up a commission of 10 men to make a single legal code, or body of laws. The work took decades, but in 565 the job was finally finished. The code was known in Latin as the *Codex Justinianeus*—Justinian's Code. The emperor sent copies to all the provinces of the empire. Everyone was to follow the code. Here are a few of its 4,562 laws.

> The sea and seashore belong to everyone. Every person in the empire is allowed to go to the beach.

> Rivers belong to everyone. Anyone in the empire can fish in the rivers without being told to leave.
>
> He who finds a jewel or other treasure washed up on the seashore may keep it for himself.
>
> A thief who steals something valuable must pay the owner four times the worth of the stolen object.
>
> If someone is trimming a tree near a road, he must call out a warning to anyone passing by. "Be careful!" he should say. "Limbs might fall on you!" If there is no warning, and a falling limb injures a traveler, it is the tree trimmer's fault. But if the traveler ignores the warning and is injured, it is not the tree trimmer's fault.

Justinian's Code helped unite the Byzantine Empire. But it was also an enduring gift to the world. Clear and consistent, the code later served as a model for the codes of law in many modern nations.

Theodora: An Empress for the Ages

Justinian achieved much as emperor, but his reign would not have been as brilliant without the actions of a woman whose name is forever linked with his own—his wife, partner, and trusted advisor, the empress Theodora (thee-uh-DOR-uh).

Few who knew Theodora could have guessed at her humble origins. Her father was said to be a bear keeper at the Hippodrome, Constantinople's equivalent of Rome's Colosseum, the place where people came to be entertained. Her mother was an actress, which was then considered a lowly profession. The beautiful young Theodora followed in her mother's footsteps.

But Theodora was not just gifted on stage. She was decisive, intelligent, brave, and compassionate. She would display all of these qualities as empress. Just how she met Justinian, we do not know. But the new empress certainly caused a stir. Why, some people clucked, she wasn't even a patrician! With the support of her husband, however, she became a patrician and placed herself at the heart of the empire's political and religious life. Justinian would benefit from her good judgment.

This spectacular mosaic of the empress Theodora adorns a church her husband Justinian built in Italy.

In 532, a mob of angry citizens battered down the palace gates. The emperor prepared to flee the city with his wife. But Theodora would have none of it. "May I never see the day when those who meet me do not call me empress," she declared, pulling around her a robe of purple, the color reserved for royalty. "As for me, I agree with the adage that the royal purple is the noblest shroud."

Theodora's boldness helped save Justinian's empire. The revolt was

suppressed, and emperor and empress proceeded with their plans for Constantinople. Theodora's plans included building hospitals for the sick and converting an old palace into a home for poor women.

Justinian and Theodora helped transform their beloved capital into a city with many magnificent churches. None was more splendid than the church known as Hagia Sophia (HAH-juh soh-FEE-uh).

The Cathedral of Hagia Sophia

The cathedral of Hagia Sophia, whose name in English means "Holy Wisdom," was an architectural wonder. Like other Byzantine churches, it was crowned by a great dome that symbolized heaven. Back when the Western Roman Empire was still mighty, it had built many domed buildings. The domed Byzantine churches linked the greatness of the new Eastern Empire with the former greatness of the West.

The roof of Hagia Sophia was huge, the dome of all domes. To support its enormous weight, the builders erected an extraordinary system of interlocking marble piers and spanning arches.

Hagia Sophia dominated the skyline of Constantinople. Surpassing in size any church in Western Europe for a thousand years, it sat like an enormous crown on a slope above the busy waters of the Bosporus. The interior of the building—ablaze with mosaics and frescoes—inspired

Above: To the faithful, the domes of Hagia Sophia symbolized the very heavens.

Right: The main dome of Hagia Sophia is 184 feet high and 102 feet across. For years it was the largest church in the world.

awe. Hagia Sophia was an achievement of which the emperor was justly proud, the most visible sign that the new Rome now surpassed the old.

"Glory be to God, who has thought me worthy to finish this work." So declared Justinian when the cathedral was completed. The emperor knew he had created a masterpiece for the ages. How great was it? Perhaps, thought Justinian, it was even grander than the Hebrew temple in Jerusalem. "Solomon," boasted Justinian, "I have outdone thee!"

In addition to building Hagia Sophia, an enormous underground aqueduct, and a fabulous palace complex, Justinian and Theodora began an industry that to this time had been found only in China. Let's imagine that we're in Constantinople in the sixth century, when China's secret traveled west to the heart of the Byzantine Empire.

Strangers from the East

Imagining the Past

"Aaaaaahhhhhhhhhh." The silk merchant clasped his hands beneath his big, round belly, leaned back, and surveyed with satisfaction the remains of his meal. A few missed crumbs of bread and cheese, a drop or two of fragrant olive oil he had failed to mop up. It was not the feast of an aristocrat—no dishes of meat in garlic sauce, no heady wine—but he was not one to complain on a full stomach. Business had been brisk this season. God was good.

From under half-closed lids he idly watched the crowds of market-goers passing by. The murmur of foreign tongues washed over him. On any given day, it was said, you could hear almost every language of the world on the streets of Constantinople.

He had just about dozed off when two monks entered his stall. Reluctantly, he raised one eyelid far enough to give them an appraising glance. Thin. Ragged. Dusty from the road. Not a gold coin between them, he was certain. Surely they could have little interest in a precious luxury item like silk. Perhaps they'd come to beg.

"Good afternoon," he said. "I wish I could invite you to share in my meal, but as you see, I just finished. Had I expected guests..." He waved his hands to show his deep regret. One must be courteous, if not sincere.

"Thank you, we've eaten."

"Ah." Hard to believe, but none of his concern. The merchant waited for the monks to move along so he could get back to the interrupted business of his nap.

Instead, the older one leaned on his walking stick. The younger one used his walking stick to point at the bolts of fabric stacked around the stall. "Nice cloth. Does it fetch a good price here in these parts?"

The merchant fought to hide his irritation. "It's *silk*," he said. "From China. Worth its weight in gold."

The older monk smiled and nodded. "And the local silk? Is it as valuable?"

Local silk? The merchant sighed at the boundless ignorance of these churchmen. "All silk comes from China," he explained. "No one outside that far-off land knows how the precious cloth is made. It is a closely guarded secret." Then curiosity overcame his annoyance. "You must be new to the city."

"We just arrived today." The old man gestured vaguely. "From the east."

Were they Armenians? the merchant wondered. Syrians? Perhaps even Persians, like himself. The merchant felt himself warming a bit toward the strangers. "Well, no matter. Wherever we come from, we're all Romans here."

He pivoted to include the younger monk in his generous welcome. In an instant, warmth gave way to panic.

"Stop!"

Startled, the young man snatched his hand back from the bolt of purple silk. "What? What's wrong?"

"You mustn't touch that. Purple-dyed silk is only for the emperor and empress." The merchant glanced around nervously. "If the imperial agents saw me selling it to foreigners, they'd have me flogged."

The monk raised an eyebrow. "Foreigners? I thought we were all Romans here." But he backed away from the forbidden cloth.

His companion shifted the conversation. "I have heard many fine things about the emperor Justinian. A pious man. A powerful leader. A reformer…"

"True, true," the merchant nodded. "When I was a boy, the legal system was a jumble. So many laws! Some long outdated, some contradicting others. The courts were filled with corruption."

"And now?"

"Now there is justice. The emperor appointed a commission to sort all the ancient laws into a single system clearly covering every aspect of modern life. Now we have the Justinian Code. Under the code, we all know where we stand."

"And when you may be flogged," the young monk added cheerfully.

The merchant frowned. "I'm a law-abiding Christian. The emperor—"

"Surely must hold you in high esteem," put in the older monk, in soothing tones. He gestured toward the purple silk. "What an honor, to be chosen to clothe the royal family. Do you often visit the palace?"

A dark flush crept up the merchant's double chins. He had never set foot in the palace. In truth, the closest he had ever been to any of the royal family was when a minor servant of the empress Theodora had stopped by to inspect his wares—and left without buying so much as a hand's width of silk.

He avoided the question by replying, "The emperor is most gracious."

The old man smiled. "We look forward to an audience."

"An audience! *You* intend to meet the emperor Justinian?"

The young monk nodded. "We think he will be very pleased with what we bring."

The silk merchant struggled to contain his feelings. Arrogant beggars! How dare they? Constantinople was the center of the world. What could these two penniless monks imagine they might have to offer the all-powerful ruler of the Roman Empire?

No longer sleepy, he pushed himself to his feet. "Come with me."

With a few quick movements, he shut down his stall. A moment later, he was pushing through the crowded market, the two strangers hurrying behind.

"Look there—ivory from Africa and India. And there—exotic spices. Furs from Russia. Jewelry. Enamel. Glassware. Silver."

The monks gazed around them with great interest, but the merchant hardly slowed down long enough to let them look.

At the edge of the market, he swung to face them. "The finest goods in the entire world sail into our port," he said. "There is nothing you could bring the emperor that he does not already have—and far better."

He folded his arms and waited for the monks to shrink with humility in the face of such splendor. But far from being abashed, the monks appeared...amused?

"Impressive indeed," said the elder. "But what we carry with us is not to be found anywhere in your market."

The silk merchant scowled. Were they making fun of him? What could these ragged travelers possess that was not sold in the market stalls of the great city?

Aha! He thought he understood their meaning. But he'd show these monks their folly.

The merchant led them through the streets, past the taverns and the public baths, past high walls carved with the names of wealthy families, past rickety wooden tenements, home to the city's poorest. He even swept past the Hippodrome, the giant stadium built by order of the emperor, where forty thousand gathered at a time to cheer the chariot races.

At last, he halted in front of a large marble building. Sweat dripped down his broad red face. "This," he announced, "is the imperial university."

"Wonderful," said the older monk. "But why have you brought us here?"

"You say you bring the emperor a gift that cannot be found in our markets. I see you carry nothing with you but your cloaks and walking sticks. Your gift must be something that can't be seen or held—such as knowledge."

The younger monk said, "Actually—"

"But you are wrong!" the merchant said triumphantly. "All the greatest Greek and Roman writings—philosophy, science, mathematics—are preserved in the libraries and schools of Constantinople. Everything worth knowing is already in the possession of the emperor."

The older monk smiled. "I'm afraid you have misunderstood us. We do not pretend to be teachers or scholars."

Puzzled, the silk merchant stared at the two strangers. What, then, could their gift be? What could they have that emperor Justinian would want?

"I know!" he said at last. "But you have come too late."

Without waiting for a reply, he caught each man by the sleeve and pulled them both through the streets.

This time, when they arrived at their destination, he didn't have to tell the monks where he had brought them. The fantastic golden dome...the splendid columns...the walls covered in mosaics made of countless tiny bits of colored glass. Of all Justinian's many ambitious—and expensive—architectural projects, the church of Hagia Sophia was by far his greatest achievement. It was dazzling. It was divine.

"You see," the merchant said, "the work is finished. The emperor has no need of your skills."

The older monk pulled his gaze away from the breathtaking spectacle. "Skills? We are not stonemasons or metalworkers. Neither are we artists."

The silk merchant was nearly beside himself. "You have no skills. You have no knowledge. You carry nothing that is valuable, nothing to be bought with gold or silver. What is this invisible gift you bring?"

The young monk laughed. "But we have all those things," he said as he tapped his walking stick on the ground.

The older monk smiled. For he knew that inside their hollow walking sticks, he and his young companion carried something worth far more than its weight in gold—the eggs of a very special kind of worm, the silkworm, and the sprigs of a special plant that silkworms feed upon. And inside their heads, they carried the skills and knowledge they had learned on their travels through China—the secrets of making silk.

"Now, if you will excuse us," said the older monk to the baffled merchant, "we are most eager to see the emperor."

Justinian himself had sent the two monks to China to obtain the secret of making silk—a secret the Chinese had guarded for centuries. The emperor soon had his workers raising silkworms and growing mulberry trees. China remained an important supplier of silk to the West, but by A.D. 600 the sale of silk brought more riches to the Byzantine Empire than any other product.

A nineteenth-century print of Mecca, birthplace of Muhammad and holiest city of Islam.

The Rise of Islam

While Christianity was spreading in Europe and the Byzantine Empire was rising to glory around the Mediterranean Sea, something momentous was happening in the land known as Arabia. It all started with the teachings of a man named Muhammad (moh-HAM-uhd). Muhammad brought to the people of Arabia a message about God, a message that would form the core of a new religion called Islam (iss-LAHM).

In a short while, the followers of Islam—known as Muslims (MUS-luhms)—were spreading their beliefs throughout much of the Mediterranean world and beyond. Muslims would go on to establish one of the greatest empires and civilizations in history. The Muslim empire is long-gone, but the religion founded by Muhammad is thriving. There are more than a billion Muslims today, many in Asia and Africa, but also in Europe and the Americas—indeed, around the world.

- Look at the map on page 460, which shows the parts of the world where Islam has more followers than any other religion.

To understand how Islam began and grew so rapidly, we need to travel back to the sixth century and visit the Arabian Peninsula—a crossroads between Asia, Africa, and Europe.

The Land of the Desert

The Arabian Peninsula, also known as Arabia, lies southeast of Europe and northeast of Africa. Since ancient times, a people known as the Arabs have lived there. They sometimes call their land the "Island of the Arabs." It's not really an island,

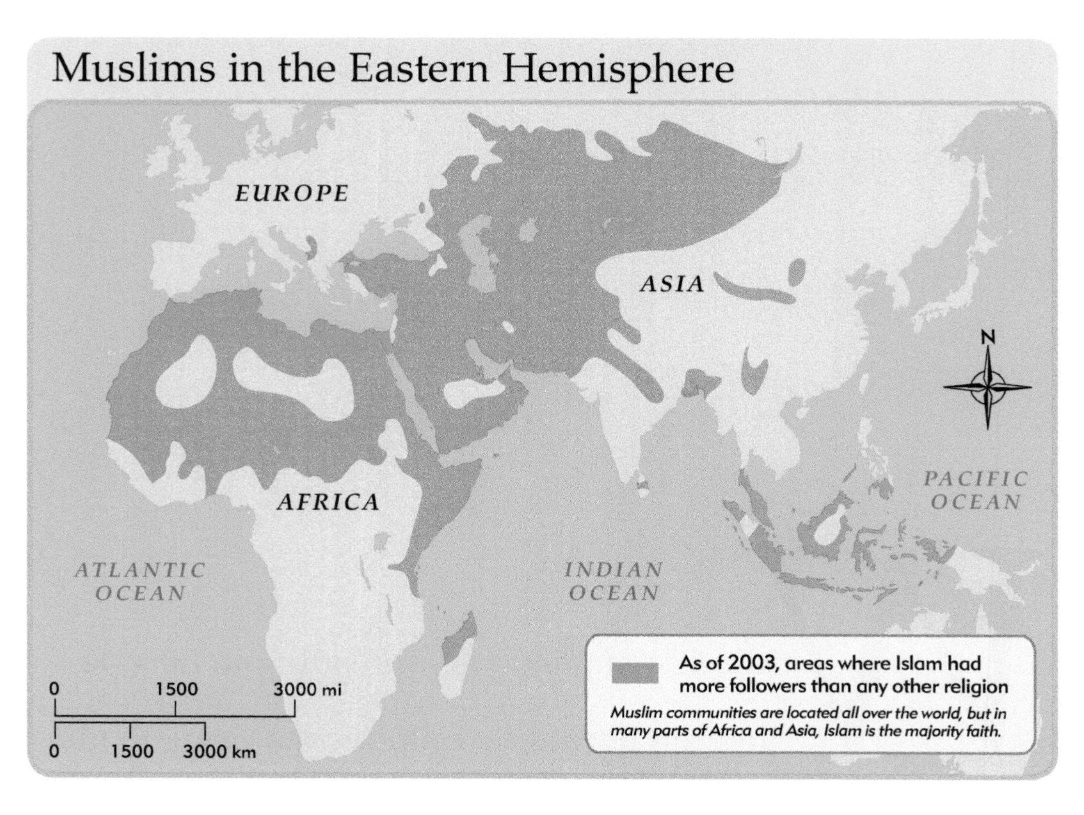

of course, but salt water does surround much of it—the Mediterranean Sea to the northwest, the Red Sea to the west, the Arabian Sea to the southeast, and the Persian Gulf to the east.

While the land is surrounded by bodies of salt water, there is little fresh water to be found. The great Arabian Desert stretches across much of the peninsula's one million square miles. This desert is a land of extremes. In the day, the sun blazes mercilessly and the temperature can climb to 120 degrees Fahrenheit or more. At night, stars fill the sky, and in some places the thermometer can drop to freezing or below.

Many parts of the desert average only two or three inches of rainfall a year. The peninsula is streaked with riverbeds, but for much of the year, they are dry. In these dry riverbeds, called wadis (WAH-deez), water sometimes flows for short periods, but only after an infrequent rain. Most of the time, people can use the wadis as roads for crossing the desert.

In the northern part of the Arabian Peninsula, intense winds sweep across the ground. Stones and pebbles cover the desert surface, with a few thin patches of grass appearing here and there. Farther south, the desert is sandy. There, winds blow the sand into dunes that look like huge waves, some piled as high as 700 feet. A vast region in the southeast, roughly the size of Texas, is called the Rub' al Khali (roob ahl KHAH-lee), or Empty Quarter. It contains the largest unbroken area of desert sand on earth.

When fierce winds whip across the desert, sand fills the air and gets into everything—shoes, shirts, pockets,

People are dwarfed by the huge sand dunes of the Arabian Desert's Empty Quarter.

hair, eyes, ears, mouths. People caught in sandstorms can hardly see or breathe. It is said that whole armies have been lost and buried beneath the sand. Little wonder that the people who manage to live in the Arabian Desert are tough, resourceful people.

- On the map below, locate the Arabian Peninsula. Find the Arabian Peninsula on a globe as well.
- On the map below, locate the Mediterranean Sea, Red Sea, Arabian Sea, and Persian Gulf. Note the areas that receive the least and most rainfall.

The People of the Desert

Since the days of the Roman Empire, a people called the Bedouin (BEH-duh-wuhn) have made a home of the Arabian deserts. The Bedouin of ancient times were nomads,

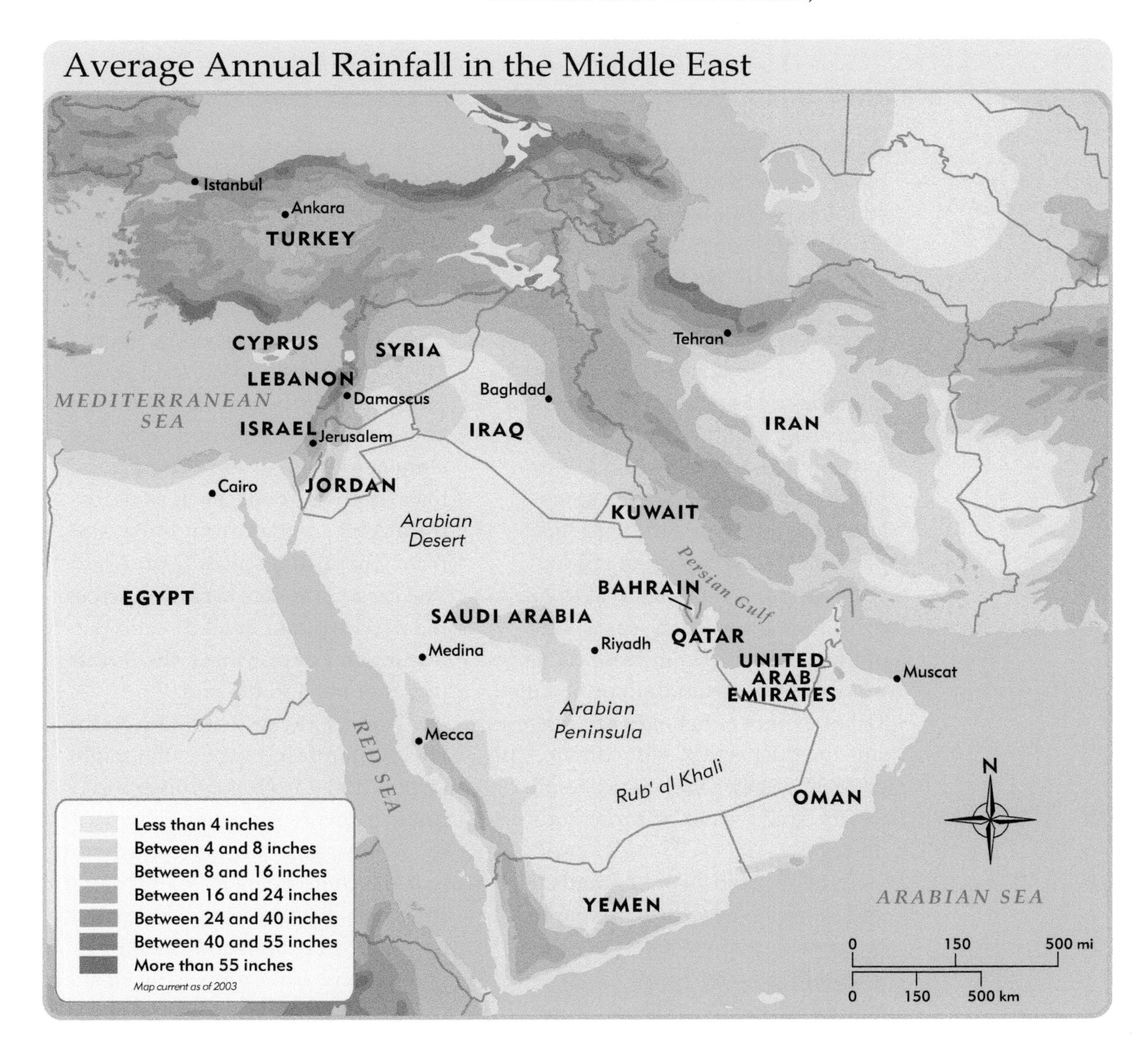

Travelers and their camels follow one of the caravan routes that crisscrossed the Arabian Peninsula.

continually moving from place to place in search of sparse vegetation and water. Their herds of livestock traveled with them and provided most of the things they needed. The Bedouin got milk and cheese from their goats. They lived in tents made of camel or goat hair mixed with plant fibers. For clothing, they used camel hair and the wool of sheep.

The Bedouin were divided into many tribes that spoke the same language but were otherwise independent. The tribes often feuded with each other. Being loyal to one's tribe, no matter what, was a code of the desert life. In defense of his tribe, an Arab would kill or be killed. Tribal members helped each other survive the harsh desert climate. The greatest disaster that could befall a desert Arab was to be turned out of his tribe.

Not all Arabs were nomads. Here and there the deserts were marked by oases, fertile places where there is usually a water supply such as a natural spring. An oasis was one of those rare spots in the desert where people could settle down, grow food, and build towns. And in a few parts of the Arabian Peninsula, enough rain fell for farmers to grow grain and sweet-smelling spices.

Farmers who wished to trade for their harvests could send their products away by caravan. Merchants in caravans—groups of people traveling across the desert—used camels to carry their goods, such as ivory from Africa, rubies from India, silk from China, and spices from Arabia. The caravan routes threaded across the parched land in all directions, leading to Egypt, Persia, the Byzantine Empire, and beyond.

Traders always had to be on the lookout for desert tribes who might swoop down from the dunes and raid a caravan or demand payment for safe passage. Crossing the desert was treacherous business, but along the routes lay the oases where travelers could stop, rest, and trade their goods. Some oases grew to be bustling centers of commerce. They were crossroads for people, products, and ideas. The most important of these towns was Mecca (MEH-kuh).

- On the map on page 461, find Mecca.

The Early Life of Muhammad

In the sixth century, the city of Mecca was both a thriving center of trade and a busy center of worship. In those days, most Arabs were polytheists. They worshipped many gods who were believed to dwell in stones, wells, springs, and trees. Each tribe had its own god, who was usually said to live in a natural stone or an idol carved of stone. The gods and goddesses represented by these idols were believed to be powerful deities, so of course people wanted to keep them happy.

One stone had become especially important to the Arabs—a meteoric black stone around which worshippers danced to gain divine favor. The Arabs placed this stone and others in a cube-shaped building called the Kaaba (KAH-buh). Once each year, tribesmen from all over Arabia traveled to Mecca to honor the stone-gods and ask them for protection. Mecca was one of the few places where, during this time of pilgrimage, tribal feuds were set aside and people could worship their gods in peace.

It was in this city that Muhammad was born around the year A.D. 570. We know few facts about his early life. His childhood was clouded with sadness—his father died before Muhammad was even born, and his mother died when he was only six years old.

Muhammad spent the first five years of his life among wandering shepherds. After his mother's death Muhammad was first cared for by his grandfather and then by an uncle. Like other Arab boys, he probably tended sheep, camels, and goats. He may also have traveled on caravan journeys with his uncle. In Mecca and along the caravan routes, he would have heard people of different faiths talk about their beliefs.

When Muhammad was almost 25, his uncle gave him some advice. He had heard about a rich widow who was sending a caravan to Syria. He urged Muhammad to go to the widow and ask for work.

The widow hired Muhammad. She had many caravans, and Muhammad journeyed with them to far-off cities, where he saw more of the world than he had ever known before. During his travels, Muhammad did more than sell spices and fine wool. He met all sorts of people, kept his ears open, and absorbed new ideas. He met Jewish people who told him that they believed in only one God. He met Christians who told him about Jesus and his teachings. As he traveled slowly across the desert, he pondered all he had seen and heard.

Soon Muhammad married the wealthy widow. Now that he had a secure income, he could spend more time considering what he had seen and heard. He hated the fact that the tribes in his land often fought with each other. Too often people seemed to think only of themselves. Most didn't try to help the poor or sick.

Surrounded by a flame-like halo, Muhammad preaches to fellow Arabs in this eighteenth-century painting.

Muhammad was troubled by their behavior. "Is this the right way to live?" he asked himself. "Could there be a better way?" The more he thought, the more he believed that the stone-gods could not give him the answer.

A Vision in a Cave

Muhammad often spent time in the hills around Mecca, where he could be alone with his thoughts. When he was about 40 years old, he retreated to a cave, where he had a vision. Muhammad said that an angel called Gabriel appeared to him. This is how Muhammad later described it: "The Angel Gabriel came to me while I was asleep. He was carrying a piece of embroidered cloth, and on the cloth there was writing. He told me to recite. I told him I did not know what to recite. Then, suddenly, the angel caught me and pressed me to him so hard I thought I was going to die."

In the end, Muhammad found that he could recite the angel's message. It was as though some words were written on his heart. The words were: "Recite in the name of your Lord." Then words seemed to flow from Muhammad's mouth as he received the first of what Muslims believe were many revelations from God.

Muhammad spent the rest of his life preaching to the Arabs. Gradually he came to the conclusion that his mission was to be the prophet of Allah (AH-luh or ah-LAH). *Allah* is the Arabic word for "God."

Muhammad told the people of Mecca that they were foolish to believe in many gods. "Allah alone created the universe," he said, "and Allah alone rules it. On the day of judgment, Allah will look at your life

Depicting the Prophet

In religious art, Muslims avoid depicting the faces of religious figures, because to do so, they believe, is to encourage people to worship images instead of Allah alone. If a Muslim artist depicts the Prophet Muhammad or another important religious figure, he will cover the face with a veil or with the image of a flame, as in the illustration on this page as well as later in this book.

and reward or punish you. He wants you to be generous and share with the poor. He wants you to stop worshipping many gods and worship only Allah."

Muhammad told people that they must give up their careless ways of living. Instead, they should surrender their whole, unmixed loyalty to Allah. From Muhammad's message came the name of a new religion—Islam. *Islam* is the Arabic word for "submission," or surrendering one's whole self to God. Muhammad's followers became known as Muslims. *Muslim* means "one who submits." Muslims believe they should submit their lives and thoughts to the will of Allah.

Muhammad never said that he was himself divine. He didn't claim the power to perform miracles. Rather, he said he was a prophet who brought a message from Allah to a world full of strife and bloodshed.

The prophet Muhammad arrives in Medina to a warm welcome. His flight to that city is known as the Hijrah.

The Flight from Mecca

Muhammad did not start out on his mission with the idea of establishing a new religion. He simply wanted the Arabs to give up their stone-gods and worship the one true God—the same God that the Jews and Christians worshipped.

For a while, the people of Mecca considered Muhammad harmless enough. But the more he preached, the more Arab leaders turned against him. They didn't like being told they were foolish and ignorant, and that their gods were not real. Besides, Meccans made a great deal of money from the thousands of Arabs who journeyed every year to worship their tribal idols at the Kaaba. All that business would disappear if pilgrims stopped coming to honor the old gods.

As Muhammad began to attract a little band of believers, troubles mounted. Mecca's rulers worried they might lose their power and riches, so they came up with a terrible plan to kill Muhammad and be rid of him forever.

When Muhammad heard about the plot, he had to make a hard decision. Should he stay in Mecca? Or should he travel to another city in Arabia where more people would listen to him? In 622, he decided to leave his birthplace and move to Medina (mah-DEE-nuh), a city some 200 miles to the north.

- On the map on page 461, locate Medina.

The journey to Medina was full of hazards. When Muhammad's enemies discovered that he was gone, they were furious. Soldiers from Mecca raced across the desert on their fastest horses, determined to catch and kill this troublemaker before he could get away. To elude his pursuers, Muhammad traveled during the darkest hours and hid during the day.

ولا تفرق بيننا وبينه حتى تدخلنا مدخله
وتوردنا حوضه وتجعلنا من رفقائه
مع المنعم عليهم من النبيين والصديقين
والشهداء والصالحين وحسن
اولئك رفيقا الحمد لله رب العالمين
ابتداء الربع الثالث
اللهم صل على محمد نور الهدى والقائد
الى الخير والداعي الى الرشد نبي الرحمة وامام
المتقين ورسول رب العالمين لا نبي بعده
كما بلغ رسالتك ونصح لعبادك وتلا اياتك
واقام حدودك ووفى بعهدك وانفذ حكمك
وامر بطاعتك ونهى عن معصيتك ووالى

Beautiful ornamentation and Arabic script mark both the Qur'an and Muslim books of prayer, as in this nineteenth-century example.

Muhammad's flight to Medina, called the Hijrah (HIJ-ruh), became a turning point in the history of Islam. *Hijrah* is the Arabic word for "migration." For Muslims, the departure from Mecca marks the beginning of the Islamic era. In the same way that the Christian calendar marks dates from the birth of Christ, the Hijrah marks the first year of the Muslim calendar.

The Prophet in Medina

The people of Medina welcomed Muhammad. Many listened eagerly to his message and became followers. Muhammad continued to have visions and believed he was being instructed by God. These instructions would develop into the religion of Islam and eventually form the Qur'an (kuh-RAN), the sacred text of Islam.

Soon Muhammad found himself the head of a community of believers. He became both a religious and political leader, and he gave people laws to help them live together—laws, he said, based on messages he received from Allah.

These laws controlled almost every part of a Muslim's life. They told the Muslims when to pray and when to fast. They also set forth rules for marriage and carrying on business. The Qur'an contained laws for regulating slavery and helping the poor. It taught that war and violence are allowable only in cases of self-defense and for the defense of Muslims if they are threatened.

Among the people Muhammad encountered in Medina, there were many Jews and Christians. Muhammad was glad to see them at first, for he believed that Allah wanted him to speak to them as well. After all, the Qur'an explained that Allah had first spoken through Abraham, Moses, and the Hebrew prophets, and later through Jesus. The message spoken by Muhammad, said the Qur'an, was coming from the last of the prophets—Muhammad himself. Muhammad thought that the Jews and Christians would be delighted to hear this message. After all, didn't they worship the same God that he worshipped?

But the more the Jews and Christians listened, the less they liked Muhammad's message. Christians believed that Jesus Christ was the Son of God. They were awaiting his return. They felt little need to heed the commands of the prophet from Mecca. And the Jews for more than a thousand years had been following their own laws, which came from Abraham, Moses, and ultimately, they believed, from God.

Some of Medina's Jews supported Muhammad, while others did not. Why was this man laying down new rules? Some Jews helped the Meccans try to oust Muhammad. When Muhammad saw that they had turned against him, he drove them out of the city and divided their lands among his followers.

Muslim warriors go into battle against their Meccan enemies.

A Triumphant Return to Mecca

Meanwhile, Muhammad's followers faced more problems. They had too little land and too little food. Some were beginning to go hungry. To get the things they needed, Muhammad began sending men into the desert to raid enemy caravans traveling to and from Mecca. As one who had led such caravans for many years, he knew the paths they would take and the best way to attack them. These battles against the "enemies of Allah" did two things for Muslims. They seemed to prove the power of Allah, and they brought some wealth to Muhammad's followers.

The leaders of Mecca, who were already angry with Muhammad, did not take kindly to these raids. The result was several long years of war between Medina and Mecca. The Meccans attacked Medina several times, but Muhammad's forces always drove them back. In one assault, the Meccans sent an army of thousands to destroy their Muslim foes. Muhammad, however, ordered his men to dig a wide, deep trench around the entire city of Medina. For about three weeks the Meccans attacked, but they couldn't cross the trench, so finally they withdrew.

In the year 630, Muhammad marched on Mecca with ten thousand soldiers and took it with scarcely a struggle. He led his followers seven times around the Kaaba, calling on Meccans to renounce their old gods and give themselves to Allah. He purified the Kaaba by emptying it of all idols, and declared the place would now be sacred as a shrine to Allah, the one God. Muhammad proclaimed Mecca the holiest city in Islam and swore that only Muslims would be allowed to enter its gates. The man who had fled Mecca with his life in danger was now the city's undisputed leader.

After entering Mecca, Muhammad purifies the Kaaba, the cube-shaped shrine that housed idols of the old religion.

Muhammad's rule over Mecca would not last long. Soon after his triumph, he grew ill. He suffered from fatigue and fever. One day in 632, he took to his bed and spoke to his wife of his readiness to leave this world and join Allah. A few hours later, Muhammad, known to his followers as the Messenger of God, breathed his last.

The Five Pillars of Islam

After Muhammad's death, Muslims collected his most important teachings in what is now the sacred book of Islam, the Qur'an. Many people say that Islam is like a building resting upon five religious duties, which are like five pillars. Muhammad wanted every Muslim to obey these duties. The Qur'an explains what these duties are.

The First Pillar:
The Declaration of Faith

All Muslims make a declaration of faith. That is, they must profess their faith in Allah, and they must say that they believe that Muhammad is Allah's prophet. Every Muslim must also believe in the Qur'an. Notice that the Muslims do not worship Muhammad. They worship only Allah. *"La ilaha illa Allah; Muhammad rasul Allah,"* Muslims declare, which means, "There is no God but Allah, and Muhammad is his prophet."

Muhammad did not want a special group of priests to stand between Allah and those who worship him. He did not want anyone—even himself—to come between them. Muhammad insisted that he was only a man who was trying to do the will of Allah. That, he said, was the highest purpose in life both for himself and for all Muslims.

The Second Pillar: Prayer

Five times a day, all Muslims are called to prayer. Five times a day, in all Muslim lands, the same sound is heard coming from the tower of a mosque (mahsk), a Muslim place of worship. The call to prayer goes out: "God is most great. I believe there is no god but Allah. I believe that Muhammad is the messenger of Allah. Come to prayer. Come to salvation. God is most great! There is no god but Allah."

When they hear this call, Muslims are supposed to stop whatever they are doing and pray. First they wash themselves, no matter where they may be. If they are in the desert, they wash themselves with sand. Then they kneel on a small prayer rug and turn toward Mecca to pray. Muhammad himself once said, "The comfort of my heart has been prayer."

The Third Pillar: Giving to the Poor

The Qur'an commands Muslims to help people in need by giving alms to the local community—money, animals, or grain given freely to help the poor. The Qur'an says, "Be good to the poor and to your neighbors, whether they are friends or strangers. Be good to fellow-travelers and to slaves." This aid to the needy reminds Muslims that their possessions are really a trust from Allah that is meant to benefit others as well as themselves.

Shoes removed as a sign of respect, modern-day Egyptians pray outside a Cairo mosque. The duty of prayer—always in the direction of Mecca—is the second Pillar of Islam.

The Fourth Pillar: Fasting

Muslims are required to fast. The Qur'an says they should give up some food and drink to help learn to fight temptation and to have compassion for those who are poor and hungry. For one month each year, Muslims cannot eat, drink, or smoke from before sunrise until after sunset. They call this month Ramadan (RAH-muh-dahn).

Ramadan is more than a time of fasting. It is also a time of additional prayer and religious study. Many Muslims break their daily fast with dates and water because that was the tradition of the Prophet Muhammad. At the end of Ramadan, Muslims celebrate with a great festival. They often feast on dried fruit, sweet buns, and little pancakes dipped in powdered sugar.

The Fifth Pillar: The Pilgrimage to Mecca

At least once before they die, Muslims must try to make a pilgrimage to Mecca and visit the Kaaba. The pilgrimage itself is called the Hajj (haj).

The Qur'an taught that both Abraham and his son Ishmael had built the Kaaba. As we have seen, the cube-shaped Kaaba once housed numerous stone idols. But Muhammad emptied the Kaaba of the idols, and declared the place a sacred shrine to Allah. It would remain an important sacred site in Mecca.

In Mecca today, one can often see great crowds of pilgrims obeying the command in the Qur'an: "Proclaim to the peoples a pilgrimage. Let them come on foot and on camel. Let them arrive in long lines."

The pilgrims first gather in a large tiled courtyard. The men are all dressed alike, in plain white robes, signifying that all are equal before Allah. The women must be covered in modest Islamic dress.

After circling the Kaaba seven times, the pilgrims move on to several days of rituals in which they

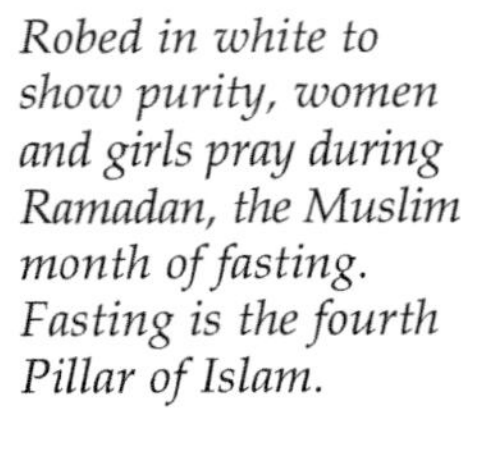

Robed in white to show purity, women and girls pray during Ramadan, the Muslim month of fasting. Fasting is the fourth Pillar of Islam.

During the Hajj, thousands of pilgrims surround the Kaaba in the city of Mecca.

worship Allah and give thanks for his mercy toward all believers. With these acts they show they have surrendered their lives to Allah.

Islam and the Brotherhood of Faith

By the time he died in 632, Muhammad had made deep changes in the lives and ideas of Arabs. He had replaced polytheistic beliefs with a monotheistic religion followed by thousands and rapidly spreading. Islam gave people laws to obey every day of their lives. And it went a long way toward unifying the Arabian Peninsula.

Remember, in Muhammad's day the Arabs had been divided into many tribes that often carried on deadly feuds. Muhammad wanted Arabs to keep their feelings of tribal loyalty, but he said that their faith in Allah must come first. Muhammad preached that all Muslims must unite and consider themselves brothers. They must not fight among themselves. Such, Muhammad said, was the will of Allah.

Muhammad replaced the "blood brotherhood" of the tribes with a "brotherhood of faith." With this new unity, Arabs found a new confidence in themselves. They even began to think about expanding Islam beyond the Arabian Peninsula.

As we'll see, in the centuries to come this brotherhood of faith would grow to include huge numbers of people, including millions who were not Arabs.

A nineteenth-century painting shows two leaders of Islam after the death of Muhammad, Abu Bakr and Umar (with faces veiled, as is customary in Islamic depictions of important religious leaders).

The Spread of Islam

In the century following Muhammad's death, Islam spread swiftly. The new faith unified Arabia. Through conquest and trade, Arabs created an empire that stretched from Spain in the west to India in the east. For the next five hundred years the Islamic Empire stood as a center of both power and learning. How did that happen?

The Caliphs Take Charge

In 632, Muhammad died without leaving an obvious successor. Who would lead the Muslims now? Muslims believed that Muhammad had been the prophet of Allah. What would happen to Islam now that he was dead?

Some Muslims turned to Muhammad's father-in-law, Abu Bakr (uh-BOO BAK-uhr), a short man who dressed in plain clothes and walked with a stoop. He had been one of the very first people to become a Muslim. During the dangerous Hijrah, when Muhammad slipped across the desert just ahead of pursuers bent on killing him, Abu Bakr had ridden at the Prophet's side. Now some Muslims began to turn to this soft-spoken and humble man who had been Muhammad's closest friend. They elected him as *caliph* (KAY-luhf), which means "successor."

The caliph did not take Muhammad's place. No one could do that. After all, Muslims believed that Muhammad had been the final prophet to bring Allah's message to the world. But the caliph did serve as the Muslim ruler. He led the army and looked after the welfare of Muslim people. He was expected to govern according to Islamic law. Muslims also looked to the caliph for spiritual leadership.

A caravan of Arab merchants.

Abu Bakr told Muslims, "People, I have been chosen by you as your leader, though I am no better than you. If I do well, give me support. If I do wrong, set me right!"

Almost at once, Abu Bakr had a fight on his hands. Several tribes refused to follow him as caliph. They said they had promised loyalty only to Muhammad. Now that the Prophet was dead, why should they follow anyone else? Other Arabian tribes had never accepted Islam in the first place. Now they hoped to destroy the power of the Muslims. Civil war broke out on the Arabian Peninsula.

Though Abu Bakr was a gentle man, he did not hesitate to send Muslim soldiers against tribes that challenged him or ignored Islamic laws. Abu Bakr's forces marched against the rebellious tribes and won. Islam became the force that unified Arabia.

Then Abu Bakr attempted to extend Muslim influence even further. He sent troops into Mesopotamia, Syria, and lands along the eastern Mediterranean coast. Each land the Muslims conquered increased the extent of the growing Islamic Empire. (The Islamic Empire is also known as the Muslim Empire. The two terms mean the same.)

Abu Bakr's reign was short. He was 60 years old when he became caliph, and he died two years later. Muslims quarreled over who should follow him. Different groups wanted different men as leaders. While Muhammad and Abu Bakr had both died naturally, the next three caliphs were murdered. As time passed, however, the power of the caliphs grew, as did the reach of the Islamic Empire.

Sunnis and Shi'ites

Not long after Abu Bakr's death, Muslims disagreed about how to choose caliphs. One group believed that the caliph should always be someone from Muhammad's family. Muhammad left no son, so this group rallied around his son-in-law, Ali, and Ali's descendants. Ali's supporters were called the Shia Ali ("the party of Ali"), or Shi'ahs (SHEE-ahs) for short. They are often referred to as Shi'ites (SHEE-iyts).

Many followers of Abu Bakr, on the other hand, said it was wrong for the leadership of Islam to stay in Muhammad's family. They said the most capable Muslim should be the caliph, and that he should rule following the Qur'an and the example of Muhammad. In Arabic, "example" is *sunna*, so these Muslims are called Sunnis (SOU-neez).

This split between Shi'ites and Sunnis sometimes caused bitter struggles within Islam. It is a division that persists to this day, although now there are far more Sunni Muslims than Shi'ite Muslims. Sunnis make up 85 percent or more of the world's Muslim population.

Muslims on the Move

Abu Bakr spread Islam across the Arabian Peninsula and beyond. The caliphs who followed called for jihad (jih-HAHD). *Jihad* is an Arabic word with several meanings. (See "The Meaning of *Jihad*" on page 475.) In its most general sense, it refers to a struggle on behalf of Islam. This struggle might be the spiritual effort of an individual Muslim to strengthen his faith. When the caliphs called for jihad, however, they were urging a holy war to extend the empire of Islam. They set their sights to the north and west. At once they ran into two great powers—the Persians and the Byzantines.

The Persians ruled territories to the north and east of Arabia, including the rich lands of Mesopotamia. The Byzantine Empire, with its capital in Constantinople, lay to the northwest. The great emperor Justinian, ruler of Byzantium, had died in 565, but his empire lived on. It still controlled Asia Minor and much of North Africa. For many years, the once-mighty Byzantine Empire had been at war with the Persians. The fighting had left both sides weak.

In 636, Muslim forces attacked a few Byzantine towns. To their surprise, they defeated the Byzantines easily. Soon Muslim armies marched into Syria and Egypt. One of their best weapons was knowledge of the barren desert, where they knew how to travel, live, and fight better than their enemies. Here is the advice one Arab general gave to his men.

> Fight the enemy in the desert. Even if you lose, you will have the familiar desert at your backs. The enemy cannot follow you there. And from there you can return again to the attack.

Muslims fought for more than riches, power, and territory. Like other people at the time, they fought for their faith. Muslims believed that those who died fighting to destroy the enemies of Islam would win a great reward in paradise, or the heavenly afterlife. As Muslim armies engaged in jihad against the enemies of Islam, their battle cry was, "Allah is most great."

This painting shows an armed Arab horseman. Such warriors extended Islamic influence far beyond the Arabian Peninsula.

People soon learned that it was wise to surrender to the Muslim armies without fighting. If they surrendered, often they had only to pay

The Meaning of *Jihad*

Jihad **is an Arabic word that means "struggle" or "battle" on behalf of Islam. Muslims believe that struggle can take place in two different ways.**

One meaning of jihad is the internal struggle that an individual faces to overcome temptation and live a good life. By praying, fasting, giving to charity, submitting to Allah, and following the Qur'an and the teachings of Muhammad, Muslims believe they can win this internal struggle.

Another meaning of jihad is as an armed struggle or holy war against people regarded as enemies of Islam. Muslims have sometimes engaged in armed jihad since the time of Muhammad, who led armies of the faithful. Those who sacrifice their lives for Islam are said to receive glory in paradise.

Today, while many Muslims think of jihad in terms of peaceful efforts for Islam, there are some who carry out armed jihad against nations and groups they view as threats to their religion.

their new Muslim rulers a tax. If they fought, the Islamic armies would probably defeat them and take their lands. Captives were often sold into slavery, a common practice in Europe, Asia, and Africa at that time.

The armies of the caliphs pressed north all the way to the Caspian Sea. They rode east through Persia, pushing as far as the Indus River. They triumphed in Egypt and gazed in wonder at the mighty pyramids. They spread west across North Africa, crossing the Strait of Gibraltar and conquering the southern part of the Iberian Peninsula. By 711, Muslim troops were crossing the Pyrenees and pressing into France. In 732, the French defeated Muslim forces and stopped the spread of Islam into Europe.

In the century from 632 to 732, Muslim forces achieved enormous victories. A hundred years after

The Islamic Empire, c. A.D. 632–732

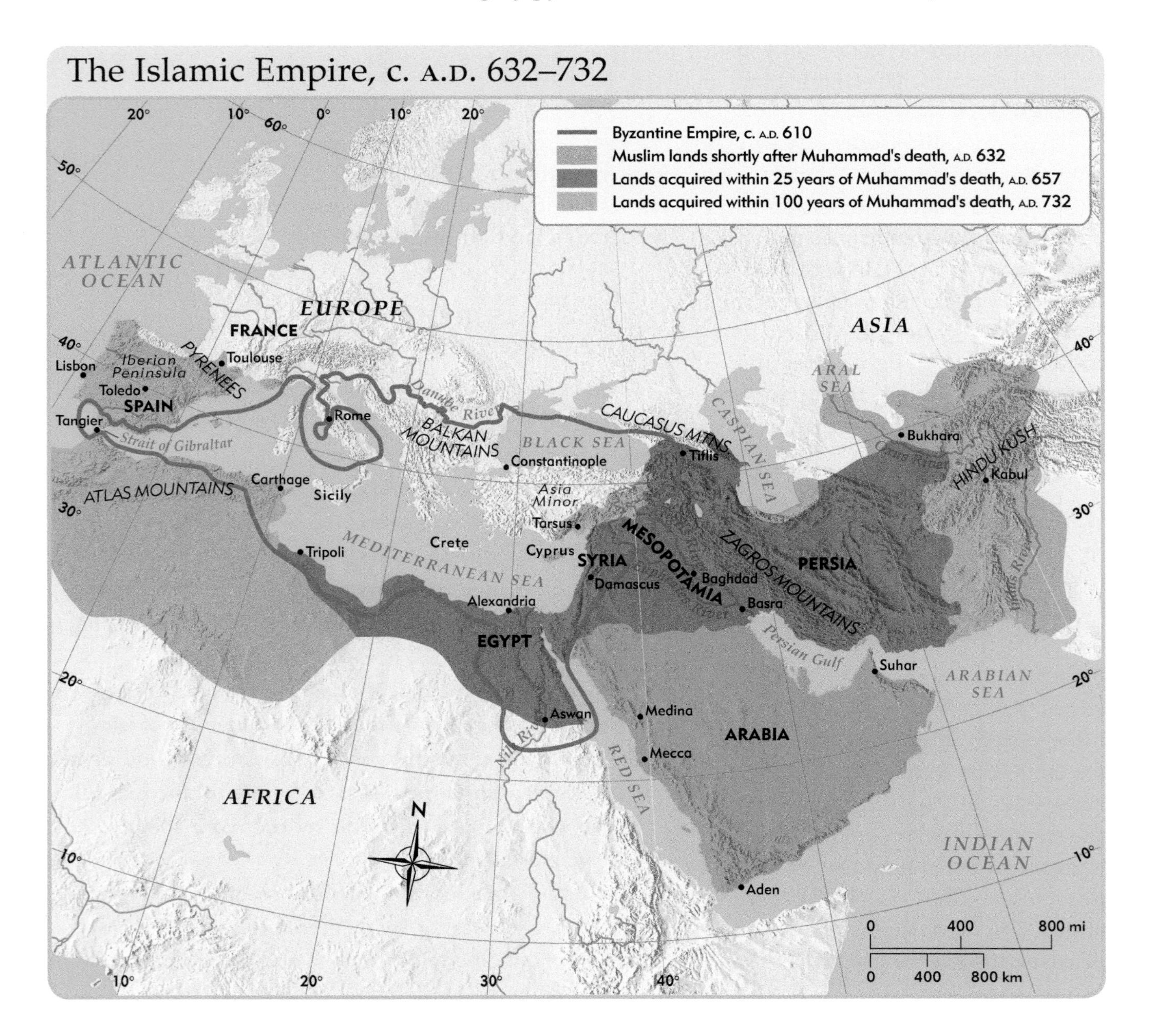

Muhammad's death, the Muslim caliphs ruled a sprawling empire. When one Muslim general reached the Atlantic, he sounded like Alexander the Great who, legend says, wept because there were no more worlds to conquer. The Muslim general cried to Allah, "If this sea were not stopping me, I would go to the unknown kingdoms of the West, conquering all nations who worship other gods than thee!"

- On the map on page 476, note the extent of the Islamic Empire shortly after Muhammad's death, within 25 years of his death, and within 100 years of his death.

The Spread of Faith and Empire

In many Byzantine and Persian cities, people hailed the Muslims not as conquerors but as liberators. These people had often been burdened by heavy taxes and corrupt governors. Many were quite content to change their old rulers for new ones. Others were not.

In lands belonging to the Islamic Empire, laws were based on the Qur'an. To the conquered people who believed in the old nature gods, the caliphs often gave a choice—they could convert to Islam or be put to death. The caliphs usually allowed Jews and Christians to follow their own religions so long as they paid a special tax. Muslims generally respected the beliefs of Jews and Christians, since they too worshipped the one God. Still, many people could not afford to pay a tax to keep their religious freedom, so over time they became Muslims.

As Muslim merchants like these traded their goods, they also spread their beliefs around the Mediterranean world.

Conquest was not the only way that Islam spread. Muslim traders followed troops through Mediterranean lands. Look again at the map of the Islamic Empire, and you'll see how geography was good for the Muslim merchants. Because the Islamic Empire lay at the crossroads of Europe, Africa, and Asia, Muslim caliphs and merchants held a commanding position over traffic between East and West.

Muslim traders carried their religion with them. They told people they met about Islam, urging the worship of Allah and adherence to the five pillars. Many who heard decided to become Muslims, too.

Islam started in the seventh century as a message proclaimed by one man, Muhammad. By the eighth century, a mere one hundred years after his death, it had become

"People of the Book"

Muslims accept many teachings from both the Jewish Torah and the Christian Gospels. They sometimes call Jews and Christians "People of the Book," a reference to a shared reverence for the Bible. All three religions honor Abraham and share many biblical heroes and stories.

much more. Through conquest and trade, it had become a thriving religion and a mighty empire.

Baghdad: Jewel of the Empire

The holy city of Islam had always been Mecca, but as the empire grew, caliphs sought a capital more central to the territories they ruled. Beginning in 661, a family from Mecca called the Umayyads (oo-MAH-yahdz) rose to power. For nearly one hundred years, the Umayyad dynasty provided caliphs for the empire. They made the city of Damascus, in Syria, their capital. It soon became a hub of intellectual and cultural life.

In 750, another family, the Abbasids (uh-BA-sids), came to power. Over the next hundred years, the Abbasid dynasty strove to rival the glories of the old Roman Empire.

The Abbasid caliphs wanted to build a new capital city—a prince of cities—in the center of their growing empire. They found a lush, green plain stretching along the Tigris River and built their capital there. This round city divided by a river flowing through the center was called Baghdad (BAG-dad).

Mecca remained the holy city of Islam, but Baghdad became home to the caliphs and the jewel of the Islamic Empire. Over time caliphs

Muslim cities such as Baghdad and Damascus (seen here) became thriving centers of trade and learning.

filled the walled city with fabulous palaces, flowering gardens, and bubbling fountains. Hundreds of busy marketplaces and thousands of public baths lined the streets. By the year 800, nearly a million people may have lived there.

- On the map on page 476, locate Baghdad.

Baghdad was ideally located for trade. Straddling the Tigris and linked to the Euphrates River by canal, it became a destination for ships sailing up the Persian Gulf from the Arabian Sea, Indian Ocean, and Red Sea. Merchants traveling by land could quickly reach the Mediterranean, Black, and Caspian Seas. Caravans paraded in and out of Baghdad. Trade routes from the city led southwest to Africa, east to Asia, and north to Europe.

Merchants came to Baghdad from all points of the compass. The city's bazaars (marketplaces) boasted goods from far and wide. Here you could buy rice from Egypt, furs from Russia, or leather from Spain. You might see peacocks, porcelain, and silks from China, spices and rubies from India, ivory and gold from Africa. You would see slaves for sale, both black and white, from Africa and other conquered lands.

Muslim traders brought back all kinds of knowledge and ideas from the lands they visited. "Seek knowledge, even unto China," was a famous saying of the Prophet Muhammad. The caliphs turned Baghdad into a great center of learning with its own university, many schools, and some of the world's first hospitals to train new doctors.

A thirteenth-century Muslim artist painted this miniature of Socrates and his students. The painting shows that Muslims revered the great Greek philosopher and classical learning.

While Muslim armies were fighting in China, they captured Chinese prisoners and brought them back to Baghdad. Several of these prisoners knew a valuable skill—how to make paper. Soon a paper mill was up and running in Baghdad, and Muslim scholars were copying books.

The House of Wisdom

Around 830, the caliphs built a great research library in Baghdad called the House of Wisdom. Here they collected scrolls, books, and manuscripts from around the Mediterranean and beyond. Merchants sought out works from Constantinople, Egypt, Persia, and India. Muslim scholars, along with learned Christians and Jews, translated the ancient works of mathematics, physics, astronomy, and philosophy into Arabic.

The scholars carefully preserved and studied the writings of the Greeks and Romans. In their hands, the philosophies of Plato and Aristotle lived on. In Europe at this time, most people had forgotten about these works. But the Muslim scholars, with their respect for learning, rescued countless writings of the past. If not for their painstaking efforts, many great ideas from ancient times might have been lost forever.

From the high towers of the House of Wisdom, when Muslim scholars peered down at the round city with its rooftops, courtyards, and gardens, their hearts surely swelled with pride. Far away to the north and west, Europe was suffering through a period sometimes called the Dark Ages, a time when Germanic tribes roamed the continent, fought for land, and the light of learning seemed to be extinguished. In Baghdad, however, the light of learning burned brightly. The Muslim scholars must have whispered to themselves—and rightfully so—that Baghdad at this time was not only the center of the Islamic Empire, but also the most splendid city in the world.

A group of Muslim scholars discuss one of the many books stacked in the wall niches of a library. Such men did much to preserve the learning of the classical world.

Across the Islamic Empire, Muslims became great preservers of ancient knowledge. They also built on what they preserved, adding important ideas and discoveries of their own. Let's look at the lives of two men who made great contributions to learning at this time.

A New Branch of Mathematics

The year is 820, and there lives in Baghdad an Arab mathematician named Al-Khwarizmi (al-KHWAHR-iz-mee). The Abbasid caliph, who knows Al-Khwarizmi's abilities well, has asked the mathematician to translate ancient Greek manuscripts at the House of Wisdom. The caliph has also asked Al-Khwarizmi to write his own works on mathematics and astronomy.

Al-Khwarizmi, a curious and tireless scholar, happily accepts these duties. Mathematics gives him no end of pleasure because, he says, numbers are so useful. After all, he writes, we must use numbers "in cases of inheritance, legacies, partition, lawsuits...trade, and in all dealings with one another, or where the measuring of lands, the digging of canals, geometrical computations, and other objects of various sorts and kinds are concerned."

Like many a Muslim scholar, he begins all his works by writing, "In the name of Allah, the Compassionate and the Merciful." He explains that mathematics is primarily a reflection of how Allah's creation is carefully arranged and made understandable to those who study it.

This Muslim scholar has written a book that makes numbers much simpler. Most people around the Mediterranean have been using Roman numerals for counting: I, II, III, IV, V, and so forth. But during their travels to India, Arabs learned that the Hindus have developed a better way. When adding or subtracting, the Hindus use a little circle or dot that the Arabs called a *sifr* (SIH-fur). *Sifr,* which means "empty," is the basis of the English word *cipher* (SIY-fur), one meaning of which is "zero." The Hindus also use the concept of place value in their number system.

Al-Khwarizmi has proposed using this Hindu system in his book. In fact, he has created a new set of numerals based on the Hindu method. He is hopeful that these new mathematical tools will become popular.

Al-Khwarizmi has also written a book about a whole new branch of mathematics that focuses on solving equations. His title is very impressive: *The Compendious Book on Calculation by Completion and Balancing.* In Arabic, part of the title is *hisab al-jabr* (hih-SAB el-JUH-bruh). *Al-jabr* means "completion." Can you see what this new branch of mathematics is? Algebra! You may soon study algebra, or you might be in the middle of a course. You can thank Al-Khwarizmi.

Scholars at the House of Wisdom and other centers of learning built on Al-Khwarizmi's work and went even further. They made breakthroughs in geometry and astronomy. Much of modern mathematics is based on their study.

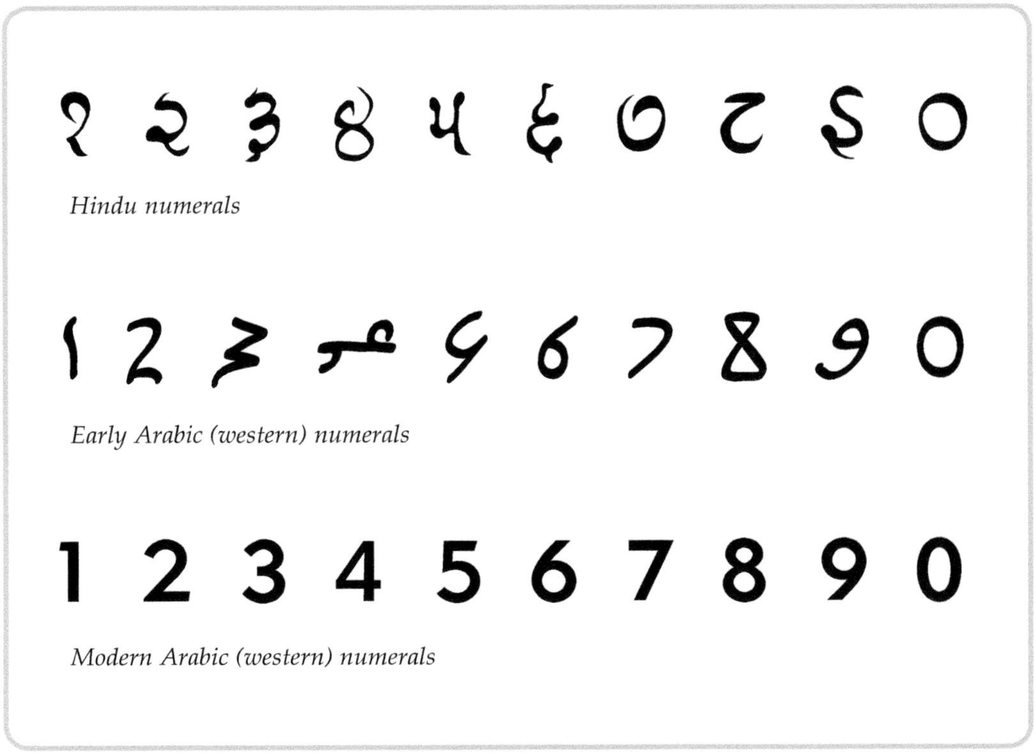

Hindu numerals

Early Arabic (western) numerals

1 2 3 4 5 6 7 8 9 0

Modern Arabic (western) numerals

Al-Khwarizmi and other Muslim scholars used Hindu numerals to create their own set of Arabic numerals, which eventually became the numerals we use today.

Above: Ibn Sina, known to his contemporaries as "The Prince of Philosophers."

Below: An open copy of Ibn Sina's Canon of Medicine, *one of the most important scientific texts of the Middle Ages. This copy dates from the 1300s.*

Ibn Sina and Advances in Medicine

Now let's leave Baghdad and zoom forward a couple of centuries. The year is A.D. 1000. The place is Persia, which is part of the Islamic Empire. It's a time when many people around the world believe that gods or demons cause illness. But Muslim doctors, who have learned from the Greeks, are studying the human body to look for natural causes of disease. Hard at work is a young Muslim scholar and doctor named Ibn Sina (IB-uhn SEE-nah).

Ibn Sina has always been a gifted student. Even when he was young, people knew of his talents. When the prince near his home fell ill, Ibn Sina managed to cure him, and he was rewarded with access to the royal library.

By the age of 18, as a physician to kings of Persia, Ibn Sina has started writing *The Book of Healing*. Soon he is at work on his *Canon of Medicine*, a book that summarizes all known diseases and treatments. He doesn't know it, but his book will later be translated and used for centuries in Europe. It is to become the single most important volume in the history of medicine.

Ibn Sina always pushes himself. Sometimes Muslim rulers want him to care for them on the road while they wage war. He even writes part of his *Book of Healing* while traveling on military campaigns.

This remarkable man of science would eventually die on one of those campaigns. But his work in medicine paved a brilliant path for others to follow.

Muslims established hospitals and traveling clinics throughout the Islamic Empire. They used surgery to treat wounds, set bones, remove eye cataracts, and fight diseases. Muslim doctors made effective medicines from plant and animal extracts.

Students traveled thousands of miles to study medicine at Muslim centers of learning. Europeans even sent their sons to study medicine with Islamic scholars. The achievements of Ibn Sina and others made Muslim medicine the wonder of medieval times.

A wall tile covered with Arabic script and the elegant leaf-and-floral designs known as arabesque.

Art in Praise of Allah

A famous Islamic saying declares, "Allah is beautiful and loves beauty." Muslim artists tried to fill the world with beautiful things that pleased the eye and reminded the faithful of Islamic teachings. As Muslims expanded their empire, they encountered artwork in Egypt, Syria, Persia, Mesopotamia, and beyond. They learned from the lands they conquered and wove the new ideas into their own distinctive style of art.

Because Muhammad had taught that Allah alone could create life, Muslims believed that it was a sin of arrogance to draw living creatures, for that would be trying to act like Allah. So Muslim artists usually did not make pictures or statues of lifelike beings. Instead, they decorated objects with complex patterns that dazzled the eye.

Often they drew on nature for inspiration. The most famous Muslim design is called arabesque (air-uh-BESK), a pattern of winding stems and abstract leaves and flowers. If you look closely, sometimes you can detect that the lines within arabesque leaf patterns aren't lines at all, but Arabic letters forming the word *Allah*.

Like the Chinese, Muslim artists turned handwriting, or calligraphy, into art. The elegant Arabic letters lent themselves to intricate patterns. Artists competed with one another to work passages from the Qur'an into clever decorations. They loved covering just about everything—walls, floors, carpets, vases, swords—with elaborate letter-patterns. Even caliphs practiced copying sayings from the Qur'an. For the Muslims, the art of calligraphy was yet another way to proclaim the glory of Allah.

Muslim crafts were a feast for the eye. Pottery glowed with the colors of a desert sunset. Jeweled pitchers shone with engraved passages from the Qur'an. Swords glistened with silver and gold arabesques. Strolling through a busy bazaar in the streets of Baghdad, you might have spotted a leather saddle and matching cloth ready to fit the finest Arabian horse, or a bronze lamp gleaming so brightly that you'd wonder if a genie made his home there.

Muslim craftsmen turned carpets into works of art. Rugs of all sizes were in great demand in the Muslim world. People sat and slept on rugs on the floor rather than on chairs or beds. Many of the faithful carried small prayer rugs with them, which they unrolled and knelt upon when they prayed in the direction of Mecca.

Muslim craftsmen covered their carpets with rich patterns made of tiny knots of colored wool or silk. A fine rug could have a thousand or more knots per square inch! They were magic carpets—not because they could fly, but because they fired the imagination with their colors and designs. Rugs from Persia were the most elaborate of all. Sometimes they looked like lush gardens, full of flowering trees, gurgling fountains, and ponds alive with ducks and fish. These designs were often inspired by Qur'anic verses that gave beautiful descriptions of paradise.

Elaborate expressions of Islamic art, such as this Persian rug, continue to be made and treasured.

Mosques for Beauty and Worship

When Muhammad was alive, his followers would gather in the courtyard of his house to pray and listen to him speak about Allah. Muhammad's house was the very first mosque. A mosque is a Muslim place of worship and the spiritual center of a Muslim community.

Muslims built mosques wherever Islam spread. The earliest ones were simple buildings made of mud brick. Muslims wanted their mosques to remind them of Muhammad's house, which had contained a courtyard. So they built each mosque around a courtyard, and inside they marked the wall nearest to Mecca so that worshippers would know in which direction to pray. Each mosque had a special place for a person to stand, lead prayers, and teach about Allah. When men wanted to call people to prayer, they simply climbed to the roof.

As the Islamic Empire grew, Muslims adopted architectural features from different lands. In Constantinople they saw the enormous, light-filled dome of the Hagia Sophia. Soon they were building domes over their mosques. From the Persians they learned to construct mosques with pointed arches.

When North African Muslims built mosques, they added towers called minarets (min-uh-RETS). Men climbed to the top of these minarets to call people to prayer.

Before long, Muslims in other parts of the empire were building minarets on their mosques.

Some mosques were humble buildings in small areas. Some were ornate, spread over acres. In the most elaborate mosques, craftsmen carved wandering arabesque designs on walls and doors. Rich carpets covered the floors. Mosaics made from millions of colored stones adorned the walkways. The finest glass lamps hung from ceilings, bringing a golden glow to the evening prayers. Fountains and gardens graced the courtyards. Mosques today continue these traditions.

Mosques varied enormously in design, but most shared and still share common features. The minaret forms the highest point, from which the call to prayer goes out five times a day. A dome often covers some part of the building. A gate in the front wall welcomes worshippers, while inside a courtyard provides a place to meditate or read. A fountain, well, or other source of water often stands in the courtyard, for it is the Muslim ritual to wash oneself before praying.

In the prayer halls, where men and women gather to worship, rugs cover the floor. A decorated niche called a *mihrab* (mih-RAHB) marks the direction of Mecca, which worshippers face to pray. Inside every mosque is a raised pulpit. Here, at Friday prayers, the *imam* (ih-MAHM), meaning "one who stands in front," gives a sermon.

From Arabia to Asia, from North Africa to Spain, wherever Muslims settled they could visit a mosque and pray. They could learn about Islam and talk with other Muslims. Visiting scholars might even live there. No matter where they went, the courtyards, minarets, domes, and mosaics were signs to Muslims that they were still in the Islamic Empire.

Top: A Muslim prays in front of the mihrab, the highly decorated wall-niche that indicates the direction of Mecca.

Above: A very different-looking house of prayer—a West African mosque built of sun-baked mud.

A: A West African mosque.

B: Sunset on the Niger River.

C: Mali's Emperor Mansa Musa.

D: A metal disc used to weigh gold dust.

E: A Muslim writing case inlaid with African gold.

Ghana and Mali: Two Medieval African Trading Empires

Muslim civilization, which had begun on the Arabian Peninsula in the seventh century, had far-reaching influence. Arab warriors united the peninsula in the name of Islam, and then pressed into Egypt and the cities of North Africa. Arab traders and merchants followed in their wake. As Islam spread, and as Arab traders extended their reach, important new empires flourished to the south in the part of Africa known as the Sudan (soo-DAN).

The Sudan is a vast, fertile grassland dotted with bushes and occasional trees. This hot, dusty region lies between the Sahara to the north and the equatorial rain forest to the south. The Atlantic Ocean washes its western edge. The upper valley of the Nile River stretches to the east.

Two of the greatest Sudanese empires lay in the western part of the region, along the banks of the crocodile-filled Senegal and Niger Rivers. One was Ghana (GAH-nuh), the place the Arabs called "the land of gold." The other was an even richer and more powerful realm, the warrior federation of Mali (MAH-lee). (A *federation* is a group of people or states united under a single authority, in which each state still retains some independence.)

These civilizations—and most of all, the powerful lords who ruled them—grew wealthy from their control of trade with the Arabs of North Africa. Contact with the Arabs, however, brought more than trade. It brought exposure to Islam, the religion many North Africans had recently adopted. In the centuries ahead, Islam would become the

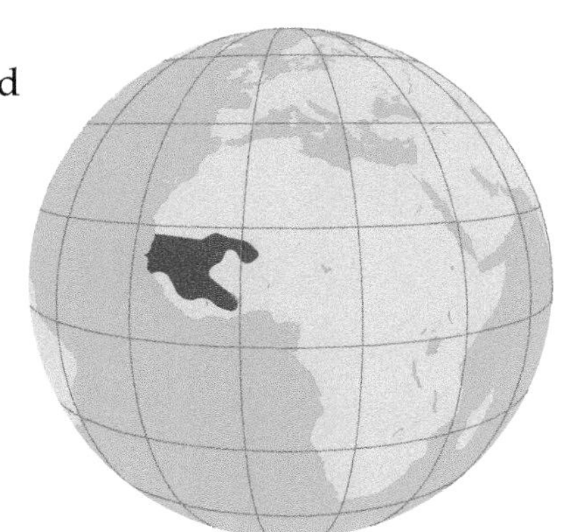

This chapter explores Ghana and Mali, two trading empires of West Africa.

dominant faith among the warriors and traders of the western Sudan.

- On the map below, locate Ghana, Mali, the Sudan, the Nile River, the Senegal River, and the Niger River.

Ghana: Traders Par Excellence

Ghana, situated on the savanna and near the headwaters of the Senegal and Niger Rivers, was the first great medieval African trading empire. Its roots may go as far back as the fourth century A.D. We know little of its first rulers, whose title of *Ghana*, or "warrior king," gave the kingdom its familiar name. We do know that this region in western Sudan was populated by Soninke (soh-NIN-kay) clans. (A *clan* is an extended family group descended from a common ancestor.) The Soninke, who were probably practicing agriculture by 3000 B.C., spoke a language called Mande (MAHN-day).

By the tenth century A.D., Ghana stood at the height of its power. At this time, its rulers controlled trade in an area approximately the size of Texas. The region was blessed with an abundance of two metals—iron and gold. Thanks to the skill and

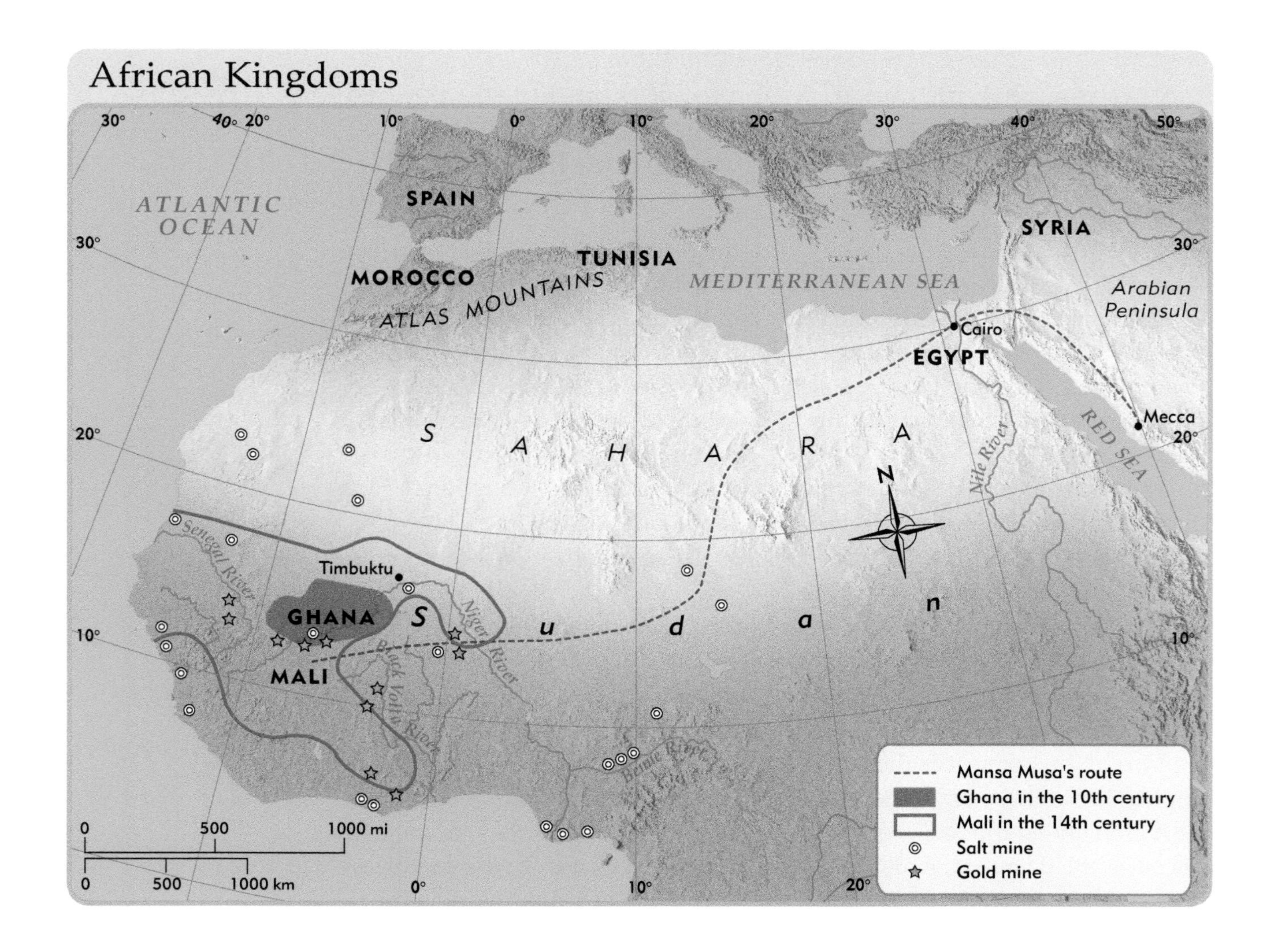

Trading in salt is still important in parts of Africa. In this photo, slabs of salt are being sold at a market in the modern-day country of Mali.

ingenuity of the Soninke traders of Ghana, these metals attracted Muslim traders from the Sahara.

The Soninke people boasted skilled blacksmiths, who crafted iron ore into tools for farming and weapons for war. Arab travelers to the kingdom of Ghana were amazed at the power of its army, which some reports—though perhaps exaggerated for effect—placed at 200,000 soldiers, 40,000 of whom were archers equipped with iron-tipped arrows. Ghana's weaker neighbors could do little to withstand the expansion of such a state. Led by one warrior king after another, Ghana grew into an imperial power.

Iron made Ghana powerful, but gold made it rich. For Ghana's traders, gold could be exchanged for many items from afar, but perhaps the most important of all was salt.

Salt? Would people actually exchange gold for something that you can now find in just about any kitchen?

Yes. Salt was vital to the Soninke people. In hot climates, like that of the western Sudan, people needed extra salt to replace that which the body naturally lost through perspiration. In Ghana, little salt was available locally, so the Soninke people had to trade for it. The salt not only fulfilled a vital bodily need; it also made food tastier and, more important, kept it from going bad.

Blacksmiths: A Class Apart

Blacksmiths were revered by the Soninke, and even thought to have magical powers. How else could they turn mere ore into precious metal? For their part, blacksmiths were careful not to reveal the secrets of their trade to others in the clan, and they became an honored class.

Two elaborately decorated tools of the West African gold trade—a weight and a spoon once used to measure gold dust.

So valuable was salt in tropical Africa that merchants would use small blocks of it as money. They wrapped "rock salt" mined in the Sahara in leaves or cloth. The wrapping kept the salt from dissolving as it was carried over long distances, even through rainy weather. In some places, merchants could exchange a weight of salt for an equal weight of gold.

To the north of Ghana, in the Sahara, salt was abundant. North African traders set out across the desert wastes in long caravans of camels laden with bars of salt. The Muslim merchants brought more than salt. As they moved south, they brought robes from Morocco, red and blue cloth from Spain, silks from all over the Islamic world, and cowrie shells from the distant Indian Ocean, which were used as currency. In exchange, Soninke traders at the Ghana market offered ivory, hides, and kola nuts from farther south, as well as slaves from their contacts in remote southern territories. For the most part, however, the Ghana trade focused on two items—gold and salt.

The rulers of Ghana made no effort to control the sources of gold, which came from remote highlands beyond their influence. It was all alluvial gold, dust and some nuggets, mined from streams at the headwaters of the Niger and Senegal Rivers.

But Ghana's lords did control sales of gold dust to desert merchants. Soninke middlemen conducted the sale of gold dust, and the king of Ghana kept all the nuggets. This trade made some African lords wealthy enough to furnish their homes with imported luxuries. They amassed followings of ministers, advisers, servants, and slaves. And they built powerful military forces of mounted knights.

The gold-for-salt exchange that so enriched the Ghana trading network frequently unfolded in a most unusual fashion. If you have ever seen how traders work today in the New York Stock Exchange, then you know it's a very noisy affair, with shouts across the floor and arms waving in the air. The gold trade of Ghana was quite the opposite. According to stories told to Arab travelers, the Soninke buyers and gold sellers never spoke to one another, but instead engaged in what was known as mute barter or silent trade.

Let's see how it might have worked, as we imagine a 13-year-old boy named Jaabe (JAH-bay) experiencing his first trade.

A Gilded Court

Ghana had many wealthy lords or princes, and a king who exacted payment from them all. The eleventh century Arab geographer al-Bakri (ahl-BAHK-ree), who came from Spain, described the glittering court of Ghana's king. Al-Bakri reported that pedigreed dogs wore gold and silver collars. The king wore a gold-embroidered cap, and his horses were covered in gold-embroidered cloth. His pages carried gold-decorated swords, and the princes of the realm braided their hair with gold.

Turning Gold into Salt

Imagining the Past

Da-da-da-rum, da-da-da-rum, da-da-da-rum!

The distinctive noise of the derba rang out. As usual, this signal from the "talking drum" made the gold miners put down their tools and prepare to leave their work.

But young Jaabe hadn't been working in the streams long, and this was the first time he had heard the beat of the drum. His father, Amma (AM-mah), had toiled there for years. Just a couple of weeks earlier, Amma had decided it was time for Jaabe to follow in his footsteps. Panning the streams of their mountainous homeland had been good to Amma and his people. The gold brought them much that they needed—especially salt.

Silently, Amma and the other men made their way toward the beating drum. But Jaabe was full of questions. "Father, what is that noise? Who's beating the drum? What do they want?"

"The traders have come," said his father.

Jaabe had heard about these traders and all the good things they brought with them.

The derba rang out again: *Da-da-da-rum, da-da-da-rum, da-da-da-rum!*

"Come on, father," said Jaabe, starting to break into a run. "Let's hurry."

Amma's restraining hand stopped Jaabe from dashing in the direction of the traders. "We must wait and watch," he told his son.

Jaabe could see nothing, and he could hear the drum no longer. But he knew to obey the words of his father.

Amma looked at his son and explained. "We must always keep secret the location of the gold. Outsiders must never find out where the gold comes from. If they do, they will take it themselves, and we will be finished."

Just then, off to his right, Jaabe saw some of the men beginning to move, quietly making their way toward the place where the drum had sounded. Amma moved, too, and Jaabe followed.

The miners made their way to a clearing beside a nearby stream. The traders were nowhere to be seen, but there on the ground lay the goods they had brought to exchange for gold. There was leather and cloth and dried fruit. And most important of all, bars of salt.

"Why have they left their goods, father?" Jaabe asked. "And where have the traders gone?"

Amma smiled. "Don't worry, they're still here. They haven't gone far."

Jaabe listened as his father and the other men assessed the value of the goods. Finally they came to an agreement. Pulling out small leaf-wrapped packets of gold dust, they laid them down beside the trade goods. Jaabe could see that they valued the salt equally with their gold and exchanged it on equal terms.

"Come on, son," said Amma.

"But father, aren't we going to take the salt and the other goods?"

"Not yet," he replied. "Come."

Puzzled, Jaabe followed his father and the other miners as they pulled back from the stream. There they sat, waited, and watched.

Jaabe was impatient—he still didn't know what he was waiting and watching for. After some time, he heard noises—human voices.

"Did they come back, father?" he asked.

"Yes, son," replied Amma. "Now the traders will decide if the gold we have left for them is enough."

Then the voices stopped. Once again, the miners cautiously made their way to the clearing. Jaabe saw that the gold, salt, and other goods remained untouched.

"Father, what's wrong?" Jaabe asked. "Will there be no trade?"

"Yes, there will be a trade, but not just yet. The traders want more gold for their wares."

Amma and the other men began to debate.

"We can offer a little more gold," said one.

"But not too much," cautioned another.

"We do need the salt, though," added a third. "Our supplies are getting low."

In the end, the miners agreed on how much more to add. One of the men bent down and placed three more packets of gold dust on the ground, and they all headed back to the place they waited.

Before long, Jaabe heard the voices of the traders again.

Then: *Da-da-da-rum, da-da-da-rum, da-da-da-rum!*

"What does that mean, father?"

"That means that the traders have concluded their business," Amma answered.

The miners made their way to the clearing. The gold was gone, while the salt and other items remained. Goods had been exchanged between the miners and the Soninke traders, but not a single word. One more silent trade—soundless except for the beating of the drum—had been successfully transacted.

The Decline of Ghana

While the story of Jaabe is fictional, the "silent barter" of gold for salt and other luxuries may well have been real. The gold-for-salt trade was the lifeblood of Ghana.

In 1076, the Soninke traders' business was disrupted by Muslim warriors from the desert, called Berbers. The Berber invasions sent the trading post at Ghana into steep decline. By the twelfth century, other traders were competing to meet an ever-greater demand for gold in the north.

Warlords in charge of mounted troops began fighting for control of the trade. Out of these contests emerged a strong warrior federation, Mali. Mali was led by wealthy and powerful horsemen who had accepted the Islamic religion brought by North African traders. The members of this federation prospered throughout the Sudan. They made their homeland, the upper valley of the Niger River, a key center of the Islamic world in the Middle Ages.

A present-day village of the Malinke people.

Mali Rising

The people of Mali are called the Malinke (muh-LING-kay). (Do you see the word *Mali* in *Malinke*?) Before Mali could succeed Ghana as the most powerful federation in the western Sudan, the Malinke had to overcome a great challenge.

The story of Sundiata comes to us largely through the songs of the griots (GREE-ohs), the story-tellers and history-keepers of many western African civilizations. In Mali, griots memorized the history and lore of their people. They recounted stories through songs that they sang over and over again, passing them down to younger generations.

Just to the north, a clan called the Sossos (SOH-sohz) had violently seized control of much of the area and made slaves of many people. To free them from the shackles of the Sossos, the Malinke would need a leader of real courage and ability. Fortunately such a leader emerged, seemingly from nowhere, when he was needed most. His name was Sundiata (sun-JAHT-ah), which means "the Hungering Lion."

There are many accounts of Sundiata, most of which mix myth and fact. Here is one story that the people of Mali later told of Sundiata.

The Triumph of the Lion

As a young boy, Sundiata bore little resemblance to a lion. He was the son of a warrior king, one of twelve children, but a sickly child, unable to walk. He could not even stand up. So when Sumanguru (soo-mahng-GOO-roo), the king of the Sossos, decided to rid Mali of anyone who posed a threat to him, he killed Sundiata's eleven brothers, but overlooked Sundiata.

"What challenge can this cripple ever be to me?" the king scoffed. "I will spare his life so that he can be a living example of the weakness of the Malinke."

Though the Sosso king could not know it, he had just made a fatal mistake.

Despite his frailty, Sundiata possessed the bright flame of intelligence. And though his legs were weak, there burned within him fierce, lion-like determination. He refused to give in to the weakness that afflicted him.

"I will walk," he told his mother and the elders of the region where he lived. "I will rise and walk."

Few believed it was possible. But Sundiata was determined.

"Go to the royal forges," he commanded a loyal servant. "And have the blacksmiths there make for me an iron rod."

The servant did as he was bid. And when he returned with the rod, a crowd gathered around Sundiata.

"Arise, young lion," his mother encouraged him. "Let the people know they have a new master."

On all fours, Sundiata crawled to the rod. Grasping the heavy iron instrument with both hands, he thrust one end into the ground and struggled to lift himself upright.

A terrible silence gripped all those present. Sweat ran down Sundiata's face. With one huge effort, he straightened himself and stood on his feet. The crowd gasped in amazement. So great had been the boy's strength that the rod of iron had bent in the middle.

After catching his breath, he threw away the rod and began to walk. As the crowd parted before Sundiata, the servant followed close behind him, crying:

Room, room, make room!
The lion has walked;
Hide, antelopes,
Get out of his way.

The lion had indeed walked. And he would continue to grow stronger. Sundiata became an expert horseman and hunter. He gathered an army around him and proved fearless in battle. Here was a leader, the people hoped, who could deliver the land from the tyranny of the hated Sossos. Sundiata prepared for that day.

Sundiata's army set out to meet the forces of Sumanguru, the usurper who had scorned the young boy years before. Sitting astride his warhorse, Sundiata raised his hand and spoke to his troops. "I salute you all, sons of Mali," he declared. "As long as I breathe, our people will never again be in slavery—rather death than slavery. We will be free because our ancestors were free. I will avenge the indignity that we have suffered."

With that, Sundiata lowered his hand. At the head of his army, he thundered off across the grassland to confront the Sossos.

This two-foot-high terra-cotta statue of a West African horseman dates from about the time of Sundiata. The mounted warriors of Mali were the most feared in the region.

Mali Takes Over the Gold Trade

It was in the year 1235 that Sundiata led his army against the Sossos. When the two sides clashed, the Sossos were crushed and their king fled in humiliating defeat. Sundiata, the Hungering Lion, was not finished. His appetite whetted, he went on to conquer the rest of the Sossos, making the Mali horsemen the most powerful figures in the western Sudan. He also converted to the Muslim religion, thus gaining favor with the Muslim merchant class.

Mali warriors now extended their control to the goldfields that had once made Ghana so wealthy. Sundiata quickly set about restoring the profitable trans-Saharan trade in gold.

The heads of the warrior federation who followed him continued to extend the range of their raids and their taxation of the trade routes. Eventually they controlled a huge area that was three times the size of

Ghana. These rulers took the title of *mansa,* which means "emperor" or "highest lord."

Mansa Musa Makes the Hajj

The most renowned of Mali's emperors ruled in the fourteenth century. He was the great Mansa Musa (MAHN-sah moo-SAH). He was named for a famous figure in the Qur'an and the Jewish and Christian Bibles. *Musa* is the Mande language word for "Moses," who led his oppressed people out of Egypt. Mansa Musa came to the throne of Mali in 1307 and ruled for the next quarter century. Previous emperors had tripled Mali's trade and expanded its territory. During the reign of Mansa Musa, Mali's fame spread throughout the Muslim world and into Christian Europe.

Mansa Musa was a Muslim, and he did much to promote Islam. One of the duties of a practicing Muslim is the *hajj,* a pilgrimage to Islam's holy city of Mecca in Arabia. In 1324, Mansa Musa led a caravan on his own hajj.

Atop his richly bedecked Arabian steed, the emperor was a striking figure. He wore a turban of many lengths of cotton wound around his head, and his robes of embroidered silk billowed gracefully in the desert winds. The royal horse was adorned in colorful padded cloths, carrying a saddle of the finest red Moroccan leather. Next to the emperor rode the royal bodyguard, their lances glinting in the sun. And beside them came the standard bearers, men who would carry the banners of Mali all the way to the holy city of Islam.

Traveling with Mansa Musa was a vast entourage of troops, slaves, family members, friends, teachers, and doctors—according to some reports, as many as 60,000 people in all. Mecca was thousands of miles from Mali, and the trip would take months to complete. To make sure the emperor had enough money for this long journey, his caravan also included 80 to 100 camel-loads of gold dust, each load weighing about 300 pounds.

With a shout, the caravan started forward across the sands of the Sahara. Searingly hot during the day and bitterly cold at night, the Sahara was a daunting obstacle. Journeying from one oasis to the next, the royal caravan pressed eastward toward Egypt, where, along the Arabian shore of the Red Sea, it turned south to Mecca.

At the outset of his pilgrimage to Mecca, Mansa Musa would have crossed the Sahara in a caravan much like the one shown in this painting.

The holy city of Mecca must have made a powerful impression on the emperor of Mali. But Mansa Musa's impression on the places he visited was surely just as great. The amazing wealth of his entourage so dazzled the local people that their descendants would talk about it a hundred years later.

No place felt the effect of the imperial presence more than Cairo, a major stopping point on the way to and from Mecca. As the emperor approached the Egyptian capital, an Arab guide informed him that he, the great Mansa Musa, would be expected to stop and pay his respects to the sultan, the ruler of Egypt.

Mansa Musa asserted that he was traveling for the hajj, and not for any other reason. Besides, as the ruler of an empire almost as large as Europe, he had no interest in going out of his way for a king whom he regarded as his equal.

The guide warned him, however, that to refuse a visit might be taken as an insult to an important Muslim brother. So Mansa Musa agreed to visit the sultan. The guide went on to inform the emperor that it was customary for all visitors to kneel

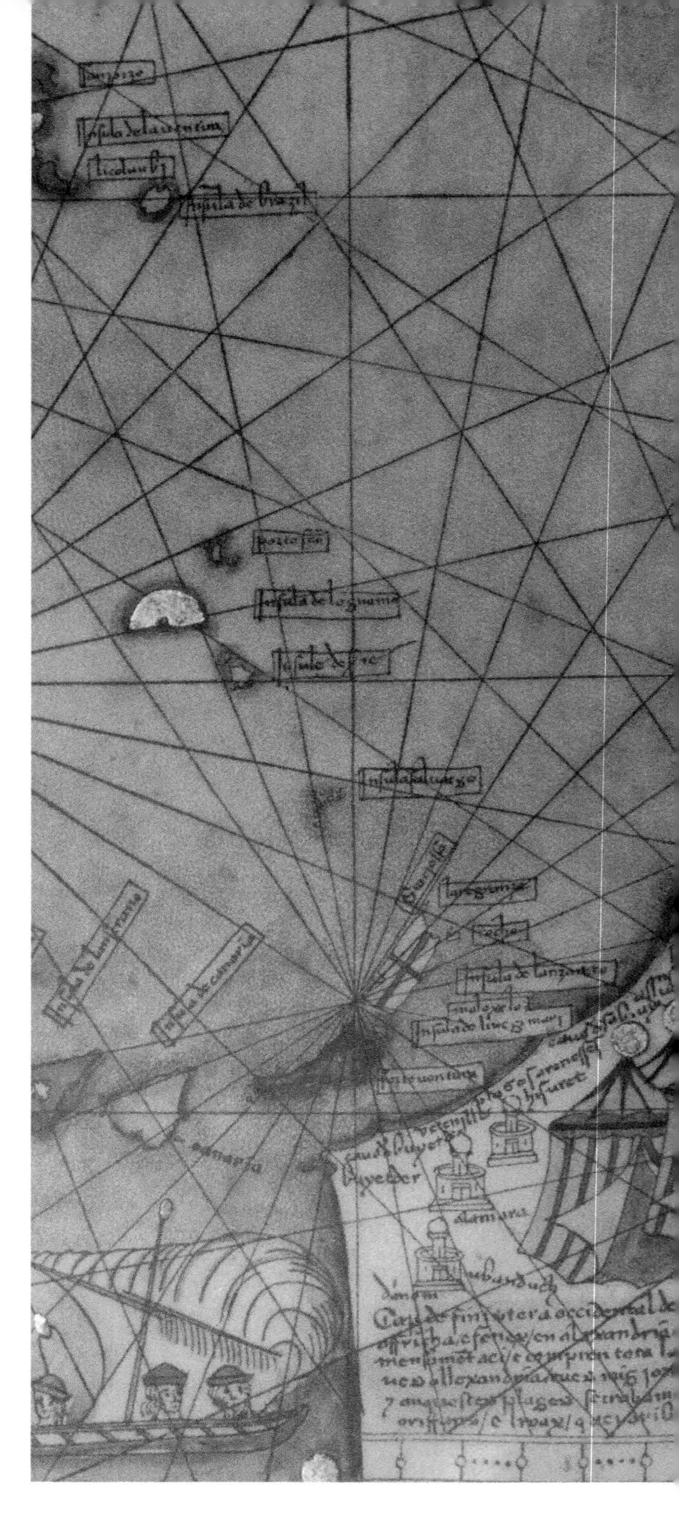

Ibn Battuta, World Traveler

One of our best sources of information about fourteenth-century Africa is the intrepid explorer, Ibn Battuta (IB-uhn bat-TOO-tah). Born in North Africa in 1304, Ibn Battuta made his own hajj to Mecca in 1326, two years after Mansa Musa. Thus began nearly three decades of travel through Arabia, Africa, Persia, India, Asia Minor, China, and Europe. Covering more than 75,000 miles, Ibn Battuta rode dromedary camels, Russian dog sleds, and Chinese junks. Once he stopped to pray in a mosque made entirely of salt blocks and roofed with camel hide. He was delighted when he sailed down the Niger and saw a hippopotamus, which he called a "water horse." He dictated a long account of his journeys and adventures. This account was later published as a book, which in English is called *The Travels of Ibn Battuta*.

About 50 years after Mansa Musa's hajj, this African map was made in Europe, where the emperor's fame had spread. It shows a seated Mansa Musa offering gold to an approaching Saharan trader.

before the sultan and kiss the ground. At the royal palace, Mansa Musa indeed knelt before the sultan and kissed the ground—but it is said that as he did so, all the while he was thinking, "I am prostrating myself before God, not this sultan—before the God who created me and brought me into this world."

The sultan responded generously to Mansa Musa's act of diplomacy. He reached out his hands to the royal visitor and beckoned him to sit beside him, a gesture that showed the two monarchs were equal.

The sultan showed much generosity to his visitor, entertaining him with feasts and dances, and housing his entourage in a fine palace. He stocked Mansa Musa's caravan with provisions for the journey to Mecca, and set up feeding stations for the camels along the route.

But all of this paled compared to the generosity of Mansa Musa. On his return from Mecca, he stopped again in Cairo. There he gave large gifts of gold to every official he met, great and small. The result was that the emperor, still far from home, found that he had run out of money and had to borrow from the city's merchants.

By freely giving out gold in Cairo, Mansa Musa put so much of the precious metal into circulation that he almost ruined the city's gold market. At a single stroke, gold was no longer as rare a commodity as it had been, and its price plummeted. Twelve years later, the market had not fully recovered from Mansa Musa's visit.

The "Pearl of Africa": Timbuktu

After seeing Islam's holiest shrines, Mansa Musa returned to Mali with a renewed faith. He also brought back a new appreciation for the architectural styles of the Arab world, as well as a man who could reproduce such majesty in Mali. Musa had met the renowned architect Es-Saheli (es-sah-HEH-lee) in Mecca, and had persuaded him to return with the royal entourage to the western Sudan. There the two men planned great mosques, libraries, and other buildings—many of them in one of Mali's grandest cities, the famed Timbuktu.

Clinging to the edge of the Sahara, just north of the great bend of the Niger River, Timbuktu was revered as the "Pearl of Africa." It attracted visitors and students from distant parts of the Muslim world and from the entire western Sudan.

Timbuktu rises from the surrounding desert in this seventeenth-century engraving. The city was a bustling center of trade and Islamic scholarship.

It had humble beginnings, as a seasonal tent settlement where nomads of the desert and people of the river met to trade. It grew to become a bustling center of commerce and Islamic learning, a place where the gold-for-salt trade flourished along with the sale of beautiful and costly manuscripts.

Here Mansa Musa set Es-Saheli to work. Drawing on his experience and skill, the architect built a mosque known as the Great Mosque for the emperor, as well as a royal palace. Es-Saheli introduced flat-topped roofs on houses and combined traditional sun-dried mud bricks with timber beams in a way that allowed construction of multistory buildings.

Timbuktu became the glory of Mali. A new university and still more beautiful mosques were built. The city blossomed as a center of trade and culture. By 1450 it was home to 100,000 people. Some 25,000 of them were scholars who had studied in Mecca or Egypt.

Mali After Mansa Musa

Mali thrived under Mansa Musa, but after his death, the empire did not fare well. Musa's successors faced competition from merchants of the eastern Niger River valley. In parts of the empire, people once controlled by the Mali warriors began to rebel. Invaders managed to attack Timbuktu.

By 1500, the Mali federation had greatly shrunk, and it lost its hold on the trans-Saharan trade. Mande-speaking people of the upper valley of the Niger continued to prosper as merchants. But the empire once known for the strength of Sundiata and the splendor of Mansa Musa had disappeared.

Left: This copy of the Qur'an, the holy book of Islam, was completed in Timbuktu in the 1500s.

Below: Built of sun-baked mud, Es-Saheli's Great Mosque still stands in Timbuktu. The poles sticking out from the walls are an important part of the building's scaffolding.

Charlemagne united a large empire during the early Middle Ages. In this sixteenth-century painting, he leads the Franks in battle against Muslims in Spain.

Europe's Early Middle Ages

Since we studied the fall of Rome, we've been looking east. We've explored Byzantium, watched the rise of a new Islamic Empire, and visited African kingdoms to the south. Now let's go back to the time of the fall of Rome, but this time focus our sights on Western Europe.

In A.D. 476, the last Roman emperor, young Romulus Augustulus, was forced from the throne. But this was the end of a long decline. For centuries, land-hungry tribes had been pressing on the Roman Empire's borders and weakened its outposts. Roman law and administration, which had brought order to a far-reaching empire, weakened under wave after wave of attacks. When the invading tribes sacked Rome and sent the child emperor into exile, the final link with the old order snapped.

The old systems of law began to disappear. So did the merchants who once crowded the trade routes from northern Britain to the Mediterranean. Much of what Rome had built—paved roads, aqueducts, and reservoirs—began to crumble. Western Europe became a dangerous place.

In later years, people called the period from the fall of Rome to the 900s the Dark Ages. Now we know there were many bright stars in that troubled time, but a very troubled time it was.

A reminder of dangerous times, this warrior's helmet dates to seventh-century England.

The Barbarian Tribes

The Romans, you may recall, had a name for the nomadic tribes that overran the Western Empire. They called them "barbarians."

The Romans got that word from the Greeks. To the ear of the ancient

Barbarian Invasions

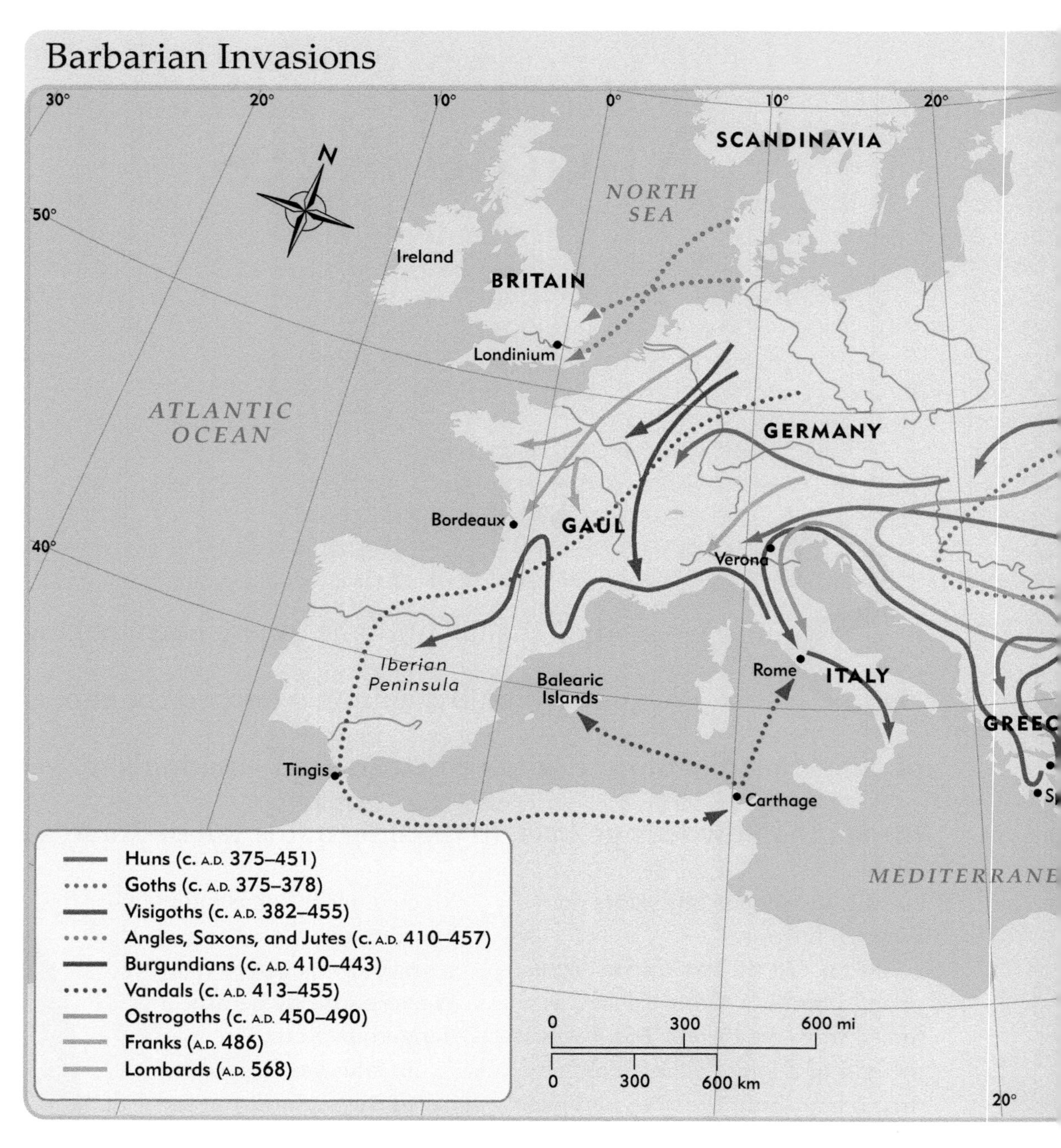

Greeks, people who did not speak their language sounded as if they were saying "ba-ba-ba." So the Greeks dubbed everyone who couldn't speak Greek "barbarians." The Romans saw themselves as heirs of Greek culture—indeed, some Romans, because of their achievements in law and empire-building, thought themselves even more civilized than the Greeks. The Romans adopted the term "barbarian" and applied it to the non-Latin speaking peoples on the fringes of their empire.

Who were these barbarians? From the east and north came fierce Germanic tribes known as Goths. Centuries before, these people had pushed into mainland Europe from Scandinavia, which is the region of northern Europe today occupied by the countries of Denmark, Sweden, and Norway. They came south in search of warmer climates. By A.D. 500,

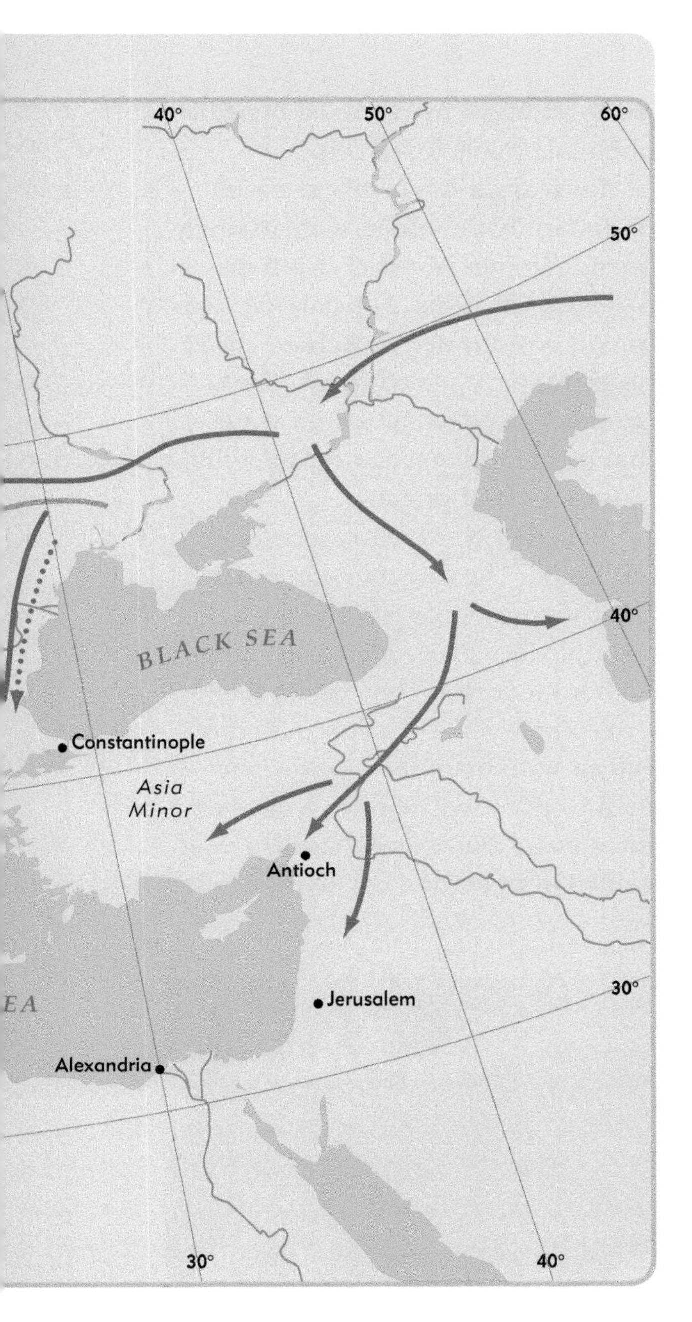

driving great herds of cattle before them, the Ostrogoths pressed south into Italy. A related tribe, the Visigoths, sacked Rome, and then headed west into Spain.

Another Germanic tribe, the Franks, invaded Gaul. They eventually gave their name to the country we now call France. Tribes known as the Angles, Saxons, and Jutes sailed from Northern Europe to the former Roman colony of Britain. There they stared in awe at the still-impressive remains of Roman buildings, and concluded that those structures must be the "cunning work of giants," as one medieval poem put it. These tribes arrived as invaders but put down roots as settlers. The land of the Angles became "Angle-land," or as it is known today, "England."

This iron axe is about 1,500 years old. It belonged to one of the Anglo-Saxon invaders of England.

- On the map to the left, locate the lands of the Ostrogoths, Visigoths, Franks, Angles, Saxons, and Jutes.

Other tribes, such as the Lombards, Burgundians, and Vandals, stormed out of their Germanic homelands to occupy former Roman lands. Each of these tribes had its own customs, its own rulers, and its own traditions. Some of them, like the Visigoths, admired Roman civilization and the Roman people. But all of them prized territory more than tradition, and that divided them against each other. Western Europe became a fractured land of warring chieftains, small kingdoms, and marauding tribes.

Germanic Tribes

Germany is a modern-day nation, but "Germanic" people existed long before the nation was born. *Germani* is the Latin name that Romans gave to warlike tribes on the Roman Empire's northern frontiers—tribes such as the Franks, Lombards, Angles, and Jutes. The vast region of northern and central Europe they inhabited was known as *Germania*. Much of that region is now part of modern Germany.

A Matter of Faith

With the fall of Rome, strong, central government seemed to vanish from Western Europe. But one great institution of the late Roman Empire remained strong and visible—the Christian Church.

The Germanic tribes that overran the old Roman Empire regarded Christian churches as good places to plunder. Still, Christianity did not disappear. It remained strong mainly because of the work of monks.

Monks were men who separated themselves from society to lead holy lives. Some banded together in small communities to live on the outskirts of cities, at first mainly in the eastern part of the Roman Empire. They lived in places called monasteries. The father of monastic communities in the West was a man named Benedict of Nursia (NOUR-see-uh).

Born around A.D. 480 to a well-to-do family in Nursia, a small town outside Rome, Benedict as a boy was a devout Christian. His parents sent him to be educated in Rome. There he grew so disgusted at his fellow students' drunken and wild ways that he literally headed for the hills to lead a life of prayer.

Benedict was twenty when he left Rome. The earnest young man came across a group of monks living a simple life. These men lived quietly without luxuries. They based their lives on prayer and work. Benedict stayed with them for a while, and then went to live alone in a cave for three years. He prayed, studied, and gained a reputation for holiness.

This sixteenth-century painting shows Benedict of Nursia, the father of early European monasticism. He prays with the monks who joined him at his first monastery, in the small Italian town of Monte Cassino.

It wasn't long before Benedict decided to form a new monastic community. *Ora et labora* (OR-ah et lah-BOR-ah)—Latin for "prayer and work"—were the principles that would guide it.

In the little town of Monte Cassino (MAWN-tay kah-SEE-noh) to the south of Rome, Benedict founded a monastery with 12 monks and himself as the abbot, that is, the leader of the monastery. Young men came to him for instruction. He wrote a book about monasticism (muh-NAS-tuh-sih-zuhm)—the monks' way of life, dedicated to prayer and work. This book, known as the *Rule of Saint Benedict*, described a daily schedule of prayer services, called offices. The brothers—as the monks called each other—were to pray together seven times a day. The *Rule* also required monks to perform manual labor, such as gardening or tending sheep.

The *Rule of Saint Benedict* helped spread monasticism all over Europe. By A.D. 600, Benedictine monasteries were springing up in more and more remote places, even in faraway Ireland. They were destined to make a big difference in the life of medieval Europe.

Monks undertook two tasks that had a lasting impact on European history. The first was spreading the Christian faith. Monks from Ireland, for example, sailed east to found monasteries in Scotland and England, and then fanned out across German territories, spreading the Christian faith to pagan tribes.

To help spread the Christian faith, the monks set up new monasteries. In these monasteries, the rigorous life of *ora et labora*—prayer and work—provided examples of serious Christian living. The monks also provided services for the people surrounding the monastery. Originally, *labora* meant agricultural labor, but in time it came to include many kinds of charitable work. Many monasteries kept a school. Monks treated the sick who came to their gates and gave food to those who needed it. The *Rule of Saint Benedict* emphasized hospitality to guests as an important monastic virtue. Armed bandits roamed highways, but monasteries offered meals and safe lodging to travelers. In this hostile time, monasteries became important sources of stability.

Soon towns grew up around monasteries. Have you heard of the city of Munich (myoo-nik), in Germany? The name Munich—or Munchen (MOUN-chuhn) in German—means "home of the monks."

These monastery ruins on England's Lindisfarne Island date from the late eleventh century. Irish missionaries first established a monastery on this site as early as the year 634.

As people came to them, the monks taught about Christianity. Little by little, the Germanic tribes converted to the Christian faith. At the same time that Islam was making converts in Arabia and North Africa, and advancing into southern Spain, Christianity was coming to dominate the European continent. By A.D. 800, there were Christian monasteries all over Europe, and the Goths and Franks were making crosses out of brass.

Preserving the Learning of Europe

Another important task of European monks was preserving the learning of Europe. With barbarian tribes raiding towns, destroying buildings, and terrorizing the countryside, people worried more about surviving than studying. Fewer and fewer people were able to read. All this turmoil threatened to extinguish the light of learning in most parts of Europe. But in their mountaintop refuges or cliffside hideaways, the monks kept learning alive.

Monasteries became *the* centers of learning in Western Europe for hundreds of years. The monastery at Monte Cassino, which Benedict himself founded, became home to a very important library. Whether in the hills of Italy or on the cliffs of Ireland, monks set out to collect and preserve every manuscript they could find.

Monks wanted to preserve scripture and prayer books, but they knew all knowledge was important. And they knew that to learn the Latin language correctly—the language of their scripture and their prayer books—they needed the best examples of Latin they could find. So they sought out classical works and sacred texts in Latin, and sometimes in Greek. Behind the stone walls of a monastery, skilled scribes worked in a writing room called a *scriptorium*. With quill and brush, they carefully wrote on parchment made from sheepskin. They copied texts about medicine, astronomy, and law, as well as religious works.

For the most important texts, copyists used gold and silver to decorate the pages with magnificent letters

Right: A monastic scribe is hard at work in a scriptorium, the monastery's writing room. Scribes copied not only the Gospels but also great works of the classical world.

In the early Middle Ages, Irish monasteries became important homes for missionaries and scholars. A missionary from Britain named Patrick had spread the Christian faith to Ireland in the 400s. As time passed, secluded Ireland became an important site of new monasteries.

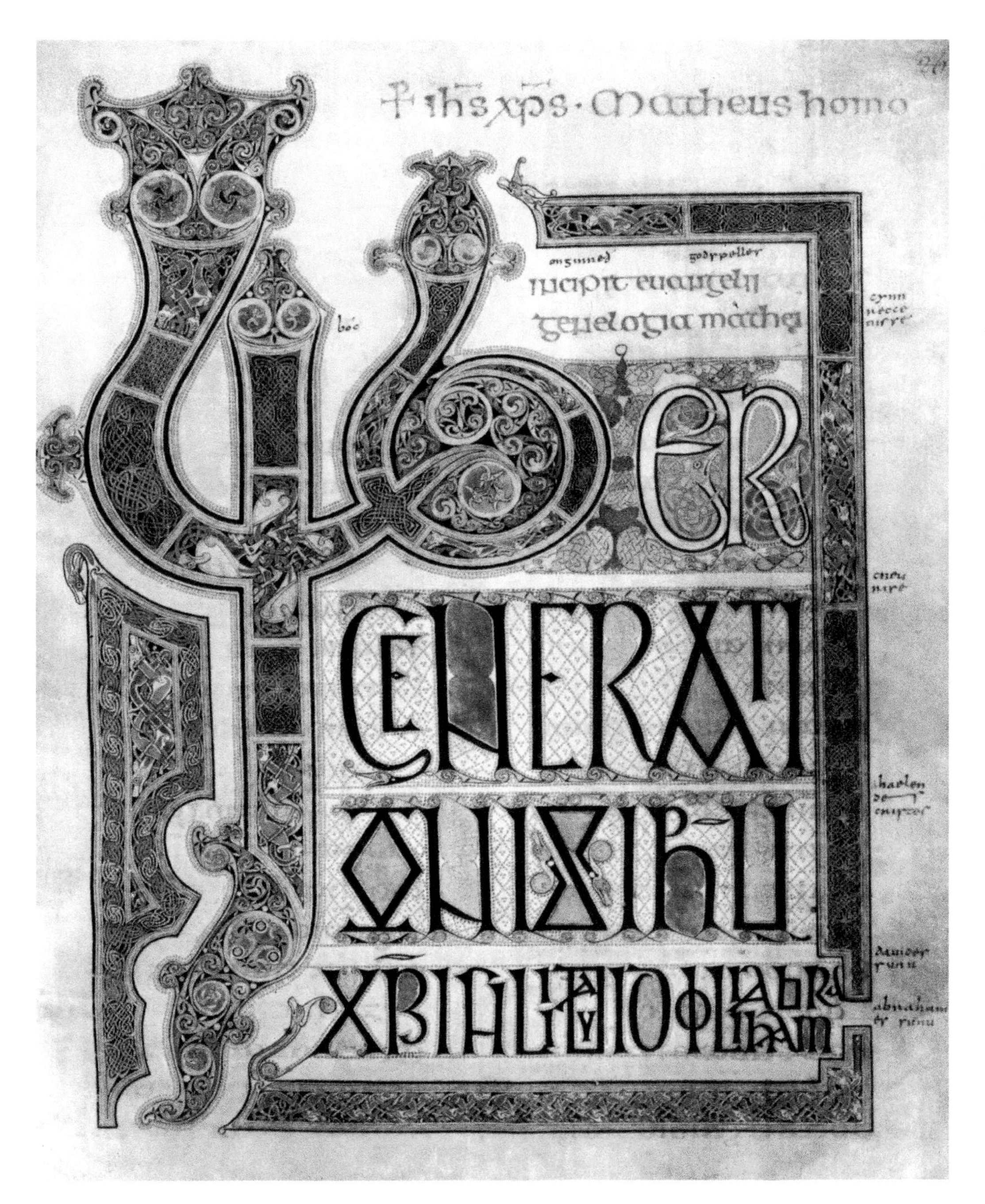

Left: The title page of the Book of Kells, *perhaps the most magnificent of the painted Gospel books of medieval Ireland.*

Below: An elaborately decorated capital B, just one of the many beautiful illuminations that adorn the Book of Kells.

and beautiful designs. These special books are called *illuminated manuscripts* because the brightly colored letters and designs light up the pages.

The illuminated manuscripts of Ireland are among the most spectacular. Monks in Ireland painstakingly wrote and preserved one of the world's most beautiful books—the famous *Book of Kells*. This illuminated manuscript contains a Latin text of the Gospels. It was produced sometime around the year 800, probably by several scribes over many years. For centuries it remained in a monastery at Kells, northwest of Dublin. Magnificent pictures, decorations, and lettering make the *Book of Kells* a masterpiece of medieval art. One thirteenth century scholar wrote, "You might believe it was the work of an angel rather than a human being."

How the Church Was Organized

By A.D. 800, Christianity had spread across much of Europe. The leader of the Christian Church was the pope, who was also the bishop of Rome. A bishop was the leader of Christians in a given region. Rome was considered the most important region because Rome had been the center of the Roman Empire, and because it was there that Peter, the first bishop of Rome, had been martyred.

The most important regions outside of Rome were led by archbishops. (*Arch* means "very important.") Each bishop or archbishop oversaw the work of many priests. Abbots oversaw the work of their monks. So priests and monks answered to their bishops and abbots. The bishops, archbishops, and abbots, in turn, answered to the pope. In that way, the pope was the leader of the whole Christian Church in Western Europe. And Christianity kept on growing.

Even though the Church was powerful, it could not provide law and order. The Christian Church had religious authority, but no armies or police. Sometimes that was a problem, such as when the pagan Lombards kept trying to attack Rome. Then the pope turned for protection to one Germanic tribe that had converted to Christianity.

Charlemagne and the Faithful Franks

Of all the tribes of Europe, one group in Gaul made a greater difference than all the others—the Franks. The Franks had ousted the Romans from central Europe, then conquered the Gauls and booted the Visigoths to Spain.

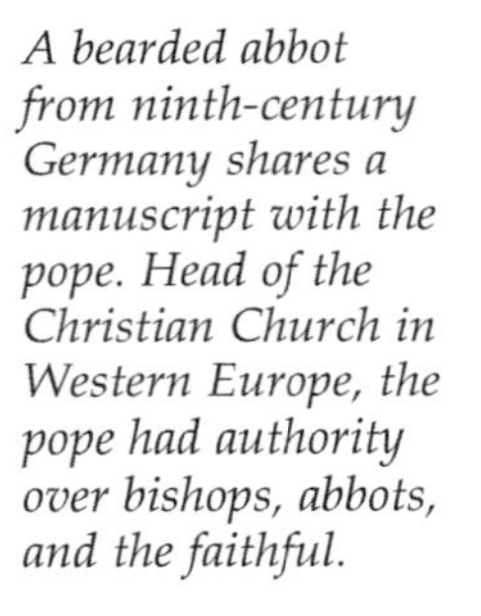

A bearded abbot from ninth-century Germany shares a manuscript with the pope. Head of the Christian Church in Western Europe, the pope had authority over bishops, abbots, and the faithful.

Pointing the way forward, the Christian king Charlemagne leads his Frankish warriors through a mountain pass. Charlemagne used his army to unite a vast territory under the Christian faith.

Their kingdom stretched from the Pyrenees Mountains in the west to the Rhine River in the east.

In about A.D. 500, under a chieftain named Clovis, the Franks embraced Christianity. Instead of destroying Christian churches, they began to worship in them. "Bow thy head, proud Frank," declared a bishop who lived among them. "Adore what thou hast burned. Burn what thou hast adored."

The Franks remained a powerful presence in Europe in the Middle Ages. They achieved the most under a Frankish king of the eighth century named Charles the Great, better known by his French name, Charlemagne (SHAHR-luh-mayn).

Charlemagne's father was known as Pépin the Short, and his mother as Big-foot Bertha. Their son, who grew to a height of six feet four inches, towered above most men of his day. He had a big bull neck, a handsome face, and a potbelly. Like his mother, he also had large feet. According to legend, our one-foot measure comes from the length of Charlemagne's feet.

Charlemagne was a skilled hunter, a lover of music and learning, a devout Christian, and a powerful

Charlemagne's Empire

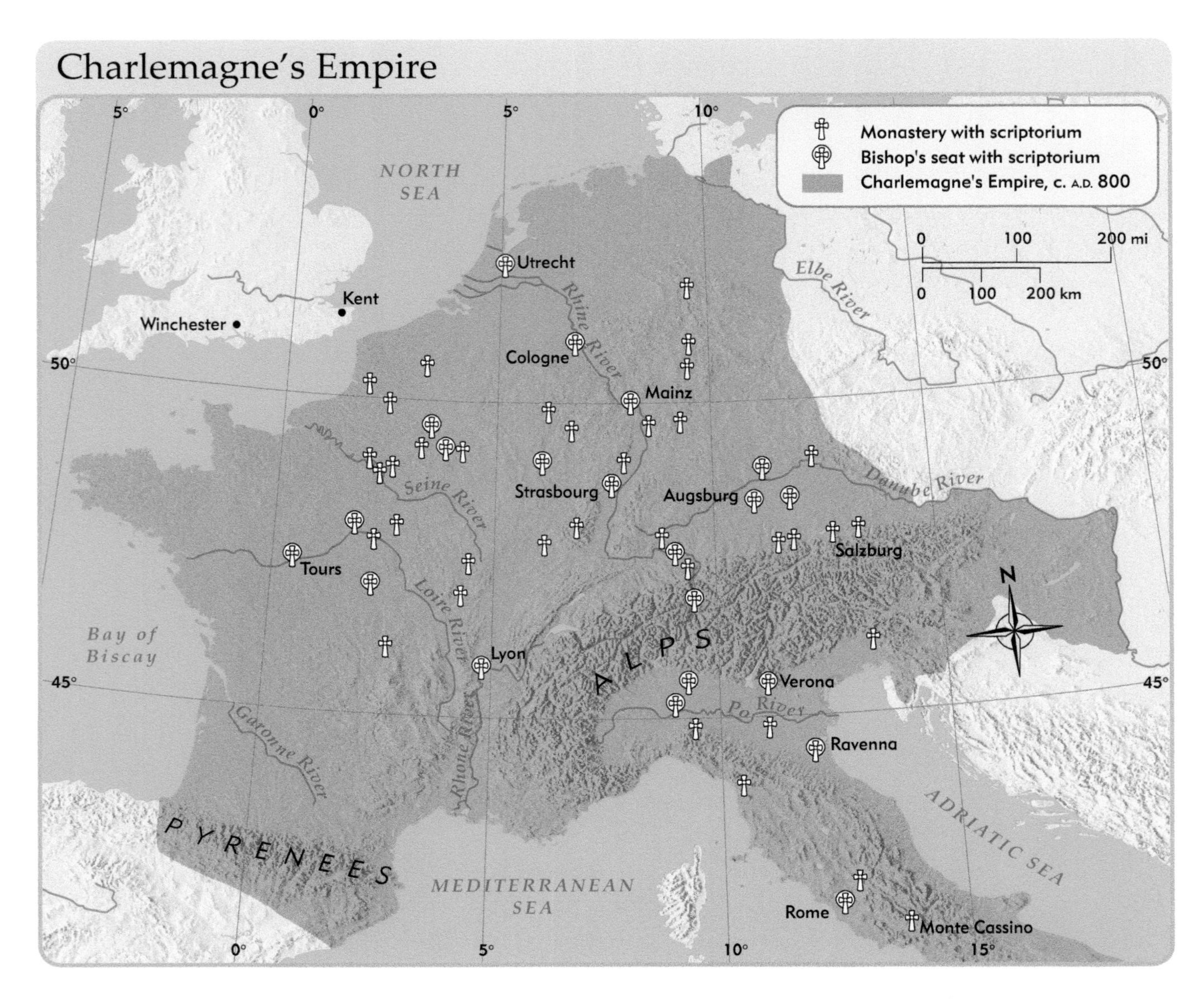

Reading the Small Print

Monks knew they had a friend in Charlemagne. One abbot told the king about a new idea to make writing easier. He said scribes were wasting a lot of time writing everything in capital letters, the way Romans used to. If scribes used a combination of large and small letters, the copying would go faster, it would be easier to read, and the words wouldn't take up as much space on parchment. Charlemagne agreed wholeheartedly, and a new kind of writing was born. It combined capital letters and small or "miniscule" letters. This new kind of writing was called Carolingian Miniscule—in Latin, the name Charles is *Carolus*. Carolingian Miniscule is the basis for the combination of large and small letters we use today.

athlete. As king of the Franks, he exuded energy in everything he did, and one thing he did was enlarge his kingdom. When this giant stretched his arms, he scattered Saxons to the northeast and Lombards to the southeast. For more than a quarter of a century, he waged war against the Saxons. When the Saxons finally surrendered, Charlemagne insisted that the tribe accept the Church and be baptized as Christians. When the Lombards threatened the pope in Italy, Charlemagne defeated them. He waged war against the Muslims in Spain, known as "Moors."

Charlemagne also valued the blessings of peace. He expanded education and learning. Though Charlemagne himself could not write, he wanted schools across his realm. He set up a palace school and brought the finest teachers to his court. There they taught students who would one day become important government officials.

Throughout his life, Charlemagne supported monasteries in their important efforts to preserve learning. He gave them funds and instructed them to care for the great classical works that they held in their libraries. With renewed vigor, monks set about their task, painstakingly copying old manuscripts and preserving them for the ages. Much of the classical literature we have today comes to us from copies of books made in Charlemagne's time.

A Crowning Glory

From Rome, Pope Leo III watched with satisfaction as Charlemagne performed his great works. He saw a Frankish king who had forged a vast empire and saved Rome from the Lombards. He saw a man of amazing energy, a Christian king devoted to the work of the Church. Was this a ruler on whom the Church could pin its hopes? Was this a leader who could restore unity and order to Europe? Yes, thought Leo—Charlemagne is just such a king.

On Christmas Day in the year 800, Leo presided over a mass in Rome. His invited guest for the occasion was Charlemagne himself. At the pope's request, the king did not wear his usual Frankish garb. For this occasion, Charlemagne donned a long Roman tunic. Around his waist he tied a golden belt, and on his feet were a pair of jeweled sandals. Charlemagne detested pomp and ceremony. But he was a Christian, and it was Christmas Day, and he was willing to humor the pope.

The church was crowded that day. Romans, Franks, Lombards, Goths, Anglo-Saxons, and even some Greeks filled the building. As the service came to an end, Charlemagne knelt in prayer. All other eyes were on Pope Leo, who approached the kneeling king. He stopped beside the altar, upon which sat a dazzling crown of gold studded with precious jewels. Suddenly, the pope picked up the crown and placed it on Charlemagne's head.

Pope Leo III crowns Charlemagne in Rome on Christmas Day in 800. The crown above is another that the king had acquired after his defeat of the Lombards.

Dating from the mid-1300s, this bust of Charlemagne is made of gold inlaid with gems. By this time, the "Emperor of the Romans" was regarded by some as first emperor of the Holy Roman Empire.

What Was the Holy Roman Empire?

In A.D. 800, Charlemagne ruled a vast realm and was crowned "Emperor of the Romans" by the pope. Charlemagne's empire broke apart after his death. About 150 years later, another pope crowned the leader of Germany, Otto I, and declared him emperor of a large area that became known as "the Holy Roman Empire."

It has been said that the Holy Roman Empire was neither very Roman nor very holy. It included most of modern Germany, Austria, and northern Italy. In these regions, ambitious nobles plotted, argued, and jealously guarded their own power. Meanwhile, the pope also wanted a say in running the empire. Despite all the disagreements, for more than eight centuries the Holy Roman Empire sprawled across a large part of Europe.

At this, the members of the congregation shouted three times. "Long life and victory to Charlemagne!" they cried. "Crowned by God as the great emperor of the Romans!" Then the pope knelt at Charlemagne's feet, kissing the hem of his Roman tunic. The king of the Franks was hailed as a new Constantine, a new Justinian. Europe, it seemed, had an emperor again.

Charlemagne claimed to be surprised and embarrassed. He insisted that he was simply king of the Franks, not any kind of emperor. But he and the pope had been talking about trying to revive the glory of the old Roman Empire. And Charlemagne had taken great strides toward that goal. He had united a vast realm under the Christian faith—indeed, people began to refer to that realm as "Christendom" (KRIH-suhn-duhm). He brought order to the empire, and made great advancements in learning. In later years, Charlemagne would come to be known as the first emperor of "the Holy Roman Empire."

Charlemagne's great empire did not last much beyond his death. His sons did not prove equal to their father. They divided his realm, fought threats from within, and faced fierce new invaders from the north.

At about the time of Charlemagne's death, the Vikings began raiding the coasts of Ireland, England, and northern France. In the next chapter, we'll learn more about the Vikings—their northern homeland, their seafaring ways, their warrior culture. For now, let's conclude this chapter by imagining what life was like around A.D. 800 when Irish monks began to encounter the Viking threat.

The Work of Angels

Imagining the Past

The wind off the sea was blowing wildly when Brother Brendan found a scholar sleeping near the mouth of a rocky cave. Brother Brendan knew the man was a scholar because of the books that spilled from the satchel by his feet.

A large rock shielded the scholar from the wind, but still he shivered, even in his sleep.

Brother Brendan shook the man gently. "Sir," he said, "are you all right?"

The scholar awoke with a start.

"Do not be afraid," Brother Brendan said. "I am a monk."

"A monk!" the scholar gasped. "Then I am near a monastery?"

Brother Brendan nodded. "You are safe, and so are the books you carry."

"Thanks be to God!"

"Amen," Brother Brendan said as he reached into his robe and pulled out a crusty piece of bread. "You look hungry. You should eat this."

The scholar took the bread in his shaking hands. "My name is Timothy," he said between bites of bread. "I have traveled such a long way—over land and sea. When I came to this place, I thought I had reached the end of the earth."

"Almost, but not quite," Brother Brendan said. "Come, I will show you the way."

He helped Timothy to his feet, picked up the satchel of books, and led him toward a wooded area.

Brother Brendan had been finding lost scholars for years. They came from all over Europe. They told stories of barbarians setting fire to great libraries. They described how they had rescued books and hidden them in their clothes on the long journey to Ireland.

They came to Ireland because they had heard about the monks who welcomed scholars and their books. But even in Ireland, monks and scholars had to hide from Vikings and other warriors looking for plunder. Monks built their monasteries—which often consisted of little more than a collection of small huts—deep in the woods, where Vikings could not see them from their ships. The monasteries were so well hidden that even some scholars had trouble finding them.

Brother Brendan led Timothy away from the rocks and into the woods. The scholar was so weak from his journey that they had to stop several times to rest.

"This monastery is a good distance," Timothy said. "What were you doing so far away?"

"I have been searching for a ewe who has gone off to lamb," said Brother Brendan.

"So you tend sheep," Timothy said. "I thought all monks were scribes."

Most scholars thought this. They all knew about the monks who carefully copied books, letter by letter and word by word, with quill pens dipped in ink. Some also knew about the monks who illustrated the text with detailed drawings and intricate scrollwork. But no one seemed to have heard of the monks who tended cattle and sheep.

"Where do you think the pages for manuscripts come from?" Brother Brendan asked. "Vellum is made from the skin of cattle, and parchment is made from the skin of sheep. There would be no pages in a manuscript if someone did not tend the animals."

Brother Brendan knew it was a sin to boast, but he considered it his duty to educate scholars.

"I did not mean that yours is not worthy work," Timothy said. "I know of no more important work than caring for God's creatures."

Brother Brendan smiled. Timothy was smarter than most scholars.

If the truth be told, Brother Brendan himself had not always understood the importance of tending animals. When he first came to the monastery as a lad, he had wanted to be a scribe. He learned to read well enough, but the quill pen seemed to jump in his hand. He tried to practice writing on the dirt floor of his hut, hoping that his hand would grow steady. But the abbot decided that he should tend animals, and Brother Brendan knew he must obey. He told himself to forget about being a scribe.

Timothy interrupted his thoughts. "I wonder whether your abbot will be pleased with the books I have brought," he said.

"Oh, he will be pleased," Brother Brendan said. "He always is."

"But I must confess," Timothy said, "the books I have brought are not religious."

"'Tis no matter," Brother Brendan said. "Our scribes copy everything.

The best scribes and illustrators work on books containing the Gospels and other sacred writings. Their work must be perfect, fit for the eyes of God. Other monks, those with less steady hands, copy less holy work."

"What have they copied with these less steady hands?" Timothy asked.

"The scribes do not talk much about their work in my presence, but sometimes I hear them speak of Plato or Cicero or Homer. And sometimes they tell stories." Brother Brendan's favorite was the story of two babes named Romulus and Remus. They were raised by a she-wolf, and they grew up to build the city of Rome.

"These scribes with less steady hands are doing the work of angels," Timothy said. "If they did not copy these books, they would be lost to the barbarians' fires."

Brother Brendan thought how nice it would be to do the work of angels. It would be especially nice on cold days when a ewe was missing and the icy wind blew off the sea.

"Sometimes," he confessed, "I wish I could be a scribe."

"Oh, I imagine it gets a little boring, staying inside all day and copying one word after another," Timothy said. "At least you get to go outside with the animals. You raise food for the monastery, you provide skins for the manuscript pages, and you even rescue lost scholars. You do important work indeed!"

Important, yes, thought Brother Brendan—but not the work of the angels.

They finally reached a clearing with several huts and a thatch-roofed chapel. Brother Brendan took Timothy to the largest hut, which belonged to the abbot. Bowing before his superior, Brother Brendan said, "Father Abbot, I have found a new scholar."

The abbot eyed Timothy. "Have you come to share knowledge, or have you come to learn?"

Timothy bowed as he produced his satchel of books. "I hope I can do both, if it pleases God."

The abbot beamed. That was the best answer a scholar could give. Then the abbot turned to Brother Brendan.

"Thank you for finding a fine scholar," he said. He then dismissed Brother Brendan, who went back to looking for the ewe.

He spent most of the day searching until he finally found her, with a healthy lamb by her side, hidden among the rocks along the shore.

"Well, well," he told her, "you did very well by yourself." Ewes often required assistance in lambing, but not this one. She was strong, and she had known what to do.

Brother Brendan was returning the sheep to the flock when he spotted, off in the distance, a ship coming toward shore. He watched for a moment until he could see the telltale sail of a Viking ship. As the ship got closer, he heard men shouting.

Brother Brendan ran into the woods, with the lamb in his arms. The ewe, worried about her baby, ran alongside him. He hoped she could keep up with him, so soon after giving birth. And he hoped the Vikings had not seen him.

With his robes flapping and the ewe at his heels, Brother Brendan ran through the woods. When he reached the monastery, he saw everyone was in the chapel, chanting their prayers before eating the last meal of the day. He knew, though, that even prayers could be interrupted with such important news.

He ran into the chapel and cried, "Vikings! On the coast!"

The abbot rose. "Go, brothers!" he ordered. "Save the manuscripts!"

The monks poured out of the chapel and ran to their huts for the manuscripts they were still working on. Timothy and other visiting scholars brought finished manuscripts from the abbot's hut. Everyone took manuscripts to the abbot, who wrapped each manuscript in cloth and put it in a cart. Brother Brendan stood ready to push the cart away.

"What will you do with the manuscripts?" Timothy asked.

"I will bury them in the ground, and I will cover the fresh earth with leaves," Brother Brendan said. "Then I will pray that the Vikings do not find them."

Timothy nodded appreciatively. "You are saving the manuscripts—and the learning of Christendom. The angels will be with you," he said, "for you are doing their work."

Brother Brendan rushed off to his task.

All across Ireland, monks like Brother Brendan hid manuscripts from Vikings and other invaders. For hundreds of years afterward, Irish farmers and children dug up these old manuscripts that had been carefully copied, beautifully illustrated, and dutifully saved by the monks of Ireland.

A Viking longship shown in stained glass.

Thunder from the North: The Viking Age

"From the wrath of the Norsemen, O Lord, deliver us!" That cry echoed in churches throughout Europe from A.D. 800 to 1100. The "Norsemen" were the Vikings. For nearly 300 years, this seafaring people raided, and then colonized parts of mainland Europe. No wonder historians have dubbed this era "the Viking Age."

The Land They Called Home

The Vikings came from the north, which is why they were also known as Norsemen. They hailed from Scandinavia, the region of northern Europe made up of the modern-day countries of Denmark, Sweden, and Norway. The starkly majestic landscape of Scandinavia is mountainous and inhospitable, a place of dark forests, unmelting ice, and deep coastal inlets called fjords (fee-AWRDS).

- On the map on pages 522–23, locate the region known as Scandinavia.
- Find Scandinavia on a world map or globe. What are the names of the seas that surround it?

Viking society was made of nobles, freemen, and slaves. Chieftains led each community, but they did not decide everything. Nobles and freemen participated in a governing council known as the Thing, or Assembly. The Thing made laws regarding, for example, sheep stealing or blood feuds. It decided when to wage war and what to do with criminals. The Vikings were not people who would unquestioningly follow one powerful leader. They were scrappy and free-spirited. Their assemblies were places where free

This chapter explores the world of the Vikings, the fearsome seaborne raiders from Scandinavia.

members of the community made themselves heard.

Members of Viking society might participate in the Thing, and they might be answerable to a chieftain. But mostly they were accountable to no one but themselves. A warrior in one of their great stories spoke words that could be the Viking motto: "I believe in my own strength."

Most Vikings were farmers. The people farmed the soil and raised livestock. Their settlements hugged the rocky Scandinavian coastline. In this rugged land, the Vikings had a hard time growing enough barley, oats, or rye to support themselves.

As the population of Scandinavia increased, farmland became scarcer. The Vikings began to look out over the waters. Across the seas lay trade, wealth, adventure—all desired by the various peoples of Scandinavia. Why not take to the seas? These hardy free spirits of the north were about to venture to the distant corners of Europe.

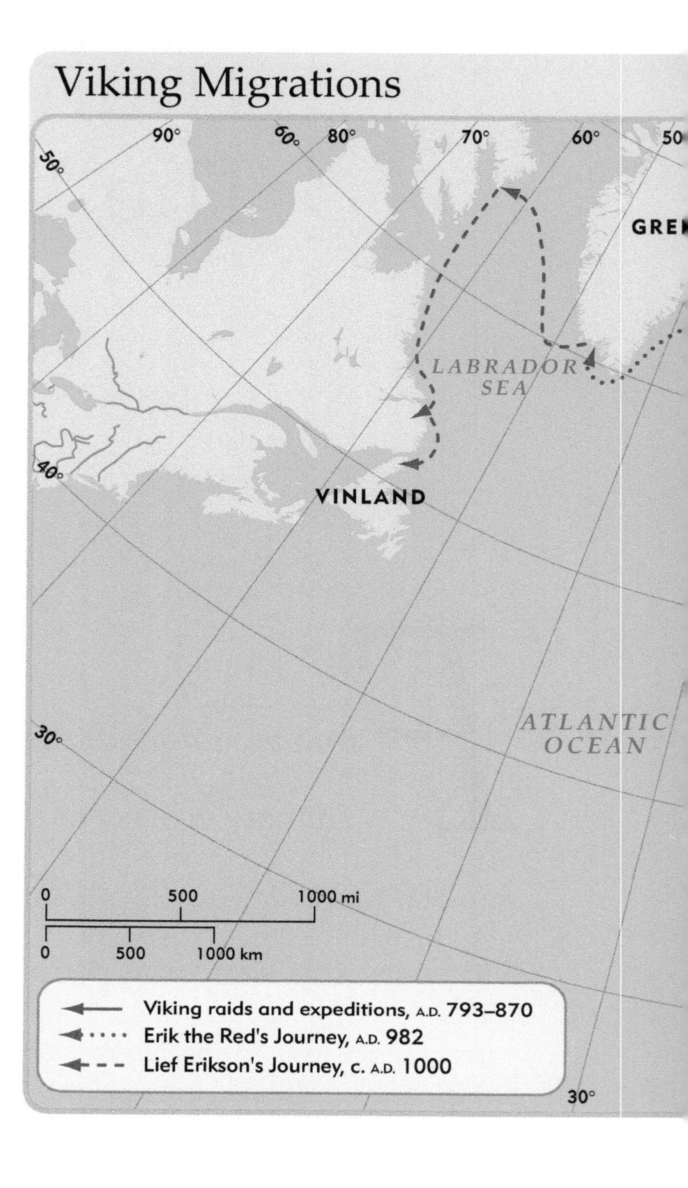

Master shipbuilders, the Vikings built strong and swift longships that skimmed the ocean waves.

The Ships They Built

To the Vikings, taking to the seas often seemed a better option than scratching out a living from the rocky land. The thick Scandinavian forests provided plenty of timber for shipbuilding—and what extraordinary ships they built!

The Viking longship was lighter, slimmer, and faster than other European vessels of the day. A typical longship measured about 70 feet long and 16 feet across at its widest point. It could carry nearly a hundred men and yet cruise the open sea with as few as 15 rowers, who sat on sea chests and pulled 18-foot oars. When

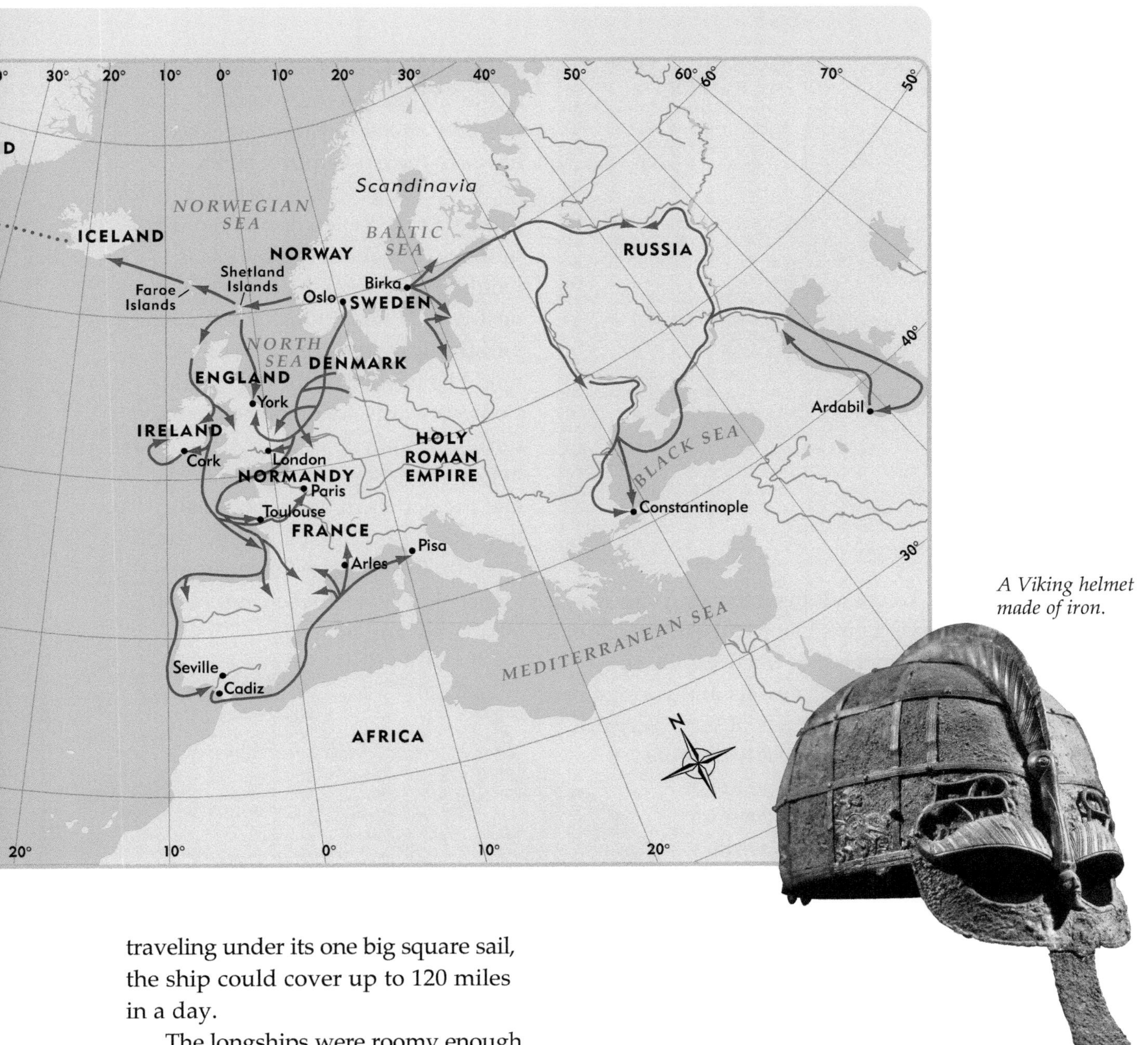

A Viking helmet made of iron.

traveling under its one big square sail, the ship could cover up to 120 miles in a day.

The longships were roomy enough to hold plunder taken in raids. They were strong enough to withstand Atlantic storms, thanks to overlapping curved planking that would "give" in a pounding sea. They were nimble enough to evade the defensive weapons of people onshore. They rode high in the water, which allowed them to sail up the rivers of Europe. They were light enough that Viking mariners could drag them overland past fortified bridges.

Take Those "Things" with You!

Vikings took their governing councils, or Things, with them to new lands they settled. When they came to Iceland in 930, they established a general assembly called the *Althing* (AHL-thing). Some form of this assembly has continued to this very day. While Viking Iceland was not a democracy, the *Althing* was perhaps the first national assembly, and has been called "the grandmother of parliaments."

Right: Built in the ninth century, this elegant vessel was excavated from a Viking burial site in Norway. The Norse believed their beloved longships would carry the dead to the afterworld.

Below: A carved dragon head that once adorned the prow of a Viking ship.

The longship opened the world to the Vikings. In these majestic vessels they sailed forth and wreaked havoc in the lands they visited.

The Vikings were so proud of their ships that they even buried nobility in them. They believed the ships would carry their occupants to the next world. The Vikings filled their burial ships with everything that might be needed in the afterworld—clothes, swords, food, kitchen tools, furniture. Sometimes they even killed horses, oxen, dogs, and servants and laid the bodies in the tomb. Then they covered the ships with mounds of earth. Buried ships have given archaeologists valuable clues about Viking life and beliefs.

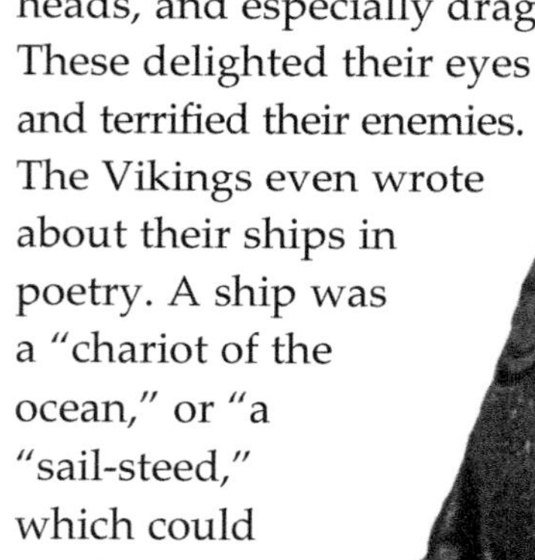

To the Vikings, the longship was a prized possession, a useful weapon, and a symbol of freedom. On the prows of their vessels, the Vikings carved figureheads of lions, serpent heads, and especially dragons. These delighted their eyes and terrified their enemies. The Vikings even wrote about their ships in poetry. A ship was a "chariot of the ocean," or "a "sail-steed," which could "gallop across the waves."

A longship noses its way along the French coast, its crew on the watch for raiding opportunities.

Raiders and Traders

The first major activity the Vikings undertook in their longships was trading. This was especially true of Viking peoples from the area that is now Sweden. Their shores faced east. Sailing across the Baltic Sea, they journeyed up the great rivers of central Europe and deep into Russia. In return for silver, glass, cloth, and weapons, the Vikings offered amber, furs, and slaves.

In time, however, the Vikings moved from trading to raiding, and then from raiding to conquest and settlement. By the ninth century, armadas of longships, with their dragonhead prows, regularly edged along the coast of Western Europe, their crews watchful for opportunities to "go a-viking"—in other words, to launch a raid.

Viking attacks were mostly hit-and-run. After beaching their ships, fearsome warriors jumped ashore,

To Go A-Viking

Known to Europeans of the time as "Norsemen," these Scandinavian tribes were later dubbed "Vikings." A *vik* was a special kind of pirate ship. When these seafaring people wanted to launch a raid, they said it was time to "go a-viking."

yelling wild battle cries and brandishing great battle-axes. Often they made straight for the local church or monastery. There they could always find booty to carry off—golden crucifixes, silver chalices, Gospels encrusted with gems. The raiders either killed the monks or carried them off as slaves. After setting fire to the buildings, the Vikings would rush back to their ships and escape before defenders arrived.

The monasteries of Ireland were a favorite target. But soon the Vikings were venturing into the Mediterranean, sacking towns from Cadiz (kuh-DIZ) in Spain to Constantinople, and menacing all points in between.

The Vikings were terrifyingly fierce in battle. Some were known as *berserkers* (bur-ZUR-kurs), from which we get our word *berserk*, which means "crazy." The berserkers wore bearshirts, shrieked blood-curdling screams, and charged into battle in a frenzy that made them blind to the dangers around them—and to their own wounds.

Eventually the Vikings began to spend the winter in the territories they raided. Rather than wasting valuable time sailing back to Scandinavia, they set up bases near their prime plundering grounds. From the rich river valleys of southern England and northern France, they could then set forth on their next missions. Following the rivers far inland, they attacked people who must have thought they lived safely beyond the reach of the raiders. Eventually some Vikings put down roots, setting up permanent colonies in the lands they had once raided.

In lands where the Vikings settled, the local rulers sometimes paid a tribute to pacify their new neighbors. Some even tried to hire Vikings to fight off other Vikings. One who did this successfully was a descendant of Charlemagne, a king with the less glorious name of Charles the Simple.

In the year 911, King Charles concluded that the Vikings were so firmly settled along the coast of northern France that there was no point in trying to drive them out.

Above: An elaborate bishop's staff of bronze and enamel, thought to have been looted from an Irish monastery in the eighth century.

Right: A modern painting depicts the Norse chieftain Rollo the Walker on the rugged coast of northern France. So many Norse settled in this area that it would later be named after them—Normandy.

So he decided to make a deal with their leader, Rollo the Walker—a man said to be so large that no horse could carry him. Charles made Rollo the duke of Normandy—the very name of the region, Normandy, came from the name of the conquering Norsemen. In return, Rollo swore allegiance to the crown. And true to his word, he helped the Franks fend off other Viking attackers.

Rollo also accepted Christianity and married a French woman. His men did the same. The Norsemen of France were gradually transforming themselves from Vikings into Normans. And the Normans would gradually transform Europe. A century later Normandy would be one of the most powerful states in Europe. And as we'll learn, a Norman duke named William the Conqueror would invade England and make it his own.

- On the map on pages 522–23, locate Normandy.

While Rollo and his followers became Christians, many Vikings held onto their beliefs in their Norse gods, who were as warlike as the Norsemen themselves. Viking mythology featured tales of courage, wit, and self-reliance, all qualities prized by the Norsemen. The Norse gods also had their share of greed, cruelty, and cunning.

Hammer raised, the thunder god Thor rides in his goat-drawn chariot.

The Vikings believed their gods lived above the earth in a land called Asgard (AS-gahrd). They feasted in great palaces thatched with silver. The three most important Norse gods were Odin (OH-dn), Thor, and Frey (fray).

Odin was the father of the gods, the spear-wielding god of battle worshiped by Viking warriors. He was the creator of the earth and the human race. Odin sat on his throne in Asgard, overlooking the world.

Thor, the god of thunder, rode the heavens in his goat-drawn chariot. The Vikings believed that Thor made it thunder when his chariot raced across the sky, and that he caused lightning when he threw his hammer. To the Vikings, Thor was a bringer of good luck. In the hope of improving their fortunes, many Vikings even carried small charms in the shape of a hammer.

A fourteenth-century Swedish copy of the Eddas, *the collection of stories that tells us much about Norse mythology and beliefs.*

The most mild-mannered of the three main deities was Frey. He was the god of fruitfulness and fertility. The people sacrificed to Thor in time of famine, to Odin in time of war, and to Frey when celebrating a wedding.

The Vikings believed that within the heavenly realm of Asgard lay Valhalla (val-HA-luh), the Hall of the Slain. This great palace was set aside for worthy humans who fought and died bravely in battle. In Valhalla they would drink mead and brawl happily among themselves forever. The hope of every Viking warrior was to spend eternity in Valhalla with Odin, Thor, and the other gods.

During the long, cold northern nights, Vikings would gather around fires and listen wide-eyed to tales about the gods of Asgard. Viking chiefs had their own poets, called *skalds*, who recited old stories of heroes slaying dragons, gods battling giants, and adventurers setting

sail for distant lands. The skalds told their stories from memory and passed them down from generation to generation. Eventually the stories were written down in two collections known as the *Eddas*. Much of what we know about Norse mythology and Viking beliefs comes from these two great medieval works.

The *Eddas* tell how Odin and his brothers made the world from a giant's body. They turned the giant's blood into the oceans, his ribs into mountains, his flesh into earth. Then they made the first man from an ash tree and the first woman from an alder. The *Eddas* also contain many short sayings to guide and warn Vikings. "A man should never move an inch from his weapons while in the fields, for he never knows when he will need his spear," says one. Another states, "A wolf that lies in its lair never gets meat, nor a sleeping man victory."

Viking Days

Tyr, the god of war.

Four of our weekdays take their names from old Norse gods. From Tyr, the god of war, we get Tyr's Day, that is, Tuesday. Odin's name was sometimes spelled Woden, and from that we get Wednesday. Thor's day is what we call Thursday. And Friday probably takes its name from Freya (FRAY-uh), the Norse goddess of love and beauty.

Erik the Red and Leif the Lucky

At a time when few European sailors ventured far from land, the Vikings made amazing journeys. Daring, determined, and hungry for land, they boldly sailed beyond their

Banished from his homeland, Erik the Red sails the treacherous waters of the North Atlantic. In the year 982 he landed in Greenland, where he set up a Viking colony.

favorite raiding spots in Ireland and northern Britain.

In the spring, when the days grew long and clear enough for sailing, these accomplished seamen set off in their longships. On the open sea, they navigated by the sun and stars. One voyage brought them to an uninhabited island in the north. Bigger than Ireland, this island of glaciers, volcanoes, and hot springs became home to the Vikings. They named it Iceland.

Iceland was the childhood home of Erik the Red. This intrepid Norseman was well named. He boasted a ruddy complexion, red hair, and a scorching-hot temper. Erik was forever exploding in murderous rages. By the time he was 35, he had been banished from Iceland three times.

The third and last time came in the year 982. He had been feuding with his neighbors, and the Thing ordered him to leave Iceland for three years. He decided to put the time to good use.

The Secret of the Runes

To write, Vikings used characters called runes, which they carved onto coins, jewelry, weapons, and other items. They also carved runes onto memorial stones, which they erected along roads and in other public places. These rune stones commemorated important events, praised chieftains, or recognized warriors killed in battle.

Archaeologists have found more than 4,000 runic writings, but they still puzzle over the meaning of many. Perhaps that's because the Vikings used the earliest runes as a secret code, to be understood by few. The word *rune*, in fact, comes from a Norse word meaning "secret."

Vikings sometimes scratched runes on the backs of their shields. They thought the runes had a magic power that would help deflect blows from even the sharpest swords. They believed that Odin discovered the meaning of the runes, and Viking priests used them in making charms and spells.

As this modern photo shows, the ice-bound coastline of Greenland must have posed a daunting challenge to Viking sailors and settlers.

Erik longed for a world of his own. He thought he knew where he could find one. Half a century earlier, a Viking sailing from Norway to Iceland had been caught in a gale that blew his vessel off course. The winds carried him several hundred miles beyond Iceland. There he claimed to have sighted a mysterious landmass in the distance. Erik set out to find that unknown land.

After several days at sea, Erik and his band of adventurers found it. Some 450 miles west of Iceland, they spotted a forbidding coastline. Huge sheets of ice seemed to cover the land. Erik sailed around the ice cliffs on the eastern coast until he saw better land in the southwest. There he selected a spot for settlement.

Winters in this new land were harsher than back in Iceland. But Erik was determined to make a success of it. He sailed back to Iceland and enlisted recruits for the colony. To make their destination sound more hospitable than it really was, he gave the landmass a flattering name. He called it "Greenland."

- On the map on pages 522–23, locate Iceland and Greenland.

Erik succeeded in building a settlement in Greenland. And because of that he is perhaps the second most famous Viking in history. But Erik had a son named Leif (leef). And for *his* achievements the son has become the best known Viking of them all.

About the year 1000, Leif Erikson sailed west from the Greenland settlement—and into the pages of history. Leif's voyage was also inspired by the report of a sailor who had lost his way in a storm. Some years earlier, an Icelandic mariner was on his way to Greenland when a northeasterly gale carried him far past his destination. He made his way back to Greenland, but not before he saw a forest-covered land far to the west. He reported his adventure to the Vikings of Greenland. Now Leif set out to retrace the man's route.

Some accounts report that Erik the Red wanted to make the journey with his son, Leif. But on the way to

the ship, he fell from his horse and injured himself. "I am not meant to discover more countries than this one we are now in," he told his son. "This is as far as we go together." So it was that, with a party of 35 men, Leif Erikson sailed from Greenland across the North Atlantic into the unknown.

They landed in a place that was pleasing to the Viking eye. It had plentiful timber. The rivers and lakes teemed with the biggest salmon the men had ever seen. The grass was green, and the winter milder than back home in Greenland. Because the land had vines bearing what Leif said were grapes, he named it Vinland, the land of grapes. Leif and his men spent the winter there before returning home.

Although their colony did not survive, the Vikings had reached North America nearly 500 years before Columbus. Leif probably came ashore in what is today Newfoundland, Canada. In fact, this area lacks the grapes he claimed to have seen, which grow only farther to the south. Leif might have seen other berries that can be used for winemaking, such as gooseberries or cranberries.

Or perhaps this was another case of "like father, like son." Leif may have been exaggerating the attractions of the new land by naming it Vinland—much as Erik the Red had stretched the truth when he gave the name Greenland to the icy land he had discovered.

In later years, other Viking explorers sailed to North America, but they did not settle there permanently. By around the year 1100, the Viking era was coming to an end. The terrifying attacks from the sea dropped off as the raiders found lands in northern Europe where they could build farms and settle permanently. Missionaries arrived, and gradually the Vikings gave up their Norse gods and accepted Christianity.

The deeds and misdeeds of the Norsemen slowly receded into people's memories. The dragon ships sailed no more, except in legends of the Vikings.

Leif Erikson stands on the shoreline of North America, which he reached about the year 1000. Though the Vikings' settlement was not permanent, their remarkable trans-Atlantic voyage is a testimony to the bravery and seamanship of this bold people.

A lord and lady lead a hunting party through the grounds of a French manor.

Of Land and Loyalty

By the tenth century, Charlemagne's empire was no more. The Vikings were raiding coastlines. Central government had broken down in what is now France, Germany, and Italy. Armed bands roamed the countryside.

Who or what could provide safety and order in this dangerous time?

Some kings still reigned in Europe in the early eleventh century, but they weren't all-powerful rulers, even in their own realms. Instead, individual noblemen grew stronger. All over Europe princes, barons, dukes, and counts ruled regions they had gained by combat or inheritance. These powerful landowners, called lords, often acted as if each ruled his own little kingdom. While a king ruled over a lord, a great lord might own more land than the king and command a larger army.

The lord of a region used his land to gain the loyalty of the people around him. He did that by granting tracts of land to lesser nobles or knights. A grant of land was called a fief (feef).

A noble or knight who received a fief became the lord's vassal (VA-suhl). As a vassal, he owed the lord certain obligations, including loyalty and the promise of military service. He swore to fight for the lord if needed. In return, he owned the fief and profited from farming the land.

This arrangement, in which a lord granted land and protection to a vassal in return for loyalty and military service, later became known as feudalism (FYOO-dl-ih-zuhm). The term comes from the French word *féodalité* (fay-oh-dah-lee-tay), which means "loyalty." Kings, nobles, and knights

A medieval knight promised to defend his lord, often in exchange for land.

throughout much of medieval Europe pledged their loyalty and recognized their duties to each other under the feudal system.

When a knight or noble swore loyalty to a lord and became his vassal, he took part in a ceremony known as homage (AH-mij). Let's drop by the great hall of a lord's house for a moment. A ceremony of homage is about to begin.

Today, if you "pay homage" to someone, it means you show great respect or high regard for that person.

Paying Homage

The knight has just arrived, looking pleased with himself, but also a little nervous. The lord's great hall is more crowded than he expected, for many members of the lord's household have gathered to witness the event. Three classes of medieval society are here, groups whose names rhyme nicely in Latin: the *oratore* (oh-rah-TOHR-ay), the *bellatore* (beh-lah-TOHR-ay), and the *laboratore* (lah-bohr-ah-TOHR-ay).

In a ceremony of homage, a knight pledges his allegiance to his new lord.

The oratore are those who pray—the clergy. We'll learn more about them in the next chapter. The bellatore are those who fight—the knights. The laboratore do some praying and fighting, too, but they're mostly known for something else—they're the ones who do the work, especially the work of providing food. Most people in the Middle Ages worked the land.

All eyes are now on the knight, who approaches the man who will be his lord. Silence falls as the knight bends to his knees. The lord gazes at him sternly.

"Do you wish, without reservation, to become my man?" the lord asks. "I wish it," the knight replies.

The lord encloses the new vassal's hands in his and seals the agreement with a ceremonial kiss. At this, a priest steps forward bearing a casket containing sacred relics of a saint, the bones or other remains of a holy person. Upon these holy objects the vassal swears his oath.

"I promise from this time forward to be faithful to my lord," he says. "And I will maintain toward him my homage."

The lord nods, and the homage ceremony comes to an end. The two men now share a bond. The lord has added one more to his army of knights. The vassal leaves satisfied as well. He's thinking of the fief he'll hold as long as he remains loyal to his lord—a broad tract of land alongside a stream. He's had his eye on it for quite some time, and now he is its lord.

The feudal system was like a chain of interlocking loyalties that held the top levels of medieval society together. Barons with much land granted fiefs to nobles, who in return pledged their loyalty and service. Those nobles, in turn, might divide their lands among lesser lords and knights, who became *their* vassals. And those lesser lords, if they had

A Little Latin

If you know a little Latin, then you can figure out the roles of each of the three classes of medieval society—the oratore, the bellatore, and the laboratore. The suffix *-tor* is added to a word to show "one who does." In Latin, *ora* is the verb for "pray, ask, beseech"; *bella* means "fight"; and, *labora* means "work" or "toil," from which, as you can see, we get our English word *labor*.

enough land, might have vassals of their own. By exchanging land, service, and protection, the nobility gained some security and order in uncertain times.

What about "those who worked," the peasants and landless laborers? They made up most of the population. They were part of a system that exchanged protection for labor. They offered their work—farming or smithing, for example—and sometimes even their freedom for permission to farm land on the lord's estate. The lord, in turn, offered the invaluable protection of his knights.

Those Who Fight: The Knights

Of the three social classes in medieval times, you have probably heard most about the bellatore—the knights. A lord often had his own army of knights on horseback, and these vassals defended the lord and his territory against raiders. Since ancient times, mounted soldiers had fought in battle. But before the Middle Ages, the soldier on horseback often wasn't an effective fighter. He lacked two very important inventions—stirrups and horseshoes.

Barbarians from central Asia, called the Huns, were the first to bring stirrups to Western Europe. Once a soldier had stirrups attached to his horse's saddle, his feet were held in place and he could sit firmly on the horse's back. This allowed him to charge against a strong line of foot soldiers, scattering them much as a bowling ball knocks down pins. Without stirrups, a soldier on horseback couldn't make this kind of charge. As soon as he bumped into

Medieval Justice

Under the feudal system, lords promised justice to their vassals. Quarrels between vassals were settled at the lord's court, where the lord himself presided. A vassal accused of wrongdoing often received judgment from his peers, that is, his social equals. The modern-day idea of a trial by a jury of one's peers came from this feudal custom.

Many medieval notions of justice wouldn't strike us as very just. Vassals sometimes settled disputes with trial by combat, even to the death. The belief was that "God defends the just man." Another way to determine guilt was trial by ordeal—for example, by making the accused person walk over hot coals. If the person's injuries healed within three days, it was taken as a sign of innocence.

Punishments in the Middle Ages could be harsh. A guilty person might be dragged behind a horse and beaten with rods. Often, however, punishment involved paying a fine to a lord or king.

the line and made contact with the foot soldiers, the horseman often ended up on the ground. It was then short work for the foot soldiers to finish him off.

After the stirrup came the horseshoe—iron shoes nailed to a horse's hooves. They helped the horse keep its footing in soft, wet ground, and gallop over hard, dry terrain. A shoed horse could carry a heavy load without damaging its hooves. And few loads were heavier than a medieval knight.

Right: A knight's weaponry included his helmet and sword.

Below: A sculpted medieval knight stands ready to do battle.

Each knight-in-armor wore a padded undergarment to protect him from ax blows. Over this undergarment he donned a tunic of iron links or "chain mail." Chain mail hoods, mitts, and leggings shielded his neck, arms, and legs, while a steel helmet covered his head. In time, knights figured out ways to protect themselves more fully by adding pieces of plate armor over the mail. Eventually, a full suit of plate armor replaced mail.

Clad in armor and mounted on his warhorse, the knight was a daunting sight to foot soldiers. Their spears and arrows could seldom pierce his armor. And blows from their swords or clubs rarely toppled him from his horse. This left the desperate foot soldiers with two options. They could try to get close enough during the battle to cut the saddle from the knight's horse. Or they could try to kill the knight's horse—unless it, too, was wearing armor.

A knight-in-armor knew how to use several deadly weapons. The most important was his lance, a long, heavy spear. In battle, knights would form a line, point their lances forward, and then, like a thundering wall of iron, rush toward their enemies. For close-in fighting, the knight could try to smash an enemy's armor with a battle-ax or a ball-and-chain. To finish the enemy off, he could use a two-handed sword or a sharp dagger to thrust between gaps in armor.

Fighting on horseback required elaborate equipment and intense training. Because both were expensive, few young men could afford to become knights.

By the 1100s, knights were practicing their skills in mock battles called tournaments. Lance in hand, knights galloped toward each other, each seeking to knock the other from his saddle or pierce his armor. Over time, these tournaments became social events with more pageantry and less bloodshed.

At first, however, the tournaments were massive contests with deadly results. In early tournaments,

Left: This sixteenth-century engraving shows a tournament. During such mock combat, knights practiced the skills they needed in battle.

Below: Chivalrous knights like the one in this fourteenth-century Italian fresco accepted rules of honorable conduct promoted by the Church.

hundreds of knights divided into two sides, then clashed head on in the countryside over several days. These first tournaments were so bloody that many called for them to end. The Church opposed them; so did many nobles and kings, who did not like the idea of all those armed men gathered in a single place, ready for combat, and maybe rebellion. Later tournaments limited combat to two knights at a time.

The Code of Chivalry

In the early Middle Ages, knights often fought among themselves for land and booty. The peasants suffered the most from these skirmishes. Warring knights trampled their fields, drove off their livestock, and killed anyone who got in their way.

The Christian Church tried many times to curb this lawlessness. Gradually priests and bishops persuaded knights throughout Europe to accept rules of honorable conduct known as chivalry (SHIH-vuhl-ree). The code of chivalry spelled out virtues knights should follow. A good knight, said the code, was loyal to God, the Church, and the lord he served. He fought bravely and could bear great suffering. Yet he was also expected to protect the weak, the poor, the helpless, and all women and children. The code of chivalry called upon the knight to be generous to all, and merciful to his enemies. A good knight was to be fair, just, kind, and truthful, and never break a promise. He never shrank from his duty—even if it meant giving up his life.

The code of chivalry described an ideal knight—charitable, kind, and loyal. It set high standards that few knights actually met. Despite the code, many knights raided and plundered when they could get away with it. While knights often acted with honor toward their lords and peers, they could be brutal toward the poor.

Still, the code of chivalry set standards for those who might try to live by them. Those centuries-old rules have helped shape our ideas of good conduct today.

Minding the Manor

There were few towns in Western Europe during the early Middle Ages. Most people lived in the countryside, often on a large estate called a manor. Every manor lay under the control of a lord. In fact, there was a saying in medieval times: "No land without a lord, and no lord without land."

Let's pay a visit to a manor. There's quite a bit to see—the lord's house, the village, and all the surrounding farmland. We'll start in the fields, where the peasants of the manor spend much of their time.

Peasants hard at work on a country estate, or manor.

The first thing we notice is that the farmland around the village has been divided into three big fields. One field has been left to lie fallow—that is, it remains unplanted. In this field, the soil is exhausted from growing crops, and the lord is giving it a rest for a year or two. In another field, he's growing wheat, and in the third, barley. After harvest time, cattle, sheep and horses can graze in these two fields.

Many peasant families live on the manor. The lord lets each family cultivate a little land in each field. They get plots laid out in long strips, which are easiest to plow. The peasants trudge miles each day to hoe or harvest the lord's fields, and then work on their own scattered strips of oats, barley, or wheat in the different fields.

Let's turn now to take a walk through the village. It isn't very big, but there's a lot going on. Here is the lord's smithy, where the blacksmith pounds out iron tools over a fire. There is the lord's mill, with a water wheel turned by a stream. In the mill, villagers are grinding grain into flour. There is the lord's bake house, where all the bread is made. And there is a wine press, and a brew house for making beer.

Like most manors, this one forms its own little world. It's isolated, with the next manor or village many miles away, so it must produce just about everything the lord and his people need to live—meat and cheese for the table, sheep's wool for clothes, even beeswax for candles. The few items the lord may need to buy from the outside world include iron for tools and salt for curing meat.

The peasants' cottages huddle together near the stream. These small, smoky huts are made of timber, thatch, and mud. Many are homes to both people and their livestock—a cow or goat, chickens, sheep, and pigs. Only the lord of the manor has his own barns and stables, near the big manor house where the lord and his family live.

The manor house is made of stone and protected by a high wall. Along with the village church, the lord's house is the center of manor life. Its great hall serves as a court. And here at special times—such as after the harvest, or at Christmastime—the lord may hold a village feast. If we could look in a window, we might see the high table where the lord and his lady sit during a banquet, while servants scurry back and forth with plates of meat and jugs of wine. But the high wall shuts off the house from prying eyes.

The lord isn't at home today. He's out hunting—perhaps with his favorite hawk, which flies after rabbits and doves in the fields, or perhaps with his hounds, which chase deer and wild boar through his woodlands. What's that sound? It's the baying of hounds approaching through the woods. The lord of the manor is returning, so we'd best be on our way.

Life in a Castle

From the manor house, a lord could rule his manor almost like a king in a castle. In fact, powerful lords who controlled one or more large manors often lived in castles that provided safety in times of danger.

The lord of this manor sets his table with gold plates and warms the stone walls of his castle with elegant tapestries showing knights in battle. The lord (seated) doesn't look very happy; perhaps the bishop (on his left) is bringing him bad news.

The first castles probably appeared in northwestern France during the ninth century, in response to frequent Viking attacks. They were made of timber and could be built quickly. Most stood on a mound of earth, surrounded by timber walls and a deep ditch called a moat. Some moats held water diverted from a nearby river, but most were dry. Even a dry moat provided a tough challenge for an attacking force. The only access over the moat was a bridge, which could be drawn into the castle.

Eventually powerful lords began rebuilding their timber castles with stone, which was stronger and more fire-resistant. Small towers spaced around the walls gave more protection from attacks. And anyone who wanted to cross the bridge had to pass through a gatehouse where watchful guards stood ready.

This aerial photo shows an Italian castle built during the Middle Ages. Such strongholds offered the lord and his people protection from all but the most determined of invaders.

Many castles boasted other defenses as well. Through slits high in the walls, archers could shoot arrows at attackers without venturing into the open. Enemies who made it past the arrows to the castle walls had better watch out. High above, jutting from the walls, there were overhangs with holes in the floors. Through these holes, defenders could drop stones or pour hot oil onto soldiers' heads!

Assaulting armies came up with ingenious ways to attack stone castles. They built tall wooden towers, rolled them up to the walls, and jumped right over. They attacked with huge rock-hurling catapults. They tried knocking down doors with battering rams. But often the most effective way to take a castle was to lay siege to it. Castles were usually stocked with food, water, and weapons, but a long siege could starve the defenders into surrender. Some sieges lasted months or even years as each side tried to outlast the other.

A castle wasn't necessarily a comfortable place to live. It could be a dark, dank, drafty home for a lord and his vassals. But in an age of raiders, bandits, and marauding armies, a castle offered something precious—a chance of safety.

Those Who Labor: Peasants and Serfs

The lord of a manor provided land and security. In return, the peasants lived hard lives of service. Nine out of every ten people in medieval Europe were peasants, that is, people who worked the land. Some were free men who owned or leased their plots of land. But many were serfs. The serfs were peasants who were tied to the land they worked; they could not leave it without the lord's permission.

Serfs spent part of their time in unpaid labor for the lord, sometimes as much as half the work week. They plowed the fields, cut and stacked the hay, and harvested the crops. If bad weather threatened, they had to gather in the lord's crops before their own. They threshed the grain, and in the surrounding woodlands they gathered firewood and looked after grazing swine.

Peasant women sometimes helped with all these tasks, in addition to completing their own duties. They spent long hours cooking and cleaning in the lord's kitchen, brewing beer, spinning wool, and churning butter.

A medieval lawyer wrote a list of duties that one group of peasants owed their lord:

> *They must wash and shear the lord's sheep for three days each summer. They must weed the lord's grain for three days, and carry the hay for him. Four times a year they must cart his grain to market. They must give him forty eggs from their hens at Easter.*

In time left over from these tasks, a serf could work the ground the lord had granted him. But if a serf sold vegetables from his own plot at market, the lord claimed a share of the profits. He allowed the peasants to use his bakehouse and his mill, but he charged them a fee for the privilege.

The life of a serf was not all drudgery. Seasonal fairs and festivals offered a break from the daily grind. When the weather was good, puppet shows made their way from village to village, or troupes of dancers, musicians, jugglers, and acrobats toured the countryside.

Wielding forks and sickles, peasants on a French manor make hay. Medieval men and women often shared this task.

But nothing could hide the fact that serfs were tied to the manor and its lord. They weren't slaves, but they were little better off. After all, if they disobeyed the lord, they could be turned off the manor, and then they might fall victim to starvation or bandits.

If they were lucky and saved their money for years, peasants could buy their way out of serfdom by purchasing a small plot of land. But most who were born serfs, died serfs. Free peasants who fell on hard times often ended up trading their freedom for serfdom, which meant years of toil on a manor they could not leave.

Serfs lived lives of toil, struggling to feed their families and fulfill their duties to their lord. For many in Europe, all they had was a hope, like a flickering candle, sometimes strong and sometimes faint—a hope that life in a world to come would be better than the life they now lived.

A gold and silver crucifix from a cathedral in northern Italy.

An Age of Faith: The Church in Western Europe

Historians sometimes call the Middle Ages an "Age of Faith." Eastern Orthodox Christianity flourished in the Byzantine Empire. In the powerful Islamic Empire, the Muslim faith knit together millions of people. In Western Europe, most people shared the common bond of Christianity.

Between A.D. 500 and 1400, the Christian Church, headed by the pope in Rome, was the great unifying force in Western Europe. In fact, people of that time didn't even refer to their land as "Europe." Most simply called it "Christendom."

Think back to how we got the term A.D. As you know, in the early Middle Ages, monks helped preserve learning. In A.D. 525, a monk named Dionysius Exiguus set out to improve the Julian calendar (the one Julius Caesar invented). He devised a new system to keep track of the years, and he decided to start with the birth of Jesus. All the years before Jesus' birth came to be called B.C. (before Christ), while the years after were labeled A.D.—*anno Domini*, Latin for "in the year of our Lord." For Dionysius Exiguus and the church leaders who put the new calendar into use, time was organized around Christ's birth. For them, Jesus stood at the center of history, as Christianity stood at the heart of Europe.

In medieval Europe, Christianity united millions. It gave people hope in hard and dangerous times, and touched almost every aspect of life in this Age of Faith.

A medieval rendering of Jesus Christ.

One Church for Western Europe

During the Middle Ages, most people in Europe lived on manors. Each manor was like its own little world. People had no reason and little opportunity to go beyond the fields where they lived and worked. If they traveled outside the manor, they might well be attacked by robbers or die of starvation. People from one region rarely encountered people from others. When they did, they often had trouble understanding each other's language.

Although they were isolated from each other, Western Europeans were held together by the Christian faith. All over this vast land, there was one Christian Church. Kings and princes came and went; armies might wipe each other out; nobles might murder one another. But the Church was always there, and it had been there as long as people could remember.

This painting sums up the importance of the Christian Church in the Middle Ages. It shows a German archbishop looming large over the smaller figures of two German princes.

At the head of the Church stood the pope in Rome. His archbishops gave direction to the bishops. The bishops, in turn, had authority to direct the priests, who looked after individual churches. The priests could direct clerks and deacons, who did everything from keep church records to assist in church services.

In an age when communication and transportation were slow, Church officials weren't always in close touch, and the Church did not run like a well-oiled machine. Still, with its structure and organization, it had vast reach.

The Church had its own laws, which were based on scripture, Church councils, and the decisions of the pope. When people broke those laws, they were tried in courts run by the Church. While most Church laws dealt with religious matters, some laws applied to legal matters in which people swore an oath. So, for example, if you were getting married, making a will, or drawing up a contract to do business with someone else, the Church had a say in how it should be done.

By the thirteenth century, the Church regulated much of daily life, and had an enormous influence on people's activities. All Christians were expected to attend church services weekly, and to confess their sins at least once a year to a priest. The priest told them how they could do penance, that is, how they could show remorse for their sins, often by praying or doing service for the Church.

The Church became the largest landowner in Europe. Kings and nobles often gave land and homes to the Church. They donated money to build cathedrals, which were great churches that served as headquarters for bishops. For their generosity to the Church, wealthy nobles hoped they would go to heaven after they died.

The Church also influenced education. Officials of the Church were about the only people who could read and write. Children who received an education were often taught by monks, who ran most schools in the Middle Ages. In the 1200s, when universities began to develop, both the students and teachers were usually priests or men preparing to be priests. The Church had a lot to say about what was taught there. Students at universities studied philosophy, law, medicine, and most of all, theology, which is the study of God. (The Greek root *theos* means "god.")

In medieval times, children lucky enough to get an education were often taught by monks, as depicted in this painting from about 1300.

The Power of the Church

The medieval Church was powerful. It owned land, charged taxes, operated courts, and ran schools. If an ambitious feudal lord challenged the Church's authority or broke its rules, the pope could "excommunicate" him, which means the pope could declare that the lord was no longer a member of the Church. An excommunicated person lost many legal rights and couldn't participate in church services until the excommunication was lifted. The threat of excommunication gave the Church power over lords who might be tempted to defy the Church's authority.

Thomas Aquinas

Thomas Aquinas (uh-KWIY-nus) was one of the greatest thinkers of the Middle Ages. He worked hard to reconcile Christian thought and Greek philosophy. Born in northern Italy around 1225, he spent much of his youth studying to enter the priesthood. In 1250, he became a priest, and a few years later he took a post as professor of philosophy and theology at the University of Paris.

Thomas Aquinas admired the works of the ancient Greeks, particularly the great philosopher Aristotle. The Greeks' confidence in the power of reason appealed to Thomas's own intellectual spirit. In his writings, he used reason, logic, and Aristotle's ideas to argue that God existed. His most famous work was *Summa Theologica* (SOO-muh thee-uh-LOH-jih-kuh), which means "summary of theology." In that work he carefully explained Christian beliefs and the logic behind such beliefs.

Right: A priest baptizes an infant.

Below: Reliquaries held the relics of Christian martyrs and saints. This elegant example was made in France in the early 1200s.

To those who knew little but daily toil and endless duty to feudal lords, the Church offered a message of hope. It promised a new and better life in the world to come. In a time when many people were haunted by fears of disease, war, starvation, and countless other hardships, the Church reassured them. Those who are faithful, said the Church, and those who live a good life, will know rest and peace with God in heaven. In a hard age, this was a comforting message.

Still, for nobles and ordinary folk alike, the greatest power of the medieval Church may have been its power to inspire. Special church ceremonies, called sacraments, marked the big occasions in people's lives. From the moment of birth to the time of death, the Church was there. The local priest baptized newborn children, which assured parents that their infant was welcomed into the fold of the Christian community. The priest also presided over marriages. He heard confessions and forgave sins in God's name. He anointed those near death with oil, which was seen as a sign that they were free from sin and thus, they believed, prepared to join God in heaven. Weekly church services, called masses, also provided a regular chance for people to pray and seek guidance.

Treasures of Faith: The Romanesque Style

The Age of Faith gave us many remarkable works of art inspired by religion—silver crosses; gold candlesticks for altars; paintings, carvings, and gilded manuscript pages; and jeweled boxes to hold relics, including bodily remains, such as pieces of bone or other objects related to saints and martyrs. Craftsmen lovingly produced all these things to express their faith in God.

Perhaps the most impressive works of medieval art are glorious churches and cathedrals. From the eleventh century to the mid-twelfth century, Europeans built in what is called the Romanesque (roh-muhn-ESK) style. Romanesque churches and monasteries were massive, fortress-like buildings, with thick walls and few windows. The thick walls were needed to support the heavy stone roofs. Huge columns and round Roman arches helped hold up the structures, which is why the style got the name "Romanesque."

Romanesque churches looked much like the castles dotting the countryside. After all, these were days when bands of thieves and unruly armies roamed the land, and people looked to the Church for protection. These buildings were constructed to be places of safety as well as places of worship.

A Romanesque church was meant to be a mighty fortress of God. The church was usually built in the shape of a Latin cross, with a long aisle down the center and two shorter aisles running off to the sides. Since it had few windows, the church was usually dark inside. But what it lacked in light, it made up in rich colors. Ceilings and columns often glowed with bright paint. Sometimes the walls themselves were painted with pictures. Sometimes they were hung with tapestries, woven with gold and silver threads forming pictures that showed scenes from the Bible stories or the lives of the saints.

Soaring Prayers in Glass and Stone: The Gothic Style

The Romanesque style of building was solid and earthbound. But from the mid-twelfth to the sixteenth centuries, a new and different style emerged, known as the Gothic style.

The Gothic style began in France, where builders began asking themselves: How can we build our cathedrals higher? The thick, massive walls of Romanesque churches could only go so high before they collapsed under their own weight. So builders had to find another solution. Soon they realized they could use tall pillars to hold up a building. And instead of the rounded Roman arches, they could use steeper, pointed arches to push a building skyward.

The Spanish cathedral of Santiago de Compostela was built in the Romanesque style.

What's a Saint?

The word *saint* comes from Latin *sanctus* and means "holy one." The medieval Christian Church taught that anyone who died and went to heaven was a saint. The Church also had a process for honoring people who had lived such holy lives that it was believed they were surely in heaven. These people were formally recognized as saints by the Church. Mary, the mother of Jesus, was revered as a saint. So too were Peter, Paul, and many of Jesus' apostles.

Perhaps the most famous Gothic cathedral of them all—Notre Dame in Paris.

The builders wanted to go even *higher*. They wanted tall spires and lofty towers. And they wanted to hold it all up without cluttering the inside of the cathedral with many stone supports. To give the walls extra strength, and to buttress—to support—the highest parts, they built supports *outside* the building. These supports took the form of stone bridges that arced through the air almost as if they were flying—which is why they are called flying buttresses.

Since the Gothic cathedrals no longer needed such thick walls, builders could open these churches to light with huge stained-glass windows. To create them, craftsmen used thousands of bits of brightly colored glass, each piece attached to the next with lead. As light came through the windows, it lit the glass like jewels. Each stained-glass window was a sparkling wall of light, taking the shape of a rose or the form of a picture that told stories of the Bible and the saints. While most people entering Gothic churches could not read, they could understand the stories in these pictures. Stained-glass windows, like painted walls in earlier churches, helped teach them about the Christian faith.

The main architectural features of Gothic cathedrals reminded people to look to God. The towers and spires that seemed to reach to the heavens; the high, pointed arches; the flying buttresses; the stained-glass windows that flooded the interiors with light—all were designed to lift Christians' sights and thoughts. The cathedrals were, in effect, attempts to recreate a heavenly city on earth.

It was a massive undertaking to build a cathedral. It usually took generations of toil. The workers who built the towers might be the great-grandchildren of the workers who set the foundations in place. There were hundreds of jobs for carpenters, stonemasons, carvers, blacksmiths, diggers, and more. And of course it all cost money. Both rich and poor gave to support the building of a local cathedral.

A cathedral was more than a great house of worship. It was a center of life. Here the bishop saw to the Church's business. On the steps outside, crowds often watched religious plays. Markets and shop-keepers' stalls clustered nearby. Great fairs drew throngs of people. Pilgrims who had journeyed from faraway lands came to see relics, and marvel at the spires that seemed to touch the clouds. A cathedral was a school and an art gallery. It was a work project for hundreds. It was a reminder of the Church's power, as well as a symbol of people's faith. And it was built to last. The soaring Gothic cathedrals still stand as the most splendid symbols of the Age of Faith.

The spectacular stained-glass windows of France's Chartres Cathedral.

A Command from the Pope

Many Europeans of the Middle Ages thought of the Church as something like an army. They felt it must fight to save souls from evil. And they felt it should take up arms to defend Christians against non-believers. So when word came from the East that the Byzantine Empire was in danger of being overrun by Muslim armies, Christendom prepared for war.

It started in 1071 with a call for help from Constantinople. Muslim warriors called Seljuk (sel-JOOK) Turks were attacking the Byzantine Empire. In battle after battle, they inched closer to the empire's capital, Constantinople. Often they left nothing but burned villages and silent,

Notre Dame Times Two

France was the center of Gothic architecture and home to two of the most magnificent Gothic churches built in the Middle Ages. Both were named for Jesus' mother, Mary, whom medieval Christians called "Our Lady," or, in French, "Notre Dame" (noh-truh DAHM). The cathedral of Notre Dame in Paris was one of the first to use flying buttresses. Rising on the banks of the Seine River, it took more than 90 years to build. Another soaring cathedral named "Notre Dame" was built at the city of Chartres (shahrt). Enormous windows of stained glass light the stone vault of the church with colored light.

smoking towns in their wake. The Byzantine emperor knew that without help, it would only be a matter of time before Constantinople fell.

The emperor knew that Western Europe was full of knights and nobles. He knew they were Christians, like the Byzantines in the East. He also knew, however, that there was a quarrel between the eastern and western branches of the Church. Still, he thought, Christians of the West might be willing to defend Christians of the East against Muslim invaders. So the emperor sent a message to the pope in Rome, asking for an army to help defend the eastern empire in the name of the Christian Church.

The pope thought long and hard about the Byzantine emperor's message. If the Byzantine Empire fell, the Islamic Empire might take up arms against the kingdoms of Western Europe next. Even if the Muslims didn't attack Western Europe, Christians might be cut off forever from the city of Jerusalem.

Palestine: The Origin of the Name

Since the time of ancient Rome, a slender strip of land along the eastern Mediterranean Sea has been known as Palestine. The ancient Hebrew people, led by Abraham, settled there and called the region Canaan. Later the Philistines came from across the Mediterranean Sea and made it their home. Greek writers called this part of the world Philistia, after the Philistines. In Latin, the language of the Romans, *Philistia* was translated as "Palaestina" or "Palestine." The region called Palestine does not have precise borders. Over the years, it has included modern-day Israel, Gaza, the West Bank, and parts of Jordan, Lebanon, and Egypt.

Jerusalem lay in a small strip of land on the Mediterranean Sea called Palestine. The area had long been important to Jews, Christians, and Muslims. To Jews, it was important as the "promised land" where Moses had led the Hebrews. To Christians, it was important as the land of Jesus' birth and death. According to Muslim belief, it was from Palestine that Muhammad's spirit traveled to heaven. Palestine was considered the Holy Land, and Jerusalem its holiest city.

- On the map on page 553, locate Christian lands, Muslim lands, Constantinople, Rome, Palestine, and Jerusalem.

For nearly 400 years, Muslims had ruled Palestine, but they allowed people of other religions to visit and live there as well. Jews in Palestine could follow their faith, and Christian pilgrims were free to come and go. But once the Seljuk Turks conquered the Holy Land, it became more dangerous for Christians to make pilgrimages there, and sometimes they were forbidden to enter the holy sites.

So it was that on a cold November day in 1095, Pope Urban II stood before thousands of people in France and called for a holy war. Speaking in the home of his historic allies, the Franks, he said it would be a war to protect Christians in the East and recapture the Holy Land from Muslim Turks. "God wills it!" the crowds cheered, and thousands volunteered to join the fight.

Many volunteers stitched a cross on their clothes. The Latin word for cross was *crux*, and the wars that would follow came to be known as the Crusades. The Crusades were wars between European Christians and Muslims over the fate of the Holy Land. There were eight of these wars in all, plus some minor expeditions, and they would last for almost two hundred years.

Saladin and Richard the Lion-Heart

The First Crusade, led by French nobles, began in 1096. Carrying banners of purple and gold, mounted on horses or walking, the crusaders set off to claim the Holy Land for Christianity. Thousands of knights, lords, peasants, workers, and priests made the 2,000-mile trek. As too often happens when angry crowds march, many in their path suffered. In this case, all non-Christians were at risk. On their way to the Holy Land, the crusaders slaughtered Jewish communities.

In 1099 the crusaders arrived at the walls of Jerusalem. To the Muslims, the crusaders did not look like a rescuing army. They looked like an invasion of enemy soldiers. After six weeks the city fell to the crusaders. Once inside the walls, the Christian soldiers killed every Muslim they could find.

That was by no means the end. Like a terrible tug-of-war, the battle for the Holy Land would go on. Both crusaders and Muslims inflicted terrible violence, with victory sometimes going to one side, sometimes the other. From these struggles emerged two famous warriors—Saladin (SAL-uh-din) and Richard the Lion-Heart.

When Saladin was born, the crusaders had been ruling Jerusalem and Palestine for years. As a boy, Saladin studied the Qur'an and faithfully prayed to Allah five times a day. When Saladin turned 14,

Above: Saladin, the great Muslim leader.

Left: Under the banner of the cross, Christian crusaders come ashore in the Holy Land.

Above: Christians capture the city of Jerusalem in this painting from the 1400s.

Below: The mighty warrior-king of England, Richard the Lion-Heart.

he became a soldier. Brave, wise, and generous, he led the Muslim armies that would take back the Holy Land.

Meanwhile, far to the north, another courageous man sat on the throne of England—King Richard I. When crowned king, he swore to honor God and the Christian Church. Then he received a pair of golden spurs and a sword to "crush evil-doers." When word reached him that Saladin had reconquered Palestine, he vowed to lead a third Crusade to the Holy Land.

Richard was the kind of general who plunged into battle with his soldiers, fighting like a lion in the midst of the fray. Though he could be fierce and cruel, he was so steadfast on the battlefield that people thought of him as a heroic knight. They called him Richard the Lion-Heart.

These two great warriors, Saladin and Richard, battled for the Holy Land. Though they were at war, they respected each other. It is said that during one battle, Saladin saw Richard without a horse. The Muslim leader sent his attendants through the raging battlefield with a new mount so the noble king would not have to fight on foot. At one point, Richard proposed that his sister marry Saladin's brother to gain peace. But the wedding never took place.

The armies of Saladin and Richard fought up and down Palestine for more than a year. At last the two leaders reached a truce. They agreed that Christians could rule the lands along the coast, while Muslims would rule inland. Muslims would also rule the city of Jerusalem, but Saladin agreed to let Christians come there to pray and worship at their holy places. It was to be a temporary solution.

The End of the Crusades

During the next hundred years, Muslim forces gradually recaptured the Christian cities along the coast. Several new Crusades set out from Europe to fight back. Many who made the long, perilous journey did so because they believed they must defend the Holy Land. Others did it as penance for their sins. Some seemed more interested in adventure and gaining riches.

In 1291, the last of the Christian cities in Palestine fell. The remaining crusaders gave up and straggled home, leaving the Holy Land under Muslim rule.

In some ways, the Crusades left the Mediterranean world a bitter place. Muslims and Christians would long blame each other for the bloody struggles. The wars also left Christians and Jews deeply divided. In their zeal to slay the "infidels" or unbelievers, crusaders massacred many Jewish communities on their way to Constantinople.

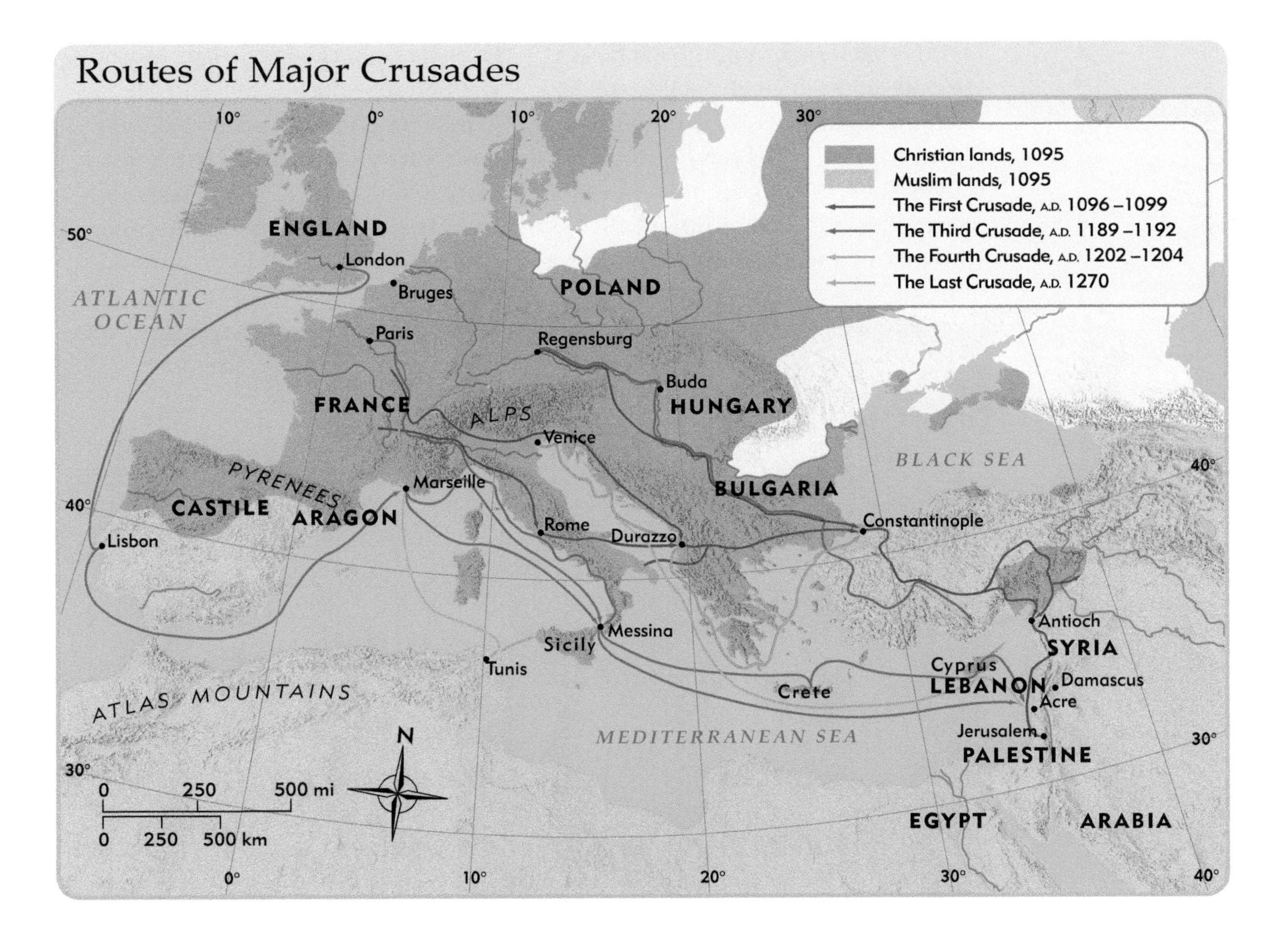

The Crusades also left Christians divided among themselves. Just before the first Crusade, you recall, the pope had urged Christians to take up arms and help their brethren in the East. But by the fourth Crusade, tensions were high between the eastern and western Church. The crusaders even ruthlessly sacked Constantinople in 1204, looting sacred treasures and carting them off to Venice. The sacking of Constantinople severely strained relations between Christians of Western Europe and Orthodox Christians of the East.

But the Crusades also kindled new interest in the East. When they returned to Europe from the Holy Land, crusaders brought back new ideas about science and medicine from the Islamic world. These ideas found a home in the new European universities. Western scholars began to translate and make copies of Al-Khwarizmi's work in mathematics, as well as Ibn Sina's books on philosophy and medicine. Greek texts from the libraries of the Islamic and Byzantine Empires came west. And goods from the East made their way to European marketplaces—lemons, sugar, rice, apricots, and fine cotton cloth. Trade slowly revived.

On a Pilgrimage

We've learned that during the Middle Ages, most people in Europe traveled very little. They lived out their lives on the manor or in the town where they were born. There were, however, exceptions to this isolation—the Crusades to the Holy Land took many people away from home. Another exception was the Christian pilgrimage. Just as Muslims went on religious journeys to Mecca, Christians sometimes showed their devotion by going on pilgrimages. They usually journeyed to famous churches where the bones of important saints were said to be buried.

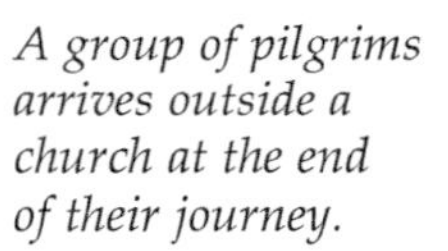

A group of pilgrims arrives outside a church at the end of their journey.

One of the most famous pilgrimage sites of the Middle Ages was the church of Santiago de Compostela (sahn-TYAH-goh thay kawm-poh-STAY-lah) in northern Spain. There, one of Jesus' original apostles, Saint James, was said to be buried. (Saint James is "Santiago" in Spanish.) Let's imagine what a Christian pilgrimage might have been like in this Age of Faith.

A Favor from Saint James

Imagining the Past

The rain beat down like angry fists. Anne tightened her grip around little Matthew and hunched forward over the horse's broad, steaming back, shielding the sleeping child with her body. Her thick woolen cloak had long since soaked through. The weight of it dragged at her shoulders like a drowning man, threatening to pull her from her slippery seat.

What sort of country is this? she wondered, not for the first time since their storm-tossed crossing. Did the sun never shine?

At first, the light twinkling up ahead seemed an illusion, another cruel trick of the endless night. It flickered, disappeared, and then reappeared, stronger. Anne pushed her streaming hair out of her eyes. "An inn! Thomas, an inn!"

The old man reined in his palfrey alongside her. "Yes, my lady." His voice betrayed no hint of feeling. "I spotted the light some time past."

Anne bit back a sharp retort. Indulging her quick temper was a sin, and there was no room for sin, however petty, on this pilgrimage. How could she expect St. James to grant her dearest wish if she would not behave like a true Christian?

***St.* is the abbreviation for "Saint."**

Still, it was just like Thomas not to tell her that shelter was nearby. The grumpy old servant had been her husband's, not her own, and it was clear he had not wanted to accompany the young widow on the long journey from England to Spain. Despite his wooden expression, she felt sure he was enjoying every moment of her misery.

With the light as a beacon, Anne urged her horse forward with renewed spirits. Almost before she knew it they had reached the inn, and she was handing Matthew down into the servant's arms. Ignoring the offered hand, she slid unassisted from the horse's back.

"Faithful Buttercup." She patted the horse's neck and turned to Thomas. "Please see that our horses are well treated. They have had a long, hard day."

The old man made no move to follow the horses. "A lady does not go into a public inn without protection."

Anne sighed. Her safety, she was certain, was of less concern to him than his own comfort. A warming fire and a tankard of ale appealed to him more than the reek of a stable.

But she said lightly, "Who will know I am a lady? In my felt hat and sandals, I look just like any other pilgrim. Only our horses show that we are privileged," she added, pointedly emphasizing the *we*. Most pilgrims traveled on foot. A servant who could ride was fortunate indeed.

She scooped the baby boy into her arms and turned her back on the old man. Surly Thomas could wait a bit longer to be warm and dry. Little Matthew could not.

Inside, the inn was crowded, but Anne noticed only the fire blazing brightly in the great stone hearth. She drew up a wooden stool and sat before it, cradling the baby on her lap. Briefly, he stirred, then settled in against her and returned to sleep.

Anne gazed down at the small, peaceful face. He seemed so fragile. And yet he had survived the fever that had carried off her husband, once so hale and strong, and so many others in their village. She knew she should be grateful. If only—

"PIE?"

The voice boomed in her ear, as a steaming meat pie thrust itself beneath her nose. Startled, she looked up. The innkeeper, a fat man with a big red face, partly hidden behind a big red beard, beamed down at her.

"Eat!" he bellowed. "You need your strength. It's a long way to Santiago de Compostela."

Anne arranged her sleeping baby on her lap, then thanked the innkeeper and bit into the savory hot pie. Delicious. For several minutes, her attention was focused entirely on eating. Finally, though, her hunger lessened, and her curiosity increased.

When the innkeeper passed again, she asked, "How did you know where I was going?"

The big man roared with laughter. "How did I know!" He turned to include everyone else in the room in the joke. "How did I know where she was going, asks the child!"

Anne felt her temper rising. Small she might be, but she was not a child. She was a grown woman, nearly sixteen years old, and the mother of a son already well past his first birthday. "What is so funny—"

A slender young man in a priest's robe turned from the fire to face her. "We are all going to Santiago de Compostela," he said gently. "This is the way."

Astonished, she forgot her anger. "All?"

She looked around. Travelers of every description filled the room. Some, like her, wore the long woolen tunic and wide-brimmed hat of the pilgrim. Others were dressed according to their social class, from the rough homespun of peasants to the fashionable silks and velvets of the wealthy.

And all of them intended to make the trek across the steep and rocky Pyrenees (PIR-uh-neez) into northern Spain, to see the burial place of St. James.

"Pilgrims throughout Christendom flock to Santiago de Compostela," said the red-faced innkeeper. He spoke boastfully, as if he himself had built the tomb and placed inside it the remains of the apostle. "Especially in this holy year."

Anne wanted to ask why this year should be holier than any other, but she was afraid he would laugh at her again.

The young priest seemed to sense her puzzlement. He waited until the innkeeper bustled off to the kitchen. Then he said, "When the feast of James falls on a Sunday, it's a holy year. Those who make pilgrimage to his tomb in a holy year will have all their sins forgiven. The Church says so."

She looked down at the sleeping baby in her lap. "I am not going there to seek forgiveness."

"Don't you want to go to heaven?" The priest smiled. "Or are you, alone among us, free from sin?"

Anne tried to smile back, but tears welled up in her eyes. Softly, she said, "I go to ask the saint a favor."

"Favor!" boomed the innkeeper, returning from the kitchen with another round of pies. "You and thousands of others. The crypt where his body lies is piled high with prayers and wishes. I wonder how he gets a moment's rest."

Heat spread across Anne's cheeks. "It's not for myself. The fever left my child lame..." Her voice broke.

Diplomatically, the young priest turned to the innkeeper. "You seem to know Santiago de Compostela well. How many times have you made the pilgrimage?"

Now it was the innkeeper's turn to flush, his face turning an even deeper red. "Me? Ah, well, I can't leave the inn. So many pilgrims to serve..."

And so much money to make? Anne added silently.

"Besides," he went on, "the way is plagued with bandits. And Spain is overrun with infidels. The Moors—"

"Rule southern Spain," the priest said. "Or so I've heard. But northern Spain is Christian."

Anne thought that she would like to see a Moor. If she had been a man, she could have ridden on Crusade and traveled to distant lands, beyond the bounds of Christendom.

But she had more immediate concerns.

"Are there really bandits?" she asked. Thomas, she thought, would be of little use against armed robbers on the road.

The young priest nodded. "That is why we pilgrims travel together, in a large group. Will you join us?"

She considered. The priest seemed kind, and it would be safer to travel with a group of pilgrims. But it also would be slower. Buttercup would have to match the pace of human travelers on foot. How long could Anne bear to wait to find out if the saint would grant her wish?

No, she must thank the priest, refuse his offer, and press on.

As she was about to speak, Matthew's eyes fluttered open. He stared at the priest. Then his face broke into a wide grin, and he reached out his arms.

Anne looked from her son to the young priest. "Yes," she said. "We will travel with you."

"Good." He smiled at Matthew. "And, by the grace of St. James, I pray you will receive the favor that you ask."

Henry II strengthened the monarchy in twelfth-century England.

Monarchs on the Rise

Through much of the Middle Ages, people in Western Europe thought of themselves as belonging to their local manor or village. Serfs who were bound to the land owed duties and labor to their lord. For them, a manor five miles away was a different world. Peasants might recognize the name of the noble who had granted their lord his fief, but most did not think of themselves as subjects of some distant, powerful emperor. It was a time of little kingdoms, not large empires like the one Charlemagne had ruled.

But as time passed, this situation began to change. Some rulers raised armies to conquer larger territories and defend their borders. These rulers began to govern wider realms. They made laws for their subjects, set up royal courts to keep the laws, and appointed officials to watch over their interests. Large kingdoms began to develop in some parts of Europe.

In the late Middle Ages, strong monarchies emerged in what would become the nations of England, France, and Spain. What is a monarchy? The ancient Greek philosopher Aristotle, in his writings on different types of governments, defined *monarchy* as rule by one man. The word *monarch* comes from the Greek roots *monos* ("alone") and *archos* ("ruler"). A monarch is a person who rules over a kingdom or empire.

In this chapter we'll look at England as an example of how monarchies grew in medieval times. Why England? Partly because it's an exciting story, and partly because what happened there set the stage for so much later history.

A coin bearing the image of William the Conqueror, who won the English throne in 1066.

To tell this story of rising monarchies, we won't start in England. First we need to make a brief trip across the English Channel, to northern France.

William the Conqueror

In the ninth and tenth centuries, as you recall, Vikings crossed the frigid North Sea in their dragon-prowed ships and landed on the coast of France. They attacked villages and burned towns. The French called these fierce raiders Normans, the French term for "north men." Eventually the newcomers settled down, began speaking French, and embraced Christianity. The region of France they inhabited came to be called Normandy, and its ruler the Duke of Normandy.

- On the map on page 564, locate Normandy. Locate England and the English Channel as well.

In 1028, a baby boy was born to the Duke of Normandy. His parents named him William. Legend says that even as a newborn he showed his strong-willed nature by clutching at the rushes covering the floor of his room and refusing to let them go. This infant, who tenaciously clung to his turf, would grow up to be known as William the Conqueror.

In 1034, William's father decided to go on a pilgrimage to the Holy Land. Before leaving, he stunned the Norman nobles by calling them together and making them swear allegiance to his young son. "He is but little, my lords," the duke proclaimed, "but he will grow, please God, into a gallant man. I hereby declare him my heir, and if I should never return from my pilgrimage, you shall accept him as your duke."

William's father never returned. He died of fever on the way back from Jerusalem. At about age eight, little William found himself Duke of Normandy.

More than once jealous nobles tried to kill the boy. For a while his mother hid him among the peasants of the Normandy forests. William grew up tall and strong. Those dangerous years gave him courage but left him with a ruthless streak. He asserted his right to rule, said one witness, by "hurling himself upon his enemies... terrify[ing] them with slaughter."

William made himself master of Normandy, but that would not be enough. He soon cast his eye across the English Channel.

England was a fertile land that, over the years, had been invaded and settled by many different peoples. The Romans had conquered part of the region. Then in the fifth century, the Angles, Saxons, and other tribes arrived from northern Germany, followed several centuries later by plundering Vikings and Danes.

In William's time, a king named Edward sat on the English throne. Edward was a distant cousin of William. When Edward died in early 1066, he left no sons or daughters. "I should be king of England," William declared.

But someone else claimed the throne as well—an English noble named Harold, Earl of Wessex. If William wanted England, he would have to fight for it.

The Battle of Hastings and the Norman Conquest

William assembled an army of more than 10,000 soldiers with 3,600 horses. He crammed them onto 700 boats, and set out across the English Channel. It is said that as he waded ashore in England, he lost his footing and fell. His knights looked at each other in dismay. It seemed a bad sign for a leader to stumble on the brink of a campaign so full of hazard. But William knew how to turn events to his advantage. Grabbing a fistful of sand from the beach, he rose shouting, "A good omen, my friends! Thus do I seize the earth of England!"

On the morning of October 14, 1066, William's Norman army met Harold's English troops near the town of Hastings. The foot soldiers, archers, and knights threw themselves at each other, the Normans crying "God helps us!" and the English shouting, "Out! Out!" The fighting lasted all day. Some sources say that Harold died when a Norman arrow struck him in the eye. By evening, the invaders held the field. William the Conqueror planted his banner in English soil.

William had won the Battle of Hastings. Now he marched on to London. The citizens of London, having no wish to put up a fight, threw open the city gates. On Christmas Day at Westminster Abbey, William was crowned William I, King of the English.

William's invasion of England would come to be known as the Norman Conquest. He spent the next several years taking control of the whole country, seizing land from the English nobles and giving it piece by piece to the Norman knights who had followed him into battle. He let his knights hold that land with an important condition—that they swear allegiance to their king. He made sure that the real power remained not in the hands of his barons or lords, but in the hands of the king.

William was a strong monarch who turned England into a well-organized feudal state. To keep control over the people, the Norman lords dotted the countryside with castles. At first they were little more than wooden forts built on mounds of earth. Later, they also built massive

It is said that William stumbled on the beach after crossing the English Channel. Holding up a handful of sand he declared, "Thus do I seize the earth of England!"

Norman knights attack English foot soldiers in this detail from the Bayeux Tapestry. The famous linen tapestry was named for the French town where it was made about 1080.

stone fortresses. From their castles the Norman lords ruled over England's serfs and peasants.

While William kept a firm grip on his feudal lords, he also listened to their opinions. He formed the Great Council, a group of nobles and church leaders who met regularly to advise the king and help him make laws. This idea of a Great Council would have tremendous influence on the history of England—and the world—in centuries to come. The Great Council was the ancestor of legislatures that represent the will of the people.

Even with his Great Council, William the Conqueror was no doubt master of England. "No one dared do anything contrary to his will," reported a scribe of the time. He united the land more firmly than ever before.

William died as he lived—as a warrior. His death seems less heroic than he might have liked. In 1087, while putting down an uprising in Normandy, he was thrown from his horse and landed in a ditch of smoldering embers. The fall proved fatal. The man who conquered England was laid to rest at an abbey in France, the land of his birth.

Henry II Strengthens the Throne

It was no easy task to rule England in the Middle Ages. Rivals were always plotting to claim the throne. Scheming lords often worked against the king while they raided each other's domains. Civil wars sometimes broke out, leaving royal authority weakened.

English Lands in the Middle Ages

Above: During his long reign, Henry II reached a long arm across England. He claimed land for himself and laid the foundations of England's modern legal system.

Left: The seal of Henry II bears the image of a horse and rider, an appropriate symbol for this royal man of action.

In his day, King William kept a strong hold, but some of his successors possessed less skill as rulers.

In 1154, however, William's great-grandson, Henry II, mounted the throne. Red-headed Henry was a bundle of energy and contradictions. One playwright described the king as "simple and royal…compassionate and hard, a man of intellect, a man of action, God-fearing, superstitious, blasphemous, far-seeing, short-sighted, affectionate, lustful, patient, volcanic, humble, overriding." This many-sided man knew how to wield power. Henry ruled for more than three decades, and during that time he turned England into one of the strongest monarchies in Europe.

As soon as he was crowned, Henry began bringing order to his troubled realm. He seized lands that he said rightfully belonged to the king. He knocked down the castles of troublesome lords. He appointed royal sheriffs to enforce his laws and collect taxes in England's counties. He set up a new system to keep accurate records.

Henry devoted his energies to establishing law and order in his realm. Perhaps his most lasting reform was the change he brought to England's legal system. In the Middle Ages, local laws and customs determined how trials were conducted. Ideas of "justice" varied from village to village. Sometimes two knights might fight each other to decide who was right or wrong. Sometimes an accused person's guilt or innocence was determined by throwing the person into a pond and seeing if he floated or sank.

Henry established a new system of justice. Rather than relying on local lords to decide guilt or innocence, he set up courts. In many cases, these courts used juries to help make decisions. He sent judges traveling around the countryside to try cases and apply the law equally throughout the land. By making the laws more uniform, Henry II made England a more unified nation.

Eleanor of Aquitaine

The Middle Ages were a time when, to a very great extent, men held power and determined the course of nations. But in this masculine world, some women wielded great political skill and power. One such woman was Eleanor of Aquitaine (A-kwuh-tayn).

Eleanor was the daughter of the Duke of Aquitaine. Aquitaine was a beautiful land of lush fields and rolling hills in southwest France. In 1137, when Eleanor was 15, she inherited Aquitaine and married Louis VII, king of France. Several years later she and Louis parted ways, and Eleanor married Henry II, king of England. Two of her sons, Richard the Lion-Heart and John, both later sat on the English throne.

In those days, noblewomen were often expected to remain in their castles and do their husband's bidding. Not Eleanor. In wartime, she pulled on boots, hopped on her horse, and galloped around the countryside, waving her sword and calling men to battle. While her son Richard was away from the throne fighting in the Crusades, Eleanor stayed behind and helped run England herself.

As Eleanor grew older, she schemed to marry her children and grandchildren to princes and princesses from other countries, so they could become kings and queens. She traveled from one end of Europe to the other, arranging royal marriages. Eleanor lived to the ripe old age of 82—a *very* long life in the Middle Ages. By the time of her death, so many of her children and grandchildren ruled parts of Europe that people called her the "Grandmother of Europe."

Eleanor of Aquitaine was not the only woman to wield power while her husband or son was away on a Crusade. The same was true in other noble families in France and England. During that time of war, while the men went off to fight, women often ran the business of manors and courts.

Henry made sure that all of the judges' decisions were carefully recorded. Thus judges trying later cases could use the earlier decisions as guides. This system became the basis for what is known as "common law"—that is, law based on rulings by judges in previous cases. English common law became the foundation of legal systems in many countries, including the United Kingdom, the United States, and Canada.

The Magna Carta

Henry II died in 1189, and the throne passed to his son Richard—the same Richard who was called the Lion-Heart. King Richard I reigned for the next 10 years, but he spent only six months of that time in England. Mostly he was away on crusades and other military adventures.

This painting shows Eleanor of Aquitaine marrying King Louis of France in 1137. Ten years later, the couple embarked on the Second Crusade (a journey represented by the ship).

While he was gone, his brother John plotted to gain power. If you've ever read any legends of Robin Hood, you've met the crafty Prince John. He tried to seize Richard's power while the Lion-Heart was off fighting Saladin. When Richard died in 1199, John became king of England, and some say he was the worst monarch ever to sit on the English throne. He was treacherous and given to savage outbursts of temper. He had his nephew thrown into prison and, according to some reports, executed to make sure the young man could never be king. And that was just the beginning.

John ignored the Great Council, the body of English nobles who gathered three times a year to advise the king and help make laws. John also quarreled with church leaders in England, as well as the pope. He got into wars, and to pay for them he raised taxes whenever he felt like it.

Finally the nobles and church leaders had had enough. They gathered their own army and threatened rebellion. Faced with a civil war, John called a truce.

In the year 1215, King John and the English nobles met at Runnymede (RUH-nee-meed), a small island in the River Thames (temz). There, on neutral ground between their two armies, the nobles presented the king with a document, the Magna Carta, which is Latin for "Great Charter." The Magna Carta stated that the nobles and church leaders had certain rights, and that the king swore to respect them. Here are some of the ideas expressed in the document:

- The Church of England should have its rights and be able to choose its own bishops.
- The great nobles should have their rights. They would not be asked to pay more taxes to the king than they had paid in the past.
- If special taxes were needed, a council must approve them. The great nobles and clergy would sit on the council.
- For a freeman to be put in jail or fined, two things were necessary. He must have broken the law of the land, and he must have been tried by a jury.

A reluctant King John signs the Magna Carta. This "Great Charter" recognized the rights of the nobility and the church—and thereby the limits of royal power.

Royal seals and noble coats of arms frame a copy of the Magna Carta. These decorative adornments symbolized the new power-sharing arrangements between the English people and their king.

The last thing King John wanted to do was sign this document. But the nobles demanded his consent or threatened civil war. Controlling his rage as best he could, John affixed the royal seal to the charter. It was done. Now the English nobles had rights that no one could take away from them, not even the king.

A year later, King John died. But the Magna Carta lived on. In fact, it helped change the English people's whole idea of justice and government.

At the time, the Magna Carta mostly benefited nobles and landholders. It barely mentioned the common people. But over the years, other Englishmen looked at the document and said, "If nobles have rights no king can take away, maybe the rest of us do, too." The Magna Carta paved the way for protecting the rights of all people living under a king.

After the Magna Carta, English kings had a much harder time ignoring the nobles and church leaders who came together in the Great Council to discuss government problems and help make laws. As time passed, English kings allowed lesser nobles, clergy, knights, and townspeople to send representatives to such councils. By the end of the thirteenth century, this council of nobles and representatives was known as the Parliament (PAHR-luh-muhnt). With Parliament, a grand idea was slowly taking shape in England, an idea with roots in ancient Greece, but until now neglected in medieval Europe—the idea that people should have a say in government.

Today the Magna Carta of 1215 is regarded as one of the great political documents of Western civilization. In many ways it is the cornerstone of modern constitutional government. The Magna Carta declared that the king could not be an all-powerful dictator. He had to rule within limits of the law. People had rights he must respect. With the passing of the centuries, these ideas would ripple across oceans and change the world.

The nobles who forced King John's hand at Runnymede took the first steps toward parliamentary government. In the painting above, Parliament's leaders gather around the empty English throne—a throne over which they now had more power.

Monarchs on the Rise

By the end of the Middle Ages, the old feudal structure was changing. The nobles—the many barons, dukes, and princes who filled castles throughout Europe—were still very strong. As we've seen, they often clashed with monarchs and even held them in check. But kings were gaining power and extending it over wider areas.

In England, William I and Henry II worked to create a powerful monarchy that they could pass on to their heirs. The same thing happened in France, and to some extent in Spain and other parts of Europe. Across much of the continent, monarchs and royal families strengthened their grip.

As the Middle Ages drew to an end, the power of the feudal lords declined. The age of isolated manors was passing away. Strong monarchies would help set the course for the evolution of Europe in the centuries to come.

Sails aloft, Emperor Yangdi's boat bobs at anchor. Yangdi was a Sui dynasty emperor of late sixth-century China.

China in the Middle Ages

The Middle Ages in Europe began as a time of uncertainty, danger, and division. Barbarian attacks splintered the aging Roman Empire. During the next thousand years, people looked for protection to the many feudal lords.

In parts of Europe, some strong monarchs did come to power, but in general, medieval Europe was a fractured continent ruled by many different kings, dukes, barons, and lords.

To the east, in China, something very different happened. The sixth century in China began, as it had in Europe, with relentless attacks from invaders to the north. But by the seventh century, a united empire was rising in eastern Asia. China emerged as the largest country in the world, a vast realm ruled by a strong centralized government. Under the Sui (sway), Tang (tahng), and Song (soong) dynasties, China cast a long shadow over much of Asia and the world beyond.

Looking Back

Do you remember Qin Shi Huangdi? He succeeded in uniting China and insisted on the title of Emperor. The name he took, Shi Huangdi, literally meant "First Emperor." By imposing new systems of standardized weights, currency, and writing, he did his best to unite his empire. By ordering the building of the Great Wall, Qin Shi Huangdi tried to protect his empire from invaders to the north.

After the First Emperor's death, his empire fell apart. But China was united again under the Han dynasty, which endured for more than 400 years. The Han prided themselves on following the teachings of the

This chapter focuses on medieval China, a great civilization of east Asia.

Two items that recall the opulence of Han-dynasty China—a painting of an elegant pavilion and a ceramic model of a watchtower that guarded the empire.

sage Confucius. They established a university in the capital for training government officials. The Han was a dynasty of innovation and trade. Merchants carried Han products—including silk, desired by many—along the Silk Road to Middle Eastern and Roman markets.

When the Han dynasty slipped from power in the third century A.D., China seemed to splinter into as many pieces as Europe. Just as the Roman Empire was pillaged by northern invaders, so China was ravaged by nomads from the north. Many different tribes roamed the northern parts of the empire. In time, some of these newcomers settled down and married the local Chinese.

A patchwork of small kingdoms sprang up in the north. These little kingdoms fought each other, but none was able to take charge. From all this chaos and conflict, however, a new empire would emerge.

The Sui Dynasty Reunites China

It began with one man, known to history as Wendi (wen-DEE). He vanquished his rivals and seized control in the north. But he wasn't content to stop there. By 581, the northern ruler had brought western regions under his control, and thus the Sui dynasty was born. Although this dynasty would last less than 40 years, it brought dramatic changes to China.

In 588, Sui dynasty forces launched a lightning attack on the south. They destroyed the southern capital, burning its palaces, temples, and homes. Then they plowed the city's land, dividing it into farmland. They tried to destroy all signs of a divided realm with two capitals.

With great energy, the Sui set about their task of uniting China. They tried to get people in the south on their side by distributing land to poor farmers. They built another capital called Chang'an (chahng-en) in the north of the country.

- On the map below, locate Chang'an. The modern name of the medieval capital is Xi'an (shee-ahn).

To unify China, the Sui also combined existing laws from north and south into a single legal code. They set up a national bureaucracy to carry out the wishes of the emperor. They returned to some Han ways, choosing many government officers on the basis of ability rather than birth, and using examinations to select some officials. The Sui tolerated different philosophies and religions in an attempt to unite people. They supported the teachings of Confucianism as well Buddhism, a religion that had spread from India to China.

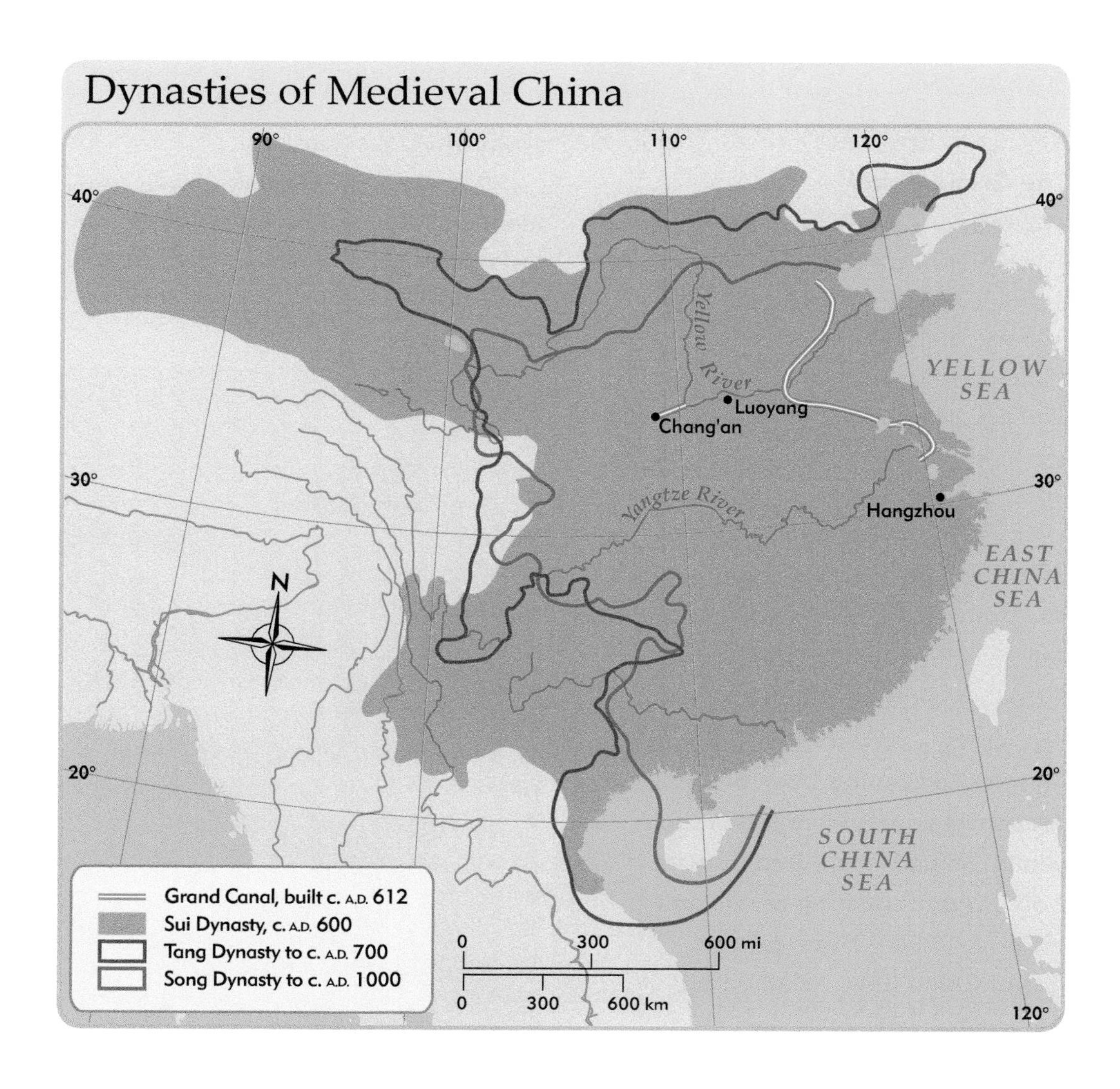

In this silk painting, Emperor Yangdi and his courtiers enjoy a horseback ride through the royal gardens.

The Grand Canal

The second Sui emperor, called Yangdi (YAHNG-dou), came to power in 604 and left a lasting mark on China's history. He was determined to complete the unification of the land. To do this, he knew he must make both north and south feel like one people.

Yangdi wanted to encourage communication, travel, and trade. Roads already connected his people. He decided to create another link—canals running between north and south.

The emperor's plans stunned government officials in the provinces. The Grand Canal system, as it was known, would join old canals to rivers and many new canals. It would connect China's two great rivers, the Yellow in the north and the Yangtze in the south. The canal system would have to cover a huge distance, about 1,200 miles in all.

Provincial officials complained that they would never be able to construct such a system. They predicted it would be a terrible waste of labor. The emperor refused to hear any criticism of his plans.

"You will build what I have commanded," he told the officials. "If you fail me, you will lose not just your jobs, but your lives."

What Is a Bureaucracy?

A bureaucracy is a group of officials who help run a government or some other organization. Bureaucrats—the members of a bureaucracy—perform many different functions, from making rules to keeping track of information. The word *bureaucracy* comes from the French word *bureau*, which means "office." The bureaucracies of some governments are huge, consisting of millions of officials. Since the days of Qin Shi Huangdi, the First Emperor, the rulers of China have relied on an extensive bureaucracy.

Tens of thousands of laborers were forced to work on the Grand Canal system—perhaps as many as had toiled on China's other great building project, the Great Wall. Thousands died in the effort.

By 611, the waterways were completed. Yangdi was right. This vast network of canals, known as the River of Transport, *did* link north and south. As many as 40,000 barges plied its waters, carrying grain from the rice-rich lands of the Yangtze to huge new granaries near Chang'an, the capital city. Imperial armies rode the canals on their way to campaigns along the empire's northern borders.

- On the map on page 573, locate the Grand Canal.

The emperor loved his canals. Periodically he took pleasure trips aboard his royal barge, a 200-foot-long canal boat in the shape of a snarling Chinese dragon. From the barge's fourth deck—at a height of 40 feet—he could survey the surrounding countryside. These trips gave the people of China a chance to see the emperor in his splendor, and they reinforced the idea of a united north and south.

Above: Small boats like this one were part of the royal flotilla that followed the emperor's barge along the Grand Canal.

Below: Modern-day barges continue to use canals that Yangdi built to unite China's north and south.

When Yangdi traveled, he traveled in style. Behind the royal barge bobbed thousands of smaller craft. These carried the emperor's attendants and servants in a flotilla that snaked along the canals for up to 65 miles.

Such extravagant spectacles left China's peasants with a strong impression of imperial might. But the emperor's achievements had come at a terrible price, and the people were tired and angry. When his armies encountered repeated defeats in the north, peasants across the empire began to rebel.

In 618, Yangdi was murdered by one of his own officials. His death brought the rule of the Sui to an end. The dynasty was short-lived, but it had brought unity to China, and changed the face of the land forever.

A Golden Age Under the Tang Dynasty

The year Yangdi died, an army general seized the capital and declared himself emperor. Thus began the Tang dynasty, which would rule for the next three centuries.

Under the Tang, China entered a golden age, a time of harmony, stability, and achievement. Government ran well under the Tang. They streamlined the imperial bureaucracy, cut the number of official posts, and sent government officials from region to region. These officers kept the emperor well informed about what was happening across the vast realm.

Meanwhile China's capital, Chang'an, grew to become the largest city in the world. It attracted merchants, adventurers, and religious pilgrims from Central Asia, Persia, and the Middle East.

The great walled capital stretched six miles from west to east and five from north to south. It boasted a population of about two million. Here were government buildings, two large street-markets, and the temples of five different religions. All were connected by great avenues that gave the city the look of a huge checkerboard. Some avenues were 500 feet wide. In New York City today, Fifth Avenue is only 100 feet wide.

In the bustling neighborhoods of Chang'an, blacksmiths, jewelers, potters, and seamstresses busied themselves making the luxury objects prized by the wealthy. And none had a greater taste for finery than the man who lived in the Great Luminous Palace—the imperial palace perched on a height called Dragon Head Plain, overlooking the rest of the city.

Known as "the Brilliant Emperor," Xuanzong (shoo-en-dzawng) ruled during the high point of China's golden age. To his court he brought the most gifted scholars, administrators, and writers of the land. From abroad came ambassadors, merchants, and religious leaders eager to pay tribute to the emperor.

Life at court was pleasant for the sons and daughters of the Tang dynasty. To entertain themselves, they threw daylong parties that featured troupes of acrobats, musicians,

Xuanzong was a man of many interests, among them horses. In this scroll painting, "the Brilliant Emperor" watches as one of his courtiers climbs onto his mount.

wrestlers, and dancers. To adorn themselves, they wore jewelry made from gold and silver. For sport they played polo, riding the most magnificent Persian steeds. And to cool off, they stood in front of mechanical fans that circulated ice-cooled air.

Under the Tang, the air at court resounded with poetry. All high imperial officials were expected to write and recite lines of verse. In fact, government examinations tested such abilities. One frequent subject of the poems was the parting of friends, which reflected a hard reality of life for officials who were routinely transferred to far-flung parts of the empire. The capital even had an academy for poets, set up by the man at the center of court life, Xuanzong, the Brilliant Emperor himself.

Let's take a trip in our imaginations back to the realm of the Brilliant Emperor.

The Brilliant Emperor's Daydreams

Imagining the Past

Standing on one of the overhanging balconies of the Great Luminous Palace, the emperor looked south across his city and smiled. The capital's thoroughfares spread out beneath him in a perfect grid, dividing Chang'an neatly into 109 neighborhoods.

"Just like the harmonious design of paradise," he thought. "A place for everything, and everything in its place."

The roofs of Buddhist temples, their eaves curling toward heaven, graced the city's skyline.

"All is as it should be," mused the emperor. "Just like my empire—all as it should be."

Absentmindedly, he reached for a porcelain wine pot that sat nearby. Over the centuries, Chinese potters had developed porcelain, a thin, hard, translucent ceramic. Their work was breathtaking. The vessels were intricately shaped and their surfaces decorated with the most delicate of carvings. If he held a piece of porcelain to the light, with a finger behind it, the emperor could see the outline of his own hand. This marvelous ceramic would one day be known for the land where it was first invented—Europeans would call it "china."

The emperor's hands ran over the wine pot—the lion's body that formed its handle, the monster's head that was its spout. Like the best of Tang porcelain, it was a beautiful creamy white.

A few lines of Chinese poetry came to the emperor's mind.

From a pot of wine among the flowers
I drank alone.
There was no one with me—
Till, raising my cup, I asked the bright moon
To bring me a shadow and make me three.

Looking out at the city again, the emperor's eyes found the city gates. Entering them each day were peasants eager to sell their wares in the markets. And exiting them, keen to escape the confines of the capital for the surrounding countryside, was often the person of the emperor himself.

On these outings he was accompanied by his current favorites among the palace ladies. Together they would recite the poetry the emperor had so encouraged. But not for him the too-familiar poems about friends parting. For these occasions, the emperor wanted words about the beauty of the landscape, or the beauty of the ladies at court. He wanted to hear the love stories that had become so popular, stories filled with tragedy, devotion, and despair.

Horses were another of the emperor's passions. He kept a troupe of dancing horses at court, as well as one of the great horse painters of the day.

Yes, for the Brilliant Emperor there was so much more to life than his obligation to rule the country. So many more things he could do with his time than occupy it with matters of state.

The emperor's belly gave a little rumble. Ah yes, food. That was another of his pleasures. His mind ran over some of his favorite dishes, a mouth-watering menu for the imperial palette. Perhaps steamed pork in garlic sauce. Or, again fingering the ceramic pot, wine-marinated white carp. Or a reliable favorite, dumplings, which came in the shapes of 24 different flowers. And of course, dessert—perhaps his favorite, flavored iced milk and rice.

A second rumble and the emperor turned away from the balcony. As he prepared to leave, he swiftly replaced the wine pot.

Crash!

The porcelain vessel tumbled to the ground and smashed into a hundred pieces.

The emperor winced. "How sad," he thought. "But they will make me another."

Little did Xuanzong know it, but his empire was heading toward a similar fate. The many pieces of China were far from "all as they should be." His realm was weakened by heavy taxation, by the luxury of palace life, and by forced labor and military service. Perhaps this leader had spent too much time enjoying court life and too little attending to his realm.

Xuanzong was overthrown by a rebellion. A bloody civil war followed, and the Tang dynasty managed to hang on to the throne. The Tang clung to power until 907, but by then the dynasty had little power left. Its glory was gone. Rebellion again threatened the state. Like the fine piece of china that fell from the emperor's hands, China itself was about to be smashed into pieces.

Portrait of a Song dynasty emperor.

The Inventive Song

After the fall of the Tang, local warlords fought each other for power. Law and order vanished. Finally, as so often happened in the course of Chinese history, a military leader seized power in the south and set up a stable government. Eventually north and south China were again united. By 960, a new dynasty had come to power. It was known as the Song.

Under the Song dynasty, China enjoyed another three centuries of relative peace and prosperity, even though the Song never reconquered the northern and western regions that the Tang had controlled. The Song rulers further refined the bureaucracy, which included more than 12,000 upper-level officials.

Each official was selected for his intellectual qualities and his understanding of the powerful moral principles of Confucianism—loyalty to authority, respect for family and traditions, and honorable behavior.

Growth was the order of the day in Song China. Trade grew and the economy boomed. Inventions abounded, such as the compass, gunpowder, paper money, and movable type. The food supply increased with the introduction of early ripening rice, which made it possible to grow two to three crops a year in the south. Cities mushroomed in size. By the early 1100s, the population of China, some 60 million when the Song came to power, had ballooned to 100 million.

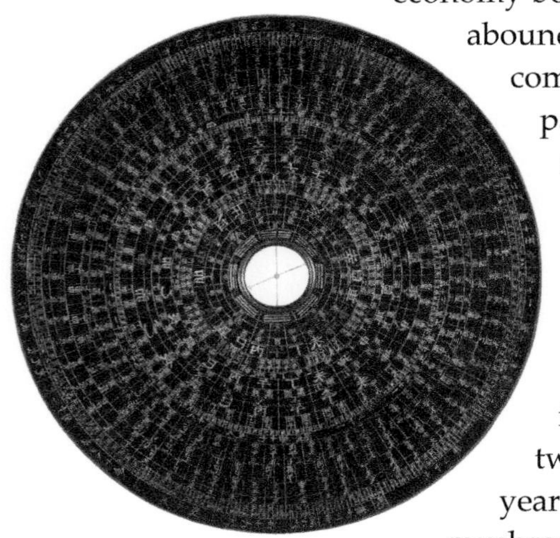

The compass was one of many Chinese inventions made during the Song dynasty. This wooden compass was used in the design of buildings.

Still, China was vulnerable to invaders from the north. The Song were aware of these threats, but they were equally aware of the danger of enlarging the army or increasing taxes. Further hardships for the peasants could again spur them to revolt. To keep the peace, the Song often negotiated treaties with northern tribal groups. These treaties usually required the wealthy Song to send payments to their northern neighbors.

Some Song emperors took seriously the ancient teachings of Confucius. Confucius had urged rulers not to overburden the peasants. "Approach your duties with reverence and be trustworthy in what you say," the great sage had advised. "Avoid excesses in expenditure and love your fellow men. Employ the labor of the common people only in the right seasons."

Other Song emperors, however, ignored Confucius' advice. Under their rule, China once again became vulnerable to conquest. In 1126, disaster struck when a wave of nomadic warriors, mounted on horses, charged down from the north.

The Imperial Dreamer

Unfortunately for China, the Song emperor at the time was not ready to meet the threat. Emperor Huizong (hwee-djoung) may have had many fine qualities, but preparing his country for war was not among them.

Like Xuanzong of the Tang dynasty, Huizong was more interested in the arts than in defense, more a poet than a warrior. He was also a painter, preferring to wield a paintbrush rather than a sword. "In my moments of leisure from the affairs of state," he declared, "I seek no other pleasure than painting."

This Imperial Dreamer, as he was known, founded China's first academy of painting and added drawing tests to the civil service exam. His own personal art collection numbered more than 6,000 works. Among them was a painting, attributed to the emperor himself, that showed 20 cranes circling over the imperial palace. Huizong had seen such a sight and had interpreted it as a positive omen, a sign of good fortune. But it did little to stop the invaders.

Faced with military defeat, Huizong left the throne in favor of one of his sons. But father and son were both taken prisoner and later died in captivity.

The rest of the Song retreated to the safety of the south, to the fertile land around the Yangtze River. There another of Huizong's sons managed to put together a southern empire, which prospered for more than a hundred years. In the early thirteenth century, however, a powerful new people emerged on the northern horizon—the Mongols (MAHNG-guls).

The mounted warriors were among the fiercest fighters ever known. They had already conquered Russia and Persia. Northern China trembled under their horses' thundering hooves. When Mongol conquerors pushed south, the Song were powerless to resist.

In 1279, the Song dynasty came to an end. For the first time in its history, as we'll see in the next chapter, all of China came under foreign rule.

Emperor Huizong probably painted this twelfth-century scroll. It shows court ladies in various stages of the preparation of silk.

Throughout the thirteenth century, mounted Mongol warriors spread terror from China in the east to Hungary and Poland in the west.

Mongols on the Move

"They have razed cities, cut down forests, overthrown fortresses, pulled up vines, destroyed gardens, killed townspeople and peasants," an alarmed European reported. These warriors, he went on to say, came riding "with the swiftness of lightning to the confines of Christendom, ravaging and slaughtering, striking everyone with terror and incomparable horror."

Who inspired such terror? The Vikings? No. Those words, written by an English monk in the 1200s, describe an even more fearsome threat—the Mongols, a band of newly united tribes from Asia.

During the thirteenth century, these mounted warriors burst from central Asia and conquered a huge empire. The disciplined Mongol troops pounded into northern China, and then rode on to vanquish the Song dynasty in the south. They charged into Muslim lands and slew the caliph in Baghdad. They thundered onto the plains of Russia and captured the city of Kiev. They threatened Constantinople and spread terror through Eastern Europe.

The Mongol Empire, which began its growth around 1207 and finally fell in 1368, was the largest land empire in history. It lasted only about 150 years, but it left its mark on the historical landscape—from China and Korea in the east to Persia and Russia in the west.

Mongolia's land and climate discouraged farming, so its people became horsemen and herders. As this photo shows, herding remains an important occupation.

Who Were the Mongols?

In east Asia, just north of China, lies the world's largest landlocked nation—Mongolia. Mongolia is a high land, most of it rising more than 3,000 feet. The air is thin and the growing season short. Much of the country is covered by grassy plains

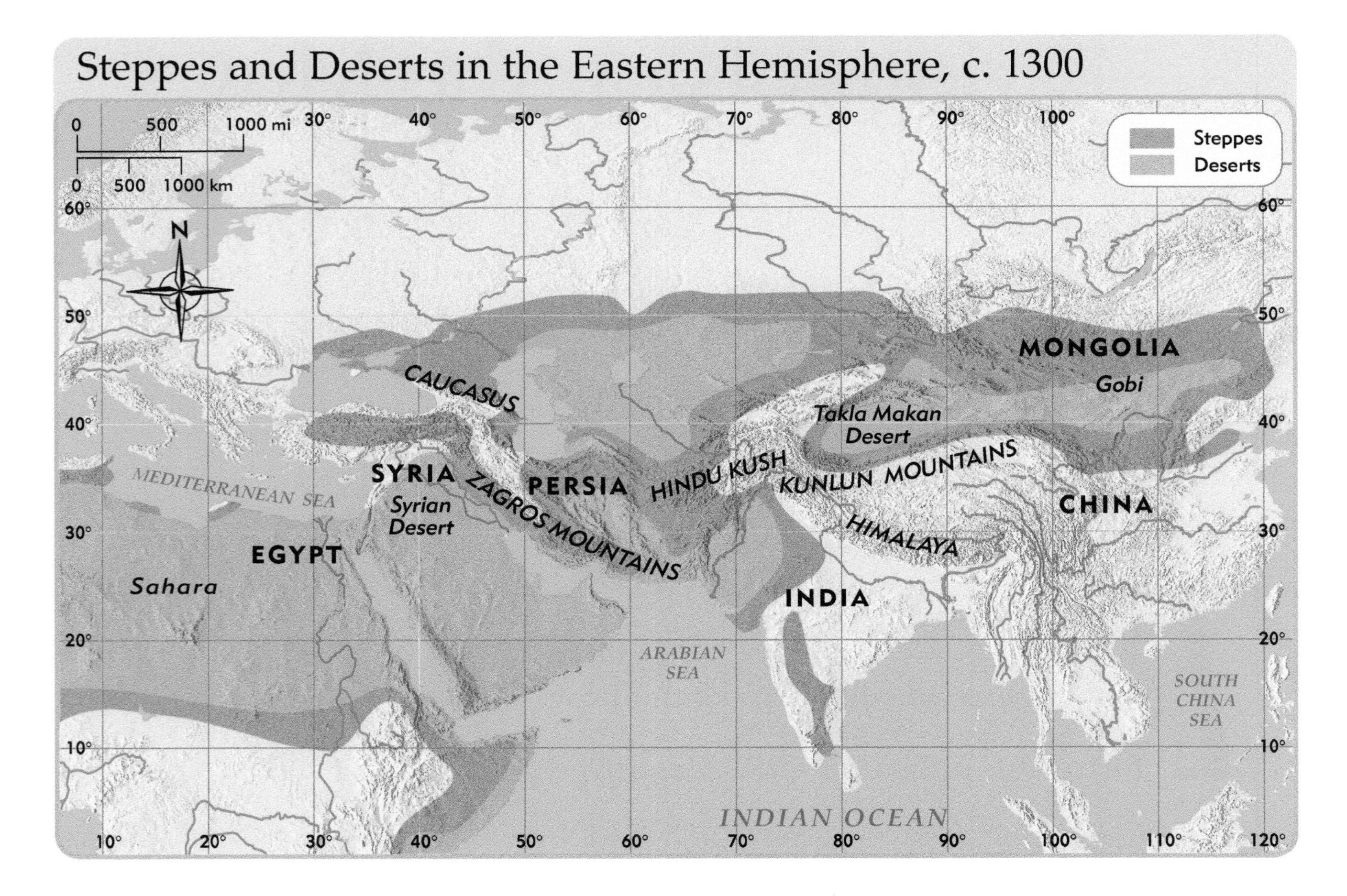

called steppes. The Gobi, a vast barren desert, blankets the southeast. Summers in Mongolia are short, the winters long and bitterly cold. Rainfall is scarce in most of the country. Throughout the year, winds blow ceaselessly across the treeless plains in this desolate land.

- On the map above, locate regions covered by steppe lands and desert.
- On a globe or world map, find the modern-day nation of Mongolia.

Mongolia has never been an easy place to live. The land and climate discourage farming, so the people who first inhabited the steppes became horsemen and herders. They tended sheep, camels, oxen, goats, ponies, and yaks. They were nomadic, moving with their herds and flocks over hundreds of miles from summer to winter pasturelands. For food they depended on the meat, cheese, and milk that their herds supplied.

The nomadic Mongols carried with them everything they owned. They even lashed their homes on the backs of pack animals or tossed them into oxcarts. These mobile dwellings, called *gers* (guhrs), were colorful round felt tents supported by wooden frames. The frames were easy to collapse and tote, and could be erected anywhere on the plains. The gers' thick sheets of felt, a sturdy cloth made of matted wool, shielded the Mongols from the unforgiving winds. Because of these dwellings, the Mongols were known to their neighbors as the "people of the felt tents."

Mongol families banded together in clans and tribes. Tribal members helped protect one another and manage the precious animals. Tribes guarded the rights to grazing grounds and often fought bitterly with enemy tribes.

To a people who moved from place to place, no animal was more important than the horse. Mongol horses were short-legged, muscular, and hardy. During severe Mongolian winters, they could break the crust of ice and snow with their hooves to forage for stunted winter grass.

A Mongol tribesman spent much of his life in the saddle. He moved his herds and family from the saddle, he hunted from the saddle, and he fought from the saddle.

Mongol horsemanship in warfare became legendary. The nomads of the steppe were among the first to use stirrups, which gave them a special advantage. Every Mongol boy learned to ride without holding the reins so he could use his bow and arrow at full gallop. There were few sights more terrifying than a band of Mongol warriors thundering across the steppes, firing their deadly arrows as they swept toward their enemies.

Genghis Khan Unites the Mongols

Around 1162, a baby boy was born on the windswept steppes. His father, the chief of a small Mongol tribe, named him Temujin (TEM-yuh-juhn), which means "made of iron."

When Temujin grew into a strong toddler, his father tied him to the saddle of a pony and taught him to ride. Later, Temujin learned to shoot arrows sure and straight as he hunted wild boar, wolves, and snow leopards. People observed that the youngster had fire in his eyes.

Temujin lived in a dangerous world. When he was still a boy, an enemy tribe poisoned his father. As the oldest son, Temujin inherited his father's position. The other families of the tribe had no desire to follow such a young chief, and they soon rode away, leaving the child, his brothers, and his mother to fend for themselves. "We have no companions except our own shadows," his mother warned.

The next several years were hard for Temujin and the few who stayed with him. They owned few sheep, camels, or horses. To survive,

Like this family gathered outside their felt tent, or ger, many Mongolians continue to lead nomadic lives.

Temujin is enthroned as ruler of the nomadic tribes of Mongolia. Later he was known as Genghis Khan, or "ruler of all men."

they had to catch fish, dig roots, and gather wild fruit. Temujin was resourceful and somehow held his little group together.

When he was about 14 or 15 years old, Temujin caught his half-brother stealing food. It is said that Temujin raised his bow and shot him through the heart. It was the kind of act that gave the broad-shouldered youth a reputation for ruthlessness.

Word spread among Mongol tribes that Temujin was a fierce and determined warrior, and soon he was attracting followers. He proved a master at organizing warrior tribes. Some had fought each other for generations. But when they joined Temujin, they put their differences aside and recognized him as their *khan* (kahn), or ruler.

The ambitious khan soon turned his warriors into an army. With this force he declared he would unite the nomadic tribes of Asia.

As his army grew he divided it into groups of tens, hundreds, thousands, and ten thousands. He chose the finest soldiers to lead each section. Wearing leather armor and thick silk undershirts, these horsemen fought pretend battles to sharpen their skills, just as knights fought tournaments in medieval Europe. They practiced firing arrows as they rode, often turning backward in the saddle and shooting with astonishing precision over their horses' tails. Temujin's troops became the most disciplined, loyal army on the Asian plains.

After many battles, Temujin succeeded in uniting many of Asia's nomadic tribes. In 1206, the tribe leaders met and chose him to be their Great Khan—the "Genghis Khan" (JEHNG-gihs KAHN), which means "ruler of all men."

Genghis Khan Sets Out to Conquer

Now that Genghis Khan had united the nomad tribes into a Mongol nation, what next? The "ruler of all men" turned his gaze toward China.

For years, nomads from the northern steppe had been nipping at the heels of the Chinese. As early as 214 B.C., China's first emperor, Qin Shi Huangdi, had ordered the building of the first Great Wall to fend off these tribes from the north. Later generations had strengthened the wall. But now, a thousand years later, under the Song dynasty, the Great Wall had fallen into disrepair. Genghis saw his chance.

The khan's warriors swept into northern China. There they found many well-fortified towns. Mongol warriors, accustomed to making lightning raids, now learned to use siege towers, scaling ladders, and catapults. In 1215—the same year King John signed the Magna Carta in England—Genghis Khan forced the city now called Beijing (bay-zhing) to surrender. The Mongol army marched through its gates and plundered the city. For weeks, cartloads of gold, silk, and jewels snaked in a triumphant caravan to Genghis's camp. He was now master of much of China.

Genghis Khan next turned west, toward the glittering cities of the Islamic Empire. Galloping across Muslim regions of Asia, his troops left destruction in their wake. They swept into Persia—lands now in Afghanistan and eastern Iran—and slaughtered tens of thousands. They demolished cities that for centuries had been centers of wealth and luxury along the great Silk Road. They even burned and destroyed the tombs of their enemies.

Genghis Khan used terror as a weapon. When he approached a city, he usually gave the inhabitants a choice—surrender or die. If they opened their gates, the Mongols would ride off with whatever food, treasures, and slaves they wanted. If the gates remained closed, the Mongol warriors would kill everyone within the city walls.

People trembled at the thought of Genghis Khan. Rumors of his cruelty flew before his army: "His warriors eat humans. His horses are big enough to eat trees. He leads an army of demons who ride on the wind!"

In 1223, Genghis's army headed for home, charging through the steppes of Russia on the way. The Mongols took the Russians completely by surprise. The writer of one Russian chronicle stated, "For our sins, unknown tribes came, whom no one exactly knows who they are, nor whence they came, nor what their faith is." The Russians called these unknown marauders Tartars.

Back in Mongolia, the aging conqueror decided to send his army once again into China. But one day in 1227, he was thrown from his horse while hunting. He lay dying for several days. Even then, his mind dwelt on war. "As long as I am still alive, keep up the slaughter," he decreed.

This fourteenth-century painting depicts Genghis Khan's Mongol horsemen fighting in the mountains of China.

Within days, the Great Khan was dead. His warriors placed his body inside a ger mounted on a huge oxcart and carried it hundreds of miles, back to the land of his birth. According to some reports, they killed everyone they met along the way. They placed the body in a secret mountain grave, which the forest eventually covered.

Genghis Khan almost lived up to his name as "ruler of all men." He had brought all the nomadic tribes together as one Mongol nation. And he had conquered more territory than any other man in all of history.

- On the map at right, locate the Mongol Empire under Genghis Khan.

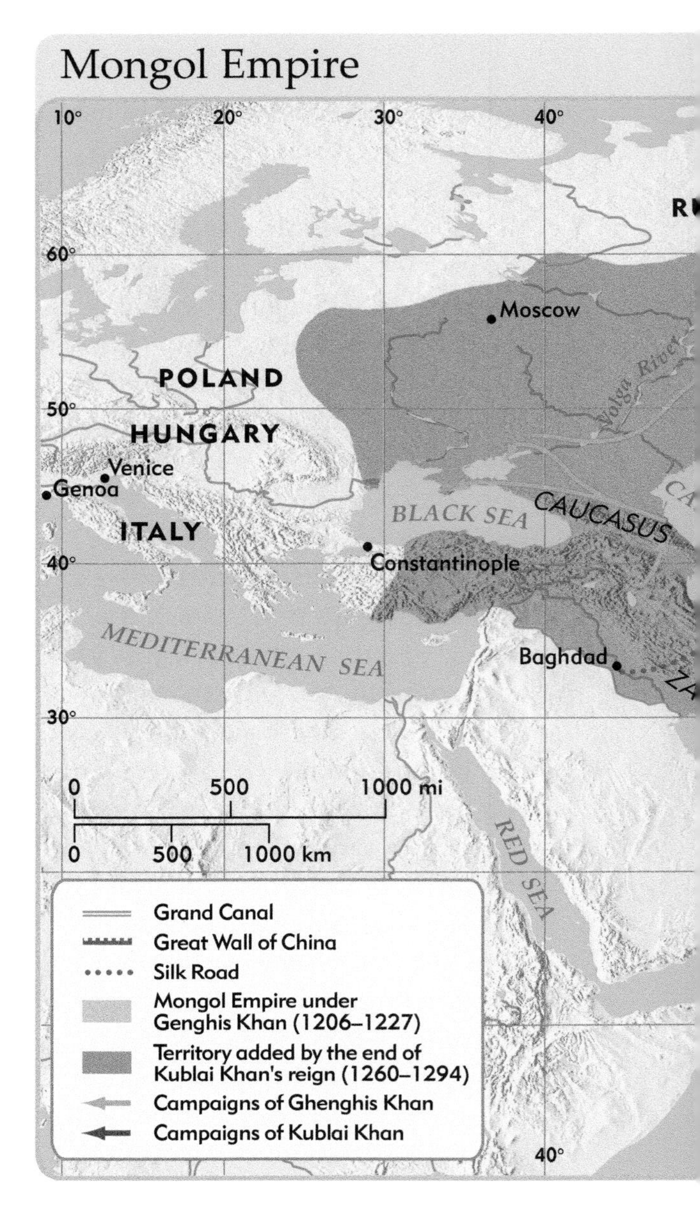

Kublai Khan: Conqueror and Builder

After Genghis died, his sons and grandsons launched more waves of conquest. They captured the small country of Korea on Asia's east coast. They smashed into Eastern Europe, easily defeating armies of knights in Hungary and Poland. They pillaged their way through Muslim lands of the Middle East, looting mosques and destroying rare books and countless works of art. In 1258, Mongols sacked the city of Baghdad and executed the caliph.

Kublai Khan, the grandson of Genghis Khan.

But Southern China, under the brilliant Song dynasty, still lay unconquered. It gleamed like a polished jade stone, waiting to be taken. That task fell to Kublai Khan (KOO-bluh KAHN), grandson of Genghis Khan, who became the ruler of the Mongol Empire in 1260.

Kublai Khan and his armies swarmed into the land south of the

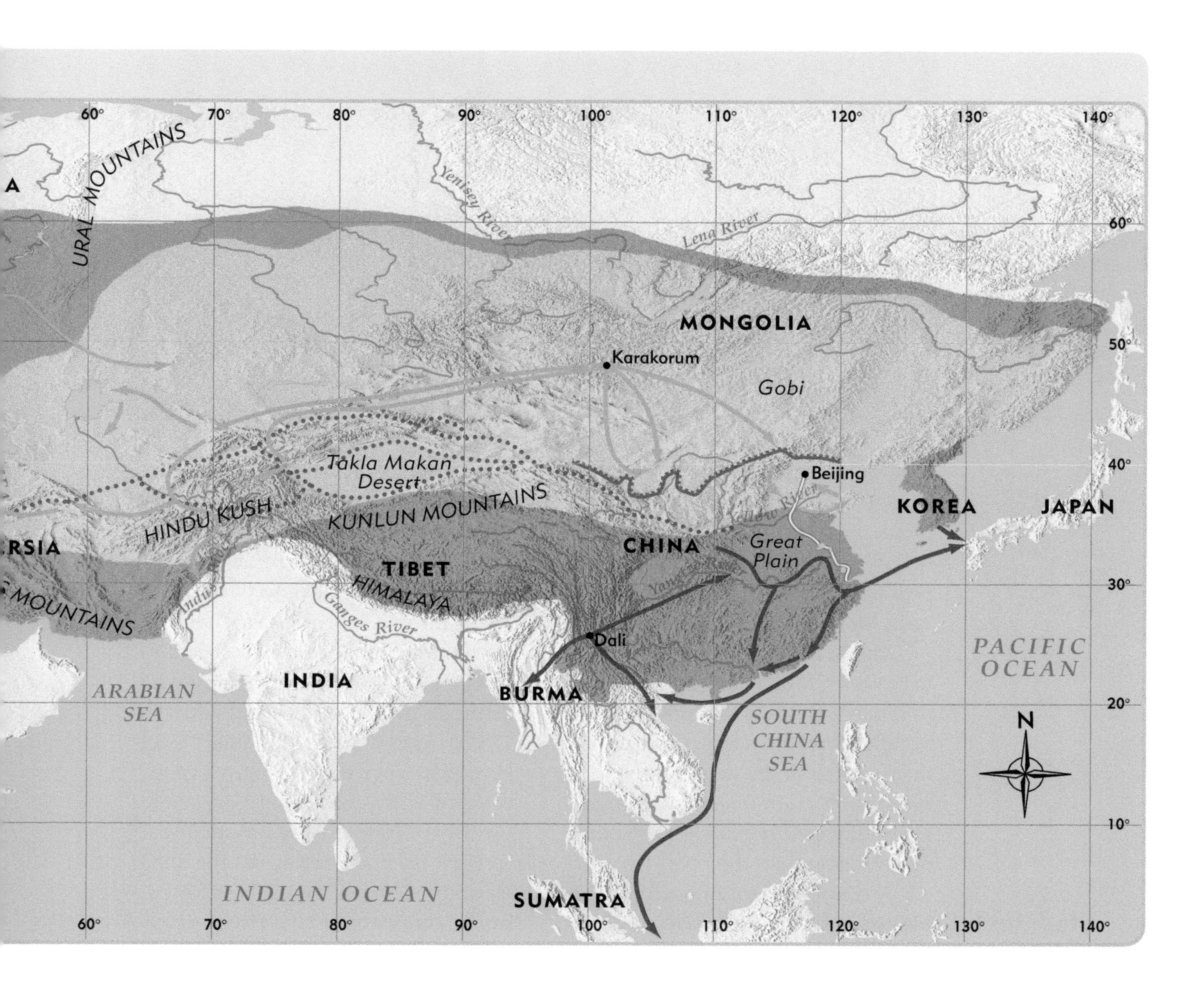

Yangtze River. By 1279, he had completed the conquest of China and ruled over the largest land empire in all of history.

- On the map above, locate the Mongol Empire under Kublai Khan.

Now that Kublai Khan was master of China, he had to think about how to rule so many people. His advisors told him, "You can conquer an empire on horseback, but you cannot govern it on horseback."

So Kublai Khan put away his soldier's armor and put on the robes of an emperor. As emperor of China, he founded a new Mongol dynasty called the Yuan (you-EN). Kublai Khan even moved the Mongol capital from central Asia to the city in China now called Beijing.

Not far from the capital, Kublai Khan built a fabulous summer palace called Shangdu (shahng-dh). There ten thousand soldiers kept guard. Paintings of birds and war scenes decorated the walls in jewel-like colors.

This fanciful European depiction of Kublai Khan hunting shows the great Mongol leader astride a horse, accompanied by a "hunting leopard," or cheetah. Marco Polo said Kublai Khan kept hundreds of cheetahs to help him on the hunt.

Close to the palace was a hill where Kublai Khan's gardeners planted the rarest, most beautiful trees in the world. A lake teeming with carp sparkled near the khan's stables, which had stalls for a thousand white horses.

Kublai Khan set to work trying to restore China from the ravages of so much war. He had Chinese workers build and repair roads. His engineers made the Grand Canal longer, bringing it all the way to Beijing. He established hospitals and some programs to help the poor.

A small Mongol minority ruled millions of Chinese subjects, so the emperor realized that he must accept some differences among his people. Under the Yuan dynasty, followers of Buddha, Confucius, and Muhammad lived side by side.

In general, Kublai Khan ruled with energy and wisdom. He invited wise men from Asia, Arabia, and Europe to help him rule his empire. He allowed traders, pilgrims, teachers, and artists to travel to China on the Silk Road. Workers built towers for observing the stars. Scholars went to work in libraries and observatories. The emperor encouraged people to become painters, writers, and calligraphers.

But Kublai Khan also made some unwise choices. Mongols living in China received special treatment. They got the biggest and best of everything, and they did not have to pay taxes. Three times a year, Kublai Khan gave them brand-new leather boots from Russia. And when he threw a birthday party for himself, he invited 12,000 high-ranking Mongols. To celebrate, he gave each of them a robe covered with jewels worth a fortune.

Most Chinese were not treated so well. Back in the days of the Song dynasty, Chinese candidates for public office could take civil service examinations, and if they passed, they could work at good jobs in the government. But Kublai Khan didn't want Chinese advisors, so he ignored the civil service exams. Instead, he hired Mongols and other foreigners to help him rule and write new laws. As for the Chinese, many had to leave their jobs and farms to work for the Mongols. They were forced to repair roads, build palaces, lengthen the Grand Canal, and pay all the taxes in China. The Chinese had never been conquered by a foreign people before, and they resented their Mongol rulers.

The End of the Mongol Empire

Kublai Khan died in 1294, and almost at once the Mongol Empire began to break into smaller parts. It was simply too vast to remain in one piece for very long.

The Mongols were fearless warriors, but they had less experience when it came to running governments. A revolution in China ended the Yuan dynasty in 1368 and put Chinese emperors back on the throne. While Mongol rulers would dominate parts of Asia for years to come, their huge empire had collapsed.

The Mongols were among the most savage conquerors in history. Genghis Khan and his successors left a trail of wreckage and terror behind them. Yet the huge Mongol Empire did increase encounters between different peoples, forcing them into contact with each other. Mongol rulers built roads to connect eastern Asia with Russia and Persia. Important Chinese inventions—gunpowder, paper, printing, and the compass—came to the West from China during the age of the khans. In Kublai Khan's time, merchants journeyed along an improved Silk Road between China and Europe.

Marco Polo Tells His Tale

One famous European merchant made Kublai Khan, the Mongol Empire, and China itself known to the West. His name was Marco Polo.

Polo was from the Italian city of Venice. In 1271, this 17-year-old boy set off with his father and uncle on a trading expedition. A few years later the young man and his party were guests of Kublai Khan at his summer palace in Shangdu.

The khan quickly recognized the talent of the Polos. Marco could speak several languages, and Kublai Khan hired him as a government official. Marco Polo would not return to Europe for 24 years.

When Marco Polo finally went home, he found Venice at war with its great rival, the Italian city-state of Genoa. Venice needed all available men, and Marco took command of a war galley. During a battle in the Adriatic Sea in September 1296, the Genoese captured him and held him prisoner.

What seemed like a terrible fate proved a wonderful opportunity. Bored prisoners passed long hours telling each other the stories of their lives. And none had a life story to tell quite like Marco Polo. For a year he shared his tales and his confinement with another Italian prisoner, a one-time professional writer named Rustichello (rus-tee-CHEH-loh).

Let's imagine we can eavesdrop on Marco Polo and Rustichello in their prison cell as they chat into the wee hours of the night.

"Seek knowledge even unto China."

These words were spoken by Muhammad, and his followers took him seriously. Muslim merchants and warriors rode east during the age of the khans. Eventually they brought Chinese prisoners back to Baghdad, who taught the Muslims how to make paper.

Paper banknote from China.

An Italian Adventurer at the Court of Kublai Khan

Imagining the Past

"Ah, Rustichello, my dreams are never as entertaining as my memories. You have no idea."

"Let me guess," said Rustichello. "Travels across desert sands and through snow-filled mountain passes."

Marco Polo raised an eyebrow. Maybe he had told this story once too often, but he never tired of repeating it. "Yes, travels on foot, on camel, and on horseback, even on the back of that magnificent long-horned creature, the yak. All the way to the ends of the earth and the court of the great Kublai Khan."

Rustichello was a good sport, and besides, what else was there to do throughout the long night? "Tell me more," he said encouragingly.

"A quarter century of sights! Past Mount Ararat (AIR-uh-rat) in Armenia, where they say Noah's ark came to rest after the Great Flood. Across the remote 'Roof of the World' in Afghanistan, where it was so cold our fires gave off no heat at all. And through the terrible Gobi, a desert filled with eerie spirit voices, which, our guides assured us, existed only in our minds."

A fifteenth-century European painting shows the Italian explorer Marco Polo on his journey home from the court of Kublai Khan. Here he arrives in Arabia after crossing the Indian Ocean.

"Marco, tell me again about Kublai Khan."

"Ah, yes," Marco responded. "The mightiest man in the world."

Rustichello looked skeptical.

"That's no exaggeration, my friend," Marco insisted. "Mightiest in number of subjects, mightiest in extent of his territory, and mightiest in amount of treasure. Three years we had been traveling to meet the Great Khan—three *grueling* years. And then, to be ushered into the imperial summer palace in Shangdu! Well, it was almost more than I could take in. The thought of it still leaves me breathless."

Marco described the summer palace—its marble walls inlaid with gold and silver, and its ceilings encrusted with rubies, amethysts, and diamonds. He regaled his friend with tales of Shangdu and of the city that lay beyond the palace walls, home to more than 100,000 people. From Shangdu, the roads led to all corners of China, each thoroughfare lined with shade trees planted at Kublai Khan's command. To bring the khan news from the most distant provinces of the empire, messengers galloped down these roads, using a relay system involving thousands of horses.

"The palace might be magnificent, and the city splendid. But most impressive of all is the great Kublai Khan himself," Marco said. "You can tell from the look in his keen eyes that he is interested in everything and has an intelligence to match anyone in his kingdom. On the day we met him he bade us welcome, and that night he gave a great banquet in our honor. For the first time in my life I ate from plates made of gold and drank from golden goblets, while fire-eaters, acrobats, and jugglers performed for our pleasure.

"I quickly learned not to drink while the khan was drinking. Each time he brought the wine to his lips, musicians would begin to play their instruments. At that signal, everyone knelt and bowed their heads to the floor until the emperor finished drinking."

"But," Rustichello interrupted, "I still don't understand how you got a job working for the khan."

Marco smiled at the recollection. "Well, I took an immediate liking to him," he explained. "And I think he felt the same about me. One day he told me he needed someone with good eyes and ears, and one who could learn languages quickly. Someone trustworthy and unafraid to face dangers."

And so it was that the Great Khan hired the young Venetian. "For the next 17 years," Marco Polo mused aloud, "I served as an envoy of the khan, traveling to the far corners of the Mongol empire, finding out what was going on all over the realm and reporting back to the emperor."

Sometimes Marco traveled with his father and uncle, and sometimes he traveled without them. During his travels he passed through many great cities. One, he claimed, had 12,000 bridges, most of them made of stone, and as many as three million inhabitants.

"In this city," said Marco to Rustichello, "for reasons of hygiene and health, the people take baths at least three times a week, and in winter every day. Every day! They heat the water with black stones that they dig out of the mountain. These black stones burn better than the wood we use in Europe; even unattended, their fires can burn from evening right through to morning."

Marco shivered at the chill night air before going on.

"And I discovered something else we don't have—paper money. That's right. They use thin, clothlike pieces of paper stamped with the Great Khan's seal on it, and they carry this around instead of bags full of gold coins. Not only is a bag of this paper money *lighter* than a bag of Venetian ducats, it's worth more, too."

By this time, Rustichello was having his own thoughts about the value of paper—paper with words on it that would tell Marco's amazing story.

But the Venetian was talking again.

"In the emperor's service, I traveled to neighboring lands that had more recently fallen to Mongol rule. To the west lies Tibet, a mysterious mountain region, the home of magicians said to possess strange powers. The emperor keeps some of these magicians in Shangdu, where they use spells to try to drive away rain-clouds so that the weather around the palace is always fine."

"To the south are the jungles of Burma and Bengal, inhabited by elephants and tigers and equally dangerous warrior-kings. Ah, my friend," Marco sighed, "the things I saw on my travels, you can't even imagine."

Rustichello listened as Marco went on to describe the unimaginable—in India, a nut as big as his head, filled with milk and sweet meat. And something that looked like it would find *him* just as tasty as he had found the nut—a huge serpent with short legs, knife-sharp teeth, and jaws wide enough to swallow a man.

In Sumatra, there was that great ugly brute as heavy as an elephant and with a single horn sticking right out of its forehead, like a unicorn. And brown hairy animals that looked like men with tails, odd creatures with hands and feet, such that at first he had expected them to open their mouths and talk.

"Ah, the sights I've seen, my dear Rustichello, the sights I've seen. For nearly 20 years I traveled across the length and breadth of the Mongol empire—observing, making notes, asking questions, recording the wonders of the East."

"What a pity you don't write all these things down in a book," replied Rustichello. "Otherwise they'll be lost to the world."

Marco was not so sure. "No one would believe me," he despaired. "They'll say I'm a liar—or a crazy man. I'll never be able to tell even the half of what I saw."

"But no one else has seen all you've seen, Marco," persisted Rustichello. "Come—tell me more."

Rustichello's arguments won the day. He convinced Marco to collaborate with him in writing a book about his experiences. A skilled writer of romances, particularly of tales about King Arthur and the Round Table, Rustichello understood the value of Marco's stories. Romance, adventure, and excitement—the stories had it all. He persuaded Marco to send for the notes of his travels, which he had safely stored in his Venice home. Then the two men set about their task, Marco dictating, Rustichello writing.

By the time Marco was freed from arrest, the book was complete. In *A Description of the World*, Marco described the places he had visited and the wonders he had seen—the burning black stones (coal), the nuts the size of a man's head (coconuts), the unicorn of Sumatra (a rhinoceros), the manlike animals with tails (orangutans), and the short-legged serpent (a crocodile).

The book became wildly popular in the Middle Ages. It was reprinted over and over again, and continued to enthrall readers in later centuries.

Among the most famous readers of the book was the explorer Christopher Columbus. Columbus's copy of the book was filled with notes written in his own hand in the margins. Using the book as one of his guides, Columbus set sail from Spain in 1492, hoping to reach the lands that Marco Polo had described—to make it to China by sailing across the Atlantic, to reach the East by sailing west.

But that, as they say, is another story.

An elderly Marco Polo reflects on his travels in the lands of Asia.

War raged in Europe during much of the 1300s—the so-called calamitous fourteenth century. Here English soldiers attack a French city.

Europe's Calamitous Fourteenth Century

As the fourteenth century dawned, medieval Europe seemed ready to thrive. The 1200s had been good years for agriculture. There was plenty of food to support more people. There were more towns and cities in which to live, work, and do business. European merchants, such as Marco Polo and his family, had extended trade to far-off lands. Venice, Marco Polo's home, and Genoa, its neighbor and rival, now claimed trading posts as far away as the Black Sea.

In some parts of Europe strong monarchs had taken charge, bringing order and even some safety to once unruly realms. Across the continent, the Christian Church provided a common bond of faith. It also inspired great works of art, such as the magnificent cathedral of Notre Dame that rose in Paris. When Marco Polo returned to Venice in 1295, he had a right to be optimistic about the future.

Instead, Europe was on the verge of what some historians have dubbed "the calamitous fourteenth century." It began with famine. For three years starting in 1315, crops failed all over Europe, and in many towns about one tenth of the population perished. Then came a century of war between England and France. Then a terrible plague struck. Death stalked the continent, felling rich and poor alike. As the Middle Ages drew to a close, it seemed to many as though the world itself might be ending.

This chapter focuses on medieval Europe.

The Hundred Years' War

By 1337, two decades of famine had taken their toll on England and France. Now war broke out between the two European monarchies. The deadly conflict would continue, on and off, until 1453. Though it lasted more than a century, we now call this conflict the Hundred Years' War.

This Anglo-French war was a fight over land and honor. Since Norman times, the English had held provinces in France. The French king wanted control of that territory. The English king, on the other hand, made claims to the French throne. Both sides were eager to defend their honor and, in a world threatened by famine, their valued land.

As in previous wars, the French continued to rely on armored knights. These warriors were almost invincible fighting machines. Their protective armor had grown heavier during the Middle Ages. Even horses rode into battle wearing chain mail.

But the great battles of the Hundred Years' War would not be won by mounted knights. Much of the glory would be garnered by lowly English peasants armed with—of all things—bows and arrows.

In England, King Edward I had learned the value of infantry (foot soldiers) during the 1200s. His troops had battled Welsh archers who used long, powerful bows to shoot arrows tipped with four-sided spikes. These spiked arrows could pierce armor. The English adopted the weapon and made the bow even longer and more deadly. By the time war with France began, the English had developed an infantry skilled at fighting with the English longbow. But could peasants wielding longbows stand up to an army of medieval knights?

In 1346, the English and French armies faced each other at the Battle of Crécy (kray-SEE) in northern France. When the French knights saw the smaller English force assembled at the crest of a hill, they immediately mounted their war horses and charged. The English expected just such an attack. In the middle of the English line, dismounted knights and men wielding pikes awaited the

English peasants armed with powerful longbows battle French knights at the Battle of Crécy.

French onslaught. On the flanks, wearing caps and sleeveless leather jackets, stood peasant archers with their six-foot longbows.

As French knights pounded up the hill, the English bowmen rained arrows on them—by some estimates as many as 48,000 per minute. From a hundred yards and more, the slim English arrowheads wounded knights and killed horses; from closer range, they punched right through the knights' armor.

The few horsemen who pounded through the English lines were quickly dispatched by the foot soldiers of King Edward III. But the French kept coming. In charge after charge—some 15 or 16 in all—the knights valiantly attacked. Each charge ended in disastrous defeat. When the French army fled from the field, the exhausted archers dropped their weapons and slept where they had fought.

After Crécy, more victories followed for the English. In 1356, led by Edward III's son, the "Black Prince," the English captured the French king at Poitiers (pwaw-tyay). Then they moved on to Paris. But the French did not lose hope.

Edward, the Black Prince

The eldest son of King Edward III, also named Edward, fought against the French at Crécy, Orléans, and Poitiers. He was one of England's finest commanders. The French dubbed him "the Black Prince" when they saw his black armor. The Black Prince was feared by the French for his battle prowess and admired by the English for his valor and chivalry. He became ruler of Aquitaine and for a while established a splendid court at Bordeaux (bor-DOH) in France. He died a year before his father. The Black Prince's son, Richard, succeeded Edward III as king of England.

Above: The French peasant girl Joan of Arc holds a sword and wears the armor of a knight.

Below: Beneath flying banners, young Joan greets King Charles and asks for his permission to lead a French army against the English.

Joan Leads and France Triumphs

Some 90 years into the on-again, off-again Hundred Years' War, a French peasant girl named Joan of Arc set out to save her land. She claimed that heavenly voices told her she should lead French troops against the English. "God sent a voice to guide me," the maid explained.

Joan traveled to southern France and managed to obtain an audience with Charles, who would soon become king of France. She persuaded the young Charles that God had called her to lead the French into battle. Donning the armor of a knight and brandishing the banner of a lily, Joan won battle after battle.

In 1429, her army routed English invaders at the city of Orléans (or-lay-AHN). Joan's forces then defeated the enemy along the Loire (lwahr) River. Charles, impressed by Joan's triumphs, insisted that she be at his side as he was crowned king of France.

Joan next marched on the French capital of Paris, which the English occupied. Her attack failed, however, and a few months later the maid-turned-warrior fell into enemy hands. The English used Church courts to try her for heresy, that is, for actions contrary to the teachings of the Church. Since Joan had claimed to hear voices, the English accused her of being a witch. The court convicted the French heroine. In the little town of Rouen (rou-AHN), the English burned her at the stake.

But the French did not forget Joan. In fact, her memory helped bring them together as one people. Inspired by her example, they continued to win battles.

As the fighting dragged on, both sides grew weary of a war that had lasted much longer than anyone could have imagined. Fortunes had been wasted, and many lives lost in the conflict.

By 1453, most of the fighting had ended. England lost all its territory on the continent of Europe, except for the port of Calais (ka-LAY) in France. The Hundred Years' War was finally over. But in the meantime, another disaster had struck. A deadly plague was ravaging Europe.

The citizens of a medieval town bury victims of the Black Death in the year 1349. The plague swept across Europe and was especially deadly in cities.

The Black Death

In October 1347, ten years after the start of the Hundred Years' War, a Genoese merchant ship docked at Messina (meh-SEE-nah) in Sicily. It had set sail from a port on the Black Sea that specialized in overland trade from China. Dying oarsmen pulled at the vessel's oars. The ill-fated ship carried not only silk and porcelain but also a hidden, deadly cargo.

When the ship docked, the townspeople of Messina were horrified at the sight of the desperately ill sailors. One after another, the sailors began to die. Terrified of catching their disease, the Sicilians drove the vessel back to sea. Historians think that before the ship left Messina, rats had scurried down the mooring ropes tied to the docks. The rats were infested with fleas that probably carried a highly contagious disease.

Within weeks, people all over the island of Sicily were dying of the plague. Three months later, the plague spread to mainland Italy. By the next year, it had reached Spain, France, and England. In 1349, an English wool ship, its crew all dead, drifted ashore in Norway. The plague had reached Scandinavia. Soon the remotest villages in Europe felt its effects.

The Black Death, as this plague is known, was an unpredictable killer. Some victims went to bed in seemingly perfect health and were dead by morning. Others suffered for up to a week before dying. Among the first signs of infection were black boils on the body, from which the disease got its name. Other symptoms of the Black Death included aches and chills, strained breathing, and bouts of coughing and sneezing.

How the Plague Spread from Asia to Europe

The plague that devastated Europe began in Asia. Eager to gain treasure and a port, Mongol forces attacked the Genoese trading post of Caffa on the Black Sea. The Mongols were ruthless in pursuit of victory. They lobbed plague-infested corpses over the city walls to spread the deadly disease. When Genoese merchants returned from Caffa to Europe, they brought the Black Death with them.

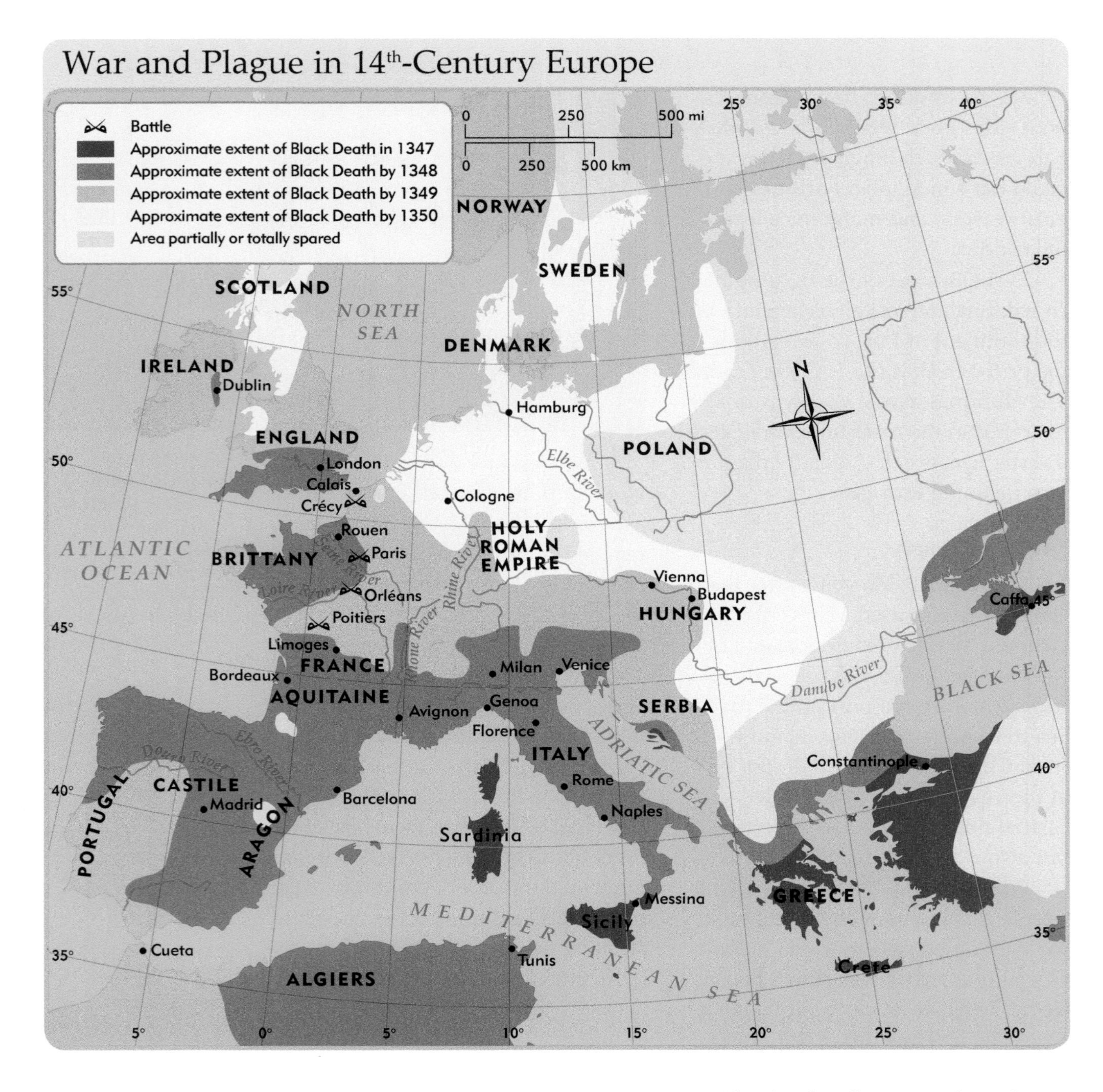

What Was the Black Death?

Historians and scientists are still puzzled by how quickly the plague spread. Was the Black Death carried by fleas in rats, or was it a rapidly spreading type of pneumonia, or something else? Experts do not know for sure. They do know that the Black Death devastated Europe, killing perhaps twenty-five million people by 1400.

The death toll mounted. In the countryside, so many peasants perished that the old social order of life on the manor began to fall apart. As labor grew scarcer, peasants left their lord's land and moved to cities in search of higher wages. But the plague was even worse in the overcrowded cities, where the disease spread like wildfire. In one five-month period alone, 96,000 people died in the Italian city-state of Florence. In London, Avignon, Paris, and many other cities, the living struggled to bury so many dead.

Science in the fourteenth century was not advanced enough to understand, much less cure, the plague. European universities had encouraged the study of theology, philosophy, and law, but knowledge of biology and natural science lagged. Scholars and doctors could not explain the plague's causes, and their medicine was powerless to stop it. In this Age of Faith, most people simply believed they were experiencing God's judgment on the sins of the world.

By the early 1350s, the Black Death had passed its peak, but there were further outbreaks in the following decades. Estimates of Europe's dead range from a third to a half of the population. No cure was ever found, and the reason for the disappearance of Europe's worst natural disaster remains unclear.

The End of an Era and the Start of Something New

The horrible famine, wars, and plague that struck Europe in the fourteenth century shook the foundations of medieval society. All this misery brought great change—some of it, surprisingly, for the better.

By the end of the century, the once-tight grip that lords held on serfs was loosening. So many people had died that there was a shortage of laborers who could plant crops and cultivate fields. Because the peasants were needed, they could demand higher wages. Serfdom in Western Europe was on its way out. A new prosperous class of peasant farmers was on the rise.

The plague wiped out many towns, but in the towns that remained, artisans often prospered. With all sorts of labor in demand, skilled craftsmen such as carpenters, stonemasons, and tailors could more easily find work.

As the Black Death disappeared, European cities showed signs of new life, particularly in northern Italy. Universities, often the beating heart of these cities, continued to emphasize the study of theology and philosophy, but the plague had changed things. Scholars now wanted to know more about the physical causes of the disease. They took new interest in medicine and the natural sciences. Important works from Muslim libraries were being translated and making their way to Europe. The writings of Aristotle and of the Muslim physician Ibn Sina were translated and studied with new urgency.

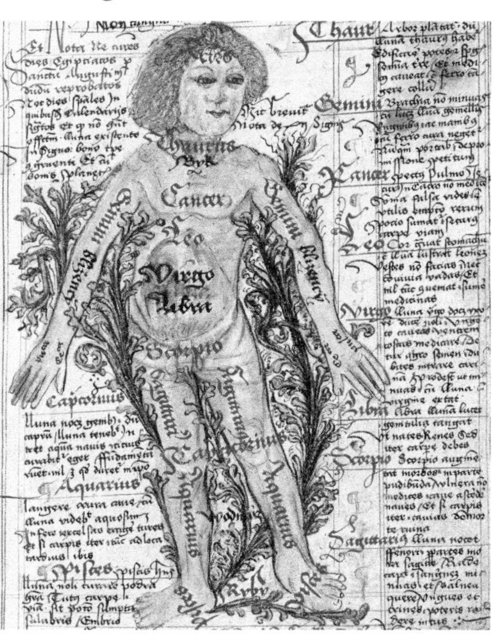

After the Black Death, scholars began to search for the physical causes of illness and disease. Despite their new interest in the body, they were still looking heavenward. This fifteenth-century manuscript examines the stars' influence on the illnesses of the human body.

In Europe, something new was in the air. The Christian Church was still strong. Faith was still a very important part of life for most people. The art and music of the time remained largely religious. But the calamitous fourteenth century was giving way to a time of new ideas, interests, and efforts. As the fifteenth century dawned, Europe seemed ready for a renewal, a rebirth.

Part 4, Conclusion

A: Chinese stoneware figures from about A.D. *600.*

B: The mosque known as the Dome of the Rock, in Jerusalem.

C: Stained-glass windows, Chartres Cathedral.

D: Muslim pilgrims en route to Mecca.

Not So "Medieval"

If you use a computer and word processor, then you might look at an old typewriter and say, "That's positively medieval." Nowadays, to call something "medieval" is to suggest that it's out of date and irrelevant. But you know that the medieval era—the thousand-year period from the fifth to the fourteenth centuries that we call the Middle Ages—has left a lasting legacy. Indeed, the Middle Ages make up one of the important foundations upon which we have built our modern world.

It's true that the period did not begin well. In much of the world, the early part of the Middle Ages was a dark and dangerous time. In Europe, barbarian tribes stormed the former Roman Empire. In Arabia, nomadic clans warred with each other. In Africa, warriors fought for dominance. In the east, China's once-powerful Han dynasty fell, leaving a fragmented collection of kingdoms.

Yet sparks of hope flickered in the darkness. In time, they kindled into an age of faith and a time of artistic creativity. Let's look back at some of the brighter medieval moments.

Byzantium's Light

In the fourth century, as barbarian tribes threatened Roman territories in Europe, the emperor Constantine made a dramatic decision. He moved the capital of the empire east, from Rome to Byzantium in Asia Minor. This move, he hoped, would keep at least part of the Roman Empire secure. The new capital, which came to be called Constantinople, became the thriving center of a new Byzantine Empire.

A mosaic of Emperor Constantine, who moved the capital of the Roman Empire from Rome to the city of Byzantium.

Madonna and child are flanked by Byzantium's founding fathers—Constantine (right) and Justinian. Symbolizing the empire's Christian foundations, Constantine offers Mary and Jesus a model of his new capital, and Justinian holds out a model of the Hagia Sophia cathedral.

While fighting ravaged the west, Constantinople became a second Rome. Merchants from Europe, Asia, and Africa gathered there to trade. Scholars preserved and reprinted countless Greek and Latin texts. In the sixth century, the emperor Justinian helped unify the Byzantine Empire by insisting on a single code of laws for all his subjects, from Asia Minor to Persia.

Under Justinian and his wife Theodora, art thrived in Constantinople. The emperor and empress—proud of their link to the Roman past, but also devout Christians—oversaw the building of Hagia Sophia, the church of the "Holy Wisdom," with its awe-inspiring dome, brilliantly glowing mosaics, and precious icons. Hagia Sophia was their gift to an empire that would last nearly a thousand years.

The Byzantine Empire became the center of Eastern Orthodox Christianity. The empire remained home to people of many faiths. But in its art, architecture, and aspirations, the identity of Byzantium was closely linked to eastern Christianity.

The Flame of Islam

To the south and east of the Byzantine Empire, on the Arabian Peninsula, another vibrant civilization emerged. During the sixth century, the nomadic tribes of this area had little to unite them. The Bedouin clans worshipped many different gods. But in the early seventh century, Muhammad, a man hailed as "the Prophet," changed everything.

Muhammad proclaimed the existence of one God, Allah. He urged his fellow Arabs to follow a new path of submission to the will of Allah. Thus the religion of Islam was born. Followers of Islam, called Muslims, were expected to abide by the Five Pillars of the faith—proclaiming faith in one God, praying, fasting, alms-giving, and making a pilgrimage to

A cross-sectional view shows the proportions of Hagia Sophia, which was for a long time the biggest church in Christendom.

Left: Turkish Muslims kneel and pray in the direction of Mecca. Daily prayer is one of the Five Pillars of Islam.

Below: Islam quickly spread from its birthplace in the Arabian peninsula. This mosque in Cairo, Egypt, dates from the year 970.

the holy city of Mecca. Islam offered Arabs a new faith and a new source of unity.

After Muhammad, leaders known as caliphs spread Islam even farther. The religion spread in part through conquest, and in part through trade as Muslim merchants carried their beliefs into different lands. A hundred years after Muhammad's death, a mighty Islamic Empire united Arabia, Mesopotamia, Persia, North Africa, and large parts of Spain.

The Islamic Empire's caliphs encouraged knowledge and learning. In the city of Baghdad, Muslim scholars translated ancient Greek and Roman texts into Arabic. The caliphs built Baghdad's House of Wisdom, a research library where scholars studied works from antiquity. Arab thinkers such as the mathematician Al-Khwarizmi and the physician Ibn Sina explored new frontiers of knowledge.

Faith became the motivation and theme of Islamic art. Muslims built domed mosques with pointed arches and slender minarets. Inside, these mosques often gleamed with intricate mosaics, swirling arabesques, and elegant Arabic script. Outside, fountains gurgled, while lush courtyards invited reflection. Medieval mosques still stand as reminders of the glory of Islamic art and architecture.

The Riches of Africa

Throughout the Middle Ages, Muslims extended their influence into Africa and as far south as the Sudan, a land ruled by two great African warrior federations, Ghana and Mali.

Between the eighth and tenth centuries, Ghana grew rich from trade with Arab merchants. The Soninke traded gold for salt and other precious items. This trade made Ghana's lords wealthy men. Ghana's king supported an army of mounted knights, as well as a court with advisors, servants, and slaves.

By the thirteenth century, Ghana gave way to Mali as the region's most powerful warrior federation. The hero Sundiata rallied his people, led them to victory, and extended his reign over a large part of western Africa. The Malinke grew wealthy from trade with their Arab neighbors to the north.

Mali imported more than salt from Muslim merchants. Its leaders adopted Islam as their faith. Mud and stick mosques soon rose along the banks of the Niger and Senegal Rivers. In 1324, Mansa Musa, emperor of Mali, made his pilgrimage to Mecca, handing out large quantities of gold as his huge caravan made its way east. Along the banks of the Niger River, Mansa Musa turned Timbuktu into a city that would become known as the "pearl of Africa." Timbuktu—with its Great Mosque, library, and bazaars—became a home to scholars and merchants from across the Islamic Empire.

Above: A pair of Arab coins made with African gold.

Right: Created in Mali about the time of Mansa Musa, this terra-cotta figure may have been used for devotional purposes.

China: The Giant of Asia

In the medieval era, China's rulers were busy building a great empire. In the early 600s, the Sui dynasty built the Grand Canal, linking the Yellow and the Yangtze Rivers. Under the Tang dynasty, which lasted from the early seventh century to the early tenth century, trade along the Silk Road brought wealth to China. Porcelain, silk painting, poetry, drama, and acrobatics all flourished.

Under the Song dynasty, which lasted until the late thirteenth century, young men who wanted to be civil servants had to prepare for rigorous examinations. They studied Chinese classics and the writings of Confucius. The Song dynasty gave us many remarkable inventions, such as paper money, the abacus, movable type, the compass, and gunpowder. China's population grew to more than 100 million people, protected only by a crumbling Great Wall to the north.

Such weak defenses could not hold back the Mongols. In the thirteenth century, these mounted warriors roared out of the windswept steppes of northern Asia, breached the Great Wall, and swept through China. They moved west, conquering large parts of Russia. They rode south, defeating the caliphs in Baghdad. The Mongols assembled the largest land empire in history.

The Mongol leader Genghis Khan and his grandson Kublai Khan proclaimed the Yuan dynasty in China. For the first time in its long history, China was ruled by foreigners. The Mongols were quick to build a new capital and fine palaces near the city now called Beijing. They learned a great deal from the people they conquered. Visiting Europeans, such as Marco Polo, learned much from them as well, and then returned home to tell amazing stories of this land of wonders.

This ceramic sculpture of a camel and its driver dates from China's Tang dynasty. The Tang were great traders, using camel caravans to transport goods east and west along the Silk Road.

Western Europe's Odyssey

During all this time, what was happening in Western Europe? Germanic tribes—such as the Visigoths, Vandals, Franks, and later the Vikings—plundered lands that had been Roman territories. As these tribes roamed and pillaged, civilization itself seemed threatened. Would all the triumphs of the classical world be lost?

One institution from the world of imperial Rome survived the barbarian attacks—the Christian Church. Headed by the pope in Rome, the Church brought some order to a turbulent Western Europe. Monks pursued a life of prayer, set up schools, and cared for the poor. In monasteries they copied the ancient works they managed to save. Gradually, the monks converted the barbarian tribes to Christianity.

Great cathedrals such as the one in Chartres, France, were designed to lift people's thoughts heavenward. During the medieval era, the Christian Church brought much-needed stability to an often turbulent world.

In particular, the Franks became devoted to the Church. They often fought battles to defend the pope. In A.D. 800, the pope placed a crown on the head of Charlemagne, thus making the king of the Franks into the emperor of a vast Christian realm. Charlemagne supported monasteries and encouraged schools. Although his empire fell shortly after his death, his efforts to preserve learning endured.

By the year 1000, Europe was a less dangerous place. Warring armies still clashed, but many people found some security behind the strong walls of cities, or under the protection of lords on the manors. Lords, their vassal knights, peasants, and serfs were all knit together in a chain of obligations. The code of chivalry promoted by the Church urged knights to defend the weak and show mercy to the poor.

In Western Europe—or Christendom, as it was often called at the time—the clergy took an active role in the lives of the faithful. Church officials presided over marriages, births, deaths, and education. Christian courts resolved quarrels. The Church owned a great deal of property and collected taxes. Bishops were often more powerful than princes, dukes, and lords.

While medieval life had more than its share of peril and suffering, the Church was able to offer some hope during this Age of Faith. The Christian faith taught people that despite their hard lives, a better world awaited those who tried to live according to the teachings of Jesus. The faithful clung to that hope.

Across medieval Europe, great cathedrals rose. They often took centuries to build. Cathedrals like Chartres and Notre Dame were meant to inspire a vision of heaven on earth. With their soaring spires, lofty towers, huge stained glass windows, and intricate stone sculptures, they symbolized the hope of something better in the next life.

During the Middle Ages, war was a constant fact of life. For more than two centuries, Christians and Muslims fought in a series of deadly Crusades. From those historic wars emerged leaders such as Richard the Lion-Heart and Saladin. These clashes, which left the Holy Land under Muslim rule, left a legacy of bitterness between Muslims and Christians. But they also made many people in each culture curious about the other, and opened the way for exchanges of goods and ideas.

By the early fourteenth century, strong monarchs were emerging in Europe, particularly in England and France. The French and English, however, were locked in the Hundred Years' War, which took its toll on both sides. Even worse, the plague spread death across Europe. The Black Death wiped out a third to a half of the continent's population. Many in Christendom believed they were experiencing the judgment of God. As the calamitous fourteenth century came to a close, many found themselves wondering: Was the end of the world at hand, or could better times be on the horizon?

A professor delivers a lecture at the University of Paris in this painting from about 1400. Such centers of learning were thriving in many European cities by the end of the Middle Ages.

Signs of New Life

Indeed, as the Middle Ages drew to a close, people had reason to hope for better times.

During the thirteenth century, many European cities had been growing. They had been hard hit by the plague, but as the Black Death disappeared at the end of the fourteenth century, cities resumed their growth and began to flourish.

Universities were thriving in cities as well. In these centers of learning, scholars gathered to study the ancient Greek and Roman texts that medieval monks had so carefully copied. Increased contact with the Muslim world brought more and more classical texts to light.

Trade resumed in many places. Merchants moved between Europe, North Africa, the Middle East, and Asia, bringing new goods and new knowledge wherever they traveled.

One fourteenth-century scholar wrote that Europeans were emerging from a time of "darkness." He prayed for a period of "rebirth" when scholars would rediscover the dignity of man and the glories of ancient Greece and Rome. This hope would give a name to the period that followed the Middle Ages—the Renaissance (REH-nuh-sahns), a term that means "rebirth."

As you will learn in future studies, the Renaissance was a time of magnificent achievement. People made exciting discoveries and gave the world amazing inventions. They took many new steps in the human odyssey. But they were steps along a path laid in the medieval era—a time when, despite extraordinary trials and challenges, religion, art, trade, and learning endured and even thrived in new ways.

Time Line (A.D. 400–1450)

A.D. 400 | A.D. 500 | A.D. 600 | A.D. 700 | A.D. 800 | A.D. 900

535
Justinian builds Hagia Sophia in Constantinople and assembles a code of laws for the Byzantine Empire.

830
Muslim caliphs build the House of Wisdom in Badhdad.

611
The Sui dynasty links the Yellow and Yangtze Rivers, and northern and southern China, with the Grand Canal.

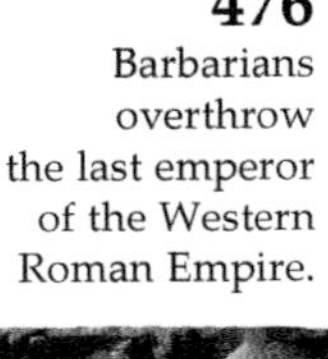

476
Barbarians overthrow the last emperor of the Western Roman Empire.

622
Muhammad flees Mecca for Medina, where he builds a community of followers.

800
Pope Leo III crowns Charlemagne as emperor of a vast Christian realm in Europe.

A.D. 1000 | A.D. 1100 | A.D. 1200 | A.D. 1300 | A.D. 1400 | A.D. 1500

1066

William the Conqueror and his Norman army invade England.

1275

Marco Polo visits Kublai Khan, ruler of the largest land empire in history.

1429

Joan of Arc defeats the English at Orléans during the Hundred Years' War.

c. 1000

Leif Erikson sails from Greenland to North America.

1347

The Black Death begins in Europe when a Genoese merchant ship carrying the plague docks at Messina, Sicily.

1190

Saladin and Richard the Lion-Heart battle for the Holy Land during the Third Crusade.

1324

Mansa Musa of Mali makes his hajj to Mecca.

1215

English nobles force King John to sign the Magna Carta.

1250

Main part of the Cathedral of Notre Dame is completed in Paris after nearly 90 years of construction.

Volume 1, Conclusion

A: Statue of what may be a high priest of the Indus River Valley civilization.

B: Prehistoric cave art.

C: The Chinese philosopher Confucius.

D: Chartres Cathedral in France.

The Ongoing Human Odyssey

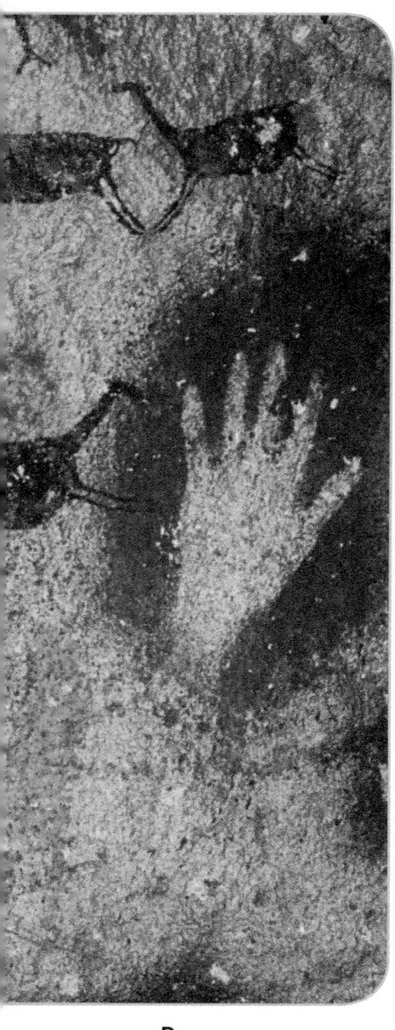

B

From cave paintings to stained glass windows. From hunters who fashioned stone tools and wore animal skins to farmers who grew their own food and wove cloth from cotton or silk. From huts on tiny plots of land to fortified cities. From ziggurats and pyramids to minarets and Gothic spires.

In our human odyssey so far, we've come a long way, making a twelve-thousand-year journey from the Ice Age to the Middle Ages. As the name "Middle Ages" suggests, we're pausing midway in this journey. There's plenty more to come. For now, let's look back and think about where we've been.

Right: The Euphrates River—so important in the development of Mesopotamian civilization—rises in the mountains of Turkey.

Geography Sets the Stage and Nature Plays a Part

A character in one of William Shakespeare's great plays once said, "All the world's a stage, and all the men and women merely players." We may be more than "merely players," but we do act on a kind of stage—on (to quote Shakespeare again) "this goodly frame, the earth." The world around us, the natural world, is the stage on which we live and breathe and act out our lives.

Over the long course of the human odyssey, geography has determined where people can live, what they can do, and what they have had to overcome. The features of the natural world can either support human life and activity or be hostile to it.

Civilization began when human beings learned to make nature work for them. Do you remember what geographic feature made the earliest civilizations possible? Yes, rivers.

The earliest cradles of civilization were all river valleys. In ancient Mesopotamia, civilization was born by the life-giving waters of the Euphrates and Tigris Rivers. In Egypt, it was the Nile; in India, the Indus and the Ganges; in China, the Yellow and Yangtze.

All these rivers were great resources that human beings learned to harness. Early people channeled flooding waters for irrigation and used the water to farm. No longer did people have to move from place to place, following the animals they hunted. Eventually they grew a surplus of food. With more than enough food to go around, people could divide the labor, stay in one place, and build cities.

The geography of a given location can be a great blessing or a hard obstacle. The people of Egypt could depend on the regular flooding of the Nile. Once the floodwaters receded, leaving behind rich silt, the Egyptians could grow the crops they needed. But in ancient Greece, the people faced rocky soil, mountainous terrain, and unreliable spring-fed streams. Even the hardest-working Greeks found it hard to coax crops from such inhospitable land. The geography of Greece is one of the main reasons why civilization developed later there than it did in Egypt.

Human beings, however, are persistent, especially in the face of challenging circumstances. The Greeks figured out how to make good use of scarce water and stony mountains. While farming was hard, the land was ideal for grazing sheep and growing olives. Civilization prospered as human beings learned how to act on the stage on which they were placed—that is, as they learned how to use the natural resources around them.

At given moments in time, however, nature has posed challenges too great for human beings to solve. A natural disaster—an earthquake, a hurricane, a flood—can unleash forces beyond human control. Or a river can dry up or change course, leaving people unable to grow the crops they need.

Or think about the role of disease in history. Three times in the course of our study so far, plagues have dramatically altered the course of events. When the Spartans battled the Athenians in the Peloponnesian Wars, Pericles and many Athenians fell victim to disease, and the course of history changed. Again, at the end of the Pax Romana, Rome suffered successive waves of plague—some historians even say that the fall of Rome was caused by germs as much as Germanic tribes. And in the fourteenth century, disease again devastated much of Europe and parts of Africa and Asia. Human beings have since learned how to battle many biological foes, but nature keeps posing new challenges.

Governments and Laws Matter

Above: In this fourth-century B.C. *relief, a figure representing democracy crowns the citizens of Athens, who pioneered rule by the people.*

Below: The "First Emperor" of China—Qin Shi Huangdi.

Civilization and government grew hand in hand. Almost since the time people began living together in groups, they faced the question: Who should rule?

In ancient Sumer, kings decided how land was distributed and who owned what. In Egypt, the pharaoh's word was law. In China, the emperor was the almighty decision-maker. The rulers of Mesopotamia and Egypt even claimed to be gods, or related to the gods.

Each of these early civilizations gave power and wealth to only a few—rulers, palace assistants, priests, and sometimes scribes. They were a lucky few. Most people had little more than the food, clothing, and shelter they needed to survive. Slavery and forced labor were common in early civilizations. All too often, the weak simply had to endure the will of the strong.

Ancient Greece and Rome supplied the first examples of democracy and republican government. These Mediterranean civilizations weren't like democracies today. They didn't give the vote to every adult in their realm, and they didn't eliminate slavery. But, for a time, they rejected monarchy (rule by a single person), and they moved away from oligarchy (rule by a small group). The classical civilizations introduced the idea of "government by the people."

Popular government wasn't easy to maintain. Greek democracies in Athens and elsewhere were short-lived. In times of trouble Romans appointed a "dictator," and eventually the Roman Republic expired under the grasping hand of Julius Caesar. But these two classical civilizations planted the seed of a great idea—that government was the business not just of rulers, but of the governed. In the Middle Ages, that idea rekindled in England when nobles forced King John to sign the Magna Carta, guaranteeing their rights.

Government is not just a matter of rulers but also of rules—that is, of laws. Under some rulers, the law was whatever the ruler said, and the ruler could change his mind at will. But civilization made a step forward when laws were written down for all to know. Written laws helped people organize their lives. They made life more predictable.

Above: An ancient cuneiform tablet with some of the 282 laws of Babylon's King Hammurabi.

Right: An artist's depiction of the Ten Commandments. These laws, central to the life of the ancient Hebrew people, have greatly influenced lawmaking in western civilization.

As early as the second millennium B.C., the great Babylonian king Hammurabi assembled the first organized code of laws for his vast realm. One of his principles was, "The strong shall not harm the weak." This is perhaps the earliest evidence we have of a human concern for justice, rather than simply a desire for order.

Great rulers have been active lawmakers ever since. Julius Caesar organized the code of Roman law, which for many years helped unite a vast realm in peace. Justinian did the same for his Byzantine Empire. In the Middle Ages, the Christian Church organized its own set of laws to apply to all.

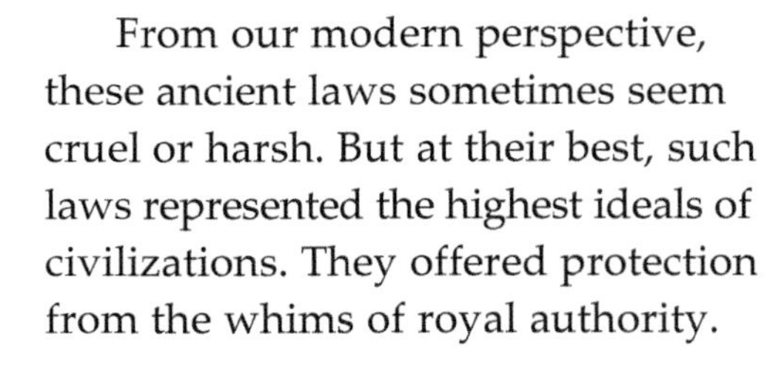

From our modern perspective, these ancient laws sometimes seem cruel or harsh. But at their best, such laws represented the highest ideals of civilizations. They offered protection from the whims of royal authority.

Beliefs and Ideas Shape History

From ancient times to medieval, the course of human history has been changed, for good and ill, by powerful ideas and religious beliefs.

Stone Age paintings on the walls of caves suggest that even very early people asked questions we still ponder now: Who made me? What is the meaning of life? Who controls human destiny? How should human beings behave? Whom should they worship?

Sumerian and Egyptian civilizations worshipped many nature gods. Their mythology, art, and artifacts reveal their beliefs about how those gods were to be worshipped, and what duties humans had toward the deities. In these ancient civilizations, people saw themselves as little more than slaves of the gods, at the mercy of their unpredictable powers. They believed the gods cared most about how and whether human beings honored them.

In the second millennium B.C., the ancient Hebrews introduced a different idea, one that lasts to this day. Their belief in one God who created all and expected people to treat each other well was a new development. The Ten Commandments were not a new code of laws, like the Code

of Hammurabi, but a new way of thinking about human obligations to God and to other people.

The Ten Commandments and other laws of Moses bound together the Jewish community. From this heritage sprang Christianity, based on the life and teachings of Jesus. During the Middle Ages, Muhammad drew on the ideas of Judaism and Christianity to found the religion of Islam. All three—Judaism, Christianity, and Islam—were monotheistic religions, and shared many ideas and stories, though this common ground did not prevent sometimes bloody conflicts between them. All three still have millions of followers today.

In the east, Hinduism and Buddhism provided other models of how one could live a good life and find peace. These two religions stressed detachment from worldly things, faithfulness to duty, compassion, and mercy. Both Hindus and Buddhists believed that human beings lived many lives and could grow spiritually in each new life. People, they thought, had a chance to act better and less selfishly at each stage of incarnation.

Sometimes religion had the power to unite empires. We've seen that Asoka wanted to extend Buddhism throughout his Indian empire. In the early Middle Ages, Constantine opened the door for the Christian faith to unite the former Roman Empire. Islam under Muhammad became the faith that united the Arabs and formed the nucleus of an empire.

It was not just religious thinkers who discussed ideas about right and wrong, or contemplated the meaning of life. You recall the great Chinese philosopher Confucius. Confucius stressed the importance of right action in human relationships. Remember also the Greek philosophers Socrates, Plato, and Aristotle. They were devoted to using the power of reason to discover the truth.

Abraham, Moses, Confucius, Buddha, Socrates, Plato, Aristotle, Jesus, Muhammad—the lasting contributions of these major figures show the power of ideas. Their ideas have inspired their followers and students. They have also inspired great writing, painting, poetry, architecture, and music.

ولا تفرق بيننا وبينه حتى تدخلنا مدخله
وتوردنا حوضه وتجعلنا من رفقائه
مع المنعم عليهم من النبيين والصديقين
والشهداء والصالحين وحسن
أولئك رفيقا الحمد لله رب العالمين
ابتداء الربع الثالث
اللهم صل على محمد نور الهدى والقائد
إلى الخير والداعي إلى الرشد نبي الرحمة وإمام
المتقين ورسول رب العالمين لا نبي بعده
كما بلغ رسالتك ونصح لعبادك وتلا آياتك
وأقام حدودك ووفى بعهدك وأنفذ حكمك
وأمر بطاعتك ونهى عن معصيتك ووالى

This page from the Qur'an, Islam's holy book, turns Arabic script into a work of art.

Individuals Make a Difference

The lives of these extraordinary people remind us of another truth of history: Individuals can make a big difference. What happens in human history is not just a matter of geography, trade systems, government, or religions. It's a matter of the particular people living at a particular time. Individuals—with their unique temperaments, strengths, weaknesses, and values—can change the course of events.

Think about how different the Greek world and everything that followed might have been if Pericles or Socrates had never lived. What if Alexander the Great had died from an illness in infancy? What if Julius Caesar had never crossed the Rubicon? What if Theodora had let Justinian flee from Constantinople during the riots? What if King John had been a generous and likable fellow, and England's nobles had never felt the need to make him sign the Magna Carta? What if Genghis Khan had been raised as a merchant instead of a warrior? What if Joan of Arc hadn't listened to her "voices"?

England's King John I signs the Magna Carta. With this act, he recognized the rights of the nobility and the Church.

In each and every one of these cases, the course of history would have been very different. Perhaps one of the most exciting and frightening lessons in human history is how much individuals matter. For better or worse, men and women have stepped forth to alter the course of our human odyssey.

Ingenuity and Creativity Are Key

Human beings are problem-solvers. We use our minds to figure out how to accomplish our goals. With ingenuity and determination, we take on great challenges, whether it's harnessing the floodwaters of the Nile or linking the Yellow and Yangtze Rivers by canal.

Knowledge and ingenuity are driving forces behind a civilization's technology. When the Romans set out to conquer a vast empire, they needed a way to unite it—and so the technology of roads was born. When the Chinese realized they were threatened by attacks from the north, they set about building a Great Wall thousands of miles long. When the Vikings realized their rocky land could not support their population, they turned to the sea, and built some of the finest ships ever to sail the ocean.

In every age, humans have found a way to express their ingenuity and creativity. Human creativity has taken visible form in extraordinary works of art. In our twelve-thousand year period of study, we've seen human beings progress from cave paintings to rose windows. We have

Left: One of the Seven Wonders of the Ancient World—the Pyramids at Giza, Egypt.

Below: In this sandstone carving, the face of the Buddha is a picture of serenity.

seen the lifelike perfection of Greek sculpture, and the dazzling elegance of Muslim calligraphy. We've seen the delicate beauty of illuminated manuscripts and the serenity on the faces of enormous statues of the Buddha.

Religion motivated some of the greatest architectural achievements in the ancient civilizations. By the third millennium B.C., the Sumerians were building ziggurats, and the Egyptians were building pyramids and sphinxes. In the fifth century B.C., the Greeks constructed elegantly proportioned temples to show their devotion to the gods. In the Middle Ages, huge domed mosques with minarets dotted the skyline in Muslim lands, while in Europe great cathedrals rose as magnificent expressions of the Age of Faith.

The Odyssey Is Ongoing

Our journey pauses now around the year 1400. The Middle Ages have drawn to a close. A new era is dawning, a time of extraordinary innovation and enterprise known as the Renaissance.

The period from the Renaissance to the present day is often called "modern history." Modern history has built on all that came before. In the next volume in this series, when we re-embark on the human odyssey, we'll see just how many important ideas, beliefs, and practices from the past continue to influence modern life.

We'll also learn about new developments—a religious upheaval in Europe, a scientific revolution, the discovery of continents that Europeans had never known existed, the formation of modern nation-states, an international movement toward democracy, an industrial revolution, and much more.

The human odyssey is ongoing and open-ended. If you can locate yourself on the map of time and find your place in history, you stand a better chance of charting a good course to the future.

Some say we study the past in order to commit ourselves to the future. What kind of ship will you captain? Which journey will be yours? Don't underestimate your role in our amazing human odyssey.

Atlas

World Physical

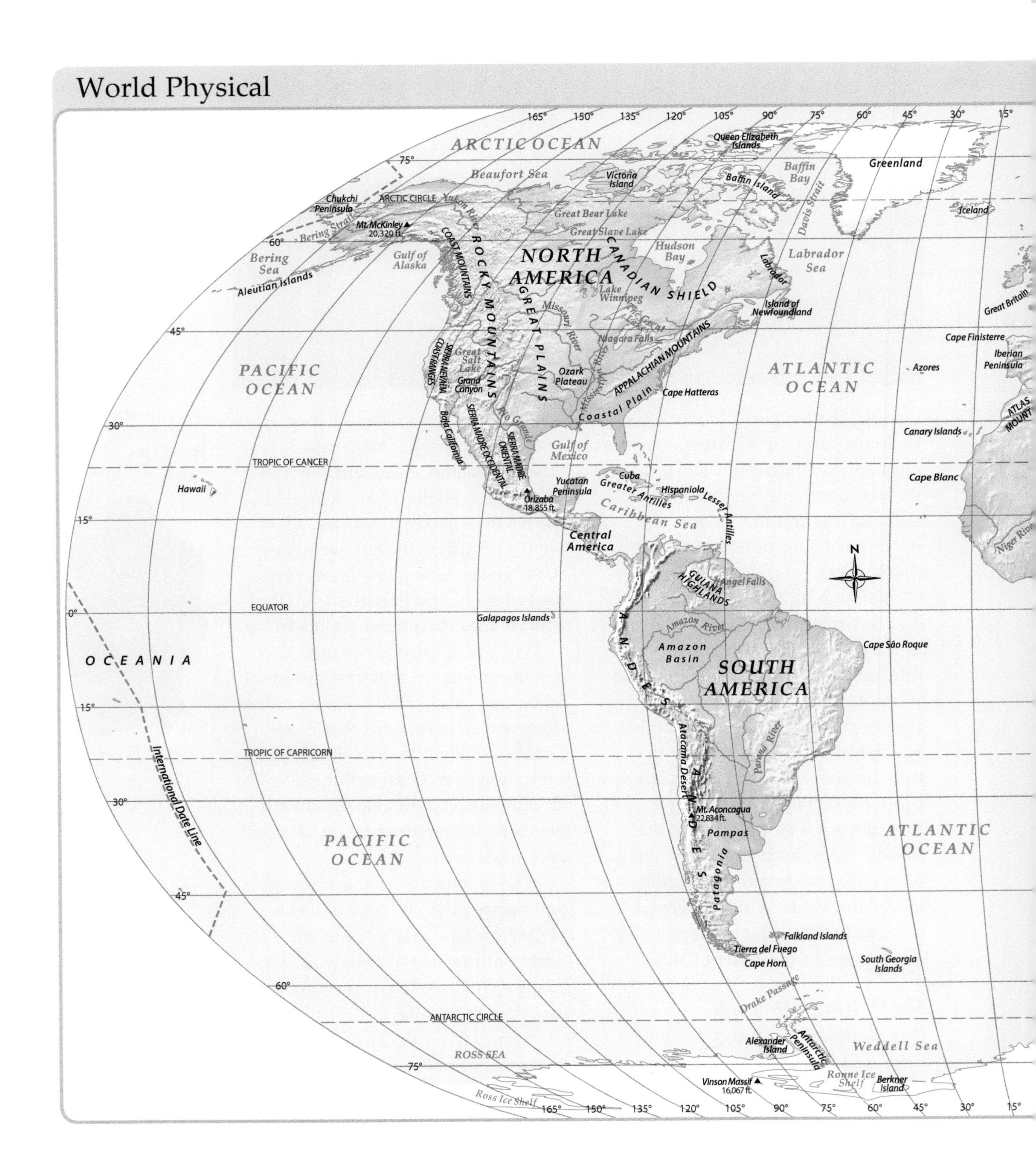

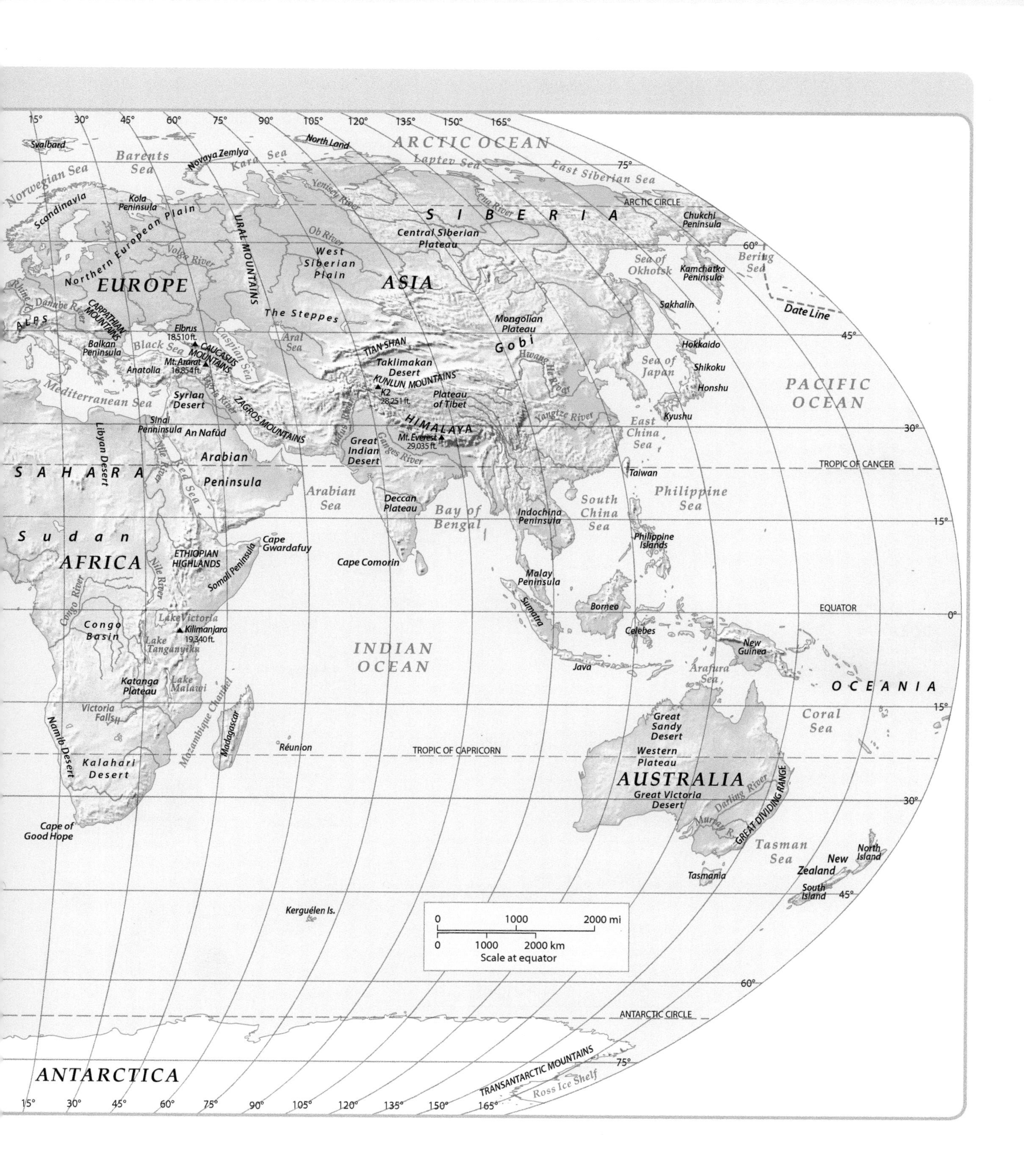
ARCTIC OCEAN
Svalbard
Barents Sea
Norwegian Sea
Novaya Zemlya
Kara Sea
North Land
Laptev Sea
East Siberian Sea
ARCTIC CIRCLE
Scandinavia
Kola Peninsula
Northern European Plain
Volga River
URAL MOUNTAINS
Ob River
Yenisey River
Lena River
SIBERIA
Central Siberian Plateau
West Siberian Plain
Chukchi Peninsula
Sea of Okhotsk
Kamchatka Peninsula
Bering Sea
EUROPE
ASIA
Rhine
Danube River
ALPS
CARPATHIAN MOUNTAINS
The Steppes
Sakhalin
Date Line
Elbrus 18,510 ft.
Caspian Sea
Aral Sea
Mongolian Plateau
Balkan Peninsula
Black Sea
CAUCASUS MOUNTAINS
TIAN SHAN
Gobi
Hokkaido
Mt. Ararat 16,854 ft.
Anatolia
Taklimakan Desert
Sea of Japan
Shikoku
Honshu
KUNLUN MOUNTAINS
PACIFIC OCEAN
Mediterranean Sea
Syrian Desert
K2 28,251 ft.
Plateau of Tibet
Hwang He River
Yangtze River
Kyushu
Sinai Penninsula
An Nafūd
ZAGROS MOUNTAINS
HIMALAYA
Mt. Everest 29,035 ft.
East China Sea
Libyan Desert
Nile River
Great Indian Desert
Indus River
Ganges River
SAHARA
Arabian Peninsula
Red Sea
Taiwan
TROPIC OF CANCER
Arabian Sea
Deccan Plateau
Bay of Bengal
Indochina Peninsula
South China Sea
Philippine Sea
Sudan
Cape Gwardafuy
Philippine Islands
AFRICA
ETHIOPIAN HIGHLANDS
Somali Peninsula
Cape Comorin
Malay Peninsula
Congo River
Sumatra
Borneo
EQUATOR
Lake Victoria
Congo Basin
Kilimanjaro 19,340 ft.
Lake Tanganyika
Celebes
New Guinea
INDIAN OCEAN
Java
Arafura Sea
Katanga Plateau
Lake Malawi
Mozambique Channel
OCEANIA
Victoria Falls
Madagascar
Great Sandy Desert
Coral Sea
Namib Desert
Réunion
TROPIC OF CAPRICORN
Western Plateau
Kalahari Desert
AUSTRALIA
Great Victoria Desert
Darling River
GREAT DIVIDING RANGE
Murray R.
Cape of Good Hope
Tasman Sea
North Island
New Zealand
Tasmania
South Island
Kerguélen Is.
0 1000 2000 mi
0 1000 2000 km
Scale at equator
ANTARCTIC CIRCLE
ANTARCTICA
TRANSANTARCTIC MOUNTAINS
Ross Ice Shelf
15° 30° 45° 60° 75° 90° 105° 120° 135° 150° 165°
0° 15° 30° 45° 60° 75°

World Political

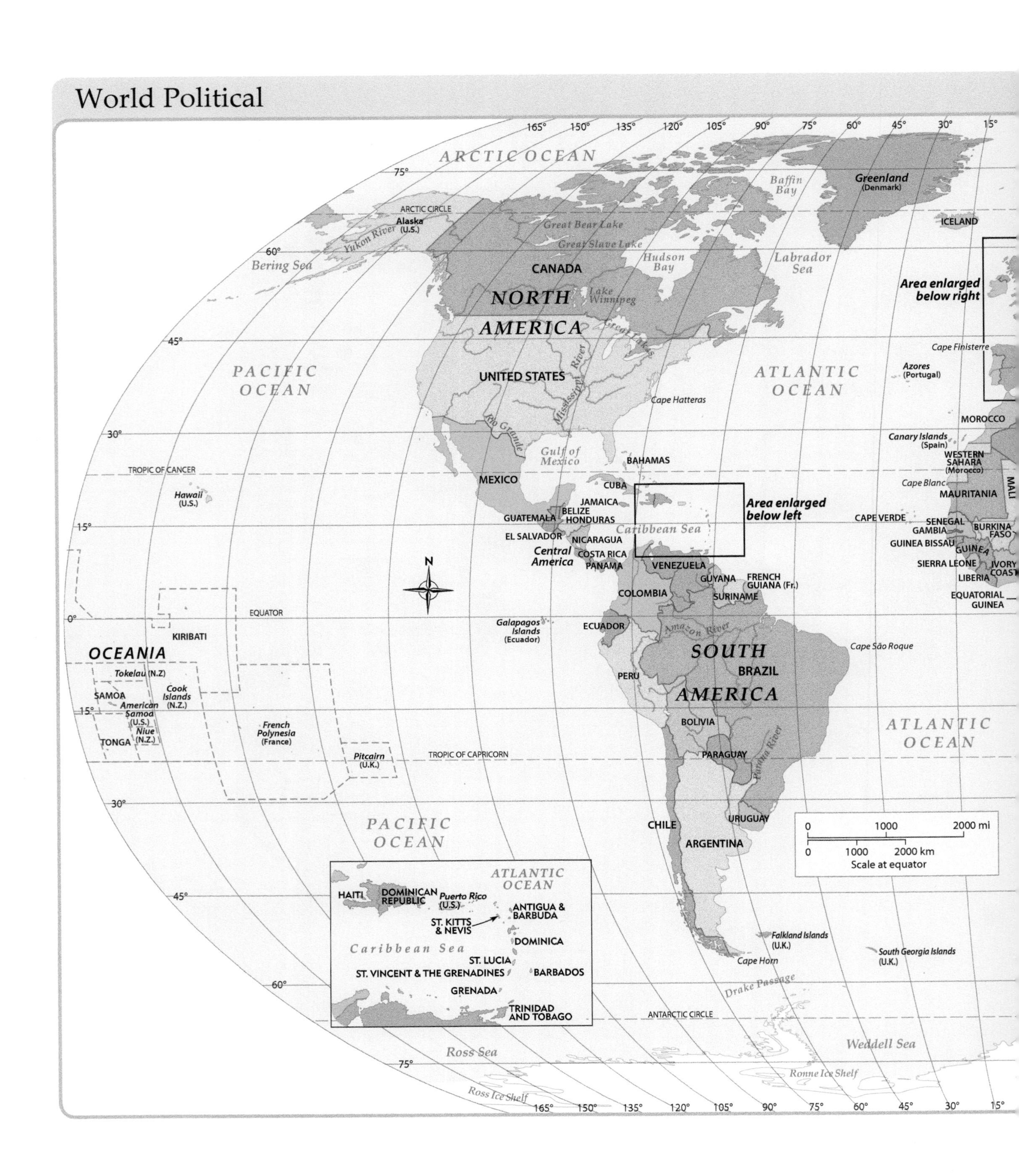

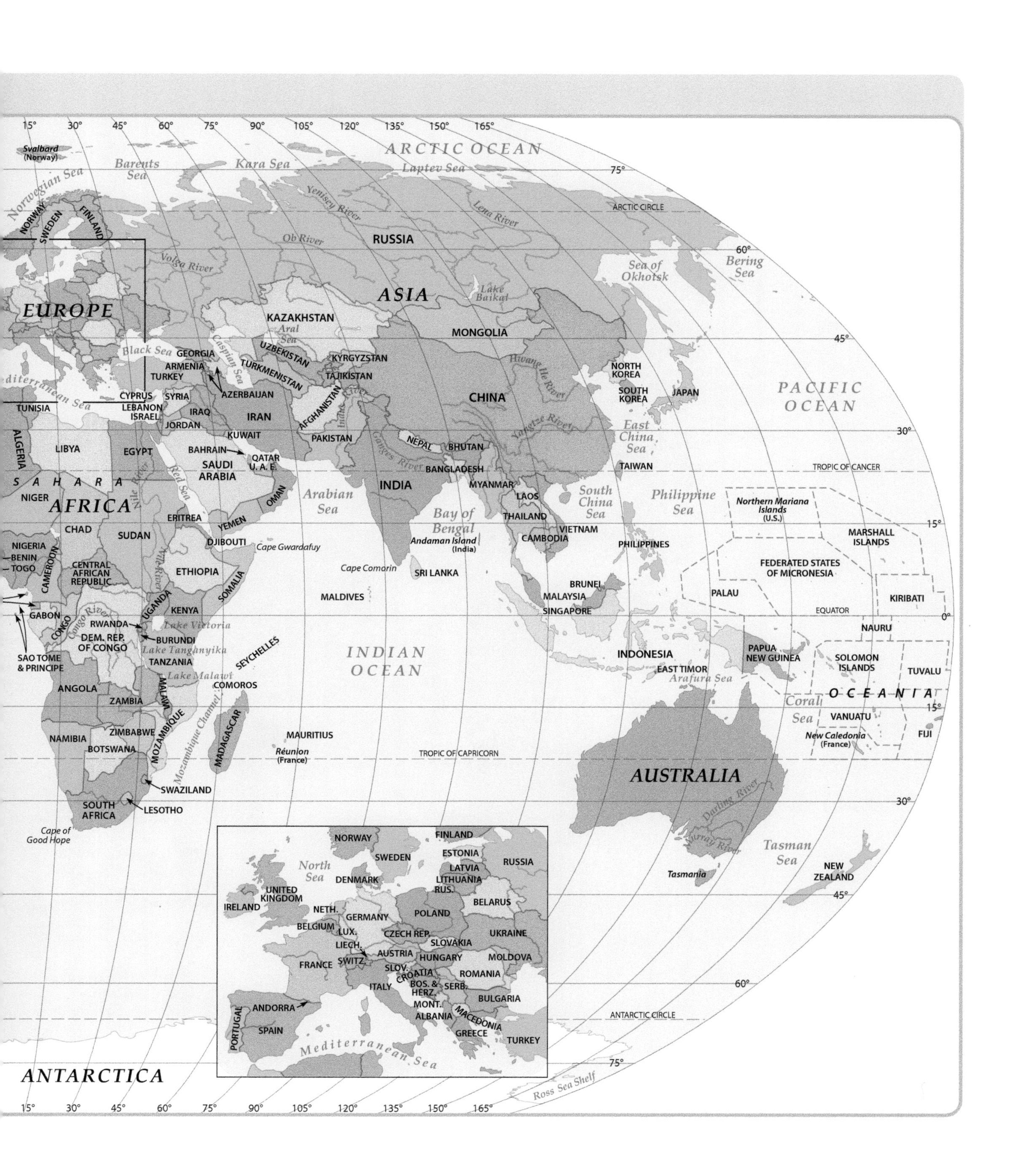
ARCTIC OCEAN
Laptev Sea
Kara Sea
Barents Sea
Norwegian Sea
Svalbard (Norway)
NORWAY
SWEDEN
FINLAND
RUSSIA
ASIA
EUROPE
Yenisey River
Lena River
Ob River
Volga River
Sea of Okhotsk
Bering Sea
Lake Baikal
KAZAKHSTAN
Aral Sea
MONGOLIA
Black Sea
GEORGIA
ARMENIA
TURKEY
UZBEKISTAN
TURKMENISTAN
KYRGYZSTAN
TAJIKISTAN
Caspian Sea
AZERBAIJAN
Mediterranean Sea
CYPRUS
SYRIA
LEBANON
ISRAEL
IRAQ
JORDAN
IRAN
AFGHANISTAN
PAKISTAN
KUWAIT
BAHRAIN
QATAR
U.A.E.
SAUDI ARABIA
OMAN
YEMEN
CHINA
Huang He River
Yangtze River
NORTH KOREA
SOUTH KOREA
JAPAN
East China Sea
PACIFIC OCEAN
TAIWAN
NEPAL
BHUTAN
Ganges River
Indus River
BANGLADESH
INDIA
MYANMAR
LAOS
THAILAND
VIETNAM
CAMBODIA
South China Sea
Philippine Sea
PHILIPPINES
Arabian Sea
Bay of Bengal
Andaman Island (India)
Cape Comorin
SRI LANKA
MALDIVES
BRUNEI
MALAYSIA
SINGAPORE
INDONESIA
EAST TIMOR
Arafura Sea
PAPUA NEW GUINEA
Northern Mariana Islands (U.S.)
MARSHALL ISLANDS
FEDERATED STATES OF MICRONESIA
PALAU
KIRIBATI
EQUATOR
NAURU
SOLOMON ISLANDS
TUVALU
OCEANIA
Coral Sea
VANUATU
New Caledonia (France)
FIJI
AUSTRALIA
Darling River
Murray River
Tasmania
Tasman Sea
NEW ZEALAND
TUNISIA
ALGERIA
LIBYA
EGYPT
SAHARA
AFRICA
NIGER
CHAD
SUDAN
Nile River
Red Sea
ERITREA
DJIBOUTI
Cape Gwardafuy
ETHIOPIA
SOMALIA
NIGERIA
BENIN
TOGO
CAMEROON
CENTRAL AFRICAN REPUBLIC
GABON
CONGO
Congo River
RWANDA
BURUNDI
DEM. REP. OF CONGO
UGANDA
KENYA
Lake Victoria
Lake Tanganyika
TANZANIA
SEYCHELLES
SAO TOME & PRINCIPE
ANGOLA
ZAMBIA
MALAWI
Lake Malawi
COMOROS
MOZAMBIQUE
Mozambique Channel
MADAGASCAR
ZIMBABWE
NAMIBIA
BOTSWANA
MAURITIUS
Réunion (France)
INDIAN OCEAN
SWAZILAND
LESOTHO
SOUTH AFRICA
Cape of Good Hope
TROPIC OF CANCER
TROPIC OF CAPRICORN
ARCTIC CIRCLE
ANTARCTIC CIRCLE
ANTARCTICA
Ross Sea Shelf
NORWAY
FINLAND
ESTONIA
SWEDEN
North Sea
DENMARK
LATVIA
LITHUANIA
RUS.
RUSSIA
UNITED KINGDOM
IRELAND
NETH.
BELARUS
GERMANY
POLAND
BELGIUM
LUX.
CZECH REP.
UKRAINE
LIECH.
SLOVAKIA
AUSTRIA
FRANCE
SWITZ.
HUNGARY
MOLDOVA
SLOV.
CROATIA
ROMANIA
ITALY
BOS. & HERZ.
SERB.
MONT.
BULGARIA
ANDORRA
ALBANIA
MACEDONIA
PORTUGAL
SPAIN
GREECE
TURKEY
Mediterranean Sea
15° 30° 45° 60° 75° 90° 105° 120° 135° 150° 165°
75° 60° 45° 30° 15° 0° 15° 30° 45° 60° 75°

Eurasia

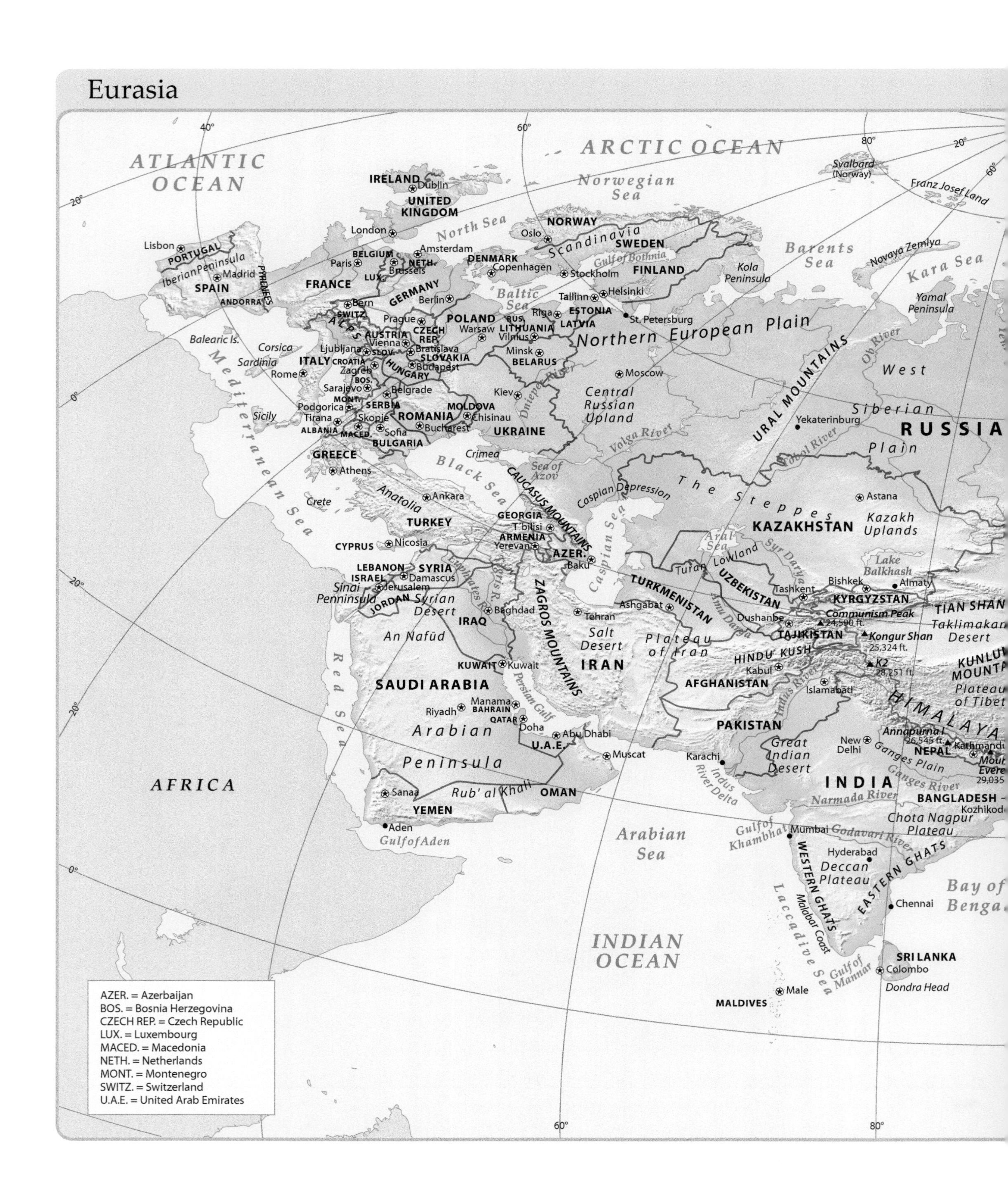

ARCTIC OCEAN
ATLANTIC OCEAN
Norwegian Sea
Svalbard (Norway)
Franz Josef Land
IRELAND
Dublin
UNITED KINGDOM
London
North Sea
NORWAY
Oslo
Scandinavia
SWEDEN
Barents Sea
Novaya Zemlya
Kara Sea
Lisbon
PORTUGAL
Iberian Peninsula
Madrid
SPAIN
PYRENEES
ANDORRA
Amsterdam
BELGIUM
NETH.
Paris
Brussels
LUX.
FRANCE
DENMARK
Copenhagen
Gulf of Bothnia
Stockholm
FINLAND
Kola Peninsula
Yamal Peninsula
GERMANY
Berlin
Bern
SWITZ.
ALPS
Baltic Sea
Tallinn
Helsinki
ESTONIA
Riga
LATVIA
RUS.
LITHUANIA
Vilnius
St. Petersburg
Prague
CZECH REP.
POLAND
Warsaw
AUSTRIA
Vienna
Bratislava
SLOVAKIA
Budapest
HUNGARY
Ljubljana
SLOV.
CROATIA
Zagreb
BOS.
Sarajevo
Belgrade
MONT.
SERBIA
Podgorica
Tirana
ALBANIA
Skopje
MACED.
Sofia
BULGARIA
ROMANIA
Bucharest
MOLDOVA
Chisinau
Minsk
BELARUS
Northern European Plain
URAL MOUNTAINS
Ob River
West Siberian Plain
RUSSIA
Balearic Is.
Corsica
Sardinia
ITALY
Rome
Mediterranean Sea
Sicily
GREECE
Athens
Crete
Moscow
Kiev
Dnieper River
Central Russian Upland
UKRAINE
Crimea
Black Sea
Sea of Azov
Volga River
Yekaterinburg
Tobol River
CAUCASUS MOUNTAINS
Caspian Depression
The Steppes
Astana
Kazakh Uplands
KAZAKHSTAN
Anatolia
Ankara
TURKEY
GEORGIA
T'bilisi
ARMENIA
Yerevan
AZER.
Baku
Caspian Sea
Aral Sea
Syr Darya
Turan Lowland
Lake Balkhash
CYPRUS
Nicosia
LEBANON
SYRIA
ISRAEL
Damascus
Jerusalem
Sinai Penninsula
JORDAN
Syrian Desert
Euphrates R.
Tigris R.
Baghdad
IRAQ
ZAGROS MOUNTAINS
TURKMENISTAN
Ashgabat
UZBEKISTAN
Amu Darya
Tashkent
Bishkek
Almaty
KYRGYZSTAN
Communism Peak
24,590 ft.
TIAN SHAN
Taklimakan Desert
Tehran
Salt Desert
Plateau of Iran
Dushanbe
TAJIKISTAN
Kongur Shan
25,324 ft.
An Nafūd
HINDU KUSH
Kabul
K2
28,251 ft.
KUNLUN MOUNTAINS
KUWAIT
Kuwait
IRAN
AFGHANISTAN
Indus River
Islamabad
Plateau of Tibet
HIMALAYA
SAUDI ARABIA
Persian Gulf
Manama
BAHRAIN
Riyadh
QATAR
Doha
Abu Dhabi
U.A.E.
PAKISTAN
Annapurna I
26,545 ft.
Kathmandu
NEPAL
Mount Everest
29,035
Arabian Peninsula
Muscat
Karachi
Great Indian Desert
New Delhi
Ganges Plain
Ganges River
Red Sea
Indus River Delta
INDIA
Sanaa
Rub' al Khali
OMAN
YEMEN
Narmada River
BANGLADESH
Kozhikode
Chota Nagpur Plateau
AFRICA
Aden
Gulf of Aden
Arabian Sea
Gulf of Khambhat
Mumbai
Godavari River
WESTERN GHATS
Hyderabad
Deccan Plateau
EASTERN GHATS
Bay of Bengal
Chennai
Laccadive Sea
Malabar Coast
INDIAN OCEAN
SRI LANKA
Colombo
Gulf of Mannar
Male
Dondra Head
MALDIVES
AZER. = Azerbaijan
BOS. = Bosnia Herzegovina
CZECH REP. = Czech Republic
LUX. = Luxembourg
MACED. = Macedonia
NETH. = Netherlands
MONT. = Montenegro
SWITZ. = Switzerland
U.A.E. = United Arab Emirates

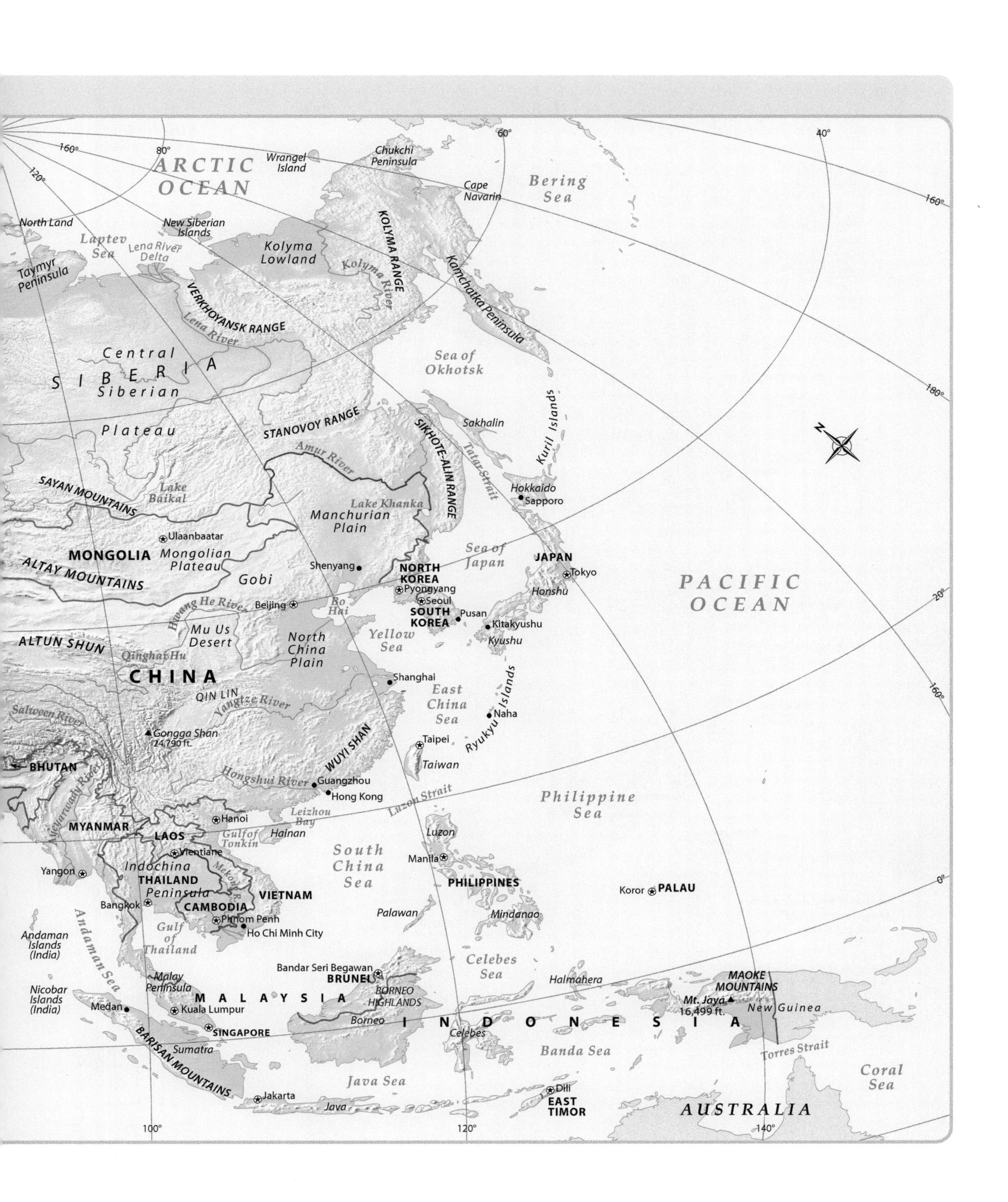
ARCTIC OCEAN
Wrangel Island
Chukchi Peninsula
Cape Navarin
Bering Sea
North Land
New Siberian Islands
Laptev Sea
Lena River Delta
Kolyma Lowland
Kolyma River
KOLYMA RANGE
Kamchatka Peninsula
Taymyr Peninsula
VERKHOYANSK RANGE
Lena River
Central Siberian Plateau
SIBERIA
Sea of Okhotsk
Kuril Islands
Sakhalin
STANOVOY RANGE
SIKHOTE-ALIN RANGE
Tatar Strait
Amur River
SAYAN MOUNTAINS
Lake Baikal
Lake Khanka
Manchurian Plain
Hokkaido
Sapporo
Ulaanbaatar
MONGOLIA
Mongolian Plateau
ALTAY MOUNTAINS
Gobi
Shenyang
NORTH KOREA
Pyongyang
Seoul
SOUTH KOREA
Pusan
Sea of Japan
JAPAN
Tokyo
Honshu
PACIFIC OCEAN
Beijing
Hwang He River
Bo Hai
Kitakyushu
Kyushu
Mu Us Desert
North China Plain
Yellow Sea
ALTUN SHUN
Qinghai Hu
CHINA
Shanghai
QIN LIN
Yangtze River
East China Sea
Naha
Ryukyu Islands
Salween River
Gongga Shan 24,790 ft.
Taipei
Taiwan
BHUTAN
Ayeyarwady River
Hongshui River
WUYI SHAN
Guangzhou
Hong Kong
Luzon Strait
Philippine Sea
Hanoi
Leizhou Bay
MYANMAR
LAOS
Gulf of Tonkin
Hainan
Luzon
Vientiane
South China Sea
Manila
Yangon
Indochina Peninsula
THAILAND
Mekong R.
PHILIPPINES
Koror
PALAU
Bangkok
CAMBODIA
VIETNAM
Phnom Penh
Ho Chi Minh City
Andaman Sea
Palawan
Mindanao
Andaman Islands (India)
Gulf of Thailand
Celebes Sea
Bandar Seri Begawan
BRUNEI
Halmahera
MAOKE MOUNTAINS
Nicobar Islands (India)
Malay Peninsula
MALAYSIA
BORNEO HIGHLANDS
Mt. Jaya 16,499 ft.
New Guinea
Medan
Kuala Lumpur
SINGAPORE
Borneo
INDONESIA
Celebes
BARISAN MOUNTAINS
Sumatra
Banda Sea
Torres Strait
Coral Sea
Java Sea
Jakarta
Java
Dili
EAST TIMOR
AUSTRALIA
160°
80°
120°
60°
40°
180°
20°
0°
100°
140°

North America

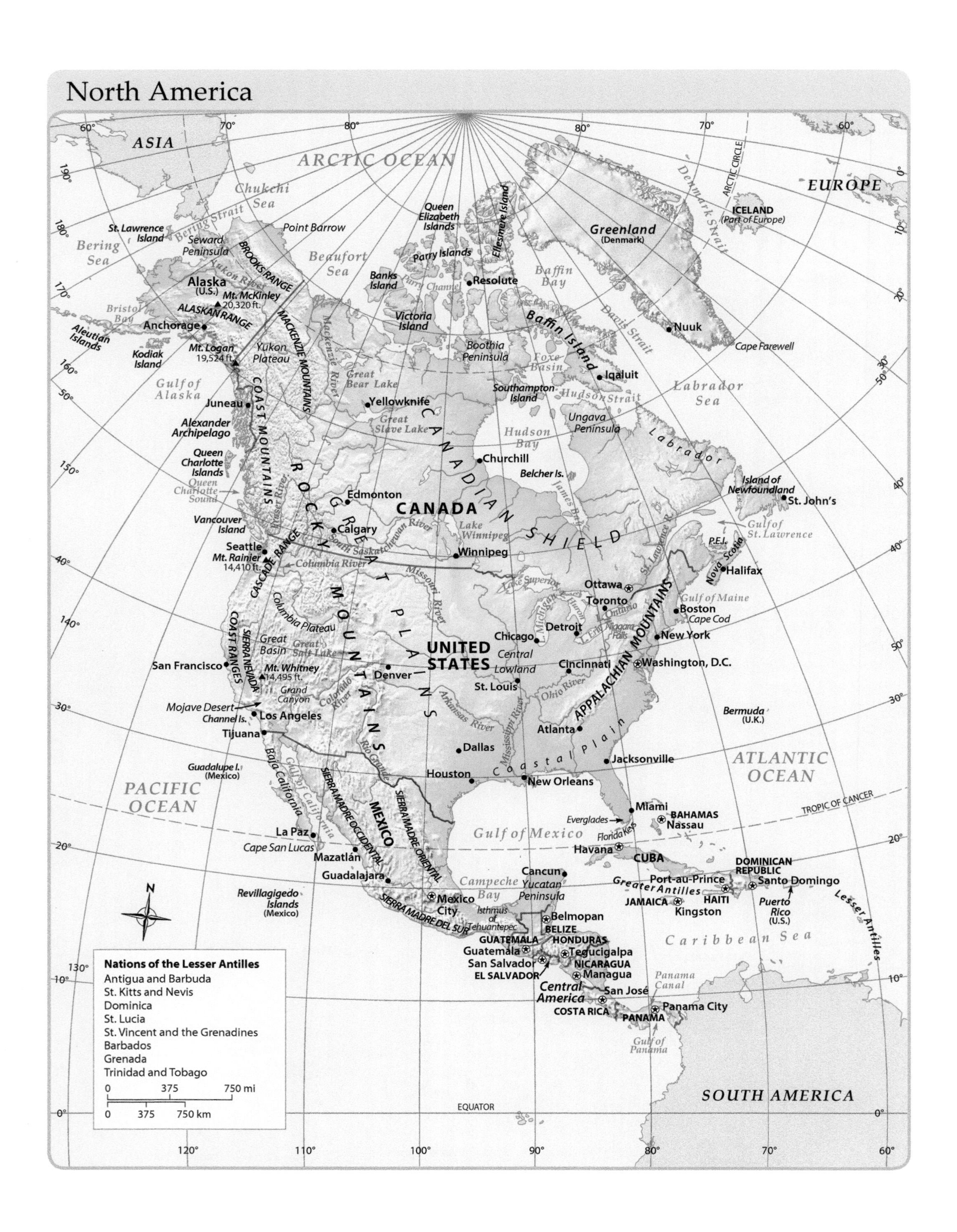

South America

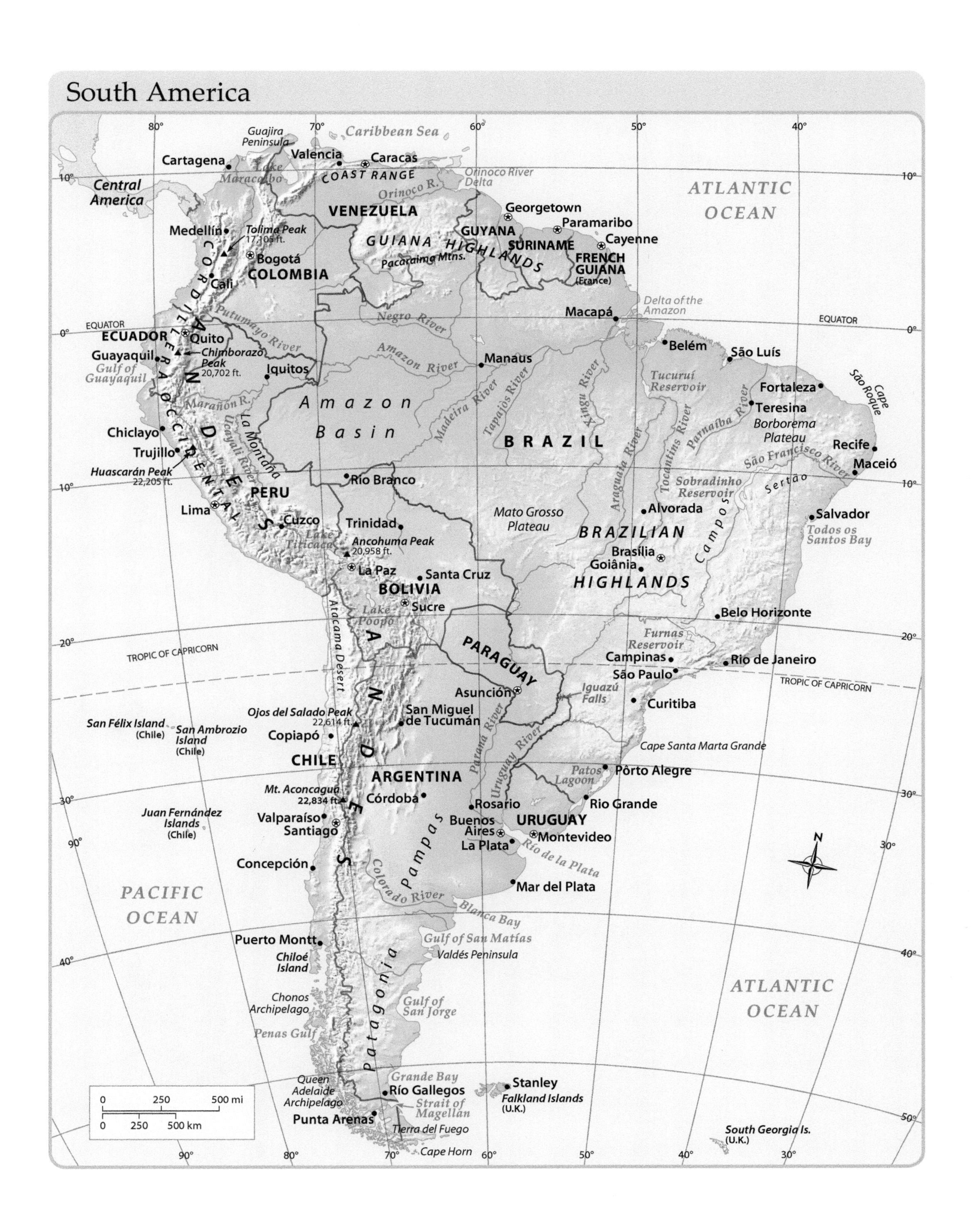

Europe
ALB. = Albania
BOS. & HERZ. = Bosnia Herzegovina
CZECH REP. = Czech Republic
LIECH. = Liechtenstein
LUX. = Luxembourg
MACED. = Macedonia
NETH. = Netherlands
RUS. = Russia
MONT. = Montenegro
SWITZ. = Switzerland
0 200 400 mi
0 200 400 km
ATLANTIC OCEAN
Norwegian Sea
North Sea
Barents Sea
White Sea
Baltic Sea
Gulf of Bothnia
Gulf of Finland
Kattegat
Skagerrak
Irish Sea
English Channel
St. George's Channel
Strait of Dover
Bay of Biscay
Mediterranean Sea
Tyrrhenian Sea
Ionian Sea
Adriatic Sea
Aegean Sea
Ligurian Sea
Balearic Sea
Black Sea
Sea of Azov
Caspian Sea
Sea of Marmara
Bosporus
Gulf of Lion
Gulf of Cádiz
Strait of Gibraltar
Donegal Bay
ASIA
AFRICA
ARCTIC CIRCLE
ICELAND
Reykjavik
Faroe Is.(Denmark)
Shetland Is. (U.K.)
Orkney Is.(U.K.)
Outer Hebrides (U.K.)
IRELAND
Dublin
Northern Ireland (U.K.)
Belfast
UNITED KINGDOM
GREAT BRITAIN
Scotland
Wales
England
Glasgow
Edinburgh
Manchester
London
Land's End
Thames R.
NORWAY
Bergen
Oslo
Trondheim
Lofoten
SWEDEN
Stockholm
Göteborg
Lake Vänern
FINLAND
Helsinki
Lake Region
Lapland
Scandinavia
DENMARK
Copenhagen
ESTONIA
Tallinn
LATVIA
Riga
LITHUANIA
Vilnius
RUS.
BELARUS
Minsk
RUSSIA
Moscow
St. Petersburg
Murmansk
Kola Peninsula
Lake Onega
Lake Ladoga
Rybinsk Reservoir
Nizhniy Novgorod
Tula
Voronezh
Volgograd
Samara
Ufa
Grozny
Kuybyshev Reservoir
Tsimlyansk Reservoir
Kama River
Ural River
Volga River
Don River
Oka-Don Plain
Volga Upland
Upper Kama Upland
Central Russian Upland
Timan Ridge
Pechora River
Northern Dvina River
URAL MOUNTAINS
Caspian Depression
KAZAKHSTAN
CAUCASUS MTNS.
Mt. Elbrus 18,510 ft.
Northern European Plain
UKRAINE
Kiev
L'viv
Donets'k
Dnieper River
Crimea
MOLDOVA
Chisinau
ROMANIA
Bucharest
Danube River Delta
BULGARIA
Sofia
TURKEY
Istanbul
GREECE
Athens
Peloponnesus
Crete (Greece)
Rhodes (Greece)
Balkan Peninsula
CARPATHIAN MOUNTAINS
Great Hungarian Plain
POLAND
Warsaw
Gdańsk
Vistula River
Oder River
GERMANY
Berlin
Hamburg
Munich
Elbe River
Rhine R.
Black Forest
Danube River
CZECH REP.
Prague
SLOVAKIA
Bratislava
AUSTRIA
Vienna
HUNGARY
Budapest
SLOVENIA
Ljubljana
CROATIA
Zagreb
Dalmatia
BOS. & HERZ.
Sarajevo
SERBIA
Belgrade
MONT.
Podgorica
MACED.
Skopje
ALB.
Tirana
NETH.
Amsterdam
BELGIUM
Brussels
LUX.
Luxembourg
FRANCE
Paris
Bordeaux
Brittany
Champagne
Seine R.
Loire River
Garonne River
Massif Central
Mont Blanc 15,780 ft.
MONACO
Riviera
Corsica (France)
SWITZ.
Bern
LIECH.
ALPS
ITALY
Milan
Venice
Rome
Palermo
Po River
Tuscany
APENNINES
SAN MARINO
VATICAN CITY
Sardinia (Italy)
Sicily (Italy)
MALTA
SPAIN
Madrid
Barcelona
Valencia
Seville
PYRENEES
ANDORRA
Iberian Peninsula
Douro River
Tagus R.
Guadiana River
Balearic Is. (Spain)
PORTUGAL
Lisbon
Cape Finisterre
Cape St. Vincent

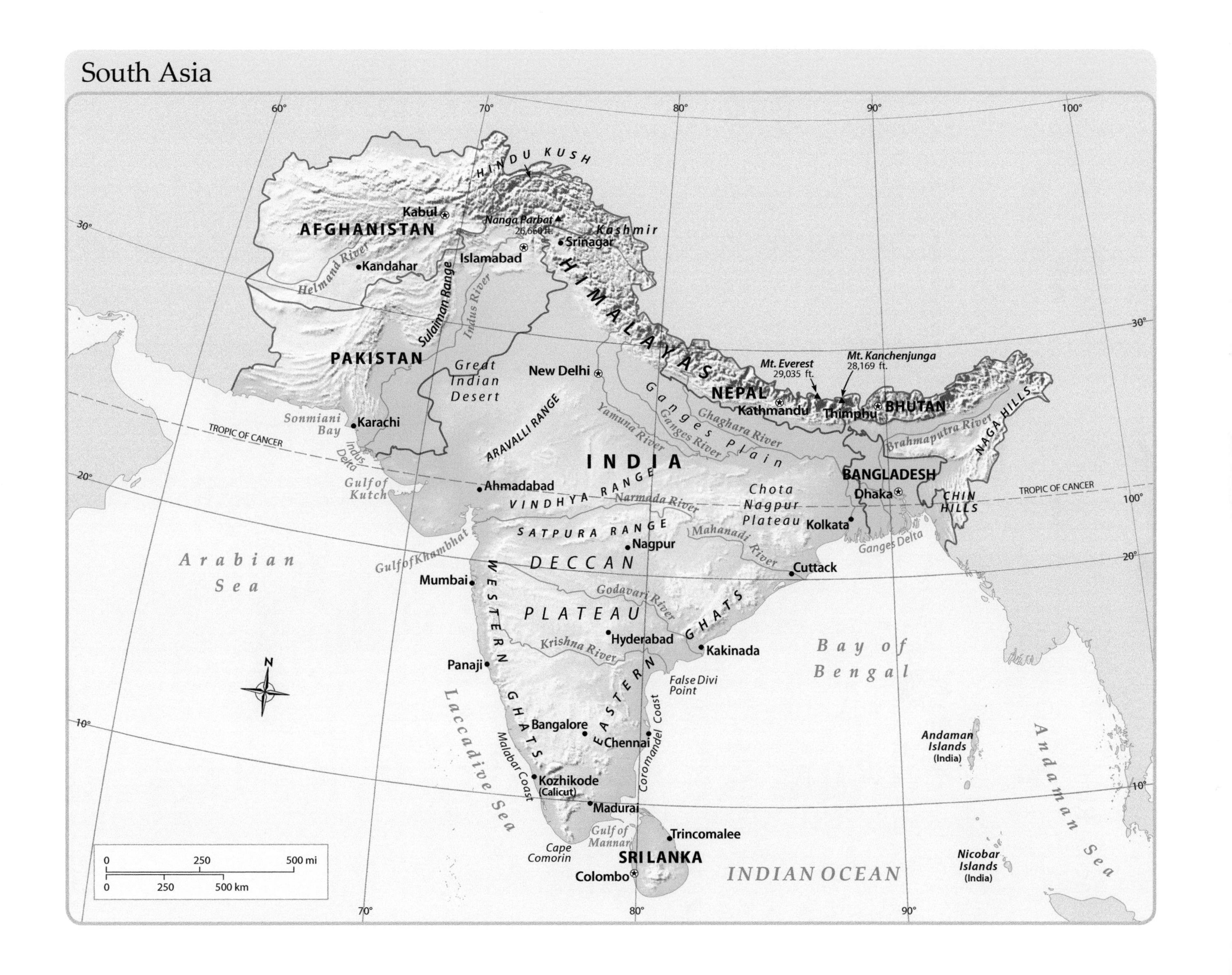

South Asia
AFGHANISTAN
PAKISTAN
INDIA
NEPAL
BHUTAN
BANGLADESH
SRI LANKA
Kabul
Kandahar
Islamabad
Karachi
Srinagar
New Delhi
Ahmadabad
Mumbai
Panaji
Nagpur
Hyderabad
Bangalore
Chennai
Kozhikode
(Calicut)
Madurai
Colombo
Trincomalee
Kakinada
Cuttack
Kolkata
Dhaka
Kathmandu
Thimphu
Mt. Everest
29,035 ft.
Mt. Kanchenjunga
28,169 ft.
Nanga Parbat
26,660 ft.
HINDU KUSH
Kashmir
HIMALAYAS
Sulaiman Range
Helmand River
Indus River
Indus Delta
Great Indian Desert
ARAVALLI RANGE
VINDHYA RANGE
SATPURA RANGE
DECCAN PLATEAU
WESTERN GHATS
EASTERN GHATS
Ganges Plain
Ganges River
Yamuna River
Ghaghara River
Narmada River
Godavari River
Krishna River
Mahanadi River
Chota Nagpur Plateau
Brahmaputra River
NAGA HILLS
CHIN HILLS
Ganges Delta
Bay of Bengal
Andaman Sea
Andaman Islands
(India)
Nicobar Islands
(India)
INDIAN OCEAN
Arabian Sea
Laccadive Sea
Sonmiani Bay
Gulf of Kutch
Gulf of Khambhat
Malabar Coast
Coromandel Coast
False Divi Point
Cape Comorin
Gulf of Mannar
TROPIC OF CANCER
TROPIC OF CANCER
N
0
250
500 mi
0
250
500 km
10°
20°
30°
60°
70°
80°
90°
100°

Pacific Rim

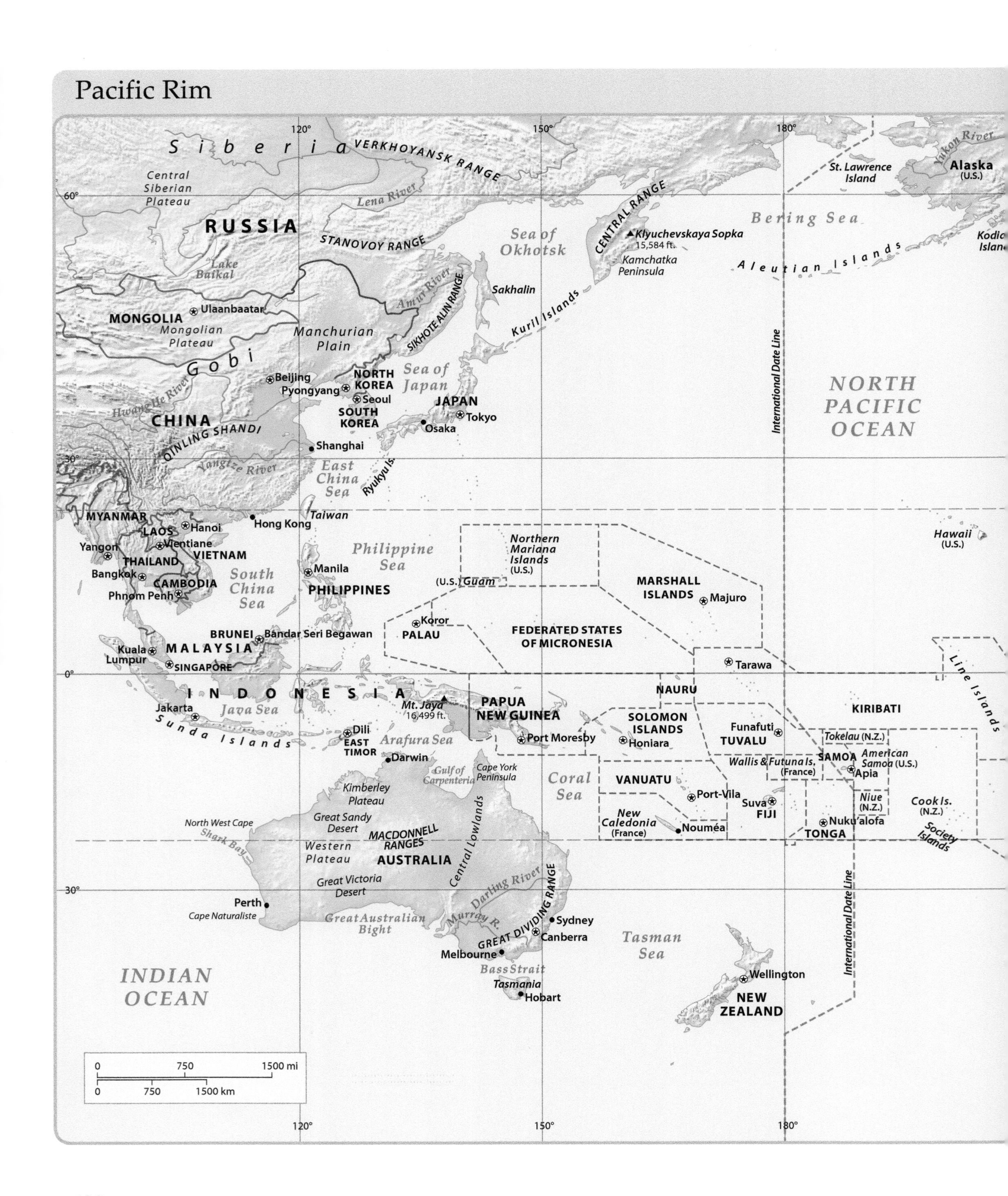

Siberia
VERKHOYANSK RANGE
Central Siberian Plateau
Lena River
RUSSIA
STANOVOY RANGE
Sea of Okhotsk
CENTRAL RANGE
Klyuchevskaya Sopka 15,584 ft.
Kamchatka Peninsula
Bering Sea
Aleutian Islands
St. Lawrence Island
Alaska (U.S.)
Yukon River
Lake Baikal
Amur River
SIKHOTE ALIN RANGE
Sakhalin
Kuril Islands
MONGOLIA
Ulaanbaatar
Mongolian Plateau
Gobi
Manchurian Plain
Sea of Japan
Beijing
Pyongyang
NORTH KOREA
Seoul
SOUTH KOREA
JAPAN
Tokyo
Osaka
Hwang He River
CHINA
QINLING SHANDI
Shanghai
Yangtze River
East China Sea
Ryukyu Is.
International Date Line
NORTH PACIFIC OCEAN
MYANMAR
LAOS
Hanoi
Hong Kong
Taiwan
Yangon
Vientiane
VIETNAM
THAILAND
Bangkok
CAMBODIA
Phnom Penh
South China Sea
Philippine Sea
Manila
PHILIPPINES
Northern Mariana Islands (U.S.)
(U.S.) Guam
MARSHALL ISLANDS
Majuro
Hawaii (U.S.)
Koror
PALAU
FEDERATED STATES OF MICRONESIA
BRUNEI
Bandar Seri Begawan
Kuala Lumpur
MALAYSIA
SINGAPORE
Tarawa
Line Islands
INDONESIA
NAURU
Jakarta
Java Sea
Sunda Islands
Mt. Jaya 16,499 ft.
PAPUA NEW GUINEA
SOLOMON ISLANDS
KIRIBATI
Dili
EAST TIMOR
Arafura Sea
Port Moresby
Honiara
Funafuti
TUVALU
Tokelau (N.Z.)
Darwin
Gulf of Carpentaria
Cape York Peninsula
Wallis & Futuna Is. (France)
SAMOA
American Samoa (U.S.)
Apia
Kimberley Plateau
Coral Sea
VANUATU
Port-Vila
Suva
FIJI
Niue (N.Z.)
Cook Is. (N.Z.)
Great Sandy Desert
North West Cape
Shark Bay
MACDONNELL RANGES
Central Lowlands
New Caledonia (France)
Nouméa
Nuku'alofa
TONGA
Society Islands
Western Plateau
AUSTRALIA
Great Victoria Desert
Darling River
GREAT DIVIDING RANGE
Perth
Cape Naturaliste
Great Australian Bight
Murray R.
Sydney
Canberra
Tasman Sea
Melbourne
Bass Strait
Tasmania
Hobart
Wellington
NEW ZEALAND
INDIAN OCEAN
0 750 1500 mi
0 750 1500 km
120°
150°
180°
60°
30°
0°

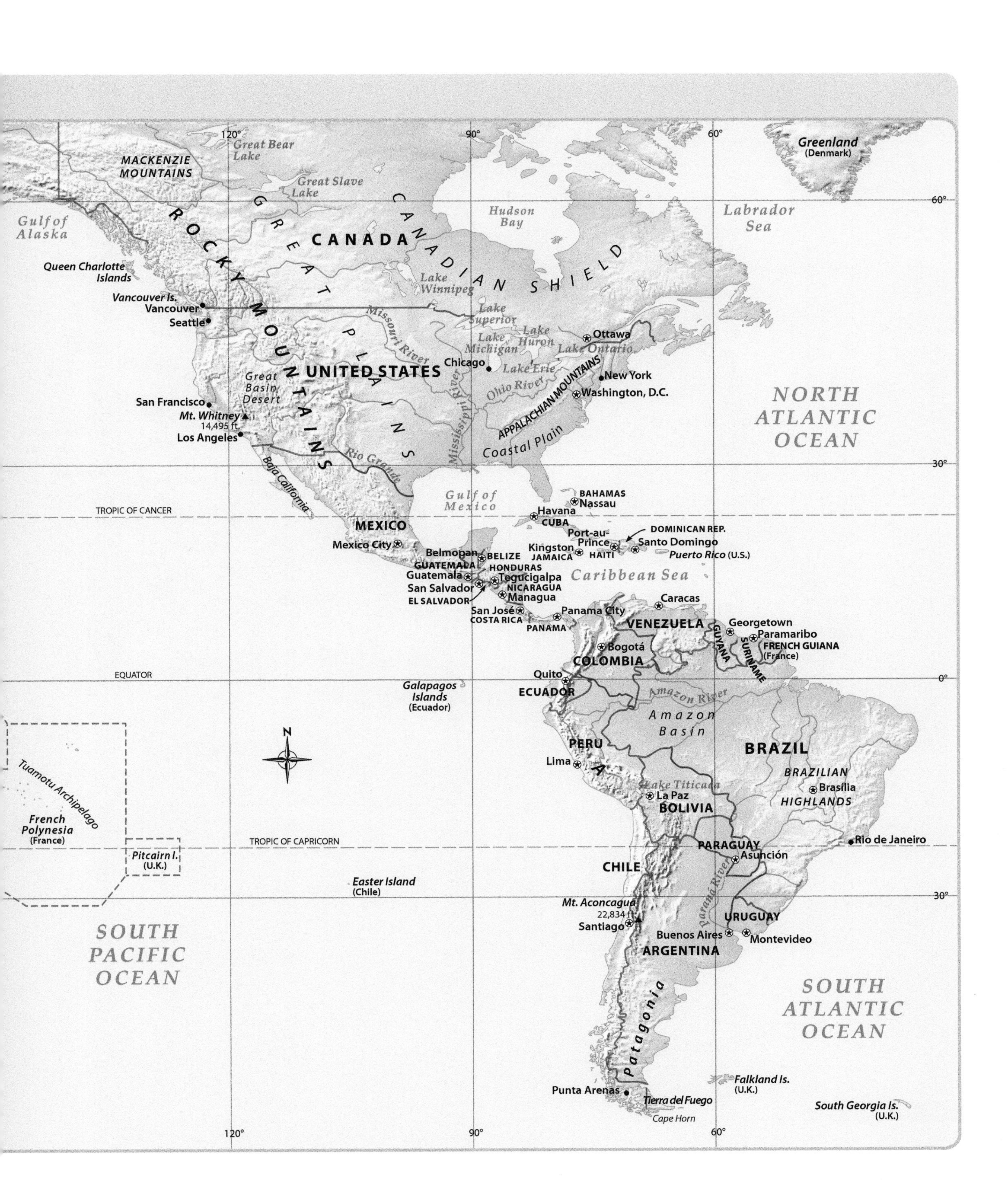

120°
90°
60°
30°
0°
Great Bear Lake
MACKENZIE MOUNTAINS
Great Slave Lake
Greenland
(Denmark)
Hudson Bay
Labrador Sea
Gulf of Alaska
ROCKY MOUNTAINS
GREAT PLAINS
CANADA
CANADIAN SHIELD
Queen Charlotte Islands
Vancouver Is.
Vancouver
Seattle
Lake Winnipeg
Missouri River
Lake Superior
Lake Michigan
Lake Huron
Ottawa
Lake Ontario
Chicago
Lake Erie
UNITED STATES
Great Basin Desert
Ohio River
Mississippi River
APPALACHIAN MOUNTAINS
New York
Washington, D.C.
San Francisco
Mt. Whitney
14,495 ft.
Los Angeles
Coastal Plain
NORTH ATLANTIC OCEAN
Rio Grande
Baja California
Gulf of Mexico
BAHAMAS
Nassau
TROPIC OF CANCER
Havana
CUBA
MEXICO
DOMINICAN REP.
Port-au-Prince
Santo Domingo
Mexico City
Belmopan
BELIZE
Kingston
JAMAICA
HAITI
Puerto Rico (U.S.)
GUATEMALA
HONDURAS
Guatemala
Tegucigalpa
Caribbean Sea
San Salvador
NICARAGUA
Managua
EL SALVADOR
Caracas
San José
COSTA RICA
Panama City
PANAMA
VENEZUELA
Georgetown
GUYANA
Paramaribo
SURINAME
FRENCH GUIANA
(France)
Bogotá
COLOMBIA
EQUATOR
Quito
ECUADOR
Galapagos Islands
(Ecuador)
Amazon River
Amazon Basin
PERU
BRAZIL
Lima
BRAZILIAN HIGHLANDS
Brasília
Lake Titicaca
La Paz
BOLIVIA
Tuamotu Archipelago
French Polynesia
(France)
Rio de Janeiro
TROPIC OF CAPRICORN
PARAGUAY
Asunción
Pitcairn I.
(U.K.)
CHILE
Easter Island
(Chile)
Paraná River
Mt. Aconcagua
22,834 ft.
URUGUAY
Santiago
Buenos Aires
Montevideo
ARGENTINA
SOUTH PACIFIC OCEAN
SOUTH ATLANTIC OCEAN
Patagonia
Falkland Is.
(U.K.)
Punta Arenas
Tierra del Fuego
South Georgia Is.
(U.K.)
Cape Horn
N

Middle East

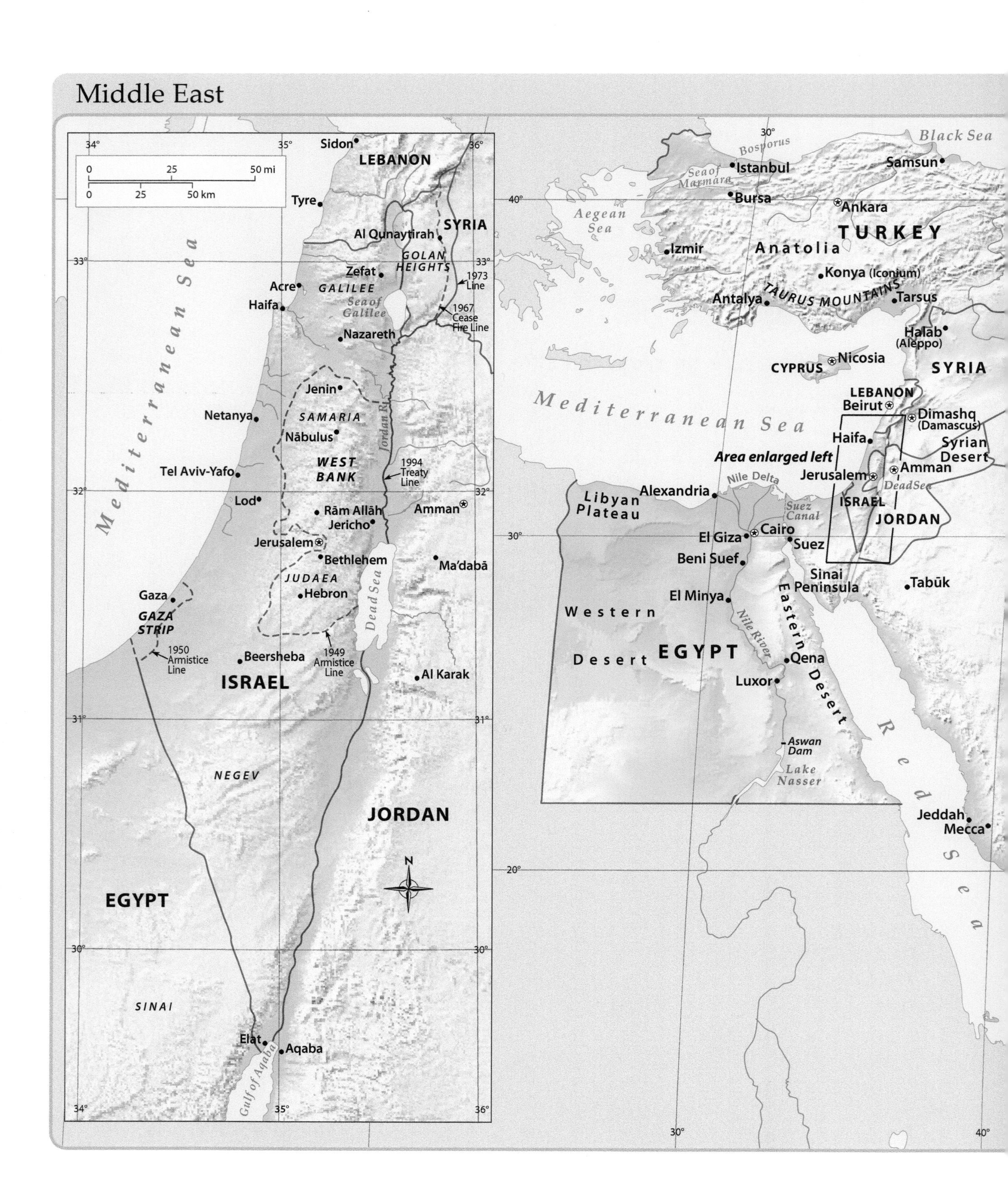

0
25
50 mi
0
25
50 km
Sidon
LEBANON
Tyre
SYRIA
Al Qunaytirah
GOLAN HEIGHTS
1973 Line
Zefat
Acre
GALILEE
Haifa
Sea of Galilee
1967 Cease Fire Line
Nazareth
Mediterranean Sea
Jenin
Netanya
SAMARIA
Nābulus
Jordan R.
WEST BANK
1994 Treaty Line
Tel Aviv-Yafo
Lod
Rām Allāh
Amman
Jericho
Jerusalem
Bethlehem
Ma'dabā
JUDAEA
Dead Sea
Hebron
Gaza
GAZA STRIP
1950 Armistice Line
Beersheba
1949 Armistice Line
Al Karak
ISRAEL
NEGEV
JORDAN
N
EGYPT
SINAI
Elat
Aqaba
Gulf of Aqaba
Black Sea
Bosporus
Sea of Marmara
Istanbul
Samsun
Bursa
Ankara
Aegean Sea
TURKEY
Izmir
Anatolia
Konya (Iconium)
TAURUS MOUNTAINS
Antalya
Tarsus
Halab (Aleppo)
CYPRUS
Nicosia
SYRIA
LEBANON
Beirut
Mediterranean Sea
Dimashq (Damascus)
Haifa
Syrian Desert
Area enlarged left
Amman
Jerusalem
Nile Delta
Dead Sea
Alexandria
Libyan Plateau
ISRAEL
Suez Canal
JORDAN
El Giza
Cairo
Suez
Beni Suef
Sinai Peninsula
Tabūk
El Minya
Western Desert
Nile River
Eastern Desert
EGYPT
Qena
Luxor
Aswan Dam
Lake Nasser
Red Sea
Jeddah
Mecca

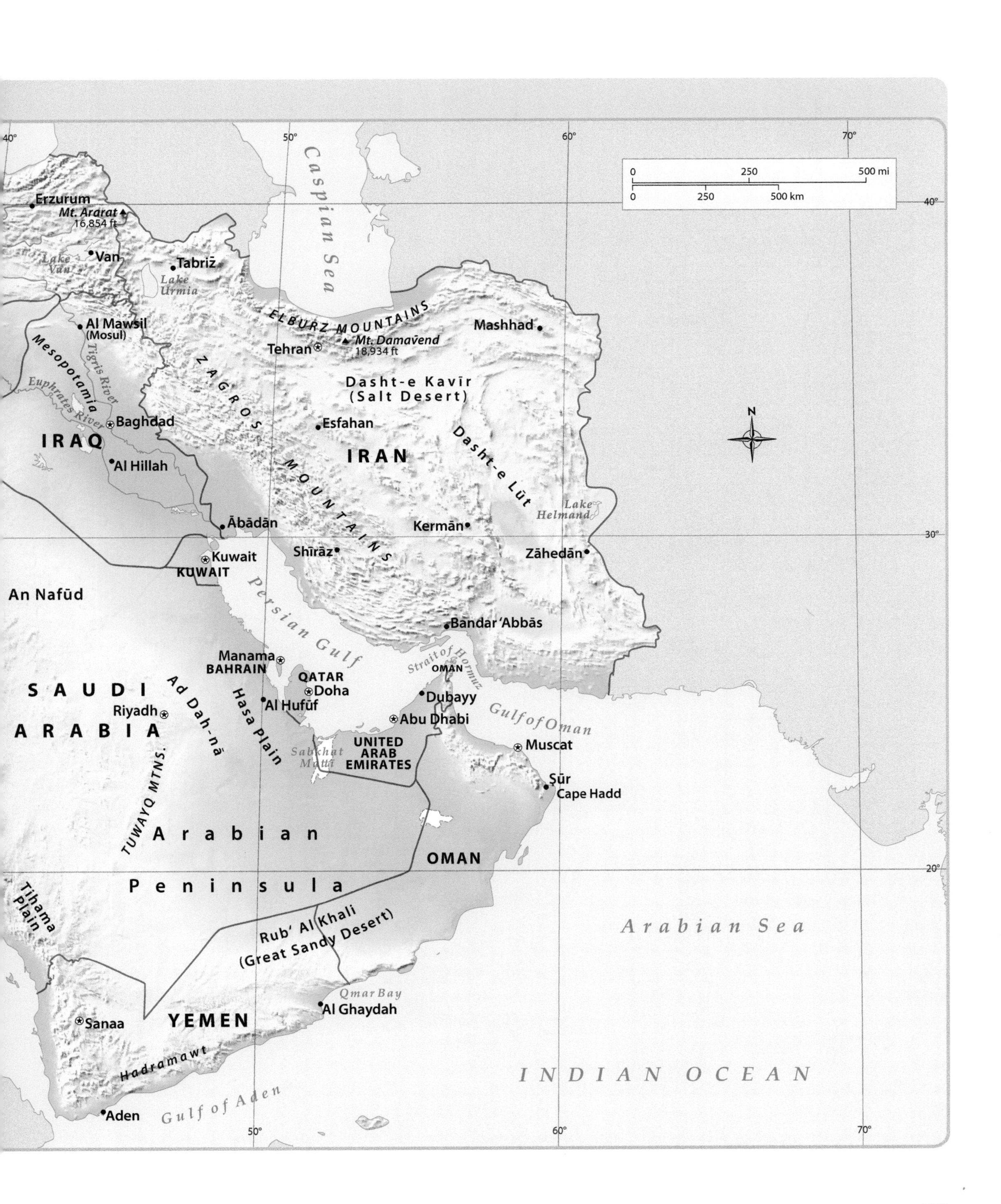
Caspian Sea
Erzurum
Mt. Ararat
16,854 ft
Lake Van
Van
Tabriz
Lake Urmia
ELBURZ MOUNTAINS
Mashhad
Al Mawsil
(Mosul)
Mt. Damavend
18,934 ft
Tehran
Mesopotamia
Tigris River
Euphrates River
ZAGROS MOUNTAINS
Dasht-e Kavīr
(Salt Desert)
Baghdad
Esfahan
IRAQ
IRAN
Dasht-e Lūt
Al Hillah
Lake Helmand
Ābādān
Kermān
Kuwait
KUWAIT
Shīrāz
Zāhedān
An Nafūd
Persian Gulf
Bandar 'Abbās
Manama
BAHRAIN
Strait of Hormuz
OMAN
QATAR
Doha
SAUDI ARABIA
Ad Dah-nā
Hasa Plain
Riyadh
Al Hufūf
Dubayy
Abu Dhabi
Gulf of Oman
Muscat
UNITED ARAB EMIRATES
Sabkhat Mattī
TUWAYQ MTNS.
Şūr
Cape Hadd
Arabian Peninsula
OMAN
Tihama Plain
Rub' Al Khali
(Great Sandy Desert)
Arabian Sea
Qmar Bay
Al Ghaydah
Sanaa
YEMEN
Hadramawt
INDIAN OCEAN
Aden
Gulf of Aden
0 250 500 mi
0 250 500 km
N
40°
50°
60°
70°
30°
20°

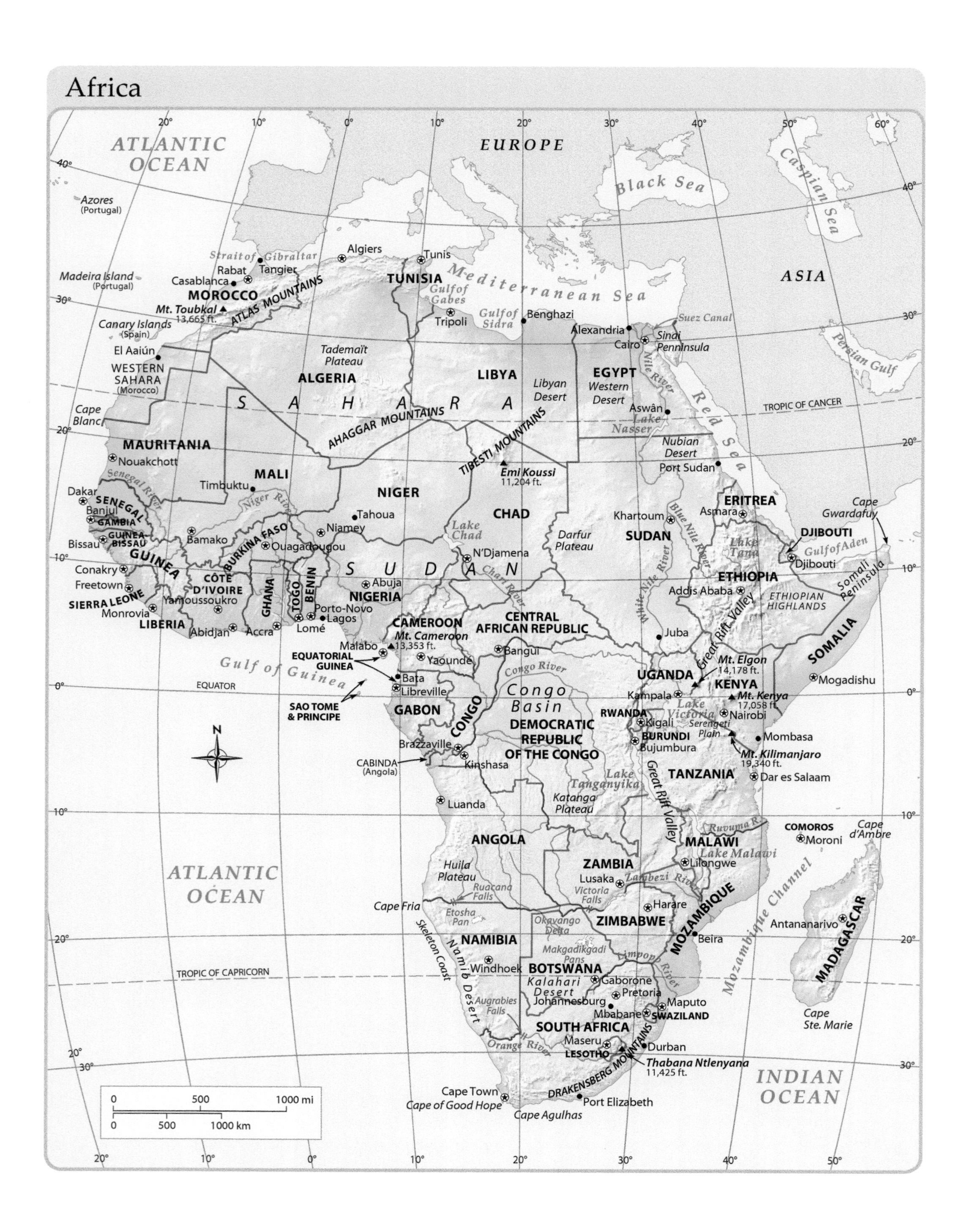

Africa
ATLANTIC OCEAN
EUROPE
Black Sea
Caspian Sea
Azores (Portugal)
Madeira Island (Portugal)
Canary Islands (Spain)
Strait of Gibraltar
Rabat
Tangier
Casablanca
Algiers
Tunis
MOROCCO
ATLAS MOUNTAINS
Mt. Toubkal 13,665 ft.
TUNISIA
Mediterranean Sea
Gulf of Gabes
Tripoli
Gulf of Sidra
Benghazi
Alexandria
Suez Canal
ASIA
Cairo
Sinai Penninsula
Persian Gulf
El Aaiún
WESTERN SAHARA (Morocco)
Tademaït Plateau
ALGERIA
LIBYA
Libyan Desert
EGYPT
Western Desert
Nile River
Red Sea
S A H A R A
AHAGGAR MOUNTAINS
TIBESTI MOUNTAINS
Aswân
Lake Nasser
TROPIC OF CANCER
Cape Blanc
MAURITANIA
Nouakchott
MALI
Timbuktu
Senegal River
Niger River
NIGER
Emi Koussi 11,204 ft.
Nubian Desert
Port Sudan
Dakar
SENEGAL
Banjul
GAMBIA
GUINEA-BISSAU
Bissau
Bamako
BURKINA FASO
Ouagadougou
Tahoua
Niamey
Lake Chad
CHAD
N'Djamena
Darfur Plateau
Khartoum
SUDAN
Blue Nile River
White Nile River
ERITREA
Asmara
Cape Gwardafuy
DJIBOUTI
Djibouti
Gulf of Aden
Lake Tana
ETHIOPIA
Addis Ababa
ETHIOPIAN HIGHLANDS
Somali Peninsula
GUINEA
Conakry
Freetown
SIERRA LEONE
Monrovia
LIBERIA
CÔTE D'IVOIRE
Yamoussoukro
Abidjan
GHANA
Accra
TOGO
Lomé
BENIN
Porto-Novo
Lagos
S U D A N
Abuja
NIGERIA
Chari River
CAMEROON
Mt. Cameroon 13,353 ft.
CENTRAL AFRICAN REPUBLIC
Juba
Great Rift Valley
SOMALIA
Malabo
EQUATORIAL GUINEA
Yaoundé
Bangui
Mt. Elgon 14,178 ft.
Mogadishu
Gulf of Guinea
Bata
Libreville
EQUATOR
SAO TOME & PRINCIPE
GABON
CONGO
Congo River
Congo Basin
UGANDA
Kampala
Lake Victoria
KENYA
Mt. Kenya 17,058 ft.
Nairobi
RWANDA
Kigali
BURUNDI
Bujumbura
Serengeti Plain
Mombasa
DEMOCRATIC REPUBLIC OF THE CONGO
Brazzaville
Kinshasa
CABINDA (Angola)
Mt. Kilimanjaro 19,340 ft.
TANZANIA
Dar es Salaam
Lake Tanganyika
Katanga Plateau
Luanda
Ruvuma R.
COMOROS
Moroni
Cape d'Ambre
ANGOLA
MALAWI
Lake Malawi
Lilongwe
ATLANTIC OCEAN
Huila Plateau
ZAMBIA
Lusaka
Zambezi River
Victoria Falls
Ruacana Falls
Mozambique Channel
Cape Fria
Etosha Pan
Harare
ZIMBABWE
MOZAMBIQUE
Beira
Antananarivo
MADAGASCAR
Okavango Delta
Skeleton Coast
NAMIBIA
Makgadikgadi Pans
Limpopo River
Windhoek
Namib Desert
BOTSWANA
Kalahari Desert
Gaborone
Pretoria
TROPIC OF CAPRICORN
Johannesburg
Maputo
Mbabane
SWAZILAND
Augrabies Falls
Cape Ste. Marie
SOUTH AFRICA
Orange River
Maseru
LESOTHO
Durban
DRAKENSBERG MOUNTAINS
Thabana Ntlenyana 11,425 ft.
INDIAN OCEAN
Cape Town
Cape of Good Hope
Cape Agulhas
Port Elizabeth
0 500 1000 mi
0 500 1000 km
N

North and South Poles

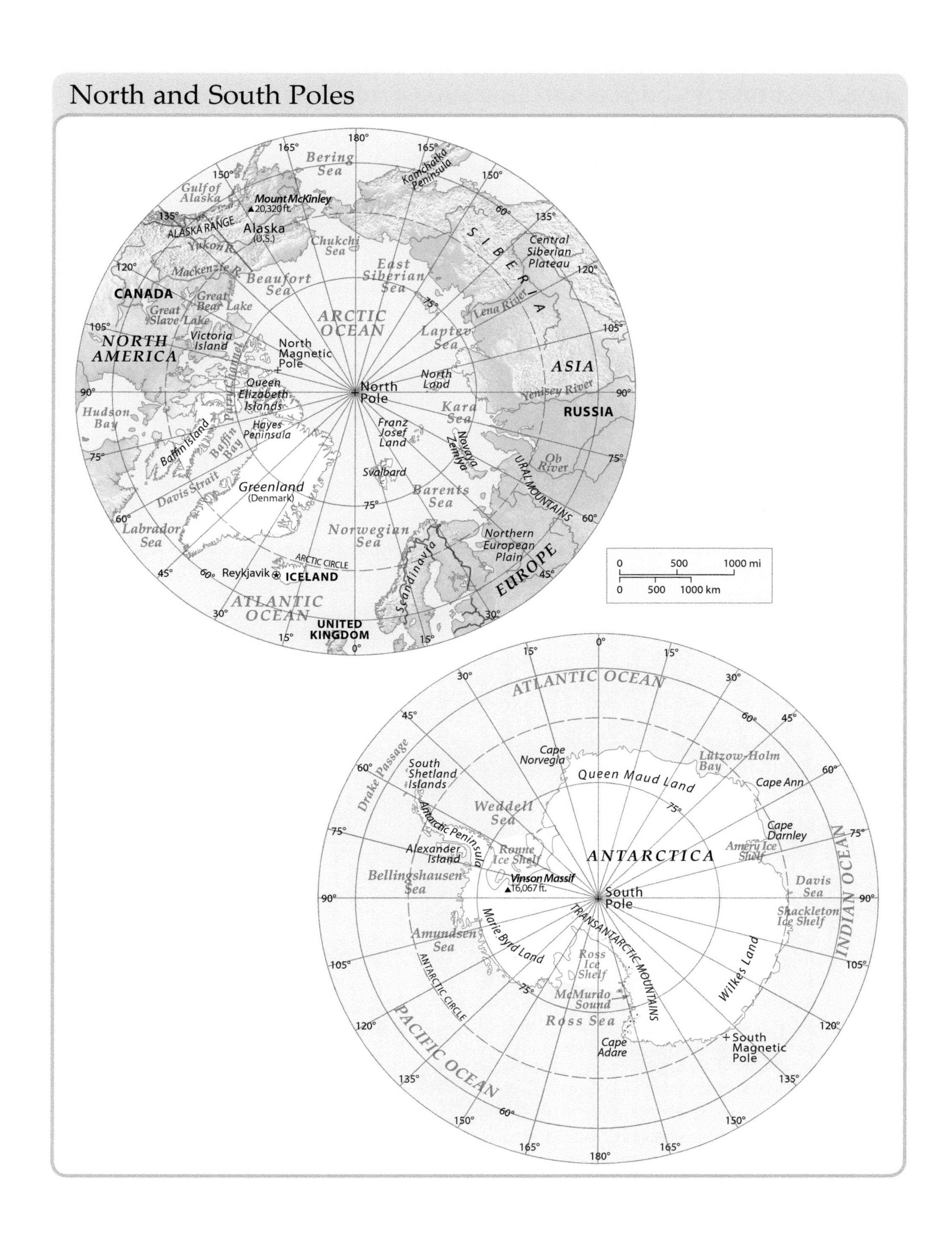

Goode's Interrupted Homosoline Projection

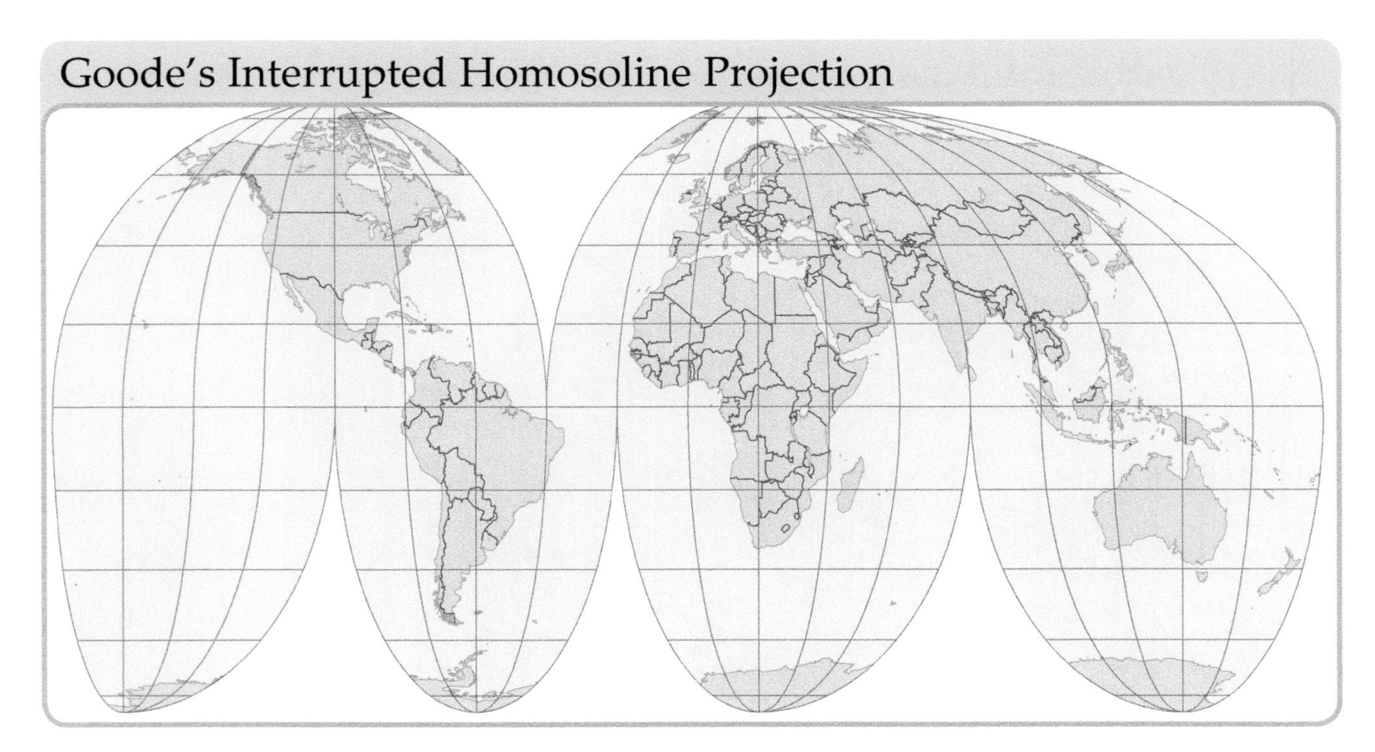

This projection, called interrupted *because it is divided into segments, minimizes distortion of scale and the shape of landforms, but breaks Antarctica, Greenland, and the oceans into pieces.*

Miller Projection

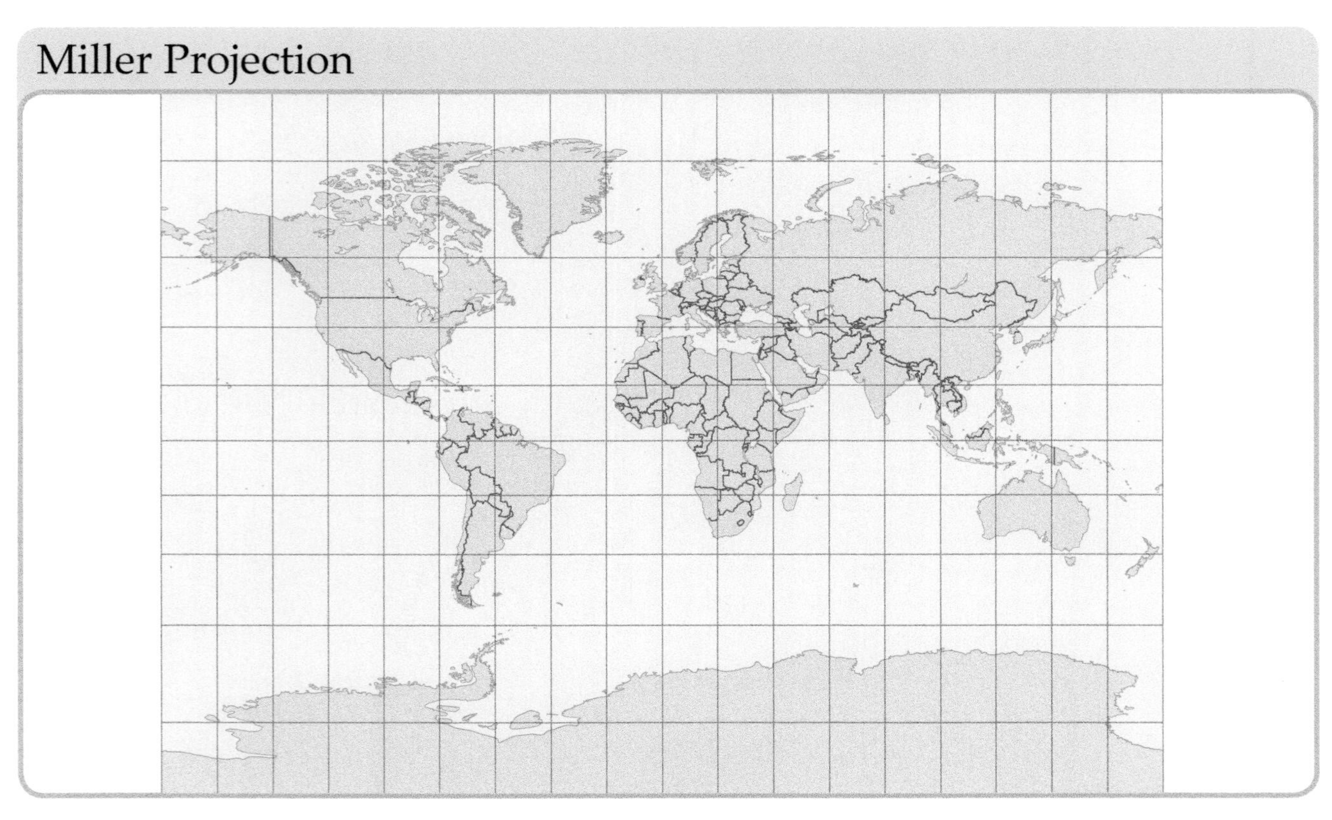

This projection, with straight meridians and parallels that meet at right angles, avoids scale exaggerations, but distorts shapes and sizes.

Mollweide Projection

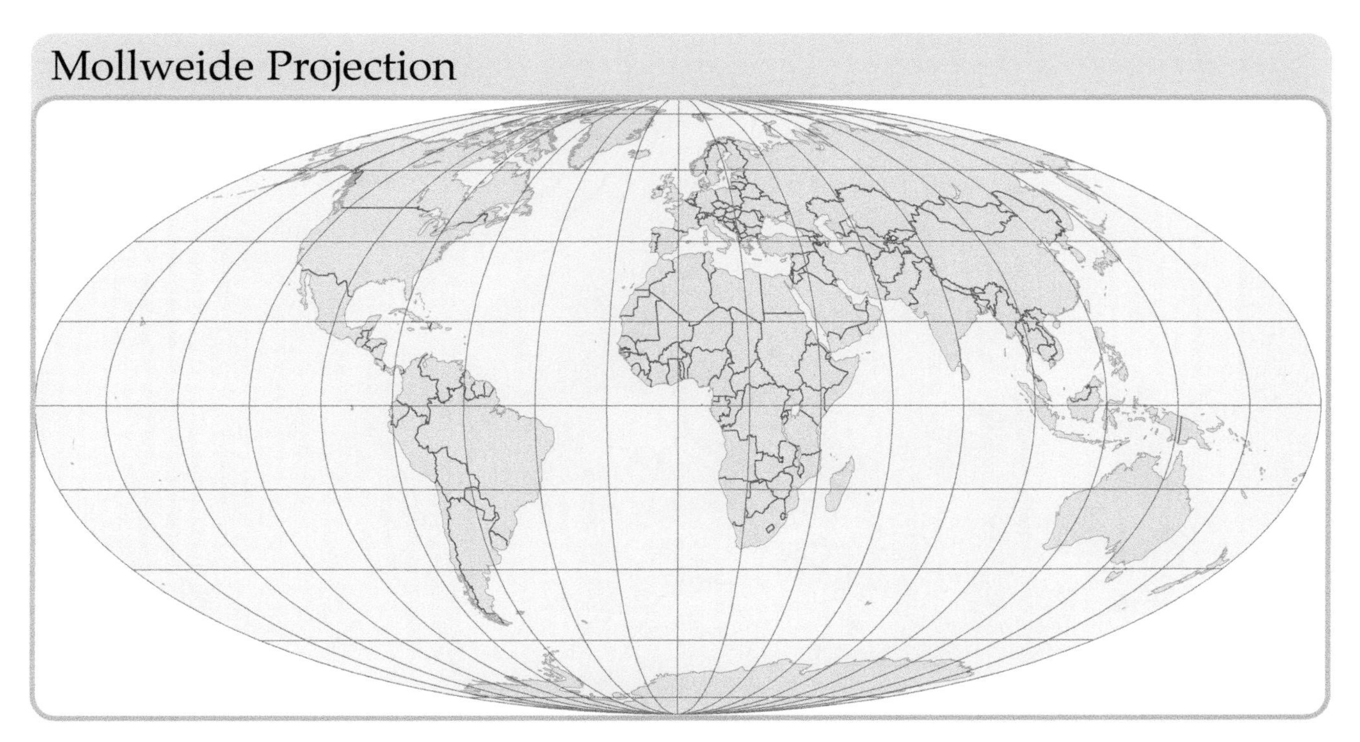

This elliptical equal-area projection, designed in 1805 by German mathematician Carl B. Mollweide, represents the size of landforms quite accurately, but distorts shapes near the edges.

Winkel Tripel Projection

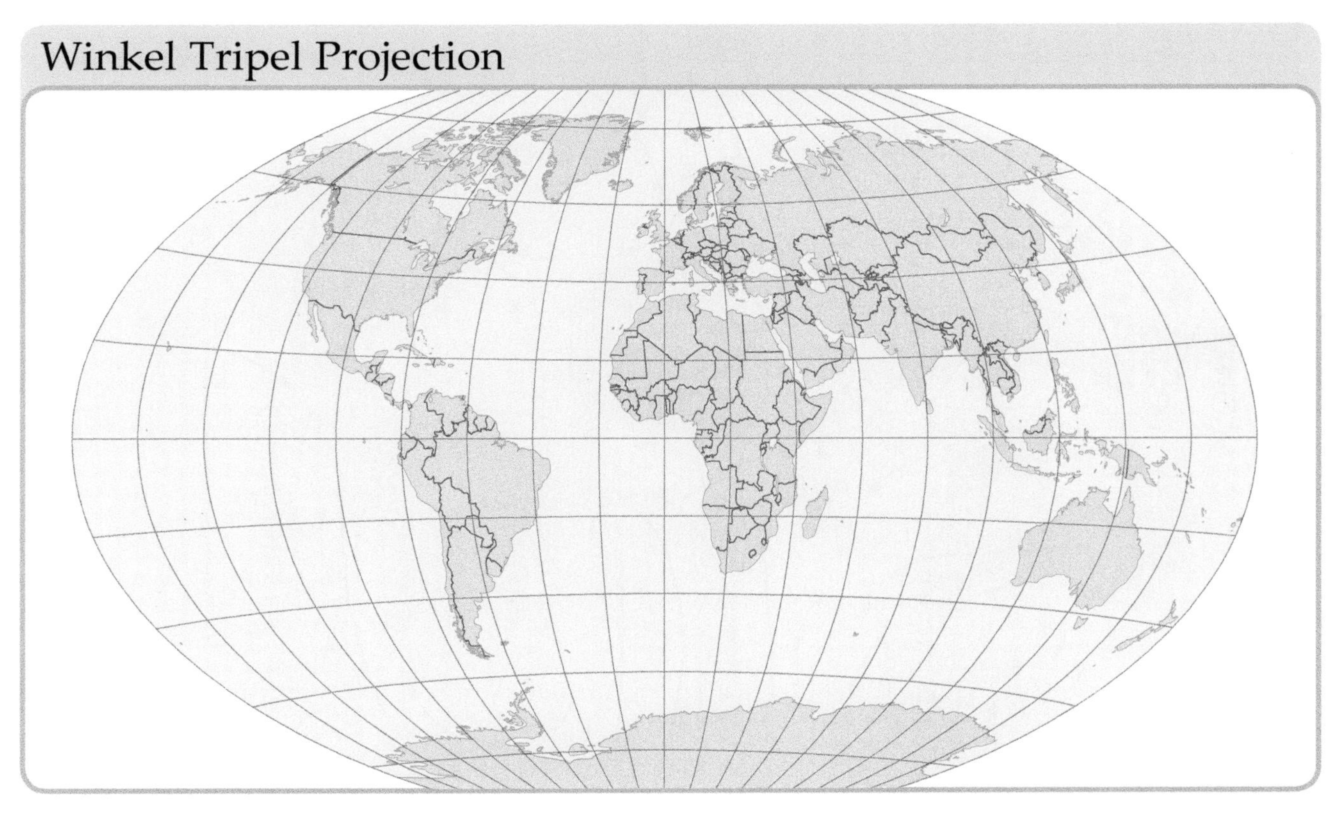

This projection, designed by Oswald Winkel of Germany in 1921, lessens the distortions of scale and shape by presenting the central meridian and equator as straight lines, and the other parallels and meridians as curved lines.

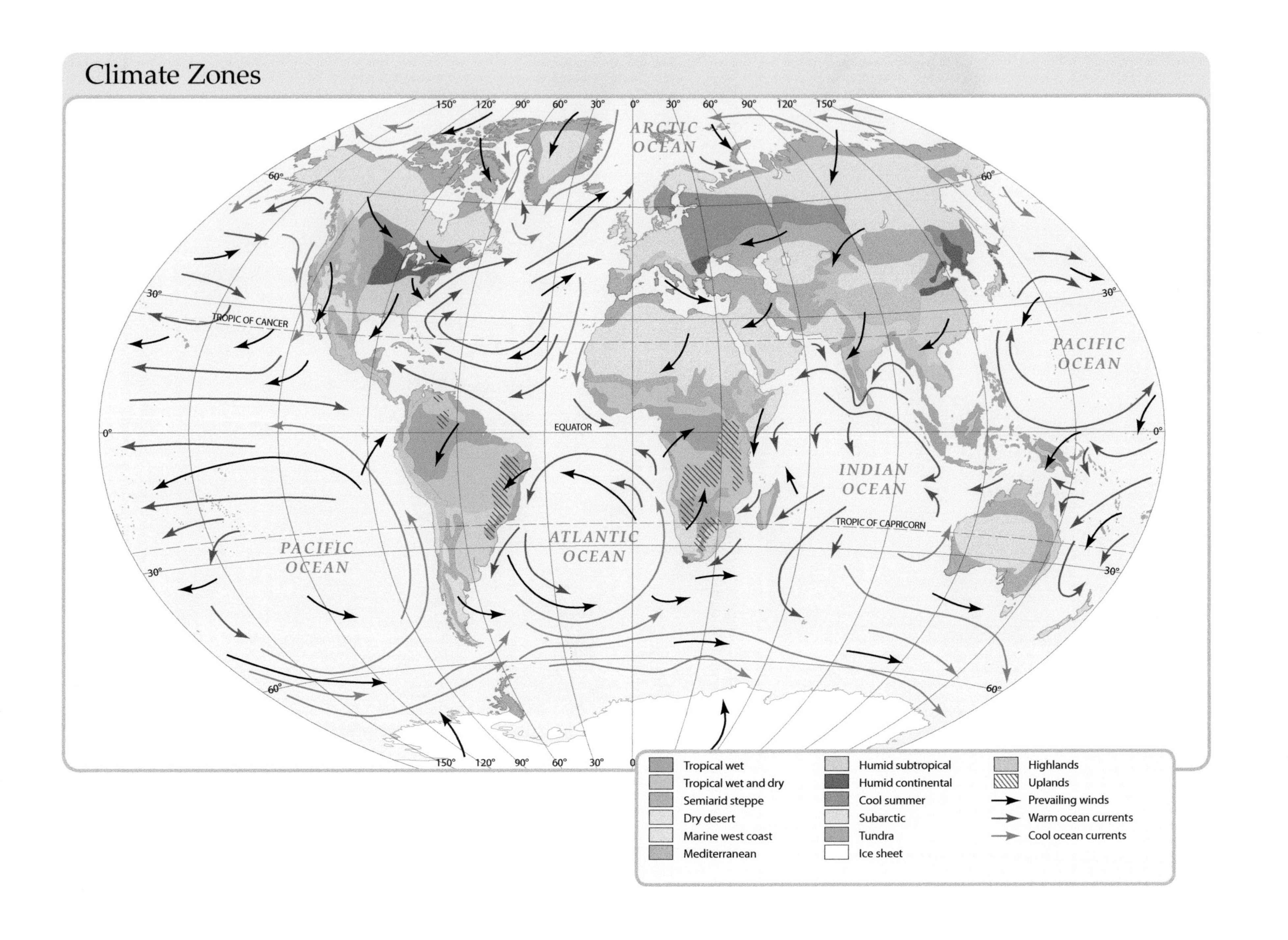
Climate Zones
ARCTIC OCEAN
PACIFIC OCEAN
ATLANTIC OCEAN
INDIAN OCEAN
PACIFIC OCEAN
TROPIC OF CANCER
EQUATOR
TROPIC OF CAPRICORN
Tropical wet
Tropical wet and dry
Semiarid steppe
Dry desert
Marine west coast
Mediterranean
Humid subtropical
Humid continental
Cool summer
Subarctic
Tundra
Ice sheet
Highlands
Uplands
Prevailing winds
Warm ocean currents
Cool ocean currents

Terrestrial Biomes

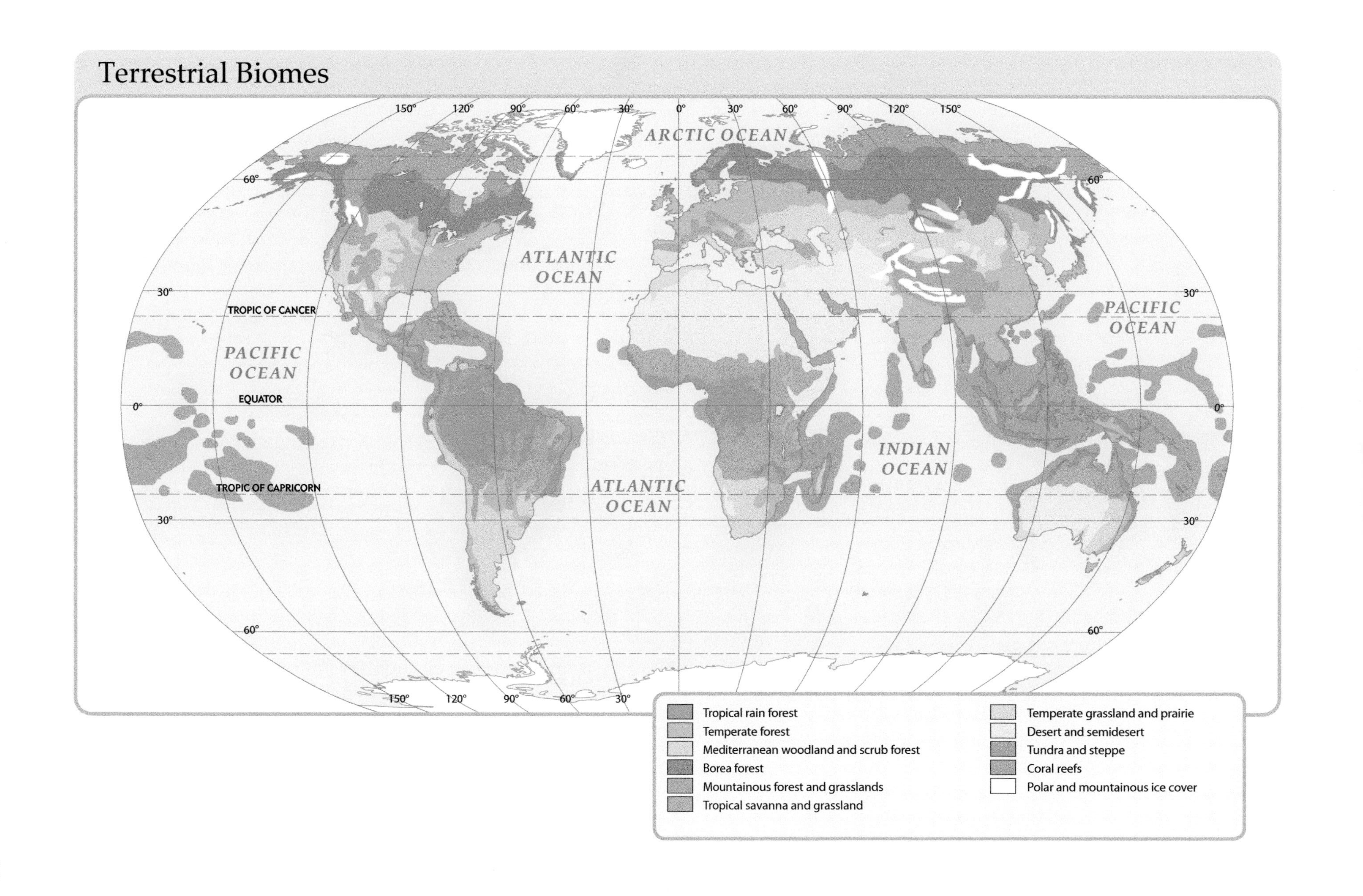

Continents

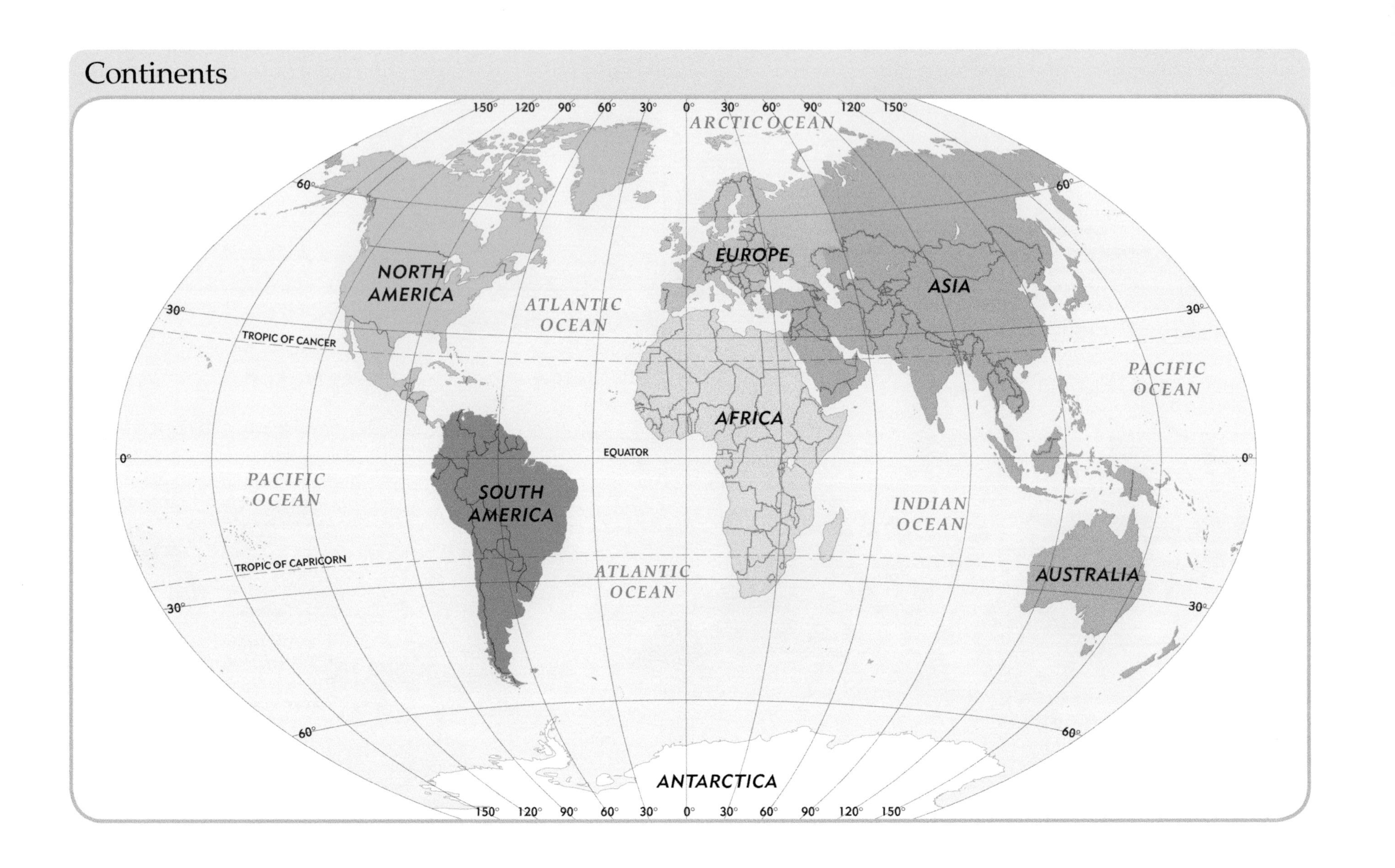
ARCTIC OCEAN
NORTH AMERICA
ATLANTIC OCEAN
EUROPE
ASIA
TROPIC OF CANCER
PACIFIC OCEAN
AFRICA
EQUATOR
PACIFIC OCEAN
SOUTH AMERICA
INDIAN OCEAN
TROPIC OF CAPRICORN
ATLANTIC OCEAN
AUSTRALIA
ANTARCTICA
150° 120° 90° 60° 30° 0° 30° 60° 90° 120° 150°
60°
30°
0°

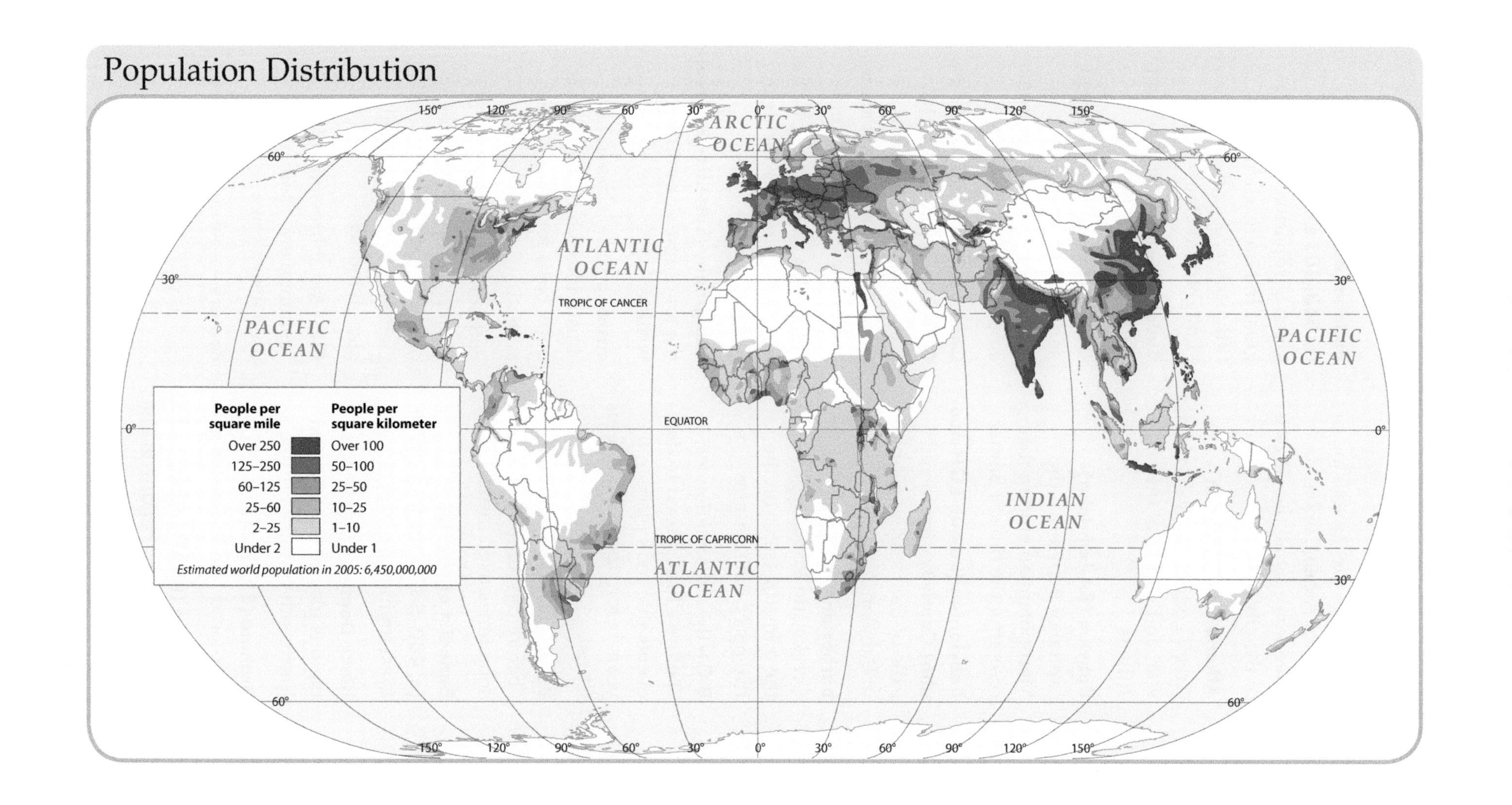
Population Distribution
ARCTIC OCEAN
ATLANTIC OCEAN
TROPIC OF CANCER
PACIFIC OCEAN
PACIFIC OCEAN
EQUATOR
INDIAN OCEAN
TROPIC OF CAPRICORN
ATLANTIC OCEAN
People per square mile
People per square kilometer
Over 250
125–250
60–125
25–60
2–25
Under 2
Over 100
50–100
25–50
10–25
1–10
Under 1
Estimated world population in 2005: 6,450,000,000

Glossary

Abraham (c. 1800 B.C.)– the "father of the Hebrews" and founder of Judaism

acropolis (uh-KRAH-puh-lus)– a fortified hill in Greek city-states where the people could take refuge in time of attack

A.D.– the abbreviation for the Latin words *anno Domini* ("in the year of the Lord"), used to date events that took place after the birth of Jesus Christ

***Aeneid* (uh-NEE-id)–** an epic poem by Virgil about the founding of Rome

Alexander the Great (356–323 B.C.)– the Macedonian ruler of Greece who built a huge empire and helped spread Greek culture

archaeology (ahr-kee-AH-luh-jee)– the scientific study of ancient ruins and artifacts in order to learn about the past

Aristotle (AIR-uh-stah-tl) (384–322 B.C.)– one of the greatest philosophers of ancient Greece; a student of Plato

Aryan– nomadic people from Central Asia who gradually conquered northern India about 1500 B.C.

Asoka (uh-SOH-kuh) (c. 269–232 B.C.)– a powerful Indian ruler who renounced war and converted to Buddhism, sponsoring missionaries across Asia

Assembly– the lawmaking body of Athens, open to attendance by all the citizens of the city-state

Athena (uh-THEE-nuh)– Greek goddess of wisdom and war, and patron of the city of Athens

Babylon (BA-buh-lahn)– capital of Babylonia, the Mesopotamian empire that rose after the time of Sumer

Babylonian (ba-buh-LOH-nee-uhn) Captivity– the forced exile of the Hebrew people in Babylon

barbarian– the name the Greeks and Romans gave to the nomadic tribes on the fringes of their empire

B.C.– the abbreviation for "before Christ," used to date events that took place in the years before the birth of Jesus Christ

B.C.E.– the abbreviation for "before the common era," sometimes used instead of B.C.

Benedict of Nursia (c. 480–547)– the founder of Western monasticism

Black Death– a highly contagious plague that ravaged fourteenth-century Europe

Brahma (BRAH-muh)– the four-faced Hindu creator god

brahman (BRAH-muhn)– a religious leader of Hinduism and member of the highest caste

Buddha (BOO-duh) (c. 563–483 B.C.)– the title given Siddhartha Gautama, great Indian teacher of the fifth century B.C.; means "Enlightened One"

Buddhism– the ideas and path set forth by the Buddha

Caesar (SEE-zuhr)– the family name of Julius Caesar, later adopted as a title of the Roman emperors

Caesar Augustus (SEE-zuhr aw-GUHS-tuhs) (63 B.C.–A.D. 14)– the title adopted by Julius Caesar's nephew Octavian after he became emperor of Rome

caliph (KAY-luhf)– the title for Muslim rulers after the death of Muhammad

calligraphy (kuh-LIH-gruh-fee)– the art of fine or beautiful writing

caste– a social class in Hinduism into which a person is born; basis for India's caste system

cathedral– the church of a bishop; in medieval times often characterized by soaring Gothic spires and stained glass windows

C.E.– the abbreviation for "common era," sometimes used instead of A.D.

century– a period of 100 years

Charlemagne (SHAHR-luh-mayn) (742–814)– the king of the Franks and emperor of a vast realm; one of the most important rulers of the Middle Ages

Christianity– world religion based on the life and teachings of Jesus Christ

city-state– an independently ruled city and the land around it

civilization– a stage of social development characterized by the building of cities, and made possible when people have a surplus of food and division of labor

classical civilization– the civilizations of ancient Greece and Rome between about 500 B.C. and A.D. 500

Code of Hammurabi (ha-muh-RAH-bee)– a set of laws assembled by the Babylonian King Hammurabi

Colosseum (kah-luh-SEE-uhm)– the huge amphitheater in Rome where gladiator contests and other events were held

Confucianism– philosophy based on the teachings of Confucius

Confucius (kuhn-FYOO-shuhs) (551–479 B.C.)– the great Chinese philosopher of the sixth century B.C., and most influential thinker in Chinese history

Constantine (KAHN-stuhn-teen) (c. 285–337)– the first Roman emperor to embrace Christianity; Constantine moved his capital from Rome to Byzantium, which became known as Constantinople

covenant (KUH-vuh-nuhnt)– a solemn, binding agreement or promise

Crusades– medieval wars fought by Christians to recapture the Holy Land from the Muslim Turks

culture– the traditions and customs of a people; their way of life and thought

cuneiform (kyou-NEE-uh-form)– ancient Sumerian form of writing that used wedge-shaped marks

Darius (duh-RIY-uhs) (550–486 B.C.)– the king of Persia who launched the Persian Wars against Greece

decade– a period of 10 years

democracy– rule by the people, originating in the city-states of ancient Greece

dynasty– a ruling family that remains in power for many years

epic– a long poem that recounts the deeds of great heroes

equator– the imaginary line that circles the Earth halfway between the North Pole and the South Pole

Erik the Red (c. 950–1000)– a Viking explorer and adventurer who started the settlement of Greenland

Exodus (EK-suh-duhs)– the journey of the Hebrew people out of Egypt, probably in the thirteenth century B.C.

feudalism (FYOO-dl-ih-zuhm)– term used to describe the political and military system of Western Europe in the Middle Ages, in which vassals exchanged military service for land

fief (feef)– a grant of land by a medieval lord to a lesser noble or knight

Five Pillars of Islam (iss-LAHM)– the five religious duties of Muslims

Four Noble Truths– four fundamental beliefs of Buddhism

Genghis Khan (JEHNG-gihs kahn) (c. 1162–1227)– the Mongol leader who united many of Asia's nomadic tribes and forged a mighty empire

Gilgamesh (GIL-guh-mesh)– a Sumerian hero whose adventures are told in the *Epic of Gilgamesh*

Gospels– the first four books of the Christian New Testament that recount the life and teachings of Jesus Christ

Gothic– a medieval style of architecture characterized by flying buttresses, pointed arches, and soaring spires

Great Wall of China– the long wall built by the Chinese to keep out invaders from the north

Hagia Sophia (HAH-juh soh-FEE-uh)– huge domed cathedral built by the Byzantine emperor Justinian in Constantinople around A.D. 535; the name means "Holy Wisdom"

Hajj (haj)– the pilgrimage to Mecca that all Muslims must make once before they die, if possible

Hammurabi (ha-muh-RAH-bee) (died c. 1750 B.C.)– a Babylonian king and lawgiver of the eighteenth century B.C.

Hanging Gardens of Babylon (BA-buh-lahn)– the elegantly terraced gardens built by King Nebuchadnezzar

Hannibal (HAN-uh-buhl) (247–183 B.C.)– a great general from Carthage who fought the Romans in the Punic Wars

Hatshepsut (hat-SHEP-soot) (reigned c. 1470 B.C.)– one of four female pharaohs who ruled Egypt

Hebrews– the first ancient peoples to develop a monotheistic religion, which today is known as Judaism

Hellenistic Civilization– the civilization of the ancient Greeks, which was spread through the Mediterranean world by Alexander the Great

Herodotus (hih-RAHD-uh-tuhs) (c. 484–425 B.C.)– a Greek historian of the ancient world, sometimes called the "father of history"

hieroglyphics (hiy-ruh-GLIH-fiks)– a form of picture-writing used in ancient Egypt

Hijrah (HIJ-ruh)– Muhammad's flight to Medina in A.D. 622, the first year of the Muslim calendar

Hinduism (HIN-doo-ih-zuhm)– world religion and major faith of India; emerged when the cultures of the Indus Valley mixed with those of the Aryan settlers

history– that period of the past for which written records exist

Homer– renowned poet of ancient Greece believed to have composed the *Iliad* and the *Odyssey*

Hundred Years' War– a long, destructive series of struggles between England and France that lasted from 1337 to 1453

Iliad (IL-ee-uhd)– Homer's epic poem about the Trojan War

irrigation– a method of watering the land by using channels and canals

Ishtar (ISH-tahr)– the Babylonian goddess of love and war, memorialized in the Ishtar Gate

Islam (iss-LAHM)– world religion based on the teachings of Muhammad; followers are called "Muslims"

Jesus Christ (c. 4 B.C.–A.D. 29)– believed by Christians to be the Messiah, the Son of God; the religion of Christianity is based on his life and teaching

jihad (jih-HAHD)– a struggle or battle on behalf of Islam that sometimes takes the form of holy war

Joan of Arc (c. 1412–1431)– French heroine who led armies against the English during the Hundred Years' War

Judaism (JOO-dee-ih-zuhm or JOO-duh-ih-zuhm)– religion of the Jews, who are descendants of the ancient Hebrews; first major religion to teach belief in one God

Julius Caesar (JOOL-yus SEE-zuhr) (c. 100–44 B.C.)– general and statesman who seized power at the end of the Roman republic

Justinian (juh-STIH-nee-uhn) (483–565)– Byzantine emperor famous for his conquests, for building Hagia Sophia, and for his code of laws

Justinian Code– the collection of Roman laws drawn up by the Byzantine emperor Justinian that has become a basis for legal codes in many modern nations

khan– the name given to the ruler of the Mongol tribes

Kublai Khan (KOO-bluh KAHN) (1215–1294)– grandson of Genghis Khan and founder of the Mongol, or Yuan, dynasty, which ruled China for nearly a century

latitude– a distance in degrees north and south of the equator

Leif Erikson (c. 980–1025)– son of Erik the Red and the founder of a temporary Viking colony in North America

levee (LEH-vee)– a bank of soil built up along the sides of a flooding river

longitude– a distance in degrees east and west of the prime, or zero, meridian

Magna Carta– document signed in 1215 by England's King John recognizing the rights of England's nobles and church leaders; a major advance in the history of constitutional government

manor– the large estate of a medieval lord

Mansa Musa (MAHN-sah moo-SAH) (died c. 1337)– a medieval ruler of Mali; *mansa* means "emperor" and *Musa* is Arabic for "Moses"

Marathon– site of a Greek victory over Persia in 490 B.C.; the modern-day marathon foot race is named for the legendary run made by a messenger who carried news of the battle to Athens

Marco Polo (1254–1324)– Venetian adventurer who traveled to China and served in the court of Kublai Khan

Mesopotamia (meh-suh-puh-TAY-mee-uh)– the region between the Tigris and Euphrates Rivers

Messiah (meh-SIY-uh)– the expected king or deliverer of the Jews; the term comes from ancient Hebrew and means "anointed one"

Middle Ages– the period between about A.D. 500 and 1400, sometimes known as the medieval era

millennium– a period of 1,000 years

Mohenjo-Daro (moh-HEN-joh DAHR-oh)– an ancient city of the Indus River Valley

monarchy– rule by one person who holds sovereign power over a kingdom or empire

monastery– a community of monks; monasteries were medieval centers of learning

monotheism (MAH-nuh-THEE-ih-zuhm)– belief in one god

Moses (14th–13th century B.C.)– led the ancient Hebrews out of bondage in Egypt; according to the Torah, Moses received the Ten Commandments from God

mosque (mahsk)– a Muslim place of worship

Mount Olympus– mythical home of the Greek gods

Muhammad (moh-HAM-uhd) (c. 570–632)– believed by Muslims to be the last great prophet; the religion of Islam is based on his life and teaching

Nebuchadnezzar (neb-yuh-kud-NEH-zur) (c. 630–562 B.C.)– the Babylonian king who built the Hanging Gardens

Nirvana (nir-VAH-nuh)– the state of freedom and peace; in Buddhism an end to the continual cycle of rebirth

nomads– people who move from place to place in search of food

Norman Conquest– the invasion of England in 1066 by William, Duke of Normandy

Odysseus (oh-DIH-see-us)– a hero of ancient Greece who, legend says, traveled for 10 years after fighting at Troy

odyssey (AH-duh-see)– a long and daring voyage; the *Odyssey* is Homer's poem about the voyage of Odysseus

oligarchy (AH-luh-gahr-kee)– a system of government in which power is held by a small group

papyrus (puh-PIY-ruhs)– a paper-like writing material made from pounded reeds and used in ancient Egypt

Parthenon (PAHR-thuh-nahn)– the huge temple to Athena that stands atop the Acropolis in Athens, Greece

patricians (puh-TRIH-shuhns)– members of the aristocratic ruling families of early Rome

Paul of Tarsus (died between A.D. 62 and 68)– Christian missionary who spread Christianity in the Roman Empire

Pax Romana (paks roh-MAH-nuh)– the "Roman Peace" or period of stability in the Roman Empire, lasting nearly two centuries

Peloponnese (PEH-luh-puh-neez)– the southern peninsula of the Greek mainland

Peloponnesian (peh-luh-puh-NEE-zhuhn) War– a war fought from 431 to 404 B.C. between two leagues of Greek city-states, one headed by Athens and the other by Sparta

Pericles (PER-uh-kleez) (c. 495–429 B.C.)– the foremost statesman of Athens during its Golden Age

Persian (PUHR-zhuhn) Wars– a series of wars between Greek city-states and the Persian Empire that lasted from about 492 to 449 B.C.; also known as the Greco-Persian Wars

pharaoh (FAIR-oh)– the title for rulers of ancient Egypt

philosophy– the study of truth, knowledge, and the things of fundamental importance in life

Plato (PLAY-toh) (c. 428–347 B.C.)– Greek philosopher; a student of Socrates

plebeians (plih-BEE-uhns)– the commoners of ancient Rome

polis (PAH-lus)– the citizen-state of ancient Greece

polytheism (PAH-lee-THEE-ih-zuhm)– belief in many gods

pope– title for the spiritual leader and head of the Christian Church in western Europe until the fifteenth century; head of the modern Roman Catholic Church

Poseidon (puh-SIY-dn)– Greek god of the seas

prehistory– the period of time before humans could write

Punic (PYOO-nik) Wars– a series of three wars between ancient Rome and the north African power of Carthage, lasting from 264 to 146 B.C. and ending with the destruction of Carthage

pyramid– the huge burial tombs of the Egyptian pharaohs, the most spectacular of which is the Great Pyramid at Giza

Qin Shi Huangdi (chin shr hwahng-dee) (c. 259–210 B.C.)– Chinese emperor who founded the Qin dynasty and unified much of China; China's "First Emperor"

Qur'an (kuh-RAN)– the sacred book of Islam

Ramayana (rah-muh-YAH-nuh)– an Indian epic poem that tells the story of Prince Rama and illustrates Hindu virtues

Ramses (RAM-seez) II (14th–13th century B.C.)– famous pharaoh of ancient Egypt

reincarnation– belief common to Hindus and Buddhists that at death the soul is reborn in the form of another living being

republic– a government in which citizens elect leaders who rule on behalf of the people

Richard the Lion-Heart (1157–1199)– the king of England who led the Third Crusade to the Holy Land

romanesque (roh-muhn-ESK)– the medieval style of architecture dominant throughout much of the Middle Ages

Rosetta Stone– a stone found near the Egyptian city of Rosetta that helped modern scholars decipher Egyptian hieroglyphs

runes– characters that the Vikings inscribed on coins, jewelry, weapons, and memorial stones

Saladin (SAL-uh-din) (c. 1138–1193)– the Muslim leader who fought against Richard the Lion-Heart during the Crusades

Sanskrit (SAN-skrit)– the language spoken by the Aryans who settled northern India around 1500 B.C.

Sargon (SAHR-gahn) (24th–23rd century B.C.)– a king of Akkad who conquered Sumer and built one of the world's first empires

serfs– peasants obliged to remain on the land of their lord and pay him with labor and rents

Shiva (SHIH-vuh)– the Hindu god of destruction, often pictured dancing in a ring of fire

Silk Road– ancient overland trade route stretching from eastern China to the Mediterranean Sea, linking East and West

Socrates (SAHK-ruh-teez) (c. 470–399 B.C.)– the first of the great Greek philosophers

Sphinx (sfinks)– a huge stone statue with a man's head and lion's body that stood guard over the pyramids

steppe– dry, treeless land blanketed by short grasses

Stone Age– the era during which humans made tools out of stone, which scientists estimate began about 2½ million years ago and ended about 3000 B.C.

stupas (STOO-puhs)– Buddhist places of worship

Sumer (SOO-mur)– the land in southern Mesopotamia that was home to the world's first known civilization

Sundiata (soun-JAH-tah) (c. 1210–1260)– founder and ruler of the Mali Empire in West Africa

synagogues (SIH-nuh-gahgs)– Hebrew places of worship and learning

Ten Commandments– according to the Torah, the 10 laws given by God to Moses for every Hebrew to obey

Theodora (thee-uh-DOR-uh) (c. 497–548)– powerful empress of the Byzantine Empire and wife of Justinian

Torah (TOHR-uh)– the first five books of the Hebrew Bible; sometimes also used to refer to the whole Hebrew Bible, or what Christians call the Old Testament

tundra (TUN-druh)– a vast, treeless plain found in the arctic and subarctic regions of the world

Tutankhamen (too-tahng-KAH-muhn) (c. 1370–1352 B.C.)– the boy-king of ancient Egypt who restored worship of traditional gods, and whose treasure-filled tomb was found almost intact in 1922

Ur (uhr)– a city in ancient Sumer

vassal (VA-suhl)– in medieval Europe, one who received land in exchange for loyalty

Vedas (VAY-duhz)– the first sacred writings of Hinduism

Virgil (VUR-juhl) (70–19 B.C.)– Roman poet and author of the *Aeneid*

Vishnu (VISH-noo)– the blue-skinned Hindu deity said to be the preserver of the world

wheel of dhamma (DUH-muh)– symbol representing the teachings of Buddha

William the Conqueror (c. 1028–1087)– Duke of Normandy who conquered England and made himself its king

Zeus (zoos)– king of the gods, as believed by the ancient Greeks

ziggurat (ZIH-guh-rat)– a stair-stepped temple built by Sumerians

Pronunciation Guide

The table below provides sample words to explain the sounds associated with specific letters and letter combinations used in the respellings in this book. For example, *a* represents the short "a" sound in *cat*, while *ay* represents the long "a" sound in *day*. Letter combinations are used to approximate certain more complex sounds. For example, in the respelling of *Rubicon*—ROO-bih-kahn—the letters *oo* represent the vowel sound you hear in *cool*, *true*, and *few*.

Vowels

a.......... short a: **a**pple, c**a**t
ay .... long a: c**a**ne, d**ay**
e, eh ... short e: h**e**n, b**e**d
ee........ long e: f**ee**d, t**ea**m
i, ih..... short i: l**i**p, act**i**ve
iy .... long i: tr**y**, m**igh**t
ah .... short o: h**o**t, f**a**ther
oh .... long o: h**o**me, thr**ow**
uh....... short u: sh**u**t, **o**ther
yoo..... long u: **u**nion, c**u**te

Letter combinations

ch .... **ch**in, an**c**ient
sh........ **sh**ow, mi**ss**ion
zh .... vi**s**ion, a**z**ure
th........ **th**in, heal**th**
th........ **th**en, hea**th**er
ur........ b**ir**d, f**ur**ther, w**or**d
us .... b**us**, cr**us**t
or........ c**our**t, f**or**mal
ehr...... **err**or, c**are**
oo .... c**oo**l, tr**ue**, f**ew**, r**u**le
ow ...... n**ow**, **ou**t
ou .... l**oo**k, p**u**ll, w**ou**ld
oy .... c**oi**n, t**oy**
aw ...... s**aw**, m**au**l, f**a**ll
ng .... so**ng**, fi**ng**er
air....... **Ar**istotle, b**arr**ister
ahr...... c**ar**t, m**ar**tyr

Consonants

b .... **b**utter, **b**a**b**y
d .... **d**og, cra**d**le
f .... **f**un, **ph**one
g .... **g**rade, an**g**le
h .... **h**at, a**h**ead
j........... **j**u**dg**e, gor**g**e
k .... **k**ite, **c**ar, bla**ck**
l .... **l**i**l**y, mi**l**e
m .... **m**o**m**, ca**m**el
n .... **n**ext, ca**n**di**d**
p .... **p**rice, co**pp**er
r .... **r**ubbe**r**, f**r**ee
s.......... **s**mall, **c**ircle, ha**ss**le
t .... **t**on, po**tt**ery
v .... **v**ase, **v**i**v**id
w .... **w**all, a**w**ay
y .... **y**ellow, ka**y**ak
z.......... **z**ebra, ha**z**e

Index

Boldface indicates illustration included on page.

C

Boldface indicates illustration included on page.

D

E

F

Boldface indicates illustration included on page.

G

H

Boldface indicates illustration included on page.

Boldface indicates illustration included on page.

M

N

Boldface indicates illustration included on page.

O

P

Q

R

Boldface indicates illustration included on page.

S

Boldface indicates illustration included on page.

Boldface indicates illustration included on page.

Illustrations Credits

Key: t=top; b=bottom; c=center; l=left; r=right

Front cover, title page: (t) The Granger Collection, New York; (b) © Réunion des Musées Nationaux/Art Resource, NY.
Back cover: © The Art Archive/John Webb.
Maps: Created by Maps.com., Brad Janke, lead cartographer.

Part 1

Introduction: 8–9 © SuperStock.
Chapter 1: 13, 15 David Shives, K12 Inc. Staff. **16** © Caves of Lascaux, Dordogne, France/ Bridgeman Art Library. **18** (l) © Bettmann/ Corbis; (r) ©AKG Images. **19** (t) © Archivo Iconografico, S.A./Corbis; (c) © Kenneth Garrett/National Academy of Sciences of Ukraine, Kiev; (b) © Erich Lessing/Art Resource, NY. **20** (t) © Kenneth Garrett/ National Museum of Prehistory, Les Eyzies-de-Tayac, France; (c) © Archives Charmet/ Bridgeman Art Library. **23** © Patrick Syder/ Lonely Planet Images. **24** © Erich Lessing/ Art Resource, NY. **25** (t) © Daniel O'Leary/ Panos Pictures; (b) © The Art Archive/ British Museum/Dagli Orti. **27** © Erich Lessing/Art Resource, NY. **31** Anton Petrov/ Deborah Wolfe Ltd. **32** © Daniel O'Leary/ Panos Pictures. **33** (t) © Georg Gerster/ Photo Researchers; (b) © Erich Lessing/Art Resource, NY.
Chapter 2: 34 © University of Pennsylvania Museum (neg. # T4-480). **36** (t) © HIP/Scala/ Art Resource, NY; (b) © G. Tortoli/Ancient Art & Architecture Collection Ltd. **37** © AKG Images. **41** (t) © Erich Lessing/Art Resource, NY; (b) © Georg Gerster/Photo Researchers. **42** (t) © Bildarchiv Preussischer Kulturbesitz/ Art Resource, NY; (b) © British Museum, London, UK/Bridgeman Art Library. **43** © Roger Wood/Corbis. **45** (t) © University of Pennsylvania Museum (neg. # T4-2100); (c) © HIP/Scala/Art Resource, NY; (b) © Scala/Art Resource, NY.
Chapter 3: 46 © The Trustees of The British Museum/Art Resource, NY. **47** © HIP/Scala/ Art Resource, NY. **48** (t, c, b) Jayoung Cho, K12 Inc. Staff. **49** © The Art Archive/Musée du Louvre Paris/Dagli Orti. **50** (t) © The Trustees of The British Museum/Art Resource, NY; (b) © The Art Archive/ Dagli Orti. **51** © Michael Yamashita. **52** (t) © HIP/ Scala/Art Resource, NY; (b) © Scala/ Art Resource, NY; **55** Anton Petrov/Deborah Wolfe Ltd.
Chapter 4: 58 © Scala/Art Resource, NY. **59** © Nik Wheeler/Corbis. **61** © Erich Lessing/ Art Resource, NY. **65** © Georg Gerster/Photo Researchers, Inc.
Chapter 5: 66 © Erich Lessing/Art Resource, NY. **67** © Louvre, Paris, France/Bridgeman Art Library. **68, 70** © Erich Lessing/Art Resource, NY. **71** © HIP/Scala/Art Resource, NY. **72** © The Art Archive/Archaeological Museum Aleppo Syria/Dagli Orti. **75, 76, 77** © Mary Evans Picture Library.
Chapter 6: 78 © Gianni Dagli Orti/Corbis. **80** © R. Sheridan/Ancient Art & Architecture Ltd. **81** (l) © The Art Archive/Musée du Louvre Paris/Dagli Orti; (b) © Gianni Dagli Orti/Corbis. **83** © R. Sheridan/Ancient Art & Architecture Ltd. **85** (t) © Erich Lessing/Art Resource, NY; (b) © SuperStock. **86** © Erich Lessing/Art Resource, NY. **87** © Réunion des Musées Nationaux/Art Resource, NY.
Chapter 7: 88 © Time Life Pictures/Getty Images. **90** © AKG Images. **91** © Dean Conger/Corbis. **92** (t) © Roger Viollet/ Getty Images; (b) © Nik Wheeler/Corbis. **93** (t) © The Detroit Institute of Arts, USA, Founders Society purchase, General Membership Fund; (b) © Snark/Art Resource, NY. **96** © Mary Evans Picture Library.
Chapter 8: 98 © Steve Vidler/SuperStock. **100** (t) © Susan Lapides/Woodfin Camp Associates; (b) © NASA/AFP photo/Getty Images. **101** (t) © HIP/Scala/Art Resource, NY; (b) © The Trustees of The British Museum/ Art Resource, NY. **103** (t) Jason Wolff, K12 Inc. Staff; (bl, br) © Mary Evans Picture Library. **104** © Samantha Lee/Ovoworks/Time Life Pictures/Getty Images. **105** (t) © Kenneth Garrett/National Geographic Image Collection; (c) © Royal Albert Memorial Museum, Exeter, Devon, UK/ Bridgeman Art Library; (b) © Ashmolean Museum, Oxford, UK/Bridgeman Art Library. **106** (t) © Courtesy of the Oriental Institute of the University of Chicago; (b) © Michael A. Hampshire/National Geographic Image Collection. **107** (t) © British Museum, London, UK/Bridgeman Art Library; (b) © HIP/Scala/Art Resource, NY. **108** (t) © The Art Archive/Dagli Orti ; (b) © Bildarchiv Preussischer Kulturbesitz/ Art Resource, NY. **109** © British Museum, London, UK/Bridgeman Art Library. **110** (t) © Gianni Dagli Orti/Corbis; (c) © Bildarchiv Preussischer Kulturbesitz/Art Resource, NY; (b) © G. Hellier. **111** © Gianni Dagli Orti/Corbis. **113** Anton Petrov/Deborah Wolfe Ltd. **114** © Bildarchiv Preussischer Kulturbesitz/Art Resource, NY.
Chapter 9: 116 © Archivo Iconografico, S.A./ Corbis. **117** © Giraudon/Bridgeman Art Library. **118** © Archivo Iconografico, S.A./ Corbis. **119** (t) © SuperStock; (b) © Hulton-Deutsch Collection/Corbis. **120** © The Art Archive/Bibliothèque des Arts Décoratifs Paris/Dagli Orti. **121** © Kenneth Garrett. **122** © Scala/Art Resource, NY. **125** © Kenneth Garrett. **126** © Private Collection/The Stapleton Collection/Bridgeman Art Library. **127** © Scala/Art Resource, NY.
Chapter 10: 128 (A) © Royal Ontario Museum/Corbis; (B) © Réunion des Musées Nationaux/Art Resource, NY; (C) © Asian Art & Archaeology, Inc./Corbis; (D) © Robert Harding; (E) © AKG Images; (F) © Scala/Art Resource, NY. **130** © Robert Frerck/Woodfin Camp Associates. **131** (t) © Borromeo/Art Resource, NY; (b) © Penny Tweedie/Panos Pictures. **133** (t, b) © Borromeo/Art Resource, NY. **134** (l) © Robert Harding; (r) © J.M. Kenoyer/Courtesy Dept. of Archaeology and Museums, Govt. of Pakistan. **136** (t) © Julia Waterlow; Eye Ubiquitous/Corbis; (b) © Liu Liqun/Corbis. **137** (t) © Fritz Polking; (b) © The Art Archive/Victoria and Albert Museum London/Eileen Tweedy; (c) © Royal Ontario Museum/Corbis. **138** (t) © Robert Harding; (b) © Carl & Ann Purcell/Corbis. **139** © Asian Art & Archaeology, Inc./Corbis.
Conclusion: 140 (A) © Giraudon/Art Resource, NY; (B) © Royal Ontario Museum/ Corbis; (C) © The Trustees of The British Museum/Art Resource, NY; (D, E) © Erich Lessing/Art Resource, NY; (F) © J.M. Kenoyer/Courtesy Dept. of Archaeology and Museums, Govt. of Pakistan. **141** © Archivo Iconografico, S.A./Corbis. **142** (l) © Erich Lessing/Art Resource, NY; (r) © Gianni Dagli Orti/Corbis. **143** © Bildarchiv Preussischer Kulturbesitz/ Art Resource, NY. **144** © Georg Gerster/Photo Researchers, Inc. **145** (t) © Bibliotheque Municipale, Poitiers, France, Giraudon/Bridgeman Art Library; (b) © The Art Archive/Dagli Orti.
Time Line: 146 (7000 B.C.) © Erich Lessing/ Art Resource, NY; (3300 B.C.) (l) © Georg Gerster/Photo Researchers, Inc.; (r) © Roger Wood/Corbis; (2900 B.C.) © The Art Archive/ Dagli Orti; (2575 B.C.) © Steve Vidler/ SuperStock. **147** (2300 B.C.) © Gianni Dagli Orti/Corbis; (2000 B.C.) © Robert Harding; (1780 B.C.) © Réunion des Musées Nationaux/ Art Resource, NY; (1700 B.C.) © Asian Art & Archaeology, Inc./Corbis; (1470 B.C.) © G.Hellier; (1360 B.C.) © Scala/Art Resource, NY; (580 B.C.) © Nik Wheeler/Corbis.

Part 2

Introduction: 148 (A) © HIP/Scala/Art Resource, NY; (B) © Araldo de Luca/Corbis;

(C) © Jack Fields/Corbis; (D) © Karen Robinson/Panos; (E) © Royalty-Free/Corbis. **150** © Image Bank/Getty. **152** © Wolfgang Kaehler/Corbis. **156** © Snark/Art Resource, NY. **157** (tl) © The Trustees of The British Museum/Art Resource, NY; (tr) © Photographer's Choice/ Getty; (b) © The Art Archive/British Library.
Chapter 1: 158 © Mary Evans Picture Library. **160** © Asian Art & Archaeology, Inc./Corbis. **161, 162** © Mary Evans Picture Library. **163** © The Art Archive/National Palace Museum Taiwan. **164** © AKG Images. **165** (t) © The Art Archive/National Palace Museum Taiwan; (b) © Private Collection/Bridgeman Art Library. **167** © Jack Fields/Corbis.
Chapter 2: 168 © The Art Archive/ Bibliothèque Nationale Paris. **169** © Burstein Collection/Corbis. **170** © HIP/Scala/Art Resource, NY. **171** Jayoung Cho, K12 Inc. Staff. **172** © Holton Collection/SuperStock. **173** © Getty/AFP PHOTO/Goh Chai Hin. **175** © ChinaStock. **176** © Keren Su/Corbis. **177** (t) © Erich Lessing/Art Resource, NY; (b) © Victoria & Albert Museum, London/ Art Resource, NY.
Chapter 3: 178 © HIP/Scala/Art Resource, NY. **180** © Ric Ergenbright/Corbis. **181** (t) © AKG London/Jean-Louis Nou; (b) © David Samuel Robbins/Corbis. **182, 183** (t) © Victoria & Albert Museum, London/ Art Resource, NY. **183** (b) © Chris Stowers/ Panos. **184** © Chris Stowers/Panos. **185** © Royalty-Free/Corbis. **188** © Victoria & Albert Museum, London/Art Resource, NY.
Chapter 4: 190 © Réunion des Musées Nationaux/Art Resource, NY. **191** © Luca I. Tettoni/Corbis. **192** © Leonard de Selva/ Corbis. **194** © The Art Archive/Musée Guimet Paris. **197** © Mary Evans Picture Library. **199** Anton Petrov/Deborah Wolfe Ltd.
Chapter 5: 200 © Chris Lisle/Corbis. **201** © Hulton Archive/Getty Images. **202** © David Samuel Robbins/Corbis. **203** (t) © Stone/Getty Images; (b) © AKG London/ Jean-Louis Nou. **204** © Kevin R. Morris/ Corbis. **205** © Hulton Archive/Getty Images. **206** (t) © The Art Archive; (b) © The Art Archive/Oriental Art Museum Genoa/Dagli Orti. **209** Anton Petrov/Deborah Wolfe Ltd.
Chapter 6: 212 © The Art Archive/National Gallery Budapest/Dagli Orti. **215** (l) © The Jewish Museum, NY/Art Resource, NY; (r) © Topham/The Image Works. **216** © The Art Archive/Musée des Beaux Arts Lyons/ Dagli Orti. **218** © Erich Lessing/Art Resource, NY. **219** © Alinari/Art Resource, NY. **220** © Agnew & Sons, London, UK/ Bridgeman Art Library. **222** © Christie's Images/Bridgeman Art Library. **224** © Musee des Beaux-Arts, Angers, France, Lauros/ Giraudon/Bridgeman Art Library. **226** © Réunion des Musées Nationaux/Art Resource, NY. **227** © Cameraphoto Arte, Venice/Art Resource, NY.
Chapter 7: 228 © The Art Archive/Dagli Orti. **229** © akg-images. **230** © Scala/Art Resource, NY. **232, 233** © The Jewish Museum, NY/Art Resource, NY. **234, 235** © Jewish Museum, New York/SuperStock. **236** © Historical Picture Archive/Corbis. **237** © AKG London/ Rabatti-Domingie. **238** © Getty Images, Inc. **239** © Richard T. Nowitz/Corbis.
Chapter 8: 240 © Rawdon Wyatt/Travel-Ink. co.uk. **242** © Scala/Art Resource, NY. **243** © Erich Lessing/Art Resource, NY. **244** (l) © R.Sheridan/Ancient Art & Architecture Ltd.; (r) © Gail Mooney/Corbis. **245** © Erich Lessing/Art Resource, NY. **246** © Wolfgang Kaehler/Corbis. **247** © Peter M. Wilson/Corbis. **249** © Index/Bridgeman Art Library. **251** (t) © Scala/Art Resource, NY; (c) © Erich Lessing/Art Resource, NY; (b) © The Art Archive/Fitzwilliam Museum Cambridge/Dagli Orti. **252** (t) © Réunion des Musées Nationaux/Art Resource, NY; (b) © Bettmann/Corbis. **253** © AKG London/ Peter Connolly.
Chapter 9: 254 © Scala/Art Resource, NY. **255** © The Trustees of The British Museum/ Art Resource, NY. **256** © Bettmann/Corbis. **257** (t) © Erich Lessing/Art Resource, NY; (b) © The Trustees of The British Museum/ Art Resource, NY. **258** © Gary M. Prior/Getty Images. **259** (t) © Nimatallah/Art Resource, NY; (b) © Erich Lessing/Art Resource, NY. **260** © Nimatallah/Art Resource, NY. **261** © Inge Yspeert/Corbis. **262** © Bettmann/ Corbis. **263** © Mary Evans Picture Library. **264** © Lebrecht Music Collection/Alamy. **269** Anton Petrov/Deborah Wolfe Ltd.
Conclusion: 270 (A) © Giraudon/Art Resource, NY; (B) © The Trustees of The British Museum/Art Resource, NY; (C) © The Art Archive/Victoria and Albert Museum London/Sally Chappell; (D) © Scala/Art Resource, NY. **271** Getty Images, Inc. **272** (t) © Christie's Images/Bridgeman Art Library; (b) © Erich Lessing/Art Resource, NY. **273** © AFP/Corbis. **274** © Simon Kwong/Reuters Newmedia Inc./Corbis. **275** © Robert Essel NYC/Corbis.
Time Line: 276 (1800 B.C.) © The Art Archive/ National Gallery Budapest/Dagli Orti; (1500 B.C.) © Victoria & Albert Museum, London/Art Resource, NY; (1400 B.C.) © Royalty-Free/Corbis; (1250 B.C.) © The Art Archive/Dagli Orti; (1200 B.C.) © Bettmann/ Corbis. **277** (776 B.C.) © Scala/Art Resource, NY; (550 B.C.) © AKG London/Rabatti-Domingie; (500 B.C.) (l) © Réunion des Musées Nationaux/Art Resource, NY; (500 B.C.) (r) © Mary Evans Picture Library; (250 B.C.) © Hulton Archive/Getty Images; (220 B.C.) © Burstein Collection/Corbis; (206 B.C.) © ChinaStock.

Part 3

Introduction: 278 (A) © Nimatallah/Art Resource, NY; (B) © The Art Archive/Dagli Orti; (C) © Mary Evans/Edwin Wallace; (D) © Bettmann/Corbis. **280** © Royalty-Free/ Corbis. **281** (t) © AP Photo/Al Stephenson; (b) © Creatas. **282** (l) © Corbis; (r) © Scala/Art Resource, NY. **283** (t) © Bettmann/ Corbis; (b) Getty/Stone Images/photo by Andy Sacks.
Chapter 1: 284 © Yann Arthus-Bertrand/ Corbis. **286, 287** © Mary Evans Picture Library. **288** (t) © Foto Marburg/Art Resource, NY; (b) © Araldo de Luca/Corbis. **289** © Bettmann/Corbis. **291** © Mimmo Jodice/ Corbis. **292** © Gilles Mermet/Art Resource, NY. **294** © Arco/C. Wermter/ImageBroker/ Alamy Images. **295** © Christie's Images/ Corbis. **296** (t) © Art Resource, NY; (b) © Erich Lessing/Art Resource, NY.
Chapter 2: 298 © AKG images. **299** © Dave Bartruff/Corbis. **302** Cole Breeding, K12 Inc. Staff. **303** (t) © Lauros/Giraudon/Bridgeman Art Library; (b) © Reuters NewMedia Inc./Corbis. **304** © Stone/Getty Images. **305** © The Art Archive/Museo Naval Madrid/Dagli Orti. **306** (t) © Hermitage, St. Petersburg, Russia/Bridgeman Art Library; (b) © Nimatallah/Art Resource, NY. **307** © Alinari/Art Resource, NY. **309** © AKG Images.
Chapter 3: 310 © Scala/Art Resource, NY. **311, 312** © Bettmann/Corbis. **313** © R. Sheridan/ The Ancient Art & Architecture Collection Ltd. **315** (t) © R. Sheridan/The Ancient Art & Architecture Collection Ltd.; (b) © The Art Archive/Agora Museum Athens/Dagli Orti. **316** © Mansell/Time Life Pictures/ Getty Images. **318** © Bildarchiv Preussisscher Kulturbesitz, Berlin. **319** (t) © Leonard de Selva/Corbis; (b) © The Trustees of The British Museum/Art Resource, NY. **320** (t) © The Art Archive/Museo Nazionale Taranto/Dagli Orti; (b) © R. Sheridan/The Ancient Art & Architecture Collection Ltd. **321** (tl) © Erich Lessing/Art Resource, NY; (tr) © Araldo de Luca/Corbis; (c) © The Art Archive/Archaeological Museum Naples/Dagli Orti; (b) © The Art Archive/ Archaeological Museum Naples/Dagli Orti. **324** Anton Petrov/Deborah Wolfe Ltd.

Chapter 4: 326 © Réunion des Musées Nationaux/Art Resource, NY. **327** © Mary Evans/Edwin Wallace. **329** © Bettmann/Corbis. **330** © AKG Images. **331** © Mary Evans Picture Library. **332** © Bildarchiv Preussisscher Kulturbesitz, Berlin. **334** (t) © Scala/Art Resource, NY; (b) © Bettmann/Corbis. **335** © Alinari Archives/Corbis. **337** (t) © The Art Archive/Jan Vinchon Numismatist Paris/Dagli Orti; (b) © Mary Evans Picture Library. **338** (t) © Erich Lessing/Art Resource, NY; (b) © Bettmann/Corbis.
Chapter 5: 340 © Gustavo Tomsich/Corbis. **343** © Scala/Art Resource, NY. **344** © Alinari/Art Resource, NY. **346** © Erich Lessing/Art Resource, NY. **348, 349, 351** © Mary Evans Picture Library. **352–53** © Erich Lessing/Art Resource, NY. **353** © Erich Lessing/Art Resource, NY. **354** (l) © The Art Archive/Museo della Civilta Romana Rome/Dagli Orti; (r) © The Art Archive/Jan Vinchon Numismatist Paris/Dagli Orti. **355** © Mary Evans Picture Library.
Chapter 6: 358 © Gianni Dagli Orti/Corbis. **359** © The Art Archive/Musée du Louvre Paris/Dagli Orti. **361** (t) © Bettmann/Corbis; (b) © The Ancient Art & Architecture Collection Ltd. **363** © Gianni Dagli Orti/Corbis. **364** © Bildarchiv Preussischer Kulturbesitz/Art Resource, NY. **364–65** © The Ancient Art & Architecture Collection Ltd. **365** © Roger Wood/Corbis. **366** © Christie's Images/Corbis. **367** (t) © The Art Archive/British Museum; (cr) © The Art Archive/Galleria degli Uffizi Florence/Dagli Orti; (cl) © Erich Lessing/Art Resource, NY; (b) © Araldo de Luca/Corbis. **369** © The Art Archive/Archaeological Museum Tipasa Algeria/Dagli Orti. **370** © Erich Lessing/Art Resource, NY. **371** © Stapleton Collection/Corbis.
Chapter 7: 372 © Scala/Art Resource, NY. **373** © The Art Archive/Musée Municipal Sémur en Auxois/Dagli Orti. **374** © Mary Evans Picture Library. **375** © Bildarchiv Preussisscher Kulturbesitz, Berlin. **377** © Bettmann/Corbis. **378** (t) © Réunion des Musées Nationaux/Art Resource, NY; (b) © Adam Woolfitt/Woodfin Camp & Associates. **379** © Macduff Everton/The Image Works. **381** © Dallas and John Heaton/Corbis. **382** (t) © Bildarchiv Preussisscher Kulturbesitz, Berlin; (c) © AKG Images; (b) © Hulton Archive by Getty Images. **383** © Charles & Josette Lenars/ Corbis. **384** (t) © Erich Lessing/Art Resource, NY; (b) © The Art Archive/Jarrold Publishing. **385** (t) © Bildarchiv Preussisscher Kulturbesitz, Berlin; (b) © Araldo de Luca/Corbis. **388** © The Art Archive/Biblioteca Estense Modena/Dagli Orti. **390** © Tate Gallery, London/Art Resource, NY.
Chapter 8: 392 © Victoria & Albert Museum, London/Art Resource, NY. **394** © Edward Owen/Art Resource, NY. **395** © Araldo de Luca/Corbis. **396** © Benjamin Rondel/Corbis. **397** © Gianni Dagli Orti/Corbis. **398** (t) © North Carolina Museum of Art/Corbis; (b) © Scala/Art Resource, NY. **399** © Erich Lessing/Art Resource, NY. **400** © Manchester Art Gallery, UK/Bridgeman Art Library. **401** © The Art Archive/San Francesco Assisi/Dagli Orti. **402** © Bildarchiv Preussisscher Kulturbesitz, Berlin. **403** © The Art Archive/Fine Art Museum Bilbao/Dagli Orti.
Chapter 9: 404 © Scala/Art Resource, NY. **405** © National Trust/Art Resource, NY. **406** (t) © Jacques Stella (1596–1657) Fitzwilliam Museum, University of Cambridge, UK/Bridgeman Art Library; (b) © Cummer Museum of Art & Gardens/SuperStock. **408** © Alinari/Art Resource, NY. **409** © The Art Archive/Pinacoteca Nazionale di Siena/Dagli Orti. **410** (t) © Giraudon/Art Resource, NY; (b) © Araldo de Luca/Corbis. **411** (t) © The Art Archive/Archaeological Museum Sousse Tunisia/Dagli Orti; (c) © Scala/Art Resource, NY; (b) © Archivo Iconografico, S.A./Corbis. **412** (t) © Bettmann/Corbis; (b) © The Art Archive/Museo di Capodimonte, Naples/Dagli Orti. **417** Anton Petrov/Deborah Wolfe Ltd.
Chapter 10: 418 © Roger Wood/Corbis. **419** © Araldo de Luca/Corbis. **420** (t) © Charles & Josette Lenars/Corbis; (b) © Bettmann/Corbis. **421** (t) © Archivo Iconografico, S.A./Corbis; (b) © Giraudon/Art Resource, NY. **422, 423** © The Art Archive/Dagli Orti. **424** (t) © Archivo Iconografico, S.A./Corbis; (b) © Philadelphia Museum of Art/Corbis. **425** © Araldo de Luca/Corbis. **426** © The Art Archive/Musée du Louvre Paris/Dagli Orti. **426–27** © Mary Evans Picture Library. **427** © Hulton-Deutsch Collection/Corbis.
Conclusion: 428 (A) © Archivo Iconografico, S.A./Corbis; (B) © Media Bakery; (C) © Stapleton Collection/Corbis; (D) © Alexander Burkatowski/Corbis; (E) © Scala/Art Resource, NY. **429** © Wonderfile. **430** © Stapleton Collection/Corbis. **430–31** © Creatas. **431** © The Art Archive/ Dagli Orti. **432** (t) © Robert Frerck/Odyssey Productions; (b) © James J. Tissot/Super-Stock. **433** © The Art Archive/Vatican Museum Rome/Album/Joseph Martin. **434** © Archives Charmet/Bridgeman Art Library. **434–35** © Scala/Art Resource, NY. **435** Photonica.
Time Line: 436 (480 B.C.) © AKG Images; (432 B.C.) © Bildarchiv Preussisscher Kulturbesitz, Berlin; (323 B.C.) © Réunion des Musées Nationaux/Art Resource, NY; (202 B.C.) © Gianni Dagli Orti/Corbis; (44 B.C.) © Scala/Art Resource, NY; (27 B.C.) © Bettmann/Corbis. **437** (A.D. 29) © Bildarchiv Preussisscher Kulturbesitz, Berlin; (A.D. 50) © National Trust/Art Resource, NY; (A.D. 80) © Dallas and John Heaton/Corbis; (A.D. 313) © Scala/Art Resource, NY; (A.D. 330) © Archivo Iconografico, S.A./Corbis; (A.D. 476) © Mary Evans Picture Library.

Part 4

Introduction: 438 (A) © Andrew Ward/Life File/Photodisc/Getty Images; (B) © Peter Willi/Bridgeman Art Library; (C) © The Granger Collection, New York; (D) © Ariadne Van Zandbergen/Lonely Planet Images. **440** (t) Private Collection/Archives Charmet/Bridgeman Art Library; (b) © Charles & Josette Lenars/Corbis. **441** © Giraudon/Art Resource, NY. **442** (l) © Scala/Art Resource, NY; (r) © Yann Arthus-Bertrand/Corbis. **443** © The Pierpont Morgan Library/Art Resource, NY.
Chapter 1: 444 © Yann Arthus-Bertrand/Corbis. **447** © Christie's Images/SuperStock. **449** (t) © Erich Lessing/Art Resource, NY; (b) © Scala/Art Resource, NY. **450** © Scala/Art Resource, NY. **451** © Bridgeman Art Library. **452** (t) © Lawrence Manning/Corbis; (b) © Topham/The Image Works. **454** Anton Petrov/Deborah Wolfe Ltd.
Chapter 2: 458 © Historical Picture Archive/Corbis. **460** © K.M. Westermann/Corbis. **462** © Christie's Images/SuperStock. **464** © The Art Archive/Turkish and Islamic Art Museum Istanbul/HarperCollins Publishers. **465** © Scala/Art Resource, NY. **466** © The Art Archive/Hazem Palace Damascus/Dagli Orti. **467** © By Permission of the British Library Or. 2936. **468** © The Art Archive/ Topkapi Museum Istanbul/HarperCollins Publishers. **469** © Josef Polleross/The Image Works. **470, 471** © Reuters NewMedia Inc./Corbis.
Chapter 3: 472 © By Permission of the British Library Or. 2936. **473** © Explorer, Paris/SuperStock. **474** © Christel Gerstenberg/Corbis. **477** © Christie's Images/SuperStock. **478** © Archivo Iconografico, S.A./Corbis. **479** Topkapi Palace Museum, Istanbul, Turkey, www.bridgeman.co.uk. **480** © Photos12.com – ARJ. **482** (t) © Archives Charmet/Bridgeman Art Library; (b) © The Art Archive/National Museum Damascus Syria/Dagli Orti. **483** © Victoria & Albert Museum, London/Art Resource, NY. **484** © Peter Harholdt/SuperStock. **485** (t) © Werner Forman/Art Resource, NY; (b) © Sandro Vannini/Corbis.
Chapter 4: 486 (A) © Ariadne Van Zandbergen/Lonely Planet Images; (B) © Jose

Azel/Aurora/PictureQuest; (C) © The Art Archive/John Webb; (D) © The Art Archive/Musée des Arts Africains et Océaniens/Dagli Orti; (E) © The Art Archive/Museum of Islamic Art Cairo/Dagli Orti. **489** © John Elk III/Lonely Planet Images. **490** © The Art Archive/Musée des Arts Africains et Océaniens/Dagli Orti. **492** Anton Petrov/Deborah Wolfe Ltd. **494, 496** © Werner Forman/Art Resource, NY. **497** © Bettmann/Corbis. **498–99** © The Art Archive/John Webb. **500** © Stapleton Collection/Corbis. **501** (t) © Robert Berger/Image State; (b) © Nik Wheeler/Corbis.

Chapter 5: 502 © Roger-Viollet, Paris/Bridgeman Art Library. **503** © British Museum, London, UK/Bridgeman Art Library. **505** © The British Museum/Topham-HIP/The Image Works. **506** © Archivo Iconografico, S.A./Corbis. **507** © English Heritage/Topham-HIP/The Image Works. **508** © SuperStock. **509** (t) © Photo 12. National Library/Snark Archives; (b) © Bildarchiv Preussisscher Kulturbesitz, Berlin. **510** © Bibliotheque Municipale, Douai, France, Giraudon/Bridgeman Art Library. **511** © The Art Archive/Musée du Château de Versailles/Dagli Orti. **513** (t) © Private Collection/Bridgeman Art Library; (b) © Archives Charmet/Bridgeman Art Library. **514** © Bildarchiv Steffens/Bridgeman Art Library. **517** Anton Petrov/Deborah Wolfe Ltd. **519** © The Board of Trinity College, Dublin, Ireland/Bridgeman Art Library.

Chapter 6: 520 © Delaware Art Museum, Wilmington, USA/Sir Edward Burne-Jones, (1833–98)/Bridgeman Art Library. **522** © Mary Evans Picture Library. **523** © Giraudon/Art Resource, NY. **524** (t) © Richard T. Nowitz/Corbis; (b) © Werner Forman/Art Resource, NY. **525** © Mary Evans Picture Library. **526** © Werner Forman/Art Resource, NY. **526–27** © The Art Archive/Aarhus Kunstmuseum Arhus Denmark/Dagli Orti. **527** © Winge, Marten Eskil (1825–96)/Bridgeman Art Library. **528** (t) © Werner Forman/Art Resource, NY; (b) © Werner Forman/Art Resource, NY. **529** (t) © Hulton Archive/Getty Images; (b) © Jason Lindsey/Alamy Images. **530–31** © The Image Bank/Getty Images. **531** © American School, (19th century)/Bridgeman Art Library.

Chapter 7: 532 © Réunion des Musées Nationaux/Art Resource, NY. **533** © The Stapleton Collection/Bridgeman Art Library. **534** © Giraudon/Art Resource, NY. **535** © Archivo Iconografico, S.A./Corbis. **536** (t) Wallace Collection, London, UK, www.bridgeman.co.uk; (c) Fishmongers' Hall, London, UK, www.bridgeman.co.uk; (b) © Mary Evans Picture Library. **537** (t) © Bibliotheque Nationale, Paris, France, Lauros/Giraudon/Bridgeman Art Library; (b) © Giraudon/Bridgeman Art Library. **538** © British Library, London, UK/Bridgeman Art library. **539** © Giraudon/Bridgeman Art Library. **540** © Alinari/Art Resource, NY. **541** © Réunion des Musées Nationaux/Art Resource, NY.

Chapter 8: 542 © A.M. Rosati/Art Resource, NY. **543** © Elio Ciol/Corbis. **544** © Mary Evans Picture Library. **545** (t) © Gianni Dagli Orti/Corbis; (b) © Réunion des Musées Nationaux/Art Resource, NY. **546** (t) © Archivo Iconografico, S.A./Corbis; (b) © Victoria & Albert Museum, London/Art Resource, NY. **547** © Robert Frerck/Odyssey/Chicago. **548** © Steve Allen/Brand X Pictures/Alamy Images. **549** © Scala/Art Resource, NY. **551** (l) © Archives Charmet/Bridgeman Art Library; (r) © SEF/Art Resource, NY. **552** (t) © Scala/Art Resource, NY; (b) © Blondel, Merry Joseph (1781–1853)/Bridgeman Art Library. **554** © Boucicaut Master, (fl. 1390–1430) Bridgeman Art Library. **558** Anton Petrov/Deborah Wolfe Ltd.

Chapter 9: 560 © National Portrait Gallery, London. **561** © Snark/Art Resource, NY. **563** © Popperfoto/Retrofile.com. **564** © Nik Wheeler/Corbis. **565** (t) © The Art Archive/Jarrold Publishing; (b) © Giraudon/Art Resource, NY. **566** © AKG Images. **567, 568** © Bettmann/Corbis. **569** © The British Library/HIP/The Image Works.

Chapter 10: 570 © Giraudon/Art Resource, NY. **572** (t) © David Forbert/SuperStock; (b) © Private Collection, Paul Freeman/Bridgeman Art Library. **574** © Snark/Art Resource, NY. **574–75** © Dean Conger/Corbis. **575** © The Stapleton Collection/Bridgeman Art Library. **576** © The Art Archive/Freer Gallery of Art. **579** © Pierre Colombel/Corbis. **580** (t) © Science Museum, London/Topham-HIP/The Image Works; (b) © Museum of Fine Arts, Boston, Massachusetts, USA/Bridgeman Art Library. **581** © Museum of Fine Arts, Boston, Massachusetts, USA/Bridgeman Art Library.

Chapter 11: 582 © Bibliotheque Nationale, Paris, France/Bridgeman Art Library/ **583** © Deborah Harse/The Image Works. **585** © Janet Wishnetsky/Corbis. **586** © Bridgeman Art Library. **587** The Art Archive/British Library/British Library. **588** © The Art Archive. **590** © Mary Evans Picture Library. **591** © Private Collection/Bridgeman Art Library. **592** © Bibliotheque Nationale, Paris, France/Bridgeman Art Library. **595** © Giraudon/Bridgeman Art Library.

Chapter 12: 596 © The Art Archive/Bibliothèque Nationale Paris/HarperCollins Publishers. **598–99** © Snark/Art Resource, NY. **599** © The Art Archive/British Library/HarperCollins Publishers. **600** (t) © Réunion des Musées Nationaux/Art Resource, NY; (b) © The Art Archive. **601** © Snark/Art Resource, NY. **603** © Giraudon/Bridgeman Art Library.

Conclusion: 604 (A) © Erich Lessing/Art Resource, NY; (B) © ImageState; (C) © Scala/Art Resource, NY; (D) © Erich Lessing/Art Resource, NY. **605** © Lauros/Giraudon/Bridgeman Art Library. **606** (t) © Erich Lessing/Art Resource, NY; (b) © Foto Marburg/Art Resource, NY. **607** (t) © Murat Ayranci/SuperStock; (b) © Erich Lessing/Art Resource, NY. **608** (l) © The Granger Collection, New York; (r) © Werner Forman/Art Resource, NY. **609** © The Art Archive/Genius of China Exhibition. **610** © Craig Aurness/Corbis. **611** © Giraudon/Art Resource, NY.

Time Line: 612 (A.D. 476) © The Art Archive/Musée du Louvre Paris/Dagli Orti; (A.D. 535) © Scala/Art Resource, NY; (A.D. 611) © Giraudon/Art Resource, NY; (A.D. 622) © Erich Lessing/Art Resource, NY; (A.D. 800) © Archives Charmet/Bridgeman Art Library; (A.D. 830) © Photos12.com–ARJ. **613** (A.D. 1066) © Snark/Art Resource, NY; (A.D. 1190) (l) © SEF/Art Resource, NY; (A.D. 1190) (r) © Blondel, Merry Joseph (1781–1853)/Bridgeman Art Library; (A.D. 1250) © Steve Allen/Brand X Pictures/Alamy Images; (A.D. 1275) © Giraudon/Bridgeman Art Library; (A.D. 1324) © The Art Archive/John Webb; (A.D. 1347) © Snark/Art Resource, NY; (A.D. 1429) © Réunion des Musées Nationaux/Art Resource, NY.

Volume 1, Conclusion: 614 (A) © Robert Harding; (B) The Granger Collection, New York; (C) © Mary Evans Picture Library; (D) © Craig Aurness/Corbis. **616** © Nik Wheeler/Corbis. **617** (t) © R. Sheridan/The Ancient Art & Architecture Collection Ltd.; (b) © Burstein Collection/Corbis. **618** (l) © Erich Lessing/Art Resource, NY; (r) © Scala/Art Resource, NY. **619** © The Art Archive/Hazem Palace Damascus/Dagli Orti. **620** © Bettmann/Corbis. **621** (l) © Steve Vidler/SuperStock; (r) © Réunion des Musées Nationaux/Art Resource, NY.

Staff for This Volume

John Agnone
Project Manager

Jeff Burridge
Text Editor

Steve Godwin
Art Director

Jayoung Cho
Bill Gordon
Designers

Meredith Condit
Photo Editor

Charlotte Fullerton
Annette Scarpitta
Jane A. Martin
Photo Researchers

Betsy Woodman
Researcher

Michelle Layer Rahal
Cartographic Editor

Megan Dubbs
Map Production

Mark Wentling
Indexer

Bud Knecht
Clean Reader

About K12 Inc.

Founded in 1999, K12 Inc. is an elementary and secondary school service combining rich academic content with powerful technology. K[12] serves students in a variety of educational settings, both public and private, including school classrooms, virtual charter schools, home schools, and tutoring centers. K[12] currently provides comprehensive curricular offerings in the following subjects: Language Arts/English, History, Math, Science, Visual Arts, and Music. The K[12] curriculum blends high quality offline materials with innovative online resources, including interactive lessons, teacher guides, and tools for planning and assessment. For more information, call 1-888-YOUR K12, or visit www.K12.com.